GREAT LAKES
CAMPING

FOGHORN OUTDOORS®

GREAT LAKES CAMPING

The Complete Guide to More Than 750 Campgrounds in Minnesota, Wisconsin, and Michigan

FIRST EDITION

Bob & Ginger Schmidt

AVALON TRAVEL

FOGHORN OUTDOORS:
GREAT LAKES CAMPING
The Complete Guide to More
Than 750 Campgrounds in
Minnesota, Wisconsin, and Michigan

First Edition

Bob and Ginger Schmidt

Published by
Avalon Travel Publishing
1400 65th Street, Suite 250
Emeryville, CA 94608, USA

Please send all comments, corrections,
additions, amendments, and critiques to:

ⒻOGHORN OUTDOORS®
GREAT LAKES CAMPING
AVALON TRAVEL PUBLISHING
1400 65th Street, Suite 250
EMERYVILLE, CA 94608, USA
email: atpfeedback@avalonpub.com
website: www.foghorn.com

Printing History
1st edition—June 2002
5 4 3 2

Text © 2002 by Bob Schmidt. All rights reserved.
Illustrations and maps © 2002 by
   Avalon Travel Publishing, Inc. All rights reserved.

Some photos and illustrations are used by permission
and are the property of the original copyright owners.

ISBN: 1-56691-399-3
ISSN: 1538-2915

Editor: Rebecca K. Browning
Series Manager: Marisa Solís
Copy Editors: Julie Leigh, Erika Howsare
Graphics Coordinators: Melissa Sherowski, Erika Howsare
Cover Design: Jacob Goolkasian
Illustrations: Bob Race
Production: Darren Alessi, Patrick David Barber Design
Map Editors: Olivia Solís, Naomi Adler Dancis
Cartography: CHK America, Chris Folks, Suzanne Service,
   Kat Kalamaras, Mike Morgenfeld
Indexer: Rachel Kuhn
Proofreader: Cynthia Rubin

Front cover photo: ©Terry Donnelly

Distributed by Publishers Group West

Printed in the USA by Arvato Services

Although every effort was made to ensure that the information was correct at the time of going to press, the author and publisher do not assume and hereby disclaim any liability to any party for any loss or damage caused by errors, omissions, or any potential travel disruption due to labor or financial difficulty, whether such errors or omissions result from negligence, accident, or any other cause.

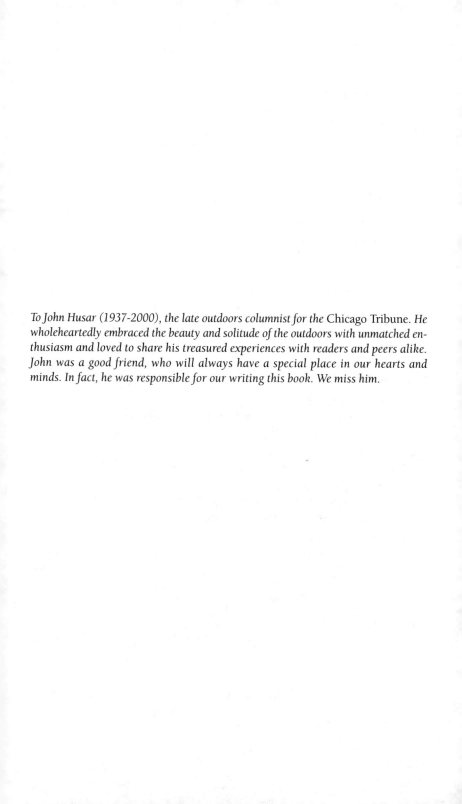

To John Husar (1937-2000), the late outdoors columnist for the Chicago Tribune. *He wholeheartedly embraced the beauty and solitude of the outdoors with unmatched enthusiasm and loved to share his treasured experiences with readers and peers alike. John was a good friend, who will always have a special place in our hearts and minds. In fact, he was responsible for our writing this book. We miss him.*

Contents

Minnesota

Wisconsin

Michigan

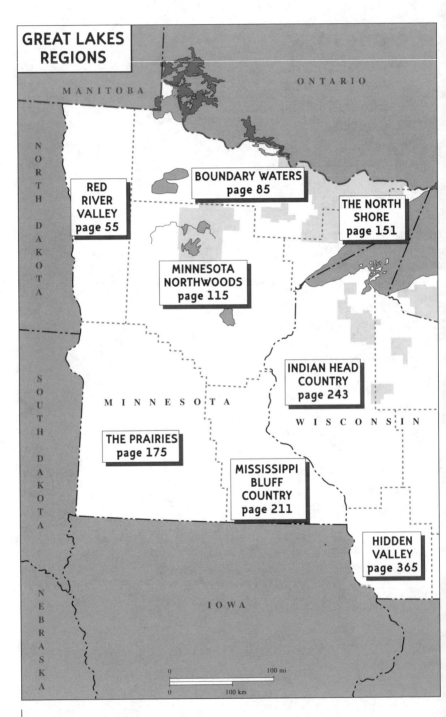

GREAT LAKES REGIONS

MANITOBA

ONTARIO

NORTH DAKOTA

RED RIVER VALLEY
page 55

BOUNDARY WATERS
page 85

THE NORTH SHORE
page 151

MINNESOTA NORTHWOODS
page 115

INDIAN HEAD COUNTRY
page 243

SOUTH DAKOTA

MINNESOTA

WISCONSIN

THE PRAIRIES
page 175

MISSISSIPPI BLUFF COUNTRY
page 211

HIDDEN VALLEY
page 365

NEBRASKA

IOWA

0   100 mi
0   100 km

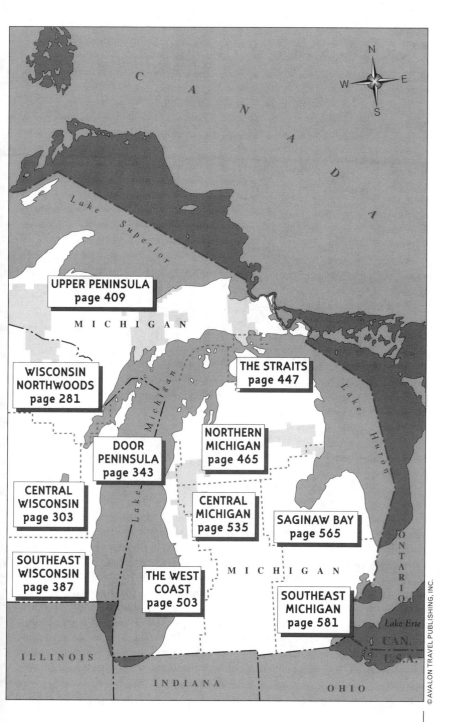

UPPER PENINSULA
page 409

THE STRAITS
page 447

WISCONSIN NORTHWOODS
page 281

DOOR PENINSULA
page 343

NORTHERN MICHIGAN
page 465

CENTRAL WISCONSIN
page 303

CENTRAL MICHIGAN
page 535

SAGINAW BAY
page 565

SOUTHEAST WISCONSIN
page 387

THE WEST COAST
page 503

SOUTHEAST MICHIGAN
page 581

How to Use This Book

Foghorn Outdoors: Great Lakes Camping is divided into three sections, one for each state: Minnesota, Wisconsin, and Michigan. Each state is then broken down into smaller chapters based on regional divisions. Maps at each chapter's beginning show where all the campgrounds in that region are located.

You can search for the ideal campsite in two ways:
1. If you know the name of the specific campground where you'd like to stay, or the name of the surrounding geographical area or nearby feature (town, national or state park or forest, mountain, lake, river, etc.), look it up in the index beginning on page 620 and turn to the corresponding page.
2. If you know the general area you want to visit, turn to the Great Lakes map and map list on pages viii–ix. Find the state or region in which your destination lies, and turn to that map at the beginning of that chapter. You can then determine which campgrounds are in or near your destination by their corresponding numbers. Opposite the map will be a chapter table of contents listing each lodging in the chapter by map number and the page number it's profiled on. Then turn to the corresponding page for the campground you're interested in.

About the Campground Profiles

Each campground in this book begins with a brief overview of its setting. Topics such as facilities, amenities, nearby or on-site recreation options, historical trivia, and ambience may also be addressed. The practical information you need to plan your trip is broken down further into the following categories:

Location—This category provides the general location of the campground by naming its proximity to the nearest major town or landmark. Following this information is the name of the map on which that campground can be found. The entire entry will be written like this: "In northwest Minnesota near Hallock, bordering Two Rivers, map 1, grid B1."

Campsites, facilities—This section provides the number of campsites for both tents and RVs and whether hookups are available. Facilities such as restrooms, picnic areas, recreation areas, laundry, and dump station will be addressed, as well as the availability of piped water, showers, playground, and stores, among others. The campground's pet policy is also mentioned here.

Reservations, fees—This section notes whether reservations are accepted, and the rates for tent sites and RV sites. If there are additional fees for parking or pets, or discounted weekly or seasonal rates, that will also be noted here.

Directions—This section provides mile-by-mile driving directions to the campground from the nearest major town.

Contact—This section provides an address, phone number, and Internet address, if available, for the campground.

Trip Notes—This section provides a brief overview of the setting, as well as information about the attractions and activities popular at the campground.

About the Icons

The icons in this book are designed to provide at-a-glance information on activities that are available on-site or near each campground. Some icons have been selected to also represent facilities available or services provided. They are not meant to represent every activity or service, but rather those that are most significant.

— Hiking trails are available.

— Biking trails or routes are available. This usually refers to mountain biking, although it may represent road cycling as well. Refer to the text for that campground for details.

— Swimming opportunities are available.

— Fishing opportunities are available.

— Boating opportunities are available. Various types of vessels apply under this umbrella activity, including motorboats and personal watercrafts (Jet Skis). Refer to the text for that campground for more detail, including mph restrictions and boat ramp availability.

— Canoeing and/or kayaking opportunities are available. Typically, canoeing is available on inland lakes and rivers, whereas kayaking is available along the coast. Refer to the text for that campground for more detail.

— Winter sports are available. This general category may include activities such as downhill skiing, cross-country skiing, snowshoeing, snowmobiling, snowboarding, and ice skating. Refer to the text for that campground for more detail on which sports are available.

— Pets are permitted. Campgrounds that allow pets may require an additional fee or that pets be leashed. Campgrounds may also restrict pet size or behavior. Refer to the text for that campground for specific instructions or call in advance.

— A playground is available. A campground with a playground can be desirable for campers traveling with children.

— Wheelchair access is provided, as advertised by campground managers. However, concerned persons are advised to call the contact number of a campground to be certain that their specific needs will be met.

— RV sites are provided.

— Tent sites are provided.

About the Maps

The maps in this book are designed to show the general location of campgrounds and are not meant to substitute for more detailed road maps. Readers are advised to take additional maps when heading out to any campground, particularly when venturing into the wilderness.

Winter Campgrounds and Winter Sports Activities

Although some campgrounds, usually state park facilities, are open all year, many campgrounds, generally private facilities, are only open to RVs, tent-campers, and backpackers from spring through fall. These dates are listed for each entry in this book. On some entries, however, a campground may include a winter sports icon and offer ski, snowshoe, and snowmobile rentals even though the campground is closed for the winter. This is because the facility has a lodge, rental cabin, or RV site that is available for winter accommodations.

Our Commitment

We are committed to making *Foghorn Outdoors: Great Lakes Camping* the most accurate, thorough, and enjoyable camping guide to this region. With this well-researched first edition, you can rest assured that every camping spot in this book is accompanied by the most up-to-date information available. However, with the change of seasons, you can bet that some of the fees listed herein have gone up, and that camping destinations may have opened, closed, changed hands, or changed their policies or procedures. It is always a good idea to call the campground ahead of time, but doubly so if you have any special needs, such as wheelchair access, or are traveling with children or pets. The time to find out the pool is closed for renovation is before you spend two hours driving to it with hot, cranky kids in the backseat.

If you would like to comment on this book, whether it's to suggest a tent or RV spot we overlooked, or to let us know about any noteworthy experience—good or bad—that occurred while using *Foghorn Outdoors: Great Lakes Camping* as your guide, we would appreciate hearing from you. Please address correspondence to:

Foghorn Outdoors: Great Lakes Camping
Avalon Travel Publishing
1400 65th Street, Suite 250
Emeryville, CA 94608 U.S.A

email: atpfeedback@avalonpub.com

INTRODUCTION

Introduction

For some people, camping is a way of life. For others, it's recreation. For centuries, nomads have traveled by day and pitched their tents at dusk. Whether you carry your shelter on your back, on a bike, or in your vehicle, when the day's activities are over, you can snuggle into bed and watch fireflies perform a miniature fireworks dance just for you.

Camping in a recreational vehicle, or RV, began in the early 1900s because people wanted more travel options than a railroad could offer. They could experience the beauty, wonder, and solitude of America's more remote areas.

Camping wasn't only an inexpensive alternative for the poor. During the 1920s, four prominent Americans—Thomas Edison, Henry Ford, Harvey Firestone, and John Burroughs—were camping enthusiasts. Known as the four vagabonds, the friends enjoyed the outdoors and camped together.

Today, many families travel in their RVs to football games, NASCAR auto races, concerts, and other events. Some have become so enamored with the nomadic lifestyle they have sold their homes and live year-round in a well-equipped RV, following the warmth of the sun across the country.

Camping can bring families closer together. It engenders responsibility in youngsters who help with camp chores. Camping is also an outdoor classroom experience; young people can explore new geographic surroundings, identify flora and fauna, or participate in wholesome sporting activities.

With the rising cost of living, camping makes it possible for families to travel more economically. Average campground fees range from $20 to $25 per night, significantly cheaper than hotel or motel rates for a family. Food budgets for a trip can be the same amount you would spend at home on groceries. All in all, camping is an outstanding vacation alternative.

The Great Lakes states of Michigan, Minnesota, and Wisconsin are beautiful areas for campers. The region may lack the awesome peaks found out West and the craggy cliffs of the northern New England shore, but it has its own natural beauty and its share of historic sites. From the pristine areas of the Northwoods, where wildlife is abundant, to the beautiful shores of Lakes Michigan and Huron, this Midwestern region's campgrounds are plentiful. You can discover them in national forests, lakeshores, and parks; state, county, and municipal parks; and in private facilities.

State Overviews

Minnesota

The origin of Minnesota's name comes from the Minnesota River, its large southern waterway. The Dakota Sioux called this river *Minisota,* meaning sky-tinted waters.

Four glaciers that eventually formed thousands of lakes and rivers once covered Minnesota. The rocky shores of Lake Superior and the St. Croix and Mississippi Rivers form the state's eastern border while the Red River of the north forms two-thirds of its western boundary. In the north, Lake of the Woods and the waters of Voyageurs National Park and the Boundary Waters Canoe Area separate Minnesota from Canada, giving the state more shoreline than California, Florida, and Hawaii combined.

Minnesota has a colorful history, ranging from the days when the Ojibwa (Chippewa) and Dakota fought frequently over territory. The victorious Ojibwa stayed in the forested north and the Dakota were forced to live in the southern prairies. French voyageurs arrived in 1654 to establish a fur trade that was later carried on by the British who took control in 1763. The British were followed by Yankee traders.

In 1819, Fort Anthony, renamed Fort Snelling in 1825, was built at the mouth of the Minnesota River to protect European settlers.

Minnesota became the 32nd state in 1858. Over the next three decades the railroad and the rich deposits of iron ore found in the Mesabi Range brought new waves of European settlers.

Today, the state remains a leading food and fiber producer. Although it was once primarily a wheat-growing region and still ranks high in the production of oats, hay and spring wheat, Minnesota has diversified its crops and added food processing to its large industries. About one-third of Minnesota is forested. It continues to be the largest single producer of forest products, although it doesn't produce at the rate or quality it once did. Mining also remains an important industry, yielding 70 percent of the iron ore mined in the United States for steel.

Thanks to the St. Lawrence Seaway and its access to the Atlantic Ocean, Duluth is the largest freshwater port in the world, shipping more than 40 million tons of waterborne cargo annually.

Wildlife flourishes in Voyageurs National Park, in the Chippewa and Superior National Forests, and in the state's 64 state parks and 55 state forests. Also Minnesota has been the home of many famous Americans as well as the legendary giant woodsman Paul Bunyan, but it is its rare and often untamed beauty that attracts campers and others who enjoy the outdoors.

State Forests

Minnesota State Forest campgrounds are rustic and designed to meet only the basic needs of campers.

Unlike state parks, state forest campgrounds do not have resident managers, organized nature programs, or modern facilities, such as showers and flush toilets.

However, they are patrolled on a regular basis to provide security and service.

Each primitive site consists of a cleared area, fire ring, and table. In addition, vault toilets, level parking spurs, garbage cans, and drinking water from a hand pump are provided at campgrounds that charge a fee.

The maximum RV length permitted in state forest campgrounds is 20 feet. Most fee campgrounds have wheelchair-accessible sites and toilets, but it is wise to call ahead for specific information.

Generally, state forestlands are open for hunting and other outdoor recreation in accordance with state laws. State game refuges within state forests are closed to hunting unless listed as open. Hunting on private land within a state forest is subject to state trespass laws.

Gathering fruits and mushrooms is allowed, but trees may not be cut without a permit. Dead wood may be gathered for campfires on site. No permit is required for recreational campfires of less than three feet in diameter in an area cleared of combustible materials for five feet around the fire.

Camping on forestlands outside of developed campgrounds is allowed with some conditions. No permit is required, but campers are urged to practice the "leave-no-trace" camping ethic. Special rules apply in developed forest campgrounds.

Camping Fees and Registration
A camping fee is charged in campgrounds with developed facilities that include drinking water, garbage containers, and toilets. Individual campsites are $9 per day. You can register by means of an envelope provided at each campground where a fee is charged. Individual sites are available on a first-come, first-served basis. No fees are charged for other recreational use of state forests.

For more information contact the Minnesota Department of Natural Resources, Information Center, DNR Building, 500 Lafayette, St. Paul, MN 55155, 651/296-6157 or 888/646-6367.

State Parks
Minnesota State Parks offer a variety of lodging and camping facilities that can be reserved ahead of time. Although 30 percent or more of the campsites in state parks are available on a first-come, first-served basis, you should reserve your campsite in advance to ensure that you have a site in the park of your choice. Campsites can be reserved from 3 to 90 days in advance if you pay by credit card or from 10 to 90 days in advance if you pay by check or money order. Lodging in state parks, particularly camping cabins, is popular and reservations are strongly recommended. These can be made 365 days in advance.

You can make reservations 24-hours-a-day by calling The Connection (952/922-9000 or 800/246-CAMP; TDD number 952/890-2883 or 800/334-7413).

For camping, the reservation fee is $7.25 and is non-refundable. The first night camping fee must be paid in advance. There is no separate reservation charge for lodging facilities, but the first night's stay must be paid in advance. Payment can be made by check, money order, or with a major credit card. Make checks payable to The Connection. Send it to: Minnesota State Parks, c/o The Connection, 11351 Rupp Dr., Burnsville, MN 55337.

If you must cancel a reservation, call The Connection.

When making a reservation, you will need to provide the following information:

- Arrival date
- Your phone number
- Name of the park where you wish to stay.
- Name of the campground (some parks have several)
- Special needs for disabled persons.
- Type of shelter you will be using (tent, RV, etc.)
- RV campers will also need to know the total length of their rig from the front of the tow vehicle to the rear of the towed vehicle.
- Length of stay
- Number of people in your party
- Number of vehicles in your party (one vehicle per site)

When you call for your reservation, have alternate campgrounds or parks in mind in case your first choice is not available. This may be necessary during summer weekends.

Camping reservations are held until 6 P.M. the day of your arrival. If you have paid the first night camping fee in advance, your reservation is held until closing time at 10 P.M.

If you have made a deposit on your camping fees and must cancel, a $5 processing fee will be deducted. There is no refund if you cancel less than eight days prior to your date of arrival.

State park information, vehicle permits, travel assistance, and gifts are available at the Explore Minnesota USA shop at the north entrance at the 500-shop Mall of America in Bloomington near the Minneapolis-St. Paul International Airport.

State Park Fees

An annual permit for a vehicle is $20. A daily permit for all vehicles is $4; a daily group permit (10-permit minimum with 24-hour notice) is $2.

The per-day fee for camping in a semi-modern site (with showers) is $12; electric hookups (where available) are an additional $3. A rustic site without showers is $8. A backpack or canoe site is $7. Half-priced camping at semi-modern and rustic sites is available Sunday through Thursday for Minnesota resident seniors or disabled campers.

Fees for lodging vary by facility. Camping cabins are $27.50; cabins with electricity are $30.

The non-refundable fee for a reservation is $7.25.

Please remember that fees are likely to change at any time so you should call ahead to check for the latest information.

For more information contact the DNR Information Center, 651/296-6157 or 888/MINNDNR (Minnesota toll free), fax 651/297-3618, TTY 651/296-5484 or 800/657-3929 (Minnesota toll free), website: www.dnr.state.mn.us.

Minnesota Driving Tours

The North Shore: A Scenic Drive Along Lake Superior
Route Location: Along U.S. Hwy. 61 northeast of Duluth
Distance: 151 miles
Travel Season: Year round
Number of Campgrounds: About 60
Description: The route, designated as the second most scenic drive in the U.S., skirts Lake Superior's western shore from Duluth to Grand Portage in Minnesota.

Although the trip can be made in about 3.5 hours, it offers so much that you should camp at two or three sites to take full advantage of the breathtaking beauty and attractions of this Northwoods wilderness, including climbing 1,600-foot Carlton Peak and viewing wondrous waterfalls like Minnesota's highest.

Here you have the opportunity to visit Superior National Forest, Isle Royale National Park, Grand Portage National Monument, no less than seven state parks, and begin an adventure on one or more major hiking trails — Superior, Sawbill, Caribou, Gunflint and Arrowhead trails—that venture into the unspoiled Boundary Waters Canoe Area Wilderness.

Even if you don't want to hike, there's plenty for campers to do, including inland fishing or Lake Superior charter boat fishing, sailing, canoeing, kayaking, excursion boats, swimming, bicycling, nature and landscape photography, wildlife-watching, art galleries, and craft and gift shops. In winter, you can choose from cross-country skiing, ice-fishing, snowmobiling, and snowshoeing.

There's plenty for history buffs, too, from the culture of early Native Americans and the French voyageurs to European settlements, which had their beginnings with the territory's exploration in the mid-1650s.

Avenue of Pines: Through the Heart of the Chippewa National Forest
Route Location: Along State Hwy. 46 from Deer River to Northome
Distance: About 48 miles
Travel Season: Year-round
Number of Campgrounds: Nine U.S. Forest Service campgrounds and one Corps of Engineers campground
Description: The "Avenue of Pines," Minnesota State Scenic Byway, covers 48 miles through the heart of the Chippewa National Forest, which encompasses more than 700 lakes and nearly 1,000 miles of rivers and streams. The forest skirts the state's fifth largest lake, Winnibigoshish, one of the state's premier northern pike and

walleye waters. Other nearby bodies of water include Island, Round, Nature's, Cut Foot Sioux, Squaw, Little Ball Club, and many smaller lakes.

About two miles of Hwy. 46 is part of the Great River Road, a national- and state-designated route that follows the Mississippi River from its headwaters in Lake Itasca State Park (218/266-2100) south to the Gulf of Mexico.

You can enjoy views of mature stands of red pine and aspen, sparkling lakes, marshland, and more. Sightings of bald eagle, deer, bear, porcupine, osprey, and other species are common.

Besides angling and wildlife-watching, other activities include boating, hiking, picnicking, swimming, and water-skiing.

Visit the Cut Foot Sioux Visitor Center on Hwy. 46 (218/246-8233) and for more information, call the Deer River Ranger District (218/246-2123).

Mississippi Bluff Country: Journey to Yesteryear
Route Location: Along State Hwy. 16 between Dexter and La Crescent
Distance: About 88 miles
Travel Season: Year-round
Number of Campgrounds: Three state park campgrounds and more than 20 private campgrounds
Description: For two-thirds of this route, you'll follow the panoramic Root River Valley to the Mississippi River. The western third showcases Minnesota's rich, rolling farmland.

The eastern two-thirds of the route winds toward the Great River Road along a trout stream and canoe route through spectacular tree-covered bluffs of hardwoods and limestone palisades. This valley, untouched by the glacier, has weathered over time to provide a picturesque setting for small towns, historic lodging places, and 35 miles of biking and hiking along the Root River State Trail. You can also canoe or kayak the Root River, motor the Mississippi, play golf, fish for trout, hunt wild turkey, and explore the state's only caves.

In the towns of Grand Meadow, Spring Valley, Preston, Lanesboro, Whalan, Peterson, Rushford, Houston, and Hokah, you'll find plenty of antique stores and bed and breakfasts. By veering off the route at Preston at Hwy. 52 and Prosper at Hwy. 44, you can take the Amish Buggy Byway. The 700-member Amish community is concentrated around Canton and Harmony. Please remember to drive carefully and avoid photographing Amish faces. It is considered extremely rude.

The route also takes you near three state parks, a fish hatchery, and a number of museums and historic sites.

For more information, contact Historic Bluff Country (800/428-2030).

Wisconsin

The same natural features that attracted the early explorers and settlers to Wisconsin make it ideal camping grounds. The shoreline of the state extends 381 miles along Lake Michigan and 292 miles along the shores of Lake Superior. In addition, the Mississippi River that creates most of the western border and more than 15,000 inland lakes and 33,000 miles of rivers and streams sustain nearly 200 species of fish. All these provide a wide variety of year-round, water-related sports.

The glaciers that scoured the terrain more than 10,000 years ago left in their wake drumlins, eskers, moraines, dames, and kettles that create uniquely beautiful land formations. Campers can follow Wisconsin's Ice Age Trails through 31 counties beginning at Potawatomi State Park on the shores of Green Bay and twist down through the Kettle Moraine stretching west and north, ending at the Dalles of the St. Croix River on the western border. This alone provides more than 600 miles of trails for hikers to explore.

Summer offers an opportunity to visit the mystique and romance of the many lighthouses that have guided sailors to Wisconsin for over 150 years. In addition, the breathtaking view of the thundering waterfalls is a photographer's delight. No one knows exactly how many there are, but the state boasts of nearly 60 waterfalls ranging from the 165-foot Big Manitou Falls to small 12-footers.

Fall is an ideal time to tour rural areas and experience the sights, smells, and flavors of country life to see how honey, mustard, or goat milk cheese are produced, pick a pumpkin or bring home buckets of red raspberries.

In 1925, Carl Eliason from the northern town of Saynor invented the snowmobile to navigate the snowdrifts of winter. Today, Wisconsin offers winter campers more than 22,000 miles of interconnected snowmobile trails, more than any other state. Many trails follow old railroad beds and cross restored trestle bridges.

Traditions of Native Americans and pioneers are preserved and re-created by the communities and their residents for visitors to see and enjoy in Wisconsin's many museums, historic districts, and state historical societies. No one can see it all, but it's fun to return again and again in an attempt to do so.

State Parks

Wisconsin state parks preserve some of the state's best scenery, plants, wildlife, and sites of archeological, geological, or historical interest. Their purpose is to offer areas for public recreation and education in conservation and nature study. They have features such as paved roads, mowed or surfaced trails, restrooms, picnic areas, campgrounds, boat ramps, and other facilities. Most are accessible to persons with disabilities. A vehicle admission sticker is required in most areas.

State Park and Trail Fees

A vehicle admission sticker is required on all motor vehicles stopping in state parks and recreation areas. Some state forests and trail parking areas also require a sticker. You can buy an annual sticker for admission to all state parks and forests for the calendar year or a daily sticker that is only valid on the date of issue. If you have only a little time to visit, a one-hour sticker is available at most state parks and forests.

The fees are as follows: Wisconsin resident, $18 annual, $5 daily, $3 one hour; Resident age 65 and older, $9 annual, $3 daily, $3 one hour; Non-resident: $25 annual, $7 daily, $3 one hour.

A trail pass is required for all people age 65 or older for biking, horseback riding, or cross-country skiing on certain designated trails. It's not required for hiking. The fee for a resident or non-resident is $10 annually or $3 daily.

Camping Fees
Camping fees vary with the facilities provided by the campground, the day of the week, season, and the camper's residency.

For a Wisconsin resident, the daily fee ranges from $7 to $10; non-resident fees range from $9 to $12. There is an additional $3 charge for electric hookup. For a reservation, the fee is $9.50. The reservation cancellation fee is $8.50.

Reserving a Campsite
You can reserve a state park campsite by accessing the ReserveAmerica website or by calling 888/947-2757, TTY 800/274-7275. The website can be used 24 hours a day, seven days a week. The call center hours are Monday through Friday 9 A.M. to 10 P.M., and weekends and holidays from 9 A.M. to 6 P.M. (CST). VISA and MasterCard are accepted.

State Wildlife Areas
State wildlife areas were acquired to preserve an important heritage of wild lands for hunters, trappers, hikers, wildlife watchers, and others interested in the outdoors. They help protect and manage important habitat for wildlife, and prevent draining, filling, and destruction of wetlands. Except for a few areas, they only have minor facility development like a small, gravel parking lot. Most don't have designated roads or trails, restrooms or vault toilets, or drinking fountains. Most don't encourage or allow camping, though some do provide primitive camping sites.

State Fishing Areas
State fishing areas protect Wisconsin waterways from improper land use due to agriculture abuse or urban runoff. They are used to preserve and manage headwaters and springs that often form the biological base for stream fisheries, and they protect and improve spawning grounds for lake fisheries.

State Flowages
State flowages—the Chippewa and Turtle Flambeau Flowages—were acquired in 1988 and 1990, respectively. They offer fishing, hunting, boating, camping, and other outdoor recreation.

State Forests

State forest properties are managed for a variety of public benefits. They provide multiple recreational uses, such as camping, fishing, hunting, hiking, and nature study. They also provide for timber resources while preserving natural areas and the scenic value of the land.

A state park sticker or fee is required at designated public use areas, including various trails, picnic areas, and campgrounds.

State Natural Areas

State natural areas are designed to protect Wisconsin's natural diversity, provide sites for research and environmental education, and serve as benchmarks for assessing and guiding use of other state lands. They are tracts of land or water that have natural communities, unique natural features, or significant geological or archeological sites.

Wildlife Viewing Areas

Most of the previous areas offer wildlife-watching opportunities. Although no area is specifically called a wildlife viewing area, those that offer the most exceptional or notable opportunities—76 of them —are designated as such in a National Watchable Wildlife Program. Such sites are also identified by the program's binocular logo symbol, and are covered in detail in the Wisconsin Wildlife Viewing Guide The guide is $10.65 payable to the Wisconsin DNR. To obtain a copy, write: Wisconsin Wildlife Viewing Guide, DNR Bureau of Wildlife Management, Box 7921, Madison, WI 53707-7921.

You can also watch for brown-and-white binocular logo signs along roadsides, which direct you to these locations.

Wisconsin Driving Tours

Wisconsin's Northwoods: Straddling the Great Divide
Route Location: Northern Wisconsin from Hayward to Glidden along State Hwy. 77
Distance: 51 miles
Travel Season: Year-round
Number of Campgrounds: Four U.S. Forest Service campgrounds and a few private facilities
Description: The Great Divide Scenic Byway takes its name from its location. Water flows down the north slopes of the Northern Highlands into the Brule, White, and Bad Rivers. It continues through to the Great Lakes and into the Atlantic Ocean. Water from the south slope flows into the Chippewa and St Croix Rivers. Then it makes its way into the Mississippi River and, eventually, the Gulf of Mexico.

Along this route you can explore the towering pines, giant hemlocks, and maples of Wisconsin's Northwoods. The byway spans 29 miles of the trip, passing through the Chequamegon National Forest with its resident black bear, timber wolves, and white-tailed deer. It crosses lakes, swamps, and bogs with beaver, loons, and bald eagles.

Once lumber camps were dominant, followed by Civilian Conservation Corps (CCC) camps in the 1930s that you can still visit today. Now, the lakes and flowages on the byways western portion are vacation destinations throughout the year.

Park your car and travel by foot, all-terrain vehicle (ATV), bike, boat, camp, canoe, hike, ride horseback, cross-country ski, snowmobile, snowshoe, or just study wildlife. In a three-county area, there are 160 miles of ATV or snowmobile trails alone.

For more information, contact the Chequamegon National Forest (715/762-2461) or District Office (715/634-4821).

Door Peninsula: County With the Most Lighthouses in America
Route Location: From Sturgeon Bay to Washington Island along State Hwy. 42
Distance: About 100 miles
Travel Season: Year-round
Number of Campgrounds: Four campgrounds in five state parks plus numerous private campgrounds
Description: Like Michigan, Wisconsin has its share of lighthouses. In fact, 75-mile-long Door County has more lighthouses than any other county in the United States along its 250 miles of shoreline, luring anglers, picnickers, and sunbathers. In many ways, the Door Peninsula combines the charm of New England fishing villages with a rugged shore of steep limestone bluffs, plunging to sandy beaches bordered by dark pine forest.

It also features five state parks, cherry and apple orchards, artist colonies, and a winery. In addition, Door County boasts an abundance of places to relax, including art galleries, golf courses, outdoor summer theater, and festivals.

Quaint communities, such as Baileys Harbor, Gills Rock, and Sister Bay, have historic sites that reflect the area's Scandinavian and other ethnic settlers. Museums showcase its rich maritime history. In Fish Creek, you can take a historical walking tour and visit the Nobel House Museum (920/868-2316). There's another pleasant walking tour in Ephraim, including the Anderson Dock and Store.

For more information, contact the Door County Chamber of Commerce (920/743-4456).

One spot you must visit is Washington Island, the largest of more than 40 islands in Door County. Take the ferry and ride the Cherry Train from the Island Ferry Dock (920/847-2546). It offers a 90-minute narrated tram trip, including stops at the museum, Schoolhouse Beach, and the Art and Nature Center. The island's past is captivating.

The Apostle Islands: Lake Superior Treasure
Route Location: By ferry from Bayfield
Distance: 36 miles
Travel Season: Year-round, especially in the fall
Number of Campgrounds: About 15 campgrounds plus those on Madeline Island
Description: This archipelago of 22 islands, jutting out into Lake Superior, is Wisconsin's northernmost landscape. Carved for more than a million years by glacial ice, wind, and waves, the Apostle Islands National Lakeshore includes 12 miles of mainland shoreline. Presumably, someone who believed there were only 12 islands named them.

In any case, the Apostle Islands offer wonderful stretches of clean sandy beach, sandstone cliffs, spectacular caves, old-growth forest, populations of black bears and bald eagles, and the National Park System's largest collection of lighthouses. There are also historic sites, including abandoned logging camps, stone quarries, farmsteads, and fishing camps.

The islands range in size from three-acre Gull Island to 10,054-acre Stockton Island.

Madeline Island, the only isle that is not part of the national lakeshore, can be reached by the Madeline Island Ferry Line (715/747-2051). It offers passenger, bicycle, and car transportation between La Pointe and Bayfield. The Historical Museum is a good place to visit.

People have used the Apostle Islands for hundreds, if not thousands, of years. Many Ojibwa legends are associated with them. Voyageurs established trading posts and settlers later built seasonal hunting and fishing camps, summer homes, and farms.

From Bayfield, you can access the national lakeshore's islands and even view the sea caves via Apostle Islands Cruise Service (800/323-7619 or 715/779-3925). There are also kayak outfitters and, if you have your own craft, you can launch at the end of Meyers Road off Hwy. 13, about 18 miles west of Bayfield. A boat ramp is available at Little Sand Bay, 13 miles north of Bayfield.

Begin your visit at the Visitor Center (715/779-3397) in Bayfield, which is in the old Bayfield County Courthouse.

Michigan

Water, water, everywhere—from Lake Superior in the north to Lake Michigan on the west and Lake Huron, Lake St. Clair, and Lake Erie on the east, Michigan is indeed a "Water Wonderland."

Michigan is the only state that is divided into two distinct parts—the Upper Peninsula (UP) is larger than Connecticut, Delaware, Massachusetts, and Rhode Island combined and comprises only one-third of the state's territory. The Lower Peninsula, often referred to as the "mitten," is connected to the UP by the Mackinac Bridge for land travelers and the Straits of Mackinac for vessels.

Michigan, whose name came from the Chippewa word *Michigama,* (great lake), has about 3,200 miles of shoreline, more than 11,000 inland lakes, and 36,000 miles of rivers and streams. This has influenced almost everything in the state, providing transportation for the rich iron and copper ore found in the UP and the timber that was harvested in both the UP and the northern part of the Lower Peninsula. Both of these rich resources played a major role in the state's development, providing the raw materials for the manufacture of steel, automobiles, chemicals, and food products. Add this to the rich soil found throughout Michigan, which has provided food products not only for its residents but also for export, and you have a state that has it all.

From the cereal on your breakfast table, the auto in your garage, the fish and berry pie that you're serving for dinner to the salt with which you flavor your meals, your family no doubt enjoys something from Michigan each day.

Michigan is also one of our leading tourist states. Both residents and visitors enjoy recreation all year. There is world-class angling in lakes and streams, boating and golfing in summer; snowmobiling, downhill and cross-country skiing, sleigh rides, and ice fishing in winter; apple, berry, and vegetable picking in their seasons. And there is always a lighthouse left on for you.

Michigan offers beauty, relaxation, and recreation for campers with thousands of acres of national parks, state parks and forests to bike, hike, and camp.

State Forests

Michigan's state forests include 7,000 miles of canoeable streams, 13,000 miles of trout waters, and 500 miles of Great Lakes shoreline. In all, these forests have some 150 campgrounds areas with about 3,000 sites.

In a state forest, a camp must be limited to six people and two tents or a tent and one wheeled camping unit. If the site is vacant, you can register as early as 8 A.M. before your overnight stay. If you cannot find a site, forestry officials will help locate one and assign it to you. You can stay up to 15 days—longer with permission from the local campground manager.

Among the regulations for state forests, pets are allowed provided they are kept on a leash of six feet or less, you can only build a campfire in a designated fire pit, and campsites cannot be left unoccupied for more than 24 hours or take up more than one site.

Camping Reservations

Michigan state forest campsites are available on a first-come, first-served basis. No reservations are accepted. In addition, campsites cannot be saved or preregistered by you or a friend. The completed registration permit is your only claim to occupy a campsite. Check-out time is 3 P.M.

To register, select a vacant site and register immediately by filling out the registration form envelope and permit. Tear off the permit and put the payment in the envelope, sealing and depositing it in the fee-collection pipe. Then attach your "paid-for" camp permit to the site's marker post.

State Forest Fees

Camping fees range from $4 to $8 per site. You can pay by check (payable to the State of Michigan) or in cash. Senior citizens who are 65 years or older may camp for half the posted fee. The fee payment is based on an honor system collection policy and is deposited in the site's fee-collection pipe.

For more information, contact Michigan Forest Management Division, State Forest Campgrounds, P.O. Box 30452, Lansing MI 48909-7952, 517/335-3338 or 517/373-1275, fax 517/373-2443.

State Parks

Michigan has 96 state parks visited by more than 25 million people annually. Seventy-three of them allow camping.

Beginning with Interlochen in 1919, the Michigan State Park system was established to protect the state's natural treasures for future generations to enjoy. The system also includes historic sites that preserve the state's rich cultural heritage. In addition to historic sites and natural features, Michigan's state parks offer a variety of outdoor recreation facilities, from modern to rustic campgrounds, to hiking and cross-country ski trails, to boat-launch sites and fishing piers.

Hunting is permitted in some state parks and recreational areas in seasons for certain species with specific weapons.

There are a number of regulations that apply to state parks and recreational lands in Michigan. For example, you cannot damage, destroy or remove trees, shrubs, wildflowers, planted grasses or other vegetation without written permission. This, however, doesn't apply to picking and removing mushrooms, berries, and edible nuts or fruits.

You can only build a fire in a designated area or in approved stoves or grills. Unless you are hunting, engaged in a field trial, or training a dog in a designated area, you cannot have a dog or other pet animal unless it's under immediate control on a leash not longer than six feet.

State park officials urge you to be a "no impact" camper by following these guidelines:
- Camp in a designated campsite.
- Carry out and recycle all garbage and litter you encounter.
- Protect water sources from contamination.

- Use biodegradable soap or try soapless hot water dishwashing, bathing, and clothes-washing.
- When using biodegradable soap and toothpaste, do so at least 100 feet from a natural or well-water source.
- Prevent forest fires and keep your fires small.
- Never leave a fire unattended.
- Have water available to extinguish a fire properly.
- Make sure ashes are cold when you leave a fire.

Camping Reservations

State park camping sites can be reserved. There is a $5 non-refundable reservation fee to book a campsite or mini-cabin. Reservation charges are $4.

When making a reservation, provide the following information:
- Campground name
- Site-specific lot number (where applicable)
- Arrival and departure states
- Alternate dates and/or parks
- Camping equipment (tents or RVs) and the size of the equipment
- Number of campers in your party

When applying by telephone, have a MasterCard or VISA credit-card number and expiration date available.

If paying by check, call 800/44-PARKS at least 15 days before the planned camping date. The operator will give you an address that your check must arrive at no later than 10 days after you call in the reservation.

If making a reservation by mail, send the information and payment to: Michigan Central Reservation System, P.O. Box 450, Cumberland, MD 21501-0450.

State Park Fees

A state park motor vehicle permit, available at each park entrance gate, DNR Operation Service Center, or at any of 1,800 retail stores in Michigan, is required at all state parks.

Campground fees at state parks vary according to the facilities offered, but range from $6 daily for a rustic campsite to $18 for a modern site with full hookups.

For more information contact Michigan Parks and Recreation Division, P.O. Box 30257, Lansing, MI 48909, 517/373-9900, State Parks Camping Reservations, 800/447-2757; website: www.dnr.state.mi.us.

Michigan Driving Tours

Lake Michigan Lighthouses: Reflections of Maritime History
Route Location: Along Lake Michigan's eastern shore from St. Joseph to Traverse City via I-94, I-96, U.S. Hwy. 31, and Hwys. 31/120.
Distance: About 270 miles.
Travel Season: Year-round.
Number of Campgrounds: More than 30 campgrounds, including six state park campgrounds.
Description: For many travelers, lighthouses are an obsession. For others they are snippets of history. For anyone, they are fascinating places to visit and Michigan has more than 120 lighthouses. A camping trip along Michigan's Lower Peninsula on Lake Michigan's eastern shore offers an ideal opportunity to see, tour, or photograph nearly 30 of the state's lifesaving beacons.

From the south, the eastern shore lighthouses begin at St. Joseph, originally named "Newburyport," and end at Petoskey near the Straits of Mackinac. The St. Joseph Historic Lighthouse and catwalk, one of Michigan's oldest, was built at the mouth of the St. Joseph River at North Pier in 1832.

Other lighthouses or stations to visit include South Haven South Pier, Holland Harbor, Grand Haven South Pier, Muskegon South Pier, White River, Little Sable Point, Ludington North Pierhead, Big Sable Point, Manistee North Pierhead, Frankfort North Breakwater, South Manitou Island, North Manitou Shoal, South Fox Island, St. James Harbor, Beaver Island, Squaw Island, Point Betsie, Grand Traverse (Cats Head Point), Old Mission Point, Charlevoix South Pier, and Little Traverse (Harbor Point).

Some lighthouses are accessible only by boat. Tour operators include Manitou Island Transit (231/256-9061) from Leland, Beaver Island Boat Co. (888/446-4095) from Charlevoix, and Bay Water Ferry and Tours (800/530-9898) from Petoskey.

Keweenaw Peninsula: A Northern Experience
Route Location: Upper Peninsula along U.S. Hwy. 41 and State Hwy. 26 from Baraga to Copper Harbor.
Distance: About 75 miles.
Travel Season: Year-round, especially spring, summer, and fall.
Number of Campgrounds: Three state park campgrounds and 36 national park campgrounds.
Description: Washed on three sides by Lake Superior, the Keweenaw Peninsula enjoys cool breezes in summer and piles of snow—nearly 400 inches—in winter. The abundant snowfall attracts hoards of cross-country skiers, snowmobilers, and other winter sports enthusiasts.

One of the archipelago's top attractions is 850-square-mile Isle Royale National Park (906/482-0984). This wilderness park, about 50 miles offshore, is a haven for hikers, lighthouse and shipwreck enthusiasts, wildlife-watchers, photographers, and anglers. There are 165 miles of scenic hiking trails and three dozen campgrounds for backpackers and recreational boaters. Ferry service is available from Grand Portage, Minnesota, and from Houghton (906/482-0984) and Copper Harbor (906/289-4437), Michigan.

In addition, the peninsula boasts three state parks—Baraga (our personal favorite), F. J. McLain and Ft. Wilkins.

The Keweenaw National Historical Park (800/338-7982) chronicles the story of the region's copper mining boom—America's first mineral "rush."

Although it's not on the peninsula, Michigan's highest point, Mount Avron (1978.82 feet), is nearby. You can drive within one-half mile of the peak. From U.S. Hwy. 41 at L'Anse, take Broad Street to Main Street (Skanie Road). From there, drive down Roland Lake Road and follow the signs. Hike the trail on the north side of the mountain. Don't expect a panoramic view because it is a forested mountain, but well worth conquering.

The Straits of Mackinaw: So Much to See and Do and So Little Time
Route Location: I-75, between Mackinaw City and St. Ignace.
Distance: About five miles.
Travel Season: Year-round, especially spring through fall.
Number of Campgrounds: One state park and numerous private campgrounds are in the area.
Description: No trip to Michigan is complete without at least one drive across the Mackinac Bridge, regarded by many as the "eighth wonder of the modern world." The Mackinac Bridge is the longest suspension bridge in the Western Hemisphere with a four-lane roadway over the Straits to link Michigan's two peninsulas. In fact, it is 950 feet longer than the Golden Gate Bridge in San Francisco. Actually, including its approaches, the span stretches about five miles over 34 water piers. Its two main towers extend 552 feet above the water. Don't worry if the thought frightens you; bridge personnel will drive you across if absolutely necessary.

Other area attractions include beautiful Mackinac Island, its 1780-acre Mackinac Island State Park, Fort Mackinac State Park—a National Historic Landmark—and the island's famed 343-room Grand Hotel. Other sights are the Marquette Mission Park and Museum of Ojibwa Culture in St. Ignace, Colonial Michimackinac, and Historic Mill Creek in Mackinaw City.

From mid-May through mid-October, costumed guides at Fort Mackinac portray early American soldiers. They perform military music presentations and rifle and cannon demonstrations. You can also tour 14 original fort buildings, housing historic exhibits.

Access to Mackinac Island is easy thanks to several ferry services, including Arnold Mackinac Island Ferry (800/542-8528), Shepler's Mackinaw Island Ferry (800/828-6157), and Star Line Mackinac Island Ferry (800/638-9892).

Camping Tips

Camping Destinations

Is that vacant lot you remember as your childhood softball field now a high-rise apartment complex? What about the corner drugstore? Is it part of a strip mall? What about the beach where you collected pebbles and a sunburn? Is it part of a marina and lined with shoreline condos? Is there any place left where you can enjoy nature?

Fortunately, some people had the vision to set aside parcels of prime land where we can still get close to nature: our national, state, and community parks. Many offer beautiful places to camp.

Although most national and state campgrounds have a lot to offer, some private campgrounds may be more convenient to interesting attractions. Also, some private facilities provide amenities not found in many national or state campgrounds, including restaurants and a variety of recreational facilities, such as swimming pools, tennis courts, and golf courses. They also might be within walking distance of retail stores.

The National Park System

Strange as it may seem, a large number of Americans do not know there is a National Park Service and that the system comprises nearly 400 areas or units. These areas of historic, cultural, natural, scenic, and scientific importance include resources that are of such national significance that they have received special protection by various acts of the United States Congress.

For example, there are less than a handful of National Lakeshores. The Apostle Islands, where Wisconsin's northernmost landscape juts out into Lake Superior, includes 21 islands and 12 miles of mainland shoreline, featuring pristine stretches of sand beach, spectacular sea caves, remnant old-growth forests, resident bald eagles and black bears, and the largest collection of lighthouses anywhere in the National Park System.

Today, most National Park units offer campgrounds that provide a range of camping experiences, from backcountry primitive sites to accommodations for the well-equipped recreational vehicle.

There are six NPS units in Minnesota, four in Michigan, and three in Wisconsin.

Great Lakes Wildlife

There are some 50 species of mammals in the Great Lakes region, including the largest population of timber wolves in the continental U.S. Other wildlife includes whitetail deer, moose, and black bears. More than 200 species of birds can be found, including the common loon, bald eagle, osprey, and great blue heron.

NPS Designations

Visitors are often confused by the numerous designations within the National Park System. The names are created in the Congressional legislation authorizing the sites or by the president, who proclaims "national monuments" under the Antiquities Act of 1906. Many names are simply descriptive—lakeshores, seashores, battlefields, scenic trails, and parkways—but others cannot be neatly categorized.

Facilities and Fees

There are 25,700 campsites in 548 campgrounds found at 77 areas of the National Park Service system. These sites can accommodate most every camping style from tent camping and recreational vehicle spaces to more primitive types of camping such as backcountry.

The largest area in the National Park System is Wrangell-St. Elias National Park and Preserve in Alaska. At 13.2 million acres, it composes 16.3 percent of the entire system. The smallest unit is Thaddeus Kosciuszko National Memorial in Pennsylvania, which is 0.02 of an acre.

Disabled persons: Many parks offer help for those who have visual, auditory, or other physical limitations. Most have parking lots, restrooms, and other features that are wheelchair-accessible.

Campsites: Campsite fees vary, so check with the campground you plan to visit ahead of time. Developed area campsites have drinking water, toilets, fire containment devices, tables, refuse containers, and limited parking spaces. Utility hookups are not usually available. *Lodging:* In-park lodges are run by individual concession contracts. Contractors operate their own reservation systems so check with the park by calling or writing for specific lodging information.

Trailers/Campers: Maximum length for trailers, campers, and motor homes vary from park to park. The average maximum length permitted is 27 feet, but some parks can accommodate vehicles up to 40 feet in length; you should check with the park you're planning to visit for specific maximum lengths so you won't be disappointed when you arrive. There are no electrical or water hookups at campsites. Some parks may have disposal stations.

Park Passports: Many National Park Service areas charge entrance fees. If your trip takes you to several parks or you go camping frequently, you can save a little by buying the *Golden Eagle Passport,* an entrance pass to national parks, monuments, historic sites, recreation areas, and national wildlife refuges that charge an entrance fee. It costs $50, is valid for one year, and admits the passholder and any accompanying passengers in a private vehicle. Where entry isn't by vehicle, it admits the passholder, spouse, children, and parents. It does not cover or reduce use fees. The Golden Eagle Passport can be bought at any NPS entrance fee area or by mail. Send a $50 check or money order to: National Park Service, Attention: Golden Eagle Passport, 1100 Ohio Dr. SW, Room 138, Washington, DC 20242.

Senior citizens are eligible for a discounted lifetime pass and disabled persons qualify for free passes. The *Golden Age Passport* is an entrance pass for those 62 years or older. It has a one-time charge of $10 and you must buy it in person, showing proof of age. You must also be a citizen or permanent U.S. resident. This passport also provides a 50 percent discount on federal use fees charged for

Bison Herds Return

Recently, 30 Plains bison were released into a 130-acre area of restored native prairie at the Big Stone National Wildlife Refuge (320/273-2191) near Odessa, Minnesota. The bison herds, once numbering 60 million animals across North America, have been absent from the Minnesota prairies for nearly 150 years. The Big Stone refuge is the only national wildlife refuge in Minnesota, and one of the only two in the Midwest, hosting bison. A herd has been also released at Blue Mounds State Park by the Minnesota Department of Natural Resources.

Like the rest of western Minnesota and Iowa, the region was once native tallgrass prairie. After European settlement, it was plowed and farmed for over a century. Coming full circle, the restored prairie is now the summer and fall home for these giant prairie icons, which can weigh up to 1,500 pounds.

facilities and services. It doesn't, however, cover or reduce special recreation permit fees or fees charged by concessionaires.

Reservations

Most parks operate their campgrounds on a first-come, first-served basis.
To make reservations, contact the National Park Service at 800/365-2267 or visit its website: www.reservations.nps.gov.

For More Information

Always plan ahead. Write to the Department of the Interior, National Park Service, Office of Public Inquiries, P.O. Box 37127, Room 1013, Washington, DC 20013-7127 or call 202/208-4747, Mon.-Fri. 9 A.M.–3 P.M. (EST) for general information or to obtain specific park brochures.

The easiest method to obtain more specific information is to contact the park directly. A park's homepage on the Internet has specific information to help you plan your trip. Also, you can visit the NPS's website at www.reservations.nps.gov and navigate its search engine for more information on campsites and availability.

If you want to avoid crowds, get a copy of *Lesser Known Areas of the National Park System*, which highlights nearly 170 areas. Send a check or money order for $1.50 payable to the Superintendent of Documents, Consumer Information Center, Department 134b, Pueblo, CO 81009.

Make the visitors center of the park you're visiting your first stop. Here, you will find information on attractions, facilities, and activities, such as scenic drives, nature trails, and historic tours. Brochures or exhibits can acquaint you with the geology, history, and plant and animal life of the area.

In general, here are some facts to keep in mind when camping within the National Park System:

- Some parks offer year-round camping while others have specific dates of operation.
- Campsite use fees vary.

- Developed area campsites have drinking water, toilets, fire containment devices, tables, refuse containers, and limited parking spaces. Generally, utility hookups are not available.
- Backcountry camping requires a permit.
- Gathering of firewood is generally restricted, except in certain areas (check with a park ranger). In some parks, the use of campfires may be restricted to protect air quality or due to extreme wild fire danger.
- In parks where bears are present, the superintendent may designate areas where food must be stored in a specified manner to prevent its loss or to avoid an encounter with a potentially dangerous wild animal.
- You must camp only in designated areas.

Other National Camping Areas

The **U.S. Department of Agriculture's Forest Service** boasts more than 4,000 campgrounds nationwide in over 150 forests, covering nearly 200 million acres of land with about 125,000 miles of trails, 128,000 miles of streams and rivers, 16,500 miles of coasts and shorelines, and 2.2 million acres of lakes. There are many National Forests in the Great Lakes region. A list of campgrounds in National Forests is available free by writing the USDA Forest Service, Public Affairs Office, P.O. Box 96090, Washington, DC 20090-6090.

There are also more than 53,000 campsites near oceans, rivers, and lakes created through **U.S. Army Corps of Engineers** projects. To get a series of brochures, write to USACE Publication Depot, 2803 52nd Ave., Hyattsville, MD 20781-1102 and indicate your region of interest. The NRRS, described above, also handles reservations for Corps projects campsites.

Reservations can be made through the National Recreation Reservation Service (NRRS), a joint program of the Forest Service and U.S. Army Corps of Engineers. With nearly 60,000 camping facilities to choose from at more than 1,700 locations, the NRRS is the largest camping reservation service in North America. It provides a one-stop resource for those who want to reserve camping facilities managed by these two agencies.

To contact NRRS, call 877/444-6777 or visit its website: www.reserveusa.com. You'll be asked for the following information:
- Campground name or state where you plan to camp
- Arrival and departure dates
- Type of site required (tent, RV, cabin, etc.)
- Your name, address, and telephone number
- Method of payment (certified check or VISA, MasterCard, AMEX, or Discover)

Camping at the more than 500 **National Wildlife Refuges** is allowed if compatible with conservation efforts at each location. A free list of refuges that permit camping is included in *National Wildlife Refuges—A Visitor's Guide,* which describes facilities and activities. You can get a copy from the U.S. Fish and Wildlife Service, National Wildlife Conservation Training Center, Shepherd Grade Rd., Rt. 1, Box 166, Shepherdstown, WV 25443, 800/344-9453.

State Forests and Parks, and Municipal Campgrounds

The administration of state forest and park campgrounds, as well as city-managed facilities, vary from state to state. Information on these sites is covered under each state section.

Private and Commercial Campgrounds

There are about 8,500 privately owned campgrounds located near national parks, forests, and tourist attractions, along Interstate routes, and in cities and small towns. Many are also vacation destinations offering family-oriented activities.

There are several campground chains. Kampgrounds of America (KOA) (550 N. 31st St., Ste. 400, Billings, MT 59101, 406/248-7444; website: www. camp-grounds.com) is North America's largest chain. In addition, there are Best Holiday Trav-L-Park Association (1310 Jarvis Ave., Elk Grove Village, IL 60007, 800/323-8899) and Leisure Systems, Inc./Yogi Bear's Jellystone Park Camp-Resorts (6201 Kellogg Ave., Cincinnati, OH 45228, 513/232-6800). Each provides directories of the location and facilities offered.

Private campgrounds along Interstate highways cater to the overnight camper and provide clean campsites and facilities. They usually offer friendly and helpful assistance. Some also provide entertainment that draws a return group of campers. Most will make allowances for the late-arriving camper with emergency spaces to park for the night.

Destination campgrounds are usually located off the beaten path—on a lake, river, or mountainside—offering campers swimming, boating, fishing, hiking, or biking opportunities. Many of these campgrounds have innovative programs that cater to families—pancake breakfasts, barbecues, hayrides, and holiday festivities. These campgrounds, however, are generally booked up during peak periods and require a reservation.

Camping Options

The most basic consideration is what kind of shelter you like and can afford to use when camping. Let's look at your options:

Tent Camping

Tents have survived the test of time. Some of the earliest recorded uses are the black goat-hair shelters used by nomadic people in Asia. Native Americans used birch bark to build wigwams, tentlike dwellings, and the skins of animals to construct teepees. Tents served as lodging for trailblazers like Lewis and Clark, and settlers moving west traveled in the Conestoga wagons—tents-on-wheels. Over the years, military units have bi-vouacked, revivals have gathered, and circuses have performed in tents. What child doesn't drape a blanket over a clothesline and camp in the backyard?

If you began your tenting days in the 1940s, your mental image may still be of a canvas tent that was sturdy, but bulky and a chore to erect. Today's geodesic dome tents, with design features including lightweight aluminum frames; strong, ripstop-nylon fabrics for siding; water-, mildew-, and puncture-resistant floors; and no-see-um netting that lets air in and keeps bugs out, are a vast improvement.

Selecting a Tent

What's the right tent for you? That depends on who's carrying the tent—you or your vehicle. If you're backpacking or biking, you want a lightweight, compact A-frame; self-supporting rectangular; or Coleman's innovative Pole Talon tent, which provides a peg-like anchor that snaps snugly into the tubular aluminum tent poles. It attaches the pole to sturdy webbing straps affixed to the tent floor corners, holding them firmly in place. These types of tents can sleep one to four people and break down into sections that are small (and light) enough to fit into bicycle panniers or a backpack.

For maximum dryness, look for tents that are made with polyurethane-coated fabric, have taped inverted seams, and come with a tapered rainfly, which keeps water from seeping through the main seam. Depending on size and style, expect to pay from $60 to $300 for a good tent. A cheap tent that leaks is no fun and no bargain.

Rapidly becoming the most popular family tent are the **umbrella** and **spider-frame** models. Supported with an aluminum or fiberglass frame, they are as easy to put up and take down as a umbrella, and the self-supporting four-pole umbrella with center "spider" provides for heights ranging from four feet, eight inches to more than seven feet. Extra features to be considered are awnings or net enclosures for sheltered meals and lounging, fly-door coverings for extra wind and rain protection, and built-in vestibules for extra storage. The more traditional **cabin tent** is still preferred by large families or groups and for dining tents because of their height and straight sides.

If you haven't slept over-night or taken shelter from bad weather in a tent, don't select one from a catalog. Go to a store that has basic styles set up and give them a try. You won't feel as silly stretching out or sitting cross-legged inside a display tent as you will trying to do this on your first camping trip. No matter what style you choose, the three most important questions to ask a salesperson are: How easy is the tent to erect? Will it last through years of regular use? and Will it keep me dry? You can count on getting all three of these functions when buying a quality tent made by major manufacturers, including American Camper, Cabela's, Coleman, or Eureka.

Selecting a Sleeping Bag

We've seen campers who spent hours trying to spread out their at-home linens only to have them crumpled into a pile during the night leaving them quite uncomfortable. Whether we camp in our tent or in a folding RV, we prefer to crawl into our sleeping bags for a cozy night's sleep.

Shapes and Sizes

Sleeping bags are classified by shape. The most popular shapes are the mummy or tapered, the modified tapered or barrel, and rectangular.

The **mummy** bag is the most efficient for saving space and keeping you comfortable because it hugs your body and eliminates the air space around you. The **modified tapered** bag offers many of the advantages of the mummy bag, but it's slightly roomier. Coleman's new OmniTemp bag can be converted from a rectangular to a mummy bag and vice versa.

The **rectangular** bag gives you the most flexibility and room. Two rectangular bags can often be zipped together to make a double-sized van bag for two people. Tapering the rectangular bag in slightly at the foot to form a **barrel** bag leaves more room inside the tent or RV and provides greater warmth. We like our Adam-and-Eve-style van bag.

In addition to shapes, sleeping bags come in various sizes. A **standard** or single bag is designed for one average-size person. A **double** bag is large enough for two people, while **tall** or oversized bags are best for the larger-than-average camper.

Insulation is an important part of a sleeping bag and is often a major factor in determining the bag's price. The primary function of insulation is to trap dead air space between you and the outside environment.

Goose down is considered the best insulation material because it traps air between the down clusters and creates hundreds of tiny dead air pockets. Most sleeping bags, however, are insulated with synthetic materials such as Quallofil, which is made of tubelike hollow fibers. These tubes trap air and make the fibers act like down. Dacron Hollofil is also a fiber with hollow spaces, but it has fewer of these "dead" air spaces; these fibers are usually used in bags designed for warmer conditions. One advantage of synthetic fibers over goose down is that they provide better insulation when damp. Synthetics also dry faster and are more mold- and mildew-resistant.

In selecting a sleeping bag, the materials and construction of the cover and lining are just as important as they are for a tent's siding and flooring. Woven nylon and polyester are popular materials for a bag's cover and lining. These materials

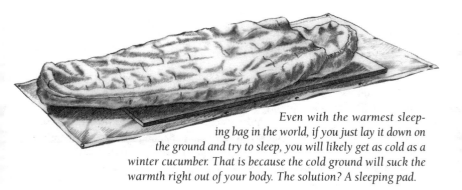

Even with the warmest sleeping bag in the world, if you just lay it down on the ground and try to sleep, you will likely get as cold as a winter cucumber. That is because the cold ground will suck the warmth right out of your body. The solution? A sleeping pad.

are comfortable, durable, and attractive. For added comfort and warmth, Coleman features a zip-in, zip-out fleece liner. If you frequently camp in damp or rainy locations, you may want to select a waterproof, breathable material like Gore-Tex.

Other Features

Some additional features to check in a quality sleeping bag are quilting, which prevents insulation from shifting and creating cold spots; a heavy-duty zipper that will work without snagging the fabric; wedges at the zipper base to keep out cold air; and baffle-fit ends for foot warmth.

Who says the ground has to be hard? Some campers place a portable cot, egg crate-pattern foam, plain polyethylene pad, or an inflatable mattress under their sleeping bags. These additions not only soften your sleeping spot, but also keep dampness and cold from reaching you.

Expect the same quality in your sleeping bag as you do in your tent. Products you can count on are made by American Camper, Bass Pro Shop's Redhead brand, Cabela's, Coleman, and Slumberjack. Your camping equipment doesn't have to be the most expensive, but quality items made by quality companies will provide many long hours of happy camping.

RV Camping

According to the Recreational Vehicle Industry Association (RVIA), the national association of RV manufacturers and component suppliers, there are about 9.3 million RVs in the United States—one in 10 vehicle-owning households owns an RV. The average owner is 48 years old, owns a home, has a household income just under $40,000, and buys an RV to travel and camp.

Your RV selection should fit the type, duration, and location of camping you plan to do as well as your budget. There are two general categories of RVs—towables (folding campers, travel trailers, fifth-wheels, and truck campers) and motorized RVs (motor homes and van conversions). Whether you purchase a used or new RV, there is a substantially larger investment than buying a tent, sleeping bag, camp stove, and a few pots and pans. Therefore, you should do your homework before rushing out to buy your first RV. Renting various types of RVs is an excellent way to get your feet wet. Some local RV dealers have rental units and Cruise America has 250 rental stations throughout America. Contact the company at 800/327-7799, fax 480/464-7321; email: info@cruiseamerica.com; website: www.cruiseamerica.com.

Begin your search at campgrounds. Why? Because RVers love to talk about their rigs. Listen to the pros and cons about various models and do some camping in a similar rental unit before you buy.

One in 10 vehicle-owning households owns an RV.

Attending a consumer show is another way to find out about RVs. A consumer show often gathers RVs of all makes and types under one roof. Manufacturer representatives are usually on hand to answer questions, and sometimes, you can get a good deal on demonstration models.

This kind of shopping is best after you've narrowed your selection down to a single type of RV and just need to compare the features offered by different manufacturers. Visit your local RV dealer for a demonstration drive.

Another option is to purchase a used model from a local dealer or individual. To make sure you get a trouble-free vehicle, look for water stains on walls or on canvas or vinyl siding. Check kitchen and bathroom water faucets, as well as the toilet, for leaks. Fill the water storage tank and gray-water (waste) tank and check for leaks. Be sure the skin or outer covering is not dented or ripped. If the RV is motorized, have an experienced mechanic check the engine's condition.

RVs You Can Tow

Towable RVs come in a wide range of styles, sizes, and prices. The most economical and easiest to pull is the folding camper. This compact little unit is lightweight, designed to make the most of space and storage, and can sleep up to eight people. It requires little maintenance and can be easily stored. Because of its light weight, there is only a small decrease in gas mileage while towing.

Although a folding camper is relatively easy to set up—usually requiring no more than 10 minutes—it can be difficult for some older people to manage. Other disadvantages might be the occasional presence of dampness, smoke, and pollens because of its screened, vinyl sides. The average cost of simple folding campers is $4,000 to $5,000.

A high-low style is becoming popular. This type, which features solid metal sides, boasts a low profile for towing, but cranks up so you can stand in it.

The most luxurious of towable RVs are the travel trailer and the fifth-wheel. Travel trailers range from 12 to 35 feet and are towed by means of a bumper or frame hitch attached to the towing vehicle. With bedroom, full bath, and living room area, these vehicles offer you all the comforts of home. A fifth-wheel RV ranges in length from 24 to 35 feet and is built with a higher forward section that fits over the bed of a full-size pickup truck where the fifth-wheel hitch is located. This type of configuration provides a bi-level floor plan. Because the pivot point is over the truck's axle, a rather large fifth-wheel trailer can be towed easily. The average cost of a travel trailer is about $13,000, while a fifth-wheel model averages $20,000 or more.

More Americans Making Road Trips

As more Americans opt for driving vacations within the United States, many are trying RVing for the first time and discovering the freedom, flexibility and control that recreational vehicles offer. Since October 2001, RV rentals have increased 30 to 40 percent for the nation's two largest RV rental agencies.

Another option is the truck camper. This type is designed to be loaded onto or affixed to a truck. Although limited in length, these are usually well-designed compact units and, like the fifth-wheel trailer, can be removed and anchored to a stand in a campground or at home. The average truck camper unit is about $10,000.

A towable RV is popular because it offers great flexibility. Keep in mind that although RVs you can tow require more driving skill than a motorized RV, the former provides you with a unit that can stay at the campground without having to unhook cords, water lines, or sewer connections to leave the site. This makes them especially suited for long-term vacationing.

Be certain, however, that your towing vehicle is compatible to the RV. Automakers offer a large selection of tow vehicles—conversion vehicles, sport utility vehicles (SUVs), light trucks, and full-size and some smaller cars. Check your auto manual for towing ratings. Most newer vehicles have engineering packages that provide more efficient towing power, superior maneuverability, and braking. If you're towing an RV in a mountainous area, getting up the mountain isn't nearly the challenge that stopping at the bottom can be.

It's rare that someone purchases a new RV and towing vehicle at the same time. If you have a fairly new towing vehicle, you need to buy an RV that matches your vehicle's towing ability. Minivans, SUVs and most six-cylinder automobiles can safely tow lightweight travel trailers and folding campers.

If you're in the market for a new vehicle and have future plans for an RV or a change in your current RV, shop for a vehicle that has a towing capacity adequate for your planned purchase. The RVIA suggests you discuss these basic factors with your RV and auto dealers when evaluating trailer/tow vehicle options: engine horsepower, transmission and axle capacity, cooling equipment, suspension, springs and shocks, power brakes, power steering, and battery capacity. Also seek advice on the type of hitch and anti-sway device to use, which are the keys to a safe towing system.

Motorized RVs
A motorized RV is built on or is part of a self-propelled vehicle chassis. This type is available in a wide range of sizes, styles, and prices. A Class A motor home is constructed on a specially designed chassis ranging from 22 to 40 feet. The average selling price is about $80,000.

Although classy-looking coming down the road, loaded with every comfort of home and easy to drive, this kind of vehicle often presents problems in parking and maneuvering in tight places, and uses more gas, an important consideration.

The Class C—mini, low profile, or compact—motor home is built on an automotive-manufactured van frame with an attached cab section. It usually ranges from 20 to 27 feet in length and offers much more living space than the van camper. While there is some reduction in gas mileage as compared to the van camper, it is not as great as a Class A motor home. Most Class C motor homes average about $45,000, which gives you luxury motorized RVing at a great price.

Another motorized RV that is gaining in popularity is the van camper, which is a panel-type truck. It may be custom-converted by the manufacturer, converted locally at a van shop, or self-converted as a family project. Ranging from about 17 to 19 feet, this kind of RV offers roominess and comfort. It is also easy to drive and park, and obtains good gas mileage as compared to most motorized RVs. The van camper is an excellent option for two people on a long sight-seeing trip because it's only needed for travel, overnight sleeping, and basic meals. They average $29,000, which offers a lot of camping for the money.

When buying an RV, consult a reputable dealer, do a lot of comparative shopping, and look for the RIVA seal. The seal is an oval-shaped emblem displayed prominently on the exterior of motor homes, travel trailers, truck campers, and folding campers. It indicates that the manufacturer has complied with more than 500 safety specifications for electrical, plumbing, and heating/fire and life safety established under the auspices of the American National Standards Institute.

A free *Getting Started* videotape with information on RV shopping, rental, and travel tips plus a list of dealers is available by calling 888/467-8464. More detailed information, including a free booklet on *Choosing and Using Your RV,* can be obtained from RVIA, P.O. Box 2999, Reston, VA 20195.

Financing and Insurance
Selecting your RV can be a lot of fun, but financing it is another story. Most RV dealerships require a 10 to 20 percent down payment with direct financing either through the manufacturer or a local bank. Some dealers offer indirect financing handled by the dealership. In most areas, expect to pay a 10to 20 percent interest rate.

Because your RV is a specialized vehicle with unique insurance needs be certain your insurance coverage is complete. A motor home policy should cover liability, comprehensive and collision coverage, emergency living expenses, furnishings, fixtures, and appliances, as well as towing and labor costs, fire department service charges, and uninsured motorist insurance against loss.

Insurance for travel trailers, truck campers, and folding campers should include all-risk comprehensive coverage, vacation liability for emergency motel and meal expenses, towing, and fire department services. Optional coverage against theft or damage to personal items should be considered.

For traveling to a foreign country, make sure your policy will cover your trip. Many insurance companies include coverage for Canada, but not for Mexico.

Winter Camping

Most people camp during their vacations or on weekends in spring, summer, and fall, but a growing number are taking advantage of the *fourth season*—winter. Depending on where you live, winter camping may seem to be a foolish endeavor, but just think about the number of people who enjoy winter outdoor recreation such as cross-country skiing, ice fishing, hunting, snowmobiling, and snowshoeing. Why not combine your favorite winter sport with winter camping?

True, it's an advanced and challenging adventure, and the winter camper has a respect for nature that the summer camper may never have. For those who have never attempted it, winter camping is difficult to explain. There is such a wonderful feeling of solitude, lying in a shelter on a cold winter night accompanied by the sound of wind howling through a forest.

Cold-weather Clothing

Dressing properly for winter conditions is vital. The key is to wear multiple layers of clothing to keep you warm and comfortable.

Modern underwear made from polyester or polypropylene is effective in moving moisture away from your skin and into outer layers where it can evaporate. These undergarments can consist of the traditional "longjohns" or t-shirts, bras, boxer shorts, or briefs. Underwear should fit snugly, but not restrict your movements. Many winter campers add a middle layer of polyester fleece (pants and top) and a windproof (just keeps out the wind), water-resistant (offers some protection against rain) or waterproof (keeps out the rain) outer layer (pants and anorak) for ultimate comfort and protection. Even if the forecast doesn't predict bad weather, be prepared for severe weather by packing a waterproof
rain jacket and pants. For true warmth in the coolest conditions, be sure your outer layer of a vest or parka is made of nylon with a waterproof PVC coating.

Because much of your body heat escapes through your neck and head, carry a hat with you for added warmth or protection from the sun.

Protecting Fingers and Toes

No matter what type of footwear your winter outdoor sport requires, Gore-Tex footwear has designed the right boot for the activity. The three- or five-layer construction of its boots provides a wafer-thin membrane with billions of minute pores. This allows body moisture, in the form of water vapor, to escape while preventing wind and rain penetration.

For comfort and blister prevention, wear two layers of socks: a thin polyester sock liner and a thicker outer sock. And be certain to bring along spare socks in case yours become soggy.

In the same way you can keep your toes toasty you can also keep your fingers cozy. There are many styles of gloves that provide warmth, such as those with Wu-lusion fleece. Durability and quick drying on the outer shell are other factors to consider. The Dry-Plus insert is 100 percent waterproof and provides extreme breathability with the dexterity needed for hikers, skiers, and ice-anglers.

Sub-zero Sleeping Bags

A sleeping bag acts as an insulator to slow the loss of body warmth. How well it does this depends on its material, construction, and amount of loft.

Choose a sleeping bag that has a temperature rating based on the conditions in which you plan to camp most often. Its rating indicates the *lowest* temperature at which an occupant would be comfortable. Keep in mind that the rating assumes the bag will be used with a ground pad. Also, some people tend to be colder than others when sleeping and might therefore want a warmer, or lower-rated, sleeping bag.

A bag rated to 0°F, with ground pad, is used for cold-weather and some winter camping. Bags rated from -15°F to -30°F, with ground pad, are suitable for most winter camping conditions.

Sleeping bags filled with down cost more and are difficult to dry when damp or wet, but contain the best natural insulators known. Since most bags come with a nylon taffeta lining, buy a fleece liner, which adds extra softness and about 15 to 20 additional degrees of warmth.

Hypothermia and Frostbite

Hypothermia and frostbite can occur when you are exposed for a prolonged time to extreme cold and the body's temperature drops below 90°F, or when extremities such as fingers, toes, ears or nose, freeze.

Watch for signs of hypothermia: uncontrolled shivering, poor motor coordination, mental confusion, and mumbling. If someone has these symptoms, get him or her into dry clothing or a sleeping bag and have the individual huddle next to a warm, dry person. Encourage warm beverages—never alcohol!

Check for signs of frostbite and pay close attention to cold feet. The first sign is white patches on the skin surface. If the skin color doesn't return to normal after applying gentle pressure, seek medical attention at once.

Winter is not the time to camp alone; always camp with others. Since winter weather is often unpredictable, plan on the unexpected, such as being snowed in—just in case. Pack an extra stove, plenty of fuel, and enough provisions to last an additional week. Keep yourself hydrated with hot soups and beverages during winter trips; caffeinated drinks are not recommended.

Tip: Leave your camping itinerary with a friend or family member and check in with them on your return.

Water, Food, and Cooking Gear

There are two basic types of camp cooking—outdoors and indoors—and there are a variety of techniques to make each of them easy.

When you are tent camping, the outdoors is your only kitchen. Many RVers also enjoy preparing some of their meals outdoors. Cooking over an open fire made in a pit or an old tire rim takes a little more talent than using a propane, charcoal, or solid-fuel camping stove. In this case, you have to cook without a knob to regulate flame height or a thermostat to control the heat. To do any camp cooking, it takes fuel, a container for the fire, and containers to hold the food.

Food Prep at Home

Preparing parts of meals before you leave home saves time. Make your favorite sauces, like spaghetti, before you even hit the road. Once the sauce has cooled, pour it into a clean, dry quart or half-gallon waxed milk carton. Fold the top down and cover with foil or freezer paper and label it. Then, freeze it until it's a solid block. This will probably thaw in a day or two in your cooler; if you need it before then, tear off the carton and place the block in a heavy pot with a small amount of water and heat until it is ready for serving. This method also provides you with blocks of ice for your cooler.

Precooking

Many meats can be precooked at home for shorter cooking times at the campsite. To do this, cook ground beef or ground turkey in a frying pan. When cooked, pour the meat into a large bowl or strainer lined with several layers of paper towels. Allow the fat to drain into the paper towels. Blot the meat, and when cool, spoon it into plastic sandwich bags. Each bag should contain enough for a casserole or sloppy joe sandwiches. Place several of these small bags of meat into a larger plastic freezer bag and freeze. Cooked meat keeps longer and saves time when you have to prepare a meal.

Preventing Spoilage

Most backpackers and bikers use dried or canned food, which is supplemented with fresh food whenever possible. Campers traveling light who need to carry a few fresh food supplies should purchase a collapsible, insulated, and leakproof chest cooler. Coleman makes one that can be carried by its handles or shoulder strap and can fold down for easy storage with the lid's elastic bands.

Tip: Create your first supply of ice at home by filling plastic half-gallon containers with water and freezing them; you'll have safe drinking water when the ice melts.

The icebox or cooler is the basic cold-storage unit for most who camp in tents or folding campers. These come in various sizes and styles, but a top-opening, chest-style storage unit is the most efficient. You'll want to use block ice, which lasts longer than cubes. To extend its life, divide a block into two pieces. Wrap each piece in several layers of newspaper and place each in a plastic bag. This slows down the melting time and will keep the water from filling the chest and softening containers. Place the two blocks on opposite ends of the cooler. You will probably need to add ice to the chest daily.

If possible, food should be frozen or cold before being placed in the cooler. Because the bottom of the chest will be colder than the top, packaged frozen meat should be placed in a single layer across the bottom followed by other frozen goods. Items that are slowest to spoil, such as eggs, cheese and produce, should be put on top.

Because meat spoils easily, precook as much of it as possible. Plan your meals so you use perishable meats first. There are many good canned meats—ham, hash, chicken, salmon, and tuna—that can be used to make delicious meals as your trip progresses. And stopping to purchase additional fresh meat or cooking the fish that you catch will add variety.

Larger RVs and many folding campers have electric refrigerators that run off your propane tank while traveling and then convert to electricity while you're in a campground. Coleman makes several thermoelectric coolers that cool to 44°F below ambient temperature or can be reversed to keep foods warmer than 100°F above ambient temperature. These models will operate off your RV transformer or with a power supply attachment that converts house current.

Cooking at Camp

Today's camper knows that camp food—whether cooked over an open fire, on a camp stove, or in the microwave—can be delicious, nutritious, and designed to follow any low-fat, low-sodium, or low-carbohydrate diet without taking the fun out of camp cooking. The basic ingredients for any hearty meal are meat (optional), vegetables—including a few starchy ones—liquid, and seasoning. The healthiest meals are made by cooking fresh vegetables and meat or by adding prepared meats to vegetable broth. Keep a lookout for produce stands or "U-Pick-Em" farms while on the road. Such stops offer a refreshing break to traveling, help conserve storage space, and offer lots of nutritious foods.

Open-pit Cooking

To build a fire for camp cooking, you'll need wood or charcoal, matches, and some means of starting the fire. There are several fire-starters available; the safest are solid-material starters such as Fat-sticks. A wood or charcoal fire does not provide instant cooking heat and they burn somewhat differently than your camp stove. Only practice makes this type of cooking perfect.

For cooking over a fire pit, you need a grate with adjustable heights. Most outfits come with a tripod stand for a large cooking pot. Cast-iron cookware, although heavy, produces the best results. Because quality pieces like those made by Lodge are expensive, but worth every penny, you can start with just a few items. A good starter set should include a Dutch oven with recessed lid, smaller pot with snap-on handle, fry pan, and a lid remover.

Use a Fire Pit

If there's a fire pit or fire ring in your campsite, use it—it will limit your impact on the environment.

When there's no fire ring, build your fire on hard-packed dirt or sandy ground, away from all vegetation. Scrape the fire site until only non-flammable soil is exposed. Bring a non-flammable cook surface like an iron frying pan or a sheet of heavy tinfoil to build a fire and protect the ground from harm and make clean-up chores easier.

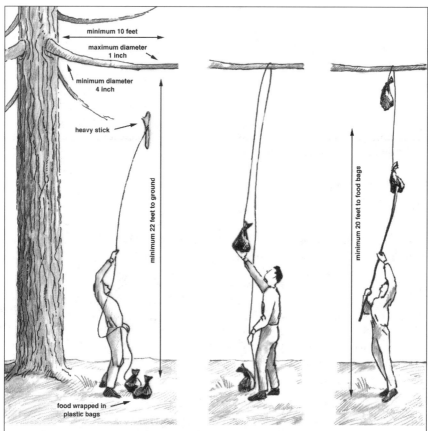

*In an area frequented by bears, a good **bear-proof food hang** is a must. Food should be stored in a plastic bag 10 feet from the trunk of the tree and at least 20 feet from the ground.*

Everything from roast duck to hunter's stew can be made in a Dutch oven placed directly on hot coals with additional coals placed on the lid. Cooking time, however, will vary with the size and heat of the fire. A meat thermometer is a must because all meat should be cooked until its internal temperature reaches 180°F. This type of cooking is slow so don't plan to eat soon after starting your fire—unless you just throw some burgers, franks, or steaks on the fire. Some foods like corn-on-the-cob can be placed directly on the coals, but keep it wrapped in its husk or in foil.

Slow-Cooking

Don't leave home without your crock pot. There's nothing like a slow-cooked stew, pot roast, chili, or homemade soup that's been cooking while you were out fishing or sight-seeing.

One of our favorite camping meals is Stone Soup. Like the little man in the children's legend who produced a meal for the disgruntled village people, you can produce a pot of the most delicious soup with almost nothing.

Start with fresh vegetables: sliced potatoes, carrots, celery with leaves, green pepper, onion, and water. Cook until all the vegetables are tender. Throw in leftover meat—even cooked hamburger is good—or leave it meatless. Add a can of tomatoes and a can of tomato soup, and/or a can of beef consommé. Adding noodles or rice is optional. Served with bread and butter, this is an all-you-can-eat meal. If you left your crock pot at home, any heavy pot on your camp stove over a very low burner will also work.

Pouch Meals

Pouch meals can be prepared over an open fire, on the stove top, or in the oven. Flank, skirt, or any thin cut of steak is excellent, as well as fish and poultry. Begin with a foil cooking pouch or several layers of heavy-duty foil. Place the meat on the bottom and layer vegetables over it, topping it off with your favorite barbecue sauce. Fold the foil together leaving an air space. Place the pouch on a grill, in a heavy pan on your stove top, or in your camp oven. Bake for about 30 minutes or until all the ingredients are tender. The pouch should puff up as it cooks.

One of our favorite pouch meals is kabobs. First, brown chunks of beef or ground meat balls in your grill's burger basket. Then, arrange the cubes of meat or uncooked fish, alternating with chunks of onion, tomato, green pepper, and mushrooms. Top with a sauce made of white wine or grape juice; brown sugar or honey; barbecue sauce; and Italian salad dressing. When cooked, serve over rice or noodles.

Camp Stoves and Fuel

Camp stoves burn several different types of fuel. **Kerosene** is probably one of the oldest and is still in use. It is the most inexpensive and performs well at all temperatures and altitudes, but it requires priming and preheating.

White gas is inexpensive and can be carried in easily refillable fuel containers. It performs well at all temperatures and altitudes. Its power output can be increased by pumping, which some campers like to do.

Butane and **propane** come in pressurized containers. This eliminates pumping. A combination of these two fuels, such as Coleman's Powermax, has become popular recently because of its ease of handling and fast cooking capability.

More recently, American Camper, a Brunswick company, has introduced a new fuel, **Magic Heat**, which uses dyethylene glycol, a non-volatile fuel that ignites only with a wick. The recyclable aluminum canister can be resealed for repeated use. An 11-pound bottle with "tree" attachment can be used to operate your camp stove and lantern simultaneously.

If you don't have outdoor cooking equipment, examine what's on the market before buying. The amount of space you have available for equipment and the amount of cooking you'll be doing should determine your choice of gear.

Backpackers, hikers, and motorcyclists have little storage space. There are some excellent fuels and mini-stoves on the market designed for these campers, including Coleman's Peak 1 Micro or Backpacker stoves.

Cleaning Up

Camping is supposed to be fun for everyone—including the cook. If you follow the KISS (Keep It Simple Stupid) principle, you can provide delicious and nutritious meals quickly and have fun doing it.

If you are camping in a small RV, you will probably have a sink that you can fill with hot water heated on the stove. Because workspace is limited, set a small plastic container of clean water on a towel on your table or the top of the stove cover (if the stove is cool). Wash dishes in the sink, rinse them in the pan, and place them on the towel to drip-dry.

Many campers use disposable tableware, having only cooking utensils to clean after a meal. There are excellent disposable products available with good coatings so gravies and other liquids won't soak into a plate or bowl. When selecting tableware, remember your storage space. Plastic is great, but cheap plastic may chip and crack with heavy use. Coleman's enamelware cleans easily and is durable. Stick to basic pieces—plates, bowls, mugs, and silverware. Most cooking utensils can be placed on the table as serving

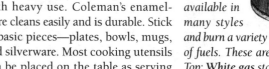

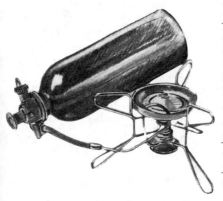

*Stoves are available in many styles and burn a variety of fuels. These are three typical examples. Top: **White gas** stoves are the most popular because they are inexpensive and easy to find; they do require priming and can be explosive. Middle: **Gas canister** stoves burn propane, butane, isobutane, and mixtures of the three. These are the easiest to use but have two disadvantages: 1) Because the fuel is bottled, determining how much fuel is left can be difficult. 2) The fuel is limited to above-freezing conditions. Bottom: **Liquid fuel** stoves burn Coleman fuel, denatured alcohol, kerosene, and even gasoline; these fuels are economical and have a high heat output, but most must be primed.*

dishes. There also are special sets of nesting cutlery if you are really short on storage space. We just use old they-don't-match-anymore knives, forks, and spoons from the kitchen.

Water Treatment

A stomachache is sometimes caused by what or how much you eat. However, it can also be caused by what you drink. Carry bottled water if you are unsure of the safety of the water.

Chemical Treatment

If you are tent camping, you will probably carry your water from the faucet to your campsite. Be certain the transporting container is clean. Rinse it out each day with a mild chlorine-and-water solution, and then keep it well capped when not in use.

If you're traveling in an RV and use a separate hose to hook up to the campsite water supply, pour a mild chlorine-and-water solution (1/4 cup chlorine per gallon of water) into the hose before each camping trip. With someone's help, lift and lower the hose so the solution runs the full length of the hose several times. Then attach it to the faucet and run water through the hose for several minutes. Or, if you're using water from your freshwater holding tank, you should sanitize your water system before the start of each camping season. Close the faucets and drain valves, and fill the water tanks with a solution of one cup of baking soda dissolved in five gallons of warm water for every 10 gallons of tank capacity. Agitate the solution by driving around for three or four miles. Drain the tank and flush with fresh water.

Water filters are a wise investment since all wilderness water should be considered contaminated. Make sure the filter can be easily cleaned or has a replaceable cartridge. The filter pores must be 0.4 microns or less to remove bacteria.

Packing Tips and Tricks

Packing and unpacking for a camping trip can be a nightmare. But if you stick with the essentials, it can be simple. For the best use of all camping storage space, think "layers" and use flexible storage bags that will conform to the shape of your space.

Because food and supplies are heavy and bulky, they

should be packed in an area that is convenient. They should also be layered. Do this by putting an assortment of nonperishable items—canned vegetables, dried fruit, and canned meats—into layers of one or two meals at a time. This will keep you from having to dig to the bottom of the boxes at each mealtime.

Place extra canned and boxed goods in can-high cardboard boxes. Keep all condiments in a separate box or container. Unless you have an airy storage area for fresh vegetables and fruits, keep them in mesh bags or old panty hose. Don't store them in plastic bags because they'll "sweat" in hot, humid places and the food will spoil.

For tent camping, Plano's large, plastic hardware boxes with drawers make excellent small, portable "kitchen cabinets." You can place plates, cups, and bowls in the spacious top section, and silverware and other utensils in the sliding drawers. When the top is closed and latched, the drawers are locked into place until you're ready to use them. If you prefer a larger storage area, buy a plastic toy or utility chest with a hinged lid. Paper napkins, silverware, cooking utensils, and condiments stored in see-through plastic containers can go straight from the utility box to the table.

If you don't have a sink, a double-sided plastic bucket provides a soapy-water wash and clear-water rinse all in one container. While traveling, damp and dry items can be stored separately in the pail.

Unless you're camping in a large RV, refrigerator or ice-box space will be limited. If you have freezer space, use it for individually wrapped frozen cooked or un-cooked meats. In an ice chest, keep items that spoil easily—mayonnaise, margarine or butter, luncheon meats—near the bottom next to the ice. When carrying liquids, put them in *screw-top* plastic containers. The movement of the vehicle makes liquids slosh around and pop-off lids will do just that: pop off.

Clothing and Weather Protection

"Camping is when I let my hair down, my shirt tail hang out, and leave my cell phone home. So why should I care what I wear?" is the common sentiment among campers. Though a camper doesn't need to go out and buy the latest camping fashions no matter what the outdoor catalogs say, there are some basic things to know about how to dress to make camping comfortable and safe.

Get Dressed

Before leaving on any camping trip, think about the expected weather conditions in your camping area and your planned activities. The biggest secret for being ready for all types of camping conditions is to think "layers."

You don't have to take lots of clothes to meet all kinds of situations and conditions. Add to your basic items (trousers, jeans, slacks, shorts, shirts, blouses, undergarments) a sweater, a jacket, and rain gear and you should be set. A well-planned outfit can take you comfortably to an unexpected, last-minute location.

When it's sunny outdoors you can throw together anything—your favorite t-shirt, shorts, and flip-flops and you're all set. No? No! Protecting our bodies from the sun's rays and from heat exhaustion is just as important as avoiding frostbite in the winter. Dark colors absorb heat and make us feel hot; on a hot day, wear light colors, especially white, which reflect heat and keep us cooler. Fabrics such as cotton or linen are made with a more open weave than knits and synthetics allowing for better perspiration absorption and airflow around the body.

Not only are light colors cooler in warm weather, they are also less attractive to stinging insects. A light covering of fabric also keeps the sun's rays from scorching your skin and leaving you with a painful sunburn.

It is also important to insulate your body against the cold when winter camping. The key to warmth is the body's "microclimate"—that layer of warm "dead" air closest to your skin. According to Gore, the manufacturer of Gore-Tex and "WindStopper" clothing, if your "microclimate" remains undisturbed, you have the sensation of "comfort." See **Winter Camping** for more information.

Waterproof: impervious to water. Though rain won't penetrate this material, if you're at all mobile you'll soon find yourself wet from perspiration that can't evaporate.

Water-resistant: resistant but not impervious to water. You'll stay dry using this material only if it isn't pouring.

Footwear

Save the flip-flops for a quick trip to the shower or pool. Your feet will thank you if they are well protected from rocks, falling objects, and long walks. Take comfortable shoes that protect and support your feet. Boots should have soles of shock-absorbing material. This is not the time to break in new shoes.

Packing Tips and Tricks

Clothing is necessary, but campers often take too much. Begin with basic slacks or jeans and matching shirts, sweaters, or sweatshirts. Top off with a jacket, preferably one that is wind- and water-resistant. Select only a few colors so everything will mix and match.

When clothes must be packed under the seats of your folding camper or in the trunk of your car, roll each item individually so it will remain wrinkle free. Place these clothing rolls and personal items in lightweight, nylon bags. The bags eliminate wasted space because they conform to the shape of most any storage place.

Towels and other linens should be packed in nylon drawstring bags that can become smaller as items are taken out. Give each member of your camping group a nylon mesh drawstring bag to store wet towels and dirty clothes after a trip to the shower/bathroom. This keeps you from losing something and provides airy storage for the laundry until it can be washed. A rubber bathtub mat is also a good idea for the floor in the dressing area of the shower room, which is often wet. The mat can be rolled and secured with a couple of rubber bands for storage.

If you must take a dressy outfit, a garment bag makes a good carrying case that can also be hung to minimize wrinkles.

Reserve the top of your vehicle or folding camper for bicycles, fishing rod case, skateboards, and surfboards—even a canoe or small boat.

Fishing rods can be easily and safely transported in hard-plastic rod cases that can be secured to the roof. Sporting goods stores like REI sell a variety of storage units for sporting equipment that will fit on top of a vehicle. These can also be obtained from U-Haul and other rental agencies.

Health and Safety

Illness, unfortunately, sometimes strikes while camping. Often, it's unavoidable, but some illnesses can be prevented by following a few healthcare rules. In the event these tips don't prevent a problem, having the proper materials and know-how can save your trip.

Insect Bites

Although they are not usually dangerous for most people, insect bites can ruin a day of hiking or fishing. You can avoid nasty stings if you keep as much of your skin covered as possible. Wear light, neutral colors, and avoid wearing perfumes, shaving lotion, or using sweet, scented soaps.

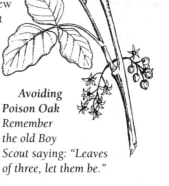

Avoiding Poison Oak Remember the old Boy Scout saying: "Leaves of three, let them be."

Repellent

Before starting an outdoor activity, apply repellent to clothing and uncovered skin. The most effective repellents contain DEET. But if you prefer natural repellents, Tender Corporation markets Natrapel, a DEET-free insect repellent. Thanks to its Controlled Flow Applicator, you can apply repellent around sensitive areas without worrying about messy hands. Simply press the sponge against the skin; a valve is activated that releases a few drops of repellent.

Just before dusk, spray your campsite, tent, and/or the sides of your folding camper with insect repellent. For evening marshmallow roasts, burn citronella candles or add wet pine needles or leaves to the campfire. This produces a light smoke that keeps the bugs at bay. Also, keep garbage and other refuse away from the campsite.

Mosquitoes, Fleas, and Gnats

Mosquito, flea, and gnat bites are rarely dangerous unless they become infected. Children are at greater risk of secondary infection from bug bites because it's difficult to keep them from scratching. Always carry an insect bite treatment. Many products contain lidocaine or benzocaine that temporarily mask the itch, but can irritate the skin because of their heavy alcohol content. The best product we've found is Tender Corporation's After Bite. The product's ammonia and mineral oil formula blocks a bite's effect.

Bees

A bee sting is more serious. Most campers come in contact with bees, which include the honeybee and bumblebee. Although not bees, the yellow jacket and wasp cause the same painful problems. To avoid attracting these buggers, never slap at a bee that is flying nearby; this may agitate it into attacking. Also, avoid wearing sweet-smelling products, keep food covered outdoors, don't smoke (the smell of tobacco smoke irritates bees while wood smoke blocks the sensory organs in bees), and wear insect repellent.

If stung by a bee, the stinger must be removed quickly because it can continue to pump venom for up to 20 minutes. Never grasp the stinger to pull it out. This may cause the venom sac to inject even more poison. Gently scrape with a thumbnail or other edged object at an angle to ease the stinger out of the wound. Immediately wash the wound with soap and water, and apply ice. Use an after-bite treatment that will not only relieve the discomfort, but will also cleanse and disinfect the sting. If you don't have an after-bite treatment, make a paste of meat tenderizer and apply it to the wound. Cover it with ice for 15 to 30 minutes.

Ticks and Lyme Disease

Although not as common as a mosquito or bee stings, the bite of a spirochete, *Borrelia borgdorferi*, is as ferocious as its name. This small deer tick can cause Lyme disease.

The tick, smaller than a common dog tick, is found in woods, tall grass, marshes, and wetlands. The ticks are spread by the animals they prey on—birds, mice, deer, and domestic animals that contract the disease themselves.

From 3 to 30 days after a tick bite, the symptoms of Lyme disease may begin with a bull's eye-shaped circular rash with a clear center, profound fatigue, stiff neck, and flu-like symptoms such as headache, chills, fever, muscle aches, swollen glands, and dizziness. Left untreated after a month or more, symptoms can include heart palpitations, light-headedness, shortness of breath, paralysis of the muscles on one or both sides of the face, encephalitis, and meningitis. Months to years later, chronic recurring arthritis, leading to erosion of cartilage and bone, may occur. Obviously, you want to avoid being bit and, if bit, receive proper medical treatment at once.

Tick season runs from April through October with peak months from May through July. When you are outdoors during these times in areas where ticks are likely to be found, wear long-sleeve shirts, long pants, and socks. Tuck shirts into pants and pants into socks. Wear shoes—not sandals. Use a tick insect repellent. After you return from your outing, shower and carefully inspect your entire body for ticks. Be sure to inspect children and pets for ticks, too.

If you find a tick, protect your hands when removing it. If the tick is still moving, it has not fed. Remove it immediately. It may take 8 to 12 hours of feeding time before enough bacteria is transmitted to cause Lyme disease. Use forceps or tweezers to remove an attached tick. Grasp the tick close to the skin and as close as possible to the tick's mouth. Without jerking, pull the tick steadily outward.

Avoid the tick's bloated abdomen, which can act like a syringe if squeezed. After removing the tick, disinfect the bite with rubbing alcohol or povidon iodine. Check the bite for 30 days. If a rash or other symptoms of Lyme disease develop, see your physician immediately.

Ticks and Your Pet

Your pet can also contract Lyme disease and get sick, too.

Deer ticks can attack a pet anywhere on its body, but the most frequent spots to check are the animal's head, neck, ears, and feet. Unlike fleas, mosquitoes, and bees, ticks cause little sensation when they bite so your pet may not let you know of its dilemma.

The risk of getting Lyme disease is directly related to the time the tick is attached. When you return from an outing, check the animal. If any ticks are noted, remove them immediately. Grasp the exposed section of its body near the pet's skin with tweezers, forceps, or a gloved hand and pull with smooth and steady pressure. Removal may leave mouthparts attached and provide skin infection and irritation.

Dispose of the tick by wrapping it in several tissues and flushing it down the toilet or put it in a small bottle of rubbing alcohol. Water won't drown a tick. Never crush, burn, or suffocate the tick; this may cause the release of infectious bacteria.

Tick repellents are available to keep ticks off your pet, but the best prevention is to vaccinate your pet. Check with your veterinarian for the best course of treatment.

If your pet seems lethargic, has difficulty moving, a fever, is slow and inactive and tender all over, take it to be vet at once. Treating the disease in its early stages greatly reduces the possibility of complications, including hospitalizing your pet.

Sun Exposure

The sun warms us, tans us, and affects many essential body processes. Sunlight causes vitamin D to be synthesized in the skin. Some people believe that sunlight can lower our blood pressure, reduce the level of cholesterol in the bloodstream, and affect our bones, numerous glands, and organs. Although it produces many healthful effects on our bodies, we've all experienced the pain that comes from overexposure, and we are aware of the serious skin problems caused by too much sun. Even on a cloudy day, the sun's rays pass through clouds.

Sunburns

The longest ultraviolet rays are UVA rays, which are the least active. They can produce a tan of short duration, but not a sunburn. On the other hand, UVB rays produce both a sunburn and a durable tan. Use a sunscreen that filters out UVB rays from your skin.

Wearing clothing made of tightly woven fabric, a hat with visor to shade the face, and a water-resistant or waterproof sunscreen with a Sun Protection Factor

(SPF) of at least 15 reduces the possibility of a painful sunburn. However, if your skin receives too much sun and becomes red and sore, use an afterburn treatment with aloe vera, which penetrates the skin quickly and carries moisture to the underlying layers of skin.

Eye Protection
Your eyes need sunglasses that provide 100 percent UV protection. Don't select sunglasses because they are fashionable. Tests on a group of 25 randomly selected sunglasses indicated that about one-third transmitted more UVA than visible light and one model actually doubled the amount of UV received. Wearing these sunglasses would be more dangerous than not shading the eyes at all. Dermatologists often advise patients to wear sunglasses to protect the sensitive skin of the eyelids and the area around eyes from UVB rays because most sunscreens aren't applied close enough to the eyes to protect these areas.

How can you tell a quality pair of sunglasses? Quality sunglasses should eliminate glare, control brightness, provide 100 percent UV protection, and have optical clarity.

Don't rely completely on sunglasses for protection; wear a hat, preferably one with a large brim, to help shield your face and eyes from sunlight or the reflective glare of water.

Digestive Ailments
A stomachache is sometimes caused by what or how much you eat. However, it can also be caused by what you drink.

Treating your water with chlorine, iodine tables, water purifiers, or by boiling are all ways to remove organisms and help prevent illness.

Wilderness Navigation
Maps
Paper maps don't rely on batteries or a clear line-of-sight to overhead satellites to help you find your way. Before trekking into wilderness areas or locations only a short distance off the beaten path, check with visitor centers or other government or private sources for detailed maps of the area you plan to explore by foot or canoe. Be sure to pack a good quality compass as well and make certain you can take into account any deviation that might affect its operation. It's also a good idea to get the advice of those who know the area and have a plan in case you lose your way.

Finding Your Way Via GPS
A growing number of travelers are taking advantage of the latest technology to find their way around the country. They are using hand-held or mobile GPS receivers. GPS refers to the $12-billion Global Positioning System, a constellation of 24 satellites that orbit the earth twice a day at an altitude of about 12,000 miles. The satellites constantly broadcast high-frequency radio signals with position and atomic

clock time data. This lets anyone with a GPS receiver determine his or her location, often within several yards, anywhere on the planet.

GPS has been used in aircraft, commercial and pleasure boats, and more recently, by anglers, climbers, hikers, hunters, and others in the outdoors.

If you plan to use a handheld GPS receiver to hike your way in the wilderness, be sure to bring along plenty of extra batteries. You'll be surprised how fast you'll go through a supply.

GPS receivers are also available for travelers in cars. Here's a sample of just three models by different makers:

- **StreetPilot GPS,** made by Garmin (website: www.garmin.com), works in an auto, truck, or van. It contains a reference base map in black and white, showing Interstate, U.S., and state highways, plus rivers and lakes in the United States, Canada, and Mexico, with main streets shown in metropolitan areas. Optional software can be uploaded into the device for street-level map detail and access to businesses and points of interest. Garmin's color-display version is called StreetPilot GPS ColorMap.
- **GlobalMap 1600,** made by Lowrance Electronics (website: www.lowrance .com), features a background map of the world with streams, ponds, highways, and roadways in North America, including the 48 contiguous states, Hawaii, southern Canada, northern Mexico, and the Bahamas. The database can be expanded with the IMS MapCreate Marine and Recreation CD-ROM, which is included. It also features U.S. city streets, rural roads, and railroads.
- The **750 NAV GPS Vehicle Navigation and Driver Information System,** made by Magellan (website: www.magellangps.com), contains all available U.S. mapping data. One coverage area is included with your purchase. Additional areas can be bought or rented with an *unlock code.* This instrument uses voice prompts and simple screen menus so you can enter your location and planned destination. It can automatically calculate a new route to your destination when you encounter traffic, closed roads, or other obstacles. Over 500,000 pre-programmed points of interest are stored in the unit.

Family Fun
Successful camping trips begin with the planning stage and should include everyone who plans to go.

Camping With Children
Whether your offspring is a toddler, entering the terrible twos, an exploring eight-year-old, or an independent teen, camping with kids can be fun—really!

Don't be afraid to go camping with a young child. Remember, the pioneers crossed the vast prairie with their babies. While on the road, don't forget to stop occasionally; get out of the vehicle and take a walk, visit a museum, have a picnic lunch, or do a little shopping.

Trip Tip

Photocopy all of your travel arrangements and leave them with a friend or relative. They will then be able to reach you at any point in your trip in case of an emergency.

When camping with infants and toddlers, be sure to take along the gear they need to make them comfortable. The market is loaded with collapsible products. Look for combination items like crib/playpen or car/booster seat.

Before taking a long trip with preschoolers, it's a good idea to make several overnight or weekend trips to nearby campgrounds. Becoming accustomed to camping equipment and camp rules are important parts of happy family camping.

Planning

It's important that youngsters participate in every aspect of a camping trip. Begin with planning. For small children, get picture and read-aloud books or magazines about the places you plan to visit. Help the youngster list things to see on the trip in a flip-type spiral-bound notebook dedicating at least one page per day. Once on the road, carry the notebook with maps and other items you will be consulting daily. Each evening let the child draw—or paste pictures from brochures—the things he or she saw that day into the notebook. This will help keep young children interested in the trip.

School-age children can get books from the local library and send for brochures to read about the places they'll be visiting. To ensure that everyone will enjoy the trip, have each family member suggest a certain number of places to visit. Encourage youngsters to keep a journal or scrapbook. They can record places they visited, what they saw, the cost of attractions, miles traveled each day, and their own feelings and reactions.

You can never start too early to develop an artist or a photographer. A book of blank paper can serve as a sketchbook for young children to draw what they see. School-age children enjoy taking pictures. A disposable camera is ideal for six- to eight-year-olds. Older campers can use a point-and-shoot camera. Art and photography offer the opportunity to learn about composition, light, and shadows without forcing youngsters to learn more complex camera techniques. It's easy for them to get "trigger-happy" so they should learn to budget their film as well as their money.

Older children will want to take an active part in planning the itinerary. You may want to arrange your trip around a certain theme such as battlefields, homes of former U.S. Presidents, places that represent a historical era (for example, Colonial Period, Civil War), or an area's natural resources. Encourage them to learn more about the areas from the excellent websites now available.

Budgeting

Budget-planning should be a family affair. Youngsters need to know not only how much money they have to spend, but also the extent of the family's travel budget. Each school-aged child should have his or her own spending money. Depending on the youngster's age, the money can be given to them daily or in advance of the trip. They should be required to stay within their personal budget.

Set up a simple system listing each category. Enter the total amount budgeted for food, fuel, lodging, and sight-seeing. List daily amounts spent and allow youngsters to figure the balance. Some amazing sharing experiences can occur when families work together to pool their resources. More than once our kids have contributed their daily allowance to permit the entire family to see an unplanned attraction.

Other mathematical lessons can be learned by calculating fuel mileage after each gas stop, computing the number of miles traveled each day using only the road map, estimating land elevation from landform maps, or figuring how much longer it will take to arrive at a destination while driving at various speeds. This also prevents the constant question, "how much longer before we get there?" If you have a GPS navigation receiver, an older teenager might want to keep track of your travels using this electronic aid. Be sure, however, to bring along plenty of extra batteries for portable units.

Playing Games

Playing games while traveling makes the miles go by. Recently, I was saddened when a local radio talk show host asked people to call in and tell them how they entertained their children while traveling. Most of the contributions listed backseat televisions/VCRs, computer games, and other expensive electronic equipment. Parents justified the cost by saying, "It was worth every penny just to keep the kids quiet."

Years ago, we developed a game of observation called "Peacock." Although we don't recall how it got its name, we remember the many hours we played it on the road. First, players must select an item. At the time, a favorite was the Volkswagen, but it can be anything—a kind of vehicle or type of building, sign, or tree. When spotted, the observer calls out "Peacock red truck" or "Peacock Jayco RV." Someone must keep score and the one with the most points at the end of a given period of time gets a treat.

The entire family can enjoy sharpening geography skills playing "Cities." The first person names a city, the next person names a city that begins with the last letter of the previous city. Of course, everyone tries to name a place like New York City. If challenged, the player must find the city on a map.

Exercise Caution

Swimmers at Hiawatha National Forest campgrounds should exercise extra caution. Swim at your own risk—lifeguards are not available at any of the forest beaches. What's more, the waters of the Upper Peninsula have unique currents, waves, and strong undertows. Swimmers and boaters should wear personal flotation devices.

A more difficult game is "States, Cites, Capitals, and Features." Again, the first person names a state, the next a city in that state, next the capital, and the last person names a feature like a river, mountain, cave, or waterfall. Then it's back to naming a state. At first, we used an atlas for help, but eventually outgrew it. If your family is really bright, you might try progressing to countries.

These games can sometimes get noisy and should be followed by a quiet time of reading, individual radio listening with earphones, or a snack. Try to stick to healthy foods and never allow bubble gum unless you want to clean it out of hair and upholstery.

Making a "trivia" game about the places you have visited can be fun, too. Take along a couple of packages of three- by five-inch index cards. In the evening, let each family member write several questions about facts they learned that day. Place the answer on the opposite side of the card. Divide into teams and combine your team's cards. Take turns selecting a card from the opposite team and work together to answer the questions. You'll be amazed at the details each person begins to observe just to win.

Don't worry about teenagers. They will sleep, eat, sleep, read, sleep, and listen to their portable CD players. At the campground they usually play video games, hunt for the opposite sex, and make new friends. However, a family that has grown up camping together will find the teenagers hanging on to their position in many of the traveling games with the younger group. They may even challenge the younger siblings to a game of Ping-Pong or, heaven forbid, a turn around a pool table.

Learning in the Great Outdoors

On one of our camping trips, before the dishes could be washed after breakfast or the boat could be launched, our youngsters ran into camp with what looked like a handful of tangled tissue paper and wanted to know what it was. After learning it was the skin of a snake shed during the molting process, they were ready to return to the wild for to discover more "treasures."

But first you have to establish a few rules. Although returning with shed snake skin is permissible, the rules of the china shop—look don't touch—are in order for wildlife-watching.

Wildlife-watching offers both youngsters and adults with the best out-of-the-classroom education for the least amount of time and money. You can enjoy this activity anytime, anywhere. Spring and summer brings new life; fall and winter find many animals wearing their winter coats or migrating to warmer climates. Each season offers a memorable show. State and national parks, forest and wildlife preserves, and other environmental sites provide some of the best settings for wildlife-watching. Many areas have interpretive or educational centers with introductory audio-visual presentations, guidebooks to assist you in talking a self-guided tour, or tour guides to help you identify what you observe.

Knowing where to go to see wildlife in your camping area is just the first step. It's also important to know *how* to watch wildlife. Before you begin you might want to attend a class taught by your state's natural resources agency or by a local nature center. The "Nature" section of your public library or bookstore has guide-books on everything from trees and flowering plants to reptiles and birds.

Often wildlife won't let you get close enough to observe it with the naked eye. A pair of binoculars is a good investment. Binoculars come in all sizes, capabilities, and prices, but for beginners, a compact pair can be purchased for less than $60.

The most important rule of wildlife-watching is that it is watching—not handling. As cute as baby raccoons are they are not accustomed to being handled by humans. Mother raccoon isn't accustomed to having her young disturbed. Therefore, a nasty scene can develop if you want to cuddle her young. The last thing a good wildlife-watcher would do is to take home a new pet whether it's a tiny toad, a turtle, a grasshopper, or a harmless snake.

So how can you continue to enjoy what you have discovered? Why not photograph it, sketch it, or describe it in words? **Photography** is fun at any age. Sometimes a photographer turns into a wildlife-watcher and, sometimes, a wildlife-watcher becomes a photographer. If you don't already have a camera bag full of equipment, you may want to consider an autofocus camera with a zoom lens. Although expensive, image stabilization in a camera is awesome. This provides the same outstanding feature that some binoculars have to hold an image steady even though you may be a little shaky. Other photographic equipment that will make a serious wildlife-watcher out of you are close-up, or macro, lenses. For birds, squirrels, and other wildlife in the trees, a telephoto lens is nice, but expensive. And, it requires a tripod to keep it rock-steady. A 75mm to 300mm zoom lens may be all you will need to take those photos.

Youngsters love to take photographs. Select a camera that they can handle depending on their age. If they are between six and eight years old, a disposable camera is suitable. Encourage them to take photos of wildlife that they can easily see through the viewer. The next step up is a point-and-shoot camera, a permanent piece of equipment to care for that gives them the options of close-up and flash photography. If they're going to become camera nuts, it won't be long before they're pestering you to take a few shots with your camera. Remember don't push; not everyone is going to be an Ansel Adams.

If you like to sketch or if you have children that are budding artists, have them draw what they see. **Drawing** their environment teaches them to observe and reproduce what they saw, and is a head start for future biology class drawings. Roger Tory Peterson, author of *Peterson's File Guide to Birds*, had no formal scientific training, but was encouraged by his seventh-grade science teacher to draw birds.

If you or one of your family members has a way with words, try **journal writing.** Put down in words what you discover. See how accurately you can describe what you find. For younger children who are beginning writers, let them talk into a pocket tape recorder and tell what the object looks like in their own words. Later, help them transcribe this in a journal. Journal entries can also identify photos and drawings.

Now that you have selected a way to record what you saw, you need to identify what you saw. It's fun to make an on-the-spot identification if possible. If not, certainly when you get home or get your photos back you will want to learn all about your findings.

Whether you focus on a specialty such as bird-watching or remain a watcher in general, wildlife-watching will bring you a lifetime of enjoyment. It will provide a quiet, relaxing outdoor adventure that introduces you to a close encounter of another kind, one where survival depends on the habitat and the preservation of that habitat depends on you.

It takes time and patience to teach youngsters how to camp, but you'll find it is worth the effort. Start them out young and you'll have a happy camper for life.

Chores

To work or not to work has always been a big question with families. In our tribe, everyone had his or her duties according to age and size. These included helping with setting up and taking down camp, walking the dog (and cleaning up after), fetching anything needed from the camp store, setting the table, and washing dishes. If your children are close in age, their capabilities may be similar and you may want to rotate duties so they don't get bored or feel they are getting picked on. If camping is going to be fun for everyone, there has to be a fair and equal amount of time at both work and play.

Camping With Felix & Fido

The warnings No Pets or Pet Restrictions are appearing in campground directory listings with increasing frequency and pet owners are to blame. An owner's best four-footed friend may not have been taught to be a good camper and a good camper is your pet's best teacher.

A cat is easier to take camping because its meows are softer than a bark, it uses an indoor litter box, and it loves to curl up in small, cozy places for long periods. Never, however, let your cat outside of your vehicle or RV without a leash. Watch the doors whenever you exit because a cat that is nervous about its strange surroundings can flee in a hurry and hide.

A dog can present more problems and should not be taken camping until you are sure it can be a good camper. Fido must learn to be collared and leashed, to sit safely in a moving vehicle, and to be quiet.

Collared and Leashed

Like it or not, your dog must wear a collar—nylon, leather, or chain. If your dog is small and has a small head, consider a harness for traveling. Often, a dog will get excited or nervous when taken for a walk and will pull backwards. It just may slip out of its collar and you will suddenly find your pet on the loose. If your dog has never worn a harness, put one on before you leave home and go for walks. It won't take long for your pet to understand that this is something it has to wear when walking.

All campgrounds require that a dog be on a leash not longer than six feet at all times. Place a stake with a leash attached in your backyard. Put the dog on it for short periods of time. At first, stay with your pet. Then leave it for a few minutes.

A Safe Seat

State laws require that children under a certain age and size must be placed in a safety seat while traveling in a vehicle. But it isn't unusual to see a dog jumping over the seats and sticking its head out the window while traveling down the road. Your dog should be taught to have a place to sit that is safe and comfortable. The plastic Comfort Ride Pet Seat is held in place by your vehicle's safety belt. The device comes with a synthetic lambskin pad for a soft ride and straps that attach to your pet's own harness. The straps are loose enough to allow it to sit or stand. This might not work for a Great Dane, but no matter the size or breed, your dog should have an assigned place to ride where it will stay during the trip.

Quiet, Please!

No dog can go without an occasional bark, nor would we want it to, but there is a big difference between a "watch dog" and a "barker." If you can't teach Fido to give a couple of barks at the approach of a stranger and then stop at your command, leave your pet at home. RV campers often like to leave their pets in their RVs while they are fishing, hiking, or sight-seeing. Pulling the shades so passersby are not as visible and leaving a TV or radio (tuned to its favorite station) playing while you are away, may keep your dog from barking. Also, be sure that there is enough air for your pooch. Do not depend on your vehicle's air-conditioning to be sufficient for ventilation. If something should happen to the power while you are away, an RV is only a big tin box that can become hot and airless quickly. Be sure that there is cross-ventilation even if the air-conditioning is operating.

If you decide to take your dog hiking or fishing, remember that it can overheat just like you do. Be sure that your pet has shade to rest in and plenty of safe drinking water to keep it cool.

Help, I'm Lost

As much as Felix or Fido love you and wouldn't leave your side, all pets have a tendency to occasionally dash out a door and, therefore, should always wear identification with the phone number of someone

Be sure to carry a good color photo of your pet. It will make searching for and identifying a lost pet much easier.

back home or where you will be visiting, as well as your vehicle's license plate information. There are many other means of identification available. These include having your pet tattooed and registered nationwide. For further information about this, call the National Dog Registry at 800/637-3547. Be sure to carry a good color photo of your pet. If lost, it will make searching for and identifying your pet much easier.

MINNESOTA
RED RIVER VALLEY

Minnesota Regions

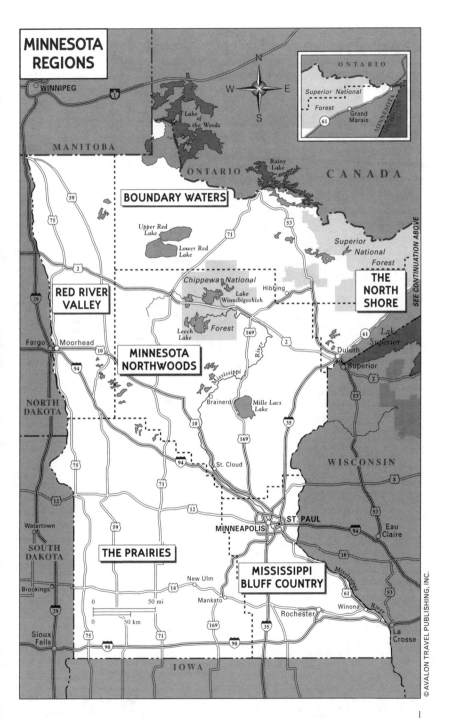

Red River Valley

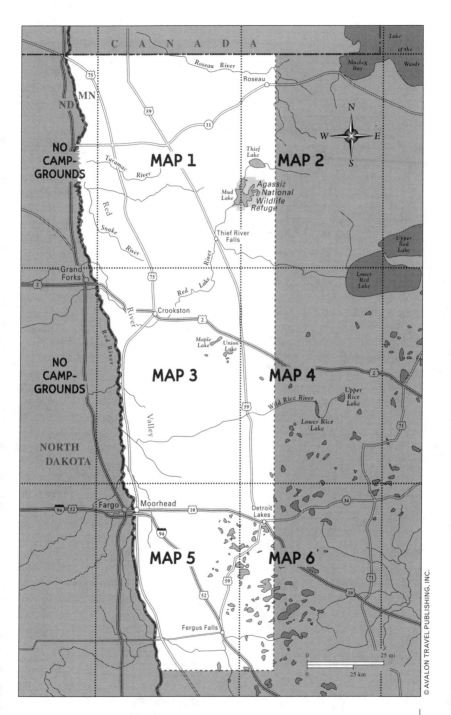

Map 1

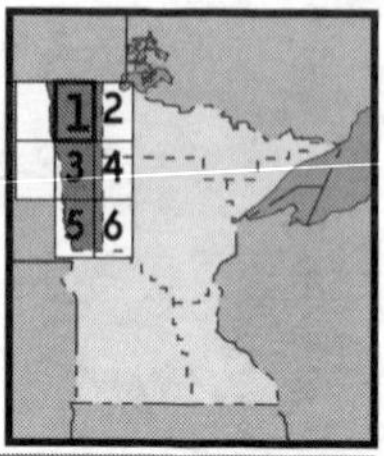

1
2
3
4
5
6

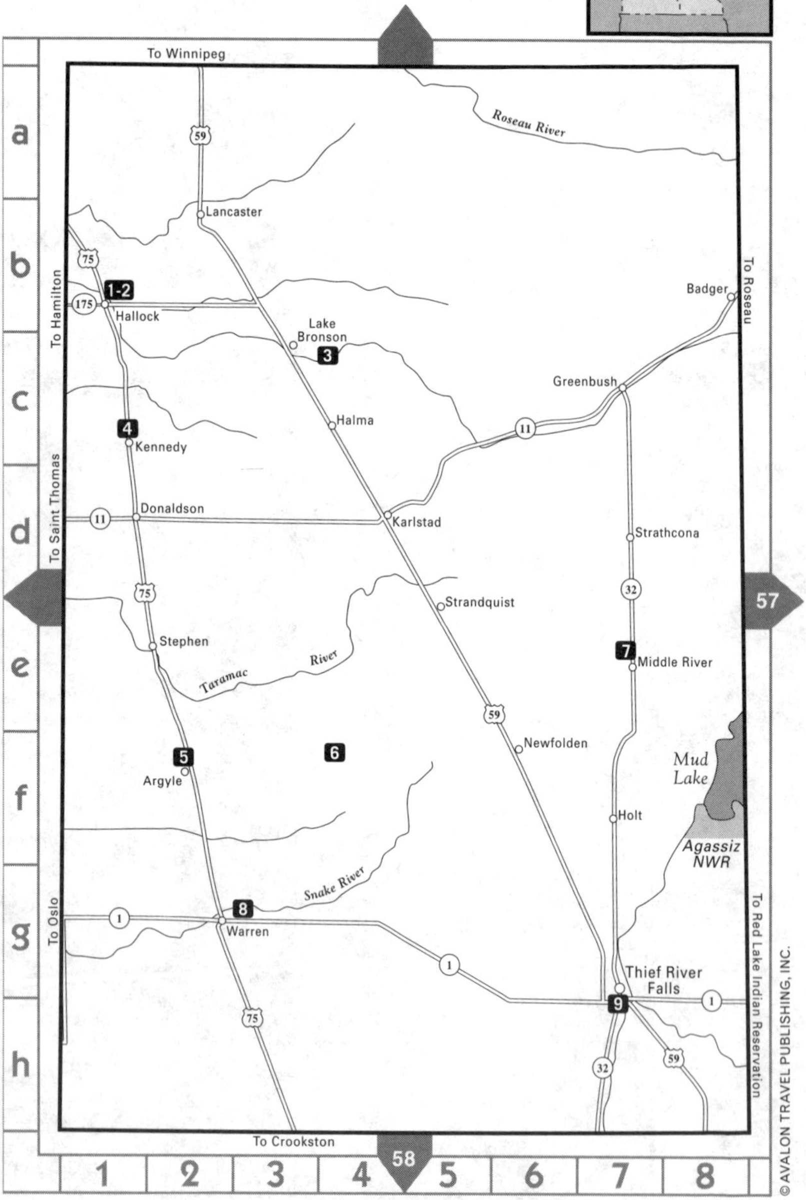

To Winnipeg
Roseau River
Lancaster
To Hamilton
Hallock
1-2
Lake Bronson
3
Badger
To Roseau
Greenbush
Halma
4
Kennedy
Donaldson
Karlstad
To Saint Thomas
Strathcona
Strandquist
57
Stephen
Taramac River
7
Middle River
Newfolden
5
6
Argyle
Mud Lake
Holt
Agassiz NWR
Snake River
8
Warren
To Oslo
To Red Lake Indian Reservation
Thief River Falls
9
To Crookston
58
a
b
c
d
e
f
g
h
1
2
3
4
5
6
7
8

Map 2

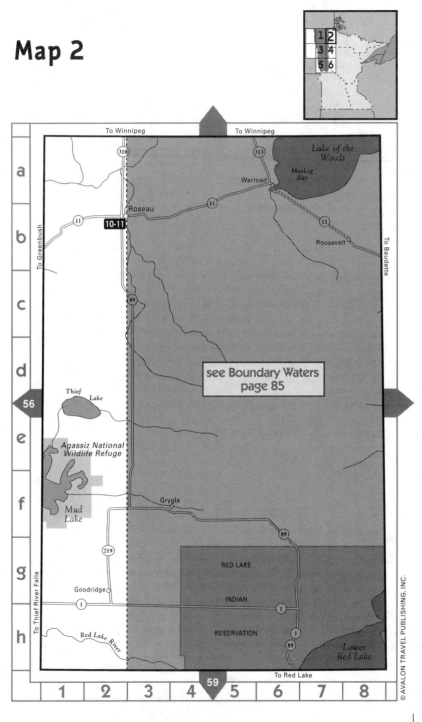

To Winnipeg

To Winnipeg

310

313

Lake of the Woods

Warroad

Muskeg Bay

11

Roseau

11

10-11

Roosevelt

11

To Greenbush

To Baudette

89

see Boundary Waters
page 85

56

Thief Lake

Agassiz National
Wildlife Refuge

Grygla

89

Mud Lake

219

RED LAKE

Goodridge

INDIAN

1

To Thief River Falls

1

RESERVATION

Red Lake River

89

Lower Red Lake

59

To Red Lake

1 2 3 4 5 6 7 8

a b c d e f g h

© AVALON TRAVEL PUBLISHING, INC.

Map 3

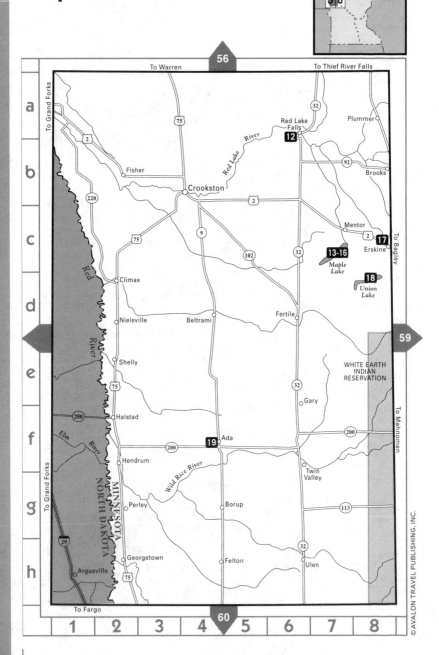

Map 4

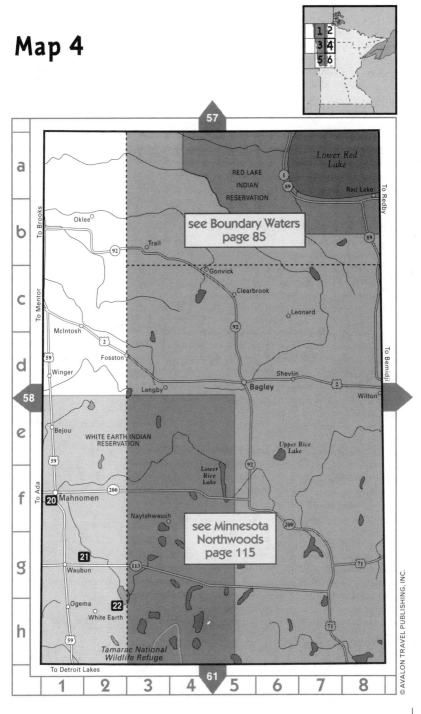

see Boundary Waters
page 85

see Minnesota
Northwoods
page 115

© AVALON TRAVEL PUBLISHING, INC.

Map 5

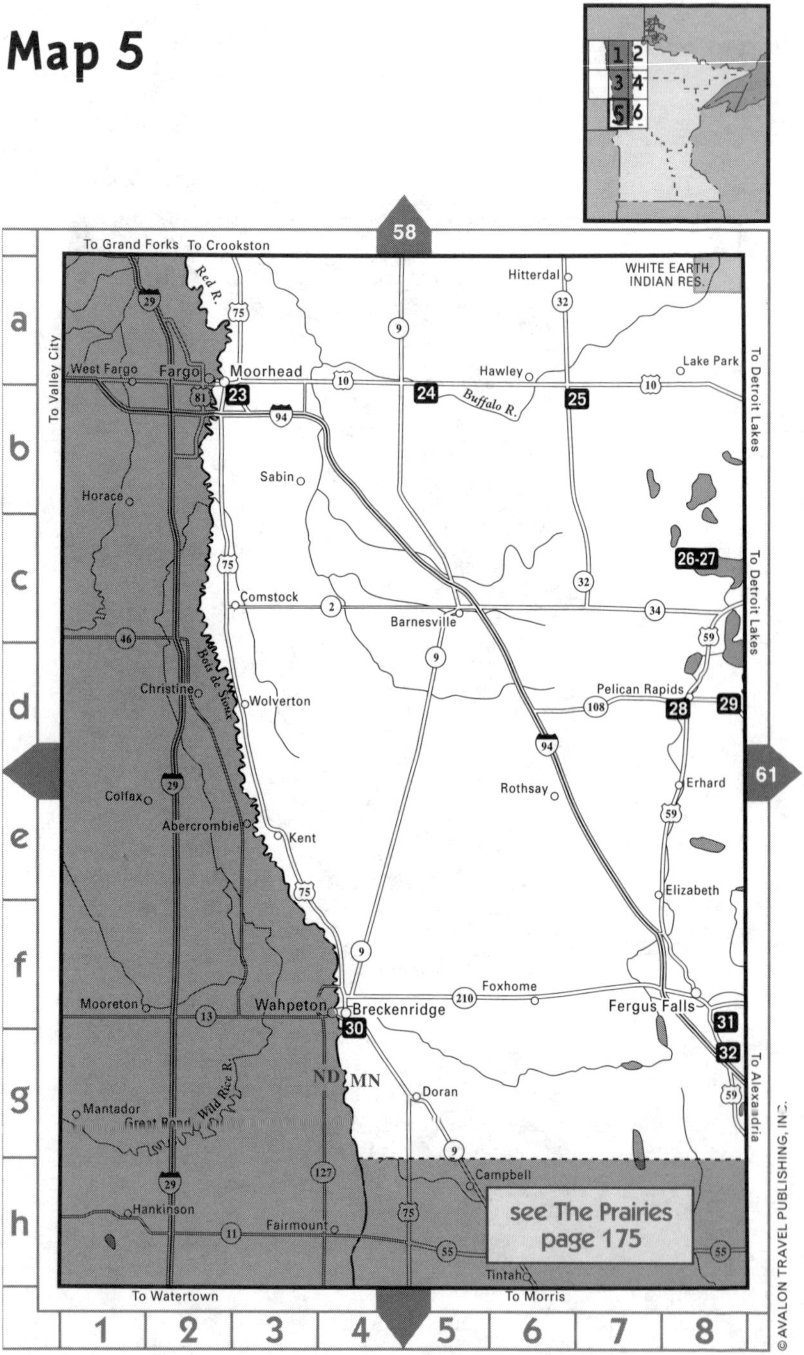

To Grand Forks   To Crookston

58

WHITE EARTH INDIAN RES.

Hitterdal

To Valley City
To Detroit Lakes
To Detroit Lakes
To Alexandria

a

West Fargo
Fargo
Moorhead
23
Hawley
Lake Park
29
75
81
94

b

Horace
Sabin
24
Buffalo R.
25
10

c

Comstock
75
Barnesville
2
32
34
59
26-27

d

Christine
Wolverton
Pelican Rapids
108
28
29
46
94
Erhard
61

e

Colfax
Abercrombie
Kent
29
75
Rothsay
59
Elizabeth

f

Mooreton
Wahpeton
Breckenridge
Foxhome
210
Fergus Falls
31
13
9
32

g

Mantador
Great Bend
Wild Rice R.
30
ND MN
Doran
59

h

Hankinson
Fairmount
Campbell
see The Prairies page 175
29
127
11
75
55
Tintah
55

To Watertown   To Morris

© AVALON TRAVEL PUBLISHING, INC.

| 1 | 2 | 3 | 4 | 5 | 6 | 7 | 8 |

60 Minnesota

Map 6

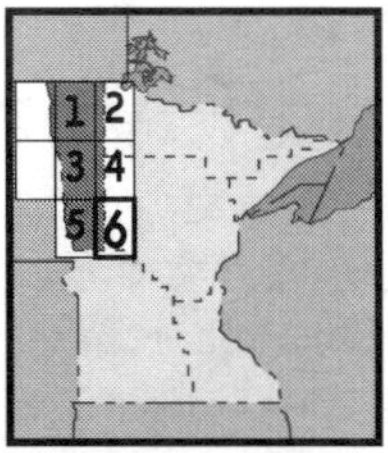

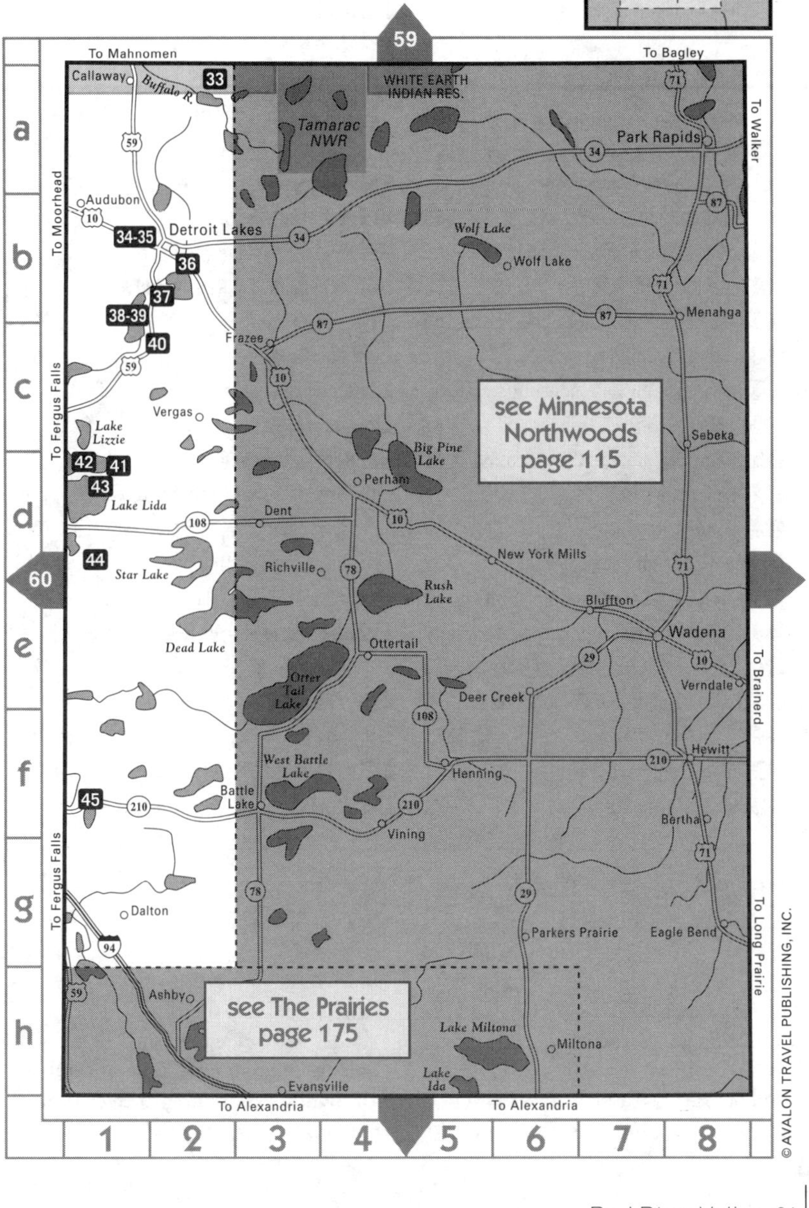

To Mahnomen

To Bagley

Callaway Buffalo R. **33**

WHITE EARTH
INDIAN RES.

71

To Walker

a

59

Tamarac
NWR

34

Park Rapids

87

b

Audubon

10

34-35

Detroit Lakes

34

Wolf Lake

Wolf Lake

71

36

37

87

87

Menahga

38-39

40

Frazee

10

c

59

Vergas

see Minnesota
Northwoods
page 115

Sebeka

Lake
Lizzie

42 **41**

Big Pine
Lake

43

Lake Lida

108

Dent

10

d

Perham

New York Mills

71

44

Star Lake

Richville

78

Rush
Lake

Bluffton

Wadena

60

Dead Lake

Ottertail

29

Verndale

10

To Brainerd

e

Otter
Tail
Lake

168

Deer Creek

Hewitt

West Battle
Lake

210

Henning

210

Bertha

45

210

Battle
Lake

71

f

Vining

78

29

g

Dalton

94

Parkers Prairie

Eagle Bend

To Long Prairie

To Fergus Falls

To Fergus Falls

To Moorhead

59

Ashby

see The Prairies
page 175

Lake Miltona

Miltona

h

Evansville

Lake
Ida

To Alexandria

To Alexandria

© AVALON TRAVEL PUBLISHING, INC.

1 2 3 4 5 6 7 8

Red River Valley

The Red River Valley, along the western border of Minnesota, is named for the Red River, which flows some 700 miles from Upper and Lower Red Lakes to Lake Winnipeg in Canada. This extremely fertile region on the fringe of the Great Plains was once covered by a vast expanse of tall prairie grass and great herds of buffalo. Several nature preserves and state parks, like Buffalo River State Park and adjacent Bluestem Prairie preserve, east of Moorhead, give you a glimpse of what the land looked like before the first settlers plowed the native prairie.

Today this agricultural area offers a wide choice of outdoor recreation for campers, from wildlife-watching to river tubing, from hunting to cross-country skiing.

Moorhead, across the Red River from Fargo, North Dakota, is the region's largest urban community. The city of 32,000 is the commercial and cultural center of northwest Minnesota.

1 Gilbert Olson Campground

Location: In northwest Minnesota near Hallock, bordering Two Rivers, map 1, grid B1.

Campsites, facilities: There are 36 campsites. Facilities include electric hookups, flush toilets, showers, wheelchair access, disposal station, golf course, tennis court, outdoor pool, and playground. There are also bike, hiking, and snowmobile trails. Seasonal campsite rentals are available. Pets are allowed.

Reservations, fees: The daily fee is $6. Open from late May through September.

Directions: Take U.S. Hwy. 75 north through Hallock. The campground is along Two Rivers.

Contact: Gilbert Olson Campground, Box 336, Hallock, MN 56728, 218/843-2737, fax 218/843-2579.

Trip Notes: Go on a biking or hiking tour of the surrounding area. The community is in the middle of some breathtaking wildlife. There's a nine-hole (par 36) public golf course with beautiful greens located at the southeast edge of town, off Hwy. 75 next to the city swimming pool.

2 Horseshoe Campground

Location: In northwestern Minnesota near Hallock, map 1, grid B1.

Campsites, facilities: There are 24 campsites. Facilities include electric hookups, flush toilets, showers, wheelchair access, disposal station, and playground. Season-

al campsite rentals are available. Pets are allowed.

Reservations, fees: The daily fee is $6. Open from late May through September.

Directions: Take U.S. Hwy. 75 north through Hallock. The campground is located along Two Rivers.

Contact: Horseshoe Campground, Box 336, Hallock, MN 56728, 218/843-2737, fax 218/843-2579.

Trip Notes: Drive on Hwy. 175 east to Hwy. 59 down to East Main Street in Lake Bronson to visit the Kittson County History Center and Museum (218/754-4100). It's considered one of the best museums in this part of Minnesota. The museum features turn-of-the-century lifestyle exhibits, agriculture machinery, a Red River ox cart, 1904 Rambler, and 1929 Harley Davidson motorcycle. Outdoors, you'll see a depot, caboose, church, country school, and log cabin.

3 Lake Bronson State Park

Location: Near the town of Lake Bronson and the south branch of Two Rivers, map 1, grid C4.

Campsites, facilities: The 2,983-acre park has 194 campsites (48 winter sites). Two are canoe-in sites. There are 35 electric hookups, flush toilets, showers, disposal station, boat ramp, wheelchair access, picnic area with shelter, swimming beach, lake and river fishing, and playground. There are 14 miles of hiking trails, five miles for mountain biking, and seven miles for skiing. Boat, canoe, and snowshoe rentals are available. Pets are allowed.

Reservations, fees: The daily fee ranges from $12 to $15. Credit cards are accepted. Open year-round.

Directions: From Thief River Falls, take U.S. Hwy. 59 northwest toward Lake Bronson. The park entrance in on County Road 28, one mile east of town.

Contact: Lake Bronson State Park, Box 9, Lake Bronson, MN 56734-0009 or 218/754-2200 or 218/754-2201, fax 218/754-6141.

Trip Notes: Set in the transition zone between the prairie land of the valley and the aspen parkland to the east, the park has a range of wildlife habitat. Climb its historic tower for a view of the surrounding area. The park supports a variety of wildlife from the prairie-dwelling upland sandpipers and sharptail grouse, to the spectacular moose. Lake Bronson is one of the few sizeable bodies of water in the area and offers you an excellent swimming beach, good fishing, and enjoyable canoeing and boating. In winter, you can ski, hike, or snowmobile its network of trails. The annual International Wood-carvers Festival (218/754-2200 for date) is usually held in August.

4 Catfish Haven Resort

Location: In Kennedy, south of Hallock, map 1, grid C1.

Campsites, facilities: The campground on the Red River has 25 sites. Facilities include RV pull-through sites, electric hookups, water, sewer, flush toilets, showers, laundry, grocery store, fishing and hunting guides, boat ramp, and playground. Seasonal campsite rentals are available. Pets are allowed.

Reservations, fees: The daily fee is $10 to $16. Open from mid-May through September.

Directions: From Crookston, take Hwy. 75 north to Kennedy and Hwy. 7 to the resort.

Contact: Catfish Haven Resort, Box 69, Kennedy, MN 56733-0069 or 218/455-3838.

Trip Notes: Be sure to drive at least a portion of the Waters of the Dancing Sky Scenic Byway, which follows MN Hwy. 11 from Karlstad to International Falls. From Kennedy, take County Road 7 to U.S. Hwy. 59. Then go south to Karlstad.

This route tracks the Minnesota-Canada border for nearly half of its length. This far-northern byway offers you an excellent chance of seeing the magnificent Aurora Borealis, better known as the Northern Lights, during an evening drive. It touches the shore of the vast Lake of the Woods, and ends at Rainy Lake.

5 Memorial Park Municipal Campground

Location: In Argyle on the Middle River, map 1, grid F2.

Campsites, facilities: There are 14 campsites, including six tent-only sites. Facilities include electric hookups, water, sewer, disposal station and playground. Seasonal campsite rentals are available. Pets are allowed.

Reservations, fees: The daily fee is $5 to $6. Open May through October.

Directions: From Crookston, take Hwy. 75 north to Argyle.

Contact: Island Park Municipal Campground, P.O. Box 288, Argyle, MN 56713-0288 or 218/437-6621 or 218/437-8463, fax 218/437-6621.

Trip Notes: Old Mill State Park is only 13 miles east of the campground down County Road 4. The old homestead's museum is at the park's campground.

6 Old Mill State Park

Location: East of Argyle on the Middle River, map 1, grid F4.

Campsites, facilities: There are 26 campsites. Facilities include electric hookups, water, flush toilets, showers, wheelchair access, swimming beach, river fishing, children's programs, and playground. There are hiking, cross-country ski, and snowmobile trails. Ski equipment and snowshoe rentals are available. Pets are allowed.

Reservations, fees: The daily fee is $12. Credit cards are accepted. Open from late May through early September.

Directions: From Argyle, take County Road 4 east for 13 miles and then one mile north to the park.

Contact: Old Mill State Park, Box 43, Rt. 1, Argyle, MN 56713-9727 or 218/437-8174, fax 218/437-8174.

Trip Notes: This 406-acre historic state park boasts an old flour mill and log cabin. It was homesteaded in 1882 by the Larson family. Beginning in 1886, a series of mills were built in and around the park. The original mill was powered by water. When it was destroyed by floods, it was rebuilt in 1889 as a wind-powered mill. That mill, too, was destroyed and rebuilt a short time later as a water-powered mill outside the park area. John Larson, the original homesteader's son, started a mill at the same location, but powered it with a Case steam engine No. A359. In 1897, both mills were moved to the area in the park where the "old mill" now stands. The mills were owned and operated by several people before being sold to the state in 1937. Rebuilt in 1958, the steam engine and mill are fired up each year as part of park special events and interpretive programs.

◼ Middle River Community Campground

Location: In the town of Middle River on the Middle River, map 1, grid E7.

Campsites, facilities: There are 10 campsites. Facilities include electric hookups, water, restaurant, and snowmobile trail. Seasonal campsite rentals are available. Pets are allowed.

Reservations, fees: The daily fee is $4 to $8. Open May through November.

Directions: From Thief River Falls, take Hwy. 32 north to Middle River and to the campground.

Contact: Middle River Community Campground, Community Center, R.R. 114, Middle River, MN 56737, 218/222-3751.

Trip Notes: Visit the nearby Felton Prairie Wildlife Management Area (218/449-4115), a bird-watching site renowned for its nesting chestnut-collared longspurs. Be sure you look for prairie birds such as Swainson's hawk, upland sandpiper, marbled godwit, sedge wren, loggerhead shrike, and numerous sparrows. There are also several tracts owned by the Nature Conservancy in the area.

◼ Holiday Park Campground

Location: In Warren on the Snake River, map 1, grid G3.

Campsites, facilities: The hotel/motel's campground has 60 sites, 20 for tents only. Facilities include electric hookups, water, sewer, flush toilets, showers, disposal station, bike trail, golf course, tennis court, outdoor pool, and playground. Seasonal campsite rentals are available. Pets are allowed.

Reservations, fees: The daily fee ranges from $8 to $12. Open from mid-May through late October.

Directions: The campground is on the northeast side of Warren alongside the Snake River. From Hwy. 75, take East Johnson Avenue to the campground.

Contact: Holiday Park Campground, Johnson Ave. East, Warren, MN 56762, 218/745-5343, fax 218/745-4344.

Trip Notes: The Wetlands Pines Prairie Audubon Sanctuary (218/745-5663) is five miles east of Warren on Hwy. 1, three miles south on Township Road, and one-half mile east. The site, which is open all year, offers a wonderful setting for bird-watching and hiking on 1.5 miles of trail. Some weekend and evening programs are offered.

An alternative is a visit to the Marshall County Historical Museum (218/745-4803) on the east side of town at the Marshall County Fairgrounds on Johnson Avenue. It features county history, farm machinery, and a "Street of Yesteryear." The museum is open from May through September.

9 Thief River Falls Tourist Park

Location: In Thief River Falls, map 1, grid H7.

Campsites, facilities: This city-owned facility has 84 campsites with 20 tent sites. Facilities include electric hookups, water, sewer, flush toilets, showers, disposal station, and wheelchair access. On the shore of Red Lake, the park offers a hiking trail and playground. Pets are allowed. The downtown area is within walking distance.

Reservations, fees: The daily fee ranges from $7 to $14. Open from mid-May through late October.

Directions: Take Hwy. 32 to Thief River Falls. The campground is at the intersection of Hwy. 32 and Oakland Park Road.

Contact: Thief River Falls Tourist Park, Hwy. 32 South and Oakland Park Rd., Thief River Falls, MN 56701-0528 or 218/681-2519, fax 218/681-8225.

Trip Notes: Visit the Peder Engelstad Pioneer Village (218/681-5767 or 218/681-4931) at 825 Oakland Park Road. Travel southeast on

Hwy. 32 South, and turn southeast on Oakland Park Road near the Evergreen Eating Emporium. The village is an authentic turn-of-the-century town that has three museums, six log houses, blacksmith shop, four old-fashioned stores, two main railroad depots and two cabooses, one-room schoolhouse, a 100-year-old church, a fully restored Victorian home, antique car, old windmill, exhibit building, and flower gardens. It's open from Memorial Day through Labor Day.

Another option is a self-guided auto or walking tour of 61,500-acre Agassiz National Wildlife Refuge (218/449-4115), established in 1937 for waterfowl production. It lies in the bed of glacial Lake Agassiz between the coniferous forests and the prairie pothole region of the Red River. It has considerable wildlife, including 280 species of birds, 49 mammals, 12 amphibians, and nine reptiles. A resident 100-plus head of moose attracts visitors from all over the world.

10 AmericInn Roseau RV Park

Location: On Hwy. 11 in Roseau, map 2, grid B2.

Campsites, facilities: This campground has only five secluded, pull-through RV sites. Facilities include electric hookups, water, sewer, cable-TV and telephone hookups, indoor pool, sauna, whirlpool, and playground. Pets are allowed.

Reservations, fees: The daily rate is $25 to $30 with a discount for extended stays. Credit cards are accepted. Open from late May through early September.

Directions: From Thief River Falls, take Hwy. 32 to Hwy. 11 northeast to Roseau. The campground is on Hwy. 11 on the west side of the town.

Contact: AmericInn Roseau, Adolph, Doris, and Jack Oseid, Hwy. 11 W, Box 39, Roseau,

MN 56751, 218/463-1045 or 800/634-3444, fax 218/463-1046, email: americin@americinn .com, website: www.americinn.com.

Trip Notes: Incorporated in 1895, Roseau was a fur trading post dating back to 1822. The Roseau County Historical Society and Museum (218/463-1918) exhibits range from the early geological formation to immigrant exploration and settlement of the region. The museum is at 110 2nd Ave., N.E. It's open Tuesday through Saturday, 9 A.M. to 5 P.M., from May 1 through October 31. In winter, it closes at 4 P.M.

11 Roseau Camping Area

Location: In Roseau on the Roseau River, map 2, grid B2.

Campsites, facilities: This 37-acre city park has 20 campsites, 10 with electric and water hookups. There are 10 tent sites. Facilities include flush toilets, showers, disposal station, playground, and biking, hiking, and horse trails. Access to river is available. Pets are allowed.

Reservations, fees: The daily fee is $5 to $10. Open from mid-May through mid-September.

Directions: From Thief River Falls, take Hwy. 32 to Hwy. 11 northeast to Roseau. The campground is on the southeast edge of town.

Contact: Roseau Camping Area, 900 11th Ave., S.E., Box 307, Roseau, MN 56751-0307 or 218/463-1542 or 800/815-1824, fax 218/463-1252, website: www.rrv.net/roseau/tourism.htm.

Trip Notes: On Hwy. 11, only about three miles west of Roseau, is the Pioneer Farm and Village (218/463-3052 for hours). This wheelchair-accessible agriculture museum includes log cabin, barn, store, church, school, blacksmith, print shop, post office, lunch counter, fellowship hall, storage shed, trappers cabin, and pioneer museum and ex-

hibit hall. Admission and parking is free. The site is open May through September.

12 Voyageurs View Campground

Location: North of Red Lake Falls, map 3, grid A6.

Campsites, facilities: There are 100 campsites with 34 tent sites. Facilities include electric hookups, water, flush toilets, showers, disposal station, boat ramp, swimming beach, grocery store, playground, and biking, hiking, ski, and snowmobile trails. Seasonal campsite rentals are available. Pets are allowed.

Reservations, fees: The daily fee ranges from $10 to $12. Credit cards are accepted. Open from late May through early September.

Directions: Go north of town on Country Road 13. The campground is less than one mile away.

Contact: Voyageurs View Campground, Rt. 2, Box 48, Red Lake Falls, MN 56750, 218/253-4329 or 218/253-2031, fax 218/253-2893.

Trip Notes: The campground offers rafting and river tubing on the Red Lake River daily from Memorial Day to Labor Day. A shuttle service is provided. There is also a 2.5-hour float trip with intermittent Class II rapids through the scenic river valley. The fee for an adult is $7; children 12 and under are $6. Group rates are also available.

13 Maple Lake Park Campground

Location: South of Mentor on Maple Lake, map 3, grid C7.

Campsites, facilities: There are 30 campsites with 20 tent sites. Facilities include electric hookups, flush toilets, disposal station, wheelchair access, boat ramp, and swimming beach. Seasonal campsite rentals are available. Pets are allowed.

Reservations, fees: The daily fee is $5 to $6. Open from mid-May through mid-September.

Directions: From Erskine, take Hwy. 2 to Mentor and turn south on the county road at the Dairy Queen to the campground on Maple Lake.

Contact: Maple Lake Park Campground, Box 27, Crookston, MN 56716-0027 or 218/574-2254 or 218/281-3952, fax 218/281-3976.

Trip Notes: Visit the Polk County Historical Museum (218/281-1038). Take U.S. Hwy. 2 to the east side of Crookston. The museum offers a free glimpse into county history with agriculture and pioneer exhibits, farm machinery, 1876 log house, and 1892 frame house. The museum is open daily from mid-May to mid-September.

14 Ullands Resort and Campground

Location: Southeast of Mentor on Maple Lake, map 3, grid C7.

Campsites, facilities: There are 47 campsites with only four tent sites. Facilities include RV pull-through sites, electric hookups, water, flush toilets, showers, disposal station, swimming beach, and playground. Seasonal campsite rentals are available. Pets are allowed.

Reservations, fees: The daily fee ranges from $15 to $20. Open May through September.

Directions: From Mentor, take Hwy. 2 about one mile east to County Road 10 and travel south on County Road 10 to the township road leading to the campground.

Contact: Ullands Resort and Campground, Rt. 1, Box 690, Mentor, MN 56736-9572 or 218/637-3252.

Trip Notes: From July 1 to September 10, visit the Bergeson Gardens (218/945-6988) near Fertile. From Mentor, take U.S. Hwy. 2 to U.S. Hwy. 59 and travel south to Mahnomen. Go seven miles west on MN Hwy. 200. Turn north on Norman County 36 and go 11 miles north to the sign and two miles west. On a self-guided tour, you'll be able to see about four acres of lawn and trees with 8,500 square feet of labeled flower beds, annuals, and perennials. The gardens are closed Sundays.

15 Oak Cove Resort

Location: South of Mentor on Maple Lake, map 3, grid C7.

Campsites, facilities: The resort has 11 campsites with four tent sites. Facilities include electric hookups, water, sewer, flush toilets, showers, disposal station, boat ramp, swimming beach, grocery store, and playground. Boat, canoe, motor, and seasonal campsite rentals are available. Pets are allowed.

Reservations, fees: The daily fee ranges from $7 to $9. Credit cards are accepted. Open May through September.

Directions: From Mentor, go west to County Road 12 and drive south to the Pavilion. Then turn left. The resort is about 500 yards from the Pavilion.

Contact: Oak Cove Resort, R.R. 1, Box 757, Mentor, MN 56736-9575 or 218/637-2124.

Trip Notes: The Agassiz Environmental Learning Center (218/945-3129), open all year, is a scenic 640-acre natural area with sand dunes, prairie oak savanna, riverine communities, and abundant wildflowers. There are 10 miles of self-guided recreation trails and 10 primitive campsites. From Mentor, take U.S. Hwy. 2 to Hwy. 32 and drive south to Fertile. Go west off Hwy. 32 onto Summit Ave., and west for about one mile to the nature center. You can contact the center at 101 Mill St., South, Fertile, MN 56540-0388.

 Lakeview Resort

Location: South of Mentor on Maple Lake, map 3, grid C7.

Campsites, facilities: The resort's campground has 50 sites, half of them for tents. Facilities include electric hookups, water, sewer, flush toilets, showers, disposal station, wheelchair access, boat ramp, swimming beach, restaurant, lounge, grocery store, laundry, and playground. Seasonal campsite rentals are available. Pets are allowed.

Reservations, fees: The daily fee ranges from $8 to $10. Open April through October.

Directions: From Mentor, take County Road 10 (Maple Lake Shore Road East) about three miles to the resort.

Contact: Lakeview Resort, Rt. 1, Box 694, Mentor, MN 56736-9573 or 218/637-6237.

Trip Notes: If you have a full day available, you might drive to neighboring North Dakota and visit the Plains Art Museum (701/232-3821) in Fargo. The non-profit museum, open year-round, features permanent collections and touring shows. Tours are about one hour. The museum is at 704 First Ave., North.

 Mobile (or Johnson's) Motel

Location: Near Erskine, map 3, grid C8.

Campsites, facilities: This campground near Erskine has only five sites with electric hookups, water, sewer, showers, and access

to a lake. Seasonal campsite rentals are available. The owners also have another nearby campground with six sites.

Reservations, fees: The daily fee ranges from $12 to $15. Open May through October.

Directions: On U.S. Hwy. 2 just north of Erskine.

Contact: Mobile Motel, Rt. 1, Box 10, Hwy 2, Erskine, MN 56535, 218/687-3500 or 218/687-3955.

Trip Notes: Drive down to Ada to visit the Prairie Village (218/784-4989 or 218/784-4141). The attraction features two churches, schoolhouse, bank, barber shop, log cabin, store with post office, depot, newspaper building, doll house, and exhibits of machinery and autos. From Erskine, take U.S. Hwy. 59 (east of Erskine) south to MN 200. Go west to Ada. The village is on the south side of the highway. It is open May through October.

 Union Lake Sarah Campground

Location: South of Erskine on Lakes Union and Sarah, map 3, grid D8.

Campsites, facilities: The small campground has only eight sites. Facilities include electric hookups, water, flush toilets, showers, disposal station, hiking trail, boat ramp, swimming beach, grocery store, and laundry. Boat, canoe, motor, and seasonal campsite rentals are available. Pets are allowed.

Reservations, fees: The daily fee ranges from $10 to $17. Open May through September.

Directions: From Erskine, take County Road 41 south to the campground.

Contact: Union Lake Sarah Campground, Rt. 2, Box 98, Erskine, MN 56535-9314 or 218/687-5155 or 218/687-3969.

Trip Notes: Visit the Rydell National Wildlife Refuge

(218/687-2224), a unique mixture of habitats, including prairie grassland, wetlands, hardwood forest, and lakes. The refuge, which attracts over 100 species of songbirds, also has a fish hatchery.

19 Norman Motel

Location: In Ada, map 3, grid F4.

Campsites, facilities: The campground has only four campsites with electric hookups, water, and sewer. Seasonal campsite rentals are available. Pets are allowed.

Reservations, fees: The daily fee is $10. Credit cards are accepted. Open April through October.

Directions: The campground is on MN 200 about five blocks west of Hwy. 9.

Contact: Norman Motel, 502 Thorpe Ave., West, Ada, MN 56510-1039 or 218/784-3781, fax 218/784-4914.

Trip Notes: Stop at the Norman County Historical Museum on Hwy. 9. It is open on Tuesday and Thursday from 1–5:30 P.M., May through October.

20 Shooting Star Casino and Hotel

Location: North of Detroit Lakes, map 4, grid F1.

Campsites, facilities: The campground, which is next to a casino/hotel, has 47 sites. Facilities include RV pull-through sites, electric hookups, disposal station, laundry, swimming pool, and sports field.

Reservations, fees: Regular RV daily fee is $12.50 ($11.25 with Good Sam card. Tent sites are $5 per day. Open mid-May through mid-October.

Directions: From the intersection of MN 200 and U.S. Hwy. 59, go one mile south on Hwy.

59. The entrance is on the right. The campground is about 35 miles north of Detroit Lakes.

Contact: Shooting Star, 777 Casino Rd., Mahnomen, MN 56557-0418 or 800/453-7827 or 218/935-2701.

Trip Notes: The Bagley Wildlife Museum (218/694-2491) on U.S. Hwy. 2, about three-quarters of one mile west of State Route 92, features more than 750 wildlife specimens, including some unusual ones such as a two-headed calf and a lamb with two bodies sharing one head. Animals range in size from tiny albino mice to an eight-foot-tall Kodiak Bear.

21 Oxbow Resort and Campground

Location: Near Waubon on Big Elbow Lake, map 4, grid G1.

Campsites, facilities: There are 25 campsites. Facilities include electric hookups, water, sewer, flush toilets, showers, laundry, lake access, boat ramp, swimming beach, grocery store, playground, and hiking and snowmobile trails. Boat, canoe, motor, and seasonal campsite rentals are available. Pets are allowed. Baby-sitting service is also available.

Reservations, fees: The daily fee ranges from $18 to $20. Credit cards are accepted. Open May through September.

Directions: From Waubon, travel east on MN 113 to Big Elbow Lake.

Contact: Oxbow Resort and Campground, 39544 Oxbow Rd., Rt. 2, Box 217, Waubun, MN 56589-9327 or 800/832-9616 or 218/734-2244, fax 218/734-2250, email: oxbow@tvutel.com.

Trip Notes: The resort was named for a hand-hewn oxen yoke found in the woods. The surrounding woodlands are a wildlife-watcher's dream. Anglers will find Big Elbow

Lake one of the state's top walleye lakes, but it also harbors abundant largemouth bass, northern pike, and panfish.

22 Cedar Crest Resort

Location: Southeast of Waubun on White Earth Lake, map 4, grid H2.

Campsites, facilities: This small campground has only three sites with electric hookups, water, sewer, disposal station, laundry, lake access, boat ramp, swimming beach, restaurant, lounge, playground, and hiking and snowmobile trails. Boat, canoe, motor, ice-fishing house, snowmobile, and seasonal campsite rentals are available. The resort also offers fishing launches and guides. Pets are allowed.

Reservations, fees: The daily fee is $20. Credit cards are accepted. Open from mid-May through September.

Directions: From Ogema on Hwy. 59, take MN Hwy. 224 to White Earth Lake.

Contact: Cedar Crest Resort, 29783 387th St., Waubun, MN 56589-9320 or 218/473-2116 or 888/492-7060, fax 218/473-2739.

Trip Notes: East of White Earth Lake is most of the White Earth State Forest. If you're around in June, you can attend the White Earth Traditional Pow-Wow (218/935-0417). You'll enjoy Native American dancing, food booths, and crafts.

23 Fargo-Moorhead KOA

Location: On the edge of Moorhead, map 5, grid A2.

Campsites, facilities: There are 100 campsites with 20 tent sites. Facilities include RV pull-through sites, electric hookups, water, sewer, flush toilets, showers, disposal station,

heated swimming pool, cable TV, and playground. Pets are allowed. Kamping Kabins are also available.

Reservations, fees: For reservations, call 800/562-0271. The daily fee for tent and RV sites for two adults ranges from $22 to $25. Credit cards are accepted. Open May 1 through October 15.

Directions: Drive southeast about two miles from the city along I-94 East. Take Exit 2. The KOA campground is on left on north I-94 Frontage Road.

Contact: Fargo-Moorhead KOA, 4396 28th Ave. South, R.R. 4, Box 168, Moorhead, MN 56560-9222 or 218/233-0671.

Trip Notes: A stay in Moorhead isn't complete without a visit to the Comstock House at 506 8th St. South (218/233-0848 or 218/291-4211), which is about one-half mile north of I-94 on Hwy. 75. The state historic site is a restored 11-room, two-story wood frame home, built in 1882-83 by Solomon Comstock. He made his fortune in the railroad and banking businesses, and helped found Moorhead State University. His home offers a close-up look at a leading Minnesota family and Red River Valley history with its original furnishings, including tapestries, china, and crystal, and varnished oak and butternut woodwork. Admission is free, but donations are welcome.

24 Buffalo River State Park

Location: On the Buffalo River east of Moorhead, map 5, grid B5.

Campsites, facilities: The 1,367-acre park has 44 campsites. Facilities include electric hookups, flush toilets, showers, disposal station, wheelchair access, 12 miles of hiking and six miles of cross-country ski trails, naturalist programs, swimming beach, and outdoor pool. Pets are allowed.

Reservations, fees: The daily fee is $12. Credit cards are accepted. Open May through mid-November.

Directions: From Moorhead, take U.S. Hwy. 10 east about 13 miles to the park. The entrance is on the right.

Contact: Buffalo River State Park, Box 352, Glyndon, MN 56547-7035 or 218/498-2124, fax 218/498-2583.

Trip Notes: This park is a wonderful spot if you love flowers. As many as 250 species of brightly colored wildflowers and grasses, including some plants now rare in Minnesota, can be found in the wooded Buffalo River Valley. The Buffalo River, which runs through the park, is bordered by a river-bottom forest of elm, ash, cottonwood, oak, and basswood. With the adjoining Nature Conservancy Bluestem Prairie Scientific and Natural Area, the park is the largest tract of native prairie in Minnesota. The site also attracts a great variety of birds. In early spring, birdwatchers come to hear "booming" prairie chickens.

25 Lee Lake Campground

Location: Near Hawley, east of Buffalo River State Park, map 5, grid B7.

Campsites, facilities: There are only seven campsites with two tent sites. Facilities include RV pull-through sites, electric hookups, water, flush toilets, showers, disposal station, laundry, wheelchair access, outdoor pool, boat ramp, grocery store, and playground. Seasonal campsite rentals are available. Pets are allowed.

Reservations, fees: The daily fee is $13 to $15. Open May through September.

Directions: From Moorhead, take U.S. Hwy. 10 east to Hawley. The campground is on the edge of Lee Lake.

Contact: Lee Lake Campground, Rt. 1, Hawley MN 56549-9801 or 218/937-5355.

Trip Notes: Minnesota State University Science Center offers two sites for visitors. One is the planetarium on the campus of MSU. It features family astronomy nights with indoor and outdoor sky-viewing as well as planetarium shows. The planetarium is in Brides Hall 167 on the campus off 11th St. South. Parking is free.

The center's Buffalo River site (218/236-2904), 16 miles east of Moorhead next to Buffalo River State Park, is a 300-acre prairie, woods, and river plot, offering a variety of science-and nature-oriented activities and experiences. Included are walking trails and cross-country skiing. It has no admission charge.

26 Pelican Hills Park

Location: On Pelican Lake, map 5, grid C8.

Campsites, facilities: There are 75 campsites, three tent-only sites, and one camping cabin. Facilities include RV pull-through sites, electric hookups, water, sewer, flush toilets, showers, disposal station, laundry, grocery store, and playground. It's located across from a public access to Pelican Lake and is adjacent to a golf course. Seasonal campsite rentals are available. Pets are allowed.

Reservations, fees: The daily fee ranges from $15 to $22. Credit cards are accepted. Open May through September.

Directions: From Pelican Rapids, drive nine miles north on County Road 9 or 2.5 miles north of Hwy. 34 on County Road 9.

Contact: Pelican Hills Park, John Morgan, Manager, 20098 S. Pelican Dr., Rt. 4, Box 218-B, Pelican Rapids, MN 56572, 218/532-3726 or 218/863-5962 (winter) or 800/430-2267, email: phprvpark@aol.com, website: www.pelican-parkhills.com.

Trip Notes: One of the major celebrations in Pelican Rapids is the Annual Turkey Festival, usually in July. Popular events are the Rotary Club turkey barbecue, Kiddie and Annual parades, volleyball tournament, street dance, and kids' carnival.

Another option is to go just across the border to Wahpeton, North Dakota, and visit the 85-acre Chahinkapa Zoo/Park (701/642-2811) at 2nd Street and 8th Avenue. It exhibits otters, bison, pheasants, mountain lemurs, lions, antelopes, zebras, and other animals. It also features a restored 1926 Spillman carousel with 20 antique wooden horses. From I-94, take MN Hwy. 210 to Wagpeton.

27 Bayview Shores Resort

Location: On Pelican Lake, map 5, grid D8.

Campsites, facilities: There are 28 campsites. Facilities include electric hookups, water, sewer, boat ramp, swimming beach, restaurant, grocery store, and playground. Boat, motor, and seasonal campsite rentals are available. Pets are allowed.

Reservations, fees: Seasonal rentals only. Credit cards are accepted. Open May through September.

Directions: From Pelican Rapids, travel north on County Road 9 to Hwy. 34. Turn right and go one-quarter mile and then turn left and resume on County Road 9 for about three miles. Then turn right and go one-half mile to the resort.

Contact: Bayview Shores Resort, Rt. 4, Box 208, Pelican Rapids, MN 56572-8825 or 218/532-2426.

Trip Notes: Wahpeton, North Dakota, is at the headwaters of the Bois de Sioux River in a rich agricultural area. The Richland County Historical Museum (701/642-3075), at Second Street North and Seventh Avenue, displays pioneer artifacts.

28 Sherin Memorial Park

Location: In Pelican Rapids, map 5, grid D8.

Campsites, facilities: There are 10 RV sites and 20 tent sites. Facilities include electric hookups, flush toilets, showers, laundry, disposal station, lake fishing, hiking trail, tennis court, golf course, outdoor pool, restaurant, grocery store, and playground. Seasonal campsite rentals are available. Pets are allowed.

Reservations, fees: The daily fee ranges from $5 to $10. Open from mid-May through August.

Directions: From Detroit Lakes, take U.S. Hwy. 59 south to Hwy. 108 East in town. Look for the Trinity Lutheran Church and the Pelican Rapids Pool and turn north. The camping area is on the left.

Contact: Sherin Memorial Park, E. Mill St. and 2-1/2 St., S.E., P.O. Box 350, Pelican Rapids, MN 56572-0350 or 800/545-3711 or 218/863-6571 or 218/863-7076, fax 218/863-7077.

Trip Notes: Visit and tour the 21-building Bagg Bonanza Farm (701/274-8909) just across the river in North Dakota. The farm is at 8015 169th Ave. S.E., 12 miles west on State Route 13. It is one of the last remaining bonanza farms, which were large, wheat-producing farms common in the

Red River Valley from the late 1870s to the early 1930s.

Cross Point Resort

Location: On Lake Lida near Pelican Rapids, map 5, grid D8.

Campsites, facilities: The resort only has five campsites. Facilities include electric hookups, water, sewer, flush toilets, showers, disposal station, wheelchair access, boat ramp, fishing guides, hiking trail, swimming beach, and grocery store. Boat, motor, ice-fishing house, and seasonal campsite rentals are available. Pets are allowed.

Reservations, fees: The daily fee ranges from $15 to $18. Open from mid-May through October.

Directions: From Pelican Rapids, take MN 108 east to Lake Lida.

Contact: Cross Point Resort, 39870 Crosspoint Ln., Rt. 3, Box 453 Lake Lida, Pelican Rapids, MN 56571-7738 or 218/863-8593.

Trip Notes: A nice drive to take is the one to Fort Abercrombie State Historic Site (701/553-8513) on the eastern edge of Abercrombie, North Dakota. It was one of the first federal forts in that state, established to protect wagon trains and river traffic. From Pelican Rapids, take MN 108 to MN 9 south to County Road 26. At I-75, go south to Kent and cross the Red River to County Road 22 to Fort Abercrombie State Park.

Welles Memorial Park and Fairgrounds

Location: On peninsula where the Bois de Sioux and OtterTail Rivers form the Red River, map 5, grid F4.

Campsites, facilities: There are only five primitive sites in the 30-acre wooded park. Facilities include two with electric hookups, flush toilets, wheelchair access, tennis court, boat ramp, arboretum, and playground. There are biking, hiking, and cross-country ski trails. Pets are allowed.

Reservations, fees: The daily fee ranges from $5 to $18. Open from mid-May through mid-October.

Directions: In Breckenridge, drive to the west end of Nebraska Avenue off 5th Street North (Hwy. 75).

Contact: Breckenridge Parks and Forestry, 420 Nebraska Ave., Breckenridge, MN 56520-0410 or 218/643-3455 or 218/643-1431, fax 218/643-1173.

Trip Notes: Visit the Wilkin County Museum at 704 Nebraska Avenue in Breckenridge. It is two blocks east of the intersection of 5th Street (Hwy. 75) and Nebraska Avenue. The museum is open from the week after Easter to Thanksgiving. There are exhibits depicting the history of the county, old newspapers from 1881 on microfilm, obituaries, and biographies. There's no fee and parking is free. There is also a self-guided walking tour of the area.

Delagoon Park and Rec Area Camp

Location: Near Fergus Falls on Pebble Lake, map 5, grid G8.

Campsites, facilities: The lakeshore campground has 44 sites with 22 tent sites. Facilities include electric hookups, water, boat ramp, and playground.

Reservations, fees: The daily fee begins at $5. Open from mid-May through September.

Directions: From Fergus Falls, take Hwy. 59 south to Pebble Lake, about one mile.

Contact: Delagoon Park and Rec Area Camp, South Hwy. 59, Fergus Falls, MN 56537, 218/739-3205.

Trip Notes: Elbow Lake on Hwys. 59 and 79, a short drive south of Fergus Falls, is a farming community whose residents are of Scandinavian heritage. The city celebrates two Scandinavian events: Syttende Mai, Norwegian Independence Day, in mid-May, and Flekkefest, a troll festival, on the first weekend in August.

32 Swan Lake Resort

Location: Near the city of Fergus Falls on Swan Lake, map 5, grid G8.

Campsites, facilities: The 18-acre resort on Swan Lake has 30 campsites (10 for RVs). Facilities include electric hookups, water, sewer, disposal station, flush toilets, showers, laundry, boat ramp, swimming beach, hiking trail, grocery store, and playground. Boat, canoe, motor, and seasonal campsite rentals are available. Pets are allowed.

Reservations, fees: The daily fee ranges from $20 to $23. Credit cards are accepted. Open mid-May through September.

Contact: Swan Lake Resort, Steph, Denny, and Amanda Frahm, 17463 Cty. Hwy. 29, Fergus Falls, MN 56537, 800/697-4626 or 218/736-4292, email: swanlk@prtel.com, website: www.swanlkresort.com.

Directions: Take I-94 to exit 61. Drive on U.S. Hwy. 59 south for three-quarters of a mile, then County Road 82 east for two miles. Then go on County Road 29 north for 1.5 miles to the resort.

Trip Notes: Swan Lake is known for its water clarity throughout the summer. Fishing is usually good with a large supply of sunfish, crappies, northern pike, and walleye. Largemouth bass are definitely the most sought

species in recent years with most released after they are weighed and photographed. Fergus Falls, about six miles away, is rich in history and recreational opportunities. This city of 12,500 people has some 500 acres of parkland. The River Walk, an especially scenic spot, stretches for three tree-lined blocks along the Ottertail River downtown.

33 Howland's Maplewood Resort

Location: North of Detroit Lakes on Little Sugar Bush Lake, map 6, grid A2.

Campsites, facilities: The resort has only four RV sites and four tent sites. Facilities include electric hookups, water, sewer, flush toilets, showers, disposal station, boat ramp, swimming beach, grocery store, laundry, and playground. Boat, canoe, motor, and seasonal campsite rentals are available. Pets are allowed.

Reservations, fees: The daily fee ranges from $15 to $30. Credit cards are accepted. Open mid-May through late September.

Directions: From Callaway, take U.S. Hwy. 59 north to County Road 14 and travel east to County Road 23. Turn south on County Road 23, drive through Richwood, and go to County Road 34. Turn left on County Road 34 to Little Sugar Bush Lake.

Contact: Howland's Maplewood Resort, 29501 Maplewood Rd., Callaway, MN 56521-9692 or 218/375-4481 or 888/881-1478.

Trip Notes: The Tamarac National Wildlife Refuge (218/847-2641) is an excellent bird-watching site for woodland and boreal species. Great gray owl, ruffed grouse, golden-winged warbler, and mourning warbler are all birds that can be found here. The refuge also features bald eagles, trumpeter swans, and many other wildlife species.. From Detroit Lakes, go eight miles east on Hwy. 34, and nine miles north on County Road 29. It's at the junction of County Road 26 and 29. This wheelchair-accessible refuge offers an auto tour or a hiking trail.

34 Forest Hills RV Resort and Campground

Location: West of Detroit Lakes, map 6, grid B2.

Campsites, facilities: Adjacent to a golf course, the campground has 150 sites. Facilities include RV pull-through sites, electric hookups, water, sewer, flush toilets, showers, sauna, hot tub, rustic trails, restaurant, laundry, grocery store, and indoor pool. Seasonal campsite rentals are available. Pets are allowed.

Reservations, fees: The daily fee ranges from $14 to $20. Credit cards are accepted. Open from mid-April through mid-October.

Directions: From Detroit Lakes, take Hwy. 10 about 3.5 miles west to the resort.

Contact: Forest Hills RV Resort and Campground, 22931 185th St., Detroit Lakes, MN 56501-7910 or 800/482-3441, fax 218/439-6471, email: dgjohnson@uswest.net, website: www.foresthillsrv.com.

Trip Notes: In August, country music fans from across the United States and Canada gather at the scenic Soo Pass Ranch for three days of music featuring Nashville's brightest stars, and four days of camping under the stars. It's called the WE Fest. The first WE Fest was held in 1983 in the middle of a wheat field on what was then a sleepy little dude ranch on the outskirts of town. The Soo Pass Ranch is anything but sleepy now. With a natural amphitheater that holds up to 50,000 people, including 5,000 reserved seats, 10 separate campgrounds with more than 7,000 campsites, and state-of-the-art production facilities, including one of the biggest stages in North America, the Soo Pass is an awesome outdoor concert facility. Contact the Detroit Lakes Regional Chamber of Commerce (800/542-3992 or 218/847-9202) for information.

35 Long Lake Campsite

Location: West of Detroit Lakes on Long Lake, map 6, grid B2.

Campsites, facilities: There are 81 campsites. Facilities include RV pull-through sites, electric hookups, water, sewer, flush toilets, showers, disposal station, boat ramp, swimming beach, grocery store, and playground. Boat, canoe, motor, and seasonal campsite rentals are available. Pets are allowed.

Reservations, fees: The daily fee ranges from $15 to $18. Reservations and credit cards are accepted. Open May through late September.

Directions: From Detroit Lakes, drive 2.5 miles west on Hwy. 10, then one-half mile south to the campground.

Contact: Long Lake Campsite, 17421 W. Long lake Rd., Detroit Lakes, MN 56501-9290 or 218/847-8920.

Trip Notes: The Detroit Lakes Wetland Management District (218/847-4431, fax 218/847-4156; email: rick_julian@fws.gov) consists of more than 39,000 acres in 159 waterfowl production areas. About 3,200 acres are regarded as native prairie. All but three areas are open to hunting during established seasons. Waterfowl and deer are the most commonly hunted species. All areas are also open for wildlife and wildflower observation.

36 American Legion Campground

Location: On the city beach in Detroit Lakes, map 6, grid B2.

Campsites, facilities: The campground, adjacent to the Legion post, has 97 sites, including primitive to full-hookup sites. Facilities include RV pull-through sites, electric hookups, water, sewer, flush toilets, showers, laundry, disposal station, fish-cleaning station, grocery store, swimming beach, and playground. Seasonal campsite rentals are available. Pets are allowed.

Reservations, fees: Reservations are accepted. The daily fee ranges from $14 to $17. Credit cards are accepted. Open May through September.

Directions: From Hwy. 59, take County Road 6 to Detroit Lake in Detroit Lakes to West Lake Drive.

Contact: American Legion Campground, Dennis and Corky Dallmann, 810 W. Lake Dr., Detroit Lakes, MN 56501, 218/847-3759, email: dallmann@tekstar.com.

Trip Notes: If you enjoy downhill skiing, Detroit Mountain (218/847-1661) is only two miles east of Detroit Lakes on MN 34. There are 15 runs, triple chair lift, double chair lift, two T-bars, handlebar tow on Bunny Hill, and snowmaking.

37 Country Campground

Location: On Glawe Lake, map 6, grid B2.

Campsites, facilities: There are 30 campsites. Facilities include 14 RV pull-through sites, electric hookups, water, sewer, flush toilets, showers, disposal station, wheelchair access, boat ramp, grocery store, laundry, bike trail, and playground. Canoe and seasonal campsite rentals are available. Pets are allowed.

Reservations, fees: Reservations are accepted. The daily fee is $18. Credit cards are accepted. Open May through mid-October.

Directions: From the intersection of Hwys. 10, 59, and 34, go two miles south on Hwy. 59, one-half mile east on County Road 6, 1.5 miles south on County Road 22, and one mile south on Township Road 5 to the campground.

Contact: Country Campground, Elwood and Lois Orner, 13639 260th Ave., Detroit Lakes, MN 56501, 800/898-7901 or 218/847-9621, or 218/847-9753, email: ccdl@lakesnet.net, website: www.lakesnet.net/ccdl.

Trip Notes: The Misty Meadows Shooting Preserve, 16 miles east of Detroit Lakes on Hwy. 34, offers three sporting clay courses. You can also hunt pheasant, chukar, and partridge on 250 acres of planted and natural cover. All hunts and clay shooting are by advance reservation only. Contact the preserve at HC 9, Box 439, Detroit Lakes, MN 56501 (218/847-4680).

38 Melissa Beach Resort

Location: On Melissa Lake, map 6, grid C1.

Campsites, facilities: There are only four campsites. Facilities include electric hookups, water, sewer, flush toilets, showers, disposal station, boat ramp, swimming beach, grocery store, and playground. Boat, canoe, motor, and seasonal campsite rentals are available. Pets are allowed.

Reservations, fees: The daily fee is $18. Credit cards are accepted. Open from mid-May through September.

Directions: From Detroit Lakes, take U.S. Hwy. 59 south to County Road 17. The resort is on the right off County Road 17.

Contact: Melissa Beach Resort, 12526 County Hwy. 17, Detroit Lakes, MN 56501-9519 or 218/847-1742, fax 218/847-3031.

Trip Notes: Enjoy birds? See a wide variety at Tamarac National Wildlife Refuge (218/847-2641) at County Roads 26 and 29 near Detroit Lakes. It's a nesting ground for bald eagles, trumpeter swans, ducks, geese, and grouse, and a sanctuary during migrations.

39 Sunset Shores Resort and Campground

Location: On Melissa Lake, map 6, grid C1.

Campsites, facilities: There are 20 campsites. Facilities include electric hookups, water, sewer, flush toilets, showers, laundry, boat ramp, swimming beach, grocery store, and playground. Boat, motor, and seasonal campsite rentals are available. A baby-sitting service is also available.

Reservations, fees: The daily fee is $19. Open May through September.

Directions: From Detroit Lakes, take U.S. Hwy. 59 south to County Road 17. The resort is on the right off County Road 17.

Contact: Sunset Shores Resort and Campground, 12436 County Hwy. 17, Detroit Lakes, MN 56501-9519 or 218/847-5851.

Trip Notes: Lake Traverse is a popular spot four miles north of Wheaton, Minnesota, on U.S. Hwy. 75, then three miles west on State Route 10. There are 15,041 acres for picnicking, boating, fishing, and winter sports. Pets are allowed, and there is a boat ramp available.

40 Cozy Corner Campground

Location: On Lind Lake south of Detroit Lakes, map 6, grid C2.

Campsites, facilities: There are 60 campsites with 40 tent sites. Facilities include electric hookups, water, sewer, flush toilets, showers, and boat ramp. Seasonal campsite rentals are available. Pets are allowed.

Reservations, fees: The daily fee ranges from $14 to $18. Open June through September.

Directions: Take U.S. Hwy. 59 south from Detroit Lakes to township road east to Lind Lake.

Contact: Cozy Corner Campground, 314 W. Lake Dr., Detroit Lakes, MN 56501-3918 or 218/847-1965.

Trip Notes: For a change of pace, the family might enjoy a day at Wild Waters Minnesota (218/847-5138), a water park that features a spectacular 450-foot flume slide, hydrotube speed slide, and water wars game. It's open from late May to early September. The park is at the intersection of Westlake Drive and Washington Avenue on (Big) Detroit Lake across from the Detroit Lakes Pavilion.

41 Frazier's Trailer Park

Location: On Crystal Lake near Pelican Rapids, map 6, grid D1.

Campsites, facilities: The facility has 27 campsites. Facilities include electric hookups, water, flush toilets, showers, and disposal station. Boat and seasonal campsite rentals are available. Pets are allowed.

Reservations, fees: The daily fee is $9. Open May through September.

Directions: From Pelican Rapids, take U.S. Hwy. 59 north for two miles to County Road 4. Turn east on County Road 4 for about five miles. Turn left on County Road 31 and drive about one mile. The trailer park is on the right.

Contact: Frazier's Trailer Park, Rt. 3, Box 171, Pelican Rapids, MN 56572-9133 or 218/863-8212.

Trip Notes: A trip to the Aniishinabe Cultural Center at 921 8th St., S.E., (218/847-3651 or 218/846-9463) in Detroit Lakes can be made at any time of the year except on Sundays and holidays. The center features a traditional round room in which Aniishinabe youth demonstrate Hoop Dancing, Traditional Dancing, and Fancy Dancing to the rhythms of Aniishinabe drum songs. Parking is free, but donations are welcome.

42 Lake Lizzie Shores Resort and Campground

Location: On Lizzie and Crystal Lakes near Pelican Rapids, map 6, grid D1.

Campsites, facilities: There are 40 campsites. Facilities include electric hookups, water, sewer, flush toilets, showers, disposal station, boat ramp, swimming beach, and playground. Boat, ice-fishing house, and seasonal campsite rentals are available. Pets are allowed.

Reservations, fees: The daily fee begins at $20. Open from mid-May through mid-September.

Directions: From Pelican Rapids, go north on U.S. Hwy. 59 for eight miles and turn east on East Lake Lizzie Road. Go one mile to the resort, which is on the right.

Contact: Lake Lizzie Shores Resort and Campground, Rt. 3, Box 213, Pelican Rapids, MN 56572-9137 or 218/863-5900.

Trip Notes: From the end of May through September, you might try tubing at Charlie's Ottertail Tubing (218/847-1480) on the Ottertail River seven miles east of Detroit Lakes on Hwy. 34. The fee includes shuttle service and free parking.

43 Crystal Lida Trailer Park and Resort

Location: On Lida and Crystal Lakes near Pelican Rapids, map 6, grid D1.

Campsites, facilities: The resort only has five RV sites (no tent camping). Facilities include electric hookups, water, sewer, bike and hiking trails, boat ramp, and swimming beach. Boat, motor, and seasonal campsite rentals are available. Pets are allowed.

Reservations, fees: The daily fee ranges from $10 to $15. Open from mid-May through September.

Directions: From Pelican Rapids, go north on U.S. Hwy. 59 for two miles and turn east on County Road 4 for six miles. The RV park is on the left.

Contact: Crystal Lida Trailer Park and Resort, Rt. 3, Box 92, Pelican Rapids, MN 56572-9121 or 218/863-8155.

Trip Notes: When the ice is thick enough, you can rent an ice-fishing house at Crystal Lida. Another spot to rent a house for ice fishing is at Buchta's Rustic Resort, 16234 Long Lake Rd., (800/393-6908 or 218/847-4159), just west of Detroit Lakes.

44 Maplewood State Park

Location: East of Pelican Rapids, map 6, grid D1.

Campsites, facilities: The 9,250-acre park has 63 campsites with three tent sites and one camping cabin. All sites are open in the winter. Facilities include electric hookups, flush toilets, showers, disposal station, wheelchair access, boat ramp, and swimming beach. There are 25 miles of hiking, 20 miles of horse, 13 miles of cross-country ski, and 15 miles of snowmobile trails. Boat and canoe rentals are available. Pets are allowed.

Reservations, fees: The daily fee is $12. Open year-round.

Directions: From Pelican Rapids, drive seven miles east on Hwy. 108.

Contact: Maplewood State Park, Rt. 3, Box 422, Pelican Rapids, MN 56572-9186 or 218/863-8383, fax 218/863-8384.

Trip Notes: Human habitation in the area goes back at least 6,000 years. Artifacts found in the park give evidence of both prairie and woodland cultures. Most artifacts, however, indicate that the site was occupied 900 to 1,200 years ago and that the residents were primarily hunters. Records of modern habitation began in the mid-1880s. The park features several fishing lakes, including Lida, Beers, and Bass Lakes. From the peak of Hallaway Hill, you can get a terrific view of the surrounding countryside, which is especially pretty in autumn when the area's maples and other hardwoods take on brilliant hues.

45 Elk's Point

Location: Near Fergus Falls on Wall Lake, map 6, grid F1.

Campsites, facilities: The shaded 25-acre campground has 10 RV sites with a large, separate area for tents. Facilities include electric hookups, water, flush toilets, showers, disposal station, boat ramp, swimming beach, and playground. Pets are allowed.

Reservations, fees: The daily fee ranges from $9 to $15. Open from mid-May through mid-September.

Directions: Take I-94 exit 57 to Fergus Falls and go on Hwy. 210 east for 7.1 miles to Elks Point Road on Wall Lake. Travel 1.2 miles to Elks Point and follow the signs to the campground.

Contact: Elk's Point, P.O. Box 502, Fergus Falls, MN 56538-0502 or 218/736-5244.

Trip Notes: Visit the Otter Tail County Historical Society Museum (218/736-6038). It is 1.25 miles east of I-94 exit 54 at 1110 W. Lincoln Avenue in Fergus Falls. The museum recreates life in an early 1900s Midwestern town with displays such as a printer's shop, dentist's office, and general store. It also has Native American and wildlife exhibits.

BOUNDARY WATERS

Boundary Waters

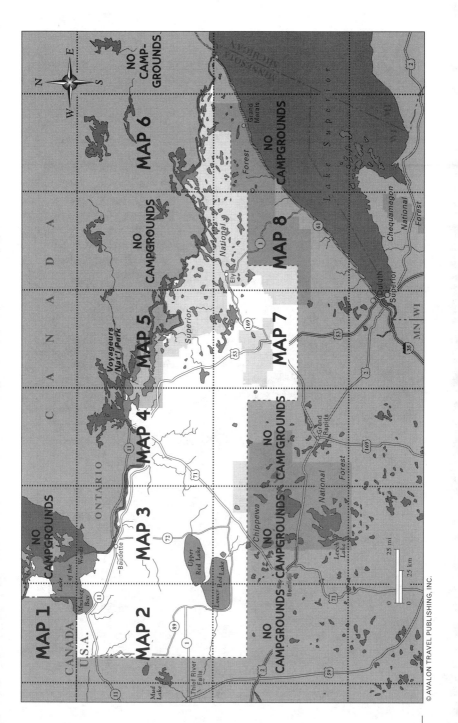

© AVALON TRAVEL PUBLISHING, INC.

Map 1

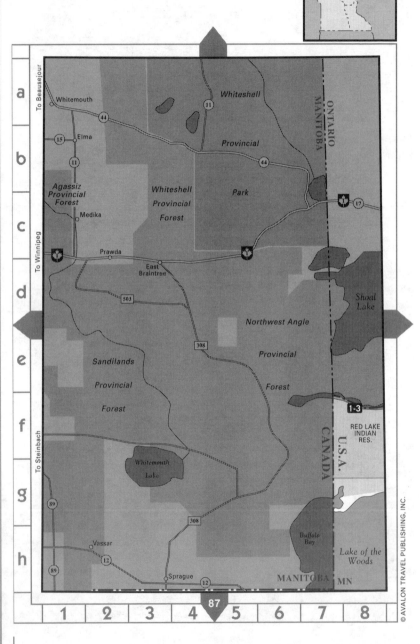

Map 2

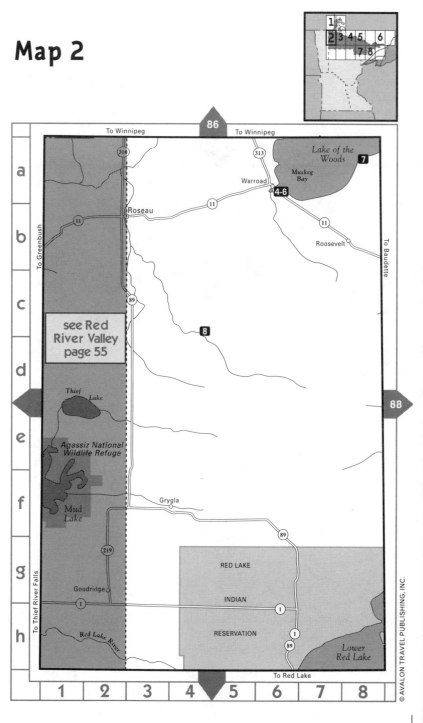

see Red River Valley page 55

Map 3

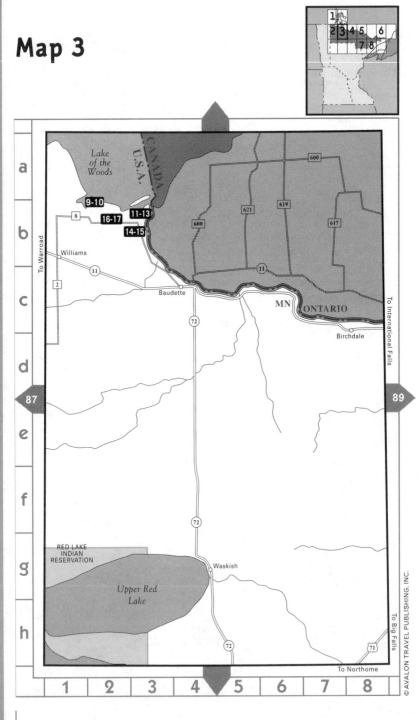

Map 4

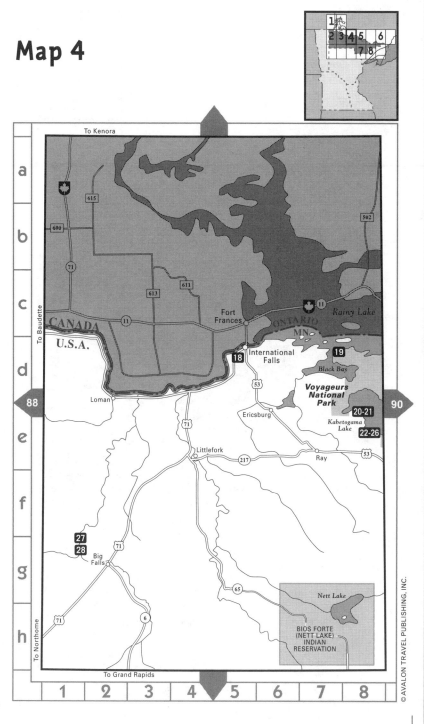

© AVALON TRAVEL PUBLISHING, INC.

Map 5

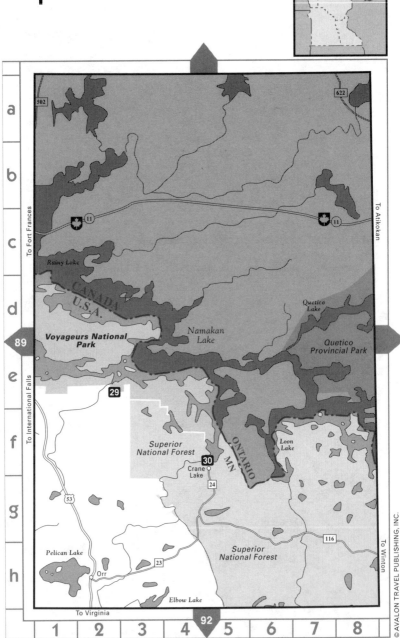

Map 6

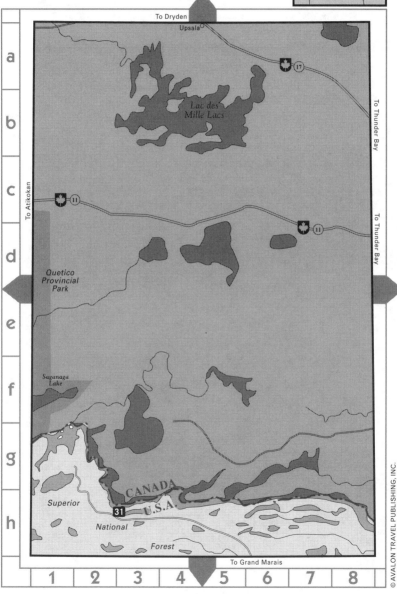

To Dryden

Upsala

17

To Thunder Bay

Lac des
Mille Lacs

To Atikokan

11

To Thunder Bay

11

Quetico
Provincial
Park

Saganaga
Lake

CANADA
U.S.A.

Superior

31

National

Forest

To Grand Marais

© AVALON TRAVEL PUBLISHING, INC.

Map 7

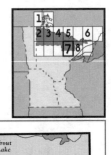

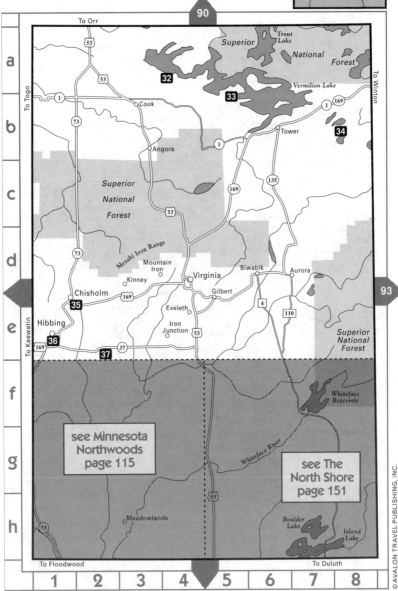

see Minnesota
Northwoods
page 115

see The
North Shore
page 151

© AVALON TRAVEL PUBLISHING, INC.

Map 8

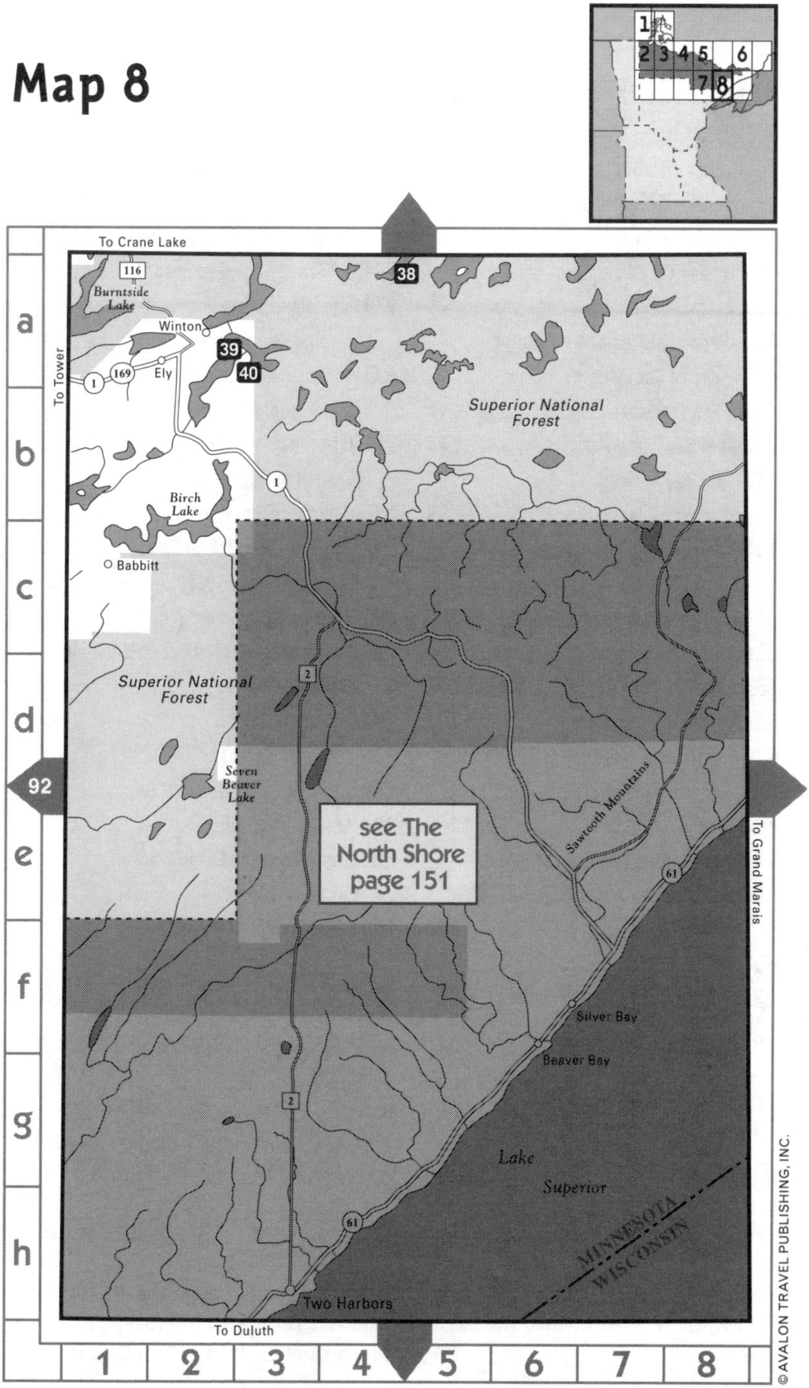

Map 8

To Crane Lake

116
Burntside Lake
Winton
Ely
1 169
To Tower

39
40

38

Superior National Forest

1

Birch Lake

Babbitt

Superior National Forest

2

Seven Beaver Lake

see The North Shore page 151

Sawtooth Mountains

61

To Grand Marais

92

Silver Bay

Beaver Bay

2

Lake Superior

61

MINNESOTA
WISCONSIN

Two Harbors

To Duluth

© AVALON TRAVEL PUBLISHING, INC.

Boundary Waters

More than two centuries ago, French-Canadian traders, called voyageurs, paddled Minnesota's northern waterway carrying loads of beaver and other fur pelts. Part of their waterway is now Voyageurs National Park, Minnesota's only national park. Voyageurs is dominated by its 30 lakes, including Rainy, Kabetogama, Namakan, and Sand Point.

This region also includes the Boundary Waters Canoe Area Wilderness (BWCAW), which contains over 1,000 pristine lakes and streams in a pine-forested, stony-cliffed wilderness. Visitors come from all over the world to experience its unspoiled beauty; the vast majority of its lakes are off-limits to motor-driven craft. In fact, the BWCAW is untouched by roads, electricity, or buildings, and visitors must have permits to enter. Lakes are linked by portages through the woods. Canoes and camping gear must be carried from lake to lake.

The Gunflint Trail, which begins on Minnesota's North Shore, is a 63-mile paved highway, offering easy access to the northern woods and lakes of the Superior National Forest and the BWCAW.

Straddling the border with Canada are the waters of Lake of the Woods, with 65,000 miles of shoreline and more than 14,500 islands.

Southeast of the border is Ely, a charming town shaped by the wilderness. It is the major western gateway to the BWCAW. To the west is Lake Vermilion, one of the area's largest and most beautiful bodies of water. It boasts 365 islands and more than 1,200 miles of shoreline.

◫ Carlson's Resort

Location: In the Northwest Angle on Lake of the Woods, map 1, grid F8.

Campsites, facilities: The campground has six campsites. Facilities include electric hookups, water, flush toilets, showers, and laundry. The resort has lake access, fishing guides, and snowmobile trails. Pets are allowed. Motors, ice fishing houses, and seasonal campsite rentals are available.

Reservations, fees: Reservations must be made far in advance. Usually the campground is filled up with seasonal campers. Credit cards are accepted. Open from early May through September.

Directions: From Warroad, take State Hwy. 313 north to Manitoba Provincial Hwy. 308. Then follow provincial 525 and State Hwy 49

to the campground. The resort is one mile from the airport.

Contact: Carlson's Resort, Rick and Beth, P.O. Box 65, Angle Inlet, MN 56711-0065 or 800/735-8961 or 218/223-8961, fax 218/223-8962.

Trip Notes: Make a driving tour of the Northwest Angle, a wooded peninsula jutting into Lake of the Woods. It's as far north as the continental U.S. reaches. Due to the 1775 surveyor's error, the Angle is separated from the Minnesota mainland by the lake and a strip of Manitoba. From Angle Inlet, take County Road 331 to Northwest Angle State Forest.

◲ Jake's Northwest Angle

Location: In the Northwest Angle on Lake of the Woods, map 1, grid F8.

Campsites, facilities: There are 32 campsites. Facilities include electric hookups, water, flush toilets, showers, disposal station, grocery store and lake access. Fishing guides and launches, motors, ice fishing houses, and seasonal campsite rentals are available. Open from mid-May through mid-October.

Reservations, fees: The daily fee for a tent is $14; $18 for a RV. Credit cards are accepted.

Directions: From Warroad, take State Hwy. 313 north to 308 in Manitoba to Provincial Hwy. 525/State Route 49. The resort is one mile from the airport.

Contact: Jake's Northwest Angle, The Colson Family, Box 38, Angle Inlet, MN 56711, 800/729-0864 or 218/223-8181, fax 218/223-8182, email: colson@jakesnorthwestangle.com, website: www.jakesnorthwestangle.com.

Trip Notes: This is a terrific spot for photographers, anglers, bird-watchers, or those who enjoy the outdoors. There is excellent fishing for walleye, muskie, and smallmouth bass. The area also boasts more than 200 species of birds, including bald eagles, osprey, wild pelicans, great grey owls, and sandhill cranes.

3 Young's Bay Resort

Location: In the Northwest Angle on Lake of the Woods, map 1, grid F8.

Campsites, facilities: The resort has 18 campsites and offers electric hookups, water, flush toilets, showers, disposal station, restaurant and lounge. Boat and motor rentals are available. Pets are allowed.

Reservations, fees: The daily fee ranges from $12 to $15. Open from early June through September.

Directions: From Warroad, take State Hwy. 313 north to 308 in Manitoba to Provincial Hwy. 525/State Route 49.

Contact: Young's Bay Resort, 7600 Young's Bay Dr. N.W., Angle Inlet, MN 56711-0127 or 218/223-8031 or fax 218/223-8032, email: ybrnwa@wiktel.com.

Trip Notes: Berry-lovers will have a field day (no pun intended) here. In June, there are plenty of wild strawberries and in July and August you can find plenty of wild blueberries and raspberries that are certain to fill you up.

4 Warroad City Campground

Location: On the shore of Lake of the Woods, map 2, grid A6.

Campsites, facilities: The grounds have 120 RV pull-through sites and 30 tent sites. The facility offers electric hookups, water, sewer, flush toilets, showers, disposal station, cable TV, wheelchair access, playground, and outdoor pool. Fishing launches and seasonal campsite rentals are available. Pets are allowed.

Reservations, fees: The daily fee ranges from $10 to $16. Open May through mid-October.

Directions: From Baudette, take State Hwy. 11 about 35 miles northwest to Lake Street. Go east on Lake St. for about one mile to the campground.

Contact: Warroad City Campground, P.O. Box 50, Warroad, MN 56763-0050 or 218/386-1004 or 218/386-1454, fax 218/386-3375, email: warroad@ruralaccess.net, website: www.ruralaccess.net/warroad.

Trip Notes: At the Warroad Museum on 202 Main St. (218/386-2500), you'll find exhibits of the history of Native Americans, commercial fishing, the Northwest Angle, pioneers, the military, lake boats, the Marvin Windows factory, the Christian Bros. hockey stick factory, the fur trade, and mink farming. It's free and open year-round, from 1–5 P.M., Monday through Saturday, and Sunday until 4 P.M.

5 Springsteel Resort and Marina

Location: On the shore of Lake of the Woods, map 2, grid A6.

Campsites, facilities: The resort has 32 RV pull-through sites and 10 tent sites. It offers electric hookups, water, sewer, flush toilets, showers, disposal station, grocery store, restaurant, lounge, snowmobile and cross-country ski trails, and fishing launches and guides. Also, boat, motor, ice fishing house, and seasonal campsite rentals are available. Pets are allowed.

Reservations, fees: The daily fee ranges from $15 to $18. Credit cards are accepted. Open from mid-May through September.

Directions: From Baudette, take State Hwy. 11 about 35 miles northwest to Lake Street. Go east on Lake St. for about one mile to the campground.

Contact: Springsteel Resort and Marina, 38004 Beach St., Warroad, MN 56763, 218/386-1000, fax 218/386-3899.

Trip Notes: If you're here in winter, by all means rent an ice fishing house where you'll be able to fish in shirt sleeves. Generally, ice fishing takes place from December to April on Lake of the Woods. If you camp in May through September, there's a charter fishing service available. One of the most popular species is walleye, but one of the most sought top predators is the elusive muskie.

⬛ Warroad Estates and RV Court

Location: On the shore of Lake of the Woods, map 2, grid A6.

Campsites, facilities: There are 32 campsites offering electric hookups, water, sewer, disposal station, fishing launches, grocery store, and restaurant. Seasonal campsite rentals are available.

Reservations, fees: The daily fee is $15. Open May through October.

Directions: From Baudette, take State Hwy. 11 about 35 miles northwest. The campground is two miles north of Hwy. 13 and two miles east on Hwy. 213.

Contact: Warroad Estates and RV Court, 111 Cedar Ct., Warroad, MN 56763-3007 or 218/386-1920.

Trip Notes: If you're in the area from June through mid-August, take in one of four summer plays at the Warroad Summer Theatre, 510 Cedar Ave., N.W. (218/386-3435). There's also a children's theater/workshop featuring the Popcorn Players, which takes place in

July with performances during the latter part of the month. The theater is located in the Warroad Mini-Theatre at Warroad High School. The box office is open daily from 1–5 P.M. Tickets are $7.50; seniors and children 12 and under are $5.50.

⬛ Arnesen's Rocky Point Resort

Location: On the shore of Lake of the Woods, map 2, grid A8.

Campsites, facilities: The campground has 50 campsites, 10 of which are open in winter. The facility offers electric hookups, water, sewer, flush toilets, showers, disposal station, grocery store, laundry, swimming beach, fishing launches and guides, restaurant, lounge, and playground. Boat, speedboat, motor, ice fishing house, and seasonal campsite rentals are available. Pets are allowed and baby-sitting is also available.

Reservations, fees: The daily fee is $24 for two adults; additional adult is $6 per day. Credit cards are accepted.

Open May through October.

Directions: Directions: From Baudette, take State Hwy. 11 to County Road 17 at Roosevelt. The campground is about 13 miles north on County Road 17.

Contact: Arnesen's Rocky Point, 6760 Rocky Point Rd., N.W., Roosevelt, MN 56673-9509 or 800/535-7585 or 218/442-7215, fax 218/442-7216, website: www.arnesens.com.

Trip Notes: Season dates may vary, but you can arrange for a guide at Arnesen's for waterfowl hunting from about mid-September through October. Other options include ice fishing on Lake of the Woods in winter or charter boat fishing in summer. Fishing charters range from about $40 to $100 per day.

8 Hayes Lake State Park

Location: South of Roseau on Hayes Lake, map 2, grid C4.

Campsites, facilities: The 2,950-acre park has 37 RV and two tent sites. Facilities include electric hookups, flush toilets, showers, disposal station, wheelchair access, swimming beach, and playground. Biking, hiking, snowmobile, and cross-country ski trails are available. Pets are allowed.

Reservations, fees: The daily fee ranges from $7 to $15. Credit cards are accepted. Open from late May through early September.

Directions: From Roseau, take State Hwy. 89 south for 15 miles and then go nine miles east on State Hwy. 4 to the park entrance.

Contact: Hayes Lake State Park, 48990 Roseau County State Aid Hwy. 4, Roseau, MN 56751, 218/425-7504, fax 218/425-7971.

Trip Notes: Hayes Lake is on the edge of the Beltrami Island State Forest, the second largest of Minnesota's 56 state forests. Because the forest has 250 miles of roads and logging trails, hiking opportunities are wonderful. As you walk the trails, look for orchids, especially the lady's slipper, the state flower. From the visitor center, pick up the "Orchids and Gentians" brochure.

9 Zippel Bay State Park

Location: On the shore of Lake of the Woods, map 3, grid B2.

Campsites, facilities: The 2,906-acre park has 57 rustic sites with disposal station, wheelchair-accessible showers and flush toilets. Firewood and ice are available. There are five miles of snowmobile, six miles of hiking, nine miles of groomed cross-country ski, and 12 miles of horse trails. The park also features picnic grounds and shelters, volleyball court, swimming beach, wheelchair-accessible fishing pier, and a naturalist. Pets are allowed.

Reservations, fees: The daily fee is $12. Credit cards are accepted. Open from mid-May through September.

Directions: Take State Hwy. 11 to Williams. Turn north on County Road 2 to Lake of the Woods Road 8 to the park entrance, which is nine miles northeast of Williams.

Contact: Zippel Bay State Park, Hwy. 8, HC 2, Box 25, Williams, MN 56686-9616 or 218/783-6252, fax 218/783-6253.

Trip Notes: To get an excellent view of Zippel Bay and the surrounding area, hike to the top of the rocky outcropping adjacent to the boat harbor. In summer, we found blueberries and strawberries, but you can also run across pin cherries, cranberries, chokeberries, and edible mushrooms along the park's trails.

10 Zippel Bay Resort

Location: On the shore of Lake of the Woods, map 3, grid B2.

Campsites, facilities: The campground has eight RV and seven tent sites. Facilities include electric hookups, water, flush toilets, showers, disposal station, fire pits, grocery store, restaurant, lounge, fishing launches and guides, hunting guides, snowmobile trails, and playground. Boat, motor, ice fishing house, canoe rentals, and baby-sitting services are available. Pets are allowed.

Reservations, fees: The daily fee is $18. Credit cards are accepted. Open from mid-April through September.

Directions: From Baudette, take State Hwy. 11 west to Williams.

Contact: Zippel Bay Resort, Nick and Deanna, 6080 39th St., N.W., Williams, MN 56686-9627 or 800/222-2537 or 218/783-6235, fax 218/783-6237, email: zippelbay@aol.com, website: www.fishandgame.com/zippel/zippel.htm.

Trip Notes: Fish the clear waters of Zippel Bay for northern pike and walleye. We strongly suggest trying the early morning or early evening hours. You can use your own boat, rent one, or go aboard one of the fishing launches available in the boat harbor.

11 Schuster's Resort

Location: At the mouth of the Rainy River on Lake of the Woods, map 3, grid B3.

Campsites, facilities: The resort has five campsites. Facilities include electric hookups, fishing launches and guides, grocery store, and lounge. There are also biking, hiking, and snowmobile trails. Boat, motor, ice fishing house, and seasonal campsite rentals are available. Pets are allowed.

Reservations, fees: The daily fee is $18. Credit cards are accepted. Open May through September.

Directions: Take Hwy. 172 from Baudette 11 miles north to the resort at the mouth of the Rainy River.

Contact: Schuster's Resort, Rt. 1, Box 165, 3140 State Hwy. 172 N.W., Baudette, MN 56623-9619 or 800/243-2412 or 218/634-2412, fax 218/634-3264, email: tom@schustersresort.com, website: www.schustersresort.com.

Trip Notes: In this area of the state, fishing is king. In the Minnesota section of Lake of the Woods, some 400,000 pounds of walleye are harvested annually. The average fish is about two pounds; northern pike of 10 pounds are common. Other species include muskie, smallmouth bass, and sauger. You can fish

aboard the resort's 27-foot launch, 20-foot airboat, 16-foot fishing boat, or aboard your own craft.

12 Wheeler's Point Resort

Location: At the mouth of the Rainy River on Lake of the Woods, map 3, grid B3.

Campsites, facilities: The campground has eight RV and two tent sites. Facilities include electric hookups, water, sewer, flush toilets, showers, disposal station, fishing launches and guides, hunting guides, grocery store, restaurant and lounge. Boat, motor, ice fishing house, and seasonal campsite rentals are available. Pets are allowed.

Reservations, fees: The daily fee is $20; $3 per pet per day. Credit cards are accepted. Open May through October.

Directions: From Baudette, take Hwy. 172 to its end at Wheeler's Point, where the Rainy River enters Lake of the Woods.

Contact: Wheeler's Point Resort, John and Tammy Fitzpatrick, 2605 River Ln., Baudette, MN 56623-9626 or 800/542-2435 or 218/634-2629, fax 218/634-1536, email: info@wheelerspoint.com, website: www.fishandgame.com.

Trip Notes: What to do? Go fishing! The resort has U.S. Coast Guard-licensed charter-boat captains who provide 8 A.M. to 5 P.M. trips for up to six people.

13 Adrian's Resort

Location: Near Baudette on the Rainy River, map 3, grid B3.

Campsites, facilities: There are 20 campsites; 12 for RVs. Facilities include electric hookups, water, sewer, flush toilets, showers, disposal station, laundry, grocery store and fishing launches. Boat, motor, and ice fishing house rentals are available. Pets are allowed.

Reservations, fees: The daily fee ranges from $14 to $17. Open from mid-May through mid-October.

Directions: From Baudette, take Hwy. 172 north for about 12 miles. There's a sign and the entrance to the resort is on the right.

Contact: Adrian's Resort, 3362 Red Oak Rd., N.W., Baudette, MN 56623, 218/634-1985, fax 218/634-1885.

Trip Notes: Visit the Lake of the Woods County Historical Museum (218/634-1200) one block south of Hwy. 11 on 8th Avenue S.E. From May through September, you can study fascinating displays on geology, natural history, Native American history, early settlement, and industry, as well as facts about the area's forest fire of 1910.

14 Morris Point Resort

Location: On Lake of the Woods, map 3, grid B3.

Campsites, facilities: There are 32 campsites. Facilities include electric hookups, water, flush toilets, showers, disposal station, fishing launches and guides, swimming beach, grocery store, restaurant and lounge. Boat, motor, and ice fishing house rentals are available. Pets are allowed.

Reservations, fees: The daily rate ranges from $15 to $20. Open from mid-May though October.

Directions: From Baudette, take Hwy. 172 north for about 10 miles to County Road 8 and turn left for three miles. At the resort sign, turn right for about two miles to the resort on the lake.

Contact: Morris Point Resort, Rt. 1, Box 228, Baudette, MN 56623-9635 or 218/634-2570, fax 218/634-2570, email: morrispoint@webtv.net.

Trip Notes: If you enjoy watching birds, the Lake of the Woods area is a paradise with almost 300 species nesting here. We discovered that a great way to observe birds is by boat. Along the shorelines you can find Canada geese, tundra swans, herons, mallards, and loons. On many islands, you can see white pelicans, double-crested cormorants, and four species of gulls and terns. Pine and Curry Islands harbor the endangered piping plover. Other species include the bald eagle, osprey, turkey vulture, sandhill crane, and pileated woodpecker.

15 Lake of the Woods Campground

Location: On the Rainy River near Lake of the Woods, map 3, grid B3.

Campsites, facilities: There are 87 campsites. Facilities include RV pull-through sites, electric hookups, water, sewer, flush toilets, showers, disposal station, laundry, fishing launches, outdoor pool, grocery store, and playground. Seasonal campsite rentals are available.

Reservations, fees: The daily fee ranges from $15 to $21. Credit cards are accepted. Open from mid-May though mid-October.

Directions: From Baudette, take Hwy. 172 about 10 miles to the sign at County Road 32. Turn right to the campground.

Contact: Lake of the Woods Campground, R.R. 1, Box 247, Baudette, MN 56623, 800/344-1976 or 218/634-1694.

Trip Notes: Take a trip to the Clementson Rapids. Every spring and summer, the Rapid River, a tributary of the Rainy River, empties over the rapids, which is a wonderful place for a picnic. There are tables and campfire spots. The rapids are eight miles east of Baudette on Hwy. 11.

16 Cyrus Resort

Location: On Bostic Bay on Lake of the Woods, map 3, grid B2.

Campsites, facilities: There are 15 campsites. Facilities include electric hookups, water, flush toilets, showers, disposal station, grocery store, fishing launches and guides, hiking trails, outdoor pool, restaurant, lounge, and playground. Boat, motor, ice fishing house, and seasonal campsite rentals are available. Pets are allowed.

Reservations, fees: The daily fee ranges from $18 to $25. Credit cards are accepted. Open May through October.

Directions: From Baudette, drive on Hwy. 172 north for about 13 miles to County Road 8. Turn west and go three miles to the resort sign. Turn right to reach the resort.

Contact: Cyrus Resort, 3298 Cyrus Rd., N.W., Baudette, MN 56623-9633 or 800/932-2924 or 218/634-2548, fax 218/634-1252, email: cyrusresort@wiktel.com, website: www.fishandgame.com/cyrus/cyrus.htm.

Trip Notes: Be sure to travel along Hwy. 11 between International Falls and Karlstad, the Waters of the Dancing Sky Scenic Byway. The drive offers excellent views of the Rainy River, Lake of the Woods, forests, and wetlands.

17 Ken-Mar-Ke Resort

Location: On Bostic Bay on Lake of the Woods, map 3, grid B2.

Campsites, facilities: There are eight RV sites. Facilities include electric hookups, water, sewer, flush toilets, showers, fishing launches and guides, grocery store, restaurant and lounge. Boat, motor, ice fishing house, and seasonal campsite rentals are available. Pets are allowed.

Reservations, fees: The daily RV camping fee is about $25 for two persons. Credit cards are accepted. Open May to mid-October.

Directions: From Baudette, take Hwy. 172 north about 10 miles to County Road 8. Turn west to sign. The resort, on County Road 271 just before Bostic Creek, is on the right.

Contact: Ken-Mar-Ke Resort, 3147 Ken-Mar-Ke Dr., N.W., Baudette, MN 56623-9631 or 800/535-8155 or 218/634-2072, fax 218/634-2072, email: info@ken-mar-keresort.com, website: www.ken-mar-keresort.com.

Trip Notes: Here you can explore the nearby Rainy River that was once home to the Laurels, an ancient people that lived along its banks more than 2,000 years ago. At the confluence of the Big Fork and Rainy Rivers on the Canadian border stands the largest Indian burial mound in the Upper Midwest. The Grand Mound Interpretive Center (218/285-3332), 45 miles east of Baudette and 17 miles west of International Falls on Hwy. 11, offers self-guided tours and a museum full of artifacts.

18 International Voyageurs RV Park

Location: Near International Falls, map 4, grid D5.

Campsites, facilities: There are 71 campsites, including 12 for tents. Facilities include electric hookups, water, sewer, flush toilets, showers, disposal station, wheelchair access, and laundry. Seasonal campsite rentals are available. Pets are allowed.

Reservations, fees: The daily fee ranges from about $12 to $20. Open from mid-May through mid-September.

Directions: Take U.S. Hwy. 53 north toward International Falls. The campground is on the right less than two miles from the city.

Contact: International Voyageurs RV Park, Box 432, International Falls, MN 56649-0432 or 218/283-3425.

Trip Notes: Cross-country skiers might like the 20-kilometer, mostly intermediate-level, Black Bay Trail (218/286-5258). From International Falls, the trail running through birch and pine forest is 11 miles east on State Hwy. 11. Turn right at the visitors center and then go one-half mile to the trailhead. There are maps along the trail.

19 Voyageurs National Park

Location: On the northern edge of Minnesota's border with Canada, map 4, grid D7.

Campsites, facilities: There are 210 water-accessible sites throughout the 218,055-acre park for either tent camping or houseboats. Sites have a mooring aid, tent pad or level area, fire ring, toilet, picnic table, and bear-proof food-storage locker. Houseboat sites include two mooring aids and a fire ring. Restaurants and grocery stores are located near the park. In addition, camping and day use are allowed on the Kabetogama Peninsula. The Cruiser Lake Trail is nine miles long; Locator Lake Trail is two miles long. Other facilities include snowmobile and cross-country ski trails, lodging, interpretive walks, children's activities, and a junior ranger program.

Reservations, fees: Currently, there is no entrance fee or any other charge for use of park facilities. Permits or reservations are not required; camping is on a first-come, first-served basis. Open year-round.

Directions: The water-based park, which is five hours by car from Minneapolis-St. Paul and three hours from Duluth, can be approached from four points along U.S. Hwy. 53 between Duluth and International Falls, which is 11 miles west. Voyageurs has four gateway communities—Ash River, Crane Lake, International Falls, and Lake Kabetogama. Visitor centers are located at Rainy Lake (218/286-5258), Kabetogama (218/875-2111), and Ash River (218/374-3221). Detailed information on camping, as well as other park resources, are available at the centers.

Contact: Voyageurs National Park, 3131 Hwy. 53, International Falls, MN 56649-8904 or 218/283-9821, fax 218/285-7407, email: voya_superintendent@nps.gov, website: www.nps.gov/voya.

Trip Notes: An unusual spot to visit is the 360-acre Vince Shute Wildlife Sanctuary in Orr (218/757-0172), just south of the park. The American Bear Association now maintains it. Instead of shooting marauding, hungry black bears, Shute, in the early 1950s, began feeding his furry neighbors and grew to know them individually, establishing a mutual trust. By the mid-1980s, "the Bear Man," as he was known, drew people to witness the unusual truce that had developed. Surprisingly, the bears accepted the presence of visitors when within the two-to three-acre area immediately surrounding his home. But when the bears left this "safe zone," most reverted back to their wild ways, showing a fear of humans.

20 Moosehorn Resort

Location: Near International Falls on Lake Kabetogama, map 4, grid E8.

Campsites, facilities: There are six RV sites on this 18-acre resort with electric hookups, water, sewer, fishing launches and guides, tennis courts, and 1,000 feet of lake frontage with swimming beach. Boat, motor, canoe, and seasonal campsite rentals are available. Pets are not allowed.

Reservations, fees: The daily fee is $25. Credit cards are accepted. Because there are so few sites, reservations must be made well in advance. Open May through mid-September.

Directions: Take Hwy. 53 to County Road 122 to the lakeside resort, which is about 25 miles southeast of International Falls.

Contact: Moosehorn Resort, Alan and Miriam Burchell, 10434 Waltz Rd., Kabetogama, MN 56669-8027 or 800/777-7968 or 218/875-3491, email: moosehorn@june.com, website: www.moosehornresort.com.

Trip Notes: Don't miss a visit to the restored Kettle Falls Hotel (888/534-6835 or 218/374-4404), which has offered lodging and meals for more than 80 years deep in the heart of Voyageurs National Park. This wilderness spot, still offering food and lodging, is only accessible by snowmobile in winter and by a 13-mile boat ride from Ash River, Crane Lake, Kabetogama, or Rainy Lake/International Falls. Tour boats run almost daily in the summer. At the Kettle Falls Dam, you can look south into Canada due to a twist in the international border.

21 Kabetogama State Forest: Woodenfrog Campground and Day-Use Area

Location: Near Lake Kabetogama, map 4, grid E8.

Campsites, facilities: There are 61 drive-in sites. Facilities include 10 picnic sites, two miles of nature trails, swimming, and fishing.

Reservations, fees: The daily fee is $9. Open year-round.

Directions: From Orr, take U.S. Hwy. 53 north for 30 miles to County Road 122 (Gamma Rd.). Turn north and follow the signs for about six miles to the campground.

Contact: Woodenfrog Campground, P.O. Box 306, 4656 Hwy. 53, Orr, MN 55771, 218/757-3274.

Trip Notes: For a change of pace, a meal at The Chocolate Moose (218/365-6343), which is at 101 N. Central Ave., in Ely, at the junction of Country Road 21 and U.S. Hwy. 169, would be a treat for the whole family. This log cabin restaurant features backwoods gourmet dishes. Try the buffalo burger and a slice of fresh fruit pie. In good weather, you can dine on the outdoor deck. Carryouts, including ice cream, are available. There's only parking on the street.

22 Tomahawk Resort

Location: Near International Falls on Lake Kabetogama, map 4, grid E8.

Campsites, facilities: There are only four campsites with electric hookups, water, sewer, fishing or hunting guides, more than 500 feet of swimming beach, and playground. Boat, motor, canoe, and seasonal campsite rentals are available. Pets are allowed.

Reservations, fees: Reservations are strongly recommended. The daily fee is $20. Credit cards are accepted. Open from mid-May through mid-October.

Directions: From U.S. Hwy. 53, take County Road 122 north 2.5 miles to the resort entrance.

Contact: Tomahawk Resort, Lee and Lori Herseth, 10078 Gappa Rd., Ray, MN 56669, 888/834-7899 or 218/875-2352, email: lherseth@geocities.com, website: www.hersethstomahawkresort.com.

Trip Notes: If you like to bicycle, it's not far to the Rainy

Lake Bike Trail (800/325-5766), a 12-mile route from International Falls to Rainy Lake, the northern gateway to Voyageurs National Park. It can also be used by walkers and—drat!—in-line skaters. The trail can be picked up about a quarter of a mile from the Convention and Visitors Bureau at 301 2nd Ave., in International Falls.

23 Ash Trail Lodge Resort

Location: On Lake Kabetogama, map 4, grid E8.

Campsites, facilities: There are 10 campsites. Facilities include electric hookups, water, sewer, flush toilets, showers, fishing guides, swimming beach, whirlpool, snowmobile trails, grocery store, playground, restaurant and lounge. Fishing boat, motor, speedboat, canoe, snowmobile, and seasonal campsite rentals are available.

Reservations, fees: The daily fee is $20. Credit cards are accepted. Open May through September.

Directions: Take Hwy. 53 from Duluth or Cloquet north to Ash River Trail on County Road 129. Turn east on County Road 129 to resort. From International Falls, take Hwy. 53 southeast to County Road 129.

Contact: Ash Trail Lodge Resort, 10418 Ash River Trail, Ash River, MN 55771, 800/777-4513 or 218/374-3131, fax 218/374-4436, email: atl@blackduck.net, website: www.ashtrail lodge.com.

Trip Notes: Take your time in exploring this park on the southern part of the Canadian Shield with some of the world's oldest exposed rock formations. The bedrock has been shaped and carved by at least four glacial periods. A thorough trek will show you that its rolling hills are interspersed among bogs, beaver ponds, swamps, islands, small lakes, and four large bodies of water. Since the last glacier, a thin topsoil supports the boreal forest ecosystem.

24 Pine Aire

Location: Near International Falls on Lake Kabetogama, map 4, grid E8.

Campsites, facilities: There are 15 campsites. Facilities include RV pull-through sites, electric hookups, water, flush toilets, showers, disposal station, swimming beach, grocery store, playground, and lounge. Boat, motor, canoe, and seasonal campsite rentals are available. Pets are allowed.

Reservations, fees: The daily fee ranges from $15 to $25. Credit cards are accepted. Open from late May through mid-October.

Directions: From U.S. Hwy. 53, take Country Road 122 north until it becomes County Road 123 at the junction of County Road 571. The resort is on the left side of County Road 123 as it runs east.

Contact: Pine Aire, 9978 Gappa Rd., Kabetogama, MN 56669, 877/875-2161, fax 218/875-2012.

Trip Notes: Take a day trip to International Falls to see the Koochiching Historical and Bronco Nagurski Museums (218/283-4316) on 6th Ave., in Smokey Bear Park. The historical museum houses materials relating to the Koochiching County and the surrounding area going back 10,000 years. The Bronco Nagurski Museum honors the 1930s and 1940s NFL legend and Hall of Fame inductee.

25 Pokorny's Resort and Campground

Location: Near International Falls on Lake Kabetogama, map 4, grid E8.

Campsites, facilities: The resort has 17 campsites. Facilities include RV pull-through sites, electric hookups, water, showers, disposal station, wheelchair access, fishing guides, snowmobile and ski trails, playground, restaurant and lounge. Boat, motor, and seasonal campsite rentals and baby-sitting services are available. Pets are allowed.

Reservations, fees: The daily fee is $18. Open from late May through September.

Directions: From U.S. Hwy. 53, take Country Road 122 north to County Road 123. Turn east on County Road 123, which then turns north to Kabetogama. Turn east (right) on Burma Road to the campground.

Contact: Pokorny's Resort and Campground, 12473 Burma Rd., Kabetogama, MN 56669, 218/875-2481 or 218/638-2528.

Trip Notes: Don't fail to enjoy a boat tour from Voyageurs National Park aboard the concession-operated *Sight-Sea-Er*. Trips offered include sunset cruises, wildlife-watching cruises and cruises to the historic Kettle Falls Hotel. Most are guided by naturalists. Reservations are suggested. Check with the Kabetogama or Rainy Lake Visitor Centers.

If you're interested in photographing large statues, don't miss the Smokey Bear statue at 3rd St. and 6th Ave. in International Falls. The 26-foot fire-fighting icon is the main attraction at this municipal park site. Another photo opportunity is the 22-foot thermometer near the park entrance.

26 Red Pine Lodge and Resort

Location: Near International Falls on Lake Kabetogama, map 4, grid E8.

Campsites, facilities: The campground has 12 campsites, including six winter sites. Facilities include electric hookups, water, sewer, flush toilets, showers, disposal station, laundry, fishing launches and guides, hunting guides, swimming beach, grocery store, playground, restaurant and lounge. There are also hiking, snowmobile, and ski trails. Boat, motor, canoe, ice fishing house, and seasonal campsite rentals are available. Pets are allowed.

Reservations, fees: The daily fee is $14. Open from mid-May through September; some sites open in winter.

Directions: From U.S. Hwy. 53, take Country Road 122 north to County Road 123. Turn east on County Road 123, which then turns north to Kabetogama. Turn east (right) on Burma Road to the resort.

Contact: Red Pine Lodge and Resort, 12443 Burma Rd., Kabetogama, MN 56669, 218/875-2441, fax 218/815-2441.

Trip Notes: If you come during June, the Lady Slipper Arts & Crafts Festival (800/524-9085 or 218/875-2621 for dates) is celebrated in Kabetogama. You'll experience orchids, food, boat tours, rock gardens, workshops, antique auction, music, and other entertainment.

27 Pine Island State Forest: Benn Linn Landing Campsites

Location: On the Big Fork River, map 4, grid G1.

Campsites, facilities: There are three drive-in sites. Facilities include access to the river and fishing.

Reservations, fees: None. Open year-round.

Directions: From Big Falls, take County Road 13 north for two miles. Turn west and follow the access road for 4.5 miles.

Contact: Benn Linn Landing Campsites, 421 Third Ave., Box 65, Littlefork, MN 56653, 218/278-6651.

Trip Notes: East on State Hwy. 11 is Baudette, home of

the 40-foot Willie the Walleye statue. Other nearby attractions include national historic sites, wilderness drives and a wildflower route.

28 Pine Island State Forest: Sturgeon River Landing Campsites

Location: On the Big Fork River, map 4, grid G1.

Campsites, facilities: There are two drive-in sites. Facilities include access to the river, swimming, and fishing.

Reservations, fees: None. Open year-round.

Directions: From Big Falls, take County Road 30 west for 3.5 miles. Turn north and follow the access road for 1.5 miles.

Contact: Sturgeon River Landing Campsites, 421 Third Ave., Box 65, Littlefork, MN 56653, 218/278-6651.

Trip Notes: International Falls, on the shore of Rainy Lake, has plenty of opportunities for water sports and cruises through Voyagers National Park. While in the area, visit Smokey Bear Park, which features a 26-foot-tall likeness of Smokey and the nearby Koochiching County Historical Museum.

29 Kabetogama State Forest: Ash River Campground

Location: On the Ash River, map 5, grid E2.

Campsites, facilities: There are nine drive-in sites. Facilities include two picnic sites, water access to the Ash River, and fishing.

Reservations, fees: The daily fee is $9. Open year-round.

Directions: From Orr, take U.S. Hwy. 53 north 26 miles to Ash River Road (County Road 126). Turn east and go five miles.

Contact: Ash River Campground, P.O. Box 306 4656 Hwy. 53, Orr, MN 55771, 218/757-3274.

Trip Notes: Take a drive north to International Falls and go on a guided tour of Boise Cascade (218/285-5011) at 2nd St. and 4th Ave. The 1.5-hour tour includes a demonstration of each step in making paper from pulp to the packaging process. Sandals and cameras are not allowed.

30 Beddow's Campground

Location: Near Orr on Crane Lake, map 5, grid F4.

Campsites, facilities: There are 25 campsites. Facilities include RV pull-through sites, electric hookups, water, sewer, flush toilets, showers, disposal station, fishing guides, and swimming beach. Boat and motor rentals are available. Pets are allowed.

Reservations, fees: The daily fee ranges from about $17 to $19. Open May through September.

Directions: From U.S. Hwy. 53, the campground is 30 miles northeast of Orr. Take County Road 23 at Orr to County Road 24 and follow it to Crane Lake.

Contact: Beddow's Campground, Joel and Bonnie Beddow, 7516 Bayside Dr., Crane Lake, MN 55725-8020 or 218/993-2389.

Trip Notes: A good way to trace the routes of the Voyageurs is to rent a houseboat. Voyagaire Houseboats, 7576 Gold Coast Rd., Crane Lake, MN 55725-8010 (800/882-6287 or 218/993-2266, email: vlhb@uslink.net, website: www.voyagaire.com), is in Crane Lake, 28 miles from Orr at the end of County Road 23. The company offers fully-equipped boats by the day or week.

Gunflint Pines Resort and Campgrounds

Location: Along the Gunflint Trail, map 6, grid H2.

Campsites, facilities: There are 209 tent and RV sites. Electrical and water hookups ($2 per night) are available along with a limited number of lakefront sites ($2 additional per night). RV length limit is 32 feet. Facilities include showers, flush toilets, disposal station, laundry, lodge, sauna, grocery store, marina with boat ramp, recreation area, restaurant, children's programs, playground, and biking, hiking and cross-country ski trails. Housekeeping cabin, boat, motor, canoe and snowshoe rentals are available. There is also a riding stable with horses for rent. Pets are allowed.

Reservations, fees: Reservations recommended and a non-refundable deposit is required. The rates are $19 per night for 1 or 2 people ($23 from late June through early September). An extra person is $1 per night. Credit cards are accepted. Open from mid-May through late September.

Directions: The campground is on Gunflint Lake along the Gunflint Trail, which begins in downtown Grand Marais. From U.S. Hwy. 61, take Country Rd. 12 about 45 miles northwest and then one mile north on County Road 50 to the site.

Contact: Gunflint Pines Resort and Campgrounds, Dick and Ronnie Smith, 217 S. Gunflint Lake Rd.; Grand Marais, MN 55604, 218/388-4454 or 800/533-5814, email: play@gunflintpines.com, website: www.gunflintpines.com.

Trip Notes: Drive part of the 63-mile, paved, two-lane Gunflint Trail to spot the area's abundant wildlife. The corridor is surrounded by the Boundary Waters Canoe Area Wilderness and Superior National Forest. It winds its way north from Grand Marais and west to Saganaga Lake at the Canadian border. Keep a camera handy because it's not uncommon to see deer, moose, fox, bear and other animals along or crossing the road. Not too many miles from here we spotted a moose sitting—yes, sitting—on the shoulder of the road.

In spring, you can fish or hike. Summer activities range from canoeing to swimming. In fall, you can venture into the alluring woods to hike or canoe, hunt grouse or fish. You can't beat winter for quiet nights, cross-country skiing, dog sledding, ice-fishing and snowshoeing.

In the evenings, go outside and look for wildlife, view the Milky Way or experience the spectacular display of Northern Lights. Listen for the howl of the timber wolf or the cry of the loon on a moonlit lake.

Wakemup Bay Campground

Location: Near Cook on Lake Vermilion, map 7, grid A4.

Campsites, facilities: There are 21 primitive sites in this Kabetogama State Forest campground. Facilities include wheelchair access, dock space, swimming beach, and hiking trails. Pets are allowed.

Reservations, fees: The daily fee is $7. Open year-round.

Directions: From Cook, take County Road 24 north to East Wakemup Village Road. Go east to the campground.

Contact: Wakemup Bay Campground, Forestry District Office, Cook, MN 55723, 218/666-5385, fax 218/666-2107.

Trip Notes: Tour the Laurentian Environmental Center (218/749-1288; email: lec@rangenet.com), which is 12 miles south of Cook (14 miles north of Virginia) on

U.S. Hwy. 53. It offers year-round family nature programs. Reservations are required.

33 Kabetogama State Forest: Hinsdale Island Campsites

Location: On Lake Vermillion, map 7, grid A5.

Campsites, facilities: There are 11 boat-in sites. Facilities include fishing.

Reservations, fees: None. Open year-round.

Directions: From Cook, take County Road 24 north to County Road 78. Turn east and go three miles to County Road 540. Continue east about six miles to the public access.

Contact: Hinsdale Island Campsites, P.O. 432, Tower, MN 55790, 218/753-4500.

Trip Notes: Be sure to visit the 1,300-acre, Soudan Underground Mine (218/753-2245) near Tower. This historic site, the state's oldest and deepest iron mine, is five miles north of State Hwy. 169 along the shore of Lake Vermilion. You can take a three-minute elevator ride 2,400 feet down to its 27th level and an electric train trip through a 3,000-foot tunnel.

34 Bear Head Lake State Park

Location: In the Vermilion Iron Range of Superior National Forest, map 7, grid B8.

Campsites, facilities: The 4,535-acre park has 74 pull-through RV sites, six tent sites, and one boat-in site. Five sites are for backpackers. Facilities include flush toilets, showers, disposal station, wheelchair access, and swimming beach. There are biking, 17 miles of hiking, nine miles of ski, and a mile of snowmobile trails. Rental boats and canoes are available. Pets are allowed.

Reservations, fees: The daily fee ranges from $7 to $12. Credit cards are accepted. Open year-round.

Directions: The park is 16 miles east of Tower. Take U.S. Hwy. 1 east to Country Road 128. Follow County Road 128 south, east and then west to the park entrance.

Contact: Bear Head Lake State Park, 9301 Bear Head State Park Rd., Ely, MN 55731-8037 or 218/365-7229, fax 218/365-7204.

Trip Notes: There are 10 lakes in the park and four are stocked with walleye and trout. Eagle's Nest and Bear Head Lakes have boat accesses. You have to portage, sometimes over a rugged trail, to the other lakes.

35 JKO Good Sampark

Location: In Chisholm, map 7, grid E1.

Campsites, facilities: There are 48 campsites, including RV pull-through sites. Facilities include electric hookups, water, sewer, flush toilets, showers, disposal station, laundry, grocery store, and restaurant. Seasonal campsite rentals are available. Pets are allowed.

Reservations, fees: The daily fee ranges from $10 to $13. Open May through September.

Directions: Take Hwy. 169 or Hwy. 73 to 6th Ave. S. in Chisholm.

Contact: JKO Good Sampark, Hwy. 73 and 6th Ave. S., Chisholm, MN 55719, 800/711-7789.

Trip Notes: In Chisholm, about one-half block from the water tower is the Minnesota Museum of Mining (218/254-5543 or 218/254-7158). It features several buildings with exhibits of mining town life, including a schoolroom, broom factory, shoemaker's shop, print shop, mining office, and simulated underground drift, on the self-guided tour. There's also a 1907 steam locomotive, 1910 steam shovel, and early mining trucks.

36 Forest Heights RV Park

Location: In Hibbing, map 7, grid E1.

Campsites, facilities: There are 40 RV pull-through sites and 20 tent sites. Facilities include electric hookups, water, sewer, flush toilets, showers, disposal station, laundry, and wheelchair access. There are also biking, hiking, ski, and snowmobile trails. Seasonal campsite rentals are available. Pets are allowed.

Reservations, fees: The daily fee ranges from $6 to $12. Open May through September.

Directions: From Virginia, take Hwy. 169 to east 25th St. in Hibbing.

Contact: Forest Heights RV Park, 2240 25th St., E., Hibbing, MN 55746, 218/263-5782.

Trip Notes: The family can have a fun day at the Ironworld Discovery Center (800/372-6437; website: www.ironworld.com) on Hwy. 169 in nearby Chisholm. The historical exhibits, research center, living history areas, and trolley offer opportunities to discover the history and ethnic heritage of the state's Iron Range. You can trolley to the edge of an open-pit mine and even operate your own remote-control ore boat.

37 Mesaba Coop Park

Location: East of Hibbing, map 7, grid E2.

Campsites, facilities: There are five RV sites and 10 tent sites. Facilities include electric hookups, flush toilets, showers, hiking trails, and swimming beach. Boat, motor, and seasonal campsite rentals are available. Pets are allowed.

Reservations, fees: The daily fee is $10. Open from mid-May through mid-October.

Directions: From Hibbing, take Hwy. 37 east to Country Road 450. Turn south down County Road 450 (Mesada Park Rd.) to campground.

Contact: Mesaba Coop Park, 3827 Mesaba Park Rd., Hibbing, MN 55746-8551 or 218/262-1350.

Trip Notes: On a rainy day, you can tour the Hibbing Historical Society and Museum (218/263-8522). It chronicles Hibbing's unique history, including the Hibbing Almanac from 1870 to present, models of old North Hibbing, and ethnic and logging exhibits. Take Hwy. 169 to 25th St. Go to 23rd St. and 5th Ave. E.

38 Canoe Country Cabins and Campground

Location: On Moose Lake near the Boundary Waters Canoe Area Wilderness, map 8, grid A4.

Campsites, facilities: There are 12 RV pull-through sites and eight tent sites. Facilities include electric hookups, water, sewer, flush toilets, showers, laundry, fishing launches and guides, canoe outfitting, hiking trails, grocery store, and playground. Boat, motor, and seasonal campsite rentals are available. Pets are allowed.

Reservations, fees: The daily fee is $16. Credit cards are accepted. Open from mid-May through late September.

Directions: From Ely, take Hwy. 169 (Country Road 18) about 20 miles east to Moose Lake Road. Turn north and drive 1.5 miles to campground.

Contact: Canoe Country Cabins and Campground, Moose Lake Rd., 629 Sheridan St., E., Box 20, Ely, MN 55731-1631 or 218/365-4046, fax 218/365-4046, website: canoecountryoutfitters.com.

Trip Notes: Visit the Ely-Winton History Museum (218/365-3226) on the east side of the Vermilion Community College Campus at 1900 Camp St. E. It depicts local history through artifacts, photos, videos, and oral histories. There are exhibits on the

Ojibwa Indians, fur trade, mining, logging, immigration, voyageurs, and the 1986 North Pole Expedition.

39 Silver Rapids Lodge and Campground

Location: On White Iron and Farm Lakes near the Boundary Waters Canoe Area Wilderness, map 8, grid A3.

Campsites, facilities: There are 34 RV sites and two tent sites on the shoreline. Facilities include electric hookups, water, sewer, flush toilets, showers, disposal station, laundry, grocery store, fishing launches and guides, canoe outfitting, swimming beach, children's programs, playground, restaurant and lounge. There are also biking, hiking, ski, and snowmobile trails. Boat, motor, ice fishing house, snowshoe, snowmobile, ski, and seasonal campsite rentals are available. Pets are allowed.

Reservations, fees: The daily fee is $28. Credit cards are accepted. Open from late May through mid-October.

Directions: From Ely, take Hwy. 69 east to Country Road 16 and turn southeast to the lodge and campground on a peninsula on White Iron and Farm Lakes.

Contact: Silver Rapids Lodge and Campground, HC 1, Box 2992, Ely, MN 55731-9336 or 800/950-9425 or 218/365-4877, fax 218/365-3540, website: www.silverrapidlodge.com.

Trip Notes: Make a two-hour round-trip by paddling a canoe through the BWCAW to see the pictographs—ancient Indian paintings on the rocks. This naturalist-led tour highlights the area's geology, ecology, and fur trading history. Beginners are welcome and canoe lessons are included. Call the Hegman Lake Pictograph Tours (218/365-5838). The cost is about $30 each with a two-person minimum.

40 Timber Trail Lodge

Location: On Farm Lake near the Boundary Waters Canoe Area Wilderness, map 8, grid A3.

Campsites, facilities: The resort on Farm Lake, part of an 11,000-acre chain of four lakes, has 18 campsites. Facilities include electric hookups, water, sewer, flush toilets, showers, fishing launches and guides, canoe outfitting, swimming beach, grocery store, children's programs, playground, and lounge. There are also biking, hiking, ski, and snowmobile trails. Boat, motor, and seasonal campsite rentals are available. Pets are allowed.

Reservations, fees: Reservations are accepted; a 50 percent deposit is required to guarantee your reservation. The daily fee ranges from $20 to $29. A pet fee is $5 per day per pet. Credit cards are accepted. Open from mid-May through September.

Directions: From Ely, take Hwy. 69 east to Country Road 16 and turn southeast to the southern shore of Farm Lake.

Contact: Timber Trail Lodge, 629 Kawishiwi Trail, Ely, MN 55731-9328 or 800/777-7348 or 218/365-4879, fax 218/365-5236, email: info@timbertrail.com, website: www.timbertrail.com.

Trip Notes: On the east edge of Ely, next to the International Wolf Center, is the Dorothy Molter Museum (218/365-4451 or 218/365-5161). It consists of two 1920s furnished cabins removed from the BWCAW in 1987 by dog teams. They were the last residences allowed in the area. Molter was widely known for her hospitality to thousands of canoeists and snowmobilers and became known as "the root beer lady" because of the homemade beverage she offered visitors.

MINNESOTA NORTHWOODS

Minnesota Northwoods

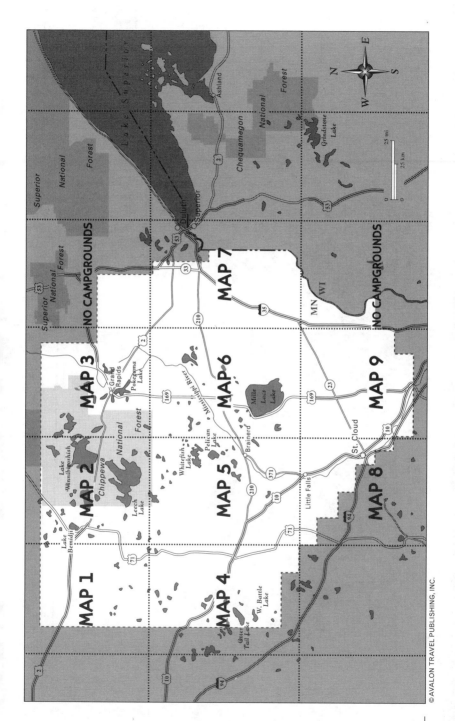

© AVALON TRAVEL PUBLISHING, INC.

Map 1

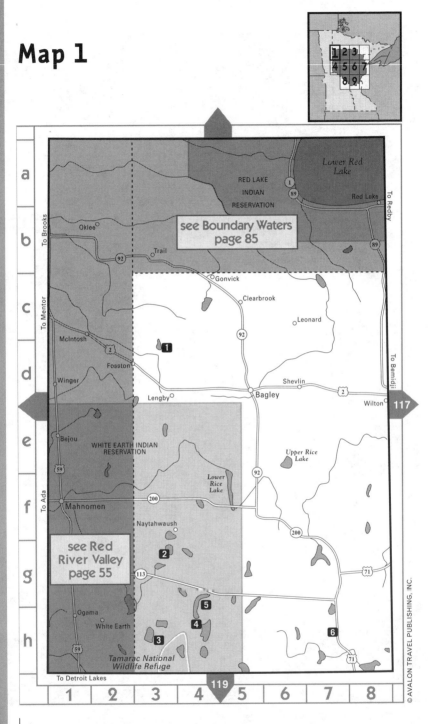

see Boundary Waters
page 85

see Red
River Valley
page 55

RED LAKE
INDIAN
RESERVATION

Lower Red
Lake

Red Lake

To Redby

To Brooks

Oklee

Trail

92

Gonvick

Clearbrook

Leonard

To Mentor

McIntosh

2

Fosston

1

Winger

Lengby

Shevlin

Bagley

Wilton

2

To Bemidji

117

Bejou

WHITE EARTH INDIAN
RESERVATION

Upper Rice
Lake

59

Lower
Rice
Lake

To Ada

Mahnomen

200

Naytahwaush

2

113

5

4

6

Ogema

White Earth

3

59

Tamarac National
Wildlife Refuge

To Detroit Lakes

119

1   2   3   4   5   6   7   8

© AVALON TRAVEL PUBLISHING, INC.

Map 2

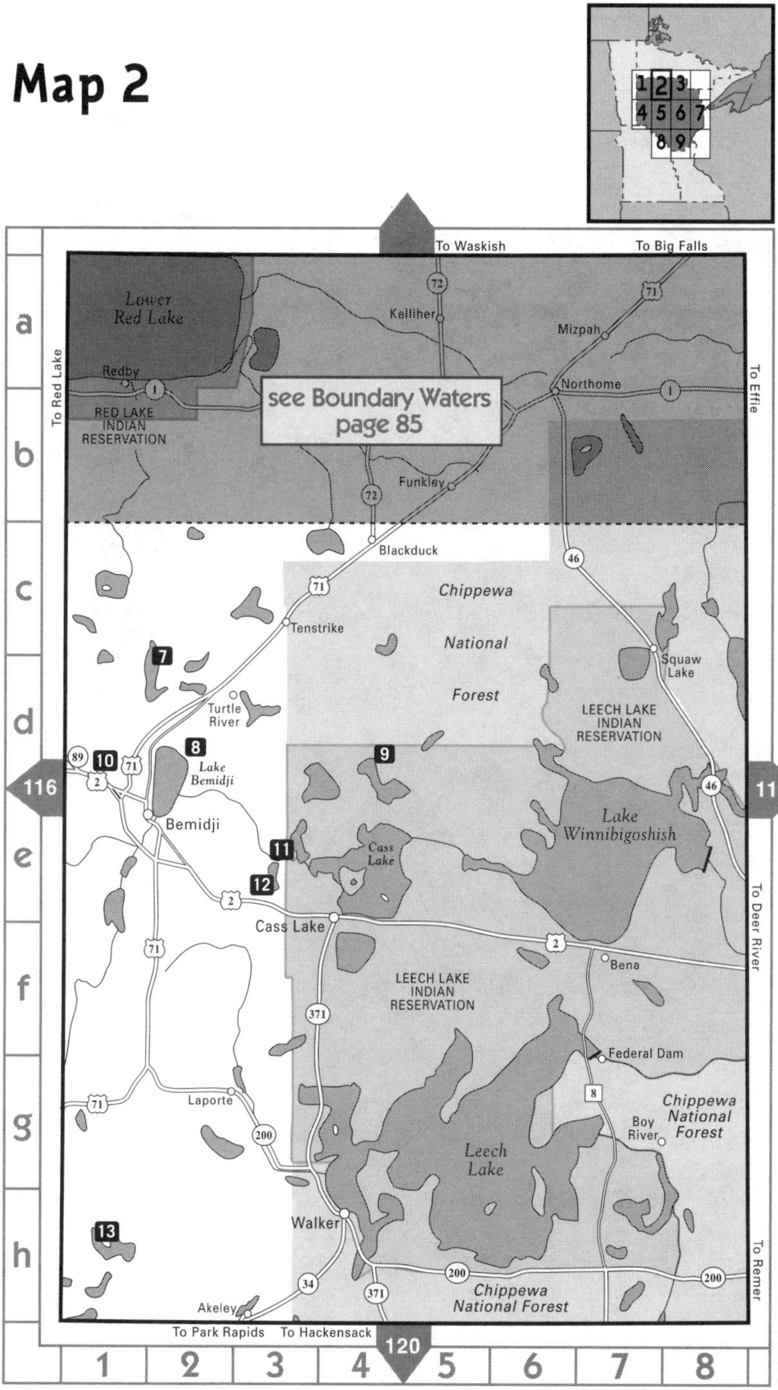

see Boundary Waters page 85

To Waskish
To Big Falls

Lower Red Lake

Kelliher
72

Mizpah

71

a

To Red Lake

Redby
1

RED LAKE INDIAN RESERVATION

Northome
1

To Effie

b

Funkley
72

Blackduck
46

c

Chippewa

71

Tenstrike

National

7

Forest

Squaw Lake

LEECH LAKE INDIAN RESERVATION

d

Turtle River

8

Lake Bemidji

9

89 10 71
2

116

Bemidji

Lake Winnibigoshish

46

118

e

11

Cass Lake

12

2

To Deer River

Cass Lake
2

Bena

f

LEECH LAKE INDIAN RESERVATION

371

Federal Dam

Chippewa National Forest

g

71

Laporte
200

8

Boy River

Leech Lake

h

13

Walker

To Remer

34 371
200

Chippewa National Forest

200

Akeley

To Park Rapids   To Hackensack
120

1   2   3   4   5   6   7   8

© AVALON TRAVEL PUBLISHING, INC.

Map 3

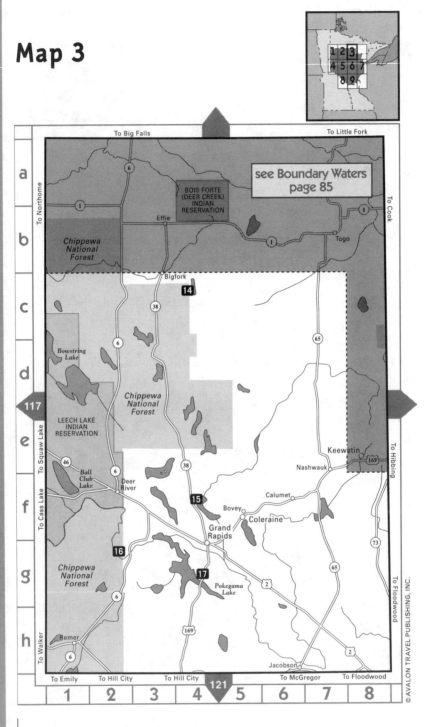

see Boundary Waters page 85

To Big Falls

To Little Fork

To Northome

6

1

BOIS FORTE
(DEER CREEK)
INDIAN
RESERVATION

Effie

To Cook

1

1

Togo

Chippewa
National
Forest

Bigfork

14

38

To Squaw Lake

Bowstring
Lake

6

65

Chippewa
National
Forest

117

LEECH LAKE
INDIAN
RESERVATION

46

38

To Hibbing

Keewatin

169

To Cass Lake

Ball
Club
Lake

6

Deer
River

Nashwauk

15

Calumet

Bovey

Coleraine

Grand
Rapids

16

Chippewa
National
Forest

6

17

Pokegama
Lake

65

2

73

To Floodwood

169

To Walker

Remer

6

2

To Emily

To Hill City

To Hill City

121

To McGregor

To Floodwood

Jacobson

2

© AVALON TRAVEL PUBLISHING, INC.

1   2   3   4   5   6   7   8

Map 4

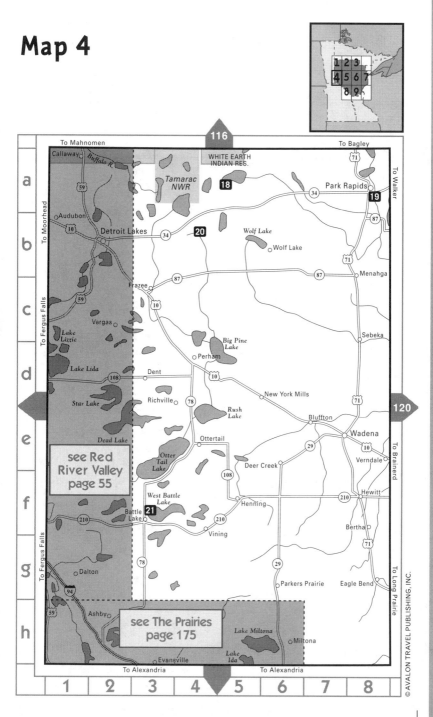

Map 5

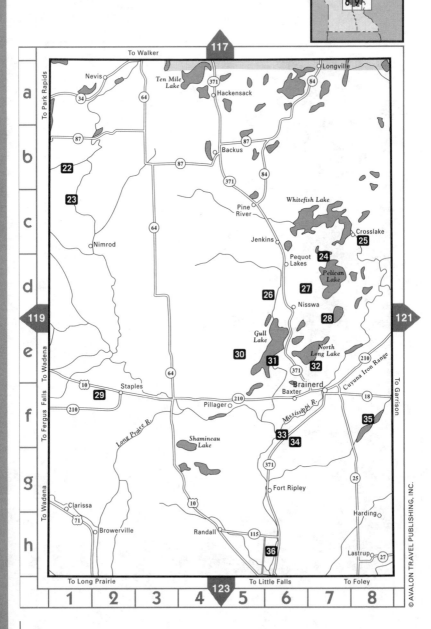

Map 6

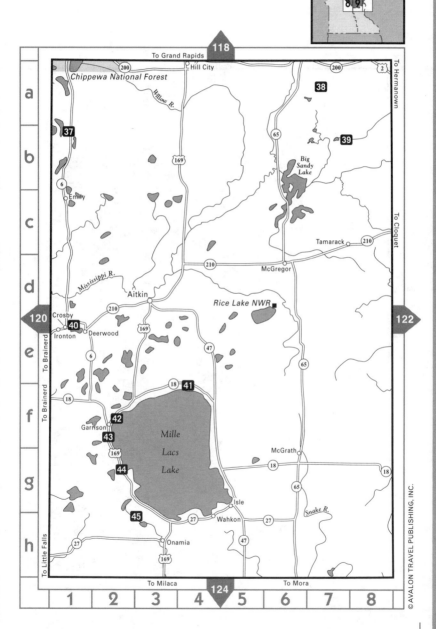

Map 7

see Indian Head Country page 243

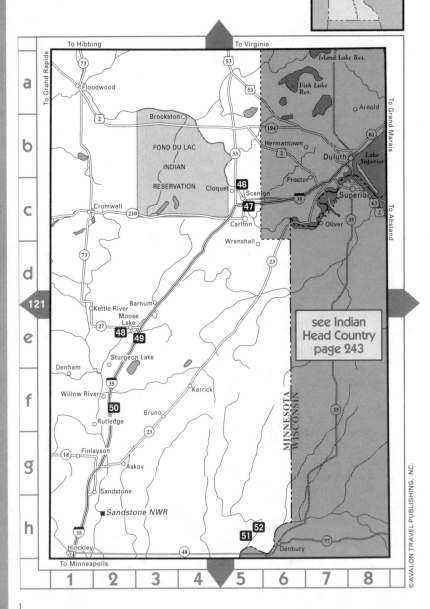

To Hibbing
To Virginia
To Grand Rapids
To Grand Marais
To Ashland

Island Lake Res.
Fish Lake Res.

Floodwood
Brookston
Arnold

FOND DU LAC INDIAN RESERVATION

Hermantown
Duluth
Lake Superior

Cloquet
Scanlon
46
47
Proctor
Superior

Cromwell
Carlton
Wrenshall
Oliver

Kettle River
Barnum
Moose Lake
48
49
Sturgeon Lake

Denham
Kerrick

Willow River
50
Bruno
Rutledge

Finlayson
Askov

Sandstone
Sandstone NWR

MINNESOTA
WISCONSIN

52
51
Hinckley
Danbury
To Minneapolis

© AVALON TRAVEL PUBLISHING, INC.

Map 8

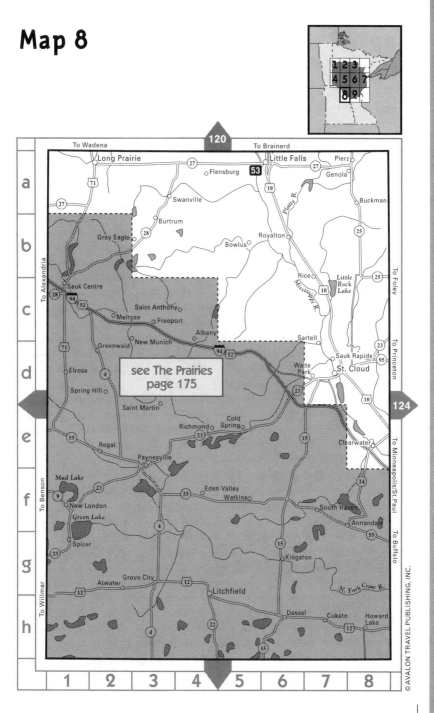

Map 8

To Wadena

120

To Brainerd

Long Prairie
27
Flensburg
53
Little Falls
27
Pierz
Genola

71
10
Buckman

Swanville

a

Burtrum

25

Grey Eagle
28
Bowlus
Royalton

b

Mississippi R.
Platte R.

To Alexandria

Rice
10
Little Rock Lake
25

Sauk Centre
28
94
52
Saint Anthony
Sartell

To Foley

c

Melrose
Freeport
Albany
94
52
Sauk Rapids
23
95

To Princeton

Greenwald
New Munich
Waite Park
St. Cloud

d

Elrosa
4
see The Prairies page 175
23
10

124

Spring Hill

Saint Martin

Cold Spring
Clearwater

To Minneapolis/St. Paul

Richmond
23
15

e

55
Regal

Paynesville

Mud Lake
24

f

9
New London
Eden Valley
Watkins
South Haven
Annandale

To Benson

Green Lake
55

55

4

15

To Buffalo

Spicer

23
Kingston

g

Grove City
12
N. Fork Crow R.

To Willmar

Atwater
Litchfield

12

Dassel
Cokato
Howard Lake

h

4
22
12

15

1 2 3 4 5 6 7 8

Map 9

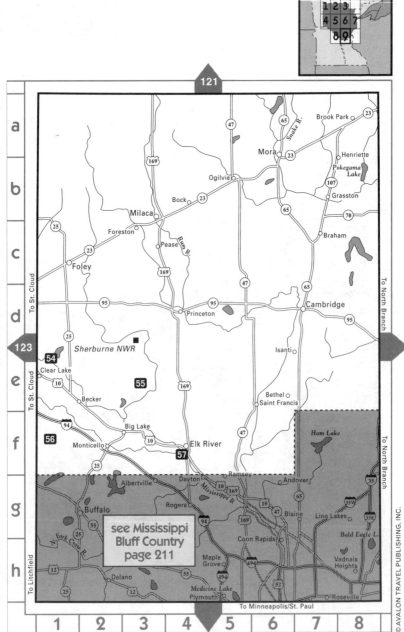

see Mississippi Bluff Country page 211

© AVALON TRAVEL PUBLISHING, INC.

Minnesota Northwoods

(CONTINUED ON NEXT PAGE)

Fragrant pine forests and dozens of crystal-clear, sandy-bottom lakes in this region evoke many happy memories. This "heartland" of Minnesota is a personal favorite because nearly 30 years ago, I (Bob Schmidt) joined Al and Ron Lindner to become one of the "founders" of *In-Fisherman* magazine, still based in Brainerd. I also was its first editor, and quickly discovered I could fish a different body of water every day for a year and not have to drive more than 50 miles in any direction. Today, the chamber of commerce boasts there are 465 sand-bottom lakes within 30 miles! I believe it.

This is also the land where the Mississippi River is born as a quiet woodland stream and flows through downtown Brainerd on its long journey to the Gulf of Mexico.

Although this area is more populated than the wilderness region to the north, it offers much to the camper in every season.

Don't care for fishing?

No matter, the woods and waters offer plenty of outdoor adventure in every season. You can go horseback riding, canoeing, golfing, cross-country skiing, snowmobiling, and bird-watching, or try biking and in-line skating on the 50-mile paved Paul Bunyan Trail.

▣ Cross Lake (Tilberg Park) Campground

Location: Northeast of Fosston on Cross Lake, map 1, grid D3.

Campsites, facilities: There are 30 campsites with 22 tent sites. Facilities include electric hookups, disposal station, and boat ramp. The facility offers access to Cross Lake. Seasonal campsite rentals are available. Pets are allowed.

Reservations, fees: The daily fee is $5 to $6. Open from mid-May through mid-September.

Directions: From Fosston, take County Road 3 east to County Road 29. Then continue east to the township road that runs south. The campground is on the west shore of Cross Lake, about one mile south of County Road 29.

Contact: Cross Lake (Tilberg Park) Campground, Box 27, Crookston, MN 56716-0027 or 218/281-3952, fax 218/281-3976.

Trip Notes: In winter, the Red Lake Falls Club Trail on County Road 13, four miles northwest of Red Lake Falls, has a 10-kilometer trail for intermediate cross-country skiers. This mostly forested trail follows some flat railroad bed and rolling hills. There are maps along the route.

◨ Elkhorn Resort and Campground

Location: Northeast of Waubun on South Twin Lake, map 1, grid G3.

Campsites, facilities: The 14-acre campground has 11 RV pull-through sites and nine tent sites. Facilities include electric hookups, water, sewer, flush toilets, showers, disposal station, boat ramp, swimming beach, grocery store, playground, and biking, hiking, and snowmobile trails. Boat, canoe, motor, and seasonal campsite rentals are available. Pets are allowed.

Reservations, fees: The daily fee ranges from $14 to $17. Credit cards are accepted. Open May through September.

Directions: From Hwy. 59, the campground on South Twin Lake is about 12 miles east on State Road 113 and four miles north on Country Road 4.

Contact: Elkhorn Resort and Campground, 2929 293rd St., Waubun, MN 56589-9482 or 218/935-5437 or 800/279-4830.

Trip Notes: Waubun is one of the towns within the White Earth Indian Reservation. Another option for hunting enthusiasts is McCollum's Hunting Preserve (218/935-2468), which operates from August through April. This public hunting preserve offers no-limit hunting for pheasant, chuckar, and bobwhites. Hunting dogs and guide and bird-cleaning are available. No license is required and overnight facilities include a cabin and clubhouse. The preserve is three miles east of Bejou on County Road 1 and one-half mile south.

◪ Woodland Trails Resort and Campground

Location: On Strawberry Lake northeast of Callaway, map 1, grid H3.

Campsites, facilities: There are 21 campsites. Facilities include RV pull-through sites, electric hookups, water, flush toilets, showers, disposal station, boat ramp, swimming beach, bike and hiking trails, laundry, grocery store, and playground. Boat, canoe, motor, ice-fishing house, and seasonal campsite rentals are available. Pets are allowed.

Reservations, fees: The daily fee ranges from $19 to $23. Credit cards are accepted. Open May through September.

Directions: From U.S. Hwy. 59 and County Road 14, drive about five miles on County Road 14, then east on County Road 21. At Richwood, go 10 miles north on County Road 34, then 1.5 miles east on County Road 143, and one mile north on a gravel road to the entrance.

Contact: Woodland Trails Resort and Campground, 33616 Loon Dr., Ogema, MN 56569-9731 or 800/879-7829 or 218/983-3230.

Trip Notes: About 20 miles northeast of Detroit Lakes on Little Sugar Bush Lake is the Maplelag Trail (800/654-7711), a 53-kilometer cross-country ski trail that winds through a maple and basswood forest and around several lakes. Trails range from beginner to expert. Ski lessons and ski and snowshoe rentals are available.

◫ Rainbow Resort

Location: Near Waubun on Little Bemidji Lake, map 1, grid H4.

Campsites, facilities: There are only eight sites here.

Facilities include electric hookups, water, sewer, laundry, grocery store, restaurant, boat ramp, fishing and hunting guides, and swimming beach. There are also biking, hiking, cross-country skiing, and snowmobile trails. Boat, canoe, motor, ice-fishing house, snowshoe, and ski equipment rentals are available.

Reservations, fees: The daily fee begins at $22. Credit cards are accepted. Open May through November.

Directions: From Waubun, take MN 113 to County Road 35 and turn south. Drive about four miles (two miles of blacktop road; two miles of gravel road) to the resort.

Contact: Rainbow Resort, 36571 County Hwy. 35, Rt. 2, Box 239, Waubun, MN 56589, 218/734-2241 or 888/734-1140, fax 218/734-2240.

Trip Notes: Spend an hour at the Becker County Museum (218/847-2938) exploring two floors of exhibits that trace the natural and social history of Detroit Lakes and Becker County. Highlights include a pioneer cabin, Ojibwa birch-bark wigwam, antique vehicles, and other historic items. Admission is free. Go two blocks south of U.S. 10 at Summit Avenue and West Front Street.

The resort is also only 20 miles from Itasca State Park, where the Mississippi River begins its journey to the Gulf of Mexico. You can find miles of hiking, biking, and skiing trails and beautiful stands of Norway pine.

⑤ Pike Lake Resort and Campground

Location: Near Waubun on Pike Lake, map 1, grid H5.

Campsites, facilities: The resort has 21 sites and offers electric hookups, water, sewer, flush toilets, showers, disposal station, laundry, lake access, hiking and snow-

mobile trails, boat ramp, swimming beach, restaurant, and playground. Boat, motor, and seasonal campsite rentals are available. Pets are allowed.

Reservations, fees: The daily fee ranges from $11 to $16. Credit cards are accepted. Open May 10 through November 30.

Directions: From Waubun, drive about 20 miles east on MN Hwy. 113 to East Elbow Lake Road, taking a left at the "Y." The campground is on Pike Lake.

Contact: Pike Lake Resort and Campground, Rt. 2, Box 235, Waubun, MN 56589-9329 or 218/734-2264 or 888/664-5750.

Trip Notes: This region has numerous bodies of water left behind by the retreating glaciers more than 10,000 years ago. Winter enthusiasts can cross-country ski on the East Frazee Trail (218/846-7307) near Detroit Lakes. The 16-km track is mostly for beginners. It's located on the east side of Frazee on County Road 150 (on the northwest side of Murphy Lake). The trail meanders through forest and meadows beside Murphy, Fischer, Evans, Albertson, Rive, and Bass lakes. A ski pass is required. Maps are placed along the trail.

⑥ Two Inlets State Forest: Hungryman Lake Campground and Day Use Area

Location: On Cedar Lake, map 1, grid H7.

Campsites, facilities: There are 14 drive-in sites, two picnic sites, access to the lake, and fishing and swimming.

Reservations, fees: The daily fee is $9. Open year-round.

Directions: From Park Rapids, take State Hwy. 71 north 10 miles to County Road 41. Turn west for 1.5 miles. Then turn north for one mile to the campground.

Contact: Hungryman Lake Campground, Box 113, 607 1st St., Park Rapids, MN 56470, 218/732-3309.

Trip Notes: About five miles east of Crookston on U.S. Hwy. 2 is the Polk County Museum (218/281-1038), which will give you a glimpse of what 19th-century life was like. It includes a chapel, agricultural building, reconstructed 1872 and 1891 homes, summer home, and 1890 schoolhouse.

7 Hamilton's Fox Lake Campground

Location: Northeast of Bemidji, map 2, grid D2.

Campsites, facilities: There are 62 RV sites and 12 tent sites. Facilities include RV pull-through sites, electric hookups, water, sewer, flush toilets, showers, disposal station, laundry, wheelchair access, grocery store, hiking trails, swimming beach, children's programs, and playground. Boat, motor, canoe, and seasonal campsite rentals and baby-sitting services are available. Pets are allowed.

Reservations, fees: The daily fee ranges from $18 to $21. Credit cards are accepted. Open from early May through mid-September.

Directions: From the junction of Hwy. 197 and Hwy. 71 north, turn north for 10 miles to Island View Dr., N.E. (County Road 22). Turn west and go four miles.

Contact: Hamilton's Fox Lake Campground, The Ducharme Family, 2555 Island View Dr., N.E., Bemidji, MN 56601-7144 or 218/586-2231.

Trip Notes: An unusual spot to visit is the Wes Westrum Baseball Museum on Main St. in the American Legion Bldg. (218/776-3933 or 218/776-3696) in Clearbrook, about 38 miles west of Bemidji. It houses memorabilia, including Westrum's uniforms, baseballs, bats, and newspaper clippings.

8 Lake Bemidji State Park

Location: On the northeast shore of Lake Bemidji, map 2, grid D2.

Campsites, facilities: This 1,688-acre park has 96 campsites. Facilities include five RV pull-through sites, electric hookups, flush toilets, showers, wheelchair access, disposal station, and swimming beach. Boat and snowshoe rentals are available. There are also six miles of biking, 15 miles of hiking, 11 miles of skiing, and three miles of snowmobile trails. Pets are allowed.

Reservations, fees: The daily fee ranges from $12 to $19. Credit cards are accepted. Open April through October.

Directions: From U.S. Hwy 71, take County Road 21 to Beltrami County State Aid Hwy. 20 for 1.7 miles to the park.

Contact: Lake Bemidji State Park, 3401 State Park Rd., N.E., Bemidji, MN 56601-8510 or 218/755-3843, fax 218/755-4073.

Trip Notes: For hundreds of years, the ancestors to the Dakota Indians fished and hunted around Lake Bemidji. Later, the westward-moving Anishinabe reached the area around 1750. Early trader records identify Lake Bemidji as Lac Traverse (French for diagonal). The Anishinabe knew the lake as Bemiji-gau-maug (cutting sideways through or diagonally). This was a reference to the path of the Mississippi River through the lake. The park features a unique boardwalk into the quiet world of a spruce-tamarack bog offering you a chance to see orchids, mosses, and insect-eating plants. There's also good walleye fishing on Lake Bemidji.

9 Pimushe Resort

Location: Near Cass Lake on Pimushe Lake, map 2, grid D4.

Campsites, facilities: There are eight wooded lakeside RV sites. Facilities include electric hookups, water, sewer, flush toilets, showers, laundry, picnic tables, fire rings, hunting guides, hiking trail, swimming beach, and playground. Boat, motor, canoe, and seasonal campsite rentals are available. No pets or jet skis are allowed.

Reservations, fees: The daily fee ranges from $20 to $25. Credit cards are accepted. Open from mid-May through mid-November.

Directions: From Cass Lake, travel six miles east then 10 miles north on County Road 10 (also County Road 39) to County Road 20 and the campground.

Contact: Pimushe Resort, Ed and Joan Fussy, 7376 Pimushe Trail, N.E., Bemidji, MN 56601-8446 or 800/450-2094 or 218/586-2094, fax 218/586-4001, website: www.mnresort vacation.com.

Trip Notes: If it's time for a "mall break" to replenish camping supplies, the Paul Bunyan Mall at 1201 Paul Bunyan Dr., N.W. (218/751-3195) is one-half mile east of the U.S. 71 intersection in Bemidji. The center has more than 30 specialty shops.

10 Bemidji KOA Kampground

Location: On the west side of Bemidji, map 2, grid D1.

Campsites, facilities: There are 62 RV sites and 25 tent sites. There are also three camping cabins. Facilities include RV pull-through sites, electric hookups, water, sewer, flush toilets, showers, disposal station, laundry, grocery store, evening entertainment, chil-

dren's programs, and playground. Seasonal campsite rentals are available.

Reservations, fees: The daily fee ranges from $19 to $27. Credit cards are accepted. Open May through mid-October.

Directions: Take U.S. Hwy. 2 toward the west side of Bemidji and exit at the 109.5 mile marker on the north side of the road.

Contact: Bemidji KOA Kampground, Mary and Keith Davidson, 5707 Hwy. 2 W, Bemidji, MN 56601-7260 or 800/562-1742 or 218/751-1792, fax 218/759-1962, email: kamp@bemidjikoa .com, website: www.bemidjikoa.com.

Trip Notes: The Tourist Information Center at 300 Paul Bunyan Dr. (800/458-2223, ext. 100 or 218/751-3541, ext. 100), in the downtown area on Hwy. 197 near the statues of Paul and Babe the Blue Ox, also features the Fireplace of States. It has a collection of Paul Bunyan artifacts and a fireplace, built in 1937, with stones from every state, except Alaska and Hawaii, and from most Canadian provinces. The center, erected in 1995, is designed after a boathouse that stood on the lakeshore in the early 1900s.

11 Oak Haven Resort

Location: Near Bemidji near the headwaters of the Mississippi River, map 2, grid E3.

Campsites, facilities: There are nine RV site and four tent sites. Facilities include electric hookups, water, sewer, flush toilets, showers, laundry, disposal station, fishing guides, hiking trail, indoor and outdoor pools, sauna, restaurant, children's programs, and playground. Boat, motor, canoe, and seasonal campsite rentals are available. Pets are allowed.

Reservations, fees: The daily fee ranges from $16 to about $20. Credit cards are accepted. Open from mid-May through early October.

Directions: From Bemidji, drive about 10 miles to County Road 75 to the Bingo Palace, then three miles to the resort on the Mississippi River.

Contact: Oak Haven Resort, 14333 Roosevelt Rd., S.E., Bemidji, MN 56601-7376 or 218/335-2092 or 877/860-9948.

Trip Notes: Over 750 mounted specimens of North American wildlife—animals, birds, fish—are displayed in natural habitat at the Bagley Wildlife Museum (218/694-2491) in Bagley, just west of Bemidji. The displays range from mouse to moose, minnow to muskie, and hummingbird to eagle. From the junction of Hwy. 2 and Hwy. 92, go one mile west on Hwy. 2. The museum is on the south side of the road. Adult admission is $3.50; students are $2.50; children are $2.

12 Big Wolf Lake Resort and Campground

Location: Near Bemidji on Big Wolf Lake, map 2, grid E3.

Campsites, facilities: There are 40 campsites. Facilities include electric hookups, water, sewer, flush toilets, showers, laundry, grocery store, swimming beach, outdoor pool, sauna, whirlpool, lounge, and playground. There are also biking, hiking, and snowmobile trails. Boat, motor, canoe, sailboat, and seasonal campsite rentals are available. Pets are allowed.

Reservations, fees: The daily fee ranges from $12 to $32. Credit cards are accepted. Open from mid-May through September.

Directions: Take U.S. Hwy. 2 six miles east of Bemidji. Go two miles north on Grace Lake Drive #46 and one mile east on Wolf Lake Drive.

Contact: Big Wolf Lake Resort and Campground, Don and Pat Miller, 12150 Walleye

Ln., S.E., Bemidji, MN 56601-7352 or 800/322-0281 or 218/751-5749, email: big@bigwolfresort.com, website: www.bigwolfresort.com.

Trip Notes: The youngsters will enjoy the Headwaters Science Center at 413 Beltrami Ave., N.W. (218/751-1110), between 4th and 5th Sts., in Bemidji. It features hands-on interactive exhibits and an interesting science and nature-oriented gift shop. Adult admission is $3, children under 12 are $2 (family is $10 maximum).

13 Paul Bunyan State Forest: Mantrap Lake Campground and Day Use Area

Location: On Mantrap Lake, map 2, grid H1.

Campsites, facilities: There are 38 drive-in sites, five picnic areas, one mile of nature trail, access to a designated muskie lake, fishing, and swimming.

Reservations, fees: There is a daily fee of $9. Open year-round.

Directions: From Park Rapids, take County Road 4 north 12 miles to Emmaville (County Road 24). Turn east for 1.5 miles to County Road 104. Then turn north and follow the signs for nearly one mile.

Contact: Mantrap Lake Campground, Box 113 607 1st St., Park Rapids, MN 56470, 218/732-3309.

Trip Notes: The Museum of Wildlife and Indian Artifacts (218/547-7251) is three blocks east on State Hwy. 200/371, in Walker's Chamber of Commerce Building. It contains wildlife dioramas and Ojibwa artifacts. A moderate fee includes admission to the Cass County Museum.

14 Scenic State Park

Location: Near Bigfork on Sandwick Lake, map 3, grid C4.

Campsites, facilities: The 3,360-acre park has 106 semi-modern RV (20 winter) and 11 tent (six winter) sites. Facilities include RV pull-through sites, electric hookups, flush toilets, showers, disposal station, wheelchair access, a naturalist, boat ramp, and swimming beach. There are two miles of biking, 14 miles of hiking, four miles of skiing and 12 miles of snowmobile trails. Boat and snowshoe rentals are available. Pets are allowed.

Reservations, fees: The daily fee ranges from $7 to $12. Open year-round.

Directions: From Bigfork, drive seven miles east on County Road 7.

Contact: Scenic State Park, 56956 Scenic Hwy. 7, Bigfork, MN 56628-9603 or 218/743-3362, fax 218/743-1362.

Trip Notes: Is this the most scenic park in the state? You be the judge. You can camp in the modern campground or trek back into one of the canoe or backpack sites on one of seven park lakes. The park is located in the Laurentian Mixed Forest landscape region, which is abundant with aspen-birch, white and Norway pine, jack pine, and mixed hardwoods. It also protects the entire virgin pine shorelands of Coon and Sandwick Lakes, plus part of the Lake of the Isles, Lake, Cedar Lake, and Pine Lake. Coon and Sandwick Lakes are the most popular places in the park and offer good fishing for walleye, northern pike, bass, and panfish.

15 Prairie Lake Campground and RV Park

Location: Northeast of Grand Rapids on Prairie Lake, map 3, grid F4.

Campsites, facilities: There are 55 campsites. Facilities include electric hookups, water, sewer, flush toilets, showers, disposal station, bike trail, boat ramp, swimming beach, and playground. Boat, canoe, and seasonal campsite rentals are available. Pets are allowed.

Reservations, fees: The daily fee ranges from $13 to $20. Open May through September.

Directions: From Grand Rapids, take Hwy. 38 north to County Road 49. Go east on County Road 49 past County Road 325 to the campground.

Contact: Prairie Lake Campground and RV Park, 30730 Wabana Rd., Grand Rapids, MN 55744-8201 or 218/326-8486.

Trip Notes: Wind your way over the hills and along the shores of 36 lakes connecting Grand Rapids, Marcell, Bigfork, and Effie in Itasca County by traveling the 41-mile Edge of the Wilderness Scenic Byway (218/326-9607), a National Scenic Byway. It begins at U.S. Hwy. 2 and trunk Hwy. 38 in downtown Grand Rapids and goes north through meadows and lakes, then through mixed hardwood and stands of conifers and aspen in the Chippewa National Forest.

16 Schoolcraft State Park

Location: Near Deer River, map 3, grid G2.

Campsites, facilities: The 295-acre park has 28 rustic tent sites (open in winter) and one canoe-in site. Facilities include a boat ramp on the Mississippi River and 1.5 miles of hiking trails. Pets are allowed.

Reservations, fees: The daily fee is $8. Open late May through early September.

Directions: From Deer River, take U.S. Hwy. 2 to Hwy. 6 and drive south to the entrance sign.

Contact: Schoolcraft State Park, 9042 Schoolcraft Ln., N.E., Calumet, MN 55716-0376 or 218/566-2383 or 218/247-7215, fax 218/247-7449.

Trip Notes: This park was named for Henry Rowe Schoolcraft, who with Anishinabe guide Ozawindib charted the headwaters of the Mississippi. Schoolcraft, who was a long-time agent for the Chippewa Indians at Sault Saint Marie, wrote several volumes of customs, legends, and history about the Indians. It was from his writings that Longfellow gathered the material for "The Legend of Hiawatha." On the field at the southern end of the park is the site of the first recorded homestead in Torrey Township. It was a stopover for early river travelers and lumberjacks. You might even find a relic of the logging days or some evidence of the Indians who camped here long before then.

An option is to drive to "Minnesota's Grand Canyon" at Hill Annex Mine State Park (218/247-7215). This historic open-pit mine was one of the nation's richest iron ore mines. A tour takes visitors down 300 feet into the spectacular pit. Fossil hunting tours are also available.

⏻ Birch Cove Resort and Campground

Location: Near Grand Rapids on 16,000-acre Lake Pokegama, map 3, grid G4.

Campsites, facilities: There are 14 campsites (four winter sites). Facilities include electric hookups, water, sewer, flush toilets,

showers, picnic tables, fire rings, boat ramp, and swimming beach. Boat, motor, and seasonal campsite rentals are available. Pets are allowed.

Reservations, fees: The daily fee ranges from $16 to $19. Credit cards are accepted. Open year-round.

Directions: From Grand Rapids, take U.S. Hwy. 169 five miles south to Southwood Road and turn east for one-half mile to resort.

Contact: Birch Cove Resort and Campground, Lori and David Wangen, 32382 Southwood Rd., Grand Rapids, MN 55744-9006 or 800/382-2498 or 218/326-8754, email: brchcove@server.northernnet.com, website: www.northernnet.com/birchcove.

Trip Notes: Bird-watchers will enjoy the Rice Lake National Wildlife Refuge (218/768-2402), among the state's best for spotting sharp-tailed grouse, great gray owl, yellow-bellied flycatcher, and boreal chickadee. From Grand Rapids, take U.S. Hwy. 2 to MN 65. Then drive five miles south from McGregor. The entrance is on the west side of the highway.

⏼ Shell Lake Resort and Campground

Location: On Shell Lake, map 4, grid A5.

Campsites, facilities: There are 30 campsites. Facilities include electric hookups, water, sewer, flush toilets, showers, disposal station, laundry, boat ramp, swimming beach, grocery store, and playground. Boat, motor, and seasonal campsite rentals are available. Pets are allowed.

Reservations, fees: The daily fee ranges from $12 to $15. Open from mid-May through mid-November.

Directions: From U.S. Hwy. 59, go east on County Road 14 to County Road 23. Turn southeast toward Richwood and take County Road 21 to County Road 26. At County Road 37, turn south to Shell Lake.

Contact: Shell Lake Resort and Campground, 25607 County Hwy. 37, Detroit Lakes, MN 56501-8112 or 800/721-6726 or 218/847-6726.

Trip Notes: The resort is nestled on 20 acres among tall pine, white birch, and other shade trees. Also, there's about 2,000 feet of lakeshore available to explore.

19 Big Pines Tent and RV Park

Location: In Park Rapids on the Fish Hook River, map 4, grid A8.

Campsites, facilities: There are 60 RV sites and 10 tent sites. Facilities include RV pull-through sites, electric hookups, water, sewer, showers, flush toilets, disposal station, biking and hiking trails, wheelchair access, and playground. Seasonal campsite rentals are available. Pets are allowed.

Reservations, fees: The daily fee ranges from $16 to $18. Open May through mid-October.

Directions: From junction of U.S. Hwy. 71 and Hwy. 34, go one-half mile east and three blocks south on Central Ave. to the campground.

Contact: Big Pines Tent and RV Park, James and Marylen Veden, 501 S. Central Ave. S., Park Rapids, MN 56470, 800/245-5360 or 218/732-4483.

Trip Notes: On 3rd St., three blocks west of Hwy. 71 in Park Rapids, is the Hubbard County Historical Museum (218/732-5237). Exhibits include a farm room, one-room schoolhouse, pioneer cabin, office and business machines, war room, clothing store, and general history room with artifacts, furniture, and Native American items.

20 Birchmere Family Resort and Campground

Location: East of Detroit Lakes on Little Toad Lake, map 4, grid B4.

Campsites, facilities: The campground—the only one on this spring-fed lake—has 30 wooded sites. Facilities include RV pull-through sites, electric hookups, water, sewer, flush toilets, showers, laundry, grocery store, boat ramp, swimming beach, and playground. Boat, canoe, motor, and seasonal campsite rentals are available. Pets are allowed.

Reservations, fees: The daily fee ranges from $16 to $18. Credit cards are accepted. Open May through September.

Directions: Take Hwy. 34 east from Detroit Lakes for about 10 miles. Then go three miles east on Little Toad Lake Road. Watch for the resort sign.

Contact: Birchmere Family Resort and Campground, Bill and Bea Purdy, 18346 Birchmere Rd., Frazee, MN 56544-8845 or 800/642-9554 or 218/334-5741, email: birchmer@ loretel.net.

Trip Notes: Does the family like rafting or river tubing? Near Detroit Lakes, Charlie's Ottertail Tubing (218/847-1480) offers tubing on the Ottertail River from mid-May through September. The location is seven miles east of Detroit Lakes on Hwy. 34. The fee includes parking and free shuttle service.

21 Glenadalough State Park

Location: East of Fergus Falls near Battle Lake, map 4, grid F3.

Campsites, facilities: There are 22 (22 winter) semi-modern, cart-in-tent and three canoe-in sites. There are also four camper cabins. Facilities include flush toilets, showers, wheelchair access, picnic grounds, hiking and cross-country ski trails, swimming beach, and playground. Boat, canoe, and snowshoe rentals are available. No gasoline or electric motors and no electronic fish-finding devices are permitted. Contact the park for other restrictions on your visit. Pets are allowed.

Reservations, fees: Reservations are recommended for weekends. The daily fee ranges from $12 to $28. Credit cards are accepted. Open year-round.

Directions: From Battle Lake go 1.5 miles north on Hwy. 78 and 1.8 miles east on Ottertail County Hwy. 16 to the entrance.

Contact: Glendalough State Park, R. R. 3, Box 28E, Ottertail County Hwy. 16, Battle Lake, MN 566515-9803 or 218/864-0110, fax 218/864-0587.

Trip Notes: The park offers a designated "Heritage Fishery" on 335-acre Anne Battle Lake. Here you can experience fishing as it was a century ago; large bass and panfish are abundant.

22 Huntersville State Forest: Shell City Landing Campground

Location: On the Shell River, joining the Crow Wing River canoe route, map 5, grid B1.

Campsites, facilities: The campground has 19 drive-in sites. Facilities include water access, fishing, and swimming.

Reservations, fees: The daily fee is $9. Open year-round.

Directions: From Menahga, take Stocking Lake Rd. east for four miles to County Road 23. Turn north one mile to 380th St. Turn east and go three miles to 199th Ave. Then turn north one mile to the campground.

Contact: Shell City Landing Campground, 30066 Huntersville Rd., Sebeka, MN 56477, 218/472-3262.

Trip Notes: The Deep Portage Conservation Reserve and Interpretive Center (218/682-2325) is a 6,300-acre facility that offers opportunities for hiking, hunting, nature study, snowmobiling and cross-country skiing. The interpretive center has a wildflower garden and exhibits on geology and wildlife. The facility is about five miles east of Hackensack on County Road 5 and then five miles east on County Road 46.

23 Huntersville Forest Landing Campground

Location: On the Crow River canoe route, map 5, grid C1.

Campsites, facilities: The campground has 17 drive-in and seven walk-in sites. Facilities include water access, fishing, and swimming.

Reservations, fees: The daily fee is $9. Open year-round.

Directions: From Menahga, take Stocking Lake Rd. east four miles to County Road 23. Turn north for one mile to 380th St. Turn east three miles to 199th Ave. Then turn south one mile to the sign and turn left and go about two miles.

Contact: Huntersville Forest Landing Campground, 30066 Huntersville Rd., Sebeka, MN 56477, 218/472-3262.

Trip Notes: Heard about the Kensington Runestone? Well, the Runestone Museum (320/763-3160) at 206 Broadway Ave., in Alexandria, has the runestone, which was found on Olaf Ohman's farm in 1898. Carvings on stone tell the journey of a band of Vikings in 1362. Although studies by runic scholars verify the stone's authenticity, there is still some controversy about whether it's genuine. There's also a 28-foot Viking statue weighing more than four tons.

24 Highview Campground and RV Park

Location: North of Brainerd on Lake Ossawinnamakee, map 5, grid D7.

Campsites, facilities: There are 100 RV pull-through sites and 32 tent sites. Facilities include electric hookups, water, sewer, flush toilets, showers, laundry, disposal station, biking and hiking trails, grocery store, swimming beach, and playground. Boat and seasonal campsite rentals are available. Pets are allowed.

Reservations, fees: The daily fee ranges from $19 to $22. Open from mid-May through September.

Directions: From Breezy Point, take County Road 11 north to Lake Ossawinnamakee.

Contact: Highview Campground and RV Park, HC 83, Box 1084, Breezy Point, MN 56472, 877/543-4526 or 218/543-4526, fax 218/543-4526.

Trip Notes: Off Hwy. 371, about six miles north of Brainerd, is The Colonel's Brainerd International Raceway (218/824-7220 for schedule; 810/249-5530 for ticket office). It has a three-mile road course for amateur and professional road racing and a straightaway for amateur and pro drag racing.

25 Crow Wing State Forest: Greer Lake Campground

Location: On Greer Lake, map 5, grid C8.

Campsites, facilities: There are 29 drive-in sites. Facilities include two picnic sites, two miles of nature trails, fishing, and swimming.

Reservations, fees: The daily fee is $9. Open year-round.

Directions: From Crosby, take State Hwy. 6 north for 12 miles to County Road 36. Turn west and go three miles to County Road 14. Turn south for 1.5 miles, then turn west and follow the signs for two miles.

Contact: Greer Lake Campground, 1601 Minnesota Dr., Brainerd, MN 56401, 218/828-2565.

Trip Notes: Brainerd and nearby Baxter are home to members of the sport fishing industry. The area is the site of In-Fisherman, a national magazine and outdoor TV program; Babe Winkelman's outdoor TV program; and the Lindy-Little Joe Tackle Company.

26 Rager's Acres

Location: North of Nisswa on Loon Lake, map 5, grid D6.

Campsites, facilities: The resort has 15 pull-through RV sites and 15 tent sites. Facilities include electric hookups, water, sewer, flush toilets, showers, disposal station, laundry, swimming beach, grocery store, playground, and biking and hiking trails. Boat, motor, snowmobile, and seasonal campsite rentals and baby-sitting services are available. Pets are allowed.

Reservations, fees: The daily fee ranges from $16 to $22. Credit cards are accepted. Open May through October.

Directions: From Nisswa, take Hwy. 371 to County Road 168. Turn west for 3.5 miles. It's the second campground on the right.

Contact: Rager's Acres, 1680 64th St., S.W., Pequot Lake, MN 56472-9319 or 218/568-8752, fax 218/568-8752.

Trip Notes: The resort is only three miles from the newly paved Paul Bunyan Biking Trail.

27 Galles' Upper Cullen Resort

Location: Near Nisswa on Upper Cullen Lake, map 5, grid D6.

Campsites, facilities: There are 40 RV pull-through sites and 10 tent sites on the 35 acres of wooded campground. Facilities include electric hookups, water, sewer, flush toilets, showers, laundry, disposal station, hiking trails, swimming beach, grocery store, and playground. Boat, motor, and seasonal campsite rentals and baby-sitting services are available. Pets are allowed.

Reservations, fees: Reservations are strongly suggested. The daily fee ranges from $18 to $25. Credit cards are accepted. Open May through September.

Directions: From Nisswa, take County Road 18 east to Old Hwy. 18 and go north to the resort on the east side of Upper Cullen Lake.

Contact: Galles' Upper Cullen Resort, Bruce and Donna Galles, Box 72, Nisswa, MN 56468-0072 or 888/872-8553 or 218/963-2249, email: vacation@uppercullen.com, website: www.uppercullen.com.

Trip Notes: The resort is on a 435-acre body of water, part of the three-lake Cullen chain, which is popular for northern pike, bass, crappie, and panfish.

28 Jolly Rogers Resort and Campground

Location: North of Merrifield on Lake Edward, map 5, grid E7.

Campsites, facilities: There are 25 campsites. Facilities include electric hookups, water, sewer, flush toilets, showers, laundry, disposal station, swimming beach, grocery store, playground, and lounge. Boat, motor, and seasonal campsite rentals are available. Pets are allowed.

Reservations, fees: The daily fee is $18. Credit cards are accepted. Open from mid-May through September.

Directions: From Merrifield, take County Road 3 to County Road 4 north to two miles south of County Road 13. The resort is on the west side of Lake Edward.

Contact: Jolly Rogers Resort and Campground, 23900 County Road 4, Nisswa, MN 56468-8552 or 218/829-6752, fax 218/825-0315, email: hoksmk@uslink.net.

Trip Notes: Experience one of the world's best high-quality paper mills in a one-hour tour at the Potlatch Paper Mill (218/828-3200, ext. 3260). See all the steps involved in manufacturing the finished product from pulp. From Brainerd, take Hwy. 210 east to Hwy. 25 north. The mill is 1.5 miles on the left.

29 Dower Lake Recreational Area

Location: West of Staples on Dower Lake, map 5, grid F2.

Campsites, facilities: There are 20 RV sites and 20 tent sites. Facilities include electric hookups, flush toilets, showers, disposal station, swimming beach, and playground. Pets are allowed.

Reservations, fees: The daily fee ranges from $10 to $15. Open from late May through mid-September.

Directions: From Staples, go two miles west on U.S. Hwy. 10 to the Dower Lake sign and travel one mile south to the municipal campground.

Contact: Dower Lake Recreational Area, 611 Iowa Ave., Staples, MN 56479-2224 or 218/894-2550, fax 218/894-2552.

Trip Notes: The New York Mills Regional Cultural Center (888/877-1969 or 218/385-3339) is dedicated to expanding creative and cultural opportunities of rural Americans. Housed in the historic 1885 structure, the center offers two art galleries and other facilities. Gallery admission and parking are free. From Staples, take U.S. Hwy. 10 northwest to 24 N. Mail Ave. in downtown New York Mills.

30 Pillsbury State Forest: Rock Lake Campground and Day Use Area

Location: West of Brainerd, map 5, grid E5.

Campsites, facilities: There are 44 drive-in and four walk-in sites. Facilities include six picnic sites, a mile of nature trail, fishing, and swimming.

Reservations, fees: The daily fee is $9. Open year-round.

Directions: From Pillager, take Hwy. 210 west for one-half mile to County Road 1. Turn north for six miles and follow the road to the campground.

Contact: Rock Lake Campground, 1601 Minnesota Dr., Brainerd, MN 56401, 218/828-2565.

Trip Notes: Just east of the forest is Brainerd, which is the heart of north-central Minnesota's lake region. The community was created by the Northern Pacific Railroad in 1871.

31 Gull Lake Dame Rec Area

Location: North of Brainerd on Gull Lake, map 5, grid E6.

Campsites, facilities: There are 39 campsites, including 18 winter sites. Facilities include electric hookups, flush toilets, showers, wheelchair access, disposal station, hiking, swimming beach, and playground. Pets are allowed.

Reservations, fees: The daily fee is $18. Open year-round.

Directions: From Brainerd, take Hwy 371 north to County Road 125. Follow County Road 125 (it becomes County Road 014 in Crow Wing County) about three miles west toward Gull Lake. At the junction, take the left road to the campground.

Contact: Gull Lake Dam Rec Area, 10867 E. Gull Lake Dr., N., Brainerd, MN 56401-9051 or 9218) 218/829-3334 or 218/829-1797, fax 218/828-0121.

Trip Notes: Camp Ripley's military museum (320/632-7374; email: mnmusem@brainerd .net; website: www.dma.state.mn.us/cripley/) is located at the National Guard Training Center. It's south of Brainerd and seven miles north of Little Falls on Hwy. 371, then west on Hwy. 115. Extensive displays include M48, M60, M4 tanks; a DUKWQ amphibious vehicle; UH-1H "Huey," OH-13 "Sioux" and "Cobra" helicopters; jeeps and a restored 1929 Reo truck. Indoor exhibits range in subject from frontier days through Operation Desert Storm.

32 Creger's Ojibwa Campground

Location: North of Brainerd on North Long Lake, map 5, grid E7.

Campsites, facilities: There are 28 campsites. Facilities include electric hookups, water, sewer, flush toilets, showers, hiking trails, and swimming beach. Pets are allowed.

Reservations, fees: Seasonal campsite rentals only. Open May through September.

Directions: From Brainerd, take Hwy. 371 north to County Road 115. Turn east to the campground.

Contact: Creger's Ojibwa Campground, 4284 Noka Trail N., Brainerd, MN 56401-8770 or 218/963-2576, fax 218/828-8836.

Trip Notes: A giant Paul Bunyan welcomes youngsters and invites them to sit on his size 80 lumberjack boots at the Paul Bunyan Amusement Center (218/829-6342) at the junction of Hwy. 371 north and Hwy. 210 in Brainerd. The park includes a logging camp and a variety of rides.

33 Crow Wing State Park

Location: Southwest of Brainerd on the Mississippi River, map 5, grid F6.

Campsites, facilities: The 2,077-acre park has 61 pull-through RV sites and one tent site. Facilities include electric hookups, flush toilets, showers, disposal station, and playground. There are also 18 miles of hiking, six miles of ski, and six miles of snowmobile trails. Boat and canoe rentals are available. Pets are allowed.

Reservations, fees: The daily fee ranges from $12 to $15. Open April through November.

Directions: From Brainerd, take Hwy. 371 about nine miles southwest to County Road 27. The entrance is one mile west.

Contact: Crow Wing State Park, 7100 State Park Rd., S.W., Brainerd, MN 56401-8237 or 218/829-8022, fax 218/828-70086.

Trip Notes: The 10-kilometer cross-country trail, with great views of the Mississippi River, is mostly for intermediate-level skiers.. There are many opportunities to spot deer. A ski pass, sold at the trailhead, is required (218/829-8022). Maps are along the trail.

34 Crow Wing Lake Campground

Location: Near Brainerd on Crow Wing Lake, map 5, grid F6.

Campsites, facilities: The campground has 100 campsites. Facilities include RV pull-through sites, concrete patios, electric hookups, water, sewer, flush toilets, showers, disposal station, wheelchair access, laundry, hiking trails, outdoor pool, grocery store, and playground. Boat, motor, and seasonal campsite rentals are available. Pets are allowed.

Reservations, fees: A credit card or deposit is required to hold a reservation. The daily fee ranges from $28 to $30. Open May through September.

Directions: From Brainerd, take Hwy. 371 11 miles south to campground.

Contact: Crow Wing Lake Campground, 8831 Crow Wing Camp Rd., S.W., Brainerd, MN 56401-9304 or 218/829-6468, email: cwcamp @brainerd.net, website: www.brainerd.net /~cwcamp/.

Trip Notes: Tour the Crow Wing County Historical Museum (218/829-3268). It features a restored sheriff's quarters and an old county jail converted into the museum. You can learn about county history, the railroad, Native Americans, and lumbering. The museum is two blocks west of Hwy. 371 and Laurel Street in Brainerd.

35 Lakeside Resort and Campground

Location: Southeast of Brainerd on South Long Lake, map 5, grid F8.

Campsites, facilities: There are 20 campsites. Facilities

include electric hookups, water, sewer, flush toilets, showers, disposal station, wheelchair access, snowmobile trails, swimming beach, grocery store, playground, restaurant and lounge. Boat, motor, ice-fishing house, and seasonal campsite rentals are available. Pets are allowed.

Reservations, fees: The daily fee ranges from $12 to $17. Open from mid-May through September. It is also open on additional dates.

Directions: From Brainerd, take Hwy. 24 east to Hwy. 18. Go east to Country Road 23 to resort.

Contact: Lakeside Resort and Campground, 4612 Old County Road 23, S.E., Brainerd, MN 56401, 218/828-1708.

Trip Notes: The 17-acre Croft Mine Historical Park (218/546-5466 or 218/546-5625), built on the site of a mine active from 1916 to 1934, features a guided, simulated underground mining tour. The original mine shaft was 630 feet deep. The museum also boasts mining artifacts, a theater, and library. It's eight blocks north of Hwy. 210 on 2nd Ave., N.E., in Crosby. A second entrance is one-half mile north of Hwy. 210 and Hwy. 6.

36 Fletcher Creek Campgrounds

Location: Near Little Falls, map 5, grid H6.

Campsites, facilities: There are 45 RV sites and five tent sites. Facilities include RV pull-through sites, electric hookups, water, sewer, flush toilets, showers, laundry, disposal station, outdoor pool, and playground. Canoes and seasonal campsite rentals are available. Pets are allowed.

Reservations, fees: The daily fee ranges from $13 to $18. Open May through October.

Directions: Off Hwy. 371 north of Little Falls.

Contact: Fletcher Creek Campgrounds, 20771 Hwy. 371, Little Falls, MN 56345-9233 or 800/337-9636 or 320/632-9636.

Trip Notes: Next to Charles A. Lindbergh State Park, two miles south of Hwy. 27 and Lindbergh Dr., is the C. A. Weyerhaeuser Memorial Museum and Morrison County Historical Society (320/632-4007). It features interpretive exhibits of local and regional history.

37 Land O' Lakes State Forest: Clint Converse Campground and Day Use Area

Location: On Washburn Lake, map 6, grid B1.

Campsites, facilities: This campground has 31 drive-in sites. Facilities include three picnic sites, a mile of nature trail, water access, fishing, swimming, and a pay telephone.

Reservations, fees: The daily fee is $9. Open year-round.

Directions: From Outing, take State Hwy. 6 north for two miles to County Road 48 (Lake Washburn Rd.). Turn west for two miles to the campground.

Contact: Clint Converse Campground, P.O. Box 27, Pequot Lakes, MN 56472, 218/568-4566.

Trip Notes: If you want to eat out, the Bar Harbor Supper Club (218/963-2568) in Lake Shore on County Road 77, about three miles west of Hwy. 371 and Country Road 18, has a good view on the Gull Lake channel and is accessible by car, boat or snowmobile. Charbroiled steaks and seafood are featured dishes. It's closed on major holidays.

38 Savanna State Forest: Hay Lake Campground and Day Use Area

Location: On Hay Lake, map 6, grid A7.

Campsites, facilities: There are 20 drive-in sites. Facilities include five picnic sites, hiking trail, swimming beach, and fishing for panfish on Hay Lake.

Reservations, fees: The daily fee is $9. Open year-round.

Directions: From Jacobson, take State Hwy. 65 south for 2.5 miles and turn east for three miles. Then turn south for one mile to the campground.

Contact: Hay Lake Campground, P.O. Box 09, Hill City, MN 55748, 218/697-2476.

Trip Notes: North on U.S. Hwy. 169 at 19 N.E. 4th St., in Grand Rapids is the Judy Garland Children's Museum. It features an interactive play station, especially areas devoted to music and art. On display is Garland film memorabilia.

39 Savanna Portage State Park

Location: Near McGregor, map 6, grid B7.

Campsites, facilities: This large 15,818-acre park has 64 RV (19 winter) sites and six tent (six winter) semi-modern sites. There are also six backpacking sites, one canoe-in site, and one camping cabin. Facilities include RV pull-through sites, electric hookups, flush toilets, showers, disposal station, wheelchair access, swimming beach, and playground. There are also 10 miles of mountain biking, 17 miles of hiking, 16 miles of skiing, and 40 miles of snowmobile trails. Boat, canoe, and motor rentals are available. Pets are allowed.

Reservations, fees: The daily fee ranges from $12 to $15. Credit cards are accepted. Open year-round.

Directions: From Grand Rapids, take U.S. Hwy. 2 south to Hwy. 65. Drive south to County Road 14. Follow County Road 14 (it's also County Road 36) east and north to the park.

Contact: Savanna Portage State Park, HCR 3, Box 591, McGregor, MN 55760-9647 or 218/426-3271, fax 218/426-4437.

Trip Notes: Walk the Savanna Portage Trail, a historic trail traveled by fur traders, Dakota and Ojibwa Indians, and explorers more than 200 years ago. The Continental Divide marks the great division of water: water to the west flows into the Mississippi River; water to the east runs into Lake Superior. You can hike the Continental Divide Trail and see forested vistas, and, in summer, enjoy swimming at Loon Lake. Bike enthusiasts can pedal on roads or on dirt trails designated for mountain bikes. With four fishing lakes and a river, anglers can fish for bass, trout, or panfish. In winter, this park offers plenty of trails for cross-country skiing and snowmobiling.

An option is to explore the Forest History Center (218/327-4482; email: foresthistory @mnhs.org; website: www.mnhs.org/places /sites/fhc/) near Grand Rapids. It features a turn-of-the-century logging camp, a floating cook shack, and a 100-foot fire tower offering a great view and educational exhibits. The center is 2.5 miles southwest on County Road 76.

40 Crosby Memorial Park Campground

Location: In Crosby on Serpent Lake, map 6, grid E1.

Campsites, facilities: There are 30 RV sites and 30 tent sites in this municipal campground. Facilities include electric hookups, flush toilets, showers, wheelchair access, swimming beach, and playground. Pets are allowed.

Reservations, fees: The daily fee ranges from $10 to $14. Open from mid-May through mid-October.

Directions: From Brainerd, take Hwy. 210 east to Crosby.

The campground is two blocks from downtown on Serpent Lake.

Contact: Crosby Memorial Park Campground, Crosby, MN 56441-1499 or 218/546-5021, fax 218/546-5686.

Trip Notes: In Crosby, one block north of Main St. on Hallett Ave., is the Cuyuna Range Historical Museum, located in the Soo Line Depot (218/546-6178 or 218/546-5435), built in 1910. It contains artifacts and memorabilia of early Cuyuna Iron Range mining, logging, and ethnic heritage.

⁴¹ Buck's Resort and Campground

Location: On Lake Mille Lacs, map 6, grid F4.

Campsites, facilities: There are 20 RV sites and 20 tent sites. Facilities include electric hookups, flush toilets, showers, disposal station, and swimming beach. Seasonal campsite rentals are available. Pets are allowed.

Reservations, fees: The daily fee begins at $15. Open from mid-May through mid-October.

Directions: From Garrison, take Hwy. 18 east to the campground on the north shore of Lake Mille Lacs.

Contact: Buck's Resort and Campground, Rt. 1, Box 284, Aitkin, MN 56431-9121 or 218/678-3787, fax 218/678-3787, email: studiocard@aol.com.

Trip Notes: The 318-acre Father Hennepin State Park (320/676-8763) off MN 27, just west of Isle, is well worth a visit. This "gateway" to Lake Mille Lacs offers a natural sand beach and boat access on the southeastern shore, as well as four miles of hiking trails.

⁴² Wilderness of Minnesota

Location: Near Lake Mille Lacs, map 6, grid F2.

Campsites, facilities: There are 60 RV pull-through sites and 10 tent sites. Fifteen RV sites are available for the winter. The facilities include electric hookups, water, sewer, flush toilets, showers, laundry, disposal station, fish-cleaning facility, biking and hiking trails, outdoor pool, and playground. Seasonal campsite rentals are available. Pets are allowed.

Reservations, fees: The daily fee ranges from $12 to $18. Open April 1 through September.

Directions: The campground, across from Lake Mille Lacs, is one-quarter mile north of the junction of Hwy. 169 and 18.

Contact: Wilderness of Minnesota, Box 387, Garrison, MN 56450-0387 or 320/692-4347 or 763/434-4155.

Trip Notes: Take a scenic drive around Lake Mille Lacs, which features 150 miles of shoreline and some 1,000 Native American burial mounds.

⁴³ Gregory's Resort

Location: On Lake Mille Lacs, map 6, grid F2.

Campsites, facilities: There are five RV sites and five tent sites. Facilities include electric hookups, water, showers, fishing launches and guides, swimming beach, and playground. Boat and seasonal campsite rentals are available. Pets are allowed.

Reservations, fees: The daily fee ranges from $5 to $15. Credit cards are accepted. Open May through October.

Directions: From Garrison, the campground is south on Hwy. 169.

Contact: Gregory's Resort, HCR 1, Box 42B, Garrison, MN 56450-9715 or 800/689-5108 or 320/692-4415.

Trip Notes: If you want to fish Mille Lacs, you can get on a launch or charter a boat at Garrison Sports and Launch Service (888/692-4480). It's one block north of the YMCA where Hwy. 169 and 18 split along Lake Mille Lacs in downtown Garrison. Fishing is available for walleye, yellow perch, northern pike, and muskie, and all tackle is provided on four-hour trips.

44 Wigwam Inn Campground and Marina

Location: On Lake Mille Lacs, map 6, grid G2.

Campsites, facilities: There are 32 RV pull-through sites and five tent sites. Facilities include electric hookups, water, sewer, flush toilets, showers, fishing launches and guides, biking and snowmobile trails, swimming beach, grocery store, and playground. Boat, ice-fishing house, and seasonal campsite rentals are available. Pets are allowed.

Reservations, fees: The daily fee ranges from $15 to $20. Open May through mid-October.

Directions: South of Garrison off Hwy. 169 on Wigwam Bay in Lake Mille Lacs.

Contact: Wigwam Inn Resort and Campground, 18271 460th St., Garrison, MN 56450-9601 or 320/692-4579 or 320/532-4527.

Trip Notes: The Wigwam Inn also offers a wide selection of live bait and LP gas.

45 Mill Lacs Kathio State Park

Location: Near Lake Mille Lacs, map 6, grid H3.

Campsites, facilities: The 10,585-acre park has 75 campsites, including 15 winter sites. Facilities include RV pull-through sites, electric hookups, flush toilets, showers, disposal station, wheelchair access, swimming beach, and playground. There are also 35 miles of hiking, 25 miles of horseback, nearly 20 miles of ski, and 19 miles of snowmobile trails. Boat, ski, and snowshoe rentals are available. Pets are allowed.

Reservations, fees: The daily rate ranges from $8 to $30. Credit cards are accepted. Open year-round.

Directions: Take U.S. Hwy. 169 about six miles northwest to County Route 26 to the park entrance.

Contact: Mille Lacs Kathio State Park, 15066 Kathio State Park Rd., Onamia, MN 56359-9534 or 320/532-3523, fax 320/532-3529.

Trip Notes: A trip to the area must include a visit to the Mille Lacs Indian Museum (320/532-3632; email: millelacs@mnhs.org; website: www.mnhs.org), which is 12 miles north of Onamia on U.S. Hwy. 169. Here you can trace the history of the Mille Lacs Band of Ojibwa. The facility features videos, computer interactives, listening stations, and objects from traditional and contemporary culture, showcasing traditions of language, music, dance, and art.

46 Knife Island

Location: On the St. Louis River, map 7, grid C5.

Campsites, facilities: Most of the 20 sites (some are pull-through sites) are in the "ghost village" of Slateville and in an old logging camp. Wooded sites have electric and water hookups and a disposal station.

Reservations, fees: Call for reservations.

Open: May through September.

Directions: Take exit 239 of I-35 and go right on Hwy. 61 for one-quarter mile to the campground, which is on the St. Louis River between Hwy. 61 and I-35.

Contact: Knife Island, 234 Hwy. 61 West (P.O. Box 361) Esko, MN 55733, 218/879-6063.

Trip Notes: Tom's Logging Camp and Trading Post (218/525-4120), 16 miles north on North Shore Drive, recreates the atmosphere of a 19th-Century logging camp. Ten buildings are furnished in the period, and a museum features authentic relics of the era.

47 Cloquet/Duluth KOA Kampgrounds

Location: In Cloquet near Duluth, map 7, grid C5.

Campsites, facilities: There are 56 RV sites and 10 tent sites. Facilities include RV pull-through sites, electric hookups, water, sewer, flush toilets, showers, laundry, disposal station, biking trails, outdoor pool, sauna, whirlpool, grocery store, and playground. Seasonal campsite rentals are available. Pets are allowed.

Reservations, fees: The daily fee ranges from $19 to $22. Credit cards are accepted. Open May through mid-October.

Directions: From I-35, take exit 239 and follow the KOA and blue camping signs.

Contact: Cloquet/Duluth KOA Kampgrounds, 1479 Old Carlton Rd., Cloquet, MN 55720-2617 or 218/879-5726.

Trip Notes: The Rushing Rapids Parkway Scenic Byway (218/384-4610), a Minnesota Scenic Byway, follows Hwy. 210 from Carlton, just south of Cloquet, to Hwy. 23, a nine-mile route. The St. Louis River plunges through waterfalls and rapids along this route, which passes through Jay Cooke State Park. We bet you'll find the Swinging Bridge awesome. There's no fee to drive through the park on Hwy. 210.

48 Moose Lake City Campground

Location: In Moose Lake, map 7, grid E2.

Campsites, facilities: There are 75 RV sites and 17 tent sites in this municipal park. Facilities include RV pull-through sites, electric hookups, water, sewer, flush toilets, showers, disposal station, biking trails, swimming beach, and playground. Seasonal campsite rentals are available. Pets are allowed.

Reservations, fees: The daily fee ranges from $14 to $16. Open from mid-May through September.

Directions: Take I-35 to MN 27 and turn right to Moose Lake.

Contact: Moose Lake City Campground, One Couillard Lane, Moose Lake, MN 55767, 218/485-4761, fax 218/485-4010.

Trip Notes: A nice day trip is the Kanabec History Center (320/679-1665; email: kanabechistory@ncis.com; website: www.kanabechistory
.com) in Mora. There are hands-on activities for the whole family and other exhibits chronicling the county's past. The center is at 805 Forest Ave., one mile west of the junction of Hwy. 65 and Hwy. 23.

49 Moose Lake State Park

Location: Southwest of Duluth on Moose Lake, map 7, grid E3.

Campsites, facilities: The 1,194-acre park has 33 RV sites and two tent sites that are open all year. Facilities include electric hookups, flush toilets, showers, wheelchair access, picnic grounds, swimming beach, and playground. There are also five miles of hiking, seven miles of skiing, and two miles of snowmobile trails. Boat rentals are available. Pets are allowed.

Reservations, fees: The daily fee ranges from $8 to $12. Open from late May through early September.

Directions: From Duluth, take I-35 west to County Road 137. Turn east on County Road 137 to the entrance.

Contact: Moose Lake State Park, 4252 County Road 137, Moose Lake, MN 55767, 218/485-5420.

Trip Notes: If you didn't bring a bicycle, try Sun Sports (800/784-8836 or 218/485-8836) in Moose Lake. It rents all types, including mountain, cross and road machines. Sun Sports is one block east of the Willard Munger Trail on Arrowhead Lane across from the Holiday grocery store.

50 General Andrews State Forest: Willow River Campground

Location: On Zelesky Lake, map 7, grid F2.

Campsites, facilities: There are 39 drive-in sites. Facilities include access to the lake and fishing.

Reservations, fees: The daily fee is $9. Open year-round.

Directions: In the community of Willow River, take North St. east to the frontage road of I-35. Turn north for one-half mile to campground.

Contact: Willow River Campground, Rt. 2, 701 S. Kenwood, Moose Lake, MN 55767, 218/485-5400.

Trip Notes: North on I-35 is the Carlton County History and Heritage Center (218/879-1938) at 406 Cloquet Ave., in Cloquet. Its free

exhibits depict the region's history from about 1860. Special exhibits focus on the 1918 fire that destroyed much of the county and the original town. Other displays include a model logging camp, and pioneer and American Indian artifacts.

51 St. Croix State Forest: Boulder Campground and Day Use Area

Location: On Rock Lake, map 7, grid H5.

Campsites, facilities: There are 21 drive-in sites. Facilities include six picnic sites, water access, fishing, swimming, and 25 miles of nature trails.

Reservations, fees: The daily fee is $9. Open year-round.

Directions: From Hinckley, take State Hwy. 48 east from I-35 for 23 miles to County Road 173. Turn left and go north on County Road 173 for five miles to the Tamarack Forest Rd. Follow the forest road for about five miles to campground.

Contact: Boulder Campground, 312 Fire Monument Rd., Hinckley, MN 55037, 320/384-6146.

Trip Notes: Visit nearby Hinckley where on Sept. 1, 1894, one of the worst recorded forest fires spread throughout east-central Minnesota and destroyed, among others, the town of Hinckley. In about four hours, more than 400 people were killed and 400 square miles of forest was wiped out. The Eastern Minnesota and St. Paul and Duluth railroads are credited with saving hundreds of lives.

St. Croix State Forest: Tamarack River Horse Campground

Location: Near Boulder Campground, map 7, grid H5.

Campsites, facilities: There are 55 campsites. Facilities include three picnic sites and 25 miles of nature trails.

Reservations, fees: The daily fee is $9. Open year-round.

Directions: From Hinckley, take State Hwy. 48 east from I-35 for 23 miles to County Road 173. Turn left and go north on County Road 173 for five miles to the Tamarack Forest Rd. Follow the forest road for about three miles and turn south two miles to the campground.

Contact: Tamarack River Horse Campground, 312 Fire Monument Rd., Hinckley, MN 55037, 320/384-6146.

Trip Notes: The Hinckley Fire Museum (320/384-7338) at 106 Old State Route 61 in Hinckley is a restored railroad depot. It commemorates the 1894 forest fire that wiped out the town. There are photographs, newspaper articles and artifacts from the fire. A depot agent's apartment is furnished in 1890s style.

Charles A. Lindbergh State Park

Location: Southwest of Little Falls on the Mississippi River, map 8, grid A5.

Campsites, facilities: The 340-acre park has 38 RV (10 winter) sites and two tent sites. Facilities include electric hookups, flush toilets, showers, disposal station, and playground. There are six miles of hiking and 5.5 miles of cross-country skiing trails. Canoe, ski, and snowshoe rentals are available. Pets are allowed.

Reservations, fees: The daily fee ranges from $8 to $16. Credit cards are accepted. Open from late May through early September.

Directions: Take County Road 52 from Little Falls one mile southwest to the park entrance.

Contact: Charles A. Lindbergh State Park, P.O. Box 364, Little Falls, MN 56345, 320/616-2525.

Trip Notes: On the outskirts of Little Falls, on the banks of the Mississippi River, is the boyhood home of famous aviator Charles A. Lindbergh Jr. Eagles, hawks, and owls can often been seen along the waterway and in the surrounding forest.

Riverwood RV Park

Location: North of Becker on Elk Lake, map 9, grid E1.

Campsites, facilities: There are 60 RV pull-through sites and 10 tent sites. Facilities include electric hookups, water, sewer, flush toilets, showers, and disposal station. Seasonal campsite rentals are available. Pets are allowed.

Reservations, fees: The daily fee is $15. Open May through September.

Directions: From Minneapolis-St. Paul, take U.S. Hwy. 10 northwest past Becker to Clear Lake. Drive on County Road 6 to Elk Lake.

Contact: Riverwood RV Park, 8170 Hwy. 10 N.W., Becker, MN 55308, 763/421-5888, fax 763/421-9334.

Trip Notes: You can step into a working 1860s farm and pick heirloom vegetables, visit the farmhands and animals, or churn butter and see what's cooking at the Oliver H. Kelley Farm (763/441-6896; email: kelleyfarm@mnhs .org; website: www.mnhs.org/places/sites /ohkf/) in Elk River. From Becker, take U.S. Hwy. 10 southeast to the farm 2.5 miles south of Elk River.

55 Sand Dunes State Forest: Ann Lake Campground and Day Use Area

Location: On Ann Lake, map 9, grid E3.

Campsites, facilities: There are 36 drive-in and six walk-in sites. Facilities include seven picnic sites, two miles of nature trails, water access, fishing, and swimming. There is also a pay telephone.

Reservations, fees: The daily fee is $9. Open year-round.

Directions: From Zimmerman, take County Road 4 west for six miles to 168th St. Turn south and follow the signs for 1.5 miles to campground.

Contact: Ann Lake Campground, 800 Oak Savanna S.W., Cambridge, MN 55008, 763/689-7100.

Trip Notes: Near this campground is Pine City (320/629-3861), just east of I-35. Once it was an American Indian village named *Chengwatana*. It is on the outlet where Cross Lake joins the Snake River. The city is built on hills of sandy clay soil and the river flows through basaltic lava flows.

56 Lake Maria State Park

Location: Near Big Lake off of the Elk River, map 9, grid F1.

Campsites, facilities: There are three RV sites and 16 tent sites. There are also remote ski- or walk-in camper cabins. All are open during winter. Facilities include wheelchair access. There are hiking, horse, and cross-country ski trails. Boat and canoe rentals are available.

Reservations, fees: Reservations recommended for weekends. The daily fee is $7. Credit cards are accepted. Open from late May through March.

Directions: From I-94, take Hwy. 9 south to County Road 29 and then drive on County Road 111 to the park.

Contact: Lake Maria State Park, 11411 Clementa Ave., N.W., Monticello, MN 56362-9725, (763/878-2325), fax 763/878-2620.

Trip Notes: Enjoy one of the few remaining stands of the "Big Woods," a maple, oak, and basswood forest that once covered part of southern Minnesota. You can stroll on the park's boardwalk that winds through a marsh or look for the Blandings turtle, easily identified by bright yellow spots on its shell. The threatened turtle makes its home in the park.

57 Wapiti Park Campground

Location: Near Elk River on the Elk River, map 9, grid F4.

Campsites, facilities: There are 109 (34 winter) campsites. Facilities include RV pull-through sites, electric hookups, water, sewer, flush toilets, showers, laundry, disposal station, grocery store, lounge, cross-country skiing, swimming beach, and playground. Canoes and seasonal campsite rentals are available. Pets are allowed.

Reservations, fees: Open year-round. The daily fee starts at $15.

Directions: From Elk River, take U.S. Hwy 10 west for 2.5 miles to the campground.

Contact: Wapiti Park Campground, Mike Glenn, 18746 Troy St., Elk River, MN 55330-1030 or 800/441-1396, or 763/441-1396.

Trip Notes: From Elk River, go northwest on I-94 to Collegeville and take the St. John's University exit. Here, you'll discover the Saint John's Hill Monastic Manuscript Library (320/363-3514), with an archive of medieval manuscripts on microfilm, books and gifts. Tours are available free of charge.

THE NORTH SHORE

The North Shore

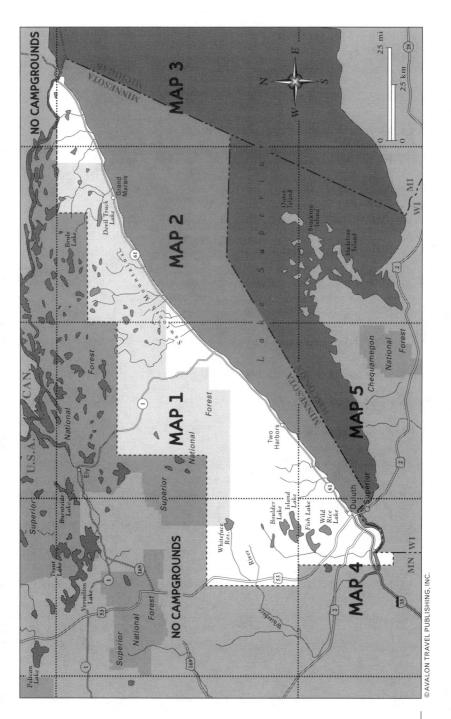

© AVALON TRAVEL PUBLISHING, INC.

Map 1

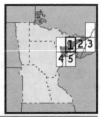

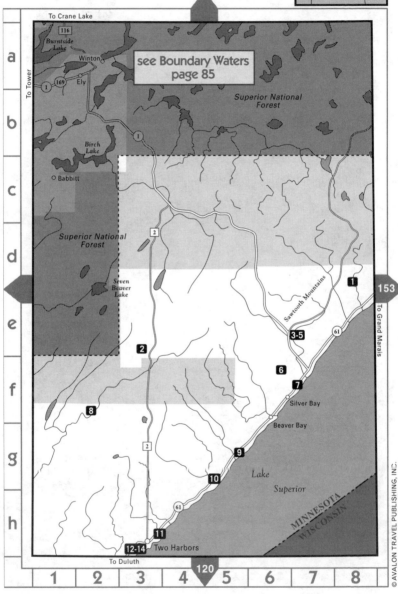

see Boundary Waters page 85

Map 2

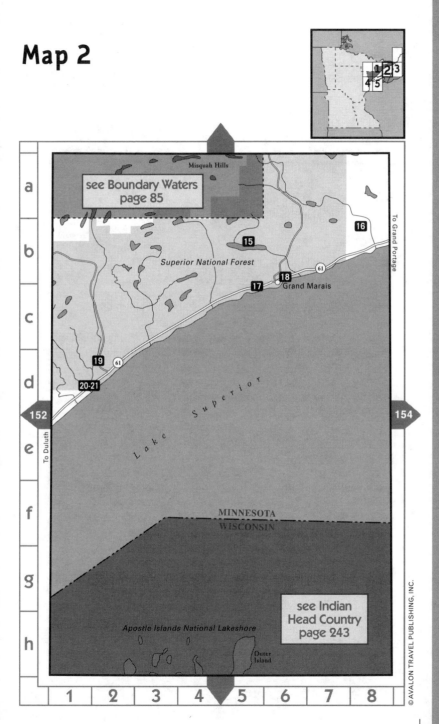

see Boundary Waters
page 85

Misquah Hills

Superior National Forest

16

15

18

61

Grand Marais

17

19

61

20-21

To Duluth

To Grand Portage

Lake Superior

152

154

MINNESOTA
WISCONSIN

see Indian
Head Country
page 243

Apostle Islands National Lakeshore

Outer
Island

© AVALON TRAVEL PUBLISHING, INC.

Map 3

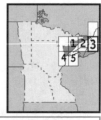

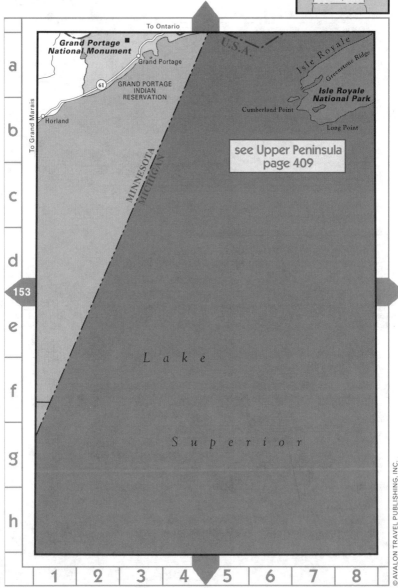

To Ontario

Grand Portage National Monument

Grand Portage

61

GRAND PORTAGE INDIAN RESERVATION

To Grand Marais

Horland

MINNESOTA

MICHIGAN

U.S.A.

Isle Royale

Greenstone Ridge

Isle Royale National Park

Cumberland Point

Long Point

see Upper Peninsula page 409

Lake

Superior

© AVALON TRAVEL PUBLISHING, INC.

Map 4

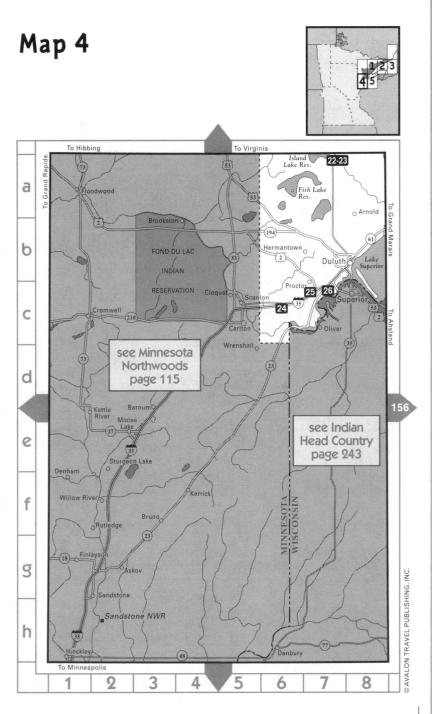

To Hibbing
To Virginia
To Grand Rapids

Island Lake Res.
22-23
Fish Lake Res.
Arnold

Floodwood
Brookston
194
Hermantown
Duluth
To Grand Marais

FOND DU LAC
INDIAN
RESERVATION
Cloquet
Proctor
25 26
Superior
Lake Superior

Cromwell
210
Scanlon
24 35
53
To Ahsland

Carlton
Oliver
35

Wrenshall

see Minnesota Northwoods page 115

Barnum
Kettle River
Moose Lake

see Indian Head Country page 243

156

Denham
Sturgeon Lake

Willow River
Kerrick

Bruno
MINNESOTA
WISCONSIN

Rutledge

Finlayson
18
Askov

Sandstone

Sandstone NWR

Hinckley
35
77
Danbury

48

To Minneapolis

© AVALON TRAVEL PUBLISHING, INC.

1 2 3 4 5 6 7 8

Map 5

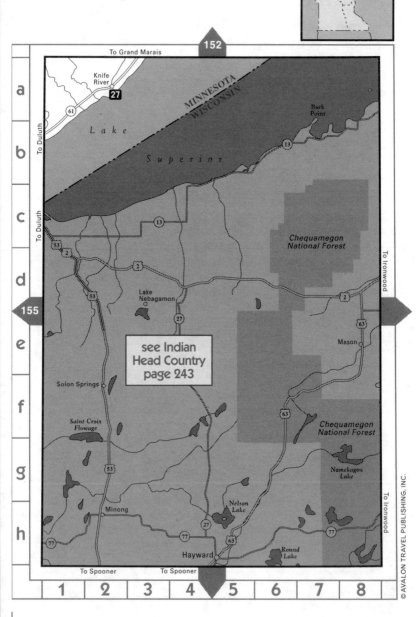

see Indian
Head Country
page 243

The North Shore

The North Shore of Minnesota is one of North America's most scenic drives. It arcs for about 150 miles along the western edge of Lake Superior. The drive is anchored by Duluth, the state's most populous city outside the Twin Cities area, and ends at Grand Portage, the port of entry into the province of Ontario.

The shining waters of vast Lake Superior form a backdrop for a spectacular trip. It meanders through quaint harbor towns and picturesque state parks where you can camp near a craggy shoreline or one of Minnesota's highest waterfalls. You can explore the region's wilderness with forests of white pine, quaking aspen, sugar maple and white birch along the Gunflint Trail. Here, rocky hillsides rise up to 1,500 feet over the lake.

Lake Superior moderates the weather along the North Shore. Spring and summer are cooler, and fall and winter are warmer than the rest of the state.

1 George H. Crosby Manitou State Park

Location: On North Shore of Lake Superior, map 1, grid E8.

Campsites, facilities: The 5,259-acre park offers 21 secluded sites (backpack tent camping only) at remote locations one-half mile to four miles from the parking area. All are open in winter. Many of these primitive sites are along the cascading Manitou River; four are near Bensen Lake. Low-impact camping is encouraged. There are no electric or water hookups; vault toilets, but no showers. There are 24 miles of hiking trails. Only carry-in boats are allowed; all motors are prohibited. The park also offers a picnic area.

Reservations, fees: The daily fee is $7. Reservations can be made 24 hours a day, seven days a week by calling The Connection 612/922-9000 in the metro Twin Cities area or 800/246-CAMP. Open all year.

Directions: From U.S. Hwy. 61, about 60 miles north of Duluth, take State Hwy. 1 to Finland and go seven miles north on Lake County Road 7 to the park entrance on the right.

Contact: George Crosby Manitou State Park, 474 Hwy. 61 East, Silver Bay, MN 55614-9612 or 218/226-6365, fax 218/226-6366.

Trip Notes: Volcanoes spewed fiery lava that cooled and built up in thick layers along the shore. Later, when glaciers moved from the north, they scraped and dislodged the rock. As the melting glaciers retreated, they left piles of rock and soil again changing the shape of the terrain. The area's last glacier left a large melt-water lake behind the shoreline ridge which drained into Lake Superior. This drainage route is now the Manitou River. Today, its rough, tumbling waters still work to change the course of the gorge through which it flows. If you like rugged backpacking to a remote campsite, this park is ideal because it offers some of the best backcountry trails in Minnesota's state parks. About five miles of the Superior Hiking Trail runs through the park. Be sure to follow the Manatee River; the River Trail follows the Manatee as it drops 600 feet. You will have plenty of fir, cedar, spruce and northern hardwoods to explore. These beautiful old-growth stands are protected as part of a Scientific and Natural Area.

2 Sullivan Lake Campground

Location: On Sullivan Lake in the Finland State Forest, map 1, grid E3.

Campsites, facilities: This state forest campground has 11 sites, two picnic sites, boat ramp and hiking trail. Pets are allowed.

Reservations, fees: No reservations are required. The daily fee is $9. Open from mid-April through October.

Directions: From Two Harbors, take County Road 2 north for 26 miles to County Road 15. Turn left (west) and go one-half mile. Then turn left (south) for about one-half mile to the campground.

Contact: Sullivan Lake Campground, 1568 Hwy. 2, Two Harbors, MN 55616, 218/834-6602, fax 218/834-6639.

Trip Notes: Lake Superior Excursions (218/226-4100) offers scenic cruises, including dinner cruises, along Lake Superior's shoreline from June through September, from 7 A.M. to 9 P.M. daily. Scenic cruises cost $8-$20; dinner cruises are about $50. Call for exact times and prices. The dock is on U.S. Hwy. 61 at Mile Post 52, in Beaver Bay, 52 miles northwest of Duluth.

3 Finland Campground

Location: On the Baptism River in the Finland State Forest, map 1, grid E7.

Campsites, facilities: This state forest campground has 39 sites and 10 picnic sites. RV length limit is 21 feet. There are no electric or water hookups, and no showers. It offers vault toilets, tables and fire rings. Pets are allowed.

Reservations, fees: No reservations are needed. The daily fee is $9. Open from about mid-May through October.

Contact: Finland Campground, 1568 Hwy. 2, Two Harbors, MN 55616, tel. 218/834-6602, fax 218/834-6639.

Directions: From Finland, take County Road 6 east along the Baptism River for one-quarter mile.

Trip Notes: See Palisade Head, a 350-foot-tall, ruddy-colored cliff soaring above Lake Superior. It's northeast of Silver Bay on U.S. Hwy. 61. The drive to the top leads to an incredible vista of the palisades, which extend easterly for 40 miles. We walked to a nearby stone wall for an excellent view of the cliff.

Another option is to visit the 3M/Dwan Museum (201 Waterfront Drive; 218/834-5798). From U.S. Hwy. 61, go seven blocks south. A tour of the museum, which chronicles the history of Minnesota Mining and Manufacturing, is conducted from the Depot Museum.

◨ Eckbeck Campground

Location: On the Baptism River in the Finland State Forest, map 1, grid E7.

Campsites, facilities: There are 30 sites open all year. RV length limit is 21 feet. There are no electric or water hookups and no showers. The campground provides vault toilets, tables and fire rings. Pets are allowed.

Reservations, fees: No reservations are required. The daily fee is $7. Open all year.

Directions: From Finland, take Hwy. 1 along the Baptism River, south for three miles to the campground.

Contact: Eckbeck Campground, P.O. Box 495, Finland, MN 55603-0495 or 218/353-7397, fax 218/353-7681.

Trip Notes: In nearby Tettegouche State Park, north of Silver Bay, visit the Baptism River, which has three waterfalls, including the highest one entirely within Minnesota. Hiking trails along the river provide views of many falls and cascades including High Falls,

the spectacular 60-foot waterfall. In addition, a section of the Superior Hiking Trail runs through the park.

◨ Wildhurst Lodge and Campground

Location: On the Baptism River, map 1, grid E7.

Campsites, facilities: There are 22 sites on the 40-acre campground (four sites with electric and water hookups; two with electric), log cabins, sleeping rooms, lodge with flush toilets and showers, disposal station, game room, bar, food/camp store. Campers have access to the North Shore Trail, and bike, horse, snowmobile, and ski trails. Five indoor units (three lodge; two cabins) are also available. Pets are allowed.

Reservations, fees: Call for reservations. The daily fee is $14; $18 with electric and water hookups. Credit cards are accepted. Open all year (winter campsites for self-contained units).

Directions: From U.S. Hwy. 61, take Hwy. 1 northwest for nine miles.

Contact: Wildhurst Lodge and Campground, 7344 Hwy 1, Finland, MN 55603-9717 or 218/353-7337, fax 218/353-7703, email: wildhurs@lakenet.com, website: www.wildhurstlodge.com.

Trip Notes: Visit the Wolf Ridge Environmental Learning Center (www.wolf-ridge.org), an accredited outdoor school. Day visitors are welcome to hike the 1,400-acre site and take self-guided tours. It's open 8 A.M. to 4 P.M. daily (closed holidays), all year. Free parking and no fees for daily visitors. From Little Marais, the center is five miles west of U.S. Hwy. 61 on Country Road 6.

6 Tettegouche State Park

Location: On North Shore of Lake Superior, map 1, grid F6.

Campsites, facilities: The 9,346-acre park has 47 sites, including 19 tent and five backpack sites; six sites are available in winter. There are also four cabins. Three sleep six each; one sleeps two. RV length limit is 60 feet. Wheelchair-accessible showers (not open in winter) and toilets are available. There are no electric sites. There are 23 miles of hiking trails, two miles of which are on the self-guided Shovel Point Trail, 1.5 miles for mountain-biking, 15.5 miles for cross-country skiing, 12 miles for snowmobiling, and four miles for skating/skiing. Also, tables, fire rings, grills, picnic area, warming house for winter activities, lake and river fishing, carry-in boats without motors, visitors center with interpretative exhibits, rental canoes and snowshoes, and gift shop. Pets are allowed.

Reservations, fees: The daily fee is $12. Reservations are not necessary in winter and early spring. Reservations can be made 24 hours a day, seven days a week by calling The Connection 612/922-9000 in the metro Twin Cities area or 800/246-CAMP. See State Park Fees. Open all year.

Directions: Take U.S. Hwy. 61, 58.5 miles northeast of Duluth. The park entrance is 4.5 miles northeast of Silver Bay; six miles southwest of Little Marais.

Contact: Tettegouche State Park, 5702 U.S. Hwy. 61, Silver Bay, MN 55614, 218/226-6365 or 218/226-6366.

Trip Notes: The Baptism River has three wonderful waterfalls, including Minnesota's highest, plus moderate-to-difficult trails that loop around four wilderness lakes. Some present day features are the result of old geologic processes. About 1.1 billion years ago, North America began to spread apart along a rift that extended from what is now Lake Superior all the way to Kansas. The deep basaltic lava that poured out of this rift formed virtually all of the bedrock of the North Shore. Removal of lava from beneath what is now Lake Superior caused the flows to tilt to the southeast. Spectacular examples of these lava flows are Palisade Head and the park's Shovel Point, which is accessible by trails to sheer-faced rock overlooks that are 170 feet above Lake Superior.

7 Northern Exposure Campground

Location: On North Shore of Lake Superior, map 1, grid F7.

Campsites, facilities: There are 70 sites, including 30 RV pull-through sites and 15 wooded sites for tent campers. Facilities include electric hookups, water, disposal station, flush toilets, showers, laundry, mini-golf, game room, playground, and grocery store. Pets are allowed.

Reservations, fees: Reservations are accepted. The daily fee begins at $16 per night. Credit cards are accepted. Open from mid-May through mid-October.

Directions: Take U.S. Hwy. 61 1-1/8 miles northeast of Silver Bay to campground.

Contact: Northern Exposure Campground, Carol and Mark Hofschulte, 5346 U.S. Hwy. 61 East, Silver Bay, MN 56614, 218/226-3324, fax 218/226-3324.

Trip Notes: Have a picnic on the Lake Superior shore at Silver Bay's Bayside Park and pick genuine agates on area beaches.

8 Indian Lake Campground

Location: On Indian Lake and the Cloquet River, map 1, grid F2.

Campsites, facilities: This state forest campground has 25 sites, including four tent sites. RV length limit is 26 feet. There are no electric or water hookups, or showers. The site offers vault toilets, tables, fire rings, and boat ramp. Campers can swim in a lake. Pets are allowed.

Reservations, fees: No reservations are required. The daily fee is $9. Open from mid-April through October (It is also open on additional dates).

Directions: From Two Harbors, go north on County Road 2 for 13 miles to County Road 14. Then, go 12 miles to Rollins in Cloquet Valley State Forest. Turn north for one mile and then left to the campground.

Contact: Indian Lake Campground, 1568 Hwy. 2, Two Harbors, MN 55616, 218/834-6602, fax 218/834-6639.

Trip Notes: We found it fascinating to watch giant ore carriers being loaded and maneuvering in and out of the port of Two Harbors from Van Hoven Park or Lighthouse Point on the waterfront. Take the tour aboard the historic coal-fired tug Edna G, built in 1896, and through the only working Light Station on the North Shore of Lake Superior.

9 Split Rock Lighthouse State Park

Location: On North Shore of Lake Superior, map 1, grid G5.

Campsites, facilities: Best known for its historic lighthouse, the 2,075-acre park has four backpack sites and 20 "cart-in" sites (park your vehicle and cart in gear in a two-wheeled cart). There are also two sites as well as showers (not available in winter) and flush toilets (available Memorial Day through Labor Day) that are wheelchaired-accessible. There are no electric sites. Split Rock offers six miles of self-guided trails, 12 miles of hiking trails, six miles for mountain-bikers, eight miles for cross-country skiing. There are also open and enclosed picnic shelters, warming house, and lake, river and stream fishing. Other facilities include visitor center, interpretive exhibits and fee-based tours.

Reservations, fees: The daily fee is $12. Reservations can be made 24 hours a day, seven days a week by calling The Connection 612/922-9000 in the metro Twin Cities area or 800/246-CAMP. Reservations for Split Rock Lighthouse State Park are not required. See State Park Fees. Open all year for tent camping only.

Directions: On U.S. Hwy. 61, 19 miles north of Two Harbors; four miles south of Beaver Bay; and 46 miles north of Duluth. The park entrance is on the right.

Contact: Split Rock Lighthouse State Park, 3755 Split Rock Lighthouse Rd., Two Harbors, MN 55616, 218/226-6377, fax 218/226-6378, email: splitrock.lighthouse@dnr.state.mn.us.

Trip Notes: From 1899 to 1906, the Merrill and Ring Lumber Company logged most of the original Norway and white pine from the area around Split Rock. During peak years, the company operated a short railroad up the river. Pilings from old wharf and dam can still be seen jutting out of the water at the mouth of the Split Rock River. In 1905, a November gale claimed the "Edenborn" and the "Madiera," a barge the "Edenborn" was towing, as well as five other ships, within a dozen miles of the river. The tragic sinking of these ships fueled the demand for a lighthouse. The fog signal building and lighthouse were completed in 1909 and commissioned one year later. For 59 years, the keepers warned ships and treacherous North Shore with its 370,000-candlepower beacon. In 1971, the federal government deeded the lighthouse station to Minnesota as a historic site. In 1976, the Minnesota Historical Society assumed operation of the site, which is one of the most photographed lighthouses in the United States. Be sure to tour the lighthouse atop a 130-foot bluff of anorthosite, the result of ancient lava flows.

10 Gooseberry Falls State Park

Location: On North Shore of Lake Superior, map 1, grid G5.

Campsites, facilities: The 1,675-acre park has 70 drive-in and three pull-through sites. Ten sites are open in winter. RV length limit is 40 feet. Two sites are wheelchair-accessible as are showers (not available in winter) and toilets. The park has a seasonal disposal station, but no electric hookups. It offers a visitor center, gift shop, naturalist programs, historic site, three picnic areas, enclosed shelter, warming house, and interpretative exhibits. Also, there are 18 miles of hiking trails (about 1.5 miles of trails are wheelchair-accessible), 12 miles of mountain bike trails, 12 miles of cross-country ski trails, and three miles for snowmobilers. Snowshoe and ski rentals available within 10 miles. Pets are allowed.

Reservations, fees: The daily fee is $12. Reservations can be made 24 hours a day, seven days a week, by calling The Connection 612/922-9000 in the metro Twin Cities area or 800/246-CAMP. See State Park Fees. Open all year.

Directions: From Duluth, take I-35 to U.S. Hwy. 61 and drive 39.5 miles north. The park, whose entrance is on the right side of the road is about 13 miles northeast of Two Harbors; about seven miles south of Split Rock Lighthouse.

Contact: Gooseberry Falls State Park, 3206 U.S. Hwy. 61 East, Two Harbors, MN 55616-9303 or 218/834-3855, fax 218/834-3787.

Trip Notes: At different times, the Cree, the Dakotah, and the Ojibwa lived along the North Shore. As early as 1670, the Gooseberry River appeared on explorer maps. The river was either named after the French explorer Sieur des Groseilliers or after the Anishinabe Indian name, "Shab-on-im-i-kan-i-sibi"; when translated, both refer to gooseberries. The waterway appeared on maps as early as 1670. This popular North Shore park features five waterfalls—two of which are 30 feet high—scenic overlooks, and superb trout fishing. The new Joseph N. Alexander Visitor Center has exhibits on Lake Superior and the North Shore, park history and area wildlife. Trails, mostly intermediate ones, run along the Gooseberry River, through aspen, cedar, spruce and pine forests. Be sure to see the lava flows at the Upper, Middle, and Lower falls, and south of the river at Lake Superior.

11 Burlington Bay Campsite

Location: On North Shore of Lake Superior, map 1, grid H3.

Campsites, facilities: There are 102 sites, many with electric hookups and water at this city campsite. It also has flush toilets, showers, disposal station, laundry and grocery store. The campground offers a boat ramp, lake fishing, hiking trails, playground and access to Lake Superior. Pets are allowed.

Reservations, fees: Call for reservations. The daily minimum fee begins at $15. Open from mid-May through mid-October.

Directions: Take Hwy. 61 north and turn on Park Road in Two Harbors toward Lake Superior. The entrance to this city park site is on the left.

Contact: Burlington Bay Campsite, 522 lst Avenue, Two Harbors, MN 55616-1504 or 218/834-2021, fax 218/834-2674.

Trip Notes: Visit the Lake County Historical Society Depot Museum (218/834-4898), which features the wood-burning "Three Spot," the first engine used in the area and a Mallett, one of the world's most powerful steam locomotives. Open daily May through October, 9 A.M. to 5 P.M.

12 Wagon Wheel

Location: On North Shore of Lake Superior, map 1, grid H3.

Campsites, facilities: This campground offers 30 shady sites with electric hookups and water. RV length limit is 35 feet. Facilities include flush toilets, showers, disposal station, tables, fire rings, playground, and sports field. Pets are allowed.

Reservations, fees: Call for reservations. The daily rate for two people begins at about $20. Open from mid-May through early October.

Directions: On U.S. Hwy. 61, 22 miles northeast of Duluth and less than two miles southwest of Two Harbors.

Contact: Wagon Wheel, Len and Judy Beardsley, 522 Old North Shore Rd., Two Harbors, MN 55616-9705 or 218/834-4901, fax 218/834-3189.

Trip Notes: Take a drive to Knife River Village, about three miles south along U.S. Hwy. 61. Originally a copper mining and logging settlement, it's renowned for its delicious smoked fish, commercial fishing and sport fishing. The Ojibwas called it "Mokomani-Zibi"

because of the sharp stones found in the riverbed and on its banks.

13 Big Blaze Campground and Cabins

Location: On North Shore of Lake Superior, map 1, grid H3.

Campsites, facilities: There are 60 sites (23 for tent campers) on 54 acres with 1,225 feet of Lake Superior shoreline. There are 12 pull-through sites for RVs, which are open in winter. Also available are full hookup sites. The wheelchair-accessible campground has sewers, flush toilets, showers, disposal station, tables, fire rings, swimming beach, boat ramp and grocery store. There are also three indoor lodging units available. Other facilities include biking, hiking, and cross-country ski trails. Snowshoe rentals are available. Pets are allowed.

Reservations, fees: Call for reservations. The daily rate is about $20. Credit cards are accepted. Open May through October.

Directions: From Duluth, take U.S. Hwy. 61 northeast for 18 miles. Turn right (east) to the campground, which is four miles southwest of Two Harbors. The entrance is on the left.

Contact: Big Blaze Campground and Cabins, Bruce and Joyce Wright, 560 Big Blaze Cir., Two Harbors, MN 55616-9705 or 218/834-2512, fax 218/834-2512, email: bigblaze@lake net.com, website: www.geocities.com /The Tropics/Cove/6191/.

Trip Notes: In Two Harbors, tour the lighthouse (800/832-5606) built in 1896. It's the oldest one in the state that is still in operation. Visit the Fog Horn Building, Assistant Keeper's House, and the pilot house from the shipwreck "Frontenac."

14 Depot Campground and Cafe

Location: Near the mouth of the Knife River, map 1, grid H3.

Campsites, facilities: The facility has 25 sites (five tent sites) with electric hookups, water, 12 pull-through sites for RVs, flush toilets, showers, disposal station, tables, and fire rings. There is also a sports field and restaurant. Pets are allowed.

Reservations, fees: Call for reservations. The daily minimum fee is about $14. Open from mid-April through about mid-October.

Directions: From the junction of U.S. Hwy. 61 and Scenic Hwy. 61, drive about seven miles south on County Road 61 to campground on left. It is adjacent to the marina.

Contact: Depot Campground and Cafe, Annamarie Peterson, P.O. Box 114, North Shore Dr., Knife River, MN 55609-0115 or 218/834-5044.

Trip Notes: In Two Harbors, you can tour the Great Lakes Fur Trade Museum & Shop (112 Waterfront Drive, 218/834-3323). From U.S. Hwy. 61 turn toward Lake Superior at the Dairy Queen on Waterfront Drive and go 5.5 blocks. The museum showcases artifacts traded to Native Americans in the 1700s and 1800s.

15 Pine Mountain Campground

Location: On Devil Track Lake, map 2, grid B5.

Campsites, facilities: There are 30 secluded sites with 11 devoted to tent campers. The campground offers electric hookups, water, disposal station, boat ramp, canoe rentals, and grocery store. Pets are allowed.

Reservations, fees: Call for reservations. The daily fee begins at $8. Open from late May through late September.

Directions: From Grand Marais, take County Road 12 (Gunflint Trail) to County Road 8 and follow County Road 8 to campground on the lake.

Contact: Pine Mountain Campground, 01 Thompson Park Dr., Grand Marais, MN 55604, 218/387-1619.

Trip Notes: Visit the Devil Track Wildlife Sanctuary on County Road 12 six miles north of Grand Marais. A brochure and signs along a short loop trail help you identify the colorful wildflowers you will find.

16 Judge C.R. Magney State Park

Location: On North Shore of Lake Superior, map 2, grid B8.

Campsites, facilities: The 4,514-acre park has 27 grassy, drive-in sites and a backpack site. RV length limit is 45 feet. Services include wheelchair-accessible showers, and flush and vault toilets. Facilities include interpretative exhibits, seven miles of hiking trails, five miles of ski trails, picnic area, and lake, river and stream fishing. Pets allowed.

Reservations, fees: The daily fee begins at $8. Camping and lodging reservations can be made 24 hours a day, seven days a week by calling The Connection (612/922-9000 in the metro Twin Cities area or 800/246-CAMP. See State Park Fees. Open all year.

Contact: Judge C.R. Magney State Park, 4051 U.S. Hwy. 61 East,
Grand Marais, MN 55604-2150 or 218/387-3039.

Directions: Take U.S. Hwy. 61 about 124 miles north of Duluth. The park entrance is off Hwy. 61, 14 miles northeast of Grand Marais; 22.2 miles southwest of Grand Portage State Park.

Trip Notes: The scenic Brule River races through the park, forming whitewater rapids and waterfalls on its way to Lake Superior. Along the lower stretches of the river are a series of spectacular waterfalls. Named for Clarence R. Magney, former Mayor of Duluth, District Judge, and Justice of the Minnesota Supreme Court, the park features two waterfalls, including the famed Devil's Kettle, where the river splits around a mass of volcanic rock. Birdwatchers will find a bonanza of warblers during the nesting months of May, June and July. Early fall is a good time to observe migrating hawks as they congregate along the shore of Lake Superior.

17 Cascade River State Park

Location: On North Shore of Lake Superior, map 2, grid C5.

Campsites, facilities: The 2,813-acre park has 40 drive-in (three pull-through), 15 tent sites, including five for backpackers; there are also two group camps. RV length limit is 35 feet. No electric or water hookups. Five sites are plowed in winter. The park offers wheelchair-accessible showers and toilets, seasonal disposal station, and 18 miles of hiking trails, 17 miles of ski trails, and two miles of snowmobile trails. There is also a warming house. The park has seven picnic areas along Lake Superior. Lake and river fishing are available as well. Pets are allowed.

Reservations, fees: The daily fee is $12. Reservations are not needed, but they can be made 24 hours a day, seven days a week by calling The Connection 612/922-9000 in the metro Twin Cities area or 800/246-CAMP. See State Park Fees. Open all year.

Directions: Take U.S. Hwy. 61, nearly 100 miles northeast of Duluth. The entrance is just off U.S. Hwy. 61 at Mile Post 101, 18 miles

northeast of Tofte; 10 miles southwest of Grand Marais.

Contact: Cascade River State Park, 3481 U.S. Hwy. 61 West, Lutsen, MN 55612-9535 or 218/387-3053, fax 218/387-3054.

Trip Notes: Aptly named, the Cascade River flows down one ledge after another for a total drop of 900 feet in the last three miles of its journey to Lake Superior. The park setting is a boreal hardwood-conifer forest of aspen, birch, fir, spruce and cedar. We stood on the footbridge that spans the river as it stairsteps through a volcanic canyon. You can also select any of the viewing spots above the river, and feel the vibration of the rushing torrent of water as it cascades down a volcanic canyon. Be certain to bring a camera. This park also has many small streams, awesome waterfalls and the Sawtooth Mountain Range. A bonus is six miles of Lake Superior shoreline. The Superior Hiking Trail, which passes through the park, provides a terrific vista of the lake, mountains and valley from the top of Lookout Mountain.

18 Grand Marais Recreation Area RV Park & Campground

Location: Municipal park on Lake Superior, map 2, grid C6.

Campsites, facilities: This city area has 300 sites (48 tent sites). There are 18 pull-through sites. Nearly 150 have full hookups—about 100 have electric and water hookups. There are also some seasonal sites. Facilities include wheelchair access, flush toilets, showers, disposal station, portable disposal, fire rings and grills. It also has a recreation hall, indoor swimming pool, sauna, whirlpool, boat ramp and rentals, playground, hiking trails and sports field. Pets are allowed.

Reservations, fees: Call for reservations. The daily fee begins at $20. Credit cards are accepted. Open from mid-May through mid-October.

Directions: Take U.S. Hwy. 61 south to 8th Avenue West in Grand Marais. The entrance is on the left on the west end of Grand Marais Harbor.

Contact: Grand Marais Recreation Area RV Park & Campground, Hwy. 61 & 8th Avenue West (P.O. Box 820), Grand Marais, MN 55604-0820 or 218/387-1712 or 800/998-0959, fax 218/387-1310.

Trip Notes: Bring your tackle and fish for brook and rainbow trout near the boiling rapids of the Brule River, which has carved unusual designs in the hard lava rock, which is believed to be as much as 3,500 feet thick.

19 Superior National Forest

Location: The Superior National Forest, which is the largest national forest in the Great Lakes region, stretches from Minnesota's North Shore area into the Northwoods and Boundary Waters regions. It includes the Boundary Waters Canoe Area Wilderness (BWCAW).

Designated in 1909, Superior National Forest encompasses 1,155,230 acres. More than 445,000 acres (695 square miles) is surface water. It has nearly 2,000 lakes, 1,500 miles of canoeing routes, and the Sawtooth Mountains, which is one of North America's oldest ranges. Map 2, grid D2.

Campsites, facilities: Campground policies vary from national forest to national forest. Sometimes, there also are variations within a national forest. This is the case at Superior where no permit is required for backcountry

camping except within the BWCAW. Also, rules can change at a moment's notice because of natural conditions like the risk of fire. Some trails may open and others may close, and fees may change. If you are uncertain about the rules, ask. And, it is worth a telephone call to check conditions.

Outside the Boundary Waters Canoe Area Wilderness, there are numerous campsites in the Superior National Forest in the North Shore region. They include:

Gunflint Ranger District Cascade River. Four sites 14 miles northwest of Grand Marais on Forest Road 158. Devil Track Lake. Sixteen sites 12 miles north of Grand Marais on County Road 8. East Bearskin Lake. Thirty-three sites 28 miles northwest of Grand Marais on Forest Road 146. Flour Lake. Thirty-five sites 30 miles northwest of Grand Marais on Forest Road 147. Iron Lake. Seven sites 38 miles northwest of Grand Marais on County Road 92. Kimball Lake. Ten sites 13 miles northeast of Grand Marais on Forest Road 140. Trail's End. Thirty-two sites 58 miles northwest of Grand Marais on Gunflint Trail.

Two Island Lake. Thirty-eight sites 15 miles northwest of Grand Marais on County Road 27.

Tofte Ranger District Baker Lake. Five sites 23 miles north of Tofte on Forest Road 1272. Crescent Lake. Thirty-three sites 27 miles northeast of Tofte on Forest Road 165. Divide Lake. Three sites six miles east of Tofte on Forest Road 172. Kawishiwi Lake. Five sites 32 miles northwest of Tofte on Forest Road 354. Little Isabella River. Eleven sites four miles west of Isabella on State Hwy. 1. McDougal Lake. Twenty-one sites 10 miles west of Isabella on Forest Road 106. Ninemile Lake. Twenty-four sites 14 miles northwest of Schroeder on County Road 7. Poplar River. Four sites 18 miles northeast of Tofte on Forest Road 164. Sawbill Lake. Fifty sites 25 miles north of Tofte on State Hwy. 2. Temperance River. Nine sites 11 miles north of Tofte on State Hwy. 2.

Reservations, fees: Although there is no fee for entry to national forests, some people are eligible for a 50percent discount on camping fees at campgrounds operated by the U.S. Forest Service or a private concessionaire. The Golden Age Passport is a $10 lifetime entrance pass for those who are 62 and older. It is free to the blind or disabled. There is also a 50 percent discount on user fees for campgrounds, parking, boat launches and other facilities operated by the Forest Service, National Park Service, and U.S. Fish and Wildlife Service.

Passports are available in person at most federally operated recreation areas, including U.S. Forest Service supervisor offices and district offices. Open all year.

Contact: U.S. Forest Service, 14th and Independence Ave., S.W.
Box 96090, Washington, DC 20090-6090 or 202/205-8333, TTY 202/205-1299.
U.S. Forest Service, Eastern Region Office, 310 W. Wisconsin Ave., Room 500, Milwaukee, WI 53203; 414/297-3646, TTY 414/297-3507.
Superior National Forest, 515 W. First St., P.O. Box 338,
Duluth, MN 55801; 218/720-5324, TTY 218/720-5433.

Directions: From Duluth on U.S. Hwy. 61, you can enter the Superior National Forest from a number of places. From the North Shore route at Tofte, you can take Hwy. 2, which is the Sawbill Trail or Hwy. 8 and 12 in Grand Marais, which is the Gunflint Trail.

Trip Notes: Carlton Peak (1,526 feet) is one of the last remaining peaks of the ancient Sawtooth Mountain Range, surviving four major glacial periods and millions of years of erosion. The peak, which offers a superb vista of Lake Superior and the surrounding area, can be reached by a two-mile round-trip hike through a maple and birch forest

from the Britton Peak trailhead on Sawbill Trail (County Road 2) near Tofte.

In Tofte, visit the North Shore Commercial Fishing Museum (218/663-7804), housed in a replica of the deep-red, twin fish house built by three Scandinavian fishermen. It's located on U.S. Hwy. 61 at Cook County Hwy. 2.

20 Lamb's Campground and Cabins

Location: On the Cross River, map 2, grid D1.
Campsites, facilities: There are 75 (50 tent) sites on 60 acres, many on the Lake Superior shoreline. There's a separate area for RVs with electric hookups; RV length limit is 36 feet. The campground offers flush toilets, showers, saunas, half-mile of beach, lake and river fishing, and biking and hiking trails. Pets are allowed. There are also 14 rustic log cabins with kitchens, baths, private yard and deck. Other facilities include recreation hall, boat ramp, restaurant, and grocery store. Pets are allowed.

Reservations, fees: Call for reservations. The daily rate begins about $20. Credit cards are accepted. Open from mid-May through mid-October.

Directions: In town at Schroeder and Cross River on U.S. Hwy. 61 at Mile Post 79, 79 miles northeast of Duluth. The entrance is on the right.

Contact: Lamb's Campground and Cabins, Skip and Linda Lamb, 4 Lamb's Way, P.O. Box 415, Schroeder, MN 55613-0415 or 218/663-7292.

Trip Notes: Visit the granite Father Baragas Cross at the base of the Cross River or view the attractive falls and gorge from the highway bridge.

21 Temperance River State Park

Location: On North Shore of Lake Superior, map 2, grid D2.

Campsites, facilities: The 539-acre park offers 55 drive-in (two pull-through) and three cart-in sites on both sides of the Temperance River. There are 18 electric sites. There are 36 campsites open during the winter. RV length limit is 50 feet. Showers and flush toilets are available. Temperance River has 22 miles of hiking trails (one-half mile is self-guided), 17 miles of cross-country ski trails, and seven miles of snowmobile trails. The park offers a picnic area, and lake and river fishing. Carry-in boats are allowed.

Reservations, fees: The daily fee begins at $12. Camping and lodging reservations can be made 24 hours a day, seven days a week by calling The Connection 612/922-9000 in the metro Twin Cities area or 800/246-CAMP. See State Park Fees. Open all year.

Directions: From Duluth, the park is 81.4 miles northeast. Take U.S. Hwy. 61, 1.4 miles north of Schroeder Village; it is 1.6 miles south of Tofte.

Contact: Temperance River State Park, 7620 Hwy. 61 East, Box 33, Schroeder, MN 55613, 218/663-7476, fax 218/663-7374.

Trip Notes: Pierre Esprit Radisson and Medard Chouart, Sier des Groselliers, were probably the first white visitors when they traveled up the shore of Lake Superior in 1660. Along with the Ojibwa Indians, the French controlled the area until 1763. The first white settlers in the area were probably clerks at American Fur Company posts along the shore in the 1830s. A story says the river got its name because, unlike other area streams, the Temperance River had no bar at its mouth. At one time, the waters of the river flowed so deep and so strong into Lake Superior that there was no build-up of debris. This meant that there was no "bar," so what else could you call a river without a bar? For an appropriate, slightly tongue-in-cheek selection, "temperance" fits ideally. In a winding gorge, the Temperance River drops 162 feet in one-half mile in a series of cascades, the last of which occurs about 100 feet from its mouth at Lake Superior. Both the North Shore Trail and the Superior Hiking Trail can be accessed from the park. You can also hike to Carlton or Britton peaks.

22 Silver Fox Lodge Resort

Location: Near the Cloquet Valley State Forest, map 4, grid A7.

Campsites, facilities: There 42 sites with electric hookups and water. Facilities include a swimming beach and boat ramp. Boat rentals are available. Pets are allowed. The resort also has four housekeeping cabins.

Reservations, fees: Call for reservations. The daily minimum fee is $14. Open May through September.

Directions: From Duluth, take County Road 4 north to Island Lake.

Contact: Silver Fox Lodge Resort, 7495 Boulder Lake Rd., Duluth, MN 55803-9222 or 218/721-4840.

Trip Notes: See the Depot at 506 W. Michigan Street (218/727-8025), a renovated 1892 railroad depot with four museums with exhibits representing 200 years of various cultures.

23 Island Beach Campground and Resort

Location: On Island Lake, map 4, grid A7.

Campsites, facilities: There are 47 sites, including RV pull-through sites. The campground features electric hookups, water, flush toilets, showers, disposal station, laundry, restaurant, playground, beach, boat ramp, grocery store and wheelchair access. Services include bike, boat, canoe and motor rentals. The facility also has four indoor lodging units. Pets are allowed.

Reservations, fees: Call for reservations. The daily minimum fee begins at $19. Credit cards are accepted. Open May through September.

Directions: From Duluth, take County Road 4 north to Island Lake.

Contact: Island Beach Campground and Resort, 6640 Fredenberg Lake Rd., Duluth, MN 55803-9468 or 218/721-3292.

Trip Notes: Visit Glensheen at 3300 London Rd. (218/724-8863), five miles north on SR 61 along Lake Superior. The 22-acre site was the 1908 estate of attorney, mining entrepreneur and state legislator Chester A. Congdon.

24 Buffalo Valley Campground

Location: Along Munger State Trail, map 4, grid C6.

Campsites, facilities: There are 80 sites (30 for tent campers) with electric hookups, water. Eight RV pull-through sites. It also has flush toilets, showers, disposal station, tables, fire rings, fishing pond, recreation area, sports field, restaurant, and biking, hiking and snowmobile trails. Seasonal campsite rentals are available. Pets are allowed.

Reservations, fees: Call for reservations. The daily minimum fee is $12. Credit cards are accepted. Open May through October.

Directions: From exit 245 on I-35, go one-quarter mile east on Hwy. 61. Then, drive one-quarter mile north on County Road 3 to Guss Road. Take Guss Road east for one-half mile. The campground is at the end.

Contact: Buffalo Valley Campground, 2590 Guss Rd., Duluth, MN 55810-2123 or 218/624-9901, fax 218/624-9901.

Trip Notes: Cruise aboard an excursion boat like those at Vista Fleet/Duluth-Superior Excursions (218/722-6218), which depart the DECC Dock on Harbor Drive. The cruises pass some of the world's largest ore docks and grain elevators, giant lake freighters and foreign vessels.

25 Spirit Mountain Ski Area and Campground

Location: On Spirit Mountain, map 4, grid C7.

Campsites, facilities: There are 73 sites including 20 winter sites with electric hookups, water, 13 pull-through sites, flush toilets, showers, disposal station, tables, grills, fire rings, wheelchair access, playground, tennis courts, restaurant, and evening entertainment. There is also access to hiking trails and cross-country and downhill ski areas. Bike and cross-country ski rentals are available. Pets are allowed.

Reservations, fees: Call for reservations. The daily minimum fee is $20. Open from mid-May through mid-October.

Directions: Take exit 249 from I-35. Go to Spirit Mountain Place.

Contact: Spirit Mountain Ski Area and Campground, 9500 Spirit Mountain Pl., Duluth, MN 55810-2029 or 218/628-2891, ext. 544, or 800/642-6377, fax 218/624-0213.

Trip Notes: The Lake Superior Zoo, located at 72nd Avenue West and Grand Avenue (218/723-3748), houses a children's zoo, nocturnal house and animals from all over the world.

26 Indian Point Campground

Location: On the St. Louis River, map 4, grid C7.

Campsites, facilities: There are 68 sites (II for tent campers), with electric hookups, water, sewer, flush toilets, showers, disposal station, laundry, playground, tables, fire rings, grills and some wheelchair access. RV length limit is 38 feet. Facilities include bike and canoe rentals, sports field, river fishing, and access to biking and hiking trails. Pets are allowed.

Reservations, fees: Call for reservations. The daily minimum fee is $14; $19 for a full hookup. Credit cards are accepted.

Open from mid-May through October.

Directions: Traveling north, take exit 251A on I-35 and drive 0.5 mile east on Cody Street, 0.25 mile south on 59th Avenue West, 1.25 miles southwest on Grand, and finally 0.25 mile southeast on 75th Avenue West. Traveling south, take exit 251B on I-35 and drive 1.25 miles southwest on Grand and 0.25 mile southeast on 75th Avenue West. The campground is at the end.

Contact: Indian Point Campground, 7000 Pulaski St., Duluth, MN 55807-2136; 218/624-5637.

Trip Notes: Take a guided tour aboard the William A. Irvin ore boat at 350 Harbor Drive (218/722-7876). The former flagship of the United States Steel fleet is named for a former company president. The 610-foot ship sailed from 1938 to 1978.

27 Duluth Tent and Trailer Camp

Location: On North Shore of Lake Superior, map 5, grid A2.

Campsites, facilities: There are 54 sites (12 sites for tent campers) near Lake Superior; 42 with electric and water hookups and 10 RV pull-through sites. Facilities include flush toilets, showers, laundry, disposal station, wheelchair access, playground, sports field, tables and fire rings. Pets are allowed.

Reservations, fees: Call for reservations. The daily minimum fee is about $15. Open May though late October.

Directions: From junction of U.S. Hwy. 61 and Scenic Hwy. 61, drive about three miles northeast to campground entrance on left.

Contact: Duluth Tent and Trailer Camp, 8411 Congdon Blvd., Duluth, MN 55804-2746 or 218/525-1350.

Trip Notes: See Minnesota Point, a narrow seven-mile peninsula with swimming beaches, seaplane base and boat clubs, at the junction of Commerce Street and Canal Park Drive. It offers excellent views of the harbor.

THE PRAIRIES

The Prairies

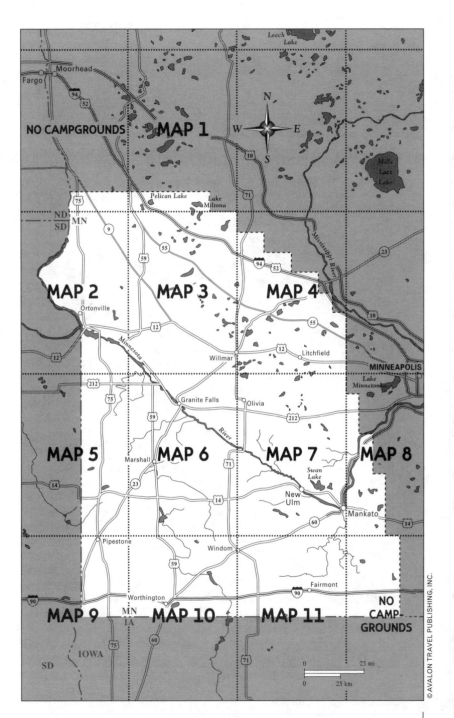

Map 1

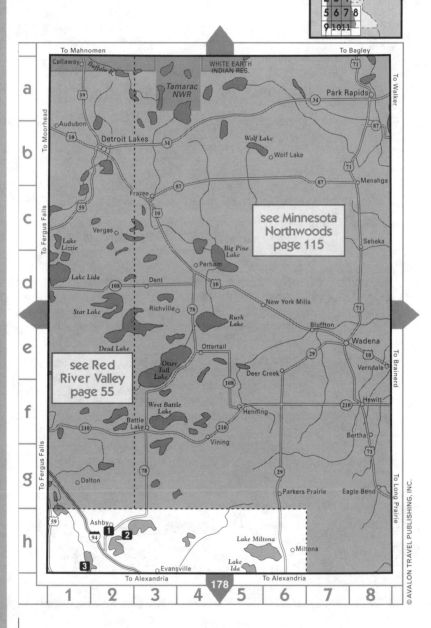

To Mahnomen
To Bagley

Callaway
Buffalo R.
WHITE EARTH
INDIAN RES.

Tamarac
NWR

Park Rapids

To Walker

a

To Moorhead

Audubon

Detroit Lakes

Wolf Lake

Wolf Lake

Menahga

b

Frazee

see Minnesota
Northwoods
page 115

To Fergus Falls

Vergas

Lake
Lizzie

Big Pine
Lake

Sebeka

c

Perham

Lake Lida

Dent

New York Mills

d

Star Lake

Richville

Rush
Lake

Bluffton

Wadena

see Red
River Valley
page 55

Dead Lake

Ottertail

Deer Creek

Verndale

To Brainerd

e

Otter
Tail
Lake

West Battle
Lake

Henning

Hewitt

f

Battle
Lake

Vining

Bertha

To Fergus Falls

g

Dalton

Parkers Prairie

Eagle Bend

To Long Prairie

Ashby

h

Lake Miltona

Miltona

Evansville

Lake
Ida

To Alexandria
To Alexandria

178

1 2 3 4 5 6 7 8

© AVALON TRAVEL PUBLISHING, INC.

Map 2

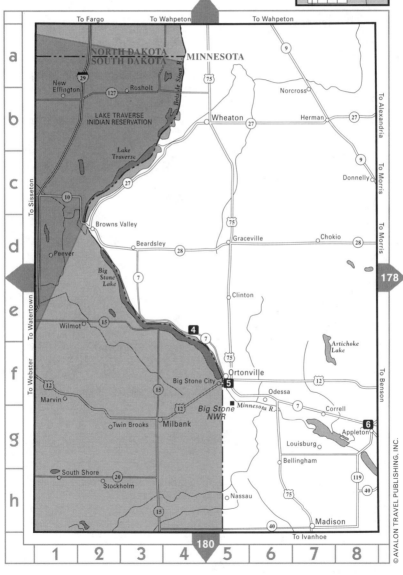

Map 3

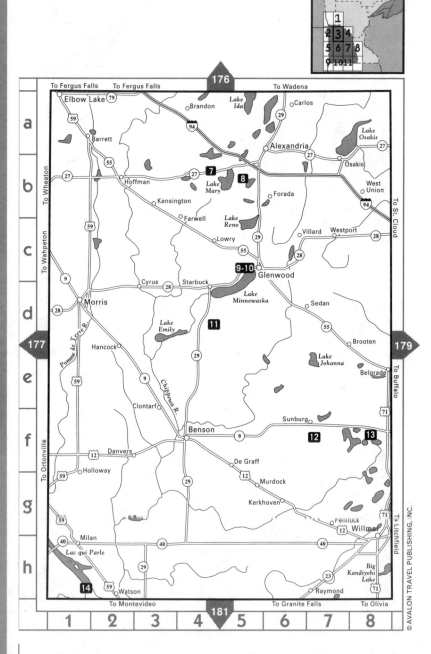

Map 3

To Fergus Falls   To Fergus Falls   **176**   To Wadena

Elbow Lake (79)
Brandon   Lake Ida   Carlos (29)

a

Barrett
Lake Osakis

To Wheaton
(55)
Alexandria (27)   (27)
(27)   Hoffman   **7**   Osakis
Lake Mary   **8**   West Union

b

Kensington
Farwell   Lake Reno   Forada   (94)

To St. Cloud
(59)
Lowry   Villard   Westport (28)
(55)   (29)
(28)

c

To Wahpeton
(9)
Cyrus (28)   Starbuck   **9-10** Glenwood

Morris   Lake Minnewaska   Sedan

d

177
(28)
Hancock   Lake Emily   **11**   (55)   Brooten

e

Pomme de Terre R.
(59)
(9)
Lake Johanna   Belgrade   To Buffalo
Clontarf   Chippewa R.   **179**
(71)

Benson   Sunburg   **12**   **13**
(9)

f

To Ortonville
(12) Danvers
De Graff
(59) Holloway   (12) Murdock

g

Kerkhoven
(29)
Pennock   (71)
(12) Willmar   To Litchfield

(59)
Milan   (40)
(40)   (40)   (40)

h

Lac qui Parle   (29)   Big Kandiyohi Lake
(23)   (71)
14 (59) Watson   Raymond

To Montevideo   **181**   To Granite Falls   To Olivia

1   2   3   4   5   6   7   8

© AVALON TRAVEL PUBLISHING, INC.

Map 4

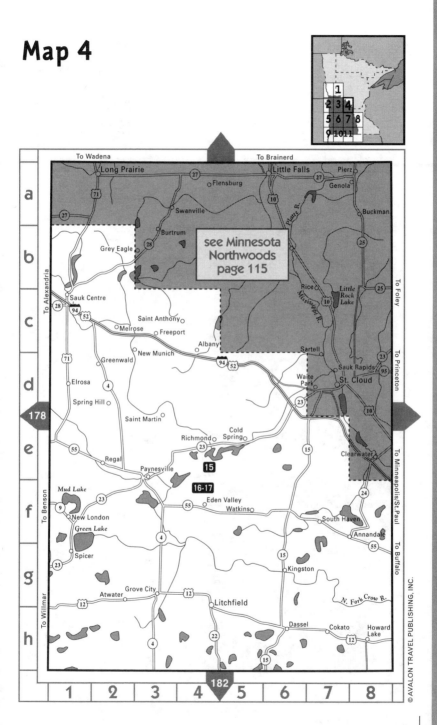

see Minnesota
Northwoods
page 115

© AVALON TRAVEL PUBLISHING, INC.

Map 5

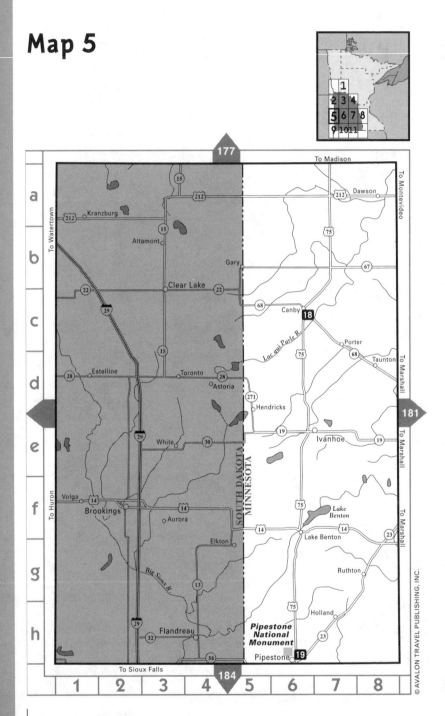

Map 6

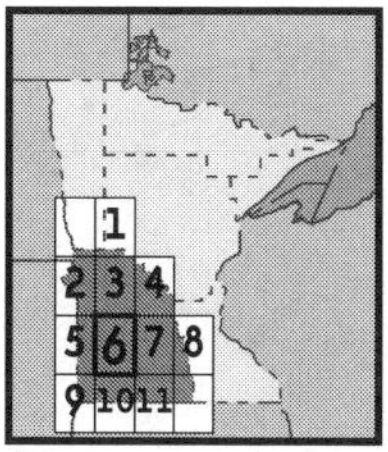

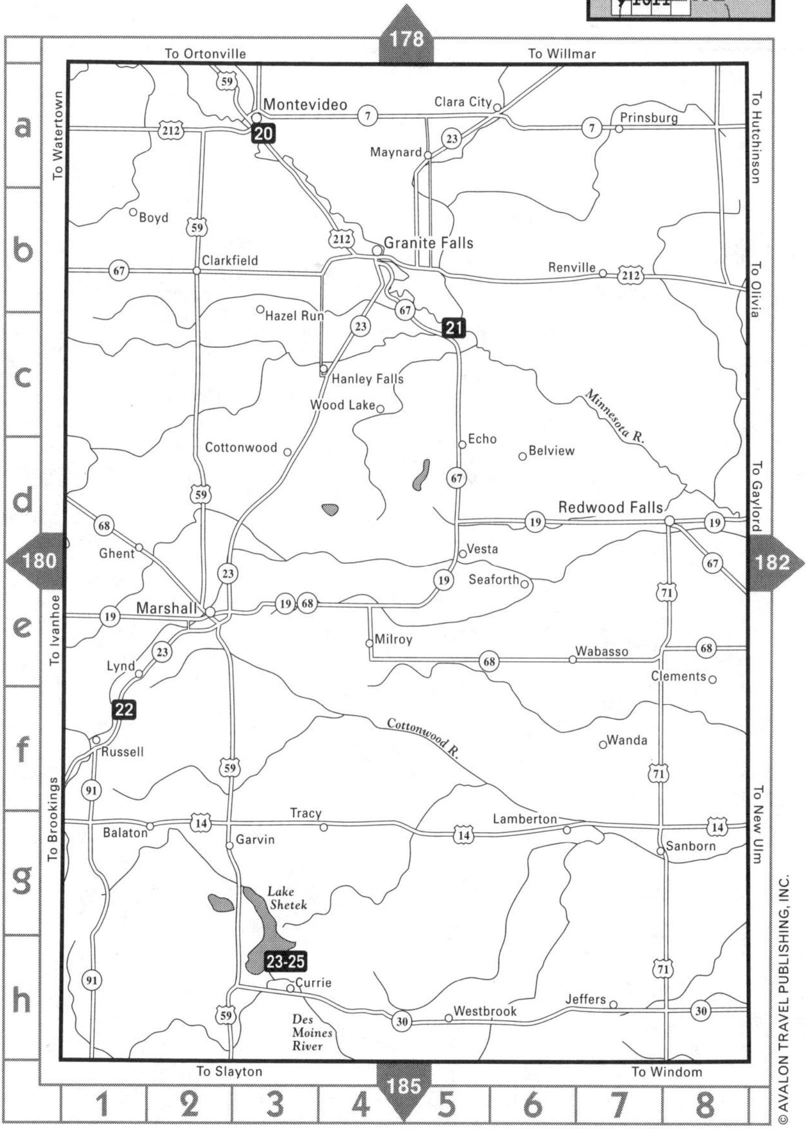

To Watertown

To Hutchinson

a
59
Montevideo
7
Clara City
212
20
Maynard
23
7
Prinsburg

To Olivia

b
Boyd
59
212
Granite Falls
67
Clarkfield
Renville
212
Hazel Run
23
67
21

To Gaylord

c
Hanley Falls
Wood Lake
Minnesota R.
Cottonwood
Echo
Belview

d
59
68
67
Redwood Falls
19
19
Ghent
Vesta
67
23
19
Seaforth
71

To Ivanhoe

e
19
Marshall
19
68
68
Lynd
23
Milroy
Wabasso
68
Clements
22

f
Russell
Cottonwood R.
Wanda
71
59

To Brookings

To New Ulm

g
91
Tracy
Lamberton
14
Balaton
14
Garvin
14
Sanborn
Lake
Shetek

h
91
23-25
Currie
71
59
Des
Moines
River
30
Westbrook
Jeffers
30

To Slayton   To Windom

Map 7

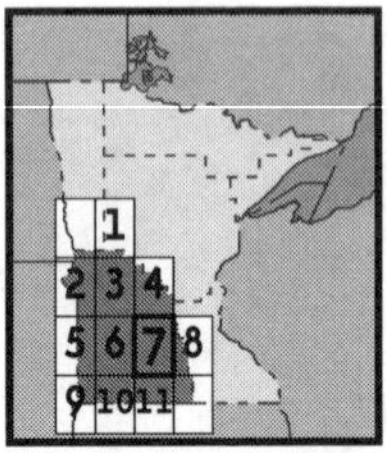

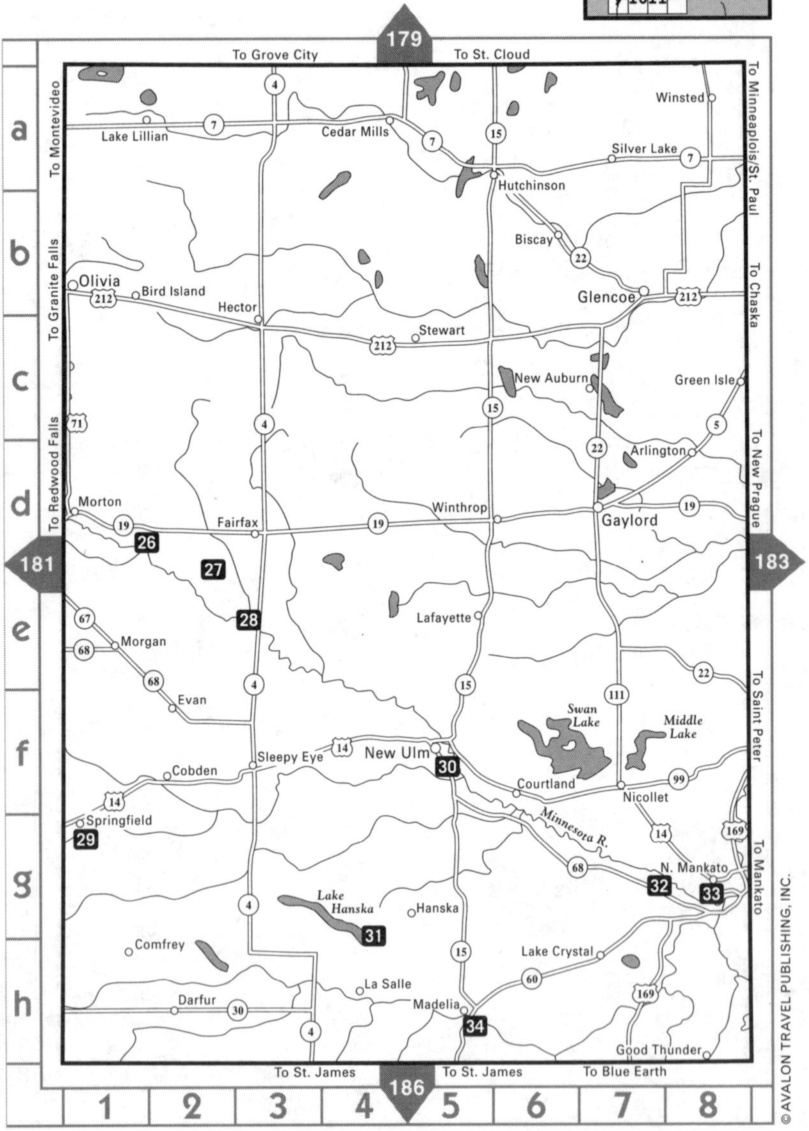

To Grove City · To St. Cloud

To Montevideo

To Minneaplois/St. Paul

Winsted

4

7 Lake Lillian

Cedar Mills

7

15

Silver Lake 7

Hutchinson

To Granite Falls

Biscay

22

Olivia

212 Bird Island

Hector

Glencoe 212

To Chaska

212 Stewart

New Auburn

Green Isle

To Redwood Falls

71

4

15

22

Arlington

5

To New Prague

Morton

19

Fairfax

19 Winthrop

Gaylord

19

181

183

26

27

67

28

Lafayette

68 Morgan

68 Evan

15

111

22

To Saint Peter

4

Swan Lake

Middle Lake

Cobden

Sleepy Eye 14 New Ulm

30

Courtland

99

Nicollet

14

169 To Mankato

14

Springfield

Minnesota R.

29

4

Lake Hanska

68

N. Mankato

32 **33**

Comfrey

Hanska

31

Lake Crystal

15

60

Darfur 30

La Salle

Madelia

169

4

34

Good Thunder

To St. James · To St. James · To Blue Earth

1   2   3   4   5   6   7   8

© AVALON TRAVEL PUBLISHING, INC.

Map 8

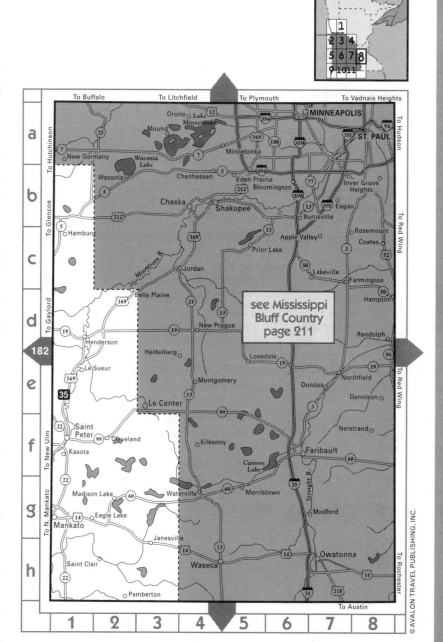

© AVALON TRAVEL PUBLISHING, INC.

Map 9

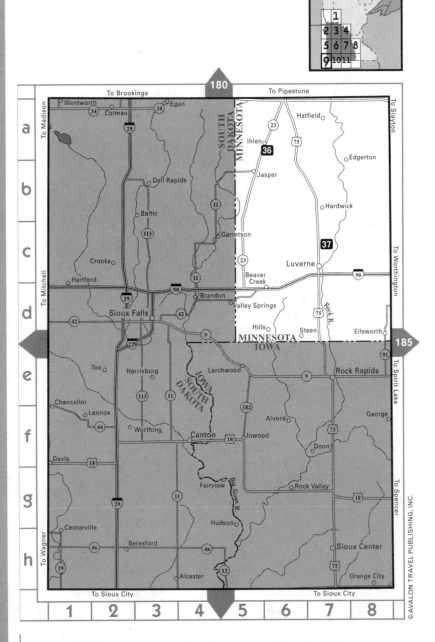

© AVALON TRAVEL PUBLISHING, INC.

Map 10

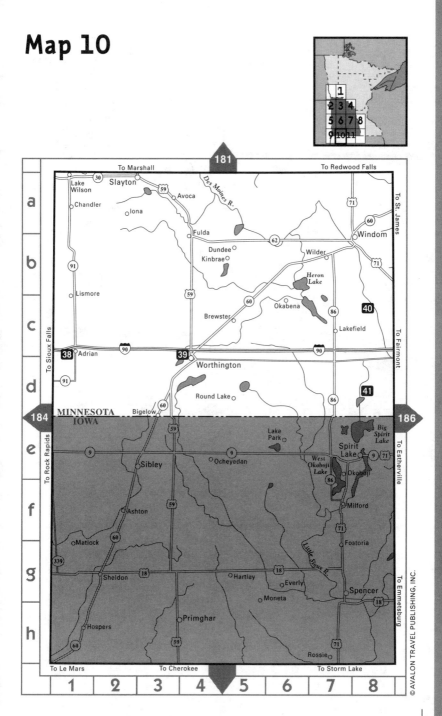

Map 11

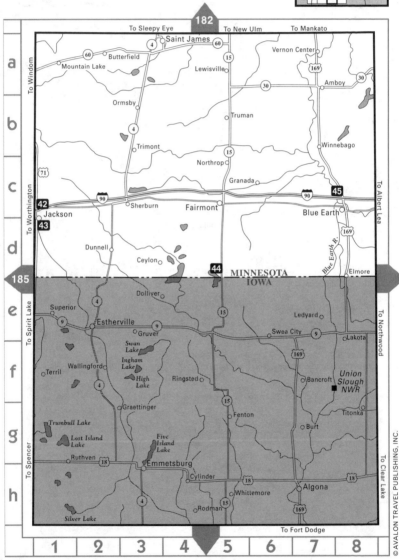

To Sleepy Eye • 182 • To New Ulm • To Mankato

To Windom

a
Saint James
60 • Butterfield
Mountain Lake
4
15
Vernon Center
169
Amboy
30
Lewisville

b
Ormsby
4
30
Truman
Winnebago

c
Trimont
71
15
Northrop
Granada
90
45 To Albert Lea
42
Sherburn
Fairmont
Blue Earth
Jackson
43
169

d
Dunnell
Ceylon
44 **MINNESOTA**
IOWA
Elmore
Blue Earth R.

To Worthington

185

e
Superior
9
Estherville
Gruver
4
15
Ledyard
Swea City
9
Lakota

To Spirit Lake

f
Terril
Wallingford
4
Swan Lake
Ingham Lake
High Lake
Ringsted
169
Bancroft
Union Slough NWR

g
Trumbull Lake
Lost Island Lake
Graettinger
4
Five Island Lake
15
Fenton
Burt
Titonka

To Spencer

h
Ruthven
18
Emmetsburg
Cylinder
18
Whittemore
Algona
18
4
15
Rodman
169
Silver Lake

To Fort Dodge

To Northwood

To Clear Lake

© AVALON TRAVEL PUBLISHING, INC.

1 2 3 4 5 6 7 8

The Prairies

When settlers from the East and Europe moved westward, the Dakota tribe lived in this part of Minnesota and the two cultures clashed in a tragic conflict. Today, the heritage of the Dakota and the pioneers who came to farm this portion of the plains that stretched beyond the horizon are honored at many historic sites and in a variety of museums.

At St. Peter, the new Treaty Site History Center focuses on the Native Americans and fur traders who used this crossing of the Minnesota River. Another historic site is Pipestone National Monument where a quarry of red stone has been used for centuries by many tribes to fashion ceremonial pipes. History here, however, goes back much further. Near Windom, the Jeffers Petroglyphs, which include more than 2,000 prehistoric rock carvings of human figures and animals, date from 3,000 B.C. to the 1700s.

By the 1850s, towns sprang up along the Minnesota River—Montevideo, Granite, and Mankato. In just a few decades, these new towns became bustling communities. For example, the river city of New Ulm, true to its German heritage, has a glockenspiel—a musical clock tower with animated figures—and a brewery. The river's headwaters are in Big Stone Lake, popular for its walleye fishing today. The area also attracts deer, small game, and waterfowl hunters each fall.

1 Sundowner Campground

Location: Southeast of Fergus Falls on Pelican Lakek, map 1, grid H2.

Campsites, facilities: There are 30 campsites. Facilities include RV pull-through sites, electric hookups, water, sewer, flush toilets, showers, and disposal station. Seasonal campsite rentals are available. Boat rentals and a golf course are nearby. Pets are allowed.

Reservations, fees: The daily fee ranges from $11 to $15. Open May through October.

Directions: From Fergus Falls, take I-94 southeast to Ashby at exit 77. Go north on Hwy 76 toward Ashby to Pelican Lake. Follow the signs to the resort.

Contact: Sundowner Campground, Carolyn Boe, Bob and Char Holtberg, Rt. 1, Box 145, Ashby, MN 56309-9801 or 218/747-2931 or 218/747-2847.

Trip Notes: If you're an architecture fan, visit the historic Christie Home Museum (320/732-2918) in nearby Long Prairie. The family of a local doctor owned the Victorian Queen Home, built in 1901. It features a carriage house and elaborate original furnishings. It's one block east of Hwy. 71 on Central Ave.

2 Ashby Resort and Campground

Location: Southeast of Fergus Falls on Pelican Lake, map 1, grid H2.

Campsites, facilities: There are 41 campsites. Facilities include RV pull-through sites, electric hookups, water, sewer, flush toilets, showers, disposal station, boat ramp, swimming beach, grocery store, restaurant, and playground. There are also biking, hiking, and snowmobile trails. Boat, motor, ice-fishing house, and seasonal campsite rentals are available. Pets are allowed.

Reservations, fees: The daily fee is $22. Credit cards are accepted. Open May through October.

Directions: From Ashby, take County Road 82 east for two miles to the campground.

Contact: Ashby Resort and Campground, Charles and Donna Frank, Box 57, Ashby, MN 56309, 800/332-9209 or 218/747-2959.

Trip Notes: Hunters, shooters, and anglers can all enjoy an outing at Elk Lake Heritage Preserve (320/986-2200; website: www.elklakeepreserve.com). The facility has a 60-round sporting clay range. There are also three privately stocked walleye lakes on the preserve overlooking scenic Torstenson Lake. Upland bird and waterfowl hunting are other options. It's located 20 miles west of Alexandria on Hwy. 27 and four miles north on Hwy. 5. The preserve is on the east side of the road.

3 Tipsinah Mounds Park Campground

Location: East of Elbow Lake on Pomme de Terre Lake, map 1, grid H1.

Campsites, facilities: There are 30 RV sites and 50 tent sites. Facilities include electric hookups, water, sewer, flush toilets, showers, disposal station, wheelchair access, boat ramp, swimming beach, biking and hiking trails, grocery store, evening entertainment, and playground. Boat, canoe, motor, and seasonal campsite rentals are available. The campground is within two miles of a golf course. Pets are allowed.

Reservations, fees: The daily fee ranges from $13 to $20. Credit cards are accepted. Open May through late September.

Directions: From I-94, take the Elbow Lake exit to Hwy. 79. Follow the signs to the municipal campground.

Contact: Tipsinah Mounds Park Campground, Scott and Jul Cleveland, Mgrs., 26527 Tipsinah Mounts Rd., Elbow Lake, MN 56531, 218/685-5114, fax 218/685-6294.

Trip Notes: Intermediate-level cross-country skiers can trace part of the historic Red River Trail used for oxcarts by the pioneers at the Andes Tower Hills Ski Area (320/965-2455). It runs through wooded hills. From Alexandria, go 11 miles west of I-94 on Hwy. 27 and 2.5 miles on County Road 15. Then drive one mile east on Andes Tower Hill Rd.

4 Big Stone Lake State Park

Location: On the Minnesota-South Dakota border, map 2, grid E4.

Campsites, facilities: There are 40 lakeside campsites, but no pads for RV campers. Facilities include electric hookups, water, flush toilets, showers, disposal station, wheelchair access, boat ramp, swimming beach, playground, and hiking and snowmobile trails. Canoe rentals are available. Pets are allowed.

Reservations, fees: Reservations are recommended for weekends. The daily fee ranges from $8 to $12. Credit cards are accepted. Open from late May through early September.

Directions: From Ortonville, go seven miles northwest on Hwy. 7. Follow the signs to the park.

Contact: Big Stone Lake State Park, R.R. 1, Box 153, Ortonville, MN 56278-9618 or 320/839-3663, fax 320/839-3676.

Trip Notes: Long ago, this area was the south end of glacial Lake Agassiz. Torrents of water cut the valley when the glacial river Warren drained Lake Agassiz. The area around Big Stone Lake State Park consists of granite and gneiss quarries. The top three inches of stone are exposed and contain the fossil remains of sharks' teeth.

Today, Big Stone Lake, the source of the Minnesota River, is 30 miles long. The northern section of this 990-acre park, the "Bonanza Area," has a picnic area and boat launch. The southern section, "Meadowbrook Area," has the campground, swimming beach, and hiking trails. The park's Environmental Education Center offers a place to discover the past and ways to preserve it.

5 Lakeshore RV Park and Fruit Farm

Location: In Ortonville on Big Stone Lake, map 2, grid E5.

Campsites, facilities: There are 40 campsites. Facilities

include RV pull-through sites, electric hookups, water, sewer, flush toilets, showers, laundry, wheelchair access, outdoor pool, whirlpool, grocery store, boat ramp, and playground. Pontoon boat and seasonal campsite rentals are available. Pets are allowed.

Reservations, fees: The daily fee ranges from $14 to $22. Credit cards are accepted. Open from mid-February through mid-October.

Directions: From Ortonville, take Hwy. 7 three miles north to the campground.

Contact: Lakeshore RV Park and Fruit Farm, Dennis, Carol, Steve and Colette Dragt, Rt. 1, Box 95, Ortonville, MN 56278, 800/936-7386 or 320/839-3701, email: mrddragt@maxminn .com, website: www.lakeshorervpark.com.

Trip Notes: If it's time for restocking, the Market Street Mall (507/532-5417) in Marshall is a half-block west of Hwy. 23 and Hwy. 19. The shopping center also features craft shows, Halloween zoo, Christmas concert, fashion shows, and other events.

6 Appleton Campground

Location: In Appleton on the Pomme de Terre River, map 2, grid G8.

Campsites, facilities: There are 25 campsites. Facilities include electric hookups, flush toilets, showers, and disposal station. Pets are allowed.

Reservations, fees: The daily fee begins at $5. Open May through October.

Directions: From Granite Falls, take U.S. Hwy. 59 northwest to Appleton. Go west on Schlieman Ave. to the campground.

Contact: Appleton Campground, 323 Schlieman Ave., W., Appleton, MN 56208, 320/289-1363, fax 320/289-1364.

Trip Notes: Take a cruise on nearby Big Stone Lake. "The Eahtonka" of Big Stone Excursions (800/519-7075 or 320/839-3824) offers

historical narration, optional island or supper club stops, and even dinner cruises. Reservations are required. From Appleton, travel west on Hwy. 7 two blocks west of Main St. to the foot of Big Stone Lake.

7 Valley Resort and Campground

Location: West of Alexandria on Mill Lake, map 3, grid B4.

Campsites, facilities: There are 40 campsites. Facilities include electric hookups, water, flush toilets, showers, laundry, disposal station, bike trail, tennis court, boat ramp, swimming beach, outdoor pool, grocery store, and playground. Boat, canoe, motor, and seasonal campsite rentals and baby-sitting services are available. Pets are allowed.

Reservations, fees: The daily fee begins at $22. Credit cards are accepted. Open May through September.

Directions: From Alexandria, take Hwy. 27 south to Mill Lake and follow the signs to the resort.

Contact: Sun Valley Resort and Campground, Jeff and Lori Carstensen, 10045 State Hwy. 27 W., Alexandria, MN 56308-6510 or 320/886-5417, email: sunvaley@ rea-alp.com, website: www.alexandriamn .com/sunvalley.

Trip Notes: The resort is on a deep, spring-fed 650-acre lake. Mill Lake has several bays and five miles of wooded shoreline. Walleye, northern pike, largemouth bass, sunfish, and crappie are abundant.

From mid-May through August, you can enjoy Saturday evenings at the Viking Speedway-NASCAR Winston Racing Series races. They are held at the Douglas County Fairgrounds (800/630-8302 or 320/762-1559) on the northwest side of Alexandria.

8 Big Foot Resort

Location: Southwest of Alexandria on Lake Mary, map 3, grid B5.

Campsites, facilities: There are 45 campsites. Facilities include RV pull-through sites, electric hookups, water, sewer, boat ramp, grocery store, and playground. Boat, motor, and seasonal campsite rentals and baby-sitting services are available. Pets are allowed.

Reservations, fees: Reservations are recommended for weekends. The daily fee begins at $20. Credit cards are accepted. Open May through September.

Directions: From Alexandria, take Hwy. 114 south just past County Road 4 to the resort.

Contact: Big Foot Resort, 8231 State Hwy. 114, S.W., Alexandria, MN 56308-6049 or 888/239-2512 or 320/283-5533, fax 320/283-5040.

Trip Notes: Visit the Carlos Creek Winery (320/846-5443), home to an orchard of 7,000 apple trees and the largest grape vineyard in Minnesota. There are daily tours and tastings. It also has one of the state's largest purebred Arabian horse facilities. You can find it on County Road 34 about three miles north of Alexandria.

9 Hobo Park Campground and Marina

Location: West of Glenwood on Lake Minnewaska, map 3, grid C5.

Campsites, facilities: There are 92 RV sites and 20 tent sites. Facilities include electric hookups, water, sewer, flush toilets, showers, disposal station, and boat ramp. Seasonal campsite rentals are available.

Reservations, fees: The daily fee ranges from $10 to $15. Open May through September.

Directions: From Starbuck, take Hwy. 29 south to Lake Minnewaska.

Contact: Hobo Park Campground, 401 E. First St., Box 606, Starbuck, MN 56381-0606 or 320/239-2525 or 320/239-2336, fax 320/239-2545.

Trip Notes: You can discover county history, farm machinery, and Native American artifacts at the Pope County Museum (320/634-3293) in nearby Glenwood. There's also a furnished pioneer log schoolhouse, the first county courthouse, a furnished pioneer log home and a Soo Line railway caboose. Go 0.75 mile south of the stoplight in Glenwood on the lake.

10 Woodlawn Resort and Campground

Location: West of Glenwood on Lake Minnewaska, map 3, grid C5.

Campsites, facilities: There are 24 RV sites and six tent sites. Facilities include electric hookups, flush toilets, showers, disposal station, boat ramp, swimming beach, grocery store, and playground. Boat, canoe, motor, and kayak rentals and baby-sitting services are available. There are two golf courses and tennis courts nearby. Pets are allowed.

Reservations, fees: The daily fee ranges from $15 to $20. Open from mid-May through September.

Directions: From Glenwood, go 2.5 miles west on County Road 54 to the north shore of Lake Minnewaska.

Contact: Woodlawn Resort and Campground, Randy and Judie Crumb, 24050 Lakeshore Dr., N, Glenwood, MN 56334-9358 or 320/634-3519 or 800/892-3619, website: www.minnewaskamn.com/woodlawn/.

Trip Notes: A resort highlight is the Woodlawn Wagon throne honor. Rides are given to the angler with lunker walleye, northern pike, bass, crappie, or yellow perch with sirens blaring, lights flashing, and bells ringing.

⑪ Glacial Lakes State Park

Location: Southwest of Alexandria, map 3, grid D4.

Campsites, facilities: There are 39 RV sites and five tent sites. All are also open in winter. Facilities include RV pull-through sites, electric hookups, flush toilets, showers, wheelchair access, disposal station, boat ramp, swimming beach, and playground. A picnic area deck overlooks Mountain Lake. There are also biking, hiking, cross-country ski, and snowmobile trails. Boat, canoe, ski equipment, and snowshoe rentals are available. Pets are allowed.

Reservations, fees: Reservations are recommended for weekends. The daily fee ranges from $12 to $19. Credit cards are accepted. Open year-round.

Directions: From Starbuck, go three miles south on Hwy. 29. Then drive two miles south on County Road 41 to the park.

Contact: Glacial Lakes State Park, 25022 County Road 41, Starbuck, MN 56381-9621 or 320/239-2860, fax 320/239-2860.

Trip Notes: The state park is located at a transition zone between the original prairie land to the west and the central hardwood forests to the east. Only about 1/10th of 1 percent of the original Minnesota prairie remains. The park preserves a portion of rare native prairie including a wide variety of grasses and plants such as the big and little bluestem grass, Indian grass, prairie clover, pasque flowers, coneflowers, and goldenrods. Common prairie shrubs include wolfberry and

rose. (Check the park office to see what wildflowers might be in bloom.) Enjoy the clear 56-acre Mountain Lake that has its entire watershed inside the park. You can also stand on top of the glacial hills here and experience vast, open prairie that once dominated Minnesota. In addition to the campground, horseback riders and backpackers can camp at the trail center and at remote sites.

⑫ Monson Lake State Park

Location: South of Sunburg, map 3, grid F6.

Campsites, facilities: There are 20 campsites. Facilities include RV pads, boat ramp, hiking trail, and picnicking. Pets are allowed.

Reservations, fees: Weekend reservations are recommended. The daily fee is $8. Open from late May through early September.

Directions: From Sunburg, take Hwy. 104 south to County State Aid Hwy. 18 to the park.

Contact: Monson Lake State Park, 1690 15th St. N.E., Sunburg, MN 56289-8118 or 320/366-3797, fax 320/354-2372.

Trip Notes: Monson Lake State Park was established in 1923 as a memorial to the members of the Broberg and Lundbergh families who died in the U.S.-Dakota Conflict of 1862. Anna Stina Broberg Peterson, the only survivor, was 16 when the settlement was attacked on August 20, 1862. Before her death in 1933, she dictated an eyewitness account of that event. Her story is available at the park office. The 187-acre park offers fishing for walleye, northern pike, bass, and sunfish in Monson Lake. Birdwatchers can spot white pelicans, herons, western grebes, and songbirds. If you bring a canoe, you can paddle the lake and make a short portage that leads from Monson Lake to West Sunburg Lake.

13 Sibley State Park

Location: West of New London on Andrew Lake, map 3, grid F8.

Campsites, facilities: There are 134 (12 winter) campsites. Facilities include RV pull-through sites, electric hookups, flush toilets, showers, disposal station, wheelchair access, boat ramp, swimming beach, and grocery store. There are also biking, hiking, cross-country ski, and snowmobile trails. Bike, boat, canoe, and motor rentals are available. Pets are allowed.

Reservations, fees: Reservations are recommended for weekends. The daily fee ranges from $12 to $16. Credit cards are accepted. Open year-round.

Directions: From Willmar, take U.S. Hwy. 71 north for 15 miles to the park entrance.

Contact: Sibley State Park, 800 Sibley Park Rd., N.E., New London, MN 56273-9664 or 320/354-2055, fax 320/354-2372.

Trip Notes: There's something in this 2,936-acre park for everyone. Climb Mount Tom, one of several high points in a 50-mile radius, and see forest, farmland, prairie knolls, and lakes. The forest is dominated by oak, red cedar, ironwood, green ash, aspen, maple, and basswood. On the knolls, remnants of prairie grasses still grow. Some of the fields, which had been cleared and farmed by settlers, have now been restored to native prairie grasslands and oak savanna. You can also canoe and portage on Henschien Lake and Swan Lake.

14 Lac Qui Parle State Park

Location: Southeast of Ortonville on Lake Lac Qui Parle, map 3, grid H1.

Campsites, facilities: There are 50 RV sites and six tent sites (20 winter sites). Facilities include electric hookups, flush toilets, showers, disposal station, wheelchair access, boat ramp, swimming beach, playground, and hiking and cross-country ski trails. Pets are allowed.

Reservations, fees: Reservations are recommended for weekends. The daily fee ranges from $7 to $12. Credit cards are accepted. Open year-round.

Directions: From Watson, take U.S. Hwy. 59 northwest to Hwy. 7 and to the park.

Contact: Lac Qui Parle State Park, Rt. 5, Box 74A, Montevideo, MN 56265-8609 or 320/752-4736, fax 320/752-4484.

Trip Notes: Lac qui Parle is a French translation of the name given to the lake by the Dakota Indians (lake that speaks). If you visit in the spring or fall, you'll know why. The lake is a stopover for thousands of migratory Canada geese and other waterfowl. You'll hear a chorus of honking, quacking, and other vocalizations. Paddle the lake, or cast a line and catch walleye, northerns, perch, or crappie. Explore one of the trails by foot or horseback. Visit historic Fort Renville and Lac qui Parle mission sites. Dr. Thomas Smith Williamson and Alexander Huggins founded the Sioux mission in 1835. They translated the Gospel and several hymns into the Dakota language and they completed the first dictionary of the language. Minnesota's first cloth was also made at the mission. Be sure to visit the 27,000-acre Lac qui Parle Wildlife Management Area, too.

15 El Rancho Mañana Campground

Location: South of I-94 on Long Lake, map 4, grid E4.

Campsites, facilities: There are 120 campsites. Facilities

include RV pull-through sites, electric hookups, water, sewer, flush toilets, showers, laundry, disposal station, grocery store, lounge, evening entertainment, boat ramp, swimming beach, hiking and cross-country ski trails, hayrides, children's programs, and playground. Boat, canoe, motor, horse, cross-country ski equipment, snowshoe, and seasonal campsite rentals are available. Pets are allowed.

Reservations, fees: The daily fee ranges from $12 to $21. Credit cards are accepted. Open May through September.

Directions: From I-94, take exit 153 at Avon and go 10 miles south on County Road 9 to the campground.

Contact: El Rancho Mañana Campground, 27302 Ranch Rd., Richmond, MN 56368-8401 or 320/597-2740, fax 320/597-2740.

Trip Notes: In winter you can go ice fishing on Minnewaska Lake. Hunt's Resort and RV Park (800/450-3323 or 320/634-33323) rents ice-fishing houses and cabins. It is 1.5 miles west of Glenwood on County Road 54 (N. Lakeshore Dr.) on the lake.

16 Morning Star Resort and Campground

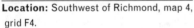

Location: Southwest of Richmond, map 4, grid F4.

Campsites, facilities: There are 100 RV sites and 30 tent sites. Facilities include electric hookups, water, sewer, flush toilets, showers, laundry, disposal station, wheelchair access, restaurant, lounge, grocery store, boat ramp, swimming beach, hiking trail, and playground. Boat, canoe, speedboat, motor, and seasonal campsite rentals are available. Pets are allowed.

Reservations, fees: The daily fee ranges from $10 to $15. Open May though early October.

Directions: From St. Cloud, take Hwy. 23 west 20 miles to County Road 43 and follow the signs to the campground.

Contact: Morning Star Resort and Campground, 22954 Green Acres Dr., Richmond, MN 56368-8500 or 320/453-7121, fax 320/453-7121.

Trip Notes: At the east end of Paynesville on Hwy. 23 is the Paynesville Historical Museum (320/243-4433 or 320/243-7547), where visitors can tour the schoolhouse, blacksmith shop, wood cabinet shop, and religious center and see the early farm implements and Native American display. Adult admission is $2; children are 50 cents. Parking is free.

17 Browns Lake Resort

Location: South of Richmond on Browns Lake and Long Lake, map 4, grid F4.

Campsites, facilities: There are 40 campsites. Facilities include electric hookups, water, sewer, flush toilets, showers, laundry, disposal station, restaurant, grocery store, boat ramp, swimming beach, and playground. Boat, canoe, and motor rentals are available. Pets are allowed.

Reservations, fees: The daily fee ranges from $18 to $25. Credit cards are accepted. Open from mid-May through early October.

Directions: From Richmond, take Hwy. 22 five miles south to Browns Lake Rd. and the resort.

Contact: Browns Lake Resort, Mike and Dave Hentges, 18091 Browns Lake Rd., Richmond, MN 56368-8508 or 320/453-2426 or 320/597-2611.

Trip Notes: If you're a hunter, the Gold Meadows Hunting Preserve (320/597-2747 or 320/685-3014) is open from August through April for pheasant hunting. The preserve is five miles north of Richmond and Cold Spring, on 260th St., off County Road 50.

18 Municipal Lake Park

Location: In Canby on Lake Sylvan, map 5, grid C6.

Campsites, facilities: There are six campsites. Facilities include electric hookups, water, flush toilets, disposal station, outdoor pool, and tennis court. Pets are allowed.

Reservations, fees: The daily fee is $10. Open from late May through early September.

Directions: In Canby, take U.S. Hwy. 75 to Sylvan Lake. Follow the signs.

Contact: Municipal Lake Park, 110 Oscar Ave., N., Canby, MN 56220-1332 or 507/223-7295, fax 507/223-5170.

Trip Notes: Southeast of Canby on Hwy. 68, visit the Museum of Natural History (800/642-0684 or 507/537-6178; email: desy@ssu.south west.msus.edu), which is open during the school year and summer sessions. It has displays of the flora and fauna of southwestern Minnesota. Admission and parking are free. It's on Hwy. 23 north of Hwy. 19 in Marshall.

19 Pipestone RV Campground

Location: In Pipestone, map 5, grid H6.

Campsites, facilities: There are 52 RV sites and 13 tent sites. Facilities include RV pull-through sites, electric hookups, water, sewer, flush toilets, showers, disposal station, laundry, wheelchair access, grocery store, heated outdoor pool, and playground. Teepees and seasonal campsite rentals are available. Pets are allowed.

Reservations, fees: The daily fee ranges from $16 to $22. Discounts are available and credit cards are accepted. Open from mid-April through October.

Directions: In Pipestone, go seven blocks north of Main St. on Hiawatha Ave. It's across the street from the Pipestone National Monument.

Contact: Pipestone RV Campground, Carl and Nancy Cowan, 919 N. Hiawatha Ave., Pipestone, MN 56164-2286 or 507/825-2455, fax 507/562-1222, email: rvcmpgrd@rconnect.com, website: www.pipestonervcampground.com.

Trip Notes: In August, Pipestone celebrates with a county fair, the "Song of Haiwatha Pageant" and the "Gathering of Sacred Pipes Sundance." Call the campground for exact dates.

Most anytime you can savor the smells and sights of an 1870s general store as you sample the wares or play a game of checkers at the Harkin Store (507/354-8666) in West Newton. When the railroad bypassed the town in 1873, the store was forced to close with unsold inventory still on the shelves where it remains today. The store is at 2 N. Broadway on County Road 21, eight miles northwest of New Ulm.

20 Lagoon Park Campground

Location: In Montevideo, map 6, grid A3.

Campsites, facilities: There are 10 campsites. Facilities include electric hookups, water, flush toilets, showers, hiking trail, and playground.

Reservations, fees: The daily fee is $10. Open May through October.

Directions: From Granite Falls, take U.S. Hwy. 212 north and continue on Hwy. 59 to Montevideo. At Hwy. 7 turn east on Canton Ave. to the campground.

Contact: Lagoon Park Campground, 103 Canton Ave., Montevideo, MN 56265-1418 or 800/269-5527 or 320/269-7572, email: chamber@maxminn.com, website: www.montechamber.com.

Trip Notes: Here's an opportunity to visit three sites—historic Chippewa City, the Swensson Farm Museum, and the Lac qui Parle Mission—near Montevideo. Chippewa City is a 23-building village replica. The farm museum is a 22-room brick home built in 1901. The Lac qui Parle Mission is where the Bible was translated into the Dakota language. Call 320/269-7636 for information and directions.

21 Upper Sioux Agency State Park

Location: South of Granite Falls, map 6, grid C5.

Campsites, facilities: There are 90 (five winter) campsites. Facilities include electric hookups, flush toilets, showers, wheelchair access, boat ramp, playground, and hiking and cross-country ski trails. Pets are allowed.

Reservations, fees: Reservations are recommended for weekends. The daily fee ranges from $12 to $14. Credit cards are accepted. Open from late May through early September.

Directions: From Granite Falls at Hwy. 212 and Hwy. 23, go south about one block to Hwy. 67. Turn east on Hwy. 67 and go about eight miles to the park entrances. The second is the main park entrance; the third is the campground entrance.

Contact: Upper Sioux Agency State Park, Rt. 2, Box 92, Granite Falls, MN 56241-9565 or 320/564-4777, fax 320/564-4838.

Trip Notes: The 1,280-acre park contains the site of the Upper Sioux or Yellow Medicine Agency and was established in 1963 to preserve the remains of the old agency site. From the river's bank visitors can fish for walleyes, northern pike, catfish, bullhead, and carp. Watch for white pelicans and great blue herons along the edges of shallow pools.

Spotted sandpipers, killdeer, and other shore birds frequently hunt for insects on the gravel bars and mud flats along the river. Red-tailed hawks, turkey vultures, and white pelicans catch the air currents above the valley. Bald eagles winter in the Minnesota River Valley. Snow enthusiasts will enjoy the park's huge sliding hill.

If you're lucky enough to book early (800/246-2267) from Memorial Day weekend on, you might get one of two teepees for rent in the park's new campground.

22 Camden State Park

Location: Southwest of Marshall, map 6, grid F1.

Campsites, facilities: There are 80 (35 winter) campsites. Facilities include RV pull-through sites, electric hookups, flush toilets, showers, disposal station, wheelchair access, boat ramp, swimming beach, and biking, hiking, cross-country ski, and snowmobile trails. Canoe rentals are available. Pets are allowed.

Reservations, fees: Reservations are recommended for weekends. The daily fee ranges from $6 to $12. Credit cards are accepted. Open year-round.

Directions: From Lynd, go three miles southwest on Hwy. 23.

Contact: Camden State Park, 1897 County Rd. 68, Lynd, MN 56157-1149 or 507/865-4530, fax 507/865-4608.

Trip Notes: The Redwood River Valley was home to prehistoric and historic people. Archaeologists discovered that people used this valley 8,000 years ago for hunting and fishing. Only 150 years ago, buffalo, elk, wolves, prairie chickens, and golden eagles were an integral part of life here. They are gone now. Today, mink, raccoons, songbirds, hawks, coyotes, and a large winter herd of white-tail deer flourish in the park. Bass and bluegill are found in Brawner Lake, and brown trout are stocked in the Redwood River each year. Other options include walking along the wooded river valley or climbing the Dakota Valley Trail to the lookout for an awesome view and stunning color panorama in fall.

23 Lake Shetek State Park

Location: North of Slayton on Shetek Lake, map 6, grid H3.

Campsites, facilities: There are 10 tent sites, which are open all winter. Facilities include electric hookups, flush toilets, showers, disposal station, wheelchair access, boat ramp, swimming beach, and playground. There are also biking, hiking, cross-country ski, and snowmobile trails. Boat and canoe rentals are available. Pets are allowed.

Reservations, fees: Reservations are recommended on weekends. The daily fee ranges from $8 to $15. Credit cards are accepted. Open year-round.

Directions: From Currie, take County Road 38 north to the park.

Contact: Lake Shetek State Park, 163 State Park Rd., Currie, MN 56123-1018 or 507/763-3256 or 507/763-3231, fax 507/763-3330.

Trip Notes: Shetek (Ojibwa for pelican) is named for the birds that visit the park during the summer and fall. Shetek Lake, the largest lake in southwestern Minnesota, forms the headwaters of the Des Moines River. You'll find excellent fishing. Visit 45-acre Loon Island, accessible by foot on a causeway. A quiet hike on one of the trails can give you a glimpse of a white-tail deer, the sounds of bobolinks in the prairie, or the flight of a white pelican overhead. The wooded shoreline of the lake offers cover for deer,

fox, mink, beaver, fox squirrels, muskrat, woodchuck, and coyote. Several wetlands in the park provide habitat for waterfowl, reptiles, and amphibians. At Eastlick Marsh interpretive signs and an observation deck with a spotting scope offer close-up views of coots, grebes, ducks, herons, and pelicans. Many species of waterfowl nest in and around the park in spring and early summer.

24 Lake Shetek Lodge

Location: Near Slayton on Lake Shetek, map 6, grid H3.

Campsites, facilities: There are 12 RV sites. Facilities include electric hookups, water, sewer, laundry, and swimming beach. Boat, canoe, ice-fishing house, and seasonal campsite rentals are available. Pets are allowed.

Reservations, fees: The daily fee ranges from $17 to $22. Credit cards are accepted. Open year-round.

Directions: From Slayton, take U.S. Hwy. 59 north to Hwy. 30. Follow the signs to the lodge.

Contact: Lake Shetek Lodge, 21 Valhalla Dr., Slayton, MN 56172-1921 or 507/763-3200, fax 507/763-3200.

Trip Notes: You can tour a working railroad yard, including a manual turntable, original Chicago & Northwestern depot, rebuilt engine house, water tower, foreman's house, coal bunker (now a picnic shelter and gift shop), general store, and one-room schoolhouse at the End-O-Line Railroad Park and Museum (507/763-3708; website: www.endoline.com) in Currie. A special attraction is an HO gauge "Hilfer's model train" with a model railroad yard. From Slayton, take U.S. Hwy. 59 north to Hwy. 30 and go east to Currie and County Road 38 (Main St.). It is at 440 N. Mill St.

25 Schreiers on Shetek Campground

Location: Near Currie on Shetek Lake, map 3, grid H3.

Campsites, facilities: There are 93 RV sites and 17 tent sites. Facilities include RV pull-through sites, electric hookups, water, sewer, flush toilets, showers, disposal station, laundry, grocery store, biking and hiking trails, boat ramp, swimming beach, and playground. Boat, motor, canoe, and seasonal campsite rentals and baby-sitting services are available. Pets are allowed.

Reservations, fees: The daily fee ranges from $12 to $18. Open May through mid-October.

Directions: From Currie, go two miles north on County Road 38.

Contact: Schreiers on Shetek Campground, Marcia Schreier, 35 Resort Rd., Currie, MN 56123, 507/763-3817, fax 507/763-3374, email: schremks@frontiernet.net.

Trip Notes: Spend some time at Minnesota's Machinery Museum (507/768-3522 or 507/768-3580; website: www.prairiewaters.com). The complex features five large buildings on a six-acre site, recapturing a century of stories about farm life. You'll see implements, tools, tractors, and gas engines in mint condition as well as rural art. Take Hwy. 23 nine miles south of Granite Falls in Hanley Falls. It's one block west of Hwy. 23 and one block north.

26 City Campground

Location: In Franklin on the Minnesota River between Redwood Falls and Fairfax, map 7, grid D1.

Campsites, facilities: There are five RV sites and seven tent sites. Facilities include electric hookups, water, flush toilets, showers, tennis court, snowmobile trail, boat ramp, restaurant, grocery store, and playground. Pets are allowed.

Reservations, fees: The daily fee ranges from $10 to $15. Open from mid-May through late October.

Directions: From U.S. Hwy. 71, take Hwy. 19 east to Franklin. Follow the signs to the campground.

Contact: City Campground, Box 326, Franklin, MN 55333-0326 or 507/557-2259.

Trip Notes: The estate of the wealthy Gilfillan family donated Gilfillan Farm (507/644-2490 or 507/249-3451) to the Redwood County Historical Society. It includes farm and home antiques, and a campground with water hookup, showers, or both. The farm is on Hwy. 67 between Redwood Falls and Morgan.

27 Valley View Campground

Location: North of Fort Ridgely State Park, map 7, grid E2.

Campsites, facilities: There are 22 RV sites and three tent sites. Facilities include electric hookups, water, flush toilets, showers, disposal station, playground, biking and hiking trails, and nearby golf courses. Seasonal campsite rentals are available. Pets are allowed.

Reservations, fees: The daily fee ranges from $13 to $15. Open from early June through late October.

Directions: From Fairfax, go west on Hwy. 19 for three miles to County Road 16. Turn south and go four miles and left at the signs.

Contact: Valley View Campground, Chuck Firle, 60861 State Hwy. 4, Fairfax, MN 55332, 507/426-7420, fax 507/426-7076.

Trip Notes: Music fan? You might drive over to the Minnesota Music Hall of Fame in New Ulm (507/354-7305). It features music memorabilia and pictures of all the inductees in the Hall of Fame. The museum is at 1st North and Broadway next to the library.

28 Fort Ridgely State Park

Location: Northwest of New Ulm on the Minnesota River, map 7, grid E3.

Campsites, facilities: There are 39 RV (four winter) sites and four (four winter) tent sites. Facilities include gravel pads for RVs, electric hookups, flush toilets, showers, playground, and hiking, cross-country ski, and snowmobile trails. Wheelchair-accessible facilities were under construction. Canoe rentals are available. Pets are allowed.

Reservations, fees: Reservations are recommended for weekends. The daily fee ranges from $8 to $12. Credit cards are accepted. Open year-round.

Directions: From Fairfax, take Hwy. 4 six miles south. Then follow the signs to the park.

Contact: Fort Ridgely State Park, Rt. 1, Box 65, Fairfax, MN 55332-9601 or 507/426-7840, fax 507/426-7112.

Trip Notes: In the spring of 1853, the steamboat "West Newton" left Fort Snelling to journey up the Minnesota River, bound for a plateau above the river in Nicollet County. It carried soldiers and their families, carpenters, and supplies to build a fort at the edge of the Dakota reservation. The fort was named "Ridgely" in honor of three men of the same name who had died during the Mexican War. Fort Ridgely was completed by 1855. You should wander historic Fort Ridgely, including its cemetery, and learn about the U.S.-Dakota Conflict of 1862, a major event in Minnesota's early history. You can also fish or ride the trails on horseback.

29 Springfield Riverside Campground

Location: In Springfield's Riverside Park, map 7, grid G1.

Campsites, facilities: There are 30 campsites. Facilities include electric hookups, water, flush toilets, showers, disposal station, wheelchair access, golf course, tennis court, outdoor pool, and playground. Biking, hiking, cross-country ski, and snowmobile trails are available. Pets are allowed.

Reservations, fees: The daily fee is $15. Open from mid-May through mid-October.

Directions: From U.S. Hwy. 14, go five blocks south on Cass Ave. to the campground.

Contact: Springfield Riverside Campground, 2 E. Central, Springfield, MN 56087-1608 or 507/723-6900, fax 507/723-6901.

Trip Notes: For a memorable photograph, take a picture of Ramsey Falls in Alexander Ramsey City Park in Redwood Falls just north of Springfield.

30 Flandrau State Park

Location: Southwest of New Ulm on the Big Cottonwood River, map 7, grid F5.

Campsites, facilities: There are 90 (five winter) campsites, including three new rustic walk-in sites. Facilities include RV pull-through sites, electric hookups, flush toilets, showers, disposal station, wheelchair access, swimming beach, outdoor pool, and playground. There are also hiking, snowshoe, cross-country ski, and snowmobile trails. Ski equipment and snowshoe rentals are available. Pets are allowed.

Reservations, fees: Reservations are recommended for

weekends. The daily fee ranges from $8 to $12. Credit cards are accepted. Open year-round.

Directions: In New Ulm, follow Broadway (Hwy. 15) to 10th St. south. Go west on 10th St. and up the hill to Summit Ave. Then turn south and go three blocks to the park entrance on the west side. The entrance is next to the New Ulm Country Club.

Contact: Flandrau State Park, 1300 Summit Ave., New Ulm, MN 56073-3664 or 507/233-9800, fax 507/359-1544.

Trip Notes: Melturate (from melting glaciers) cut through 150 feet of rock, sand, clay, and gravel deposited by glaciers during the Ice Age and formed the valley that is the Big Cottonwood River and Flandrau State Park today. Under this glacial material is sandstone, which was laid down millions of years ago by the great seas that once covered North America. Fossilized plant material and orange-colored iron-oxide bands can be seen in the exposed sandstone near the park's eastern boundary.

You can't leave New Ulm without hearing the Glockenspiel (888/463-9856), one of the world's few, free-standing carillon clock towers. It plays at noon, 3 P.M., and 5 P.M. You'll find it at 4th North and Minnesota St.

You can also visit the A. Schell Museum of Brewing, south of Broadway on 17th St., South. It's on the grounds of the brewing company, which has remained in continuous operation for more than 140 years. The tour concludes with a tasting overlooking the gardens.

31 Lake Hanska County Park

Location: On Lake Hanska southwest of New Ulm, map 7, grid G4.

Campsites, facilities: There are 12 RV sites and 10 tent sites. Facilities include electric hookups, flush toilets, showers, disposal station, wheelchair access, swimming beach, and playground. There are also biking, hiking, and cross-country ski trails. Pets are allowed.

Reservations, fees: The daily fee ranges from $8 to $10. Open May through September.

Directions: From New Ulm, take Hwy. 15 south to Hwy. 257 (County Road 20) and travel west to County Road 11 and the park.

Contact: Lake Hanska County Park, 10977 County Rd. 11, Hanska, MN 56041-9708 or 507/439-6411.

Trip Notes: This Brown County park, about 17 miles southwest of New Ulm, has a variety of historic highlights, including a log cabin built in the 1850s, a fort site, and interpretive signage. There is also Minnesota Department of Natural Resources public lake access.

32 Minneopa State Park

Location: West of Mankato on Minneopa Creek, map 7, grid G8.

Campsites, facilities: There are 62 (four winter) campsites. There is also one camping cabin. Facilities include electric hookups, flush toilets, showers, wheelchair access, boat ramp, and biking, hiking, and cross-country ski trails. Pets are allowed.

Reservations, fees: Reservations are recommended on weekends. The daily fee is $12. Credit cards are accepted. Open year-round.

Directions: From Mankato, take U.S. Hwy. 169 west to Hwy. 68 (Royal Rd.) to the park entrance.

Contact: Minneopa State Park, 54497 Gadwall Rd., Mankato, MN 56001-8219 or 507/389-5464, fax 507/389-5174.

Trip Notes: Minneopa comes from the Dakota language (water falling twice). It refers to the beautiful waterfalls of Minneopa Creek, a favorite spot for weddings and reunions. You can walk the trail encircling the falls, which leads down a limestone stairway to the valley below. You can also visit Seppmann Mill, a wind-driven gristmill.

The entire park lies within the banks of the Glacial River Warren, which drained Glacial Lake Agassiz some 15,000 years ago. These banks are easily viewed if you look north and south from Seppmann Mill. You can also see many large boulders scattered on the prairie grassland. The boulders, known as "glacial erratics," are made of parent material entirely different than that commonly found in this area.

33 Land of Memories Campground

Location: In Mankato near the Minnesota and Blue Earth Rivers, map 7, grid G8.

Campsites, facilities: There are 47 campsites. Facilities include electric hookups, flush toilets, showers, disposal station, boat ramp, and playground. There are also biking, hiking, and cross-country ski trails. Seasonal campsite rentals are available. Pets are allowed.

Reservations, fees: The daily fee ranges from $11 to $13. Open from mid-April through mid-October.

Directions: In Mankato, take U.S. Hwy. 169 south to Hawley St. Follow the signs to the campgrounds.

Contact: Land of Memories Campground, Doug Elling, P.O. Box 3368, Mankato, MN 56001-3368 or 507/387-8649, fax 507/387-5195.

Trip Notes: The Blue Earth County Historical Society's Heritage Center (507/345-5566) highlights the settlement, development, history, and culture of the county and city, and includes hundreds of artifacts. From U.S. Hwy. 169 go east onto the bridge that crosses the river (Main St. bridge), and continue on

Mulberry St. up to south 5th St. for five blocks until you reach Cherry St.

34 Watona Park

Location: Southwest of Mankato, map 7, grid H5.

Campsites, facilities: There are 32 campsites. Facilities include electric hookups, water, sewer, flush toilets, showers, disposal station, golf course, tennis court, cross-country ski and snowmobile trails, boat ramp, outdoor pool, and playground. Seasonal campsite rentals are available.

Reservations, fees: The daily fee ranges from $10 to $14. Open from mid-April through mid-October.

Directions: In Madelia, go to the southwest corner of town next to the golf course to find the campground.

Contact: Watona Park, 116 W. Main St., Madelia, MN 56062, 507/642-3245 or 877/302-1875, fax 507/642-8556.

Trip Notes: Built in 1902 and run by the Sleepy Eye Area Historical Society (507/794-5053), the Depot completed its last renovation in 1996. It has a display of Chicago and Northwestern artifacts and is custodian to the grave site of Chief Sleepy Eye, a Sisseton-Dakota and signer of several treaties ceding southern Minnesota, Iowa, and eastern North and South Dakota to the U.S. government. It's in Sleepy Eye, one block north of Hwy. 14 on 1st N. and Oak St.

35 Peaceful Valley Campsites

Location: North of Mankato, map 8, grid E1.

Campsites, facilities: There are 50 campsites, including 19 tent-only sites. Facilities include electric hookups, water, sewer, flush toilets, showers, disposal station, grocery store, and two playgrounds. Seasonal campsite rentals are available. Pets are allowed.

Reservations, fees: The daily fee begins at $15. Credit cards are accepted. Open from mid-April through mid-October.

Directions: From Le Sueur, go 1.5 miles south on U.S. Hwy. 169. Then travel 0.25 mile west on Peaceful Valley Rd. to the campground.

Contact: Peaceful Valley Campsites, Len and Judy Schollen, 213 Peaceful Valley Rd., Le Sueur, MN 56058-9626 or 507/665-2297, fax 507/665-4104, email: pvcamps@aol.com.

Trip Notes: What do the Mayo Clinic and the Green Giant Co. have in common? Both stories began in Le Sueur (Have you seen the name on a can of peas?). Visit the W. W. Mayo House (507/665-3250), the early home of the Mayo Clinic founders, which was hand-built by Dr. William Worrall Mayo in 1859. In 1874, the Cosgrove family moved in. Carson Nesbit Cosgrove served as the head of the Minnesota Valley Canning Co., which became the Green Giant Co. in 1950. The State Historic Site is at 118 N. Main St.

36 Split Rock Creek State Park

Location: Near Pipestone, map 9, grid A6.

Campsites, facilities: There are 26 RV sites and seven tent sites. All are open in winter. Facilities include electric hookups, flush toilets, showers, disposal station, wheelchair access, swimming beach, and playground. There are also biking, hiking, cross-country ski, and snowshoe trails. Boat, canoe, and snowshoe rentals are available. Pets are allowed.

Reservations, fees: Reservations are recommended for weekends. The daily fee ranges from $10 to $13. Open from late May through early September.

Directions: From Pipestone, take Hwy. 23 seven miles southwest to the park.

Contact: Split Rock Creek State Park, Rt. 2, Box 102, Jasper, MN 56144-9802 or 507/348-7908, fax 507/348-8940.

Trip Notes: Split Rock Lake is the largest body of water in Pipestone County. Stop by the Beach Side Trail Center for an excellent view and learn more about the area. Three major ice movements during the ice age deposited a thick layer of sand, gravel, rocks, and clay called till, which is several hundred feet in some areas. Under the till lies a hard, pink bedrock known as Sioux quartzite. This hard metamorphic rock was quarried in the area for use as a building material, including the dam in the park, which was constructed in 1938.

37 Blue Mounds State Park

Location: Near Luverne in southwestern Minnesota, map 9, grid C7.

Campsites, facilities: There are 73 RV sites and 14 tent sites. All are open in winter. Facilities include electric hookups, flush toilets, showers, disposal station, wheelchair access, swimming beach, rock-climbing, and playground. There are also hiking, cross-country ski, and snowmobile trails. Canoe rentals are available. Pets are allowed.

Reservations, fees: Reservations are recommended for weekends. The daily fee ranges from $8 to $12. Credit cards are accepted. Open year-round.

Directions: From Luverne, take Hwy. 75 north to County Road 20. Turn east on County Road 20 and go one mile to the park entrance.

Contact: Blue Mounds State Park, R.R. 1, Box 52, Luverne, MN 56156-9610 or 507/283-1307, fax 507/283-1306.

Trip Notes: You'll find surprises here. A Sioux quartzite cliff rises 100 feet from the plains, a bison herd grazes on the prairie, and prickly pear cactus blooms in June and July. Stop at the interpretive center, once home of author Frederick Manfred, to discover the natural history of the area. The large rock outcrop appeared blue to settlers going west in the 1860s and 1870s. They named the prominent landmark the Blue Mound. The mystery of the Blue Mound is not restricted to the cliffs. At the Mound's southern end is a 1,250-foot-long line of rocks aligned in an east-west direction. Who built it and why is unknown. However, it is known that on the first day of spring and fall, the sunrise and sunset are aligned on the stones.

38 Adrian Municipal Campground

Location: On the northeast edge of Adrian, map 10, grid C1.

Campsites, facilities: There are 80 RV sites and 40 tent sites. Facilities include RV pull-through sites, electric hookups, water, sewer, flush toilets, showers, laundry, disposal station, hiking trails, outdoor pool, playground, and nearby golf course. Seasonal campsite rentals are available. Pets are allowed. Also nearby are drug, grocery, and hardware stores.

Reservations, fees: The daily fee ranges from $11 to $17. Open from mid-May through September.

Directions: From I-90, take exit 26 and go one block south and two blocks west.

Contact: Adrian Municipal Campground, Box 187, Adrian, MN 56110-0187 or 507/483-2820, fax 507/483-2005, email: adrianch@frontier net.net.

Trip Notes: Take time out for some culture. World-renowned nature photographer Jim Brandenburg has an exclusive display of prints from his *National Geographic* magazine articles, "Wolf Encounters" and "90 Day Journal," at the Brandenburg Gallery (888/283-4061 or 507/283-1884) in Luverne. There's no admission fee. To get there, drive from the intersection of I-90 and U.S. Hwy 75 to the stoplight at Main St. Turn right and go 4.5 blocks. The gallery is on the north side of the street.

39 Olson Park Campground

Location: In Worthington on Lake Okabena, map 10, grid D4.

Campsites, facilities: There are 61 campsites. Facilities include RV pull-through sites, electric hookups, flush toilets, showers, laundry, disposal station, bike and hiking trails, playground, and nearby golf course. Pets are allowed.

Reservations, fees: The daily fee ranges from $13 to $17. Open May through October.

Directions: From I-90, take Hwy. 266 south to County Road 35 and go west for one mile to County Road 10. Then go south for two miles to the city campground.

Contact: Olson Park Campground, Box 279 (County Road 10), Worthington, MN 56187, 507/372-8650, fax 507/372-8651.

Trip Notes: You can tour 45 turn-of-the-century buildings, including a school, general store, train depot, church, and farm house at the Nobles County Pioneer Village (507/376-3125 or 507/376-4431). It's located at 501 Stower Dr., next to the fairgrounds in northeast Worthington.

40 Kilen Woods State Park

Location: Near Lakefield on the Des Moines River, map 10, grid C8.

Campsites, facilities: There are 33 RV sites and seven tent sites. All sites are open in winter. Facilities include RV pull-through sites, electric hookups, flush toilets, showers, disposal station, wheelchair access, boat ramp, swimming beach, and playground. There are also hiking, cross-country ski, and snowmobile trails. Pets are allowed.

Reservations, fees: Reservations are recommended for weekends. The daily fee ranges from $11 to $16. Credit cards are accepted. Open from late May through early September.

Directions: From Lakefield, drive four miles north on Hwy. 86 until you reach the junction of Hwy. 86 and County Road 24. Then go five miles east on County Road 24 to the park.

Contact: Kilen Woods State Park, 50200 860th St., Lakefield, MN 56150-9566 or 507/662-6258, fax 507/662-5501.

Trip Notes: For a quiet, relaxing time, you can't beat this state park. You can hike the cool woodland trail that meanders along the Des Moines River or enjoy the view of the river valley from the Dinosaur Ridge Overlook. If you enjoy wildflowers or birds, you won't be disappointed. The Des Moines River provides aquatic habitat for beaver and muskrat. Resourceful anglers catch walleye, northern pike, catfish, and bullhead from the river's pools and numerous snags. Wood ducks nest in tree cavities along the river's edge while herons quietly stalk the shallows and backwaters. Deer, squirrels, and woodpeckers are abundant. Red admiral butterflies are seen all summer long, while swallowtail butterflies are present during late summer.

41 Loon Lake Campground

Location: Near I-90 and U.S. Hwy. 71, map 10, grid D8.

Campsites, facilities: There are 77 campsites. Facilities include RV pull-through sites, electric hookups, flush toilets, showers, disposal station, playground, and biking and hiking trails. Seasonal campsite rentals are available. Pets are allowed.

Reservations, fees: The daily fee begins at $10. Open April through October.

Directions: From I-90, take U.S. Hwy. 71 south to Jackson. Then go five miles west on CSAH 4 to the campground.

Contact: Loon Lake Campground, 405 4th St., Jackson, MN 56143-0064 or 507/847-2240, fax 507/847-4718.

Trip Notes: In Jackson, at the intersection of Hwy. 71 and County Road 34, you'll find Fort Belmont (507/847-5840), a replica of the 1860 fort built to protect settlers. It includes a mill, church, sod house, blacksmith shop, moonshine still, museum, and gift shop. Each spring and fall, the Mountain Man Rendezvous is held here. The site is open from Memorial Day through Labor Day.

42 Jackson KOA Kampground

Location: Near I-90 and U.S. Hwy. 71, map 11, grid C1.

Campsites, facilities: There are 50 RV sites and 10 tent sites. There are also two camping cabins. Facilities include RV pull-through sites, electric hookups, water, flush toilets, showers, sewer, disposal station, laundry, wheelchair access, grocery store, heated outdoor pool, and playground. Bike rentals are available. Pets are allowed.

Reservations, fees: The daily fee ranges from $16 to $22. Credit cards are accepted. Open May through September.

Directions: From I-90, take exit 73 to U.S. Hwy. 71. Go north on Hwy. 71 to County Road 34 and enter across from County Road 34.

Contact: Jackson KOA Kampground, 2035 U.S. Hwy. 71 North, Jackson, MN 56143-9308 or 800/562-5670 or 507/847-3825.

Trip Notes: A short drive north is the Sod House Exhibit (507/723-5138). There are two sod houses on the prairie near Sanborn on the Laura Ingalls Wilder Historic Highway. The exhibit is one mile east of the junction of Hwy. 71 and Hwy. 14.

43 Brown Park Campground

Location: Near I-90 and U.S. Hwy. 71, map 11, grid D1.

Campsites, facilities: There are 50 campsites. Facilities include electric hookups, showers, disposal station, hiking trail, and playground. Seasonal campsite rentals are available.

Reservations, fees: The daily fee ranges from $10 to $11. Open April through October.

Directions: From I-90, take U.S. Hwy. 71 south to Jackson. At West Ashley (Country Road 14), go west one block to 4th St. and turn north to the campground.

Contact: Brown Park Campground, 405 4th St., Jackson, MN 56143-0064 or 507/847-2240, fax 507/847-4718.

Trip Notes: Visit the Birch Coulee Battlefield (507/697-6310), where volunteer soldiers and civilians were surrounded and attacked by the Dakota in the late summer of 1862. A self-guided tour takes you through the 36-hour siege. The site is three miles north of Morton, at the junction of Renville Co. Hwy. 2 and Hwy. 18, off U.S. Hwy. 71.

44 Dawson's Lakeside Campground

Location: Near I-90 and Hwy. 15 on South Silver Lake, map 11, grid D5.

Campsites, facilities: There are 116 RV sites and 24 tent sites. Facilities include RV pull-through sites, electric hookups, water, sewer, flush toilets, showers, laundry, disposal station, wheelchair access, swimming beach, outdoor pool, whirlpool, grocery store, and playground. Boat, canoe, motor, and seasonal campsite rentals are available. Pets are allowed.

Reservations, fees: The daily fee ranges from $15 to $20. Credit cards are accepted. Open May through September.

Directions: From I-90, take exit 102. Go 10.5 miles south on Hwy. 15. Turn west for two miles on County Road 8 (MM #2). Then go one-half mile south to the campground.

Contact: Dawson's Lakeside Campground, 248 Cottonwood Rd., Fairmont, MN 56031-9404 or 507/235-5753.

Trip Notes: If your family members are racing fans, the Jackson Speedway (507/847—2084 or 712/336-3016) south of I-90 on Hwy. 71 on the Jackson County Fairgrounds is the place to go on Saturday evenings from May through Labor Day. It's a one-half mile dirt racetrack that attracts IMCA hobbies, stock cars, and modifieds, as well as the Wissota Championship sprints.

45 Faribault County Fairgrounds

Location: In Blue Earth north of I-90, map 11, grid C8.

Campsites, facilities: There are 150 RV sites and 50 tent sites. Facilities include RV pull-through sites, electric hookups, water, sewer, flush toilets, showers, disposal station, hiking trails, and playground. Pets are allowed.

Reservations, fees: The daily fee is $5. Open April through October.

Directions: From I-90, take U.S. Hwy. 169 north to Blue Earth and the Faribault County Fairgrounds.

Contact: Faribault County Fairgrounds, 125 W. 6th St., Blue Earth, MN 56013-1960 or 507/526-2916 or 507/526-4733.

Trip Notes: At any time of year be sure to stop at the Etta Ross Historical Museum (507/526-5421) in Blue Earth. It includes the James B. Wakefield House and the Good Shepherd Episcopal Church. During the summer at the fairgrounds, exhibits expand to include Woodland School, Krosch Log House, Blacksmith Shop, and the Guckeen Post Office. Admission and parking are free. Go west on 7th Street at junction of U.S. Hwy. 169 and County Road 16. Cross the railroad tracks and go right one block. Turn left to the museum.

MISSISSIPPI BLUFF COUNTRY

Mississippi Bluff Country

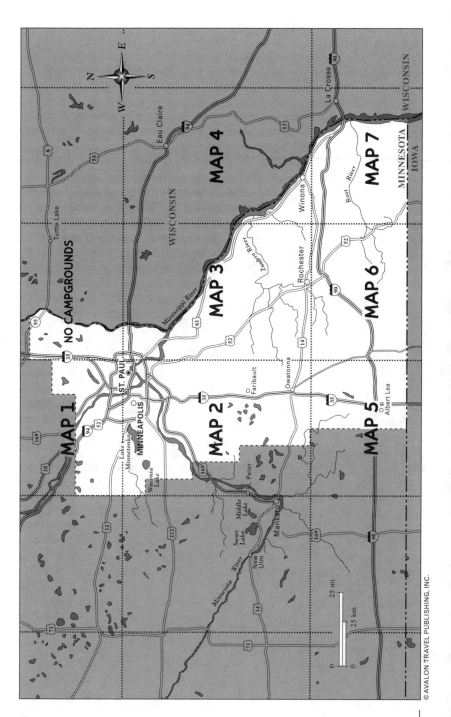

© AVALON TRAVEL PUBLISHING, INC.

Map 1

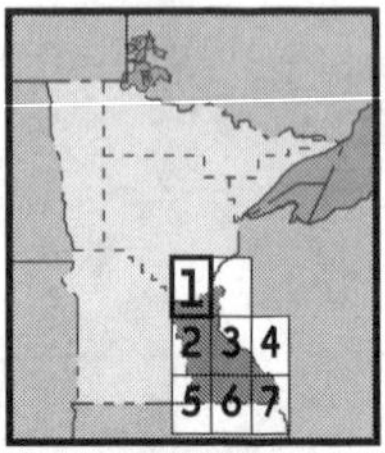
1
2
3
4
5
6
7

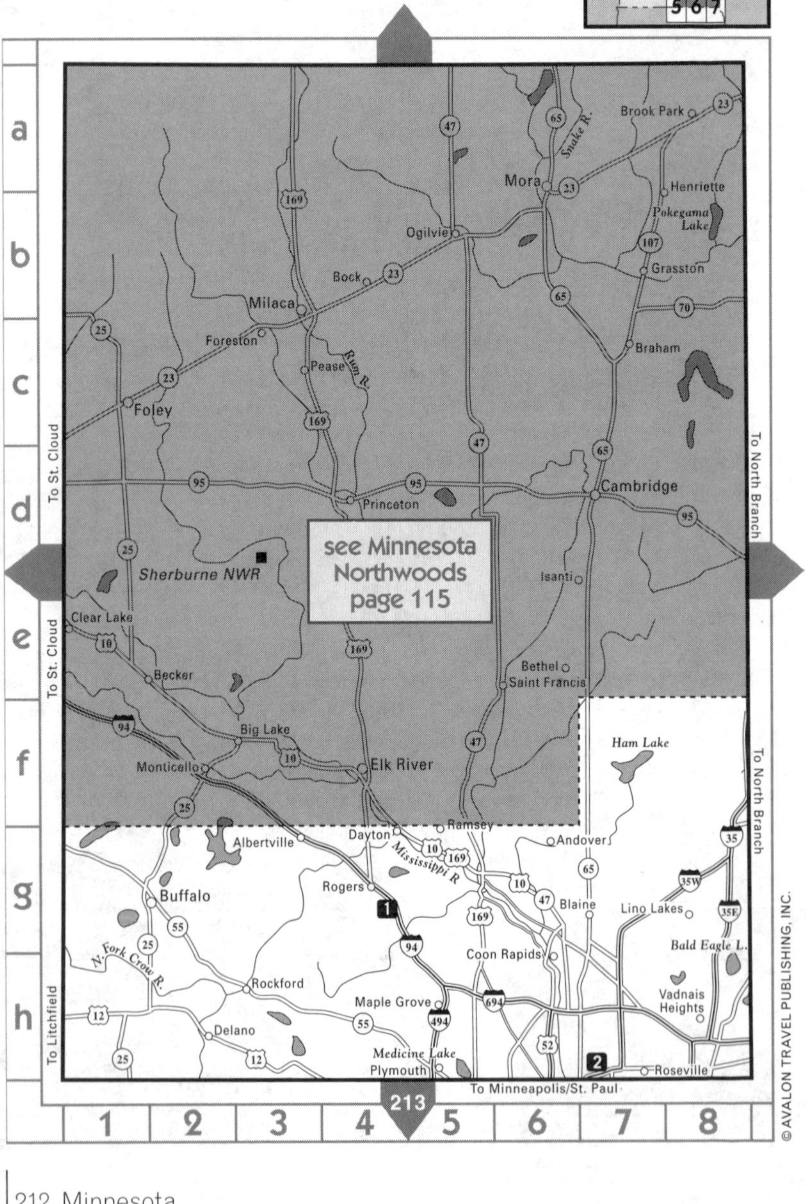
a
b
c
d
e
f
g
h
1
2
3
4
5
6
7
8
Brook Park
Mora
Snake R.
Henriette
Pokegama Lake
Ogilvie
Grasston
Bock
Milaca
Foreston
Braham
Pease
Rum R.
Foley
Cambridge
Princeton
see Minnesota Northwoods page 115
Sherburne NWR
Isanti
Clear Lake
Becker
Bethel
Saint Francis
Ham Lake
Big Lake
Monticello
Elk River
Albertville
Dayton
Ramsey
Andover
Mississippi R
Rogers
Buffalo
Blaine
Lino Lakes
Coon Rapids
Bald Eagle L.
N. Fork Crow R.
Rockford
Maple Grove
Vadnais Heights
Delano
Medicine Lake
Plymouth
Roseville
To St. Cloud
To St. Cloud
To Litchfield
To North Branch
To North Branch
To Minneapolis/St. Paul
213
© AVALON TRAVEL PUBLISHING, INC.

Map 2

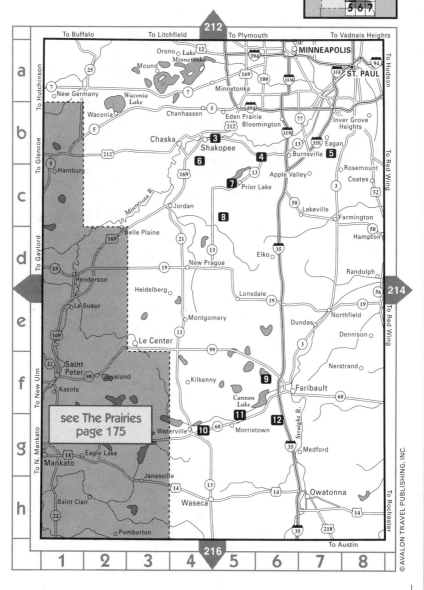

212

a

To Hutchinson

Orono *Lake Minnetonka* 12

Mound

MINNEAPOLIS

25

394

100 35W

ST. PAUL

To Hudson

New Germany 7 169

Minnetonka

Waconia Lake

To Glencoe

Waconia 5

Chanhassen 5

Eden Prairie 494

Bloomington 77

Inver Grove Heights

b

Chaska **3**

212 35W

13 35E Eagan

Shakopee **6**

4

Burnsville **5**

5

Hamburg 212

169

7 13

Apple Valley Rosemount

Coates 52

c

Minnesota R.

Jordan **8**

Prior Lake

50

Lakeville

Farmington 50

Belle Plaine

169 21

13

Elko 35

Hampton

To Gaylord

19 19

New Prague

Randolph

d

Henderson

Heidelberg

Lonsdale 19 56 **214**

To Red Wing

Le Sueur

Montgomery

Dundas Northfield 19

e

169 13

Le Center

Dennison

To New Ulm

Saint Peter 22

99 Cleveland

Kilkenny 99

Faribault

Nerstrand

f

Kasota

Cannon Lake **9** 60

see The Prairies page 175

11

12

g

To N. Mankato

22 14 Eagle Lake

Waterville **10** 60 Morristown

Straight R.

Medford 35

Mankato

Janesville

To Rochester

h

Saint Clair 14 13

14 Owatonna 14

22

Waseca 218

Pemberton 35

To Austin

216

1 2 3 4 5 6 7 8

Map 3

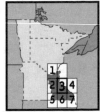

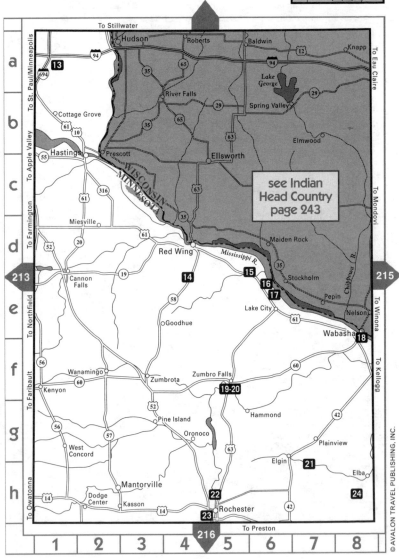

see Indian Head Country page 243

© AVALON TRAVEL PUBLISHING, INC.

Map 4

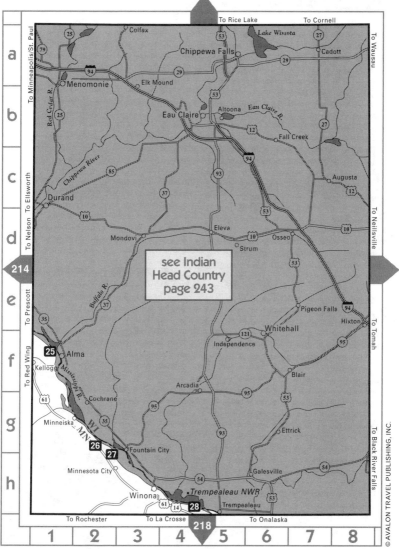

To Rice Lake   To Cornell

Colfax

Lake Wissota

Chippewa Falls

Cadott

To Wausau

To Minneapolis/St. Paul

To Ellsworth   To Nelson

To Prescott

To Red Wing

a

b

c

d

e

f

g

h

Menomonie

Elk Mound

Red Cedar R.

Eau Claire

Altoona

Eau Claire R.

Fall Creek

Chippewa River

Augusta

Durand

To Neillsville

Eleva

Mondovi

Osseo

Strum

see Indian
Head Country
page 243

214

Buffalo R.

Pigeon Falls

Hixton

To Tomah

Whitehall

Alma

Independence

Kellogg

Mississippi R.

Blair

Arcadia

Cochrane

MN   WI

Minneiska

Ettrick

Fountain City

Minnesota City

Galesville

To Black River Falls

Winona

Trempealeau NWR

Trempealeau

To Rochester   To La Crosse   To Onalaska

218

© AVALON TRAVEL PUBLISHING, INC.

1   **2**   **3**   **4**   **5**   **6**   **7**   **8**

Map 5

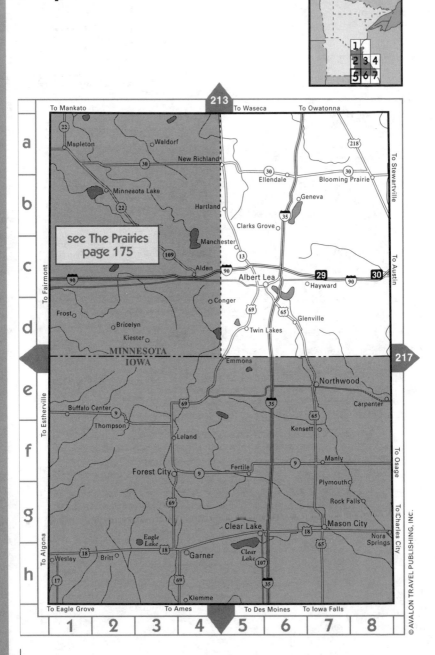

Map 6

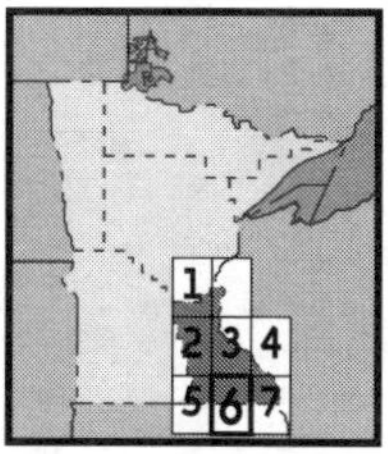

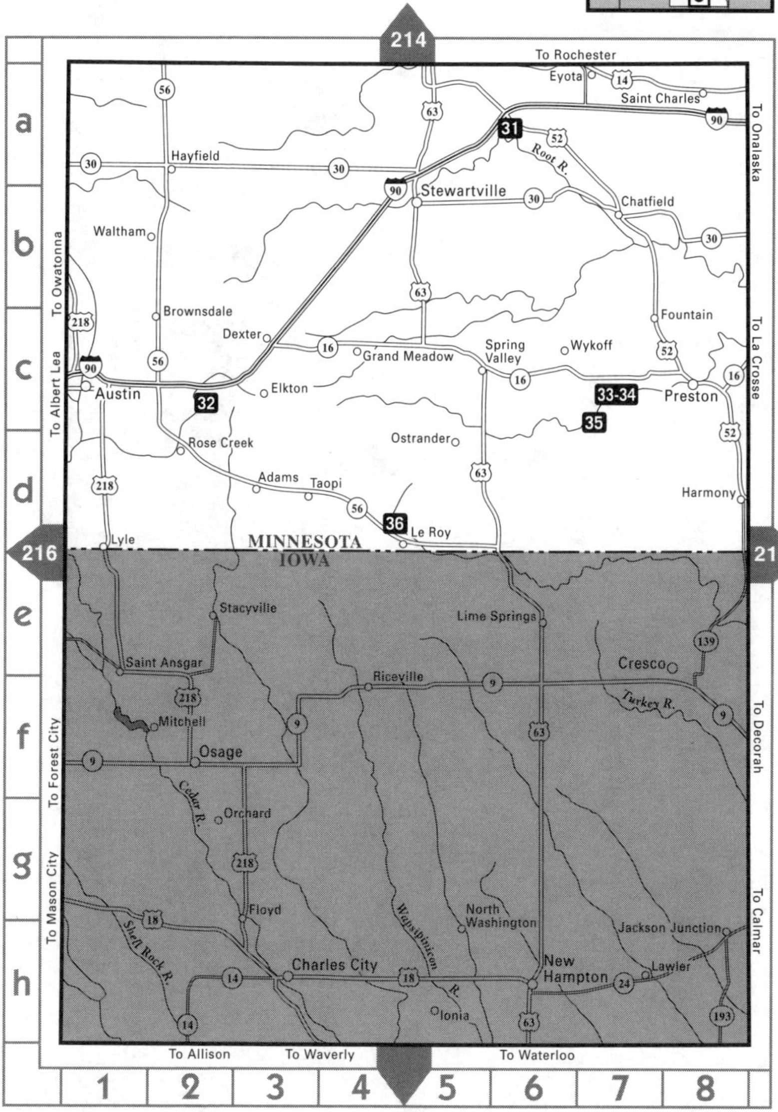

© AVALON TRAVEL PUBLISHING, INC.

Map 7

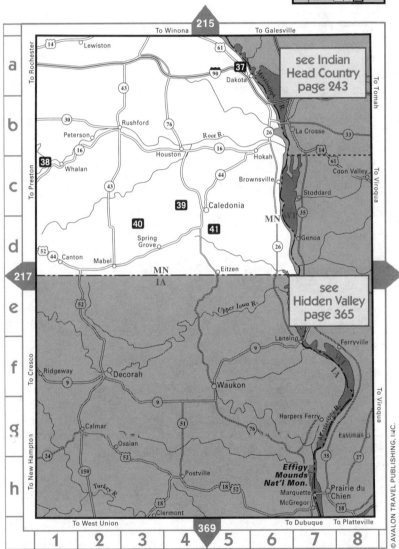

To Winona
215
To Galesville

see Indian
Head Country
page 243

14 Lewiston

61

90 37

Dakota

To Rochester

43

30 Rushford 76

Peterson

Root R.

26 La Crosse 33

16 16

Houston Hokah

14

38 61

Whalan

44 Coon Valley

43 Brownsville

Stoddard

39 Caledonia

40 MN WI 35

Spring 41 Genoa
Grove

52 44 Canton Mabel

26

Eitzen

MN

IA

217

52

Upper Iowa R.

see
Hidden Valley
page 365

Lansing Ferryville

9

To Cresco

Ridgeway Decorah

9

Waukon

9

To Viroqua

Calmar 51

76 Harpers Ferry

Ossian

52 35 27 Eastman

To New Hampton 24

150 Postville

Effigy
Mounds
Nat'l Mon.

Turkey R. 18 52

Prairie du
Chien

18 Marquette

McGregor 18

Clermont

To West Union
369
To Dubuque
To Platteville

1 2 3 4 5 6 7 8

© AVALON TRAVEL PUBLISHING, INC.

Mississippi Bluff Country

Some of the most scenic areas in several Midwestern states lies along the Mississippi River, and Minnesota is no exception. You'll discover tall, wooded bluffs looming over the historic waterway in this picturesque corner of the state. Gentle rolling countryside dips into ravines and valleys where quiet creeks meander through emerald pastures. You'll also encounter charming river towns—Winona, Wabasha, Lake City, and Red Wing—and bluff hamlets—Lanesboro, Canton, and Harmony—with 19th-century architecture and historic inns. Throughout the Mississippi Bluff Country, there are trout streams just begging for anglers, rivers inviting canoeists, and trails beckoning for.

bicyclists and hikers to wind their way through forested hillsides. You can also take a step back in time at historic sites, visit Amish communities, and even venture underground to explore Minnesota's only caves.

No matter how old and experienced, writers like us are always learning new things—like how water-skiing was invented in 1922 on Lake Pepin, the widest part of the Mississippi, by an adventurous teenager who was sometimes towed by a low-flying airplane.

◱ Minneapolis N.W./ I-94 KOA Campground

Location: On I-94, 15 miles northwest of Minneapolis, map 1, grid G4.

Campsites, facilities: There are 145 RV sites and 28 tent sites. Facilities include RV pull-through sites, electric hookups, water, sewer, flush toilets, showers, laundry, disposal station, grocery store, biking and hiking trails, outdoor pool, sauna, horse stable, children's programs, and playground. Seasonal campsite and horse rentals are available. Pets are allowed.

Reservations, fees: The daily fee ranges from $22 to $38. Credit cards are accepted. Open April through mid-October.

Directions: From I-94, take exit 213 and go two miles west on County Road 30. Then drive one mile north on Hwy. 101 to the campground.

Contact: Minneapolis N.W./I-94 KOA Campground, P.O. Box 214, Rogers, MN 55374-0214 or 800/562-0261, ext. 10, or 763/420-2255, fax 763/493-4679.

Trip Notes: Spend some time at the Ellingson Car Museum (763/428-7337). It boasts more than 100 different cars, trucks and motorcycles arranged by decades. Historic

videos and memorabilia accompany each display. There's also a version of a 1950s drive-in movie with old film clips, a speed shop, and a replica of 1960s drag strip. The museum, at 20950 Ribers Dr., also has a gift shop and ice cream parlor. From I-94 take Hwy 101.

◲ Lowry Grove Partnership Campground

Location: In Minneapolis, map 1, grid H7.

Campsites, facilities: There are 64 campsites. Facilities include electric hookups, water, sewer, flush toilets, showers, and disposal station. Seasonal campsite rentals are available.

Reservations, fees: The daily fee ranges from $20 to $24. Open year-round.

Directions: From I-35W, take exit 22 (St. Anthony Blvd.) off I-35W and go north to Silver Lake Rd. Then turn left and drive two blocks to the campground.

Contact: Lowry Grove Partnership Campground, 2501 Lowry Ave., N.E. St. Anthony Village, MN 55148-4414 or 612/781-6167 or 612/781-3148.

Trip Notes: We found the Raptor Center at the University of Minnesota (612/624-4745; email: raptor@cvm.umn.edu) a captivating place to visit. This facility specializes in the treatment and rehabilitation and research of owls, hawks, eagles, and falcons. Open all year, you can reserve a tour. The center is on the school's St. Paul campus, near the state fairgrounds near Larpenteur and Cleveland.

◳ Shakopee Valley RV Park

Location: In Shakopee, map 2, grid B4.

Campsites, facilities: There are 96 RV sites and six tent sites. Facilities include RV pull-through sites, electric hookups, water, sewer, flush toilets, showers, wheelchair access, laundry, disposal station, grocery store, biking and hiking trails, indoor pool, sauna, whirlpool, and playground. Seasonal campsite rentals are available. Pets are allowed.

Reservations, fees: The daily fee ranges from $17 to $25. Credit cards are accepted. Open year-round.

Directions: From I-35W, go four miles west on Hwy. 13 south to Shakopee exit #B (by I-35). Then drive five miles west on Hwy. 101 north to the campground.

Contact: Shakopee Valley RV Park, Rosie and Al Jones, 1245 E. Bluff, Shakopee, MN 55379-4908 or 952/445-7313, fax 952/445-7457.

Trip Notes: If you haven't been there yet, you must visit the massive Mall of America in Bloomington (952/883-8800 or 952/883-8843; website: www.mallofamerica.com), which is open every day except Thanksgiving and Christmas. It's the largest fully enclosed retail and entertainment complex in the United States. It even has a roller-coaster ride in the largest indoor family theme park. The mall is off I-494 at 24th Ave., South.

⁴ Town and Country Campground

Location: Southwest of the Twin Cities, map 2, grid B5.

Campsites, facilities: There are 61 campsites. Facilities include RV pull-through sites, electric hookups, water, sewer, flush toilets, showers, laundry, disposal station, grocery store, outdoor pool, whirlpool, and playground. Seasonal campsite rentals are available. Pets are allowed.

Reservations, fees: The daily fee ranges from $20 to $26. Credit cards are accepted. Open April through October.

Directions: From I-35W, exit on Hwy. 13 south and travel 4.5 miles. Follow Hwy. 13 south for one block and drive west on 126th St. and one-half mile south on Boone Ave. into the campground.

Contact: Town and Country Campground, David and Jill Olmstead, 12630 Boone Ave., S., Savage, MN 55378-1008 or 888/300-2267 or 952/445-1756.

Trip Notes: Nearby is the Murphy Hanrahan Park Reserve (952/447-6913 or 763/559-9000), offering 19.4 kilometers of track for skating or skiing. Be warned that the trails are mostly expert-level. The facility is one mile west of County Road 5 on County Road 42. Then drive one mile south. Ski passes, which are required, are sold at the trailhead.

⁵ Lebanon Hills Campground

Location: South of the Twin Cities and east of Minnesota Zoo, map 2, grid B7.

Campsites, facilities: There are 93 RV and tent sites at this campground on Gerhardt Lake. Facilities include electric hookups, water, sewer, flush toilets, showers, laundry, wheelchair access, disposal station, grocery store, and swimming beach. There are also hiking, cross-country ski, and snowmobile trails. Seasonal campsite rentals are available. Pets are allowed.

Reservations, fees: The daily fee ranges from $14 to $23. Credit cards are accepted. Open from mid-February through mid-October.

Directions: From the junction of I-494 and I-35E in Eagan, go south on I-35 for five miles to Cliff Rd., and turn east for 0.75 mile to Johnny Cake Ridge Rd. Then drive south for just over one mile to the campground.

Contact: Lebanon Hills Campground, 12100 Johnny Cake Ridge, Apple Valley, MN 55124-8151 or 952/454-9211, website: www.co.dakota.m.n.us.

Trip Notes: You shouldn't overlook the Minnesota Zoo (800/366-7811 or 952/431-9500; website: www.mnzoo.com), directly west of the campground. It features more than 2,400 animals and natural habitat trails.

6 Minneapolis S.W. KOA (Jordan/Shakopee KOA)

Location: South of Shakopee, map 2, grid B4.

Campsites, facilities: There are 103 RV sites and eight tent sites. Facilities include RV pull-through sites, electric hookups, water, sewer, flush toilets, showers, laundry, wheelchair access, disposal station, grocery store, indoor pool, and playground. Seasonal campsite rentals are available. Pets are allowed.

Reservations, fees: The daily fee ranges from $21 to $50. Credit cards are accepted. Open April through mid-October.

Directions: From Shakopee, take Hwy. 169 south toward Jordan, exiting between mile markers 102 and 103 on the east side of the highway.

Contact: Minneapolis S.W. KOA, Richard and Joanne Conaway, 3315 166th St., W. Jordan, MN 55352-9376 or 952/492-6440, fax 952/492-3884, email: mplsswkoa@aol.com, website: www.koakampgrounds.com.

Trip Notes: We think the Minnesota Valley State Recreation Area (952/492-6400) is one of Minnesota's best-kept secrets. This park has outstanding natural resources close to the Twin Cities. Canoeing is popular on the river. There are also 37 miles of hiking, 31 miles of horseback-riding, four miles of cross-country ski, and 34 miles of snowmobile trails. A daily permit is $4. From U.S. Hwy. 169 west of Jordan, drive west on County Road 9 to Township 57 and travel south for three miles.

7 Dakotah Meadows Campground

Location: Southwest of the Twin Cities, map 2, grid C5.

Campsites, facilities: There are 48 campsites. Facilities include RV pull-through sites, electric hookups, water, sewer, flush toilets, showers, laundry, disposal station, wheelchair access, grocery store, restaurant, on-site casino, and playground. Seasonal campsite rentals and baby-sitting services are available. Pets are allowed.

Reservations, fees: The daily fee is $24. Credit cards are accepted. Open March through October.

Directions: From the Twin Cities, take I-35 to County Road 42. Travel west on County Road 42 to CR83. Go south for one mile to the campground.

Contact: Dakotah Meadows Campground, 2341 Park Pl., Prior Lake, MN 55372, 952/445-8800, website: www.mysticlake.com.

Trip Notes: In Belle Plaine, southwest of Shakopee on Hwy. 169, is a middle-late Victorian house (952/873-6109) with a large lawn and attractive gardens. What sets it apart from most residences is that it features the only attached two-story outhouse in Minnesota and possibly the United States! Go to Main St. and turn right on Cedar and drive to the end of the street.

8 Fish Lake Acres Campground

Location: On Fish Lake, south of Prior Lake, map 2, grid C5.

Campsites, facilities: There are 50 RV sites and 47 tent sites. Facilities include electric hookups, water, sewer, flush toilets, showers, disposal station, hiking trails, swimming beach, boat ramp, and playground. Boat, canoe, and seasonal campsite rentals are available. Pets are allowed.

Reservations, fees: The daily fee ranges from $17 to $21. Open from mid-May through late October.

Directions: From I-35W, take exit 81 and go 10 miles on Hwy. 13 to County Road 8 to Fish Lake.

Contact: Fish Lake Acres Campground, 3000 210th St. E., Prior Lake, MN 55372-8707 or 952/492-3393

Trip Notes: There's old-fashioned fun at Historic Murphy's Landing (952/445-6901), a unique, 88-acre, living history museum that interprets 19th-century life in the Minnesota River Valley. The self-guided walking tour includes 40 period buildings with costumed interpreters along the banks of the Minnesota River. It's one mile east of Shakopee on Hwy. 101, 25 miles from the Twin Cities.

⑨ Roberds Lake Resort and Campground

Location: On Roberds Lake, northwest of Faribault, map 2, grid F6.

Campsites, facilities: There are 31 RV sites and 19 tent sites. Facilities include electric hookups, water, sewer, flush toilets, showers, laundry, disposal station, grocery store, swimming beach, and playground. Boat, motor, canoe, and seasonal campsite rentals are available. Pets are allowed and baby-sitting service is available.

Reservations, fees: The daily fee ranges from $18 to $24. Credit cards are accepted. Open May through mid-October.

Directions: From I-35, take exit 56 and follow camping signs to Roberds Lake area, which is northwest of the downtown area.

Contact: Roberds Lake Resort and Campground, Bob and Shermayne Cross, 18192 Roberds Lake Blvd., Faribault, MN 55021-7784 or 800/879-5091 or 507/332-8978, fax 507/333-2795, email: roberds.cross@deskmedia.com, website: www.roberdslakeresort.com.

Trip Notes: About one-half mile east of downtown Faribault off Hwy. 60 is the River Bend Nature Center (507/332-7151), 700 acres of woods, prairie, river, and ponds. There are also eight miles of biking and hiking trails, and five miles of cross-country skiing trails. Other features include an observation deck and bird-feeding station. Admission is free; just follow the brown "Nature Center" signs.

⑩ Sakatah Lake State Park

Location: East of Mankato on Sakatah Lake, map 2, grid G4.

Campsites, facilities: There are 63 campsites and one camping cabin (most sites are open in winter). Facilities include electric hookups, flush toilets, showers, and disposal station. There are also biking, hiking, cross-country ski, and snowmobile trails. Boat and canoe rentals are available. Pets are allowed.

Reservations, fees: Reservations are recommended on weekends. The daily fee ranges from $12 to $15. Credit cards are accepted. Open all year-round.

Directions: From Waterville, take Hwy. 13 south to Hwy. 60. Drive east to the park entrance.

Contact: Sakatah Lake State Park, Rt. 2, Box 19, Waterville, MN 56096-9505 or 507/362-4438 or 507/362-4950.

Trip Notes: Members of the Dakota Nation, the Wahpekita (Wapacoota) tribe inhabited the area that is now the park. They named the area Sakatah (Singing Hills), hence the name for the state trail. Bikers can access the Sakatah-Singing Hills State Trail in the park. It stretches 39 miles to Faribault. The paved route offers hikers, bikers, skiers, and snowmobilers beautiful scenery through Minnesota's hardwood forests. The Cannon and other area rivers served as an important water route between south-central Minnesota and Wisconsin. Numerous trading posts and Indian villages existed along the route. A village site is believed to have existed in the area of the point separating Sakatah and Lower Sakatah Lakes. In 1862, Alexander Faribault, a trader, established a post on the northeast shore of Cannon Lake—one of the first white settlements in the area.

11 Camp Maiden Rock

Location: West of Faribault, map 2, grid G5.
Campsites, facilities: There are 110 RV sites and 15 tent sites. Facilities include electric hookups, water, sewer, flush toilets, showers, laundry, disposal station, grocery store, outdoor pool, playground, and biking and hiking trails. Canoe and seasonal campsite rentals are available. Pets are allowed.
Reservations, fees: The daily fee ranges from $17 to $21. Credit cards are accepted. Open from mid-May through October.
Directions: From I-35, take exit 56 in Faribault and go eight miles west on Hwy. 60. The campground is at Morristown on the north side of the highway.
Contact: Camp Maiden Rock, 22661 Dodge Ct., Faribault, MN 55021, 800/657-4776 or 507/685-4430, email: cmrfern@clear.lakes.com.

Trip Notes: The campground, located on the Sakatah Singing Hills State Bicycle Trail, has two campground sites on each side of the Cannon River and connected by the bike trail. If you need some camping gear or other sporting goods, a big Cabela's store is only 15 minutes away in Owatonna.

12 Camp Faribo

Location: South of Faribault, map 2, grid F6.
Campsites, facilities: This Good Sam Park has 71 campsites. Facilities include RV pull-through sites, electric hookups, water, sewer, flush toilets, showers, laundry, disposal station, grocery store, outdoor pool, and playground. Seasonal campsite rentals are available. Pets are allowed.
Reservations, fees: The daily fee ranges from $18 to $22. Credit cards are accepted. Open from mid-April through mid-October.
Directions: From Faribault, take I-35 south to exit 56. Go east to Western Ave. (County Road 93) and south for 1.75 miles.
Contact: Camp Faribo, Chuck and Fern Kubalsky, 21851 Bagley Ave., Faribault, MN 55021-7863 or 800/689-8453 or 507/332-8453.
Trip Notes: Take a trip back through history when yarns were hand spun, hand dyed, and made into unique toys or gifts at Hirschey's Canna Lily Farm (800/255-6725, ext. 8246, or 507/332-8932). You see natural colored sheep and a variety of farm animals. Watch demos of wool spinning and weaving. Cost is $2 per person. From Faribault, take Hwy. 60 east for eight miles and turn north at Jacobs Ave. or County Road 24 for one mile. It's the third house on the right.

13 St. Paul East KOA

Location: East of St. Paul, map 3, grid A1.

Campsites, facilities: There are 71 RV sites and five tent sites. There are also five camping cabins. Facilities include RV pull-through sites, electric hookups, water, sewer, flush toilets, showers, laundry, wheelchair access, disposal station, grocery store, outdoor pool, and playground. Pets are allowed.

Reservations, fees: The daily fee ranges from $22 to $50. Credit cards are accepted. Open from mid-April through mid-October.

Directions: From the I-494/694 interchange on I-94, take exit 251 or 253 and go south, following the blue camping signs. The campground is one mile on Frontage Rd.

Contact: St. Paul East KOA, Richard and Susan Poss, 568 Cottage Grove Dr., Woodbury, MN 55129, 800/562-3640 or 651/436-6436.

Trip Notes: Youngsters of any age will love the Twin City Model Railroad Museum, a converted 100-year-old train car shop, at 1021 Bandana Blvd., E. Bandana Square in St. Paul (651/647-9628; email: tcmrc@mtn.org). This is an awesome 3,000-square-foot O-scale model railroad layout of the 1930s, 1940s, and 1950s, featuring Twin Cities rail landmarks. The museum is in Bandana Square. It's between Snelling and Lexington on Energy Park Drive, just south of Como Park.

14 Hay Creek Valley Campground

Location: On Hay Creek, south of Red Wing, map 3, grid E4.

Campsites, facilities: There are 100 (five winter) campsites. Facilities include RV pull-through sites, electric hookups, water, flush toilets, showers, disposal station, laundry, grocery store, heated outdoor pool, playground, state-stocked trout stream, restaurant, lounge, and hiking and snowmobile trails. It's near a state forest with hiking and horse trails. Seasonal campsite rentals are available. Pets are allowed.

Reservations, fees: The daily fee ranges from $18 to $22. Open year-round.

Directions: From Red Wing, take Hwy. 58 south for six miles to the campground.

Contact: Hay Creek Valley Campground, George O'Neill, 31673 Hwy. 58 Blvd., Red Wing, MN 55066-9804 or 888/388-3998 or 651/388-3998.

Trip Notes: You can stroll through the orchard at Frontenac Hills Apple Farm in the bluffs overlooking the Mississippi River Valley. Pick apples, pumpkins, and other produce, and browse the country store. Kids can play in the calico corn maze and climb a haystack. From Red Wing, take U.S. Hwy. 61 east to County Road 21 (Flower Valley Rd.). Drive one-half mile to Circle Rd. and to the farm (following the blue road signs).

15 Frontenac State Park

Location: Southeast of Red Wing on Lake Pepin (Mississippi River), map 3, grid D6.

Campsites, facilities: There are 58 RV (11 winter) sites and four tent sites. Facilities include electric hookups, flush toilets, showers, wheelchair access, and disposal station. There are also 14.5 miles of hiking, eight miles of snowmobile, and six miles of ski trails. Pets are allowed.

Reservations, fees: The daily fee is $16. Credit cards are accepted. Open year-round.

Directions: From Red Wing, take U.S. Hwy. 61 for 10 miles.

Then drive one mile north on Goodhue County Road 2.

Contact: Frontenac State Park, 29223 County 28 Blvd., Frontenac, MN 55026, 651/345-3401, fax 651/345-3694.

Trip Notes: You can enjoy magnificent views of Lake Pepin as you hike along the wooded slopes of this 2,773-acre park. Since the turn of the century, Frontenac has had a reputation for great bird-watching. Some 260 species of birds make the park their home for part or all of the year, while others just stop by on their way up or down the Mississippi River flyway. Bald eagles are commonly seen in the fall, winter, and spring. A few eagles even nest in the area. Several species of warblers visit every year, particularly the first part of May.

16 Hok-Si-La Municipal Park

Location: In Lake City on Lake Pepin, map 3, grid E6.

Campsites, facilities: There are 41 tent sites. Facilities include water, flush toilets, showers, swimming beach, and playground. There are also hiking and cross-country ski trails. Pets are allowed.

Reservations, fees: The daily fee ranges from $15 to $20. Open May through October.

Directions: From Red Wing, take U.S. Hwy. 61 south along the Mississippi River. As you approach Lake City, look for a sign to the campground, which is on the left.

Contact: Hok-Si-La Municipal Park, 2500 N. Hwy. 61, Lake City, MN 55041-0066 or 651/345-3855.

Trip Notes: Visit the Wabasha County Museum (651/345-3987), which is a four-room, brick 1870 schoolhouse with displays (clamming, lumbering, early river transportation), antique farm machinery, exhibit on Laura Ingalls Wilder, antique quilts, Native American artifacts, and military and clothing exhibits. The museum has also acquired the Reads Landing Post Office. Take U.S. Hwy. 61 southeast to Reads Landing. The museum is one block south of Hwy. 61. Adult admission is $2; children are 50 cents. There's free parking.

17 Lake Pepin Campground and MHP, Inc.

Location: Near Lake Pepin (Mississippi River), map 3, grid E6.

Campsites, facilities: There are 60 RV sites and 25 tent sites. Facilities include RV pull-through sites, electric hookups, water, sewer, flush toilets, showers, disposal station, nearby boat ramp, grocery store, and playground. Seasonal campsite rentals are available. Pets are allowed.

Reservations, fees: The daily fee ranges from $9 to $15. Open from mid-April through mid-October.

Directions: Located on High St., one mile from downtown Lake City.

Contact: Lake Pepin Campground, 1818 High St., N., Lake City, MN 55041-9048 or 651/345-2909, fax 651/345-2909.

Trip Notes: Nearby is Mount Frontenac (800/488-5826 or 651/388-5826), a downhill ski area featuring 11 runs and a 420-foot vertical drop. The longest run is 5,000 feet. It also boasts one of the best mogul runs, which has been reshaped for a greater challenge, in the area. Wildlife—eagles, deer, and fox—is abundant here. From Red Wing, take U.S. Hwy. 61 nine miles south to the ski area.

18 City of Wabasha Campground

Location: In Wabasha on the Mississippi River, map 3, grid F8.

Campsites, facilities: There are 28 campsites. Facilities include electric hookups, water, flush toilets, showers, and access to the river. Seasonal campsite rentals are available. Pets are allowed.

Reservations, fees: The daily fee begins at $20. Open May through October.

Directions: From Lake City, take U.S. Hwy. 61 south to Wabasha.

Contact: City of Wabasha Campground, 900 Hiawatha Dr., E., P.O. Box 268, Wabasha, MN 55981, 651/565-4558, fax 651/565-4569.

Trip Notes: How about renting a houseboat? Great River Houseboats, 1009 Main St., E., P.O. 247, Wabasha, MN 55981 (651/565-3376), offers fully equipped boat rentals on Lake Pepin and the Mississippi River. The company's located at the Wabasha Marina about one-half mile south of the Minnesota-Wisconsin Interstate bridge.

19 Zumbro Valley Sportsmans Park

Location: Northwest of Rochester, map 3, grid F5.

Campsites, facilities: There are 40 campsites. Facilities include playground, river access, boat ramp, and canoe rentals. Pets are allowed.

Reservations, fees: The daily fee ranges from $5 to $10. Open from mid-May through September.

Directions: Take U.S. Hwy. 63 to the south side of Zumbro Falls to the campground.

Contact: Zumbro Valley Sportsmans Park, P.O. Box 91, Zumbro Falls, MN 55991-9768 or 507/753-2568.

Trip Notes: Minnesota's only remaining original covered bridge is north of downtown Zumbrota on Main St. (Hwy. 58), where it spans the Zumbro River in the 65-acre Covered Bridge Park (507/732-7318). The park is also home to the town's other historic treasures, a Milwaukee Road Railroad Depot and an original one-room country schoolhouse.

20 Bluff Valley Campground

Location: Northwest of Rochester, map 3, grid F5.

Campsites, facilities: There are 275 campsites. Facilities include RV pull-through sites, electric hookups, water, flush toilets, showers, disposal station, biking and hiking trails, swimming beach, outdoor pool, playground, children's programs, and evening entertainment. Canoe and seasonal campsite rentals are available. Pets are allowed.

Reservations, fees: The daily fee ranges from $26 to $33. Credit cards are accepted. Open from mid-April through early October.

Directions: From U.S. Hwy. 63, take Hwy. 60 west for two miles to the campground, which is located on the river.

Contact: Bluff Valley Campground, R.R. 1, Box 194 Bluff Valley Rd., Zumbro Falls, MN 55991-9744 or 800/226-7282 or 507/753-2955, fax 507/753-3055.

Trip Notes: Housed in a limestone church dating to 1869 is the Dodge County Historical Society Museum (507/635-5508). It features Native American artifacts and a Civil War collection. From Zumbro Falls, take U.S. Hwy. 63 south to Rochester and pick up U.S. Hwy. 14 west to Hwy. 57. Then go north to

Mantorville. The museum is at 615 N. Main St., in the downtown area.

21 Carley State Park

Location: South of Plainview on the North Branch of the Whitewater River, map 3, grid H7.

Campsites, facilities: There are 20 campsites. Facilities include wheelchair access, five miles of hiking trails, six miles of cross-country ski trails, picnic area, and playground. Pets are allowed.

Reservations, fees: The daily fee is $8. Open from late May through early September.

Directions: From Plainview, go four miles north on County Road 4.

Contact: Carley State Park, Rt. 1, Box 256, Altura, MN 55910-9754 or 507/534-3400 or 507/932-3007, fax 507/532-5938.

Trip Notes: The Dakota Indians once hunted, farmed, and gathered wild food in and around the Whitewater River Valley. They gave the Whitewater River its name because it turned a murky white color in spring as high water eroded the light-colored clay of the valley floor. In 1851, the United States government and the Dakota Indians signed a treaty that opened most of southern Minnesota for European settlers. The nearest settlement to the park, Plainview, was named for the large, upland fields of prairie grass that surrounded the valley. The land for the park was donated to the state in 1948 by State Senator James A. Carley and the Ernestina Bolt family in hopes of preserving an outstanding grove of native white pines. In spring, the 204-acre park is a woodland filled with the colors of bluebells. It features excellent bird-watching and fishing.

22 Silver Lake RV Park

Location: In Rochester on the Zumbro River near Silver Lake, map 3, grid H5.

Campsites, facilities: There are 63 campsites. Facilities include electric hookups, water, sewer, flush toilets, showers, laundry, and wheelchair access. Seasonal campsite rentals are available. Pets are allowed.

Reservations, fees: The daily fee is $24. Open from April through October.

Directions: From the north, take U.S. Hwy. 63 to the park, which is on Broadway (also Hwy. 63), near Silver Lake.

Contact: Silver Lake RV Park, 1409 N. Broadway (Hwy. 63), Rochester, MN 55906, 507/289-6412.

Trip Notes: Take the youngsters to the Olmsted County History Center (507/282-9447), featuring interpretive exhibits on Rochester's history and the surrounding area. It's 1.5 miles west of Apache Mall, at the corner of County Roads 255 and 22 S.W.

23 Brookside RV Park

Location: On the west side of Rochester, map 3, grid H5.

Campsites, facilities: There are 26 RV sites and three tent sites. All are open during winter. Facilities include RV pull-through sites, electric hookups, water, sewer, flush toilets, showers, laundry, and wheelchair access. Seasonal campsite rentals are available. Pets are allowed.

Reservations, fees: The daily fee is $21. Credit cards are accepted. Open year-round.

Directions: Take U.S. Hwy. 52 (17th Ave. N.W. parallels the highway) south and exit after it joins U.S. Hwy. 14.

Contact: Brookside RV Park, 516 17th Ave., N.W., Rochester, MN 55901-1861 or 800/658-7050 or 507/288-1413, fax 507/288-3316.

Trip Notes: Located off 14th St. N.W., and 11th Ave. N.W., is the Assisi Community Center (507/280-2180 or 507/282-7441, ext. 180). One-hour tours of Assisi Heights, a building of Italian Romanesque architecture are offered. It's a retreat location for the sisters of St. Francis and Assisi Community Center.

24 Whitewater State Park

Location: South of Elba on the Whitewater River, map 3, grid H8.

Campsites, facilities: There are 107 RV sites and four tent sites. Facilities include electric hookups, flush toilets, showers, disposal station, wheelchair access, and swimming beach. There are also 10 miles of hiking and 10 miles of cross-country ski trails. Snowshoe rentals are available. Pets are allowed.

Reservations, fees: The daily fee is $14. Credit cards are accepted. Open year-round.

Directions: From Elba, take State Hwy. 74 three miles south to the park entrance.

Contact: Whitewater State Park, Rt. 1, Box 256, Altura, MN 55910-9754 or 507/932-3007, fax 507/932-5938.

Trip Notes: Nearly 450 million years ago, shallow seas covered most of North America, including southeastern Minnesota. On its bed, sediment accumulated that turned into rock hundreds of feet thick. When the sea withdrew, erosion carved through the bedrock, creating the original valleys and bluffs found in what is now Whitewater State Park. More recently, glacial meltwaters sculpted the cliffs and valleys.

The park is remarkable in another respect. It has no mosquitoes! Yep, these blufflands don't have any. The 2,700-acre park also features six scenic overlooks and good trout fishing in the spring-fed Whitewater River and Trout Run Creek.

25 Pioneer Campsite

Location: On the Mississippi River near Wabasha, map 4, grid F1.

Campsites, facilities: There 198 RV sites and 22 tent sites. Facilities include electric hookups, water, sewer, flush toilets, showers, laundry, disposal station, biking and hiking trails, outdoor pool, grocery store, and playground. Canoe and seasonal campsite rentals are available. Pets are allowed.

Reservations, fees: The daily fee ranges from $13 to $17. Open from mid-February through mid-October.

Directions: From Wabasha, take U.S. Hwy. 61 south to Midland Junction, just north of Kellogg. Go east on County Road 24 to the campground.

Contact: Pioneer Campsite, Ray and Lorriane Logan, 130 Pioneer Dr., Wabasha, MN 55981-3214 or 651/565-2242.

Trip Notes: You'll be able to study a complete Winchester gun collection (one of each model from 1866 to 1982, including commemorative models) at the Arrowhead Bluffs Museum (651/565-3829) in Wabasha. Take U.S. Hwy. 61 or Hwy. 60 west to the museum.

26 John Latsch State Park

Location: Near Winona along the Mississippi River, map 4, grid G2.

Campsites, facilities: There are 12 tent sites. Facilities include hiking trails. Pets are allowed.

Reservations, fees: The daily fee is $8. Open year-round.

Directions: From Winona, take Hwy. 61 north for 12 miles to the park.

Contact: John Latsch State Park, Rt. 1, Box 256, Altura, MN 55910-9754 or 507/932-3007, fax 507/932-5938.

Trip Notes: The park offers three overlooks towering more than 500 feet above the Mississippi River. Steamboat captains relied on a trio of rocky-headed bluffs called "Faith," "Hope," and "Charity" to navigate their way up and down the Mississippi. In the 1850s, a busy steamboat landing and logging town was established below these bluffs. The logging operations supplied cut timber for the sawmills in the new town of Winona. For many years, the area was only visited by a few ambitious hikers who hiked the steep hills for a bird's-eye view of the valley. John A. Latsch, a local businessman, purchased some of these blufflands and persuaded an adjacent landowner to donate, along with him, approximately 350 acres to the state for a park in 1925. Latsch loved to fish in the waters below the bluffs. Adjacent to Whitman Dam, the facility provides good views of the waterway's Pool 5. Also, a one-half mile trail leads to the top of Mt. Charity.

27 Pla-Mor Campground

Location: South of Wabasha on the Mississippi River, map 4, grid G3.

Campsites, facilities: There are 23 RV sites and 12 tent sites. Facilities include RV pull-through sites, electric hookups, water, showers, disposal station, grocery store, hiking trail, swimming pool, and playground. Canoe and seasonal campsite rentals are available. Pets are allowed.

Reservations, fees: The daily fee is $17 to $22. Credit cards are accepted. Open from mid-April through October.

Directions: From I-90, take Hwy. 43 north toward Winona to the campground.

Contact: Pla-Mor Campground, Gordie and Ann Rasmussen, R.R. 6, Box 18-1, Winona, MN 55987, 877/454-2267 or 507/454-2851.

Trip Notes: Be sure to visit the Julius C. Wilkie Steamboat Center (507-454-1254) at Levee Park. It's an actual-size replica of a steamboat offering a museum, river history, and miniatures of steamboats.

28 Winona KOA

Location: South of Winona on the Mississippi River, map 3, grid H4.

Campsites, facilities: The campground offers 62 RV sites and 10 tent sites. There are also two camping cabins. Facilities include RV pull-through sites, electric hookups, water, flush toilets, showers, laundry, disposal station, grocery store, outdoor pool, hiking trails, playground, and evening entertainment. Canoe and seasonal campsite rentals are available. Pets are allowed.

Reservations, fees: The daily fee ranges from $17 to $22. Credit cards are accepted. Open from mid-April through October.

Contact: Winona KOA, R.R. 6, Box 18-1, Winona, MN 55987-4387 or 877/454-2267 or 507/454-2851.

Directions: From I-90 take Hwy. 43 north to Winona. Take a right on Hwy. 61 and drive to mile marker 20.

Trip Notes: The Bunnell House Museum (507-454-2723), about five miles south of Winona on Hwy. 61 in Homer, is a rural, gothic wood-frame house built in the 1850s. The museum, overlooking the Mississippi River, is on the National Register of Historic Places. Adult admission is $3; students $1; ages six and under are free, as is parking.

29 Albert Lea/Austin KOA Campground

Location: East of Albert Lea, map 5, grid C7.

Campsites, facilities: There are 84 RV sites and 26 tent sites. Facilities include RV pull-through sites, electric hookups, water, sewer, flush toilets, showers, laundry, disposal station, grocery store, hiking trails, golf course, outdoor pool, and playground. Seasonal campsite rentals are available. Pets are allowed.

Reservations, fees: The daily fee ranges from $15 to $22. Credit cards are accepted. Open from mid-April through mid-October.

Directions: From I-90, take exit 166 (County Road 46) and go right for one-half mile.

Contact: Albert Lea/Austin KOA Campground, R.R. 3, Box 15, Hayward, MN 56043-9705 or 507/373-5170.

Trip Notes: Visit an Amish homestead with Amish Country Tours (507/886-2303; email: amish@means.net). You can see the lifestyle of the 1800s where horse and buggies, kerosene lamps, and wood-burning stoves are still in use. The company is on the Village Green in the Old Train Depot in Harmony.

30 Nelson's Wheel Estates MHP

Location: On the west side of Austin, map 5, grid C8.

Campsites, facilities: There are 21 campsites (three are open in winter). Facilities include RV pull-through sites, electric hookups, water, sewer, flush toilets, showers, disposal station, laundry, and playground. Pets are allowed.

Reservations, fees: The daily fee begins at $20. Open year-round.

Directions: From I-90, take exit 175 and go west on County Road 46 to 37th Street. Turn south to the campground.

Contact: Nelson's Wheel Estates, 3700 3rd Pl. S.W., Austin, MN 55912-1205 or 507/433-3134.

Trip Notes: You can't overlook the Hormel First Century & Spam Museum (800/444-5713 or 507/437-4563). It has free displays, photos, and artifacts from the first 100 years of the company's operation. It's at the northwest corner of the Oak Park Mall in Austin on I-90 and 14th St. N.W.

31 Rochester KOA

Location: South of Rochester, map 6, grid A6.

Campsites, facilities: There are 65 RV sites and eight tent sites. There are also two camping cabins. Facilities include RV pull-through sites, electric hookups, water, sewer, flush toilets, showers, laundry, wheelchair access, disposal station, grocery store, outdoor pool, and playground. A golf course and the Root River Bike Trail are nearby. Pets are allowed.

Reservations, fees: The daily fee ranges from $19 to $22. Credit cards are accepted. Open from mid-March through October.

Directions: From I-90, take exit 218 and travel south for one-quarter mile on U.S. Hwy. 52.

Contact: Rochester KOA, Roger and Barb Philip, I-90 and U.S. 52 South, 5232 65th Ave., S.E., Rochester, MN 55904, 800/562-5232 or 507/288-0785, fax 507/252-1993.

Trip Notes: Nearby is the internationally famous Mayo Clinic (507/284-2511). Did you know it offers free 1.5-hour tours Monday through Friday at 9:40 A.M.? Artwork tours, featuring unique art throughout the clinic, are held Tuesday, Wednesday, and Thursday at 1:30 P.M.

32 Beaver Trails Campground

Location: East of Austin, map 6, grid C2.

Campsites, facilities: There are 200 campsites. Facilities include RV pull-through sites, electric hookups, water, sewer, flush toilets, showers, disposal station, laundry, wheelchair access, grocery store, restaurant, hiking trails, heated outdoor pool, stocked fish pond, playground, children's programs, and evening entertainment. Canoe and seasonal campsite rentals are available. Pets are allowed.

Reservations, fees: Reservations are advised and a deposit is required to hold a site. The daily fee ranges from $21 to $25. Credit cards are accepted. Open from mid-April through mid-October.

Directions: From I-90, take exit 187 to County Road 20 and turn south to the campground.

Contact: Beaver Trails Campground, 21943 630th Ave., Austin, MN 55912-9118 or 800/245-6281 or 507/584-6611, fax 507/584-6661, email: camping@beavertrails.com, website: www.beavertrails.com.

Trip Notes: Visit the J. C. Hormel Nature Center (507/437-7519), with 278 acres of woods and prairie and nine miles of walking trails to explore. There's also an interpretive building with touch-and-see exhibits of area wildlife. The center is one-quarter mile north of I-90 east on exit 180B at 21st St. N.E.

33 Maple Springs Campground

Location: West of Preston on Forestville Creek, map 6, grid C7.

Campsites, facilities: There are 49 campsites. Facilities include electric hookups, water, grocery store, fishing, and hiking trails. Pets are allowed.

Reservations, fees: The daily fee ranges from $13 to $16. Open mid-April through October.

Directions: From Preston, take Hwy. 16 west toward Spring Valley. Look for the sign to the campground.

Contact: Maple Springs Campground, Rt. 2, Box 129B, Preston, MN 55965, 507/352-2056.

Trip Notes: The Arches Museum of Pioneer Life (507/523-2111 or 507/454-2723) is well worth a visit. It features exhibits on pioneer and agricultural history. The site includes a one-room schoolhouse, log house, log barn, and a covered bridge. From Winona, go about nine miles west on Hwy. 14 between Lewiston and Stockton.

34 Old Barn Resort

Location: West of Preston on the Root River, map 6, grid C7.

Campsites, facilities: There are 130 RV sites and 40 tent sites. Facilities include RV pull-through sites, electric hookups, water, sewer, flush toilets, showers, disposal station, laundry, grocery store, canoe rentals and outfitting, biking and hiking trails, indoor pool, downhill ski area, restaurant, lounge, children's programs, playground, and evening entertainment. Pets are allowed.

Reservations, fees: The daily fee ranges from $17 to $26. Credit cards are accepted. Open April through October.

Directions: In Preston, take County Road 17 east for about 2.5 miles. Turn right at the blue sign and travel nearly one mile to the campground.

Contact: Old Barn Resort, Rt. 3, Box 57, Preston, MN 55965-9036 or 800/552-2512 or

507/467-2512, fax 507/467-2382, website: www.bluffcountry.com.

Trip Notes: The Allis Barn on the 220-acre property is a National Historic Site. Built in 1884-1885 and rebuilt in 1988-1990, it's the centerpiece of the resort. Also, about a mile of the Root River passes through the site and is an excellent designated trout stream. Nearby, too, is the Root River State Trail, which is regarded by many as Minnesota's most scenic. It offers more than 60 miles of blacktop that winds through woods and rivers for bikers, hikers, and those darn in-line skates.

Forestville/Mystery Cave State Park

Location: Near Wykoff, map 6, grid C7.

Campsites, facilities: There are 73 semi-modern and 26 rustic sites; 60 are tent-only sites. There are also four sites available in winter. Facilities include electric hookups, flush toilets, showers, disposal station, wheelchair access, seasonal naturalist programs, and evening entertainment. There are 11 miles of cross-country ski, 5.5 miles of snowmobile, and 17 miles of hiking and horseback trails. Pets are allowed.

Reservations, fees: Reservations are recommended on weekends. The daily fee ranges from $12 to $16. Credit cards are accepted. Open year-round.

Directions: From I-90, take exit 193 and Hwy. 16 east toward Wykoff. Go south on Fillmore County Road 5 for four miles. Then go two miles east on Fillmore County Road 118 to the park entrance.

Contact: Forestville/Mystery Cave State Park, Rt. 2, Box 128, Preston, MN 55965-9535 or 507/352-5111 for main park, 507/937-3251 for Mystery Cave, fax 507/352-5113.

Trip Notes: In the center of the park, along the South Branch of the Root River, is the restored site of Forestville, maintained by the Minnesota Historical Society. Founded in 1853, the village emerged as a rural trade center, typical of hundreds that emerged across southern Minnesota during the 1850s. Area farmers came here to trade their farm produce for goods and services. By 1858, Forestville's population was about 100 and it had 20 buildings, including two general stores, gristmill, brickyard, two hotels, school, and mechanics of several trades. Forestville prospered until the first area railroad, the Southern Minnesota, bypassed the community in 1868. Residents watched their town struggle to survive, while towns served by the railroad boomed. By 1890, Thomas J. Meighen, son of one of the town's founders, owned the entire village. The 50 remaining residents earned their living on Meighen's farm. In return, his employees received housing, board, and credit in his store. Meighen also maintained a post office, school, feed store, and sawmill.

You can also enjoy the constant 48-degree Fahrenheit temperature in Mystery Cave—the state's longest—at this 3,112-acre park.

Lake Louise State Park

Location: Near Le Roy on Lake Louise, map 6, grid D4.

Campsites, facilities: There are 22 campsites (four winter sites). Facilities include electric hookups, showers, disposal station, lake and river fishing, boating (electric motors only), and swimming beach. There are also one mile of biking, 11.6 miles of hiking, 10 miles of horseback riding, 2.2 miles of cross-country ski, and 9.3 miles of snowmobile trails. Pets are allowed.

Reservations, fees: The daily fee ranges from $8 to $12. Credit cards are accepted. Open from late May through early September.

Directions: From Le Roy, take County Road 14 1.5 miles north to the entrance.

Contact: Lake Louise State Park, Rt. 1, Box 184, 12385 766th Ave., Le Roy, MN 55951-9743 or 507/324-5249, fax 507/324-5249.

Trip Notes: This area was lightly glaciated by the first two of four ice ages about 400,000 years ago. As a result, the limestone bedrock is close to the surface and only a thin layer of glacial soil covers the bedrock. In some places, the soft, porous limestone has dissolved, creating a depression in the landscape. Despite these few rather interesting depressions, the 1,168-acre park's terrain is relatively level and ideal for the novice cross-country skier and horseback rider. You might bring a canoe for a leisurely paddle around Lake Louise and the Little Iowa and Upper Iowa Rivers. Spring flowers are abundant in April and May, and this is a great place to watch birds during spring and fall migrations. There is also a 1.5-mile paved Shooting Star Recreation Trail from Le Roy to the park, which we discovered to be among the state's more quiet ones.

37 Great River Bluffs State Park

Location: Near Winona on the bluff overlooking the Mississippi River, map 7, grid A5.

Campsites, facilities: There are 31 campsites (four winter sites). Facilities include flush toilets, showers, wheelchair access, picnic area, playground, and 6.5 miles of hiking and 9.2 miles of cross-country ski trails.

Snowshoe rentals are available. Pets are allowed.

Reservations, fees: The daily fee ranges from $8 to $12. Credit cards are accepted. Open from late May through early September.

Directions: From I-90, take exit 266 at County Road 12. County Road 12 leads into Winona County Hwy. 3 (Apple Blossom Dr.). Take this road to the park entrance.

Contact: Great River Bluffs State Park, Rt. 4, Winona, MN 55987-9804 or 507/643-6849, fax 507/643-6849.

Trip Notes: You can easily reach the scenic overlooks at this 2,835-acre park, formerly O.L. Kipp State Park, by walking trails. You'll see oak and hickory woods, pine plantations, and prairies. The park attracts more than 35 species of mammals, 17 species of reptiles and amphibians, and well over 100 species of birds. Rabbits, mice, and ground squirrels are common in the patches of prairie in the park. Predators include red-tailed hawks, great horned owls, and red foxes. The hardwood forest provides habitat for opossums, skunks, Indigo buntings, ruffed grouse, and wild turkeys. In winter, visitors report seeing bald eagles. The prairie also draws uncommon species: a lizard, the six-lined racer; and a prairie bird, the bobolink.

38 Sylvan Park/Riverview Campground

Location: On the Root River in Lanesboro, map 7, grid C1.

Campsites, facilities: There are 45 RV sites and 50 tent sites. Facilities include electric hookups, water, flush toilets, showers, disposal station, canoe outfitting, tennis courts, and playground. There are also biking, hiking, and cross-country ski trails. Canoe and seasonal campsite rentals are available. Pets are allowed.

Reservations, fees: The daily fee ranges from $10 to $17. Open April through November.

Directions: From Hwy. 250, from the north, or from Hwy. 16, from the south, turn on Parkway Ave. in Lanesboro.

Contact: Sylvan Park/Riverview Campground, 202 Parkway Ave., Box 333, Lanesboro, MN 55949, 800/944-2670, fax 507/467-2557.

Trip Notes: Need recreation gear? The Little River General Store 800/944-2943 or 507/467-2943) at 104 and 106 Parkway North in downtown Lanesboro probably has it. It offers bike, canoe, kayak, tube, and cross-country ski rentals.

39 Beaver Creek Valley State Park

Location: Near Caledonia on Beaver Creek, map 7, grid C4.

Campsites, facilities: There are 26 RV sites and 22 year-round tent sites. Facilities include electric hookups, showers, disposal station, wheelchair access, children's wading pool, and playground. There are also eight miles of hiking trails, as well as snowmobile and cross-country ski trails. Pets are allowed.

Reservations, fees: The daily fee ranges from $8 to $12. Credit cards are accepted. Open from late May through early September.

Directions: From I-90, take Hwy. 76 south for 24 miles. Then, drive four miles on Houston County Rd. 1 to the park.

Contact: Beaver Creek Valley State Park, 15954 County 1, Caledonia, MN 55921-9615 or 507/724-2107, fax 507/724-2107.

Trip Notes: The 695-acre park is an excellent place to view wildflowers and it also boasts a blue-ribbon trout stream. The great diversity of plant species contributes to a great diversity of wildlife. If you are observant, you might spot deer, raccoon, muskrat, mink, badger, red and gray fox, an occasional beaver, and wild turkey. Another interesting animal that resides in the park is the timber rattlesnake, which is seldom seen. If you encounter one, please leave it alone; although venomous, they offer little threat. Bird-watchers flock to the park to see the treasured Acadian flycatcher and the Louisiana waterthrush.

40 Supersaw Valley Campground

Location: Southeast of Preston, map 7, grid D3.

Campsites, facilities: There are 91 RV sites and 15 tent sites. Facilities include RV pull-through sites, electric hookups, water, sewer, flush toilets, showers, laundry, disposal station, grocery store, hiking trails, outdoor pool, and playground. Seasonal campsite rentals are available. Pets are allowed.

Reservations, fees: The daily fee ranges from $19 to $23. Open from early May through September.

Directions: Take Hwy. 44 to Mabel and turn north on Hwy. 43 for about five miles. Where Hwy. 43 goes west, turn east on County Road 18 for about three miles.

Contact: Supersaw Valley Campground, R.R. 2, Spring Grove, MN 55974-1210 or 507/498-5880.

Trip Notes: Be sure to bring a fly rod. The 200-acre campground is on the banks of Riceford Creek, which is stocked with trout.

41 Dunromin Park Campground

Location: Near Caledonia on Winnebago Creek, map 7, grid D5.

Campsites, facilities: There are 92 RV sites and 16 tent sites. Facilities include RV pull-through sites, electric hookups, water, flush toilets, showers, laundry, disposal station, grocery store, hiking trails, nearby trout fishing, outdoor pool, evening entertainment, children's program, and playground. Pets are allowed.

Reservations, fees: The daily fee ranges from $15 to $28. Credit cards are accepted. Open May through October.

Directions: From Spring Grove, take Hwy. 44 to Hwy. 76 south at Caledonia and go about 4.5 miles. A sign for the campground is on the right; the campground entrance is on the left.

Contact: Dunromin Park Campground, Rt. 1, Box 146, Caledonia, MN 55921-9734 or 800/822-2514 or 507/724-2514, email: dunromin@means.net.

Trip Notes: Cross-county skiers will like the 14.2 km Wet Bark Trail near Caledonia. It travels from Houston 4.8 miles southwest on County Road 13. In the state forest, you'll find wooded bluffs with some hilltop fields and scenic overlooks. Maps are along the trail.

WISCONSIN
INDIAN HEAD COUNTRY

Wisconsin Regions

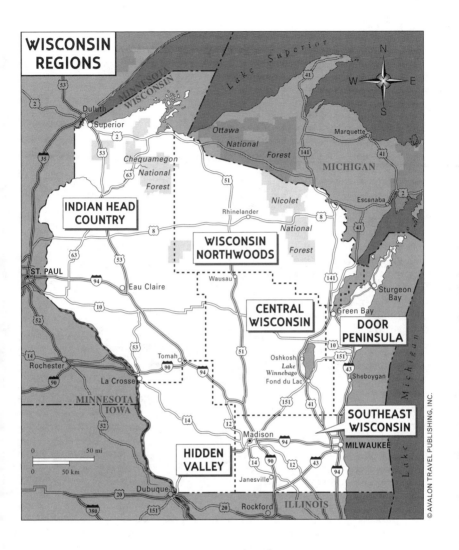

Indian Head Country

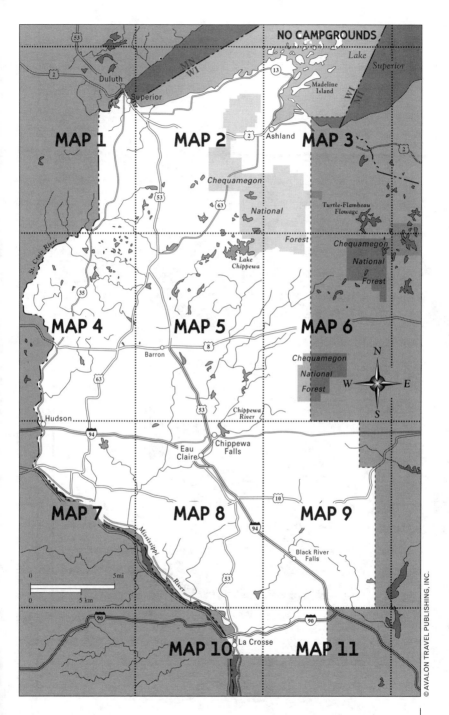

© AVALON TRAVEL PUBLISHING, INC.

Map 1

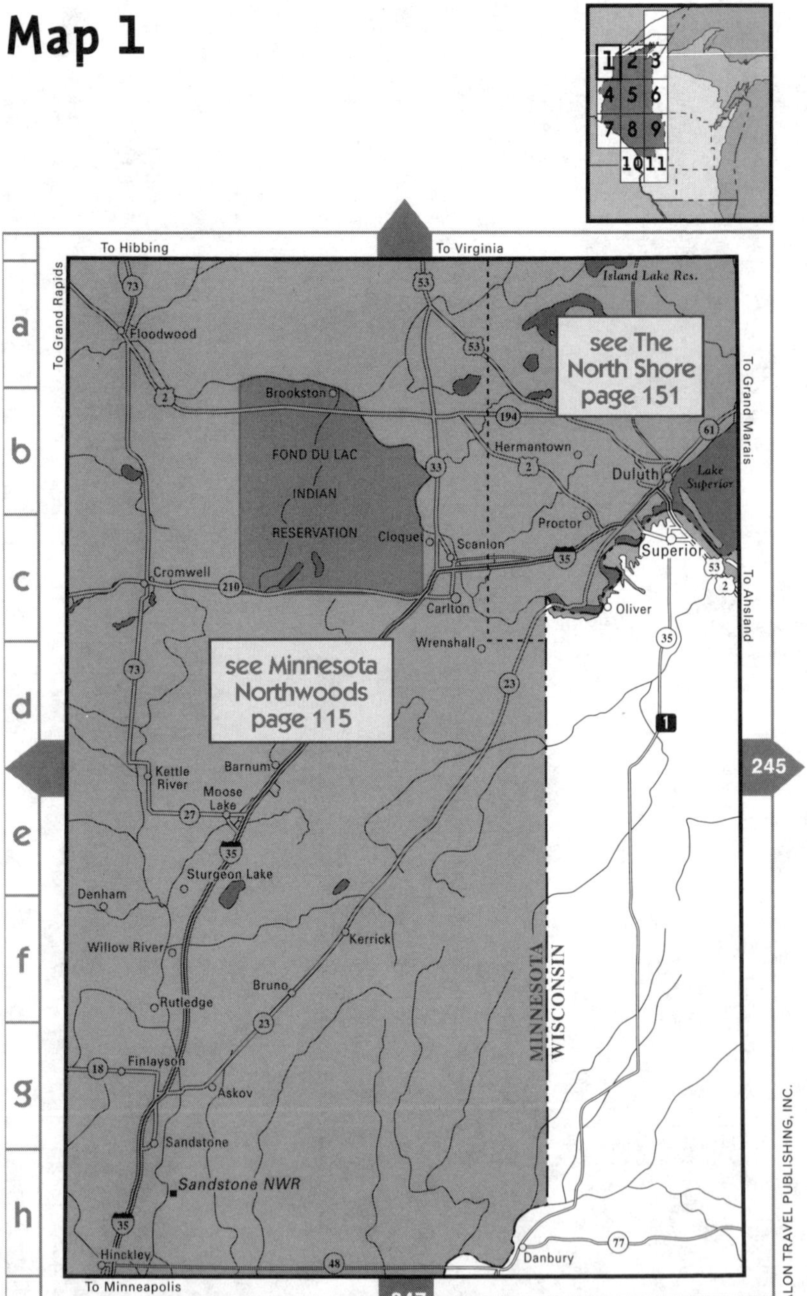

To Hibbing
To Virginia

a

see The
North Shore
page 151

b

c

see Minnesota
Northwoods
page 115

d

e

f

g

h

Island Lake Res.

Floodwood

Brookston

FOND DU LAC

INDIAN

RESERVATION

Hermantown

Duluth

Lake
Superior

Cloquet
Scanlon

Proctor

Superior

Cromwell

Carlton

Oliver

Wrenshall

To Grand Rapids
To Grand Marais
To Ashland

Barnum

Kettle
River
Moose
Lake

Sturgeon Lake

Denham

Willow River

Kerrick

Rutledge

Bruno

Finlayson

Askov

Sandstone

Sandstone NWR

Hinckley
Danbury

To Minneapolis

MINNESOTA
WISCONSIN

245

247

© AVALON TRAVEL PUBLISHING, INC.

Map 2

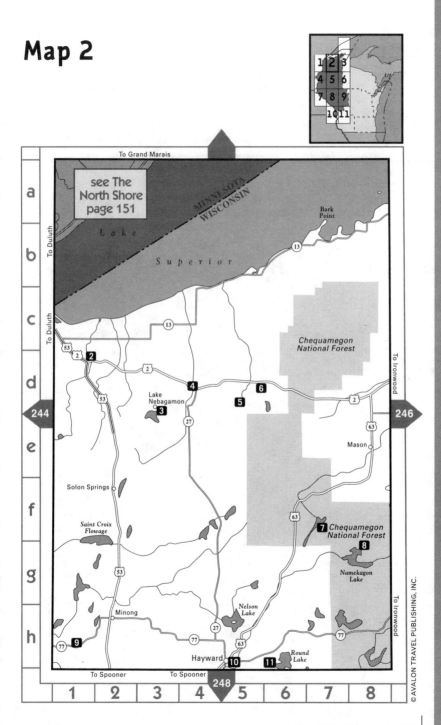

see The North Shore page 151

To Grand Marais

MINNESOTA
WISCONSIN

Bark Point

Lake

Superior

To Duluth

To Duluth

Chequamegon National Forest

To Ironwood

13

53

2

2

2

4

Lake Nebagamon

3

5

6

2

63

Mason

27

Solon Springs

Saint Croix Flowage

63

7 Chequamegon National Forest

8

Namekagon Lake

53

To Ironwood

Minong

Nelson Lake

27

77

77

63

9

Hayward

10

11

Round Lake

77

To Spooner

To Spooner

© AVALON TRAVEL PUBLISHING, INC.

Map 3

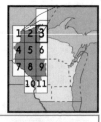

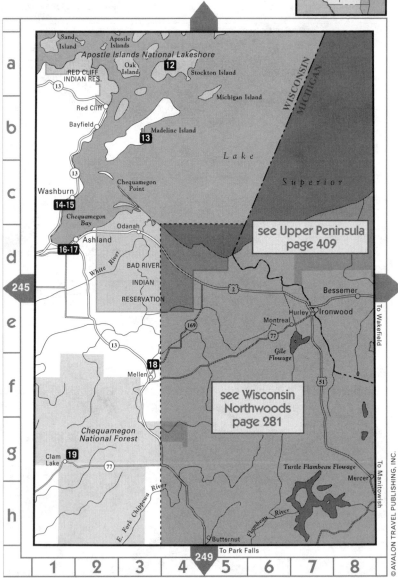

Sand Island
Apostle Islands
Oak Island
12
Stockton Island
Apostle Islands National Lakeshore
RED CLIFF INDIAN RES.
13
Michigan Island
Red Cliff
Bayfield
Madeline Island
13
WISCONSIN
MICHIGAN
Lake Superior
Washburn
Chequamegon Point
14-15
Chequamegon Bay
Odanah
16-17
Ashland
White River
BAD RIVER INDIAN RESERVATION
see Upper Peninsula
page 409
2
Bessemer
245
169
Hurley Ironwood
Montreal
77
To Wakefield
13
Gile Flowage
51
Mellen
18
see Wisconsin Northwoods
page 281
Chequamegon National Forest
Clam Lake
19
77
Turtle Flambeau Flowage
Mercer
To Manitowish
E. Fork Chippewa River
Flambeau River
River
Butternut
249
To Park Falls

© AVALON TRAVEL PUBLISHING, INC.

Map 4

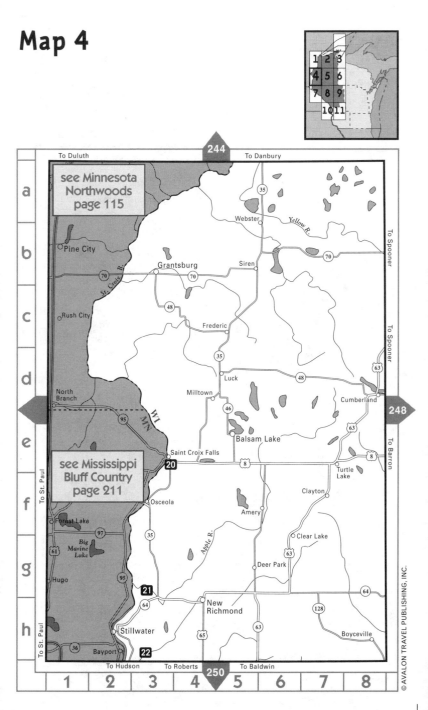

To Duluth **244** To Danbury

see Minnesota Northwoods page 115

To Spooner

35

Webster

Yellow R.

Pine City

70

Grantsburg

Siren

70

St. Croix R.

48

Rush City

Frederic

35

Luck

48

Cumberland

63

To Spooner

North Branch

95

WI / MN

Milltown

46

248

To Barron

Balsam Lake

63

see Mississippi Bluff Country page 211

Saint Croix Falls

8

8

Turtle Lake

8

20

To St. Paul

Osceola

Amery

Clayton

63

Clear Lake

Forest Lake

97

Apple R.

Big Marine Lake

61

35

Deer Park

Hugo

95

64

21

New Richmond

128

64

Stillwater

64

65

63

Boyceville

36

Bayport

22

To St. Paul

To Hudson   To Roberts   **250**   To Baldwin

1 2 3 4 5 6 7 8

© AVALON TRAVEL PUBLISHING, INC.

Map 5

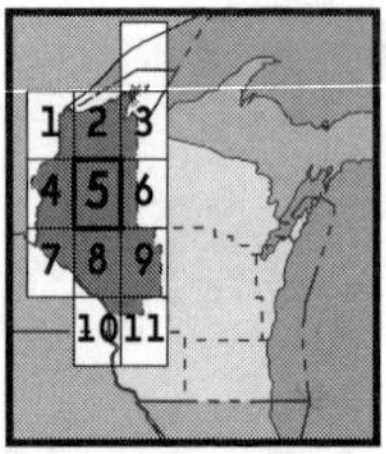

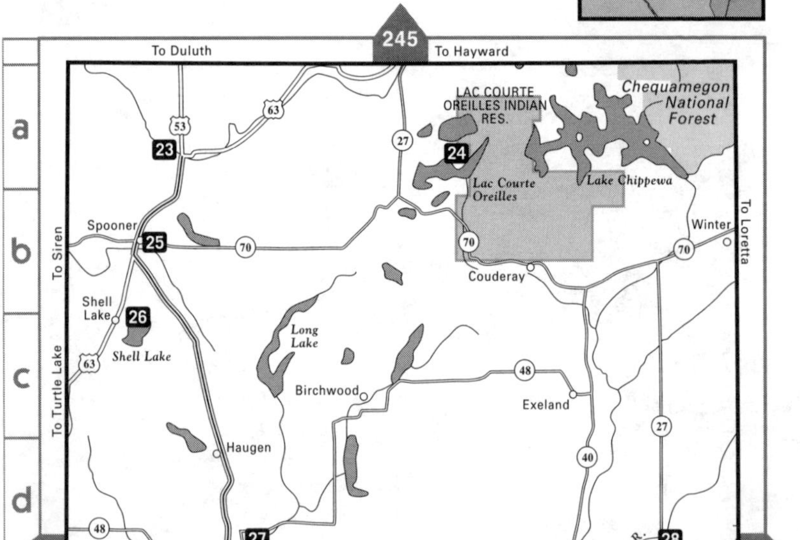

▼ 245

To Duluth
To Hayward

LAC COURTE
OREILLES INDIAN
RES.

Chequamegon
National
Forest

53
63
23
27
24

Lac Courte
Oreilles

Lake Chippewa

To Loretta

a

Spooner
25
70
70
Winter
70

To Siren

b

Shell
Lake
26
Long
Lake

Co:Couderay

Shell Lake
63

c

Birchwood
48
Exeland
27

Haugen
40

d

48
27
Thornapple R.
28
8

To Turtle Lake

To Rhinelander

Rice Lake
Bruce
Ladysmith

e

Cameron
Weyerhaeuser

8
Barron

f

25
Chetek
Lake
Chetek
40
Flambeau R.

29-30
Holcombe
Flowage

Dallas

Prairie Farm
53

To New Richmond

g

Ridgeland
New Auburn
31
64
Cornell

To Gilman

64
25

h

Wheeler
Bloomer
40
27

To Menomonie
To Eau Claire
To Cadott

▼ 251

To Turtle Lake ◄ 247
249 ►

© AVALON TRAVEL PUBLISHING, INC.

1   2   3   4   5   6   7   8

Map 6

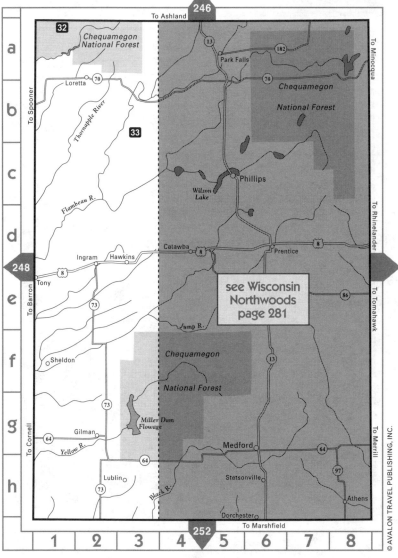

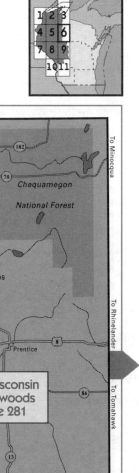

To Ashland

32

Chequamegon
National Forest

a

Loretta 70

To Spooner

b

Thornapple River

33

c

Flambeau R.

Wilson
Lake

Phillips

13

182

Park Falls

70 Chequamegon

National Forest

To Minocqua

d

Ingram Hawkins

Catawba 8

Prentice 8

To Rhinelander

248

8

Tony

To Barron

73

e

Jump R.

86

To Tomahawk

f

Sheldon

Chequamegon

National Forest

13

g

73

Gilman

64

Miller Dam
Flowage

64

Medford

64

To Merrill

Yellow R.

97

h

Lublin

73

Black R.

Stetsonville

Athens

Dorchester

To Marshfield

252

see Wisconsin
Northwoods
page 281

© AVALON TRAVEL PUBLISHING, INC.

| 1 | 2 | 3 | 4 | 5 | 6 | 7 | 8 |

Map 7

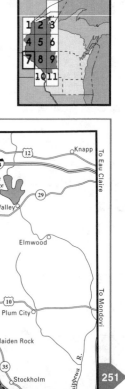

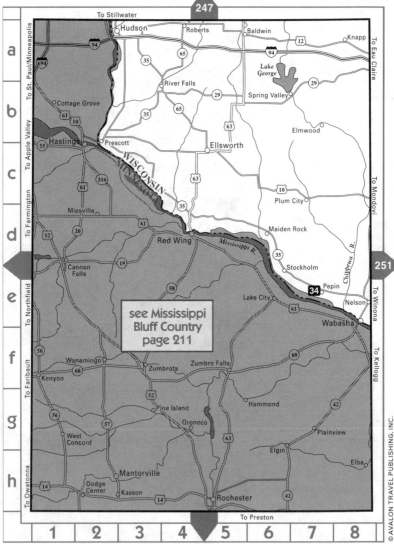

see Mississippi
Bluff Country
page 211

247

251

To Stillwater

To St. Paul/Minneapolis
To Eau Claire

Hudson
Roberts
Baldwin
Knapp

94
12

65
94

35

River Falls
Lake
George

To Apple Valley

29
Spring Valley
29

65
63

Cottage Grove
Elmwood

61
10

Hastings
Prescott
Ellsworth

55

WISCONSIN
MINNESOTA

316
63
10

61
Plum City

Miesville
35

61
Maiden Rock

52
20
Red Wing
Mississippi R.
35

Stockholm

Cannon
Falls
19
Pepin
34
Nelson

58
Lake City
Wabasha

61

To Northfield

56
60
Zumbro Falls
60

Wanamingo
Zumbrota

Kenyon
60

52
Hammond
42

Pine Island
57
Oronoco
Plainview

56
63
Elgin

West
Concord
Elba

To Faribault

Mantorville
42

14
Dodge
Center
Kasson
Rochester

14
To Preston

To Owatonna
To Kellogg

To Winona

To Mondovi

To Farmington

To Stillwater

Chippewa R.

© AVALON TRAVEL PUBLISHING, INC.

Map 8

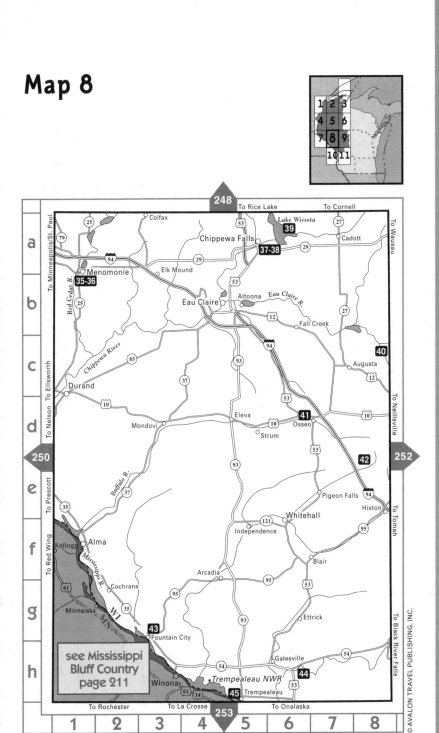

To Rice Lake   To Cornell

To Wausau

Colfax
Lake Wissota
25
39
53
Chippewa Falls
27   Cadott
37-38
29
79
94
29

Elk Mound
53
Menomonie
35-36
Altoona   Eau Claire R.
25
Eau Claire
12   Fall Creek
27

Chippewa River
85
94
12
93
Augusta
40
37
Durand
53
10
12
Eleva
10   Osseo
Mondovi
41
Strum
53

250   93   42   252

Buffalo R.
37
Pigeon Falls
94
35   Whitehall   Hixton
121
Independence   95
Kellogg   Alma
Mississippi R.   Blair
61   Arcadia   95   53
Cochrane
95
Minneiska   35   93   Ettrick
43
Fountain City
54
see Mississippi
Bluff Country
page 211   Galesville   54
Winona   Trempealeau NWR   44
61   14   Trempealeau   53
45
To Rochester   To La Crosse   To Onalaska

To Minneapolis/St. Paul
To Ellsworth
To Nelson   To Prescott
To Red Wing

Red Cedar R.

WI
MN

To Neillsville
To Tomah
To Black River Falls

© AVALON TRAVEL PUBLISHING, INC.

253

a
b
c
d
e
f
g
h

1 2 3 4 5 6 7 8

Map 9

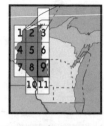

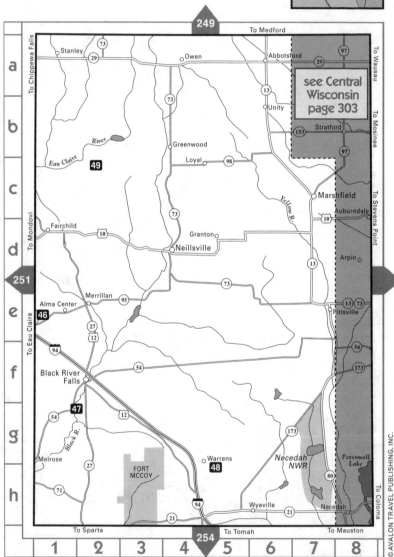

Map 10

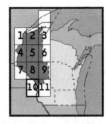

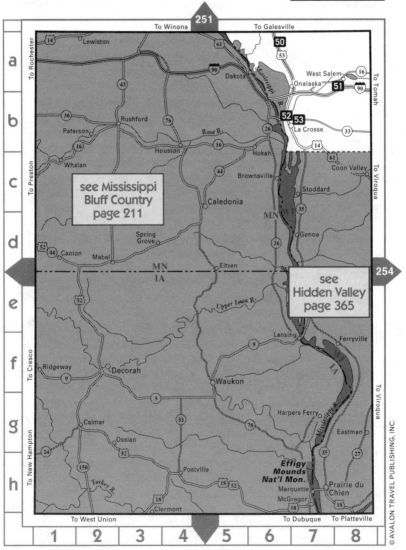

To Winona   **251**   To Galesville

To Rochester

a

To Tomah

14   Lewiston

50

53

West Salem   16

90   Dakota   Onalaska   **51**

43   Mississippi R.

b

30   Rushford   76   Roof R.   26   **52 53**   La Crosse   33

Peterson   16   Houston   16   Hokah

To Preston   16   61   Coon Valley

Whalan   44   Brownsville

c   **see Mississippi Bluff Country page 211**   Stoddard   To Viroqua

Caledonia   MN WI   35

52 44 Canton   Mabel   Spring Grove   Genoa

d   MN IA   Eitzen   26   **254**

52   **see Hidden Valley page 365**

e   Upper Iowa R.

Lansing   Ferryville

To Cresco   9

Ridgeway   Decorah

f   9   Waukon

WI IA

To Viroqua

9   Harpers Ferry

Calmar   51   76   Eastman

g   Ossian   35   27

To New Hampton   24   52   Mississippi R.

150   Postville   ***Effigy Mounds Nat'l Mon.***

h   Turkey R.   18 52   Marquette   Prairie du Chien

18   McGregor

Clermont   18

To West Union   **1 2 3 4 5 6 7 8**   To Dubuque   To Platteville

Map 11

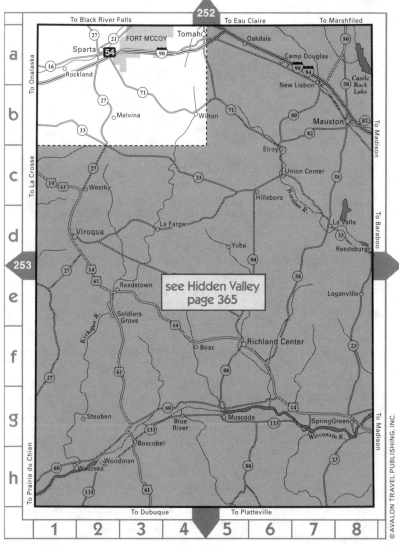

see Hidden Valley page 365

© AVALON TRAVEL PUBLISHING, INC.

Indian Head Country

From the shores of Lake Superior, where thousand-foot ships come into Superior to load cargoes of iron ore and grain, to the picturesque bluffs along the Mississippi River on Wisconsin's western border, Indian Head country is a diverse and fascinating place to visit.

Why is the region called "Indian Head"? Simply because its shape resembles the profile of an Indian looking westward.

The state's northernmost landscape juts out into Lake Superior as the scenic archipelago known as the Apostle Islands. This national lakeshore includes 22 islands and a dozen miles of mainland shoreline.

Lakes and rivers dominate much of the rest of Indian Head territory. Many bodies of water provided the transportation routes for logging and many communities—for example, Rice Lake, Ladysmith, and Hayward—grew along their shores. Today, they offer a variety of recreational opportunities for residents and visitors alike.

◻ Pattison State Park

Location: Superior, on the Black River, map 1, grid D8.

Campsites, facilities: There are 62 campsites. Facilities include electric hookups, showers, disposal station, lake boating, canoeing, swimming, river fishing, nature center, and hiking and cross-country ski trails. Pets are allowed. In winter, there are one plowed site and 61 backpack campsites without water.

Reservations, fees: Reservations are accepted. Campsite reservations are available.

See State Park Camping Fees and Reserving a Campsite. Open year-round.

Directions: From Superior, go 13 miles south on Hwy. 35 to the park entrance.

Contact: Pattison State Park, 6294 S. State Rd. 35, Superior, WI 54880-8326 or 715/399-3111.

Trip Notes: One of Wisconsin's cornerstone parks, Pattison features the Black River's 165-foot Big Manitou Falls, the highest waterfall in Wisconsin.

If you'd like to see the home of the person for whom the park was named, tour the Fairlawn Mansion and Museum (715/394-5712; website: www.visitsuperior.com/newmuseums.html), which was built in 1890 for lumber baron Martin Pattison. The 42-room Victorian mansion faces Lake Superior and includes a city block as its grounds. The exterior and first floor have been restored to their original 1890s beauty and recall the early days of Great Lakes Victorian elegance, maritime commerce, and Native American lore.

◻ Amnicon Falls State Park

Location: Superior, on the Amnicon River, map 2, grid D1.

Campsites, facilities: There are 36 campsites. There are no hookups or showers, but the campground has vault toilets, river fishing, and a hiking trail. Pets are allowed.

Reservations, fees: Reservations are accepted. Campsite reservations are available. See State Park Camping Fees and Reserving a Campsite. Open May through September.

Directions: From Superior, go 10 miles east on U.S. Hwy. 2, then one-half mile north on County Road U to the park entrance.

Contact: Amnicon Falls State Park, 6294 S. State Rd. 35, Superior, WI 54880-8326 or 715/398-3000 or 715/399-3111 off-season.

Trip Notes: This park features a series of delightful waterfalls and rapids along the Amnicon River and you can see or photograph them from a covered foot bridge.

In Superior, you might like to tour the "S.S. Meteor" (715/394-5712), the last remaining whaleback freighter. Another possibility is the Old Firehouse and Police Museum (715/394-5712), a former fire station featuring exhibits of police and fire memorabilia.

❸ Waskos Lakeshore Campground

Location: Lake Nebagamon, south of Superior, map 2, grid D3.

Campsites, facilities: There are 116 campsites. Facilities include RV pull-through sites, electric hookups, water, sewer, flush toilets, showers, disposal station, laundry, grocery store, boat ramp and dock, lake boating, canoeing, fishing, swimming, and hiking trail. Boat and seasonal campsite rentals are available. Pets are allowed.

Reservations, fees: The daily fee ranges from $12 to $18. Open May through September.

Directions: From the junction of U.S. Hwy. 53 and County Road L, go 3.5 miles east on County Road L. Then drive one mile north on County Road P to the campground entrance.

Contact: Waskos Lakeshore Campground, 8441 S. County Rd. P, Lake Nebagamon, WI 54849, 715/374-3514.

Trip Notes: Lake Nebagamon is a 3,227-acre body of water with plenty of northern pike, walleye, and panfish.

An interesting place to visit is the White Winter Winery (715/372-5656 or 800/697-2206), which specializes in mead (honey wine). There are free weekend tours and daily wine-tastings. It's at 402 S. George Street in Iron River. Call for hours.

❹ Brule River State Forest Campground

Location: Brule, on the Bois Brule River, map 2, grid D4.

Campsites, facilities: There are 40 campsites. There are no hookups or showers. Facilities include vault toilets, river canoeing, and fishing. There are also biking, hiking, horseback riding, and cross-country ski trails.

Reservations, fees: Reservations are accepted. Campsite reservations are available. See State Park Camping Fees and Reserving a Campsite. Open from April through October.

Directions: From the junction of Hwy. 27 and U.S. Hwy. 2, go one mile west on Hwy. 2, then one-half mile west and one mile south on Ranger Road to the forest campground entrance.

Contact: Brule River State Forest, 6250 S. Ranger Rd., Brule, WI 54820, 715/372-5678.

Trip Notes: The Bois Brule River flows into Lake Superior and is an excellent trout stream. If you want to see fish "up close and personal," take a self-guide tour of the nearby Brule Rearing Station (715/372-4820), which has a fish and wildlife display and features live brook, brown, and rainbow trout, and steelhead. The station is on Hatchery Road off Hwy. 27, south of Brule.

❺ Top O the Morn Resort and Campground

Location: Iron River, on Iron Lake, map 2, grid D5.

Campsites, facilities: There are 54 campsites. Facilities include electric hookups, water, sewer, flush toilets, showers, disposal station, laundry, lake boating, canoeing, fishing, swimming, boat ramp and dock, playground, and planned activities. Boat and seasonal campsite rentals are available. Pets are allowed.

Reservations, fees: The daily fee ranges from $11 to $12. Open year-round. Facilities are fully operational from early May through mid-October.

Directions: From the junction of County Road A, go two miles west on U.S. Hwy. 2, then drive two miles south on Deep Lake Road to the campground entrance.

Contact: Top O the Morn Resort and Campground, 6080 Iron Lake Rd., Iron River, WI 54847, 715/372-4546.

Trip Notes: The Chequamegon National Forest is a mountain biker's playground thanks to an excellent trail system (800/533-7454 or 715/634-4821). There are 28 trails with more than 300 miles of riding in the forest and surrounding region. Just follow the blue-and-white CAMBA signs. The Namekagon Trail winds through beautiful stretches of forests. The Lynch Creek Overlook reveals a vast, gorgeous area of streams, bogs, and tamarack trees.

6 Wildwood Campground

Location: Iron River on Peterson Lake, map 2, grid D5.

Campsites, facilities: There are 25 campsites. Facilities include electric hookups, water, sewer, flush toilets, showers, disposal station, grocery store, lake boating, canoeing, fishing, swimming, and hiking trail. Boat and seasonal campsite rentals are available. Pets are allowed.

Reservations, fees: The daily fee ranges from $14 to $16. Open from mid-May through mid-October.

Directions: From the junction of U.S. Hwy. 2 and Wayside Road, go almost three miles south on Wayside Road, then drive one-half mile east on Wildwood Drive to the campground entrance.

Contact: Wildwood Campground, Carl and Sandra Westlund, Rt. 2 Box 18, Iron River, WI 54847, 715/372-4072, email: wildcamp@win.bright.net

Trip Notes: Off U.S. Hwy. 2 in Ashland, east of Iron River, is the Superior Water-Logged Lumber Co. (715/685-9663; website: www.old logs.com) at 2200 E. Lakeshore Drive. The business recovers and saws rare, old-growth logs from Lake Superior for purchasers who make fine wooden furniture and other items from the wood. The timber was felled and then sank while being rafted to lumber mills across the United States. This "logging boom" era coincided with America's westward growth in the 1800s. Many of these timbers were seedlings when the first explorers reached America's shores in the 15th century.

7 Two Lake Campground

Location: Drummond, southwest of Ashland on Lake Owen, map 2, grid F7.

Campsites, facilities: There are 94 campsites. Facilities include water, vault toilets, disposal station, wheelchair access, two boat ramps, two swimming beaches, and an interpretative hiking trail. The campground also provides lake boating, canoeing, and fishing. Pets are allowed.

Reservations, fees: Reservations are accepted. The daily fee is $12. Open May through October.

Directions: From Drummond, go five miles southeast on Forest Road 213 and 216. Then go east and continue on FR 213 for two miles.

Travel on FR 214 and travel one-half mile to the campground entrance.

Contact: Chequamegon National Forest, Two Lake Campground, 10650 Nyman Ave., Hayward, WI 54843, 715/634-4821 or 715/373-2667, website: www.camptwolakes.com.

Trip Notes: Located on the east side of beautiful 1,323-acre Lake Owen, this campground has shaded sites under towering pines and hardwoods. Anglers can fish for northern pike, walleye, bass, trout, and panfish. In addition, the North Country National Scenic Trail and Porcupine Lake Wilderness are near the campground.

⑧ Namekagon Lake Campground

Location: Near Cable, on Namekagon Lake, map 3, grid G8.

Campsites, facilities: There are 34 campsites. Facilities include water, vault toilets, picnic area, grocery store, boat ramp, fishing pier, swimming beach, and hiking trails.

Reservations, fees: Reservations are accepted. The daily fee is $12. Open May through November.

Directions: From the junction of U.S. Hwy. 63 and County Road M, go 12 miles east on County Road M, then 5.5 miles north on County Road D. Finally, drive about one-third mile north on Forest Road 209 to the campground entrance.

Contact: Chequamegon National Forest, Namekagon Lake Campground, 10650 Nyman Ave., Hayward, WI 54843, 715/634-4821 or 715/373-2667.

Trip Notes: This campground is situated on large Namekagon Lake, the headwaters of the Namekagon River. Recreational opportunities here include excellent fish, wildlife viewing, bike trails, and hiking on the North Country National Scenic Trail. The gently rolling terrain includes hardwood and hemlock forest and wetlands. Numbered posts correspond with a free trail booklet that covers such topics as habitats, the importance of trees, animal adaptations for protection from weather and predators, specialized plants, and geological features.

⑨ Eagle Lodge Campground and Resort

Location: Minong, on Chicog Lake, map 2, grid H1.

Campsites, facilities: There are 70 sites. Facilities include electric hookups, water, flush toilets, showers, disposal station, laundry, boat ramp and dock, and swimming. Cabin and seasonal campsite rentals are available. Near Spooner and Hayward there are many cross-country ski trails. Pets are not allowed.

Reservations, fees: The daily fee ranges from $12 to $25. Open year-round. The facility is fully operational from mid-May through September.

Directions: From the junction of U.S. Hwys. 53 and 77, go seven miles west on Hwy. 77, then 2.5 miles north on Chicog Lake Road to the entrance.

Contact: Eagle Lodge Campground and Resort, W8234 Bald Eagle Dr., Trego, WI 54888, 800/352-1984.

Trip Notes: It is less than 25 miles to Hayward where you can visit the six-acre Fresh Water Fishing Hall of Fame (715/634-4440), noted for its five-story-high muskie-shaped building, a research library, hundreds of mounted fish, 30,000 square feet of displays of classic angling artifacts, 500 outboard motors, 800 fishing reels, 6,000 lures, and hundreds of fishing rods and other tackle.

Nearby you can also enjoy a boat tour of the Chippewa Flowage aboard the "Denum Lacey" at Chippewa Queen Tours (715/462-3874).

10 Hayward-KOA

Location: In Hayward, on the Namekagon River, jap 2, grid H5.

Campsites, facilities: There are 160 campsites. Facilities include RV pull-through sites, electric hookups, water, sewer, flush toilets, showers, disposal station, laundry, grocery, swimming pool, stream fishing, hiking trail, playground, and planned weekend activities. Bike, canoe, tube, and cabin rentals are available, as are canoe and tube float trips. Pets are allowed.

Reservations, fees: The daily fee ranges from $19 to $27. Credit cards are accepted. Open from early May through early October.

Directions: From the junction of U.S. Hwy. 63 and Hwy. 27, go three miles northeast on Hwy. 63 to the campground entrance.

Contact: Hayward-KOA, 11544 N. U.S. Hwy. 63, Hayward, WI 54843, 715/634-2331, email: winkles@hotmail.com.

Trip Notes: At the Appa-Lolly Ranch Riding Stables (715/634-5059) you can take the family horseback riding on guided trails.

11 Lake Chippewa Campground

Location: Near Hayward, on Lake Chippewa, map 2, grid H6.

Campsites, facilities: There are 160 campsites. Facilities include RV pull-through sites, electric hookups, water, sewer, flush toilets, showers, disposal station, laundry, grocery store, swimming, boat ramp and dock, hik-

ing trail, and planned weekend activities. Boat, cabin, and seasonal campsite rentals are available. Horseback riding is available nearby. Pets are allowed.

Reservations, fees: The daily fee ranges from $15 to $25.

Directions: From the junction of U.S. Hwy. 63 and Hwy. 27, go one-half mile south on Hwy. 27, then 13 miles east on County Road B. Finally, drive five miles south on County Road CC to the campground entrance.

Contact: Lake Chippewa Campground, Don and Judy Robinson, 8380 N. County Road CC, Hayward, WI 54843, 715/462-3672, email: lakechip@winmbright.net, website: www.lakechip.com.

Trip Notes: Relive the days of lumbering at the Lumberjack World Championships (800/724-2992) held each year in late July.

12 Presque Isle-Stockton Campground

Location: Stockton Island, off Bayfield, map 3, grid A4.

Campsites, facilities: There are 21 campsites. There are no hookups or showers, but it does have vault toilets, boating, fishing, swimming, and hiking trails. Pets are allowed.

Reservations, fees: No daily fee, just a $15 camping permit (applies to any campground in the Apostle Islands National Lakeshore for a 14-day period). Open year-round.

Directions: The island is accessible by excursion boat during the months of July and August or by private boat.

Contact: Presque Isle-Stockton Campground, 415 Washington Ave., Bayfield, WI 54814, 715/779-3397, website: www.nps.gov /apis.

Trip Notes: The Bayfield Peninsula is the gateway to the stunning Apostle Islands National Lakeshore, which has 22 gem-like coastal islands and 12 miles of mainland Lake Superior shoreline. This area, especially beautiful during the color season in fall, features pristine stretches of sand beach, spectacular sea caves, remnant old-growth forest, resident bald eagles and black bears, and the largest collection of lighthouses anywhere in the National Park System.

13 Big Bay State Park

Location: Madeline Island, one of the Apostle Islands in Lake Superior, map 3, grid B3.

Campsites, facilities: There are 60 campsites. There are no hookups. Facilities include showers, nearby disposal station, nature center, hiking and cross-country ski trails, nearby lake boating, canoeing, fishing, and swimming. Pets are allowed. In winter, there are up to 30 campsites with no electric hookups and only hand-pumped water.

Reservations, fees: Reservations are accepted. Campsite reservations are available. See State Park Camping Fees and Reserving a Campsite. Open year-round.

Directions: Take the ferry about three miles offshore to Madeline Island, then go five miles east on County Road H to the entrance.

Contact: Big Bay State Park, 141 S. 3rd St., Box 589, Bayfield, WI 54814-0589 or 715/747-6425 or 715/779-4020.

Trip Notes: Located on Madeline Island, the park features picturesque sandstone bluffs, lake caves, and 1.5 miles of Lake Superior shoreline.

Scenic, guided cruises of the Apostle Islands are available from the Apostle Islands Cruise Service (715/779-3925; website: www.apostleisland.com). Open daily from mid-May through mid-October, but reservations recommended.

Stop at the Madeline Island Museum (715/747-2415). Historically, the island is the spiritual home of the Ojibwa Indians, and was an important fur-trading center for the French in the 17th century. Over the next 300 years, the island saw the arrival of missionaries, loggers, fishermen, boat builders, and miners. The log museum and Casper Center capture the island's history.

14 West End Park

Location: Washburn, on Lake Superior's Chequamegon Bay, map 3, grid C1.

Campsites, facilities: There are 46 campsites. Facilities include electric hookups, showers, disposal station, lake boating, boat ramp and dock, canoeing, fishing, swimming, hiking trail, and playground. Pets are allowed.

Reservations, fees: The daily fee ranges from $11 to $15. Open from mid-April through mid-October.

Directions: From the junction of Hwy. 13 and 8th Avenue, go four blocks south on 8th Avenue to the park entrance.

Contact: Washburn Recreation Center, West End Municipal Park, P.O. Box 638, Washburn, WI 54891, 715/373-6174.

Trip Notes: The Washburn Historical Museum (715/373-5591), which is housed in an historic bank building, features changing fine art exhibits, local and regional history, and dioramas. It's at 1 E. Bayfield Street.

15 Memorial Park

Location: Washburn, on Lake Superior's Chequamegon Bay, map 3, grid C1.

Campsites, facilities: There are 51 campsites. Facilities include electric hookups, showers, disposal station, lake boating, canoeing, fishing, and swimming. Pets are allowed.

Reservations, fees: The daily fee ranges from $11 to $15. Open from mid-May through mid-October.

Directions: From Washburn, go north on Memorial Park Lane to the park entrance.

Contact: Washburn Recreation Center, Memorial Municipal Park, P.O. Box 638, Washburn, WI 54891, 715/373-6174.

Trip Notes: The Washburn area offers class-A trout streams, sandy beaches, and a well-equipped marina.

While you're in the area, be sure to visit the Northern Great Lakes Visitors Center (715/685-9983), three miles west of Ashland on U.S. Hwy. 2, just west of the intersection with Hwy. 13. It features an observation tower; 100-seat theater; and regional visitor information center for Wisconsin, Minnesota, and Michigan's Upper Peninsula. There are also historic exhibits, educational programs, and a boardwalk trail. The center is next to Whittlesey Creek National Wildlife Refuge.

16 Prentice Park

Location: Ashland on Chequamegon Bay on Lake Superior, map 3, grid D1.

Campsites, facilities: There are eight campsites for small RVs and 10 campsites for tents. Facilities include electric hookups. There are no showers. The campground provides lake boating, canoeing, swimming, lake/pond fishing, playground, and hiking trail. Pets are allowed.

Reservations, fees: This municipal park does not accept reservations. The daily fee is

$10 for RVs and $7 for tents. Open May through October.

Directions: The west city limits off U.S. Hwy. 2 is the park entrance.

Contact: Prentice Park, City of Ashland, 601 Main St. W., Ashland, WI 54806, 715/682-7071.

Trip Notes: Several interesting places to visit are the Northern Great Lakes Center and Northern Wisconsin History Center (715/685-9983); the South Shore Brewery, a microbrewery in the fully-restored Soo Line Deport (715/682-4200); and the Superior Water-Logged Lumber Company, which salvages and saws 100-year old logs from Lake Superior (715/685-9663).

17 Kreher RV Park

Location: Ashland on Chequamegon Bay on Lake Superior, map 3, grid D1.

Campsites, facilities: There are 36 campsites for RVs only. Facilities include electric hookups, water, disposal station, flush toilets, and showers. The campground provides lake boating, canoeing, fishing, swimming, playground, and hiking trail. Pets are allowed.

Reservations, fees: This municipal park does not accept reservations. The daily fee for RVs is $15. Open from mid-May through mid-October.

Directions: In Ashland off U.S. Hwy. 2.

Contact: Kreher RV Park, City of Ashland, 601 Main St. W., Ashland, WI 54806, 715/682-7071.

Trip Notes: Take a scenic ride along the Lake Superior shore to Bayfield and the Bayfield Maritime Museum (715/779-3925). Here, you'll find hands-on demonstrations and exhibits on commercial fishing, lighthouses, sailor crafts, shipwrecks, and more. The museum is at 131 S. 1st Street.

18 Copper Falls State Park

Location: Mellen, on the Bad River, map 3, grid F3.

Campsites, facilities: There are 55 campsites. Facilities include electric hookups, vault toilets, showers, disposal station, and grocery store. The campground also provides lake boating, canoeing, swimming, lake and river fishing, and bike, hiking, and cross-country ski trails. Pets are allowed. In winter, there are four campsites with electric hookups and water.

Reservations, fees: Reservations are accepted. Campsite reservations are available. See State Park Camping Fees and Reserving a Campsite. Open year-round.

Directions: From the junction of Hwys. 13 and 169, travel two miles northeast on Hwy. 169 to the park entrance.

Contact: Copper Falls State Park, Rt. 1, Box 17AA, Mellen, WI 54546, 715/274-5123.

Trip Notes: Ancient lava flows, deep gorges, and a spectacular waterfall that drops 40 feet into the Bad River make this one of the state's most scenic state parks. Log buildings from the CCC era in the 1930s add a special charm. For bikers, there are three terrific bike trails to ride. The Takesin is a single-track trail with views of the Bad River. The Vahtera Trail rolls through a birch and maple forest. The North Country National Scenic Trail skirts Loon Lake and crosses the marshland and woods to Mellen.

19 Day Lake Campground

Location: Near Clam Lake on Day Lake, map 3, grid G1.

Campsites, facilities: There are 52 campsites. Facilities include water, vault toilets, grocery store, boat ramp, swimming beach, fishing pier, and playground.

Reservations, fees: Reservations are accepted. The daily fee is $12. Open from late May through early December.

Directions: From Clam Lake, travel one mile north on County Road GG, then three-quarters of a mile west on Forest Road 1298 to the campground entrance.

Contact: Chequamegon National Forest, Day Lake Campground, 10650 Nyman Ave., Hayward, WI 54843, 715/634-4821 or 715/264-2511.

Trip Notes: Towering pines shade the campsites at Day Lake, which features a one-mile interpretive trail that provides tree and plant information. The 632-acre lake features excellent muskie fishing and legal-sized fish have been caught off the fishing pier. The campground is also known for eagles, loons, and deer visiting near the campsites.

20 Interstate State Park

Location: St. Croix Falls, on the St. Croix River, map 4, grid E3.

Campsites, facilities: There are 85 campsites. There are no hookups. Facilities include showers, disposal station, lake swimming, and boat ramp. There are hiking, self-guided nature, snowmobiling, and cross-country ski trails. Pets are allowed.

Reservations, fees: Reservations are accepted. Campsite reservations are available. See State Park Camping Fees and Reserving a Campsite. Open April through mid-November.

Directions: From St. Croix Falls, go one mile south on Hwy. 35 to the park entrance.

Contact: Interstate State Park, P.O. Box 703, St. Croix Falls, WI 54024, 715/483-3747.

Trip Notes: A deep forge, called the "Dalles of the St. Croix," is the scenic focus of Wisconsin's oldest state park. The park's Ice Age Interpretive Center features photographs, murals, and other information about the great glaciers. For the serious biker, hiker, and snowmobiler, the Gandy Dance State Bike Trail (715/349-2157) begins at St. Croix Falls and runs along the 47-mile railway bed trail north to Danbury. A second 51-mile segment through Minnesota connects Danbury to Superior, Wisconsin.

21 Apple River Campground

Location: Somerset, on the Apple Falls Flowage, map 4, grid G3.

Campsites, facilities: There are 465 campsites. Facilities include electric hookups, water, flush toilets, showers, disposal station, grocery store, two swimming pools, river canoeing, fishing, hiking trail, and playground. Pets are allowed.

Reservations, fees: The daily fee ranges from $20 to $45. Open from late May through August.

Directions: From the junction of Hwys. 64 and 35, go one-half mile north on Hwy. 35 to the campground entrance.

Contact: Apple River Campground, Box 307, Somerset, WI 54025, 800/637-8936.

Trip Notes: The first half of the canoe trip down the Apple River offers relaxed family floating. The last half features a wild rapids area with a walkway along the side of the river for the less adventurous. A number of outfitters around Somerset provide rentals and transportation for this popular river trip.

22 Willow River State Park

Location: Hudson, on Willow River and Willow Falls, map 4, grid H3.

Campsites, facilities: There are 78 campsites. Facilities include electric hookups, showers, disposal station, lake swimming, boat ramp, and river fishing. Biking, hiking, self-guided nature and cross-country ski trails are available. In winter, there are six plowed campsites and 72 backpack sites. All have electric hookups and water. Pets are allowed.

Reservations, fees: Reservations are accepted. Campsite reservations are available. See State Park Camping Fees and Reserving a Campsite. Open year-round.

Directions: From the junction of I-94 and U.S. Hwy. 12, go three miles north on Hwy. 12 to Country Road A to the park entrance.

Contact: Willow River State Park, 1034 County Road A, Hudson, WI 54016, 715/386-5931.

Trip Notes: A lake trout stream, sandy beach, prairie remnants, and a nature center are featured on 2,891 acres of rolling countryside. Spectacular views of the historic Willow Falls and the Willow River Gorge can be seen and photographed.

23 Bay Park Resort and Campground

Location: Northwest of Trego, on Trego Lake, map 5, grid A2.

Campsites, facilities: There are 75 campsites with a separate tent area. Facilities including RV pull-through sites, electric hookups, water, sewer, flush toilets, showers, disposal station, laundry, grocery store, swimming pool, boat ramp, hiking trail, shuffleboard courts, playground, and planned activities. Boat and cottage rentals are available. Two cross-country ski trails are nearby.

Reservations, fees: The daily fee ranges from $20 to $24. Open year-round. The facility is fully operational April to November.

Directions: From Trego, go three miles west on County Road E, then three miles north on County Road K to the campground entrance.

Contact: Bay Park Resort and Campground, Dan and Anita Frase, N8347 Bay Park Rd., Trego, WI 54888, 715/635-2840.

Trip Notes: There are two outstanding cross-country ski trails—Leisure Lake Trail (800/234-6635 or 800/367-3306) and Trego Lake Trail (715/635-8346). Trego is the place to arrange a canoe or tube trip down the Namekagon River. If that's too wild and wooly for you, drive south to Sarona and visit the Hunt Hill Audubon Sanctuary, a residential environmental learning center on more than 500 acres of forest, meadows, and glacial lakes (800/367-3306).

24 Trail's End Resort and Campground

Location: Near Hayward, on Lac Courte Oreilles, map 5, grid A5.

Campsites, facilities: There are 65 campsites. Facilities include RV pull-through sites, electric hookups, water, sewer, flush toilets, showers, disposal station, boat ramp and dock, swimming, and playground. Boat and cottage rentals are available. Pets are allowed.

Reservations, fees: The daily fee ranges from $15 to $30. Open May through mid-October.

Directions: From the junction of U.S. Hwy. 63 and Hwy. 27, go six and three-quarter miles

south on Hwy. 27, then six and one-quarter miles east on County Road K to the entrance.

Contact: Trail's End Resort and Campground, Mike and Michelle Horman, 8080 N. Country Road K, Hayward, WI 54843-2161 or 715/634-2423, website: www.haywardlakes.com/trail send.htm

Trip Notes: Near Hayward, you'll find the Sawyer County Historical Society Museum (715/634-8053; website: www.sawyercounty hist.org) at 15715 Cty. Hwy. B East. The three-story 1939 building has two floors of exhibits about the Lac Courte Oreilles Reservation, the logging industry, and the CCCs. There's a gift shop with many books on local history.

25 Scenic View Campground

Location: Spooner, map 5, grid B1.

Campsites, facilities: There are 45 campsites. Facilities include electric hookups, water, flush toilets, showers, disposal station, grocery store, boat ramp and dock, and hiking trail. Boat and seasonal campsite rentals are available. Pets are allowed.

Reservations, fees: The daily fee ranges from $20 to $25. Open May through September.

Directions: From the junction of U.S. Hwy. 63 and Hwy. 70, go nine and one-quarter miles west on Hwy. 70, and then one-half mile south on Scenic View Lane to the campground entrance.

Contact: Scenic View Campground, Carol Haseltine, 24560 Science View Ln., Spooner, WI 54801, 715/468-2510, email: cline@space star.net, website: www.scenicviewcamp ground.com.

Trip Notes: Have you been trying to catch a big muskie? If you haven't had the best of luck at least you can see how these large predators are raised at the Governor

Tommy G. Thompson State Fish Hatchery (715/635-4147), the largest muskie-rearing hatchery in the world. You can also see walleye or northern pike at the facility.

26 Red Barn Campground

Location: Shell Lake, south of Spooner, map 5, grid C1.

Campsites, facilities: There are 90 campsites. Facilities include electric hookups, water, sewer, flush toilets, showers, mini-golf, playground, hiking trail, horseback riding, and horse-drawn hayrides. At the Shell Lake Memorial Park nearby, you can swim, boat, canoe, and fish. It also has a boat ramp. Seasonal campsite rentals are available. Pets are allowed.

Reservations, fees: The daily fee ranges from $15 to $23. Open from late May through August.

Directions: From Shell Lake, go one-half mile north on U.S. Hwy. 63, then two miles east on County Road B to the entrance.

Contact: Red Barn Campground, Lee and Dotty Swan, W6820 Country Rd. B, Shell Lake, WI 54871, 715/468-2575 or 877/468-2575, website: www.redbarncampground.com.

Trip Notes: Shell Lake is a 2,580-acre lake that harbors muskie, walleye, smallmouth bass, and panfish.

Don't miss the Museum of Woodcarving (715/468-7100; website: www.roadsideamerica.com/museumofwoodcarving) on Hwy. 63 N, in Shell Lake. It has 100 life-sized carvings depicting the life of Christ, as well as 400 miniature carvings.

27 Rice Lake-Haugen KOA

Location: Rice Lake, on Rice Lake, map 5, grid D3.

Campsites, facilities: There are 106 campsites. Facilities include electric hookups, water, sewer, flush toilets, showers, disposal station, laundry, grocery store, swimming pool, lake swimming, boat ramp and dock, and hiking trail. Bike, boat, cabin, and cottage rentals are available. Pets are allowed.

Reservations, fees: The daily fee ranges from $20 to $26. Open May to mid-October.

Directions: From the junction of U.S. Hwy. 53 and Hwy. 48, go 10 miles north on Hwy. 53, then one mile east on the campground driveway to the entrance.

Contact: Rice Lake-Haugen KOA, Dave and Mary Johelson, 1876 29-3/4 Ave., Rice Lake, WI 54866, 715/234-2360 or 800/562-3460, email: ricelakekow@aol.com, website: www.koa.com/where/wi/4908htm.

Trip Notes: Rice Lake, which was founded as a logging camp in the 1850s, has the Pioneer Village Museum (800/523-6318), just south of town. It re-creates what life was like during the logging era.

Also, the nearby Tuscobia State Trail (715/634-6513) offers 74 miles of biking, hiking, snowmobiling, and cross-country skiing from Rice Lake to Park Falls.

28 Thornapple River Campground

Location: Ladysmith, on the Thornapple River, map 5, grid D8.

Campsites, facilities: There are 25 campsites, including a separate tent area. Facilities include RV pull-through sites, electric hookups, water, flush toilets, showers, disposal station, river swimming, canoeing, fishing, hiking trail, and a playground. Nearby Lake Flambeau and the Flambeau River also provide boating and fishing. Cottage rentals are available. Pets are allowed.

Reservations, fees: The daily fee ranges from $12 to $17. Open May through September.

Directions: From the junction of Hwy. 27 and U.S. Hwy. 8, go four miles north on Hwy. 27 to the campground entrance.

Contact: Thornapple River Campground, Carolyn Kenny, N6599 Hwy. 27, Ladysmith, WI 54848, 715/532-7034.

Trip Notes: Lake Flambeau and Flambeau River contain 1,745 acres with muskie, walleye, and smallmouth bass.

For something different, you might enjoy a train ride aboard Ladysmith Rail Excursions (715/532-2642 or 800/535-RUSK; website: www.2719.com).

29 Ken's Kampsite

Location: Chetek, on Prairie Lake, map 5, grid F3.

Campsites, facilities: There are 60 campsites, including a separate tent area. Facilities include electric hookups, water, flush toilets, showers, disposal station, boat ramp, and lake swimming. Boat and seasonal campsite rentals are available. Pets are allowed.

Reservations, fees: The daily fee ranges from $17 to $18. Open May through September.

Directions: From the junction of U.S. Hwy. 53 and County Road I, drive one-half mile east on County Road I, then three-quarters of a mile north on County Road SS. Then go two miles north on County Road M, 1.5 miles northwest on Gregarson Slough Road, and

one-half mile east on Bronstad Beach Lane to the entrance.

Contact: Ken's Kampsite, Bea Pfaff, P.O. Box 222, Chetek, WI 54728, 715/859-2887.

Trip Notes: You might enjoy visiting Sarona, just north of Rice Lake. There is a 500-acre wildlife sanctuary, the Hunt Hill Nature Center and Audubon Sanctuary (715/635-6543). It has wooded glacial hills, three clear lakes, old-growth forest, and northern bogs. You can see nesting osprey and loons, as well as many other species.

30 Chetek River Campground

Location: Chetek, on the Chetek River, map 5, grid F3.

Campsites, facilities: There are 100 campsites. Facilities include electric hookups, water, sewer, flush toilets, showers, disposal station, swimming pool, river swimming, fishing, boating (no motors), dock, shuffleboard courts, mini-golf, and a playground. Canoe rentals are available. Pets are allowed.

Reservations, fees: Reservations are recommended. The daily fee ranges from $18 to $20. Open May through September.

Directions: From the junction of U.S. Hwy. 53 and County Road I, go one-quarter mile west on County Road I, then three-quarters of a mile west on River Road to the entrance.

Contact: Chetek River Campground, Christine Gay and Jan Gebhardt, 590 24th St., Chetek, WI, 54728, 715/924-2440, email: camp @chetekriver.com, website: www.chetek river.com.

Trip Notes: Fish the Chetek Chain of Lakes; it's noted for its northern pike, walleye, bass, and panfish.

If you're feeling more adventurous, the Indianhead Sport Parachute Club (715/289-4440; website: www.skydiverwissota.org) is located on County Road K near Chippewa Falls. You can take skydiving lessons April through October, weather permitting, and see part of Wisconsin from the air.

31 Brunet Island State Park

Location: Cornell, in the middle of the Chippewa and Fisher Rivers, map 5, grid G7.

Campsites, facilities: There are 69 campsites. Facilities include electric hookups, disposal station, river swimming, and boat ramp and dock. There are also hiking, snowmobiling, and cross-country ski trails. Pets are allowed.

Reservations, fees: Reservations are accepted. Campsite reservations are available. See State Park Camping Fees and Reserving a Campsite. Open May through September.

Directions: From Cornell, go one mile north on Park Road to the park entrance.

Contact: Brunet Island State Park, 23125 255th St., Cornell, WI 54732, 715/239-6888.

Trip Notes: Framed by the Chippewa and Fisher Rivers just northwest of Cornell, this 1,030-acre island park's bay and lagoons offer you a quiet respite. The main park development lies on an island in the Chippewa River.

For a side trip, see the Chippewa Falls Museum of Industry and Technology (715/720-9206, website: www.execpc.com/~cfmit/). There's a great deal to explore in various changing exhibits.

32 Black Lake Campground

Location: Winter, on Black Lake, map 6, grid A1.

Campsites, facilities: There are 29 campsites, including three walk-in sites. Facili-

ties include water pumps, vault toilets, picnic area, two boat ramps, swimming beach, fishing, and a four-mile interpretive hiking trail along a wooded shoreline.

Reservations, fees: The daily fee is $10. Open May through late October.

Directions: From Hayward, travel east on Hwy. B for 26 miles to the intersection of Hwy. B, Hwy. W and Fishtrap Road. Turn north (left) on Fishtrap Road and drive 4.9 miles to the intersection of Forest Road 173 and drive nearly one-half mile to the entrance. Turn east (right) on the campground road and go one-half mile.

Contact: Chequamegon National Forest, Black Lake Campground, 10650 Nyman Ave., Hayward, WI 54843, 715/634-4821.

Trip Notes: The four-mile Black Lake Interpretive Trail features logging history starting with the white pine era of 1880-1900, moving to the hemlock-hardwoods era of 1909-1924, and ending with selective cutting under the U.S. Forest Service. Stops include a white spruce plantation, the site of a pine-era logging camp, and an abandoned Stout Spur of Edward Hines Lumber Company's railroad.

33 Connor's Lake Campground and Lake of the Pines Campground

Location: Both campgrounds are at Winter and each one is on a lake, map 6, grid B3.

Campsites, facilities: Each campground has 30 sites. Facilities include vault toilets. Connor's Lake provides a disposal station. Both campgrounds offer lake boating, canoeing, fishing, swimming beach, and hiking trail.

Reservations, fees: Reservations are accepted. Campsite reservations are available.

See State Park Camping Fees and Reserving a Campsite. Connor's Lake is open June through early September. Lake of the Pines is open year-round.

Directions: Take Hwy. 8 to Hawkins. Then, drive down County Road M north for 18 miles to County Road W. Turn west (left) and go about three-quarters of a mile to Lake of the Pines Road. Go north (right) about two miles to campgrounds.

Contact: Flambeau State Forest, Connor's Lake/Lake of the Pines, W1613 County Rd. W, Winter, WI 54896 715/332-5271.

Trip Notes: Both campgrounds are at opposite ends of adjacent lakes. About 30 miles west of Winter is Couderay where you can visit "The Hideout" (715/945-2746), once the Northwood's retreat of Chicago gangster Al Capone. It's now a restaurant and offers tours of the complex.

34 Lake Pepin Campground

Location: Pepin, on the Mississippi River/Lake Pepin, map 7, grid E7.

Campsites, facilities: There are 47 campsites. Facilities include electric, water, and sewer hookups on all sites, flush toilets, showers, and disposal station. The campground also offers a playground and outdoor activities. The Mississippi River and Lake Pepin provide boating, canoeing, and fishing. Pets are allowed.

Reservations, fees: The daily fee ranges from $10 to $14. Open April through November.

Directions: From the junction of Hwy. 25 and Hwy. 35, go 6.5 miles northwest on Hwy. 35 and then 500 feet north on Locust Street to the campground entrance.

Contact: Lake Pepin Campground, 305 Elm St., Pepin, WI 54759, 715/442-2012.

Trip Notes: If you tuned in each week to watch one of America's favorite prairie families on "Little House on the Prairie," you'll enjoy a visit to the Laura Ingalls Wilder—the author—Wayside and Cabin to see a replica of the now-famous "Little House in the Big Woods" (715/442-3161). Or, you might enjoy a visit to the Pepin Railroad Depot Museum in Laura Ingalls Wilder Park to see exhibits detailing the area's logging, steamboating, and railroad history (715/442-3011).

35 Edgewater Acres Campground

Location: Menomonie, on the Red Cedar River, map 8, grid A1.

Campsites, facilities: There are 69 campsites, including a separate tent area. Facilities include electric hookups, water, flush toilets, showers, disposal station, grocery store, swimming pool, boat ramp and dock, river and lake boating and canoeing, fishing, and playground. A biking and hiking trail are nearby. Boat rentals are available. Pets are allowed.

Reservations, fees: The daily fee ranges from $13 to $16. Open May through mid-October.

Directions: From the junction of I-94 and Hwy. 25, take exit 41 and go two miles north on Hwy. 25. Then drive 1.5 miles east on County Road BB and three-quarters of a mile south on Cedar Falls Road to the campground.

Contact: Edgewater Acres Campground, Tina King, E5468 670th Ave., Menomonie, WI 54751, 715/235-3291, email: info@mycamp ground.com, website: www.my campground .com.

Trip Notes: Campers can go hiking, biking, snowmobiling, or cross-country skiing on the 14.5-mile Red Cedar State Trail (888/523-3866) from Menomonie to the Chippewa River Valley that includes an 846-foot former railroad bridge and connects to the 20-mile Chippewa River State Trail in Dunnville.

36 Twin Spring Camping Resort

Location: Menomonie, on the Red Cedar River, map 8, grid A1.

Campsites, facilities: There are 75 campsites. Facilities include RV pull-through sites, electric hookups, water, sewer, flush toilets, showers, disposal station, laundry, grocery store, swimming pool, boat ramp, lake and river boating, canoeing, fishing, hiking trail, and playground. Biking, hiking, snowmobiling, and cross-country ski trails are nearby. Cabin rentals are available. Pets are allowed.

Reservations, fees: The daily fee ranges from $16 to $24. Open year-round. The facility is fully operational May through September.

Directions: From the junction of I-94 and Hwy. 25, take exit 41 and go one block north on Hwy. 25, then two miles east on Cedar Falls Road to the campground entrance.

Contact: Twin Spring Camping Resort, John and Lillian Statz, N6572 530th St., Menomonie, WI 54751, tel.715/235-9321.

Trip Notes: The Wilson Place Museum (800/826-6970 or 715/235-2283) will take you back in time to the area's lumbering days with displays of local history and the furnishings of lumber baron Joseph Knapp.

37 O'Neil Creek Campground and RV Park

Location: Chippewa Falls, north of Eau Claire, map 8, grid A5.

Campsites, facilities: There are 360 campsites. Facilities include RV pull-through sites, electric hookups, water, sewer, flush toilets, showers, disposal station, laundry, grocery store, river swimming, boat ramp and dock, lake and river fishing, mini-golf, hiking trail, playground, and planned activities. Bike, boat, cabin, and seasonal campsite rentals are available. Pets are allowed.

Reservations, fees: The daily fee ranges from $11 to $20. Credit cards are accepted. Open from mid-April through mid-October.

Directions: From the junction of Hwy. 124 and U.S. Hwy. 53, go five miles north on Hwy. 53, then two miles east on County Road S. Drive two miles north on Hwy. 124 and three-quarters of a mile east on 105th Avenue to the campground entrance.

Contact: O'Neil Creek Campground and RV Park, Mike and Judy Rabska, 14956 105th Ave., Chippewa Falls, WI 54729, 715/723-6581.

Trip Notes: Bikers, hikers, and snowmobilers will want to experience the scenic Old Abe State Trail (715/723-0331 or 866/723-0331) that runs along the Chippewa River for about 20 miles from Chippewa Falls to Cornell. It follows agricultural and undeveloped lands between Lake Wissota State Park and Brunet Island State Park at Cornell. A parallel horse trail connects with Lake Wissota State Park.

38 Duncan Creek Campground

Location: Chippewa Falls, on Duncan Creek, map 8, grid A5.

Campsites, facilities: There are 42 campsites. Facilities include electric hookups, water, flush toilets, showers, disposal station, stream fishing, and playground. Lake boating, canoeing, fishing, swimming, and hiking and biking trails are nearby. Pets are allowed.

Reservations, fees: The daily fee is about $20. Open May through September.

Directions: From the junction of Hwy. 53 and County Road S, take exit 105, then go one mile east on County Road S and one mile north on County Road Q to the campground entrance.

Contact: Duncan Creek Campground, 12374 102nd Ave., Chippewa Falls, WI 54729, 715/720-4686.

Trip Notes: Chippewa Falls is a charming old town that has preserved its buildings. The city's oldest business is the Leinenkugel Brewing Company (715/723-5557), established in 1867. You will want to visit the brewery and gift shop. Tours, which include the brewery museum and tasting room, may be arranged by appointment.

❸❾ Lake Wissota State Park

Location: Chippewa Falls, on Lake Wissota, map 8, grid A6.

Campsites, facilities: There are 81 campsites. Facilities include electric hookups, showers, disposal station, lake boating, canoeing, fishing, swimming, and nature center with programs. There are also biking, hiking, horseback riding, snowmobiling, and cross-country ski trails. Pets are allowed.

Reservations, fees: Reservations are accepted. Campsite reservations are available. See State Park Camping Fees and Reserving a Campsite. Open April through September.

Directions: From the junction of U.S. Hwy. 53 and County Road S, go seven miles east on County Road S and two miles east on County Road O to the park entrance.

Contact: Lake Wissota State Park, 18127 County Road O, Chippewa Falls, WI 54729, 715/382-4574.

Trip Notes: This park has 1,062 acres of primarily young forest and open prairie on a 6,300-acre man-made lake. It attracts hikers, campers, recreational boaters, and anglers, who fish for walleye, muskie, and bass.

❹⓿ Coon Fork Lake Park

Location: Augusta, on Coon Fork Lake, map 8, grid C8.

Campsites, facilities: There are 88 campsites in this county park. Facilities include electric hookups, showers, disposal station, lake swimming, boating (electric motors only), canoeing, fishing, boat ramp, hiking trail, and a playground. Boat rentals are available. Pets are allowed.

Reservations, fees: The daily fee ranges from $11 to $15. Open year-round.

Directions: From Augusta, go one mile east on U.S. Hwy. 12, then four miles north on County Road CF (Coon Fork Road) to the park entrance.

Contact: Eau Claire County Parks and Forests, Coon Fork Lake Park, 227 First Ave., West, Altoona, WI 54720, 715/839-4738.

Trip Notes: Augusta has an Amish settlement of more than 150 families. Guided tours of the community are available and handcrafted Amish goods are sold at the Wood Shed (715/286-5404). If you've never seen how our forefathers ground their grain into flour, you'll also want to visit the Dells Mill Museum (715/286-2714), a five-story, water-powered historic grist mill.

❹❶ Osseo Camping Resort

Location: Osseo, Southeast of Eau Claire, map 8, grid D7.

Campsites, facilities: There are 100 campsites, including a separate tent area. Facilities include electric hookup, water, sewer, flush toilets, showers, disposal station, laundry, grocery store, swimming pool, mini-golf, nature trail, and planned weekend activities. Fishing and a golf course are nearby. Pets are allowed.

Reservations, fees: The daily fee ranges from $15 to $20. Credit cards are accepted. Open from mid-April through mid-October.

Directions: From the junction of I-94 and U.S. Hwy. 10, take exit 88 and go one-quarter mile east on Hwy. 10, then one-quarter mile south on Oak Grove Road to the entrance.

Contact: Osseo Camping Resort, Tom and Joy Levake, 50483 Oak Grove Rd., Osseo, WI 54758, 715/587-2102 or 888/349-6399, email: osseocmp@win.bright.net.

Trip Notes: The campground is about 20 miles southeast of Eau Claire where you can visit the Paul Bunyan Logging Camp, an authentic reproduction of an 1890s logging camp located in 134-acre Carson Park (715/835-6200).

42 Triple R Resort

Location: Northfield, on Lake Mariah, map 8, grid E8.

Campsites, facilities: There are 25 campsites, including a separate tent area. Facilities include electric hookups, water, flush toilets, showers, disposal station, grocery store, lake swimming, boat dock (no motors allowed), and hiking trail. Biking, hiking, and snowmobile trails are nearby. Boat rentals are available. Pets are allowed.

Reservations, fees: Reservations are requested. The daily fee ranges from $12 to $21. Credit cards are accepted. Open year-round. The facility is fully operational April through November.

Directions: From I-94, take exit 98 and go 500 feet east on Hwy. 121 and then one mile north and northeast on Ellingson Road. Follow the signs to the campground entrance.

Contact: Triple R Resort, the Reinkes, N11818 Hixton Levis Rd., Hixton, WI 54635, 715/964-8777 or 888/963-8777, email: rrrresort @aol.com.

Trip Notes: There is excellent biking, hiking, snowmobiling, cross-country skiing, and horseback riding on the Black River State Forest Trails. If you wish, you can visit antique and craft shops near this campground.

43 Merrick State Park

Location: Fountain City, on the Mississippi River, map 8, grid G2.

Campsites, facilities: There are 67 campsites. Facilities include electric hookups, vault toilets, showers, disposal station, river swimming, boating, canoeing, marina, fishing pier, and nature center. There are also hiking and cross-country ski trails. Pets are allowed.

Reservations, fees: Reservations are accepted. Campsite reservations are available. See State Park Camping Fees and Reserving a Campsite. Open year-round.

Directions: From Fountain City, go three miles north on Hwy. 35 to the park entrance.

Contact: Merrick State Park, S2965 State Rd. 35, Box 127, Fountain City, WI 54629-0127 or 608/687-4936.

Trip Notes: Located on the backwaters of the Mississippi River, the park is a year-round haven for anglers. Its marshy bayous are home to egrets and herons.

River's Edge Campground

Location: Galesville, on the Black River, map 8, grid H6.

Campsites, facilities: There are 150 campsites. Facilities include electric hookups, flush toilets, showers, disposal station, grocery store, swimming pool, river boating, canoeing, fishing, mini-golf, shuffleboard courts, hiking trail, and planned weekend activities. Pets are allowed.

Reservations, fees: The daily fee ranges from $14 to $17. Open May through October.

Directions: From the junction of Hwys. 54 and 53, go about three and one-quarter miles south on Hwy. 53, and then one-third mile southeast on Pow Wow Lane to the entrance.

Contact: River's Edge Campground, W16751 Pow Wow Ln., Galesville, WI 54630, 608/582-2995.

Trip Notes: Drive to Trempealeau and visit the 5,600-acre Trempealeau National Wildlife Refuge (608/539-2311), featuring nature trails and a five-mile driving tour.

Perrot State Park

Location: Trempealeau, at the confluence of the Trempealeau and Mississippi Rivers, map 8, grid H5.

Campsites, facilities: There are 98 campsites. Facilities include electric hookups, showers, disposal station, boat ramp, canoeing, and fishing. There are also biking, hiking, and cross-country ski trails. Pets are allowed.

Reservations, fees: Reservations are accepted. Campsite reservations are available. See State Park Camping Fees and Reserving a Campsite. Open year-round.

Directions: From Trempealeau, go one mile northwest on River Road to the park entrance.

Contact: Perrot State Park, W26247 Sullivan Rd., P.O. Box 407, Trempealeau, WI 54661-0407 or 608/534-6409.

Trip Notes: The park's 1,243 acres are nestled among 500-foot bluffs where the Trempealeau and Mississippi Rivers meet. It features breathtaking river vistas and ancient Indian burial mounds.

 Hixton-Alma Center KOA

Location: Alma Center, west of the Trempealeau River, map 9, grid E1.

Campsites, facilities: There are 66 campsites, including a separate tent area. Facilities include electric hookups, water, sewer, flush toilets, showers, disposal station, laundry, grocery store, swimming pool, pond fishing, and hiking trail. Cabin rentals are available. Lake and river boating, canoeing, fishing, and biking, snowmobiling, and cross-country trails are located nearby. Pets are allowed.

Reservations, fees: The daily fee ranges from $18 to $24. Credit cards are accepted. Open April through November.

Directions: From the junction of I-94 and Hwy. 95, take exit 105 and go 3.5 miles east on Hwy. 105 to the campground entrance.

Contact: Hixton-Alma Center KOA, Jim and Donna Rankin, N9657 State Rd. 95, Alma Center, WI 54611, 715/964-2508 or 800/562-2680 for reservations, email: koajimdj@cuttingedge.net.

Trip Notes: There is good fishing nearby on Lakes Wazee and Arbutus. The Trempealeau River is an excellent trout stream with many feeder tributaries.

47 Lost Falls Resort and Campground

Location: Black River Falls, on the Black River, map 9, grid F1.

Campsites, facilities: There are 30 campsites, including a separate tent area. There are also some riverside sites. Facilities include electric hookups, water, sewer, flush toilets, showers, grocery store, river swimming, boating, fishing, canoe landing, and hiking trail. Boat, trailer, and cabin rentals are available. Pets are allowed in camping area. No pets or smoking in cabins.

Reservations, fees: The daily fee ranges from $17 to $22. Open May to mid-October.

Directions: From the junction of I-94 and Hwy. 54, take exit 116 and go 10.5 miles west and south on Hwy. 54, then one-quarter mile south on Sunnyvale Road to the entrance.

Contact: Lost Falls Resort and Campground, Rose and Ed Schaper, N2974 Sunnyvale Rd., River Falls, WI 54615, 715/284-7133 or 800/329-3911, website: www.lostfalls.com

Trip Notes: In Neillsville, about 20 miles north, there are two unusual museums—the 1897 Jail Museum (715/743-6444) and the Wisconsin Pavilion from the 1964 World's Fair, which features "Chatty Belle," a larger-than-life talking cow (715/743-2222).

48 Yogi Bear's Jellystone Park Camp Resort-Warrens

Location: Warrens, southeast of Black River Falls, map 9, grid H5.

Campsites, facilities: There are 463 campsites. Facilities include electric hookups, water, sewer, flush toilets, showers, disposal station, laundry, grocery store, swimming pool, water slide, pond swimming, boat dock, canoeing, fishing, mini-golf, shuffleboard and tennis courts, hiking trail, and planned activities. Cabin rentals are available. Pets are allowed.

Reservations, fees: The daily fee ranges from $28 to $38. Credit cards are accepted. Open year-round. The facility is fully operational from mid-April through mid-October.

Directions: From the junction of I-94 and County Road E, take exit 135 and go one-half mile east on County Road E to the entrance.

Contact: Yogi Bear's Jellystone Park Camp Resort-Warrens, Steve Stenklyft, P.O. Box 67, Warrens, WI 54666, 608/378-4977, email: steve@yogiwarrens.com, website: warrens jellystone.com.

Trip Notes: Cranberries are not just for Thanksgiving, so stop at the Cranberry Expo (608/378-4878) and visit the museum and gift shop dedicated to cranberries.

49 Rock Dam Resort

Location: Greenwood, east of Eau Claire, map 9, grid C2.

Campsites, facilities: There are 98 campsites. Facilities include electric hookups, water, sewer, flush toilets, showers, disposal station, laundry, and grocery store. This campground provides lake boating, canoeing, fishing, swimming, and hiking trail. Pets are allowed.

Reservations, fees: The daily fee ranges from $10 to $13. Open from mid-April through November.

Directions: To reach Rock Dam Resort from Greenwood, go 16 miles west on County Road G and GG, then 2.5 miles west on Willard Road to the entrance.

Contact: Rock Dam Resort, W10666 Camp Globe Rd., Willard, WI 54493, 715/743-5140.

Trip Notes: Marshfield is less than 30 miles east of Greenwood and it is a town with a relaxed, friendly atmosphere. It is the home of Wisconsin's fourth largest zoo (800/422-4541), featuring more than 200 animals and birds including snow monkeys, grizzly bears, buffalo, and a large aviary.

50 Sandman's Campground

Location: Holmen, southeast of Trempealeau, map 10, grid A7.

Campsites, facilities: There are 60 campsites. Facilities include RV pull-through sites, electric hookups, water, flush toilets, showers, disposal station, hiking trail, and playground. Lake and river boating, canoeing, and fishing are nearby. You can also bike or hike the nearby Great River State Trail from Onalaska to Marshland. Pets are allowed.

Reservations, fees: The daily fee is $14. Open May through mid-October.

Directions: From the south junction of Hwy. 35 and U.S. Hwy. 53, go 7.5 miles north on Hwy. 53 to the campground entrance.

Contact: Sandman's Campground, N8905 Hwy. 53, Holmen, WI 54636, 800/526-4958.

Trip Notes: While you're in the area you can take a sight-seeing, lunch, or dinner cruise on one of several cruise ships, including those from La Crosse Queen Cruises (608/784-2893) or Julia Belle Swain (800/815-1005) from La Crosse.

51 Neshonoc Lakeside Campground

Location: West Salem, on Lake Neshonoc, map 10, grid A8.

Campsites, facilities: There are 240 camp-

sites. Facilities include RV pull-through sites, electric hookups, water, sewer, disposal station, laundry, grocery store, swimming pool, lake swimming, boat ramp and dock, fishing, playground, and weekend activities. Boat, cabin, and cottage rentals are available. Pets are allowed.

Reservations, fees: The daily fee ranges from $17 to $22. Credit cards are accepted. Open from mid-April to mid-October.

Directions: From the junction of I-90 and County Road C, take exit 12 and go 1.5 miles north on County Road C through the village, then 1.5 miles east on Hwy. 16, and 1,000 feet south on Neshonoc Road to the campground entrance.

Contact: Neshonoc Lakeside Campground, Bob and Paula Martell, N5334 Neshonoc Rd., West Salem, WI 54669, 608/786-1792, email: neshcamp@aol.com.

Trip Notes: The La Crosse River State Park offers a 21-mile route alongside an active rail line to La Crosse and joins the Great River State Trail, adding another 24 miles for biking, hiking, and snowmobiling.

52 Pettibone RV Park

Location: La Crosse, on the Mississippi River, map 10, grid B6.

Campsites, facilities: There are 160 campsites. Facilities include electric hookups, water, flush toilets, showers, disposal station, laundry, grocery store, swimming pool, boat ramp and dock, fishing, and hiking trail. Cottage rentals are available. Pets are allowed.

Reservations, fees: The daily fee ranges from $20 to $22. Open year-round. The facility is fully operational from mid-April through October.

Directions: From the junction of I-90 and U.S. Hwys. 14/61, take exit 275 on the Minnesota side and go five miles south on Hwys. 14/61 to the entrance.

Contact: Pettibone RV Park, Mark Pretasky, 333 Park Plaza Dr., La Crosse, WI 54601, 608/782-5858, email: pettiboneresort@prodigy .net, website: www.pettiboneresort.com.

Trip Notes: Even if you don't have a little girl in the camper, you will enjoy the La Crosse Doll Museum (608/785-0020), which has nearly 6,000 dolls on display, including a large Barbie doll collection.

53 Goose Island Park

Location: La Crosse, on the Mississippi River, map 10, grid B7.

Campsites, facilities: There are 400 campsites in this county park. Facilities include electric hookups, flush toilets, showers, disposal station, laundry, grocery store, river swimming, boat ramp and dock, fishing, hiking trail, playground, and planned weekend activities.

Boat rentals are available. There are restrictions on pets.

Reservations, fees: The daily fee ranges from $14 to $16.50. Open April through November.

Directions: From the south junction of U.S. Hwys. 14/61 and Hwy. 35, go 1.5 miles south on Hwy. 35, then one mile west on County Road GI to the park entrance.

Contact: Goose Island Park, W6488 County Rd. GI, Stoddard, WI 54658, 608/788-7018.

Trip Notes: For the nature-lover a visit to Hixon Forest Nature Center (608/784-0303)

offers 720 acres of nature preserve with a Nature Center and hiking trails.

54 Leon Valley Campground

Location: Sparta, northeast of La Crosse, map 11, grid A2.

Campsites, facilities: There are 90 campsites. Facilities include electric hookups, water, flush toilets, showers, disposal station, grocery store, swimming pool, and playground. Sleeping cabin rentals are available. The Elroy-Sparta State Trail and Great River State Trail offer biking, hiking, canoeing, fishing, snowmobiling, and cross-country skiing. Pets are allowed.

Reservations, fees: The daily fee ranges from $16 to $20. Open year-round.

Directions: From the junction of I-90 and Hwy. 27, go four miles south on Hwy. 27, then one and one-quarter miles east on Jancing Avenue to the entrance.

Contact: Leon Valley Campground, Bernie and Joann Waege, 9050 Jancing Ave., Sparta, WI 54656, 608/269-6400, email: leonvalley @centuryinter.net, website: www.campleon calley.com.

Trip Notes: As you enter Sparta you will be greeted by the world's largest bike—an old-fashioned high-wheeler made of fiberglass. It indicates that the community calls itself the "Bicycling Capital of America." This is because the Elroy-Sparta State Trail (608/269-4123 or 800/354-3453), the first rails-to-rails bicycle route in the country begins here.

WISCONSIN NORTHWOODS

Wisconsin Northwoods

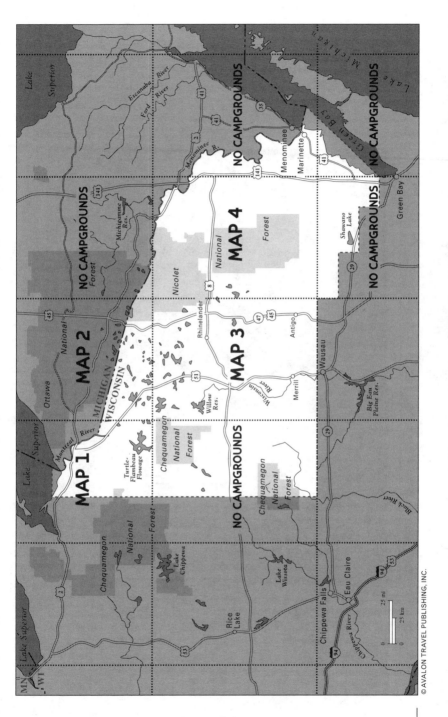

Map 1

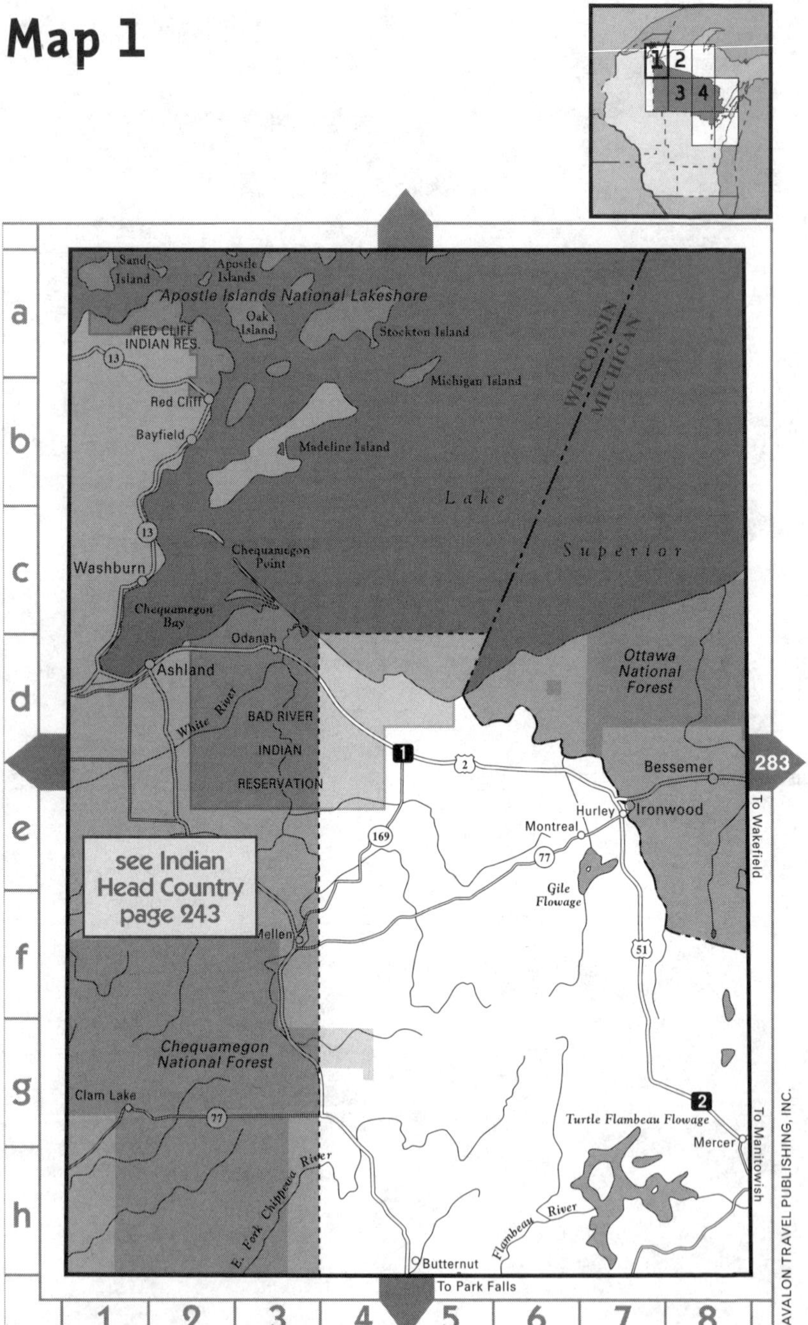

see Indian Head Country page 243

© AVALON TRAVEL PUBLISHING, INC.

Map 2

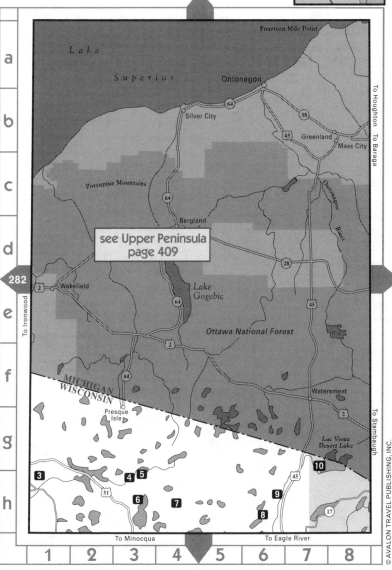

see Upper Peninsula
page 409

Map 3

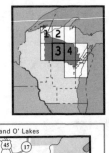

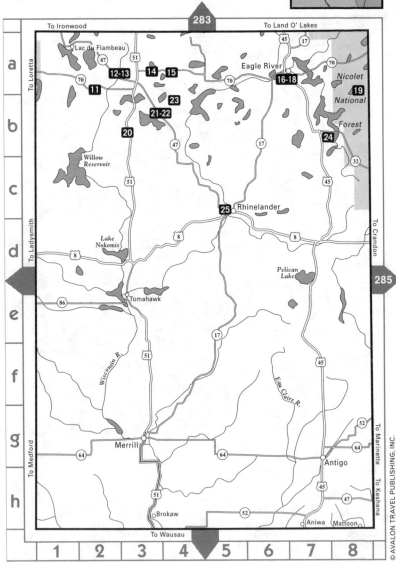

Map 4

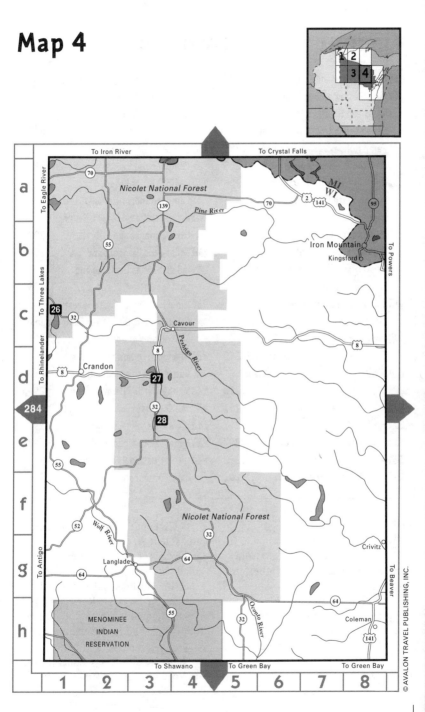

To Iron River
To Crystal Falls

a

70

Nicolet National Forest

139

Pine River

70

2 141

MI
WI

95

b

55

Iron Mountain

Kingsford

To Powers

To Eagle River

To Three Lakes

To Rhinelander

c

26 32

Cavour

8

d

8 Crandon

27

Perhsigo River

8

284

32

e

28

55

f

52 Wolf River

Nicolet National Forest

32

Crivitz

g

52

64 Langlade

64

32

64

To Antigo

To Beaver

h

MENOMINEE
INDIAN
RESERVATION

55

32

Oconto River

Coleman

141

To Shawano
To Green Bay
To Green Bay

1 2 3 4 5 6 7 8

© AVALON TRAVEL PUBLISHING, INC.

Wisconsin Northwoods

Since the earliest settling of northern Wisconsin, life has been influenced by a combination of natural resources—ore, timber, and water. Early pioneers came to extract the minerals from the earth and fell the pine and other trees for lumber. Today, some reminders of these early days remain for visitors to view; like Hurley's Historic Silver Street, where the boisterous, weary miners and lumberjacks went to have a good time and put aside their woes.

The days of the timber trail can be recalled with visits to the Ghost Town of Emerson, Springstead Historical Districts, or the Round Lake Logging Dam in the Chequamegon National Forest. Today, the woods and waters offer a haven for campers and others.

There are all sorts of trails through the Northwoods—ATV, mountain bike, hiking, nature, ski, snowmobile, snowshoe, and automobile—that can take you through breathtaking wilderness or quiet, quaint communities.

With vast forestland, shimmering bodies of water, and crisp clean air, the Northwoods is a camper's delight.

◻1 Frontier Bar and Campground

Location: Saxon, west of Lake Superior and northwest of the Giles Flowage, map 1, grid D4.

Campsites, facilities: There are 25 campsites. Facilities include RV pull-through sites, electric hookups, water, sewer, flush toilets, showers, disposal station, grocery store, restaurant and hiking trail. Boating, canoeing, and fishing in Lake Superior and in the Giles Flowage are nearby. Pets are allowed.

Reservations, fees: The daily fee ranges from $12 to $16. Credit cards are accepted. Open year-round. The facility is fully operational May through mid-October.

Directions: Drive to the junction of U.S. Hwy. 2 and Hwy. 169.

Contact: Frontier Bar and Campground, Ban Innes, HC 1, Box 477, Saxon, WI 54559, 715/893-2461, email:frontierbar@skynet.net.

Trip Notes: The campground is conveniently located near Lake Superior, the Montreal River, and the Giles Flowage for excellent muskie, walleye, or panfish angling.

You might also drive to Hurley (715/561-4334; website: www.hurleywi.com), which boomed with the discovery of iron ore in 1879.

◻2 Big 6 Resort and Campground

Location: Mercer, on Grand Portage Lake, map 1, grid G8.

Campsites, facilities: There are 40 campsites. Facilities include RV pull-through sites, electric hookups, water, sewer, flush toilets, showers, disposal station, laundry, boat dock and fishing. Boat rentals are available. Pets are allowed.

Reservations, fees: The daily fee ranges from $12 to $18. Open May through September.

Directions: From the junction of Hwy. 51 and Clinic Street, go one block northeast on Clinic Street, then one block west on Margaret Road to the entrance.

Contact: Big 6 Resort and Campground, Phil Tack and Peter Szleszinski, P.O. Box 426, Mercer, WI 54547, 715/476-2466.

Trip Notes: The campground is near the Turtle-Flambeau Flowages, which are noted for great northern pike, walleye, and smallmouth bass fishing. In nearby Hurley, tour the Iron County Historical Museum (715/561-2244). It features three floors of intriguing, nostalgic and educational exhibits, including logging, mining, farming, weaving, clothing, and home furnishings. The museum is at 303 Iron Street.

◻3 Northern Highland State Forest: Sandy Beach Lake Campground

Location: Manitowish Waters, on Sandy Beach Lake, map 2, grid H1.

Campsites, facilities: There are 37 campsites. Facilities include vault flush toilets, showers, disposal station, swimming beach, boat ramp, and fishing. Hiking trails are nearby.

Reservations, fees: Reservations are accepted. Campsite reservations are available. See State Park Camping Fees and Reserving a Campsite. Open from late May through late August.

Directions: From the junction of U.S. Hwy. 51 and Hwy. 47, go eight miles southeast on Hwy. 47 to the entrance.

Contact: Sandy Beach Lake Campground, 4125 CTH M, Boulder Junction, WI 54512, 888/947-2757 or 715/385-2727.

Trip Notes: While camping in the area nature-lovers will want to visit the 66-acre North Lakeland Discovery Center (877/543-2085 or 715/543-2085). It is a former Department of Natural Resources camp that now offers nature trails, hiking, cross-country skiing, snowshoeing, wildlife watching, and interpretive programs.

◪ Camp Holiday

Location: Boulder Junction, on Rudolph Lake, map 2, grid H3.

Campsites, facilities: There are 160 campsites. Facilities include electric hookups, water, sewer, flush toilets, showers, disposal station, laundry, grocery store, swimming beach, boat ramp, lake fishing, shuffleboard courts, and hiking trail. Boat and seasonal campsite rentals are available. Pets are allowed.

Reservations, fees: The daily fee ranges from $17 to $21. Credit cards are accepted. Open May through October.

Directions: From the junction of U.S. Hwy. 51 and Country Road H, go three miles northeast on County Road H and then about 500 feet east of Rudolph Lake Lane to the campground entrance.

Contact: Camp Holiday, Al and Lila Vehrs, P.O. Box 67, Boulder Junction, WI 54512, 715/385-2264, email: campholiday@centurytel.net, website: www.boulderjct.org/holiday.htm.

Trip Notes: Finding good fishing in this area is like wanting the weather to change, just wait a few minutes or move to the next lake nearby for excellent muskie, northern pike, walleye, and bass fishing.

◱ Birchwood Campground

Location: Boulder Junction, on the Manitowish River, map 2, grid H3.

Campsites, facilities: There are 60 campsites. Facilities include electric hookups, water, sewer, flush toilets, showers, disposal station, lake and river swimming, boating, canoeing, fishing, and hiking trail. Boat rentals are available. A bike trail is nearby. Pets are not allowed.

Reservations, fees: The daily fee is $12. Open May through mid-October.

Directions: From the junction of County Road M and County Road K, go 2.5 miles west on County Road K and then three-quarters of a mile north on Lucas Lane to the entrance.

Contact: Birchwood Campground, 5540 Lucas Ln., Boulder Junction, WI 54512, 715/385-2882.

Trip Notes: Boulder Junction, according to town officials, probably has more miles of bike trails per capita than any place in the country. Several years ago local people formed B.A.T.S. (Boulder Junction Area Trail System) and put signage on a 10-mile bike loop of local snowmobile and cross-country trails. The town opened a paved trail running south to a picnic area on Trout Lake. For the mountain biker, the loop through the dense forest is highlighted by small streams and lakes. A short spur runs north to Fishtrap Dam.

❻ Northern Highland/American Legion State Forest: Big Lake-South Trout Lake and Upper Gresham Lake

Location: Boulder Junction, on Big, Trout and Gresham Lakes, map 2, grid H3.

Campsites, facilities: There are 72 campsites at Big Lake, 24 at South Trout Lake, and 27 at Upper Gresham Lake. Facilities at all three campgrounds include vault toilets, lake swimming, boat ramps and fishing. Pets are allowed.

Reservations, fees: Reservations are accepted. Campsite reservations are available. See State Park Camping Fees and Reserving a Campsite. Big Lake and Upper Gresham Lake are open all year. South Trout Lake is open from the end of May through August.

Contact: Northern Highland/American Legion State Forest

Big Lake, South Trout Lake, or Upper Gresham Lake, 4125 CTH M, Boulder Junction, WI 54512, 888/947-2757 or 715/385-2727.

Directions: To Big Lake: From Boulder Junction, go eight miles west on County Road K, then one mile north on County Road P to the entrance. To South Trout Lake: From Boulder Junction, go six miles south on County Road M to the entrance. To Upper Gresham Lake: From the junction of U.S. Hwy. 51 and County Road H, go 1.5 miles northeast on County Road H to the entrance.

Trip Notes: Boulder Junction has over 190 lakes and is known as the "Muskie Capital of the World," but this is nothing compared to the colorful splendor of the region in autumn. The area provides many fall celebrations. For dates and locations, contact Vilas County Tourism (800/236-3649).

❼ Northern Highland State Forest: Firefly, Razorback Lake, Starrett Lake Campgrounds

Location: Sayner, south of Boulder Junction, map 2, grid H4.

Campsites, facilities: Firefly Campground has 70 campsites, Razorback has 55 campsites, and Sarrett Lake has 46 campsites. Facilities at all three campgrounds include vault toilets, showers, disposal stations, swimming beaches, boating, canoeing, and fishing. Razorback has a boat ramp. Pets are allowed.

Reservations, fees: Reservations are accepted. Campsite reservations are available. See State Park Camping Fees and Reserving a Campsite. Firefly is open May through October. Razorback and Sarrett Lakes are open all year.

Directions: To Firefly Campground: From Sayner, go three miles west on County Road N to the entrance. To Razorback Lake: From Sayner, go two miles west on County Road N and then five miles north on Razorback Road to the entrance. To Starrett Lake: From Sayner, go two miles west on County Road N and then three miles northwest on Razorback and Musky Roads to the entrance.

Contact: Northern Highland/American Legion State Forest-Firefly Campground, Razorback Lake and Starrett Lake Campgrounds, 4125 CTH M, Boulder Junction, WI 54512, 888/947-2757 or 715/385-2727.

Trip Notes: Be sure to visit the Vilas County Historical Museum (715/542-3388) in Sayner to view the displays of local history and the world's first snowmobile.

In nearby St. Germain is the International Snowmobile Racing Hall of Fame and Mu-

seum (715/542-4488; website: www.snow
mobilehalloffame.com). Here you'll find historic machines, uniforms, videos, and biographies. Take Hwy. 51 north to Hwy. 70 east
and follow Hwy. 70 east for 12 miles.

8 Buckatabon Lodge and Lighthouse Inn

Location: Conover, on Lower Buckatabon
Lake, west of Eagle River, map 2, grid H6.

Campsites, facilities: There are 61 campsites, most of which are seasonal rentals.
Facilities include electric hookups, water,
sewer, flush toilets, showers, grocery store,
swimming beach, and boat ramp.

Boat and cottage rentals are available. Golf
and horseback riding are located nearby.
Pets are allowed.

Reservations, fees: Reservations are required. The daily fee ranges from $16 to $19.
Open year-round. The facility is fully operational from mid-April through October.

Directions: From the junction of U.S. Hwy.
45 and County Road K, go 2.25 miles west on
County Road K. Then drive 1.25 miles south
on East Buckatabon Road and nearly one-
half mile west on Rush Road to the entrance.

Contact: Backatabon Lodge and Lighthouse
Inn, the Boehm family, 5630 Rush Rd.,
Conover, WI 54519, 715/479-4660, email:
btabnldg@nnex.net.

Trip Notes: In Eagle River, visit Carl's Wood
Art Museum (715/479-1883) to see the displays of unique wooden works of art, including chainsaw sculptures.

Another stop might be Aquarius Fisheries
(715/479-7472), which offers fishing with
poles and bait provided. The facility at 8458
Hwy. H also features a Japanese koi display
pond and gift shop.

If youngsters are along, don't miss the
Northwoods Children's Museum (715/479-
4623). There are 14 exhibits, including a mini-
log cabin and fishing pond. The museum is at
346 W. Division Street.

9 Northern Highland State Forest: East Star Lake Campground

Location: Conover, on Star Lake, west of
Eagle River, map 2, grid H6.

Campsites, facilities: There are 30 campsites. Facilities include vault toilets, showers,
boat ramp, hiking trails, swimming beach,
and fishing. Pets are allowed.

Reservations, fees: Reservations are accepted. Campsite reservations are available.
See State Park Camping Fees and Reserving
a Campsite. Open year-round.

Directions: From Conover, go nine miles
west on County Road N to the entrance.

Contact: East Star Lake Campground, 4125
CTH M, Boulder Junction, WI 54512, 888/947-
2757 or 715/385-2727.

Trip Notes: Whether you've been on a sleigh
ride before or this is your first time, Eagle
River's Bit's N Wheels Ranch (715/479-1552)
will take you through scenic wooded trails.

10 Nicolet National Forest: Lac Vieux Desert Campground

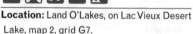

Location: Land O'Lakes, on Lac Vieux Desert
Lake, map 2, grid G7.

Campsites, facilities: There are 31 campsites. Facilities include vault toilets, boat
ramp and dock, picnic area, hiking trail, lake
swimming and fishing. A bike trail is nearby. Pets are allowed.

Reservations, fees: The daily fee is $10. Open from early May through mid-October.

Directions: From the junction of U.S. 45 and County Road E, go three miles east on County Road E, then 1.75 mile north on Forest Road 2205 to the entrance.

Contact: Nicolet National Forest, Lac Vieux Desert Campground, 68 S. Stevens St., Rhinelander, WI 54501, 715/479-2827.

Trip Notes: The 2,853-acre lake (shared with Michigan's Upper Peninsula) is at the headwaters of the Wisconsin River, and has been "home" to Chippewa (Ojibwa) Indians for centuries. Border angling regulations apply. Lac Vieux Desert is known for its muskies, walleye, bass, and northern pike.

If you like to bike and have good strong legs, you'll want to tackle the 25-mile Lac Vieux Desert Tour that will give you a roller coaster ride through the Northwoods from Land O'Lakes to Phelps. The route is one of hundreds of miles of recommended on-road and off-road routes shown on the new VAM-BASA (Vilas Area Mountain Bike and Sky Association) map. The route is full of bicycle excitement through a delightful mix of maple, birch, balsam, and black spruce forest.

11 Patricia Lake Campground

Location: Minocqua, south of Woodruff, map 3, grid A3.

Campsites, facilities: There are 100 campsites. Facilities include electric hookups, water, sewer, flush toilets, showers, disposal station, laundry, grocery store, swimming beach, boating (electric motors only), fishing, boat dock, shuffleboard courts, hiking trail, and playground. Pets are allowed.

Reservations, fees: The daily fee ranges from $15 to $21. Open May through mid-October.

Directions: From the junction of U.S. Hwy. 51 and Hwy. 70, go 2.5 miles west on Hwy. 70, then one-half mile south on Camp Pinemere Road to the entrance.

Contact: Patricia Lake Campground, David and Joy Taber, 8505 Camp Pinemere Rd., Minocqua, WI 54548, 715/356-3198, email: patlake@newnorth.net.

Trip Notes: If you are interested in the area's history, be sure to stop at the Minocqua Museum Bolger Memorial Building (715/356-7666).

If you're looking for something different, visit the Riverside Raceway (715/479-5981) west of Eagle River. Take Hwy. 70 to Cloverland Drive. Races on the one-third-mile clay, semi-banked, tri-oval track are held on Tuesdays, but be certain to call for current information.

12 Fox Fire Campground

Location: Woodruff, on Brandy Lake, map 3, grid A3.

Campsites, facilities: There are 97 campsites. Facilities include RV pull-through sites, electric hookups, water, sewer, flush toilets, showers, laundry, grocery store, swimming beach, and playground. Boat and seasonal campsite rentals are available. Golf courses and biking trails are nearby. Pets are allowed.

Reservations, fees: The daily fee ranges from $16 to $23. Open May through mid-October.

Directions: From the junction of U.S. Hwy. 51 and Hwy. 47, go 1.25 miles north on Hwy. 51 to the entrance.

Contact: Fox Fire Campground, Jeanette Krueger, 11180 Fox Fire Rd., Arbor Vitae, WI 54568, 715/356-6470, email: foxfire@new north.net.

Trip Notes: Did you ever try to swing an ax or chop wood? Visit the Scheer's Lumberjack

Shows (715/634-5010) and see how the pros do long rolling, chopping, sawing, and climbing.

13 Hiawatha Trailer Resort

Location: Woodruff, on Lake Arrowhead, map 3, grid A3.

Campsites, facilities: There are 170 campsites. Tents are not permitted. Facilities include electric hookups, water, sewer, flush toilets, showers, disposal station, laundry, grocery store, swimming beach, hiking trail, shuffleboard courts, playground, and planned activities. Boat rentals are available. Pets are allowed.

Reservations, fees: The daily fee is $24. Credit cards are accepted. Open May through mid-October.

Directions: From the junction of U.S. Hwy. 51 and Hwy. 47, go one-quarter mile east on Hwy. 47 and then one-half mile north on Balsam Street to the entrance.

Contact: Hiawatha Trailer Resort, Johnnie Kuehneman, P.O. Box 590, Woodruff, WI 54568, 715/356-6111 or 888/429-2842, email: namenheuk@aol.com.

Trip Notes: For a bit of local history and a look at early medicine in this area, visit the Dr. Kate Museum (715/356-6896) and see how this early Wisconsin pioneer doctor worked.

14 Arbor Vitae Campground

Location: Woodruff, near Big Arbor Vitae Lake, map 3, grid A3.

Campsites, facilities: There are 100 campsites. The facilities include electric hookups, water, sewer, flush toilets, showers, disposal station, grocery store, swimming beach,

playground, and hiking trail. Boat rentals are available. Pets are allowed.

Reservations, fees: The daily fee ranges from $13 to $20. Open May through mid-October.

Directions: From the junction of U.S. Hwy. 51 and Hwy. 47, drive 1.75 miles north on Hwy. 51, then 1.5 miles east on Hwy. 70. Finally, drive one-half mile north on Big Arbor Vitae Drive to the entrance.

Contact: Arbor Vitae Campground, 10545 Big Arbor Vitae Dr., Arbor Vitae, WI 54568 715/356-5146.

Trip Notes: It's fascinating for the entire family to see how fish are raised to stock lakes and streams. Stop by the Art Oehmcke Hatchery (715/356-5211)) and take a free tour of the facilities. It specializes in rearing muskies, walleye, lake trout, and suckers. The hatchery is on County Road J, two miles east of Woodruff.

15 Lynn Ann's Campground

Location: St. Germain, on Big St. Germain Lake, map 3, grid A4.

Campsites, facilities: There are 90 campsites. Facilities include electric hookups, water, sewer, flush toilets, showers, disposal station, laundry, grocery store, swimming beach, boat ramp and dock, shuffleboard courts, and playground. Boat rentals are available. Pets are allowed.

Reservations, fees: The daily fee ranges from $19 to $22. Credit cards are accepted. Open from early May to mid-October.

Directions: From the junction of Hwys. 70 and 155, go two miles west on Hwy. 70, then one-half mile north on Normandy Court, and one-quarter mile east on South Shore Drive to the entrance.

Contact: Lynn Ann's Campground, Heather and Mike Davidson, P.O. Box 08, St. Germain, WI 54558, 715/542-3456, email: bigst camp@aol.com, website: www.lynnanns campground.com.

Trip Notes: A visit to the International Snowmobile Racing Hall of Fame and Museum (715/359-9917) will give you an excellent background of historic racing snowmobiles, uniforms, videos, and biographies of the inductees.

16 Nicolet National Forest: Franklin Lake Campground, Luna-White Deer Campground, and Spectacle Lake Campground

Location: Eagle River, on Franklin, Luna and Spectacle Lakes, map 3, grid A7.

Campsites, facilities: Franklin Lake has 77 campsites, Luna-White Deer has 37 sites, and Spectacle Lake has 34 sites. Facilities include vault toilets, swimming beach, picnic areas, boat ramps, and hiking trails. Pets are allowed.

Reservations, fees: The daily fee ranges from $10 to $12. Franklin Lake and Luna-White Deer are open May through mid-October. Spectacle Lake is open mid-May through early September.

Directions: To Franklin Lake: From Eagle River, go nine miles east on Hwy. 70. Then drive two miles south of Forest Road 2178 and six miles east on FR 2181. To Luna-White Deer: From Eagle River, go 14.5 miles east on Hwy. 70 and then 4.5 miles south on FR 2176. Finally, go one mile northwest on FR 2188 to the entrance. To Spectacle Lake: From Eagle River, go eight miles east on Hwy. 70 and three miles north on FR 2178.

Then travel two miles north on FR 2465, two miles north on FR 2196, and one mile east on FR 2572 to the entrance.

Contact: Nicolet National Forest, Franklin Lake, Luna-White Deer, and Spectacle Lake Campgrounds, 68 S. Stevens St., Rhinelander, WI 54501, 715/479-2827.

Trip Notes: The Franklin Lake Campground is the beginning and end of a one-mile interpretive trail that crosses Franklin-Butternut Creek and passes under a natural arch to Hemlock Cathedral's evergreen canopy abundant with sugar maples, raspberry, elderberry, and an esker ridge. The Lund-White Deer Trail is four miles and circles White Deer Lake. Campers at 174-acre Spectacle Lake can take the Spectacle Lake-Kentuck Lake Trail—three miles of gentle trail through a hardwood forest.

17 Pine-Aire Resort and Campground

Location: Eagle River, on the Eagle Chain of 28 lakes, map 3, grid A7.

Campsites, facilities: There are 136 campsites. Facilities include electric hookups, water, sewer, flush toilets, showers, disposal station, laundry, grocery store, swimming beach, boat ramp and dock, tennis courts, and planned activities. Boat and cottage rentals are available. In the winter you can fish through the ice, cross-country ski, and snowmobile. Pets are allowed.

Reservations, fees: The daily fee ranges from $23 to $39. Open year-round. The facility is fully operational May through September.

Directions: From the junction of Hwy. 70 and U.S. Hwy. 45, go three miles north on Hwy. 45, then one-eighth mile east on Chain O'Lakes Road to the entrance.

Contact: Pine-Aire Resort and Campground, Ron and Cindy Meinholz, 4443 Chain O'Lakes Rd., Eagle River, WI 54521, 715/479-9208 or 800/597-6777, email: vacation@pine-aire.com, website: www.pine-aire.com.

Trip Notes: This campground has it all. You can boat, fish, swim, or just relax. You can even take the family out to dinner at their Logging Camp Kitchen and Still Restaurant.

In Pence, a few miles southwest of Hurley on Hwy. 77, is the Plummer Mine Headframe (715/561-2922; website: www.ironcounty wi.com) that opened in 1904. The shaft angles down following a vein of ore to a depth of 2,367 feet. The mine closed in 1924 and is the last such headframe standing in Wisconsin.

18 Chain O'Lakes Resort and Campground

Location: Eagle River, on Cranberry Lake, map 3, grid A7.

Campsites, facilities: There are 100 campsites. Facilities include electric hookups, water, flush toilets, showers, disposal station, swimming pool, boat ramp, and tennis and shuffleboard courts. Boat rentals are available. There is a golf course nearby. Pets are allowed.

Reservations, fees: Reservations are required. The daily fee is $25 (two persons; $1 per each additional person. Open May through September.

Directions: From Eagle River, go four miles east on Hwy. 70, then south on East Cranberry Road and follow the signs to the entrance.

Contact: Chain O'Lakes Resort and Campground, Gordon and Lois Parnitzke, 3165 Campground Rd., Eagle River, WI 54521, 715/479-6708, email: colcamp@nnex.net

Trip Notes: Everyone will enjoy a visit to Trees for Tomorrow Natural Resources Education

Center (715/479-6456 or 800/838-9472) as they tour a former CCC-era camp demonstration forest and wildlife trail.

19 Nicolet National Forest: Sevenmile Lake Campground

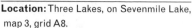

Location: Three Lakes, on Sevenmile Lake, map 3, grid A8.

Campsites, facilities: There are 27 campsites. Facilities include vault toilets, swimming beach, boat ramp and dock, and hiking trails.

Reservations, fees: The daily fee is $10. Open from mid-May through early September.

Directions: From Three Lakes, go 5.5 miles east on Hwy. 32, then four miles north on Forest Road 2178. Then drive two miles east on FR 2179 and one mile south on FR 2435 to the entrance.

Contact: Nicolet National Forest, Sevenmile Lake Campground, 68 S. Stevens St., Rhinelander, WI 54501, 715/479-2827.

Trip Notes: The campground, 15 miles southeast of Eagle River, is high on a ridge overlooking Sevenmile Lake. There is a two-mile walking trail on a high bluff that passes two ponds, red pines, and blueberry patches. There's a boardwalk through the wetlands area.

20 Cedar Falls Campground

Location: Hazelhurst, on the Willow Flowage, map 3, grid B3.

Campsites, facilities: There are 42 campsites. Facilities include electric hookups, water, flush toilets, showers, disposal station, laundry, grocery store, boat ramp, swimming beach, fishing, and hiking trails. Pets are allowed.

Reservations, fees: Registration at Wilderness Cruises. The daily fee is $18.

Directions: From the junction of U.S. Hwy. 51 and County Road Y, go nine miles west on County Road Y and then west on Willow Dam Road, following the signs.

Contact: Cedar Falls Campground, 4973 Willow Dam Rd., Hazelhurst, WI 54531, 715/356-4953.

Trip Notes: You will surely want to take a sight-seeing cruise, a luncheon, or dinner Wilderness Cruise (715/453-3310 or 800/472-1516) through the Willow Reservoir.

An option is to drive northeast to Conover and Rohr's Wilderness Tours (715/547-3639; website: www.rwtcanoe.com). It offers canoe rentals as well as canoe day trips, weekend, and extended outings to the headwaters of the Wisconsin River and guided trips to a number of other rivers, too. It's located at 5230 Razorback Road.

21 Indian Shores Camping and Cottage Resort

Location: Woodruff, on Tomahawk Lake, map 3, grid B3.

Campsites, facilities: There are 213 sites. Facilities include electric hookups, water, sewer, flush toilets, showers, disposal station, laundry, grocery store, swimming pool, swimming beach, boat ramp, mini-golf, tennis and shuffleboard courts, hiking trail, and planned activities. Boats, cabin, and seasonal campsite rentals are available. Pets are allowed.

Reservations, fees: The daily fee ranges from $28 to $34. Credit cards are accepted. Open May through October.

Directions: From the junction of U.S. Hwy. 51 and Hwy. 47, go nearly five miles southeast on Hwy. 47 to the entrance.

Contact: Indian Shores Camping and Cottage Resort, Richard Giebel and George Denis, P.O. Box 12, Woodruff, WI 54568-0012 or 715/356-5552, fax 715/356-1146, email: ind shore@networth.net.

Trip Notes: Children of all ages love animals. A trip to Jim Peck's Wildwood Wildlife Park (715/356-5588) will provide the whole family with the opportunity to pet a porcupine, feed a deer, and see hundreds of other woodland animals.

22 American Legion State Forest: Buffalo Campground, Clear Lake Campground and Indian Mounds Campground

Location: Near Woodruff on Buffalo, Clear and Tomahawk Lakes, map 3, grid B3.

Campsites, facilities: Buffalo Lake has 52 campsites, Clear Lake has 100 sites, and Indian Mounds has 39 sites. Facilities include vault toilets and showers. Buffalo and Clear Lake have disposal stations, boat ramps, and docks. They all offer swimming beaches, boating, canoeing, and fishing. Pets are allowed. In winter, Clear Lake has six plowed sites with water, but no electric hookups.

Reservations, fees: Reservations are accepted. Campsite reservations are available. See State Park Camping Fees and Reserving a Campsite. Open year-round.

Directions: To Buffalo Lake: From Woodruff, go six miles east on County Road J to the entrance. To Clear Lake: From Woodruff, go four miles southeast on Hwy. 47 to the entrance. To Indian Mounds: From Woodruff, go five miles southeast on Hwy. 47 to the entrance.

Contact: Buffalo Lake, Clear Lake, and Indian Mounds Campgrounds, 4125 CTH M,

Boulder Junction, WI 54512, 888/947-2757 or 715/835-2727.

Trip Notes: If you want to get an overview of this area's spectacular wildlife and habitat, you can take a wilderness cruise at Hazelhurst on the Will Reservoir (715/453-3310 or 800/472-1516).

23 American Legion State Forest: Cunard Lake Campground

Location: Lake Tomahawk, on Cunard Lake, map 3, grid B4.

Campsites, facilities: There are 34 campsites. Facilities include vault toilets, showers, disposal station, boat ramp, swimming beach, fishing, and hiking trails. Pets are allowed.

Reservations, fees: Reservations are accepted. Campsite reservations are available. See State Park Camping Fees and Reserving a Campsite.

Directions: From the junction of County Road D and County Road E, go two miles west on County Road E to the campground entrance.

Contact: American Legion State Forest, Cunard Lake Campground, 4125 CTH M, Boulder Junction, WI 54512, 888/947-2757 or 715/358-2727.

Trip Notes: Drive over to Hazelhurst to the Warbonnet Zoo (715/356-5093) to enjoy the petting zoo and amusement park.

24 Mann's Harbor Campground

Location: Three Lakes, on Spirit Lake, k map 3, grid B7.

Campsites, facilities: There are 45 campsites. Facilities include electric hookups, water, sewer, flush toilets, showers, disposal station, swimming beach, boat ramp and dock, hiking trails, and playground. Boat rentals are available. Pets are allowed.

Reservations, fees: The daily fee ranges from $15 to $23. Open May through September.

Directions: From the junction of U.S. Hwy. 45 and Hwy. 32, go nearly three miles east on Hwy. 32 to the campground entrance.

Contact: Mann's Harbor Campground, 1021 Hwy. 32, Three Lakes, WI 54562, 715/546-3520.

Trip Notes: Tour the Three Lakes Winery and see how wine is made and even have a little taste (800/944-7534), or drive to Minocqua to the Northwoods Wildlife Center (715/356-7400). The center has a wildlife hospital and wildlife and environmental education program. Tours are offered when the facility is open. The center is at 8683 Blumenstein Road. Take Hwy. 51 to Hwy. 70 west and go one-half mile to Blumenstein Road. It's on the left.

25 The Outpost

Location: Rhinelander, on Lake Nokomis, map 3, grid C5.

Campsites, facilities: There are 270 campsites with a separate tent area. Facilities include electric hookups, water, sewer, flush toilets, showers, disposal station, laundry, grocery store, restaurant, swimming beach, boat ramp, shuffleboard courts, and playground. A state biking trail is nearby. Boat and cottage rentals are available. Pets are allowed.

Reservations, fees: The daily fee ranges from $23 to $30.

Directions: From U.S. Hwy. 51, take exit U.S. Hwy. 8 west and go 12 miles west on County Road L to County Road N. Then travel three miles north on County Road N to the entrance.

Contact: The Outpost, Lou and Kitty Miller, 9507 Hwy. N, Tomahawk, WI 54487, 715/453-3468.

Trip Notes: There are more than 230 lakes within a 12-mile radius of Rhinelander. In the town's past, access to water routes made Rhinelander a logging center. This heritage is preserved at the Logging Museum Complex (715/362-2193) where there is a full-scale reproduction of the 19th-century logging camp with a narrow-gauge railroad.

26 Hiles Pine Lake Campground

Location: Hiles, on Pine Lake, map 4, grid C1.

Campsites, facilities: There are 80 campsites. Facilities include electric hookups, water, sewer, flush toilets, showers, disposal station, swimming beach, boat ramp and dock, hiking trail, and weekend planned activities. Boat, campers, mobile home, and seasonal campsite rentals are available. Pets are allowed.

Reservations, fees: The daily fee ranges from $12 to $18. Open year-round. The facility is fully operational May through September.

Directions: From the junction of U.S. Hwy. 8 and Hwy. 32, go 14 miles north on Hwy. 32, then one-half mile south on West Pine Lake Road to the entrance.

Contact: Hiles Pine Lake Campground, Joan and Bill Ferris, 8896 W. Pine Lake Rd., Hiles, WI 54511, 715/649-3319.

Trip Notes: Drive to nearby Laona and visit the Holt and Balcolm Logging Camp (715/276-7561) built in 1880. It is Wisconsin's oldest logging camp still on its original site.

Or, you can devote much of a day at Peck's Wildwood Wildlife Park and Nature Center (715/356-5588; website: www.peckswildwood.com). The center has more than 500 animals and birds, including zebra, wallaby, elk, bobcat, lynx, and lemur. There is also a muskie pond and a nature walk. The center is two miles west on Hwy. 70 west in Minocqua.

27 Ham Lake Campground

Location: Laona, on Ham Lake, map 4, grid D3.

Campsites, facilities: There are 46 campsites. Facilities include electric hookups, water, sewer, flush toilets, showers, disposal station, laundry, grocery store, swimming beach, boat dock, mini-golf, hiking trail, and playground. Boat, cabin, and cottage rentals are available. Pets are allowed.

Reservations, fees: The daily fee ranges from $15 to $19. Open May through mid-October.

Directions: From the junction of U.S. Hwy. 8 and Hwy. 32, go four miles south on Hwy. 32 to the entrance.

Contact: Ham Lake Campground, Judy and Terry Collins, RR 1 Box 434, Wabeno, WI 54566, 715/674-2201, fax 715/674-5028, email: hamlake@newsnorth.net

Trip Notes: Would you want to take a ride on an old-fashioned lumberjack train? If so, visit the Lumberjack Special Steam Train and Camp Five Museum (715/674-5028 or 800/774-3414).

28 Nicolet National Forest: Bear Lake Campground

Location: Laona, on Bear Lake, map 4, grid E3.

Campsites, facilities: There are 27 campsites. Facilities include vault toilets, swimming beach, picnic area, and boat ramp. Pets are allowed.

Reservations, fees: The daily fee is $10. Open May through October.

Directions: From the junction of U.S. Hwy. 8 and County Road T, go three miles east on County Road T and then four miles east on Forest Road 2136 to the campground entrance.

Contact: Nicolet National Forest, Bear Lake Campground, 68 S. Stevens St., Rhinelander, WI 54501, 715/674-4481.

Trip Notes: If you want a quiet campground and excellent northern pike fishing, this campground is for you. The nearby Pestigo and Rat Rivers offer good trout fishing.

Northeast of Laona is Catwillow Creek Trail. Named for a local stream, this 11-mile route crosses the Catwillow Wildlife Management Area and is used for hiking and snowmobiling. There are bogs, marshes, abandoned railroad grades, and wildlife watering holes.

CENTRAL WISCONSIN

Central Wisconsin

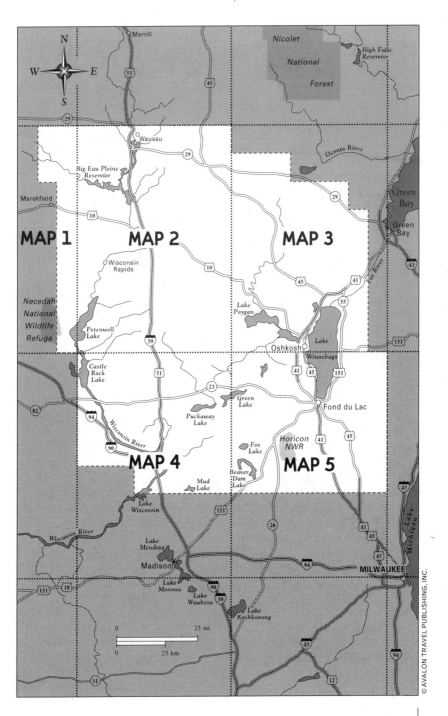

© AVALON TRAVEL PUBLISHING, INC.

Map 1

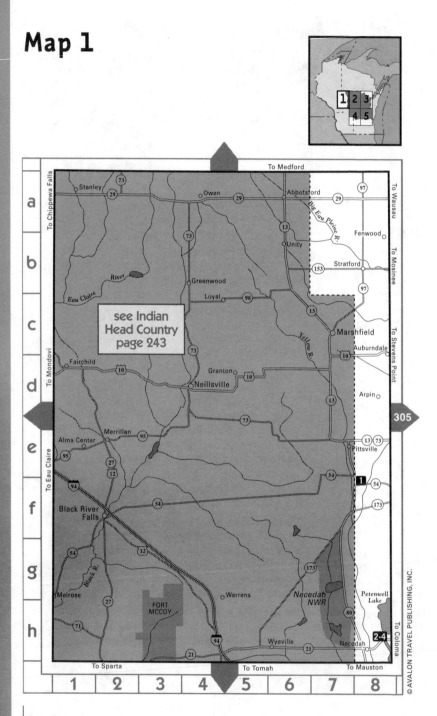

see Indian Head Country page 243

305

1

2-4

© AVALON TRAVEL PUBLISHING, INC.

Map 2

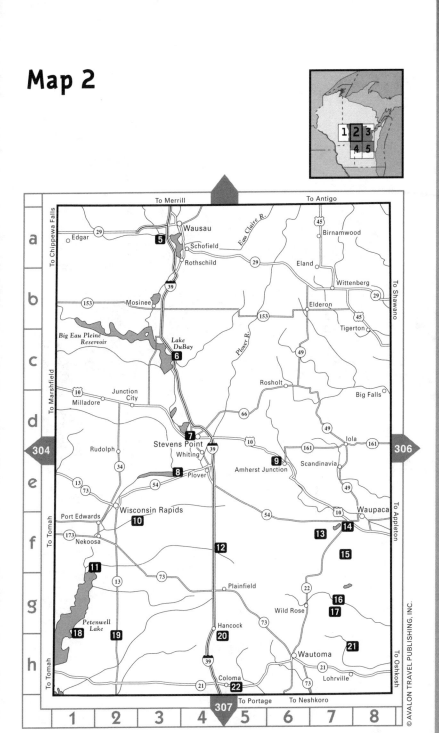

a
Edgar Wausau
Schofield
Rothschild

b
Birnamwood
Eland
Wittenberg
Mosinee
Elderon
Tigerton

Big Eau Pleine
Reservoir
Lake
DuBay

c
Rosholt
Big Falls

d
Junction
City
Milladore
Stevens Point
Whiting
Iola

Rudolph
Amherst Junction
Scandinavia

e
Plover
Waupaca

Wisconsin Rapids

f
Port Edwards
Nekoosa

g
Plainfield
Wild Rose

Petenwell
Lake
Hancock

h
Wautoma
Lohrville
Coloma

© AVALON TRAVEL PUBLISHING, INC.

Map 3

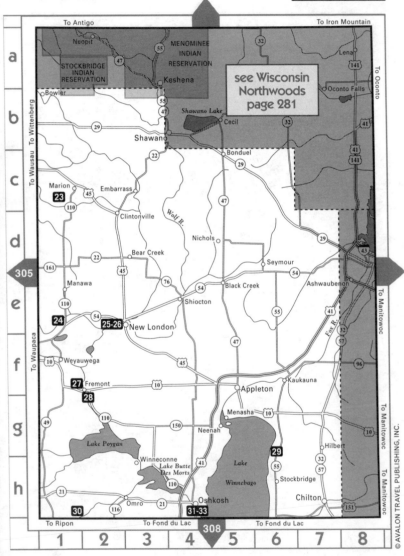

see Wisconsin Northwoods page 281

To Antigo

To Iron Mountain

Neopit

MENOMINEE INDIAN RESERVATION

STOCKBRIDGE INDIAN RESERVATION

Lena

Keshena

Oconto Falls

Bowler

To Oconto

Shawano Lake

Cecil

To Wausau To Wittenberg

Shawano

Bonduel

Marion

Embarrass

Clintonville

Wolf R.

Nichols

Seymour

Bear Creek

Manawa

Black Creek

Ashwaubenon

Shiocton

New London

Weyauwega

To Waupaca

Fremont

Appleton

Kaukauna

Menasha

Neenah

Lake Poygan

Hilbert

Winneconne

Lake Butte Des Morts

Lake Winnebago

Stockbridge

To Manitowoc

To Manitowoc

Omro

Oshkosh

Chilton

To Ripon

To Fond du Lac

To Fond du Lac

Fox R.

© AVALON TRAVEL PUBLISHING, INC.

305

308

a b c d e f g h

1 2 3 4 5 6 7 8

23 24 25-26 27 28 29 30 31-33

Map 4

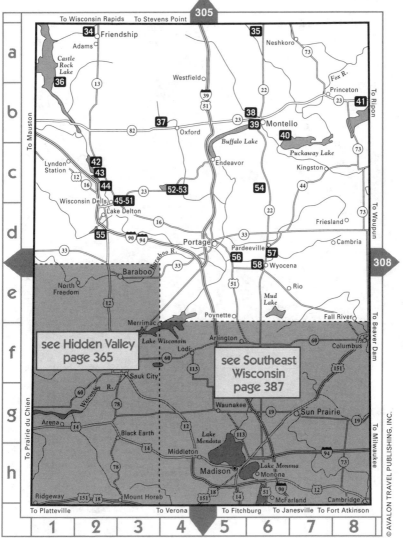

To Wisconsin Rapids   To Stevens Point

a

34 Friendship
35

Adams

Neshkoro

Castle Rock Lake

36

Westfield

Fox R.

13

Princeton

b

39

51

Oxford

37

82

Endeavor

38

23

39 Montello

40

Buffalo Lake

Puckaway Lake

73

Kingston

To Mauston

Lyndon Station

42

43

44

52-53

54

44

16

12

23

To Ripon

41

23

73

c

Wisconsin Dells

45-51

Lake Delton

16

22

73

Friesland

d

55

90 94

Portage

Pardeeville

57

33

Cambria

To Waupun

56

58 Wyocena

308

e

North Freedom

Baraboo

Rio

33

33

12

51

Mud Lake

Fall River

Merrimac

Poynette

f

see Hidden Valley
page 365

Lake Wisconsin

Lodi

Arlington

60

Columbus

To Beaver Dam

60

113

151

see Southeast
Wisconsin
page 387

Sauk City

g

78

Waunakee

19

Sun Prairie

19

To Milwaukee

To Prairie du Chien

Arena

14

Lake Mendota

113

Wisconsin R.

60

Black Earth

12

h

14

Middleton

94

73

78

Madison

Lake Monona
Monona

Ridgeway

151 18

Mount Horeb

151 18

14

51

McFarland

12

Cambridge

To Platteville

To Verona

To Fitchburg   To Janesville   To Fort Atkinson

1   2   3   4   5   6   7   8

© AVALON TRAVEL PUBLISHING, INC.

Map 5

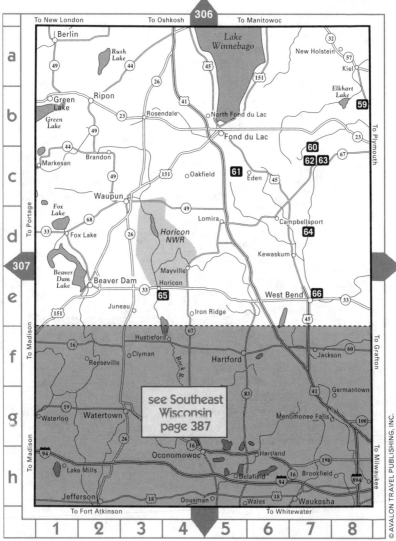

To New London   To Oshkosh   **306**   To Manitowoc

Berlin

Rush Lake

Lake Winnebago

New Holstein

Kiel

49

Green Lake

Green Lake

Ripon

Rosendale

North Fond du Lac

Elkhart Lake

59

To Plymouth

Markesan

Brandon

Fond du Lac

60

62 63

Waupun

Oakfield

61

Eden

To Portage

Fox Lake

Fox Lake

Lomira

Horicon NWR

Campbellsport

64

Kewaskum

307

Beaver Dam Lake

Beaver Dam

Mayville

Horicon

65

Juneau

Iron Ridge

West Bend

66

To Madison

Hustisford

Reeseville

Clyman

Rock R.

Hartford

Jackson

To Grafton

see Southeast Wisconsin page 387

Germantown

Waterloo

Watertown

Menomonee Falls

Oconomowoc

Hartland

To Madison

Lake Mills

Delafield

Brookfield

To Milwaukee

Jefferson

Dousman

Wales

Waukesha

To Fort Atkinson   To Whitewater

© AVALON TRAVEL PUBLISHING, INC.

Central Wisconsin

(CONTINUED ON NEXT PAGE)

The heart of Wisconsin has an abundance of relatively small cities and towns surrounded by rugged natural beauty. Many communities are near or on the shores of bodies of water, offering a cornucopia of adventures or interesting sights for campers.

For example, around Wausau on the Wisconsin River, you can still see the remnants of the lumbering days of the 1800s. An observation tower at nearby Rib Mountain State Park gives you a breathtaking view of one of the oldest geological formations on earth, as well as the Wisconsin River Valley.

To the west is Wisconsin Rapids, where early settlers harnessed the river to power a sawmill and later built a pulp mill. Since then, Wisconsin Rapids, Port Edwards, and Nekoosa have been a center of the state's papermaking industry.

In the southern part of this region, Green Lake's deep, cool waters offer excellent trout fishing, and nearby Ripon is the birthplace of the Republican Party.

Appleton, on the shores of Lake Winnebago, is Wisconsin's largest inland lake and the hometown of magician Harry Houdini; Oshkosh, the site of the world's largest aviation event at the EAA Air Adventure's annual fly-in; and Fond du Lac (French for foot of the lake) features an antique carousel in 400-acre Lakeside Park and a magnificent collection of German woodcarvings in St. Paul's Cathedral.

No matter where you camp in Central Wisconsin, you're certain to be captivated by natural beauty and fascinated by man-made achievements.

■ Dexter Park

Location: Pittsville, on the Yellow River, map 1, grid E8.

Campsites, facilities: There are 90 campsites in this county park. Facilities include electric hookups, flush toilets, showers, disposal station, boat ramp, tennis court, hiking trail, river swimming, and playground. Pets are allowed.

Reservations, fees: The daily fee ranges from $12 to $15. Open May through November.

Directions: From the junction of Hwy. 80 and Hwy. 54, go one mile west on Hwy. 54 to the park entrance.

Contact: Dexter Park, 715/421-8422.

Trip Notes: Drive the Cranberry Highway (715/422-4861 or 800/554-4484; website: www.visitwisrapids.com), which runs about 50 miles through south Wood County. In addition, there are guided marsh tours and bike trails, ranging from 24 to 53 miles through the largest inland cranberry-growing region in the world.

If you're into golf or tennis, it's worth the short trip to Steven's Point to visit the SentryWorld Sports Center (715/345-1600). Open daily, it includes a tennis complex and an 18-hole world-class golf course.

❷ Buckhorn Campground Resort

Location: Necedah, west of Lake Petenwell, map 1, grid H8.

Campsites, facilities: There are 147 campsites. Facilities include electric hookups, water, sewer, flush toilets, showers, disposal station, grocery store, swimming pool, and playground. Nearby there is lake boating, canoeing, and fishing. Pets are allowed.

Reservations, fees: The daily fee is $20. Open year-round. Facilities are fully operational from mid-April through mid-October.

Directions: From the junction of I-90/94 and Hwy. 58, go eight miles north on Hwy. 58, then four miles northeast on County Road G to the campground entrance.

Contact: Buckhorn Campground Resort, Rick and Carrie Gorski, N8410 Country Road G, Necedah, WI 54646, 608/565-2090.

Trip Notes: If you're looking for fun boating, canoeing, or fishing, this campground is a short distance from Lake Necedah and Lake Petenwell.

Nearby is the Necedah National Wildlife Refuge (608/565-2551), a 44,000-acre facility that's home to the world's largest population of endangered Karner blue butterflies. You can spot sandhill cranes, migrating waterfowl in the fall, wild turkeys, bald and golden eagles in the winter, and shorebirds and songbirds in the spring. The refuge also offers hiking and ski trails, observation towers, and routes to drive along. It's on Hwy. 21 west of Necedah or Hwy. 21 east of Tomah.

❸ St. Joseph Resort

Location: Necedah, west of Lake Petenwell, map 1, grid H8.

Campsites, facilities: There are 40 campsites. Facilities include RV pull-through sites, electric hookups, water, flush toilets, showers, disposal station, laundry, pond swimming, hiking trail, and playground. Nearby there is lake boating, canoeing, and fishing. Cabin and cottage rentals are available. Pets are allowed.

Reservations, fees: The daily fee is $18. Open from mid-April through November.

Directions: From the junction of Hwy. 80 and Hwy. 21, go one mile east on Hwy. 21 to the resort entrance.

Contact: St. Joseph Resort, Tammy and Mike Istvanek, P.O. Box 467, Necedah, WI 54646, 608/565-7258.

Trip Notes: If you're a racing fan, the Golden Sands Speedway (715/423-4660; website: www.goldensandsspeedway.com) in Wisconsin Rapids might be the ticket. The speedway, a fast, high-banked one-third mile asphalt track, offers variety of racing, including Super Late Model, Super Stock, Pure Stock, and Four-Cylinder competition.

❹ Wilderness County Park

Location: Necedah, on Lake Petenwell, map 1, grid H8.

Campsites, facilities: There are 159 campsites. Facilities

include electric hookups, flush toilets, showers, disposal station, lake swimming, boating, canoeing, fishing, hiking trail, and playground. Pets are allowed.

Reservations, fees: The daily fee ranges from $10 to $12.50. Open year-round. Facilities are fully operational May 1 through November 30.

Directions: From the junction of County Road Q and Hwy. 21, go one mile east on Hwy. 21, then nine miles north on County Road G and 2.5 miles east on 9th Street to the park entrance.

Contact: Wilderness County Park, N14054, 21st Ave., Necedah, WI 54646, 608/565-7285.

Trip Notes: Hunting, snowmobiling, and cross-country skiing are available at nearby Buckhorn State Park and an adjacent wildlife area, which are on a 2,512-acre peninsula on the Castle Rock Flowage of the Wisconsin River.

5 Rib Mountain State Park

Location: Wausau, near Lake Wausau, map 2, grid A3.

Campsites, facilities: There are 40 campsites. Facilities include only two electric hookups, flush toilets, showers, and downhill skiing. There are also scenic overlooks, as well as hiking and snowshoeing trails. Nearby at Lake Wausau you can swim, boat, canoe, and fish. Pets are allowed.

Reservations, fees: Reservations are accepted. Campsite reservations are available. See State Park Camping Fees and Reserving a Campsite. Open year-round.

Directions: Take U.S. Hwy. 51 and go five miles southwest to the park entrance.

Contact: Rib Mountain State Park, 4200 Park Rd., Wausau, WI 54401, 888/947-2757 or 715/842-2522.

Trip Notes: The billion-year-old hill in the 1,172-acre park is one of the oldest geological formations on earth. The top of the 60-foot observation tower, which rises 700 feet above the surrounding plain, gives you some spectacular views.

Nearby is Rustic Road #1, which was laid out in 1895. It is the first official rustic road in Wisconsin and one of the first in the nation to be preserved for its rustic and scenic characteristics. It winds for about five miles through outstanding forested glacial topography.

6 Lake DuBay Shores Campground

Location: Near Knowlton, on Lake DuBay and the Wisconsin River, map 2, grid C3.

Campsites, facilities: There are 150 campsites with a separate tent area. Facilities include RV pull-through sites, electric hookups, water, sewer, flush toilets, showers, disposal station, laundry, grocery store, boat ramp and dock, lake and river fishing, lake swimming, hiking trail, playground, and planned weekend activities. Canoe, RV, and seasonal campsite rentals are available. Pets are allowed.

Reservations, fees: The daily fee ranges from $13 to $24. Credit cards are accepted. Open year-round. Facilities are fully operational from April 1 through mid-October.

Directions: From the junction of U.S. Hwy. 51 and Hwy. 34, take exit 175 (Hwy. 34) and go two miles south on Hwy. 34. Then drive about 600 feet east on DuBay Drive to the entrance.

Contact: Lake DuBay Shore Campground, Gene Carmin, 1713 Dubay Dr., Mosinee, WI 54455, 715/457-2484, email: pooh@tznet.com.

Trip Notes: On Lake DuBay and the Wisconsin River there is outstanding fishing for muskies, walleyes, northern pike, bass and panfish. Other nearby options are the Mead Wildlife Area and five golf courses.

7 River's Edge Campground

Location: Stevens Point, on the Wisconsin River, map 2, grid D4.

Campsites, facilities: There are 115 campsites with a separate tent area. Facilities include electric hookups, water, flush toilets, showers, disposal station, grocery store, restaurant, swimming pool, river swimming, boat ramp, and playground. Seasonal campsite rentals are available. Pets are allowed.

Reservations, fees: The daily fee ranges from $16 to $20. Open year-round. Facilities are fully operational from mid-April through mid-October.

Directions: From the north on U.S. Hwy. 51, take exit 165 and go one-third mile east on County Road X, then 2.5 miles north on Sunset Drive, one-half mile west on Maple Drive, and one mile north on Campsite Drive to the entrance. From the south on U.S. Hwy. 51, take exit at County Road DB and go one-half mile east on County Road DB, then 4.5 miles south on Sunset Drive, one-half mile west on Maple Drive, and one-quarter mile north on Campsite Drive to the entrance.

Contact: Rivers Edge Campground, Jerry Fahrner, 3368 Campsite Dr., Stevens Point, WI 54481, 715/344-8058.

Trip Notes: Take the family to visit the George W. Mean Wildlife Area (715/457-6771), which is preserved and managed for waterfowl, fur bearers, deer, prairie chickens, ruffled grouse, and other game and non-game species. Bird-watching, limited fishing, hunting, and hiking are available.

Another option is the 220-acre Schmeeckle Reserve, a nature preserve at the University of Wisconsin-Stevens Point, 2419 N. Point Dr.

(715/346-4992). The visitors center includes the Wisconsin Conservation Hall of Fame.

8 Ridgewood Campground

Location: Plover, on the Wisconsin River, map 2, grid E4.

Campsites, facilities: There are 70 campsites. Facilities include electric hookups, water, flush toilets, showers, disposal station, grocery store, swimming pool, boat ramp and dock, river/pond fishing, and playground. Boat and seasonal campsite rentals are available. Pets are allowed.

Reservations, fees: The daily fee ranges from $15 to $21. Open from late May through August.

Directions: From the junction of Business U.S. Hwy. 51 and Hwy. 54, go four miles west on Hwy. 54, then three-quarters of a mile north on River Ridge Road to the campground entrance.

Contact: Ridgewood Campground, Art and Joan Langlois, 4800 River Ridge Rd., Plover, WI 54467, 715/344-8750.

Trip Notes: Everyone is sure to enjoy Rainbow Falls Family Fun Park (800/321-2228 or 715/345-1950), which is an aquatic park with water slides, wave pool, and "lazy river."

For adults, the Stevens Point Brewery at 2617 Water Street (800/369-4911; website: www.pointbeer.com) offers an interesting tour and tasting.

9 Lake Emily Park

Location: Amherst Junction, on Lake Emily, map 2, grid E6.

Campsites, facilities: There are 49 campsites in this

county park. Facilities include electric hookups, water, flush toilets, showers, disposal station, lake swimming, boat ramp and dock, hiking trail, and playground. Pets are allowed.

Reservations, fees: The daily fee ranges from $11 to $13. Open year-round.

Directions: From Amherst Junction, go one mile west on Old U.S. Hwy. 18 to the park entrance.

Contact: Lake Emily Park, 3961 Park Dr., Amherst Junction, WI 54407-9514 or 715/824-3175 or 715/346-1433.

Trip Notes: This is a great area for winter sports. For example, at Stevens Point you can find places for downhill skiing, snowboarding, and cross-country skiing at Standing Rocks (715/346-1433); cross-country skiing at Iverson Park (715/346-1531) and Schmeeckle Reserve (715/346-4992); and plenty of snowmobiling trails (715/343-6277).

🔟 South Wood County Park

Location: Wisconsin Rapids, on Wazeecha Lake, map 2, grid F3.

Campsites, facilities: There are 75 campsites. Facilities include electric hookups, flush toilets, showers, lake swimming, boating, canoeing, fishing, and playground. Pets are allowed.

Reservations, fees: The daily fee ranges from $11 to $15. Open May through October.

Directions: From Wisconsin Rapids, go five miles southeast on Hwy. 13 and County Road W to the campground entrance.

Contact: South Wood County Park, P.O. Box 8095, Wisconsin Rapids, WI 54495, 715/421-8422.

Trip Notes: Do you know how paper is made? If you want to see this process in action, visit Consolidated Papers at 231 1st Avenue N. (715/422-3789) and see papermaking

machines longer than a city block. Tours are available Wednesdays, Thursdays, and Saturdays beginning at 10 A.M.

🈁 Deer Trail Park Campground

Location: Nekoosa, on Ross Lake, map 2, grid F1.

Campsites, facilities: There are 160 campsites. Facilities include electric hookups, water, flush toilets, showers, disposal station, laundry, grocery store, swimming pool, boat ramp, tennis court, and playground. Boat, cabin, trailer, and seasonal campsite rentals are available. Pets are allowed.

Reservations, fees: The daily fee ranges from $16 to $19. There's a special rate from mid-April to mid-May and from mid-September to mid-November. Open from mid-April through mid-November.

Directions: From Hwy. 173 and Hwy. 73, go one-half mile east on Hwy. 73, then three miles south on County Road Z to the campground entrance.

Contact: Deer Trail Park Campground, Sharon and Rob Rose, 13846 County Road Z, Nekoosa, WI 54457, 715/886-3871, email: deertrl@wctc.net, website:www.gocamping america.com/deertrailpark.

Trip Notes: With its wooded, rolling hills, Wisconsin has been described a having the best natural golf course terrain in the country. If you want to play a round while camping here, visit Lake Arrowhead Golf Course (715/325-2929).

If you prefer something different, drive to nearby Rudolph, which is eight miles north of Wisconsin Rapids, to the Rudolph Grotto Gardens and Wonder Cave at 6957 Grotto Avenue (715/435-3120 or 715/435-2456). You'll see floral walkways and gardens, as well as folk art memorials, shrines, and a museum.

In Wisconsin Rapids, there's Down on the Farm Harvest and Craft (715/423-5678), a fall harvest-and-craft sale held on a 1940s-style farm. It specializes in fall, Halloween, Thanksgiving, cranberry and everyday produce, supplies, and crafts. There are farm animals to feed, pet, and photograph. It's between Washington Street and County Trunk W on 48th Street South, about 1.5 miles from Hwy. 54.

12 Vista Royalle Campground

Location: Bancroft, south of Stevens Point, map 2, grid F4.

Campsites, facilities: There are 180 campsites. Facilities include electric hookups, water, sewer, flush toilets, showers, disposal station, laundry, grocery, pond swimming and fishing, mini-golf, hiking trail, and planned weekend activities. Pets are allowed.

Reservations, fees: Reservations appreciated. The daily fee ranges from $19 to $25. Open from mid-April to mid-October.

Directions: From the junction of U.S. Hwy. 51 and County Road W, take exit 143 and go three-quarters of a mile east on County Road W. Then drive one mile north on Isherwood Road to the campground entrance.

Contact: Vista Royalle Campground, Jim and Judy Kollock, 8151 County Hwy. BB, Bancroft, WI 54921, 715/335-6860.

Trip Notes: There are five golf courses nearby, including Sentry World (715/345-1600) in Stevens Point.

If golf isn't for you or your family, there's the South Wood Historical Museum at 540 Third Street S., (715/423-1580; website: www. swch-museum.com) in Wisconsin Rapids. It documents local history with re-creations of a general store, doctor's office, and more.

Or, you might drive to New London to the Mosquito Hill Nature Center (920/779-6433; website: www.newlondonwi.org/mosquito_hill.htm), a 430-acre environmental education center two miles east of New London. There are hiking trails, indoor exhibits, and a variety of weekend programs, including birdwatching. It's open all year.

13 Hartman Creek State Park

Location: Waupaca, on the upper Waupaca Chain O' Lakes, map 2, grid F7.

Campsites, facilities: There are 101 campsites. There are no hookups, showers, or disposal station, but the campground provides swimming pool, lake swimming, boat ramp, boating (electric motors only), canoeing, fishing, and playground. There are biking, hiking, horseback riding, snowmobiling, snowshoeing, and cross-country ski trails. Pets are allowed.

Reservations, fees: Reservations are accepted. Campsite reservations are available. See State Park Camping Fees and Reserving a Campsite. Open year-round.

Directions: From Waupaca, go six miles west on Hwy. 54, then two miles south on Hartman Creek Road to the park entrance.

Contact: Hartman Creek State Park, N2480 Hartman Creek Rd., Waupaca, WI 54981-9727 or 888/947-2757 or 715/258-2372.

Trip Notes: Located on the beautiful, Waupaca Chain O' Lakes (there's 22 spring-fed bodies of water), the park is a quiet and friendly natural gem that's ideal for a picnic or an afternoon of swimming or fishing in one of the park's lakes.

There are excursion boat cruises. You can also bike,

hike, and, in winter, ski. Join a guided hike or evening program.

If you're in the mood to shop or browse, there's Waupaca's Art Barn Gallery and Gardens at N2241 Country Lane (715/256-1150), which is open all year. You'll discover art galleries and studios, folk art, and specialty shops.

14 Waupaca Camping Park

Location: Waupaca, on Old Taylor Lake, map 2, grid F8.

Campsites, facilities: There are 105 campsites. Facilities include electric hookups, water, sewer, flush toilets, showers, disposal station, laundry, grocery store, swimming pool, lake boating (no motors), canoeing, fishing, and playground. Pets are allowed.

Reservations, fees: The daily fee ranges from $19 to $23. Open from mid-April through mid-October.

Directions: From the junction of Hwy. 10/22S and Country Road K, go one-third mile south on Hwy. 22 S., then one-third mile west on South Western Avenue. Finally, follow the signs on Holmes Road to the park entrance.

Contact: Waupaca Camping Park, Ed and Gwein Berg, E2411 Holmes Rd., Waupaca, WI 54981, 715/258-8010, fax 715/258-8930, email: waupacacamp@pitnet.net.

Trip Notes: You can do it yourself and take a float trip or paddle down the Crystal River from Ding's Dock/Crystal River Canoe Trips (715/25-2612) or just sit back and enjoy a cruise on the Chief Waupaca, a sternwheeler, or the Lady of the Lakes, a motor launch, at Clearwater Harbor/Chief Waupaca Cruises (715/258-2866; website: www.clearwater harbor.com).

15 Rustic Woods Campground

Location: Waupaca, southeast of Stevens Point on private Little Rustic Lake, map 2, grid F8.

Campsites, facilities: There are 169 campsites. Facilities include electric hookups, water, sewer, flush toilets, showers, disposal station, laundry, swimming pool, lake boating (no motors), canoeing, fishing, tennis and shuffleboard courts, mini-golf, and planned weekend activities. Seasonal campsite rentals are available. Pets are allowed.

Reservations, fees: The daily fee ranges from $18 to $21. Open year-round. Facilities are fully operational mid-April to mid-October.

Directions: From the junction of U.S. 10 and Hwy. 49 and Country Road A, go three miles south on County Road A, then one-quarter mile west on County Road EE. Finally drive two and one-quarter miles west on Lake Spencer Road, one-half mile south on County Road E, and 500 feet east on Southwood Drive to the campground entrance.

Contact: Rustic Woods Campground, David and Kathy Thibaudeau, E2585 Southwood Dr., Waupaca, WI 54981, 715/258-2442.

Trip Notes: Photography enthusiasts will love capturing the 40-foot lattice-design covered bridge, featuring 400 handmade oak pegs used in its construction. It can be seen three miles south on County Road K near the Red Mill Colonial Shop in Waupaca.

Another site in Waupaca is the Hutchinson House Victorian Museum (715/258-5958) in South Park. It was the first wood frame building erected in the community. Moved to this site, it had become the local historical society's museum, showing how homes were decorated and outfitted in the mid-1850s. Guided tours are available for a small fee. Go to South Park at the south end of Main Street.

16 Patzer's Last Resort and Campground

Location: Wild Rose, on Wilson Lake, map 2, grid G7.

Campsites, facilities: There are 80 campsites. Facilities include electric hookups, water, flush toilets, showers, disposal station, lake swimming, boating, canoeing, fishing, and playground. Pets are allowed.

Reservations, fees: The daily fee is $15. Open from mid-May through mid-October.

Directions: From the junction of Hwy. 22 and County Road H, go three and one-quarter miles east on County Road H, then one-half mile east on Archer Lane to the campground entrance.

Contact: Patzer's Last Resort and Campground, 920/622-3490.

Trip Notes: Did you know that Marathon County is a center for the buying and selling of ginseng? In fact, it's the world leader in the production of this medicinal root highly valued in the Orient. If you're interested, go to Hsu's Ginseng Enterprises (715/675-2325) at T6819 County Hwy. W. in Wausau. There you can browse a gift shop that offers a variety of ginseng-related items.

17 Evergreen Campsites

Location: Wild Rose, on Kusel Lake, map 2, grid G7.

Campsites, facilities: There are 400 campsites. Facilities include electric hookups, water, sewer, flush toilets, showers, disposal station, laundry, grocery store, restaurant, lake swimming, boating, canoeing, fishing, mini-golf, hiking trail, and planned weekend activities. Boat, cabin, and seasonal campsite rentals are available. Pets are allowed.

Reservations, fees: The daily fee ranges from $18 to $20. Credit cards are accepted. Open year-round. Facilities are fully operational from mid-April through mid-October.

Directions: From the junction of Hwy. 22 and County Road H, go three miles east on County Road H, then 1.5 miles east on Archer Lane to the campground entrance.

Contact: Evergreen Campsites, Jim and Dawn Button, W5449 Archer Ln., Wild Rose, WI 54984, 920/787-3601, email: evergrn @wirural.net, website: www.evergreencamp sites.com.

Trip Notes: Campers of all ages will be enlightened by a visit to the Wild Rose Hatchery (920/622-3527) to see how fish are hatched and reared to stock Wisconsin lakes and rivers. The facility specializes in brown trout, chinook salmon, pure and hybrid muskie, northern pike, suckers, walleye, and lake sturgeon.

If history is more interesting to you, the Wild Rose Historical Museum on Main Street has guided tours of eight buildings and displays the tools, arts and crafts of Welsh, Norwegian, and English immigrants who came to the area in the 1850s.

18 Petenwell Park

Location: Friendship, southeast of Necedah, map 2, grid G2.

Campsites, facilities: There are 500 campsites in this county park. Facilities include electric hookups, flush toilets, showers, disposal station, lake swimming, boat ramp and dock, canoeing, fishing, hiking trail, and playground. Pets are allowed.

Reservations, fees: The daily fee ranges from $10 to $14. Open from mid-April through October.

Directions: From the junction of Hwy. 13 and Hwy. 21, go six miles west on Hwy. 21, then five miles north on County Road Z and one mile west on Bighorn Drive to the park entrance.

Contact: Petenwell Park, 2004 Bighorn Dr., Arkdale, WI 54613, 608/564-7513.

Trip Notes: If you're a ski enthusiast, the Skyline Ski Area (888/933-3361 or 608/339-0754) near Friendship is for you. You'll find five miles of cross-country ski trails over wooded, hilly, and flat areas, as well as snow-boarding areas. In addition, there are nine downhill ski runs with the longest at 4,000 feet and a vertical drop of 335 feet.

19 Pineland Camping Park

Location: Big Flats, north of Wisconsin Dells, map 2, grid H2.

Campsites, facilities: There are 162 campsites. Facilities include electric hookups, water, sewer, flush toilets, showers, disposal station, laundry, swimming pool, tennis court, hiking trail, and playground. Nearby are several lakes and rivers for boating, canoeing, and fishing. Pets are allowed.

Reservations, fees: The daily fee ranges from $18 to $19. Open year-round. Facilities are fully operational mid-April through December 1.

Directions: From the junction of U.S. Hwy. 51 and County Road V, go two miles south on County Road V, then 10 miles west on County Road C and one mile north on Hwy. 13 to the entrance.

Contact: Pineland Camping Park, Randy, Jolynn, and Cierra Bakovka, 916 Hwy. 13, Big Flats, WI 54613, 608/564-7818.

Trip Notes: This campground is close to Castle Rock and Pentenwell Flowage. Castle Rock, Wisconsin's fourth largest lake, is one of the state's best fishing lakes, providing walleye, northern pike, bass, and a large variety of panfish.

20 Tomorrow Wood Campground

Location: Hancock, on Fish Lake, map 2, grid H5.

Campsites, facilities: There are 170 campsites. Facilities include electric hookups, water, sewer, flush toilets, showers, disposal station, laundry, grocery store, lake swimming, boat dock, canoeing, fishing, and playground. Boat and seasonal campsite rentals are available. Pets are allowed.

Reservations, fees: The daily fee ranges from $16 to $20. Open from mid-April through mid-October.

Directions: From the junction of U.S. Hwy. 51 and County Road V, take the Hancock exit and go one and one-quarter miles east on County Road V, then two miles southeast on County Road GG. Finally, drive one-half mile south on 7th Drive to the campground entrance.

Contact: Tomorrow Wood Campground, Ed and Bonnie Zdroik, N3845 7th Dr., Hancock, WI 54943, 715/249-5954.

Trip Notes: The campground is located on Fish Lake, which is an excellent lake for fishing.

Spend a day at Tomah, where you might visit Amish Country Corner (608/372-3222; website: www.amishcountrycorner.com), where you'll find a variety of Amish shops.

Or drive north to Waupaca and the Cottage Garden Farm Gift Shops (715/256-0638) on Hwy. 54 a few miles west of town on the south side of the road (directly east of Hwy. 54 and County Road Q). The specialty stores include 2,500 square feet of shopping in a turn-of-the-century granary, atrium, and stone cellar brimming with rustic garden charm. You'll find quilts, furniture, pottery, folk art, artificial flowers, candles, garden art, and more.

21 Flanagan's Pearl Lake Campsite

Location: Redgranite, on Pearl Lake, map 2, grid G8.

Campsites, facilities: There are 306 campsites. Facilities include electric hookups, water, flush toilets, showers, disposal station, laundry, grocery store, pond swimming, mini-golf, hiking trail, planned weekend activities, and playground. Boating, canoeing, and fishing are available nearby. Seasonal campsite rentals are also available. Pets are allowed.

Reservations, fees: The daily fee ranges from $15 to $18. Open from mid-April through mid-October.

Directions: From the junction of Hwy. 21 and County Road E/EE, go three miles north on County Road EE and then about 500 feet west on Pearl Lake Road to the entrance.

Contact: Flanagan's Pearl Lake Campsite, Pat and Dianne Flanagan, W4585 S. Pearl Lake Rd., Redgranite, WI 54970, 920/566-2758, email: plcamp@vbe.com, website: www.pearl akecampsite.com.

Trip Notes: Take Hwy. 21 east to Main Street in Omro, where you can tour the Downtown Historic District. It consists of 14 late-19th century and early 20th century one-to three-story brick commercial buildings. They form the commercial core of the city, which was once known for trapping, trading, and boat-

ing on the historic Fox River, which flows through the city.

22 Coloma Camperland

Location: Coloma, northeast of Wisconsin Dells, map 2, grid H5.

Campsites, facilities: There are 82 campsites. Facilities include electric hookups, water, sewer, flush toilets, showers, disposal station, laundry, grocery store, swimming pool, shuffleboard courts, and playground. Nearby there is river boating, canoeing, and fishing. Pets are allowed.

Reservations, fees: The daily fee ranges from $14 to $20. Open year-round. Facilities are fully operational mid-April through mid-October.

Directions: From the junction of U.S. Hwy. 51 and Hwy. 21, go one-quarter mile east on Hwy. 21, then one mile south on County Road CH to the entrance.

Contact: Coloma Camperland, Chris and Carole Johnson, N1130 5th Rd., Coloma, WI 54930, 715/228-3611, email: colomarv@union tel.net, website: www.colomacamperland .com.

Trip Notes: The Mecan River runs next to Coloma and offers anglers good trout fishing.

If you enjoy horseback riding, the Enchanted Oaks Stable (715/228-2360) at W11687 State Road 21 offers guided trail rides and beginner lessons. Reservations are required.

23 Kastle Kampground

Location: Near Marion, on Kinney Lake, map 3, grid C1.

Campsites, facilities: There are 175 campsites in this county campground. Facilities include electric hookups, water, flush toilets, showers, disposal station, laundry, grocery store, boat ramp and dock, lake swimming, mini-golf, tennis court, planned weekend activities, and hiking trail. Boat rentals are available. Pets are allowed.

Reservations, fees: The daily fee is $19. Open year-round. Facilities are fully operational from the end of April through October.

Directions: From the junction of U.S. Hwy. 45 and Hwy. 110, go 2.5 miles south on Hwy. 110, then 3.5 miles west on County Road G and one-quarter mile north on Kinney Lake Road to the entrance.

Contact: Kastle Kampground, 715/754-5900.

Trip Notes: Just to the east of Marion is the Navarino Wildlife Area (715/526-4226). This wetland was once part of a glacial lake bed formed 12,000 years ago. Birds include a resident population of sandhill cranes, black terns, wood ducks, mallards, and yellow-headed blackbirds.

Other alternatives include a stop and a tour at Dupont Cheese (715/754-6525), where you can buy fresh curbs, Colby, Cheddar, Monterey Jack, and other cheeses. Ah, the power of cheese! The store is six miles south of Marion on Hwy. 110. Or you can visit the Marion A-MAZE-ment Park (toll-free 866/754-6293), a 30,000-square-foot series of walkways, towers, and platforms that twist through the maze. It's one of only five places like it in the country. The maze is two blocks off Hwys. 110 and 45, at the intersection.

24 Bear Lake Campground

Location: Manawa, on Bear Lake, map 3, grid E1.

Campsites, facilities: There are 150 campsites. Facilities include RV pull-through sites, electric hookups, water, flush toilets, showers, disposal station, laundry, grocery store, lake swimming, and mini-golf. Pets are allowed.

Reservations, fees: The daily fee ranges from $17 to $24. Open from mid-May through mid-October.

Directions: From the junction of County Road N and Hwy. 22/110, go four miles south on Hwy. 22/110 to the campground entrance.

Contact: Bear Lake Campground, Bridget and Ryan Conroy, N4715 Hwy. 22/110, Manawa, WI 54949, 920/596-3308.

Trip Notes: Bear Lake, which is a 200-acre body of water, offers fishing, boating, water-skiing, and swimming. Nearby you can enjoy water slides, tubing, canoeing, and golfing.

If you're in the area in winter, the L S Stables (800/983-7557 or 920/982-7557) on Fuerst Road in New London offers rides on a sleigh pulled by Belgian horses. There's a warming house, bonfire, and snacks. In fall, you can take a hayride.

25 Huckleberry Acres Campground

Location: New London, northwest of Appleton, map 3, grid E2.

Campsites, facilities: There are 200 campsites. Facilities include electric hookups, water, flush toilets, showers, disposal station, grocery store, lake swimming, boating (no motors), canoeing, fishing, mini-golf, shuffleboard court, and playground. Pets are allowed.

Reservations, fees: The daily fee ranges from $16 to $18. Open year-round. Facilities are fully operational from May 1 through mid-October.

Directions: From the junction of U.S. 45 and Hwy. 54, go one-half mile west on Hwy. 54, then four miles south on County Road D.

Then drive two miles west on Manske Road, one-quarter mile south on a paved unnamed road to the entrance.

Contact: Huckleberry Acres Campground, 920/982-4628.

Trip Notes: Treat the family to a hayride or, in winter, an old-fashioned sleigh ride. Royal Dome Percheron Farm (920/982-4382) provides rides, bonfires, hot chocolate, and snacks. There is also a carriage for hire. It's at N4788 Otto Road in New London.

26 Wolf River Trips and Campgrounds

Location: New London, on Little Wolf River and Big Wolf River, map 3, grid E2.

Campsites, facilities: There are 118 campsites. Facilities include electric hookups, water, sewer, flush toilets, showers, disposal station, grocery store, boat ramp, river swimming and fishing, boating, canoeing, tennis and shuffleboard courts, and hiking trail. Canoe rentals are available. Pets are allowed.

Reservations, fees: The daily fee ranges from $15 to $17. Open May through September.

Directions: From the junction of U.S. 45 and Hwy. 54, go four miles west on Hwy. 54, then one mile south on Larry Road and two blocks west on County Road X to the park entrance.

Contact: Wolf River Campgrounds, Janet Koplien, Gary and Mark Flease, E8041 Country Road X, New London, WI 54961, 920/982-2458, email: rivertrips@yahoo.com.

Trip Notes: You won't get stung if you visit the Mosquito Hill Nature Center, but in July and August you will see hundreds of live Wisconsin butterflies in the Butterfly House filled with native plants (920/779-6433).

An alternative is a visit to the New London Heritage Historical Society (920/982-5186) at 612 W. Beacon Street.

27 Blue Top Resort and Campground

Location: Fremont, on Partridge Lake, map 3, grid F2.

Campsites, facilities: There are 50 campsites. Facilities include electric hookups, water, sewer, flush toilets, showers, disposal station, laundry, pond swimming, boat ramp, lake and river boating, canoeing, lake/river fishing, and playground. Boat and cottage rentals are available. Pets are allowed.

Reservations, fees: The daily fee ranges from $14 to $18. Open from mid-April through mid-October.

Directions: From the east at junction Hwy. 110 and U.S. Hwy. 10, go two miles west on U.S. Hwy. 10, then drive about 200 feet east on County Road U to the campground entrance. It's about 1.5 miles west of the Wolf River bridge on Hwy. 10.

Contact: Blue Top Resort and Campground, Ron Gramer, 1460 Wolf River Dr., Fremont, WI 54940, 920/446-3343, website: www.blue topresort.com.

Trip Notes: The campground is on Partridge Lake, which connects to the Wolf River, an excellent spot to catch trout. In spring and fall, the area is packed with anglers fishing the run of white bass and walleye.

28 Yogi Bear Jellystone Park Camp Resort

Location: Fremont, on Lake Partridge and the Wolf River Flowage, map 3, grid F2.

Campsites, facilities: There are 240 campsites with a separate tent area. Facilities include electric hookups, water, sewer, flush toilets, showers, disposal station, laundry, grocery store, heated swimming pools, lake/river boating, canoeing, fishing guides, mini-golf, shuffleboard court, and hiking trail. Bike, boat, and cabin rentals are available. Pets are allowed.

Reservations, fees: The daily fee ranges from $25 to $42. Open from mid-April through mid-October.

Directions: From the junction of County Road H and U.S. Hwy. 10, go 1.5 miles west on U.S. Hwy. 10 to the resort entrance.

Contact: Yogi Bear Jellystone Park Camp Resort, John and Alyssa Harlan, P.O. Box 497, Fremont, WI 54940, 920/446-3420, email: mail@fremontjellystone.com, website: www.fremontjellystone.com.

Trip Notes: If you've never been tubing, get the thrill of your life on a tubing trip from Wolf River Trips (920/982-2458) in New London.

If fishing or tubing doesn't interest you or your family, visit the Hearthstone Historic House Museum (920/730-8204) at 625 W. Prospect Avenue in Appleton for its current exhibits.

From New London, take Hwy. 54 to County Road C and turn north to Seymour and the Hamburger Hall of Fame (920/833-9522) at 126 Main Street. It's packed with hamburger artifacts and memorabilia.

29 Calumet County Park

Location: Stockbridge, on the eastern shore of Lake Winnebago, map 3, grid H6.

Campsites, facilities: There are 71 campsites. Facilities include electric hookups, flush toilets, showers, disposal station, laundry, grocery store, boat ramp and dock, lake swimming, and hiking trail. Pets are allowed.

Reservations, fees: The daily fee ranges from $14 to $20. Open April through October.

Directions: From Stockbridge, go two miles north on Hwy. 55 then two miles west on County Road EE to the park entrance.

Contact: Calumet County Park, N6150 County Road EE, Hilbert, WI 54129, 920/439-1008.

Trip Notes: Lake Winnebago has 160,000-plus acres of water filled with northern pike, walleye, bass, and panfish. It's a terrific body of water for the angler.

If birds interest you more, drive up to the Kaytee Avian Education Center (800/699-9580, ext. 211; website: kaytee.com) on Clay Street in nearby Chilton. This exotic bird aviary features interactive exhibits, educational videos, and baby birds. While you're there, a stop at the Ledge View Nature Center (920/849-7094) is worth your while. Located in a 100-acre preserve at W2348 Short Road, it offers three miles of trails, a nature center, observation tower, and a variety of birds. From late May through November, you can also tour one of the facility's natural caves.

30 Eureka Dam Campsite

Location: Omro, on the Fox River, map 3, grid H1.

Campsites, facilities: There are 50 campsites. Facilities include electric hookups, water, vault toilets, disposal station, river boating, boat ramp and dock, canoeing, and fishing. There are no showers. Boat rentals are available. Pets are allowed.

Reservations, fees: The daily fee is about $12. Open April through November. Facilities are fully operational from mid-April through mid-October.

Directions: From the junction of Hwy. 116 and Hwy. 21, go 4.5 miles west on Hwy. 21, then two and three-quarters miles south on County Road K. Finally, drive one and three-quarters miles west on Eureka Lock Road to the entrance.

Contact: Eureka Dam Campsite, 920/834-5441.

Trip Notes: This is a great spot to camp if you want to fish the Upper Fox River.

If you're the adventurous sort, Skydive Adventure (920/685-5122; website: www.skydiveadventure.com) offers static line, tandem, and accelerated free-fall jump programs, which include instruction and your first jump the same day, weather permitting. The facility is at 4028 Rivermoor Road in Omro.

31 Circle R Campground

Location: Oshkosh, near Lake Winnebago, map 3, grid H4.

Campsites, facilities: There are 132 campsites with separate tent area. Facilities include RV pull-through sites, electric hookups, water, sewer, flush toilets, showers, disposal station, laundry, grocery store, nature trail, and playground. Lake swimming, boating, canoeing, and fishing are available nearby. Seasonal campsite rentals are also available. Pets are allowed.

Reservations, fees: The daily fee ranges from $15 to $19. Open May through October.

Directions: From the junction of Hwy. 41 and Hwy. 26, go one block northeast on Hwy. 26, then one mile east on County Road N. Finally, drive one and one-quarter miles south on Old Knapp Road to the entrance.

Contact: Circle R Campground, the Streblow Family, 1185 Old Knapp Rd., Oshkosh, WI 54902, 920/235-8909, email: circle@vbe.com, website: www.circle-r-camp.com.

Trip Notes: If you're camping in early July, plan on visiting Sawdust Days, which is a celebration to commemorate the region's lumbering era.

For a radical change of pace, visit the Grand Opera House (920/424-2355; website: www.grandoperahouse.org) at 100 High Avenue. Designed by William Waters and built in 1883, it reflects the architecture and opulence of the Victorian era. Restored in the 1980s, the 660-seat opera house features historic ladies' and men's warming rooms, and Victorian-style paintings around the auditorium chandelier, over the proscenium, and in the coves. There are also fine woodwork beams, wainscotting, and moldings.

32 Hickory Oaks Fly-In and Campground

Location: Oshkosh, near Lake Winnebago, map 3, grid H4.

Campsites, facilities: There are 50 campsites. Facilities include electric hookups, water, disposal station, and pond swimming and fishing; there are no restrooms. Lake boating, canoeing, fishing, and swimming are nearby. Pets are allowed.

Reservations, fees: The daily fee ranges from $15 to $18. Open May through mid-October.

Directions: From the junction of U.S. Hwy. 41 and Hwy. 110, go one-eighth mile south on Hwy. 110. Then drive 1.5 miles east on Snell Road and one-half mile south on Vinland Road to the entrance.

Contact: Hickory Oaks Fly-In and Campground, Robert Gallinger, 555 Glendale Ave., Oshkosh, WI 54901, 920/235-8076, email: flyin camp@aol.com.

Trip Notes: A visit to the EAA Air Adventure Museum (920/426-4818) to see the historic civilian and military aircraft exhibits and plane rides aboard an antique Stinson Tri-Motor should thrill the entire family.

There is also a 22-mile stretch of the Wiouwash State Trail (920/232-1960) in Oshkosh. Don't forget to obtain a state trail pass if you plan to use the trail.

33 Kalbus' Country Harbor

Location: Oshkosh, on Lake Winnebago, map 3, grid H4.

Campsites, facilities: There are 50 campsites. Facilities include electric hookups, water, sewer, flush toilets, showers, disposal station, laundry, boat ramp and dock, and lake swimming. Boat rentals are available. Pets are allowed.

Reservations, fees: The daily fee ranges from $16 to $30. Open May through October.

Directions: From the junction of U.S. Hwy. 41, Hwy. 26, and County Road N, go three miles east on County Road N, which becomes Fisk Road. Then drive 1.5 miles south on U.S. Hwy. 45. Go one-half mile east on Nekimi Avenue and one-quarter mile north on Lake Drive to the entrance.

Contact: Kalbus' Country Harbor, Gerald L. Kalbus, 5309 Lake Rd., Oshkosh, WI 54902, 920/426-0062.

Trip Notes: Make a visit to the Paine Art Center and Arboretum, (920/235-6903), a Tudor-revival house with European and American paintings and sculpture, changing art exhibits, and arboretum and display gardens.

In nearby Oxford, there's Elusive Dream Balloons (608/985-7722), which lets you experience the Wisconsin Dells from a unique perspective—high in the sky in a hot-air balloon. It's breathtaking any time of the year. Flights are by appointment only, so call for reservations.

34 Roche-A-Cri State Park

Location: Friendship, southeast of Necedah, map 4, grid A2.

Campsites, facilities: There are 40 campsites. Most sites have no hookups, showers, or a disposal station. The campground does offer hiking and cross-country ski trails. Nearby there is lake boating, canoeing, and fishing.

Reservations, fees: Reservations are accepted. Campsite reservations are available. See State Park Camping Fees and Reserving a Campsite. Open May through September.

Directions: From Friendship, go two miles north on Hwy. 13 to the park entrance.

Contact: Roche-A-Cri State Park, 1767 Hwy. 13, Friendship, WI 53934, 608/339-6881 or 608/565-2789 off-season.

Trip Notes: Roche-A-Cri is a French name that refers to the 300-foot-high rock outcropping that is the central feature of this quiet park. Climb the stairway to the top for a panoramic view of the prairie.

You can swim, boat, and fish at nearby Castle Rock and Petenwell Parks.

Farther south in Mauston, you can get away from the crowds at Red Ridge Ranch Riding Stable (608/847-2273). North of the Wisconsin Dells, this stable offers a scenic one-hour guided trail ride through 250 acres of rolling farmland and wooded hills along the Lemonweir River. There are also pony rides available. Take I-90/94 to Mauston exit 69 and go two miles east on Hwy. 82. It's open daily.

35 Lake of the Woods Campground

Location: Wautoma, on Pine Lake and the Mecan River, map 4, grid A6.

Campsites, facilities: There are 270 campsites. Facilities include electric hookups, water, flush toilets, showers, disposal station, laundry, grocery store, restaurant, swimming pool, swimming, river boating (no motors), canoeing, lake and river fishing, mini-golf, shuffleboard courts, and planned weekend activities. Boat, trailers, and seasonal campsite rentals are available. Pets are allowed.

Reservations, fees: The daily fee ranges from $18 to $22. Open year-round. Facilities are fully operational mid-April through mid-October.

Directions: From the junction of Hwys. 73, 21 and 22, drive eight miles south on Hwy. 22, then one mile west on County Road JJ and one and one-quarter miles south on 14th Avenue to the entrance.

Contact: Lake of the Woods Campground, Jack and Sue Scimeca, N9070 14th Ave., Wautoma, WI 54982, 920/787-3601, email: lotw3601@aol.com, website: www.lakeofthewoodswi.com.

Trip Notes: You can ski or just watch while enjoying a meal in the restaurant or cafeteria at the Nordi Mountain Ski Area (920/787-3324 or 800/253-7266).

Another possibility is Kusel Lake (920/787-7037; website: www.1waushara.com), a park that's the starting point for about six miles of cross-country and skating trails with a mixture of hills and other scenery. From Wild Rose, drive 4.5 miles east on County Road A and turn south on 24th Avenue and go about one mile.

In the spring, summer, and fall, The Vintage Shoppes (920/787-2303) might entice you. Specialty stores sell furniture, needlework, prints, Amish folk art, and gifts.

36 Castle Rock Park

Location: Friendship, southeast of Necedah, map 4, grid A1.

Campsites, facilities: There are 200 campsites in this county park. Facilities include electric hookups, flush toilets, showers, disposal station, lake swimming, boat ramp and dock, canoeing, fishing, hiking trail, and playground. Pets are allowed.

Reservations, fees: The daily fee ranges from $10 to $14. Open from mid-April through October.

Directions: From the junction of County Road J and Hwy. 13, go 3.5 miles south on Hwy. 13, then six miles west on County Road F and one-half mile south on County Road Z to the park entrance.

Contact: Castle Rock Park, 2397 County Hwy. Z, Rt. 2, Friendship, WI 53934, 608/339-7713.

Trip Notes: Near Castle Rock Lake, the Quad D Ranch Riding Stable (800/RANCH-75 or 608/339-6436) offers scenic horse trails, pony rides, horse-drawn hayrides, and wintertime sleigh rides.

If it's raining, head for the Boorman House (website: www.juneaucountytourism.com) in Mauston. Off I-90/94, take Hwy. 82 to Union Street. The historical museum is near the corner.

37 Coon's Deep Lake Campground

Location: Oxford, on Coon Lake, map 4, grid B3.

Campsites, facilities: There are 50 campsites. Facilities include RV pull-through sites, electric hookups, flush toilets, showers, disposal station, laundry, grocery store, and lake swimming. A boat ramp and hiking trails are nearby. Pets are allowed.

Reservations, fees: The daily fee ranges from $15 to $18. Open from mid-April through mid-October.

Directions: From the junction of County Road A and Hwy. 82, go four miles west on Hwy. 82, then about 1,000 feet north on a paved road to the campground entrance.

Contact: Coon's Deep Lake Campground, Delores and George Benich, Scott and Elizabeth Rockwell, 348 Fish Ln., Oxford, WI 53952, 608/586-5644.

Trip Notes: Just northeast of the Wisconsin Dells there is much to see and do. Drive down to see the MH Ranch (608/296-2171), which breeds miniature horses. The one-hour tour displays more than 100 mini-horses.

In Portage, a short drive south on U.S. Hwy. 51 is the Zona Gale Civic League (800/474-2525 or 608/742-6242; website: www.portagewi .com). The 1921 Pulitzer prize-winning dramatist, author, and social activist built this house in the Greek Revival style for her parents in 1906. She lived there until 1928. On her death, William Breese, her husband, deeded it to the Women's Civic League, which she had founded in 1932 to promote education and civic and social improvement.

38 Kilby Lake Campground

Location: Montello, on Kilby Lake, map 4, grid B6.

Campsites, facilities: There are 123 campsites. Facilities include electric hookups, water, sewer, flush toilets, showers, disposal station, laundry, grocery store, swimming pool, boat dock, lake swimming, hiking trail, and planned weekend activities. Boat, cabin, and trailer rentals are available. Pets are allowed.

Reservations, fees: The daily fee ranges from $16 to $23. Open from mid-April through November.

Directions: From the junction of Hwy. 22 and Hwy.23, go two miles west on Hwy. 23, then

one-half mile north on Fern Avenue to the campground entrance.

Contact: Kilby Lake Campground, Jim and Sharon Caulfield, N4492 Fern Ave., Montello, WI 53949, 608/297-2344 or 877/497-2344, email: klcg@yahoo.com, website: www.kilby lake.com.

Trip Notes: You must take a drive east on Hwy. 23 to Ripon to see the Little White Schoolhouse (920/748-6764; website: www .ripon-wi.com). This historic building, a National Historic Landmark that's on the National Register of Historic Places, is the birthplace of the Republican Party. You can also learn more about the founding of Ripon and what school was like for children in the 1800s. The site is on Hwy. 23 (Blackburn Street), one block east of downtown Ripon.

39 Buffalo Lake Camping Resort

Location: Montello, on Buffalo Lake, northeast of Wisconsin Dells, map 4, grid B6.

Campsites, facilities: There are 130 campsites. Facilities include electric hookups, water, sewer, flush toilets, showers, disposal station, laundry, grocery store, swimming pool, boat ramp and dock, lake boating, and planned weekend activities. Bike, cabin, and seasonal campsite rentals are available. Pets are allowed.

Reservations, fees: The daily fee ranges from $14 to $22. Open from mid-April through mid-October.

Directions: From the junction of Hwy. 22 and Hwy. 23, go west on Hwy. 23, then one mile west on County Road C to the campground entrance.

Contact: Buffalo Lake Camping Resort, Linda and Gary Doudna, 555 Lake Avenue, Montello, WI 53949, 608/297-2915 or 888/297-

2915, email: lake@maqs.net, website: www.go campingamerica/buffalolake.

Trip Notes: Buffalo Lake is a 2,210-acre lake that is a catfisherman's delight. If you don't fish, visit Amish House (608/296-2728) at W1886 White Lake Court. It's open all year.

40 Lake Arrowhead Campground

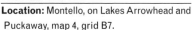

Location: Montello, on Lakes Arrowhead and Puckaway, map 4, grid B7.

Campsites, facilities: There are 225 campsites. Facilities include electric hookups, water, sewer, flush toilets, showers, disposal station, laundry, grocery store, boat ramp, lake swimming, heated swimming pool, and planned activities. Bike, boat, motor, and seasonal campsite rentals are available. Pets are allowed.

Reservations, fees: The daily fee ranges from $25 to $30. Open from mid-April through mid-October.

Directions: From the junction of northbound Hwy. 22 and Hwy. 23, go one-eighth mile east on Hwy. 23, then six miles east on County Road C. Then drive about 1,000 feet east on Fox Court to the entrance.

Contact: Lake Arrowhead Campground, Phil and Linda Malsack, W781 Fox Ct., Montello, WI 53949, 920/295-3000, website: www.lake arrowheadcampground.com.

Trip Notes: Ever see a Clydesdale ranch? Here's your chance to visit one at Larson's Famous Clydesdales (920/748-5466; website: www.larsonsclydesdales.com) near Ripon. There's a 90-minute show that includes a tour, a presentation on how the horses are prepared for showing, and a demonstration. The kids can pet a baby Clydesdale and tour a museum and gift shop. The ranch is 17 miles west of Fond du Lac and four miles south of Ripon on Reeds Corners Road.

41 Green Lake Campground

Location: Green Lake, northeast of the Wisconsin Dells, map 4, grid B8.

Campsites, facilities: There are 300 campsites. Facilities include electric hookups, water, sewer, flush toilets, showers, disposal station, laundry, grocery store, swimming pool, pond swimming, hiking trail, mini-golf, playground, and planned activities. Lake boating, canoeing, fishing, boat ramps, and golf courses are nearby. Pets are allowed.

Reservations, fees: The daily fee ranges from $24 to $30. Open from mid-April through mid-October.

Directions: From the junction of Hwy. 23 and Hwy. 49, go 3.5 miles west on Hwy. 23 to the campground entrance.

Contact: Green Lake Campground, Rick Pierce, W2360 Hwy. 23, Green Lake, WI 54941, 920/294-3543, email: glcamp@itol.com, website: www.wisvacations.com/greenlake campground.

Trip Notes: This campground is a golfer's delight with three golf courses nearby and a nine-hole, par 3 course that is free to guests.

If you lack recreation gear, Zephyr Kayak and Recreation (920/294-3949) has kayaks, bikes, and sailing equipment for charter or rental with instruction available. You can tour lakes, rivers, and scenic areas with their custom outfitting and delivery and support service. The facility is on the north end of Mill Street in downtown Green Lake next to the Chamber of Commerce and across from the grocery store.

42 Holiday Shores Campground and Resort

Location: Wisconsin Dells, on the Wisconsin River, map 4, grid C2.

Campsites, facilities: There are 325 campsites with a separate tent area. Facilities include electric hookups, water, flush toilets, showers, disposal station, grocery store, restaurant, swimming pool, boat ramp, river swimming, hiking trail, and playground. Bike, boat, cabin, and seasonal campsite rentals are available. Pets are allowed, but no pets are permitted in rental units.

Reservations, fees: Deposit is required on reservations. The daily fee ranges from $27 to $30. Credit cards are accepted. Open May through mid-October.

Directions: From the junction of I-90/94 and Hwy. 13, take exit 87 and go seven miles east on Hwy. 13. Then drive about 100 feet northwest on County Road Q and 500 feet north on River Road to the resort entrance.

Contact: Holiday Shores Campground and Resort, the Ward Family, 3901 River Rd., Wisconsin Dells, WI 53965, 608/254-2717, website: www.wisvations.com/holidayshores.

Trip Notes: Believe it or not, there really is a place to experience the wacky and weird. Visit Ripley's Believe It or Not! Museum (608/253-7556) to witness the strange, the unbelievable, the bizarre, and downright loony. There are eight galleries, two sit-down theaters, and seven video presentations. The museum is at 115 Broadway.

43 Stand Rock Campground

Location: Wisconsin Dells, near the Upper Dells, map 4, grid C2.

Campsites, facilities: There are 225 campsites. Facilities include electric hookups, water, sewer, flush toilets, showers, disposal station, laundry, grocery store, swimming pool, pond fishing, mini-golf, hiking trail, playground, and planned activities. Boating, canoeing, and fishing are nearby. Pets are allowed. No motorcycle campers.

Reservations, fees: The daily fee ranges from $24 to $27. Credit cards are accepted. Open from mid-April through mid-October.

Directions: From the junction of I-90/94 and U.S. Hwy. 12/16, take exit 85 and go about 600 feet east on Hwy. 12/16. Then drive one mile northeast on 60th Street and about 600 feet north on Stand Rock Road to the campground entrance.

Contact: Stand Rock Campground, the Krahn family, N570 Hwy. N., Wisconsin Dells, WI 53965, 608/253-2169, website: www.stand rock.com.

Trip Notes: A visit to Storybook Gardens (608/253-2391; website: www.dells.com/storybook.html) will fascinate the child in every camper. Meet live storybook characters in the Land of Once-Upon-a-Time. The family can also pack and bring along a picnic basket or enjoy lunch at the Gingerbread House. Storybook Gardens is at 1500 Wisconsin Dells Parkway.

44 Rocky Arbor State Park

Location: Wisconsin Dells, near the Upper Dells, map 4, grid C2.

Campsites, facilities: There are 89 campsites. Facilities include electric hookups, showers, disposal station, self-guided nature trails, and hiking trails. Boating, canoeing, and fishing are nearby. Pets are allowed.

Reservations, fees: Reservations are accepted. Campsite reservations are available.

See State Park Camping Fees and Reserving a Campsite. Open from late May through early September.

Directions: From Wisconsin Dells, go one mile northwest on U.S. Hwy. 12 to the park entrance.

Contact: Rocky Arbor State Park, E10320 Fern Dell Rd., Baraboo, WI 53913, 608/254-8001, summer, and 608/254-2333, off-season.

Trip Notes: This 225-acre state park, a quiet, secluded escape just 1.5 miles from Wisconsin Dells, features beautiful pine tree forest and sandstone bluffs.

45 K and L Campground

Location: Wisconsin Dells, on a private lake, map 4, grid C2.

Campsites, facilities: There are 96 campsites. Facilities include electric hookups, water, sewer, flush toilets, showers, disposal station, grocery store, swimming pool, lake swimming, and "whiffle ball" golf. Bike, boat, and cottage rentals are available. Pets are allowed, but no pets or smoking in rental cottages.

Reservations, fees: The daily fee ranges from $20 to $25. Open May through mid-September.

Directions: From Wisconsin Dells, take Hwy. 23 and go east to County Road G, then go six miles north on County Road G to the campground entrance.

Contact: K and L Campground, Katy and Lynn Eder, 3503 County Road G, Wisconsin Dells, WI 53965, 608/586-4720, email: threes@maqs.net.

Trip Notes: You can take a guided 20-or 50-minute horseback ride through a wildlife refuge at Beaver Spring Riding Stable (608/254-2707).

Fun for the whole family is a visit to the American UFO and Sci-Fi Museum (608/253-5055).

Here you can see characters from Star Wars, the Terminator, E.T., and other films. Learn more about UFO sightings and "contacts" in the UFO Research Gallery and video theater. The museum is at 740 Eddy Street.

46 Arrowhead Resort Campground

Location: Wisconsin Dells, near the Wisconsin River, map 4, grid C2.

Campsites, facilities: There are 274 campsites. Facilities include electric hookups, water, sewer, flush toilets, showers, disposal station, laundry, grocery store, swimming pools, mini-golf, shuffleboard courts, hiking trail, and playground. Boating, canoeing, and fishing are nearby. Pets are allowed.

Reservations, fees: The daily fee ranges from $23 to $39. Open from mid-April through November. Facilities are fully operational mid-April through early October.

Directions: From the junction of I-90/94 and Hwy. 12/16, go one mile west on Hwy. 12/16, then one and one-quarter miles south on Arrowhead Road to the entrance.

Contact: Arrowhead Resort, Karl Weber, P.O. Box 295, Wisconsin Dells, WI 53965, 608/254-7344.

Trip Notes: If you're looking for a thrill a minute, be sure to see the Tommy Bartlett Thrill Show (608/254-2525), featuring professional water-skiers and daredevil entertainers who perform on water, on stage, and high in the air.

Another option is the Beaver Springs Aquarium (608/254-2735), which features more than 1,000 live fish and other aquatic creatures. Large tanks surround you with more than 50,000 gallons of water on display. There are also touch-and-feel areas

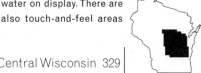

that give visitors the chance to interact and feed fascinating fish. It is located (naturally) at 600 Trout Road.

47 Dell Boo Campground

Location: Wisconsin Dells, near Mirror Lake, map 4, grid C2.

Campsites, facilities: There are 138 campsites. Facilities include electric hookups, water, sewer, flush toilets, showers, disposal station, laundry, grocery store, swimming pool, tennis and shuffleboard courts, hiking trail, and planned activities, including movies. Boating, canoeing, and fishing are nearby. Bike and cabin rentals are available.

Reservations, fees: The daily fee ranges from $26 to $34. Open May through September.

Directions: From the junction of I-90/94 and U.S. Hwy. 12, take exit 92 and go one and one-quarter miles southeast on Hwy. 12, then three-quarters of a mile west on Shady Lane Road to the entrance.

Trip Notes: You can ride your own horse or take a horse-drawn carriage ride through a scenic sandstone canyon at the Lost Canyon Tours (608/253-2781).

48 Erickson's Tepee Park Campground

Location: Wisconsin Dells, map 4, grid C2.

Campsites, facilities: There are 119 campsites with a separate area for tents. Facilities include electric hookups, water, sewer, flush toilets, showers, disposal station, grocery store, swimming pool, mini-golf, and playground. Boating, canoeing, and fishing are nearby. Bike and cabin rentals are available. Pets are allowed.

Reservations, fees: Reservations are required. The daily fee ranges from $19 to $26. Credit cards are accepted. Open from mid-April through mid-October.

Directions: From the junction of I-90/94 and Hwy. 13, go one-quarter mile east on Hwy. 13 to Trout Road, then go two miles southwest on Trout Road to the campground entrance.

Contact: Erickson's Tepee Park Campground, Georgine, Greg, and Russ Erickson, E10096 Trout Rd., Wisconsin Dells, WI 53965, 608/253-3122, fax 608/253-6211, website: www.geocities.com/tepeepark.

Trip Notes: Have you ever ridden a duck? If not, then you need to take a duck tour at Original Wisconsin Ducks (608/254-8751; website: www.wisconsinducktours.com), which uses amphibious World War II landing craft to cruise through the Lower Dells and Lake Delton. You'll get a close look at the rocky cliffs along the river. There's also the Dells Army Duck Tours (608/254-6080), which also has a game farm where you can feed white-tail deer, turkeys, peacocks, goats, and rabbits.

49 Wisconsin Dells KOA

Location: Wisconsin Dells, near the Wisconsin River, map 4, grid C2.

Campsites, facilities: There are 140 campsites. Facilities include electric hookups, water, sewer, flush toilets, showers, disposal station, laundry, grocery store, swimming pool, playground, and planned activities. Boating, canoeing, and fishing are nearby. Bike and cabin rentals are available. Pets are allowed, but they are not permitted in cabins.

Reservations, fees: The daily fee ranges from $21 to $30. Open from mid-April through mid-October.

Directions: From I-90/94, take exit 87 and go north on Hwy. 13 to the third stoplight and turn left on Stand Rock Road to the campground entrance.

Contact: Wisconsin Dells KOA, Ed and Jill Brennan, S235 Stand Rock Rd., Wisconsin Dells, WI 53965, 800/254-4177 or 608/254-4177, website: www.koacampground.com.

Trip Notes: Take the family to Noah's Ark Water Park (608/254-6351), which is America's largest water theme park and enjoy the water slides and wave pools.

50 Sherwood Forest Camping and RV Resort

Location: Wisconsin Dells, near the Wisconsin River, map 4, grid C2.

Campsites, facilities: There are 200 campsites. Facilities include electric hookups, water, sewer, flush toilets, showers, disposal station, laundry, swimming pool, hiking trail, and playground. Boating, canoeing, and fishing are nearby. Cabin and RV rentals are available. Pets are allowed.

Reservations, fees: The daily fee ranges from $22 to $30. Open May through September.

Directions: From the junction of I-90/94 and Hwy. 13, take exit 87 and go one mile east on Hwy. 13, then one-half mile northwest on Hwys. 12/16 to the resort entrance.

Contact: Sherwood Forest Camping and RV Resort, Bob and Barbara Gussel, S 352 Hwys. 12/16, Wisconsin Dells, WI 53965, 608/254-7080.

Trip Notes: Would you like to pretend you are Mark Twain and lazily cruise the Upper Dells? Then take the Mark Twain Dells Tours (608/254-6080), which is a one-hour tour of the Upper Dells from Kilbourn Dam to Louise Bluff.

51 Yogi Bear's Jellystone Park Camp Resort

Location: Wisconsin Dells, map 4, grid C2.

Campsites, facilities: There are 358 campsites. Facilities include electric hookups, water, sewer, flush toilets, showers, disposal station, laundry, grocery store, restaurant, swimming pool, boat dock, boating (electric motors only), shuffleboard courts, hiking trail, and playground. Boat, cabin, and cottage rentals are available. Pets are allowed. No motorcycle campers.

Reservations, fees: The daily fee ranges from $18 to $55. Credit cards are accepted. Open from mid-April through mid-October.

Directions: From the junction of I-90/94 and U.S. Hwy. 12, take exit 92 and go one-half mile northwest on Hwy. 12. Then drive one mile west on Gasser Road to the campground entrance.

Contact: Yogi Bear's Jellystone Park Camp Resort, P.O. Box 510, Wisconsin Dells, 53965, 800/462-9644, ext. WAC, email: yogi bear@ chorus.net, website: www.dells.com/yogibear.

Trip Notes: Want to meet some celebrities? Visit the Wax World of the Stars (608/254-2184; website: www.wisdells.com) and see more than 100 personalities, including Elvis, Marilyn, Dolly, Lucy, and the Duke, figures so lifelike you'll expect them to speak. The museum is at 105 Broadway next to the Ripley's Believe It Or Not! Museum.

52 Wagon Wheel Campground

Location: Briggsville, on Lake Mason, map 4, grid C4.

Campsites, facilities: There are 150 campsites. Facilities

include electric hookups, water, sewer, flush toilets, showers, disposal station, grocery store, swimming pool, boat ramp and dock, lake swimming, and playground. Boat rentals are available. Pets are allowed.

Reservations, fees: The daily fee is $16. Open May through October.

Directions: From the junction of County Road A and Hwy. 23, go 1.5 miles west on Hwy. 23 and then about 500 feet north on a paved road to the campground entrance.

Contact: Wagon Wheel Campground, 4106 First Dr., Briggsville, WI 53920, 608/981-2161.

Trip Notes: Just a few miles south to Portage is the Fox-Wisconsin Portage Site (800/474-2525 or 608/742-6242; website: www.portagewi.com), the original portage or carrying place. It's a narrow strip of land between the north-flowing Fox and the south-flowing Wisconsin Rivers. Father Marquette and Louis Joliet recorded using the portage on June 14, 1673. By the 1780s, it became a rendezvous point for the trading of furs and supplies. Native Americans controlled and used the portage for hundreds of years until the Treaty of 1828. The route, now city street Wauona Trail, is listed on the National Register of Historic Places.

53 Lake Mason Campground

Location: Briggsville, on Lake Mason, map 4, grid C4.

Campsites, facilities: There are 174 campsites. Facilities include electric hookups, water, sewer, flush toilets, showers, disposal station, laundry, grocery store, swimming pool, boat ramp and dock, lake swimming, and playground. Boat rentals are available. Pets are allowed.

Reservations, fees: The daily fee ranges from $14 to $18. Open May through October.

Directions: From the junction of Hwys. 13, 16, and 23, go 6.5 miles east on Hwy. 23 and 1.5 miles north on County Road G. Then drive two miles east on Golden Avenue and one-third of a mile south on First Lane to the campground entrance.

Contact: Lake Mason Campground, 4035 First Ln., Briggsville, WI 53920, 608/981-2444.

Trip Notes: In Portage, you can visit the Historic Indian Agency House (608/742-6362), built by the U.S. government in 1832 for John Harris Kinzie, the agent to the Winnebago Nation. His wife, Juliette Magill Kinzie, wrote WauBun. The structure is near the site of Fort Winnebago, facing the Portage Canal. It's furnished with antiques dating to pre-1833.

54 Wilderness Campground

Location: Montello, on the banks of three private lakes, map 4, grid C6.

Campsites, facilities: There are 300 campsites. Facilities include RV pull-through sites, electric hookups, water, sewer, flush toilets, showers, disposal station, laundry, grocery store, boat ramp, swimming pool, lake swimming, boating (no motors), hiking trail, mini-farm, and mini-golf. Bike and boat rentals are available. Pets are allowed.

Reservations, fees: The daily fee ranges from $18 to $32. Credit cards are accepted. Open from mid-April through mid-October.

Directions: From the junction of Hwy. 23 and Hwy. 22, go seven miles south on Hwy. 22 to the campground entrance.

Contact: Wilderness Campground, Bea Weiss, N1499 Hwy. 22, Montello, WI 53949, 608/297-2002, email: wildrnes@palacenet.net, website: www.wildernesscampground.com.

Trip Notes: In winter, a short trip south to Portage, 30 miles north of Madison off I-90/94, is the Cascade Mountain Ski and Snowboard

Area (608/742-5588; website: www.cascade mountain.com). The site features a large beginner area. There's also a new Snowtubing Park, with four chutes and a surface tow, and the Daisy Warming Chalet, with cafeteria and sundeck. The area's high-speed, detachable quad chairlift gets you to the top in less than three minutes. Other amenities and services include restaurant, lounges, and ski shop.

55 Mirror Lake State Park

Location: Lake Delton, on Mirror Lake, map 4, grid D2.

Campsites, facilities: There are 147 campsites. Facilities include electric hookups, showers, disposal station, lake swimming, boating, canoeing, fishing, and biking, hiking, and cross-country ski trails.

In winter, the southern unit has 40 sites with electric hookups and hand-pumped water at Ottawa Lake. Reservations here are not required.

Reservations, fees: Reservations are accepted. Campsite reservations are available. See State Park Camping Fees and Reserving a Campsite. Open year-round.

Directions: From Lake Delton, go one mile southeast on Hwy. 12 to the park entrance.

Contact: Mirror Lake State Park, E10320 Fern Dell Rd., Baraboo, WI 53913, 608/254-2333.

Trip Notes: Just three miles from Wisconsin Dells, this park has a picturesque lake that is nearby surrounded by sandstone bluffs. There are plenty of wooded campsites.

When you're this close to Baraboo, you can't overlook the Circus World Museum (608/356-8341; website: www.circusworldmuseum.com), the world's largest relating to the circus. The 50-acre complex is at the Ringling Bros. Circus original winter quarters, a National Historic Landmark. Be among the

200,000 who tour the facility each year. It's great fun for the entire family. The museum is at 426 Water Street (Hwy. 113), just 15 minutes from I-90/94.

56 Pride of America Camping Resort-Lake George

Location: Portage, on Lake George, map 4, grid D5.

Campsites, facilities: There are 311 campsites with a separate tent area. Facilities include electric hookups, water, sewer, flush toilets, showers, disposal station, laundry, grocery store, swimming pool, lake swimming, boat dock, boating (motors are not allowed), canoeing, fishing, and playground. Boat, cabins, and RV rentals are available. Pets are allowed.

Reservations, fees: The daily fee ranges from $24 to $29. Credit cards are accepted. Open from mid-April through mid-October.

Directions: From the junction of I-90/94 and Hwy. 33, take exit 106 and go four miles east on Hwy. 33. Then drive two and three-quarters miles southeast on Hwy. 16/51 and two and one-quarter miles northeast on County Road G to the campground entrance.

Contact: Pride of America Campground-Lake George, Sheldon Hanson, P.O. Box 403, Portage, WI 53901, 800/236-6395 or 608/742-6395, website: www.camppoa.com.

Trip Notes: The community of Portage marks an ancient overland portage that was a strategic link between the Fox and Wisconsin Rivers. Tour the city's downtown historic district and the waterfront. You can obtain a map to guide you to 23 historic buildings from the Chamber of Commerce at 301 W. Wisconsin Street. Each building has a number plaque on the front that's visible from the street to help you match the structure to historical photographs.

Also, be sure to get to the Museum at the Portage (804 MacFarlane Road, 608/742-6682), which honors the history of the third oldest city in Wisconsin.

57 Indian Trails Campground

Location: Pardeeville, on a private lake, map 4, grid D6.

Campsites, facilities: There are 300 campsites. Facilities include electric hookups, water, sewer, flush toilets, showers, disposal station, laundry, grocery store, swimming pool, lake swimming, boating (motors are not allowed), mini-golf, shuffleboard courts, planned weekend activities, and playgrounds. Boat and seasonal campsite rentals are available. Pets are allowed.

Reservations, fees: The daily fee ranges from $20 to $24. Open from mid-April through mid-October.

Directions: From the junction of Hwys. 44 and 22, go one and one-quarter miles north on Hwy. 22, then one mile west on Haynes Road to the campground entrance.

Contact: Indian Trails Campground, Fritz and Myrna Meierdirk, W6445 Haynes Rd., Pardeeville, WI 53954, 608/429-3244, email: itcinfo@ndntrls.com.

Trip Notes: Be sure to stop and see LaReau's World of Miniature Buildings (608/429-2848). It's a fascinating collection of 100 miniature buildings built to scale. They include the White House, Statue of Liberty, and more.

58 Duck Creek Campground

Location: Pardeeville, on Duck Creek, map 4, grid D6.

Campsites, facilities: There are 125 campsites. Facilities include electric hookups, water, flush toilets, showers, disposal station, laundry, grocery store, restaurant, pond swimming, pond or stream fishing, and planned weekend activities. Lake boating, canoeing, and fishing are nearby. Cabin rentals are available. Pets are allowed.

Reservations, fees: The daily fee ranges from $19 to $20. Credit cards are accepted. Open May through mid-October.

Directions: From the junction of Hwys. 16 and 22, go one-half mile north on Hwy. 22, then one mile west on County Road G to the campground entrance.

Contact: Duck Creek Campground, Tom and Judy Buchta, W6560 County Road G, Pardeeville, WI 53954, 608/429-2425, website: www.duckcreekcampground.com.

Trip Notes: Take a few minutes to drive to Poynette to see the MacKenzie Environmental Center (608/6335-8110) and see deer, buffalo, and wolves; view exhibits in the interpretive center; walk through the nature trails and arboretum; and ascend the observation tower.

59 Plymouth Rock Camping Resort

Location: Elkhart Lake, on Little Elkhart Lake, map 5, grid B8.

Campsites, facilities: There are 486 campsites. Facilities include electric hookups, water, sewer, flush toilets, showers, disposal station, laundry, grocery store, restaurant, swimming pool, boat ramp, lake swimming, lake boating, hiking trail, shuffleboard courts, mini-golf, and movies. Bike and cabin rentals are available. Pets are allowed.

Reservations, fees: Reservations are recommended. The daily fee ranges from $23 to $38. Open from mid-May through mid-October.

Directions: From the junction of Hwy. 23 and Hwy. 67, go three miles north on Hwy. 67 to the campground entrance.

Contact: Plymouth Rock Camping Resort, Sandi Thuecks, P.O. Box 445, Elkhart Lake, WI 53020, 920/892-4252, email: plymouth rock@excel.net, website: plymouthrock campingresort.com.

Trip Notes: Elkhart Lake is the home of Road America (800/365-7223; website: www.road-america.com), an internationally famous motor sport track that draws the world's top drivers for a series of prestigious races throughout the summer. It's also the site for national tire testing, vehicle introductions, TV commercials, films, and car club events.

Other noteworthy area attractions are Henschel's Indian Museum (920/878-3193), one of the state's most complete Indian museums, which contains a collection of Native American copper, pottery, and other artifacts dating back to 8000 B.C.; and Rolling Meadows Sorghum Mill and Brooms (920/876-2182). Established in 1984, Rolling Meadows produces brooms by hand with broomcorn grown and processed on site. Tours by appointment.

60 Westward Ho Camp-Resort

Location: Fond du Lac, southeast of Lake Winnebago, map 5, grid C7.

Campsites, facilities: There are 250 campsites. Facilities include electric hookups, water, sewer, flush toilets, showers, disposal

station, laundry, grocery store, heated swimming pool, pond fishing, mini-golf, hiking and exercise trails, arts and crafts, three playgrounds, and planned activities. Lake boating, canoeing, and fishing are nearby. Pets are allowed.

Reservations, fees: Reservations are recommended. The daily fee ranges from $25 to $36. Credit cards are accepted. Open from mid-May through September.

Directions: From the junction of U.S. Hwy. 41 and Hwy. 23, go 16 miles east on Hwy. 23 and three miles south on County Road G. Then go one-half mile east on County Road T and follow the signs to the entrance.

Contact: Westward Ho Camp-Resort, Joanne Sussex, N5456 Division Rd., Glenbeulah, WI 53023, 920/526-3407.

Trip Notes: The Convention and Visitors Bureau rents an audio tape, "Talking Country Roads," which describes rural points of interest in Fond du Lac County (920/923-3010 or 800/937-9123). You might pay a visit to the Kristmas Kringle Shoppe (920/922-3900 or 800/721-2525), a two-story Bavarian-style building that houses many Christmas shops and is open all year.

61 KOA-Fond du Lac Kampground

Location: Fond du Lac, at the south end of Lake Winnebago, map 5, grid C5.

Campsites, facilities: There are 149 campsites. Facilities include electric hookups, water, sewer, flush toilets, showers, disposal station, laundry, grocery store, swimming pool, pond swimming, mini-golf, hiking trail, playground, and planned weekend activities. The campground is close to the southern end of Lake Winnebago for boating, canoeing, and fishing. Cabin rentals are available. Pets are allowed.

Reservations, fees: The daily fee ranges from $20 to $27. Open from mid-April through mid-October.

Directions: From the junction of Hwy. 151 and U.S. Hwy. 41, go 5.25 miles south on U.S. Hwy. 41, then 1.5 miles east on County Road B to the entrance.

Contact: KOA-Fond du Lac, David and Nancy Evans, P.O. Box 356, Eden, WI 53019, 920/477-2300.

Trip Notes: When you're in Fond du Lac, be sure to visit the Galloway House and Village (800/937-9123), a restored 30-room Victorian mansion and a village of late 1800s buildings, including a working gristmill. It's located at 336 Old Pioneer.

If you still have energy, take a hike at the Horicon Marsh (920/887-9899; website: www.fws.gov/horicon.html). Don't forget to bring your binoculars or borrow some from the 47-acre Marsh Haven Nature Center, which is on Hwy. 49, three miles east of Waupun. This facility, on the northern edge of the Horicon Marsh, is dedicated to research, rehabilitation, and education.

62 Benson's Century Camping Resort

Location: Campbellsport, on Long Lake, map 5, grid C7.

Campsites, facilities: There are 250 campsites. Facilities include electric hookups, water, flush toilets, showers, disposal station, grocery store, boat ramp and dock, and lake swimming. Boat rentals are available. Pets are allowed.

Reservations, fees: The daily fee ranges from $16 to $30. Open from mid-May through mid-October.

Directions: From the junction of U.S. Hwy. 45 and Hwy. 67, go six miles northeast on Hwy. 67 to the resort entrance.

Contact: Benson's Century Camping Resort, Nancy Benson, N3845 Hwy. 67, Campbellsport, WI 53010, 920/533-8597 or 920/533-8150.

Trip Notes: It's worth making the short trip to Adell to see the Pleasure Valley Llamas (920/994-9294), take in a one-to two-hour indoor llama show, spin wool, and get a kiss (eek!) from a llama (presumably they don't kiss like a camel does). Call for a reservation.

63 Long Lake Campground: Kettle Moraine State Forest North Unit

Location: Campbellsport, in Kettle Moraine State Forest, map 5, grid C7.

Campsites, facilities: There are 200 campsites. Facilities include only three sites with electric hookups, showers, and a disposal station. The campground provides lake swimming, boat ramp, boating, canoeing, fishing, and hiking trails.

Reservations, fees: Reservations are accepted. Campsite reservations are available. See State Park Camping Fees and Reserving a Campsite. Open May through mid-October.

Directions: From Campbellsport go eight miles north on Hwy. 67 to Kettle Moraine Drive and the campground entrance.

Contact: Kettle Moraine State Forest, Northern Unit, Long Lake Campground, N1765 County Road G, Campbellsport, WI 53010, 262/626-2116.

Trip Notes: The 29,000-acre area is a gift of the glacier. Be sure to visit the Henry S. Reuss Ice Age Visitor Center (920/533-8322) to view the interpretive displays and the 20-minute video on the Ice Age.

Another interesting place is the Kettle Moraine Springs Hatchery (920/528-8825), which rears steelhead (rainbow) trout and coho (silver) salmon. Take Hwy. 28 north from Batavia, turn west on Cherry Hill Road to Trout Spring Road. Then turn right.

64 Mauthe Lake Campground: Kettle Moraine State Forest-North Unit

Location: Kewaskum, south of Campbellsport, map 5, grid D7.

Campsites, facilities: There are 137 campsites. Facilities include electric hookups, vault toilets, showers, disposal station, lake swimming, boating, canoeing, lake fishing, hiking trails, planned activities, and playground. Canoe rentals are available. Pets are allowed.

In winter, there are 10 campsites with electric hookups and water, plus six backpacking sites. Reservations are required.

Reservations, fees: Reservations are accepted. Campsite reservations are available. See State Park Camping Fees and Reserving a Campsite. Open year-round.

Directions: From Kewaskum, drive seven miles north on County Road GGG to the campground entrance.

Contact: Kettle Moraine State Forest, Northern Unit, N1765 County Road G, Campbellsport, WI 53010, 262/626-2116.

Trip Notes: You can take a trail ride through the state forest with the Bar-N-Ranch (262/626-4096), which is open weekends from mid-April to Memorial Day and from Labor Day to mid-November. The ranch is at N1639 County Road GGG.

An alternative is to drive 1.5 miles west of Waupun on Hwy. 49 to the Tom Dooley Orchard (920/324-3664). Here you can buy many different kinds of apples. The store also has apple cider, apple pies, apple turnovers, carmel apples, and a large variety of craft items, many of which are supplied by local crafters.

65 Playful Goose

Location: Horicon, on the Rock River, map 5, grid E3.

Campsites, facilities: There are 199 campsites with a separate tent area. Facilities include electric hookups, water, sewer, flush toilets, showers, disposal station, laundry, swimming pool, boating (motors are not allowed), canoeing, river and pond fishing, shuffleboard courts, and hiking trail. The 32-mile-long Wild Goose Hiking and Biking Trail (920/929-3135) is three miles away. Boat rentals are available. Pets are allowed.

Reservations, fees: The daily fee ranges from $19 to $27. Open May through mid-October.

Directions: From the junction of Hwys. 26 and 33, go three miles east on Hwy. 33. Then go one-half mile south on Main Street to the campground entrance.

Contact: Playful Good Campground, 2001 South Main St., Horicon, WI 53032, 920/485-4744, email: andy@internetwis.com.

Trip Notes: The Horicon Marsh covers 32,000 acres of Dodge County with the Horicon National Wildlife Refuge (800/937-9123 or 920/324-5818). Horicon is the headquarters and education center for the Wisconsin Department of Natural Resources with observation windows and displays.

66 Lake Lenwood Beach and Campground

Location: West Bend, on Lake Lenwood, map 5, grid E7.

Campsites, facilities: There are 110 campsites. Facilities include electric hookups, water, sewer, flush toilets, showers, disposal station, lake swimming, boating (electric motors only), canoeing, fishing, hiking trail, and playground. Boat and cottage rentals are available. Pets are allowed.

Reservations, fees: The daily fee ranges from $22 to $26. Open from mid-April through mid-October.

Directions: From the junction of U.S. Hwy. 45 and County Road D, go one mile east on County Road D. Then drive one mile north on Hwy. 144 and one block west on Wallace Lake Road to the campground entrance.

Contact: Lake Lenwood Beach and Campground, Mike and Mary Dricken, 7053 Lenwood Dr., West Bend, WI 53090, 262/334-1335.

Trip Notes: Take the two-hour wagon ride through Shalom Wildlife Sanctuary (262/338-1310) to view deer, elk, and buffalo.

In Waupun, there are eight bronze sculptures at various places around the city. Check at the Chamber of Commerce for a brochure showing the locations and descriptions of each.

DOOR PENINSULA

Door Peninsula

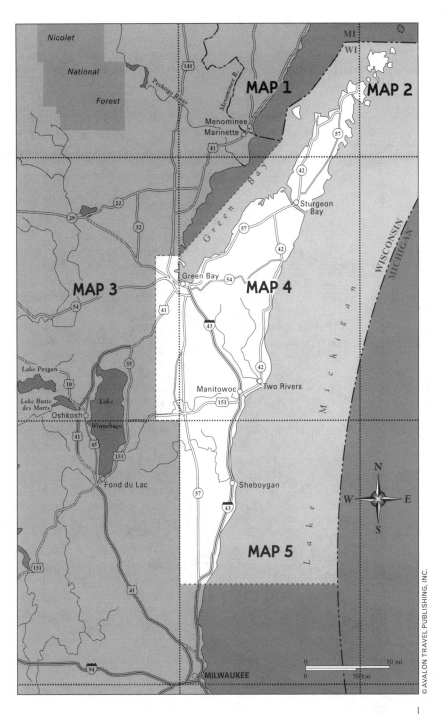

Map 1

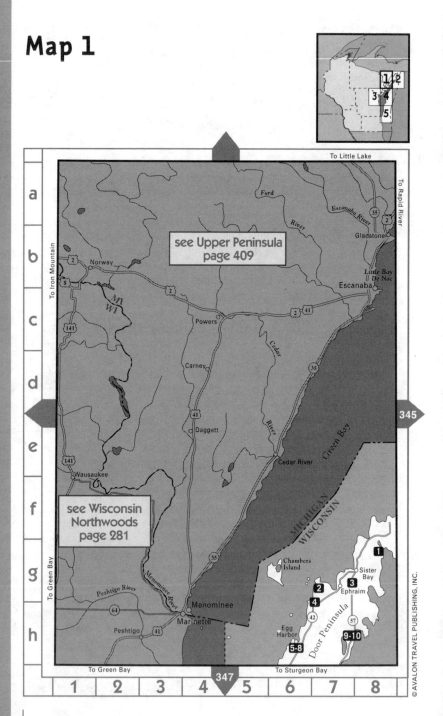

To Little Lake

To Rapid River

Ford

River

Escanaba River

Gladstone

see Upper Peninsula page 409

To Iron Mountain

Norway

Little Bay De Noc

Escanaba

MI
WI

Powers

Cedar

Carney

River

Daggett

Cedar River

Green Bay

see Wisconsin Northwoods page 281

Wausaukee

MICHIGAN
WISCONSIN

To Green Bay

Chambers Island

Sister Bay

Peshtigo River

Menominee River

Ephraim

Menominee

Egg Harbor

Door Peninsula

Peshtigo

Marinette

To Green Bay

To Sturgeon Bay

345

347

© AVALON TRAVEL PUBLISHING, INC.

Map 2

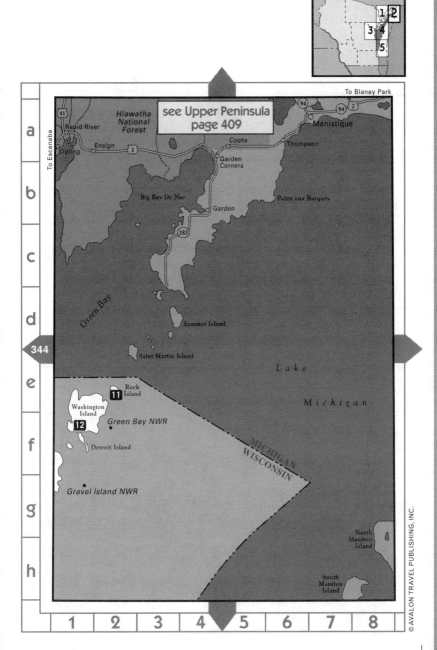

see Upper Peninsula page 409

Hiawatha National Forest

Rapid River

To Escanaba

Kipling

Ensign

Cooks

Garden Corners

Thompson

Manistique

Big Bay De Noc

Garden

Point aux Barques

Green Bay

Summer Island

Saint Martin Island

Lake Michigan

Rock Island

11

Washington Island

12

Green Bay NWR

Detroit Island

MICHIGAN

WISCONSIN

Gravel Island NWR

North Manitou Island

South Manitou Island

© AVALON TRAVEL PUBLISHING, INC.

344

Map 3

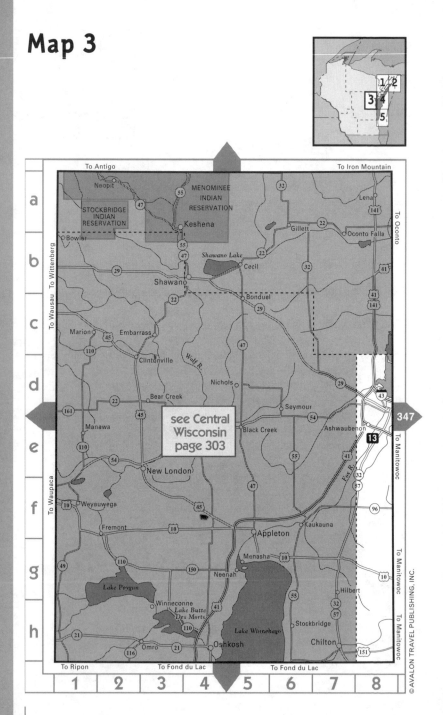

To Antigo   To Iron Mountain

Neopit

MENOMINEE INDIAN RESERVATION

STOCKBRIDGE INDIAN RESERVATION

Keshena

Lena

Bowler

Gillett

Oconto Falls

Shawano Lake

Cecil

Shawano

Bonduel

Marion   Embarrass

Clintonville

Wolf R.

Nichols

Bear Creek

see Central Wisconsin page 303

Seymour

Manawa

Black Creek

Ashwaubenon

New London

Weyauwega

Fremont

Appleton

Kaukauna

Menasha

Neenah

Lake Poygan

Winneconne
Lake Butte
Des Morts

Hilbert

Lake Winnebago

Stockbridge

Omro

Oshkosh

Chilton

To Ripon   To Fond du Lac   To Fond du Lac

To Wausau   To Wittenberg

To Waupaca

To Oconto

To Manitowoc

To Manitowoc

To Manitowoc

347

13

347

Map 4

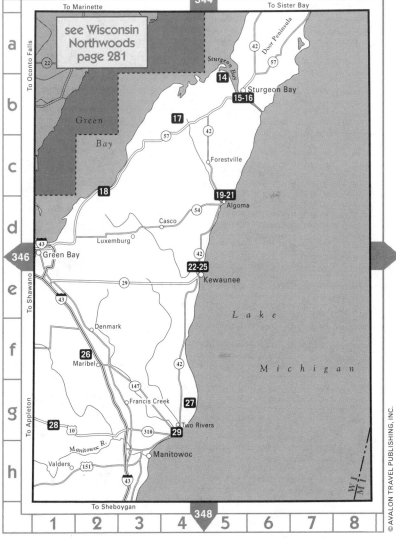

see Wisconsin
Northwoods
page 281

To Marinette

To Sister Bay

344

To Oconto Falls

Door Peninsula

Sturgeon Bay

14

15-16

Sturgeon Bay

17

Green

Bay

57

42

Forestville

18

19-21

54

Algoma

Casco

Luxemburg

43

346

Green Bay

42

22-25

To Shawano

29

Kewaunee

43

Denmark

L a k e

26

Maribel

42

147

M i c h i g a n

Francis Creek

27

To Appleton

28

10

310

Two Rivers

29

Manitowoc R.

Manitowoc

Valders

151

43

To Sheboygan

348

a b c d e f g h

1 2 3 4 5 6 7 8

© AVALON TRAVEL PUBLISHING, INC.

Map 5

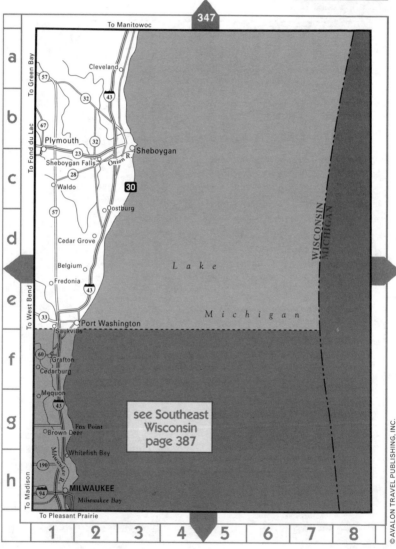

To Manitowoc

347

a

To Green Bay

Cleveland

57

b

To Fond du Lac

32

43

67

Plymouth

32

c

23

Sheboygan

Sheboygan Falls

Onion R.

28

Waldo

30

57

Oostburg

d

Cedar Grove

L a k e

Belgium

Fredonia

43

e

To West Bend

33

M i c h i g a n

Port Washington

Saukville

WISCONSIN
MICHIGAN

f

60

Grafton

Cedarburg

g

Mequon

43

see Southeast
Wisconsin
page 387

Fox Point

Brown Deer

Milwaukee R.

Whitefish Bay

h

190

To Madison

94

MILWAUKEE

Milwaukee Bay

To Pleasant Prairie

1 2 3 4 5 6 7 8

© AVALON TRAVEL PUBLISHING, INC.

Door Peninsula

abbing into Lake Michigan like a thumb is the Door Peninsula, which separates the waters of Lake Michigan from Green Bay. It offers the camper more than 250 miles of scenic, often awesome, shoreline, five state parks, cherry and apple orchards, and artist colonies.

You can begin your journey in Green Bay, Wisconsin's oldest community, which was originally settled as a French fur-trading center. Today, it's home of the National Football League's Green Bay Packers. You must not miss a chance to visit the Green Bay Packer Hall of Fame, Lambeau Field, and other area sights.

Taking a leisurely drive up the 10-mile-wide and 75-mile-long peninsula. You'll enjoy one picturesque community after another and sample a wide variety of activities from cherry picking to exploring some of the 10 lighthouses dating back to the 1800s, ending at the tip with a wonderful ferry boat cruise to Washington Island. There, on the island, you can bicycle for hours.

Working your way back you will see that the art and industry of shipbuilding is still practiced in Sturgeon Bay where commercial ships, private yachts, and military vessels are under construction. The lore of the Great Lakes can be relived at the new Door County Maritime Museum.

Traveling farther south, you'll reach Wisconsin's Maritime Capitol of Manitowoc. A major builder of submarines during World War II, the community retains an important role as a shipbuilder. It is also home of the largest maritime museum on the Great Lakes.

Undoubtedly, the Door County region is one of Wisconsin's most scenic, most interesting, and most popular areas.

❶ Wagon Trail Campground

Location: Near Ellison Bay on the northern side of the Door Peninsula, map 1, grid G8.

Campsites, facilities: There are 141 campsites. Facilities include electric hookups, water, sewer, flush toilets, showers, disposal station, laundry, grocery store, RV storage, separate tent area, lake swimming, lake and river fishing, hiking trail, and playground. Cabins and seasonal campsite rentals are available.

Reservations, fees: The daily fee ranges from $21 to $33. Open from early May through late-October.

Directions: From the junction of Hwy. 42 and County Road ZZ, go six miles northeast on County Road ZZ to the campground entrance.

Contact: Wagon Trail Campground, Cheri Ault and Richard Bartlett, 1190 Hwy. ZZ, Ellison Bay, WI 54210, 920/854-4818.

Trip Notes: This quiet campground is our personal favorite whenever we're in the area. If you love art, you will want to stop at The Clearing, an arts, humanities, and nature schoolhouse. At various rebuilt Scandinavian pioneer log and stone houses you can see classes at work (920/854-4088).

❷ Peninsula State Park

Location: Fish Creek, on the northern side of Door Peninsula, map 1, grid G7.

Campsites, facilities: There are 469 campsites in four separate campgrounds. Facilities include electric hookups, showers, disposal station, boat ramp, lake swimming, boating, canoeing, fishing, tennis court, golf course, and nature center. There are also hiking, mountain bike, snowmobile, and cross-country ski trails. In winter, there are nine campsites with electric hookups and water.

Reservations, fees: Reservations are accepted. Campsite reservations are available. See State Park Camping Fees and Reserving a Campsite. Open year-round.

Directions: From Hwy. 42, go one mile northwest on Shore Road to the park entrance.

Contact: Peninsula State Park, 9462 Shore Rd., Box 218, Fish Creek, WI 54212-0218 or 920/868-3258.

Trip Notes: Humans have inhabited the Door Peninsula for about 11,000 years. These early people were hunters and gatherers and eventually established small seasonal villages. A village site dating back to 500 BC was established at today's Nicolet Bay Beach. Various cultures occupied the site until 1300 AD. State Archaeologist Victoria Dirst conducted a dig at Nicolet Bay in 1994 and dated artifacts to the Early, Middle, and Late Woodland and Oneota Native American cultures (400 BC).

Mixed villages of Potawatomi and other native groups covered Door County and its islands through the mid-1800s. At that time, following treaties and the Indian Removal Act, the U. S. government relocated native people outside of Door County. Today, about 2 percent of Door County's population are identified as Native American.

High bluffs, sand and cobble beaches, a challenging 18-hole golf course (920/854-5791), and professional summer theater make this 3,776-acre park, which juts out into the waters of Green Bay, extremely popular. Don't miss a guided tour of 125-year-old Eagle Bluff Lighthouse.

3 Aqualand Camp Resort

Location: Sister Bay, on the northern side of Door Peninsula, map 1, grid G8.

Campsites, facilities: There are 150 campsites. Facilities include electric hookups, water, flush toilets, showers, disposal station, swimming beach, pool, shuffleboard courts, and playground. Seasonal campsite rentals are available. Pets are allowed.

Reservations, fees: The daily fee is $22. Open from early May through late-October.

Directions: From the junction of Hwy. 42 and Hwy. 57, go 2.5 miles south on Hwy. 57, then one-quarter mile east on County Road Q to the resort entrance.

Contact: Aqualand Camp Resort, Mike McAndrews, Box 538, Sister Bay, WI 54234, 920/854-4530.

Trip Notes: Remember the days of the drive-in movie theater? Well, you can enjoy a night out with your favorite camping partner or family at the Skyway Drive-In Theater on Hwy. 41 (920/854-9938), a short drive away.

4 Path of Pines Campground

Location: Fish Creek, on the northern side of Door Peninsula, map 1, grid G7.

Campsites, facilities: There are 95 campsites. Facilities include RV pull-through sites, electric hookups, water, flush toilets, showers, disposal station, laundry, grocery store, hiking and biking trails, and a playground. Lake boating, canoeing, fishing, and swimming are nearby. Seasonal campsite rentals are available.

Reservations, fees: The daily fee ranges from $22 to $28. Credit cards are accepted. Open from mid-May through mid-October.

Directions: From the junction of Hwy. 42 and County Road F, go one-half mile east on County Road F to the campground entrance.

Contact: Path of Pines Campground, Tim and Janet Johnson, 3709 Hwy F, Fish Creek, WI 542212, 800/868-7802 or 920/868-3332, email: crimp@dcwis.com.

Trip Notes: Want a little entertainment? Take in a professional musical performance in the outdoor amphitheater at the American Folklore Theatre (920/868-9999).

5 Door County Camping Retreat

Location: Egg Harbor, on the northern side of Door Peninsula, map 1, grid H6.

Campsites, facilities: There are 212 campsites. Facilities include electric hookups, water, flush toilets, showers, disposal station, laundry, grocery store, swimming pool, nature trails, playground, and planned weekend activities. Lake swimming, boating, canoeing, and fishing are nearby. Bike, cabin, and cottage rentals are available. Pets are allowed.

Reservations, fees: The daily fee ranges from $20 to $25. Credit cards are accepted. Open May through October.

Directions: From the junction of County Road E and Hwy. 41, go three and three-quarter miles south on Hwy. 42, then one-quarter mile east on Sunny Point Road. Finally, go one-half mile north on Court Road to the campground entrance.

Contact: Door County Camping Retreat, John and Marty Maravec, 4906 Court Rd., Egg Harbor, WI, 54209, 920/868-3151, email: office @doorcountycamp.com, website: www.door countycamp.com.

Trip Notes: Go see the Cana Island Lighthouse. Take County Road Q at the north edge of Bailey's Harbor to Cana Island Road and follow the signs for about 2.5 miles to the end of the road to view the lighthouse. However, do not take a big rig down there because there is a small turn-around area. Whether this lighthouse was built on a peninsula or an island depends on the lake. The only access is a causeway of rock and gravel, which at times must be waded, but it's well worth getting your knees wet. This is probably the most photographed, painted, and videotaped lighthouse in Door County.

6 Monument Point Camping

Location: Egg Harbor on the northern side of Door Peninsula, map 1, grid H6.

Campsites, facilities: There are 84 campsites. Facilities include electric hookups, water, flush toilets, showers, disposal station, grocery store, hiking trail, and playground. Lake swimming, boating, canoeing, and fishing are nearby. Pets are allowed.

Reservations, fees: The daily fee ranges from $18 to $20. Open May through October.

Directions: From the junction of Hwy. 42 and Hwy. 57, go eight miles north on Hwy. 42, then one and one-quarter miles northwest on Monument Point Road to the campground entrance.

Contact: Monument Point Camping, Doug and Deb Krauel, 5718 W. Monument Point Rd., Sturgeon Bay, WI 54235, 920/743-9411.

Trip Notes: If you want to really see the lighthouses of Door County, take a 90-minute Lighthouse Cruise to offshore islands or the Sunset-Shipwreck Cruise from Gills Rock (920/854-2606).

7 Frontier Wilderness Campground

Location: Egg Harbor, on the northern side of Door Peninsula, map 1, grid H6.

Campsites, facilities: There are 240 campsites. Facilities include electric hookups, water, flush toilets, showers, disposal station, laundry, grocery store, swimming pool, hiking trail, mini-golf, and playground. Lake boating, canoeing, and fishing are nearby. Seasonal campsites are available. Pets are allowed.

Reservations, fees: The daily fee ranges from $19 to $21. Open May through October.

Directions: From the junction of County Road E and Hwy. 42, go 2.5 miles south on Hwy. 42, then 1.5 miles east on Hillside Road to the campground entrance.

Contact: Frontier Wilderness Campground, 4375 Hillside Rd., Egg Harbor, WI 54209, 920/868-3349.

Trip Notes: Want to spend a day on Washington Island? Take the Island Clipper or the Yankee Clipper (920/854-2972) and get a narrated cruise out to the island. There's plenty to see and do when you get there. If you're tired of walking, you can take a tram tour.

8 Camp-Tel Family Campground

Location: Egg Harbor on the northern side of Door Peninsula, map 1, grid H6.

Campsites, facilities: There are 121 campsites. Facilities include electric hookups, water, flush toilets, showers, disposal station, laundry, grocery store, swimming pool, and playground. Boating, canoeing, fishing, and hiking trails are nearby. Pets are allowed

Reservations, fees: The daily fee ranges from $16 to $18. Open from mid-May through mid-October.

Directions: From the junction of County Road E and Hwy. 42, go 1.5 miles north on Hwy. 42 to the park entrance.

Contact: Camp-Tel Family Campground, The Irmen Family, 8164 Hwy. 42, Egg Harbor, WI 54209, 920/868-3278, email: camptel@dcmail.com.

Trip Notes: Take time out from your outdoor activities or from your shopping in the quaint boutiques in the area to have the world's largest and best ice cream cone at Wilson's in Ephraim.

9 Bailey's Bluff Campground

Location: Bailey's Harbor, on the southern coast of Door Peninsula, map 1, grid H7.

Campsites, facilities: There are 83 campsites. Facilities include electric hookups, water, flush toilets, showers, disposal station, laundry, grocery store, tent area, biking trail, and playground. Boating, canoeing, fishing, and hiking trails are nearby. Pets are allowed.

Reservations, fees: The daily fee ranges from $20 to $26. Credit cards are accepted. Open April through mid-October.

Directions: From the junction of Hwy. 57 and County Roads F/EE go three-quarters of a mile west on County Road F/EE, then one-quarter mile west on County Road EE to the campground entrance.

Contact: Bailey's Bluff Campground, Bob and Cheryl Hook, P.O. Box 338, Bailey's Harbor, WI 54202, 920/839-2109 or 886/722-5333.

Trip Notes: On County Road Q off Hwy. 57 West and one-half mile north of Bailey's Har-

bor, is the Ridges Sanctuary with 800 acres of natural landscapes. The Nature Center is an 1880 log building housing an information center, store, and the sanctuary, which includes hiking trails and an abundance of native Arctic plants.

10 Bailey's Grove Travel Park

Location: Bailey's Harbor on the southern coast of the Door Peninsula, map 1, grid H7.

Campsites, facilities: There are 68 campsites. Facilities include electric hookups, water, sewer, flush toilets, showers, disposal station, laundry, swimming pool, and playground. Boating, canoeing, fishing, and hiking and biking trails are nearby. Pets are allowed.

Reservations, fees: The daily fee ranges from $22 to $26. Open May to mid-October.

Directions: From the junction of Hwy. 57 and County Road EE/F, go one-half mile west on County Road EE/F to the campground's entrance.

Contact: Bailey's Grove Travel Park, P.O. Box 198, Bailey's Harbor, WI 54202, 920/839-2559, email: campnowwi@yahoo.com.

Trip Notes: Be sure to visit the Bjorklunde Chapel (920/839-2216), a replica of a 15th-century Norwegian Stavkirke on the grounds of Bjorklunde Vid Sjon (Birch Forest by the Water). It is located on a 405-acre estate that includes meadows, woods, and more than a mile of Lake Michigan shoreline.

11 Rock Island State Park

Location: Rock Island in Lake Michigan, map 2, grid E2.

Campsites, facilities: There are 40 campsites. There are no hookups, but facilities include vault toilets, showers, boat dock, canoeing, fishing, and hiking trails. The campground offers lake boating only if you boat out to the island.

Reservations, fees: Reservations are accepted. Campsite reservations are available. See State Park Camping Fees and Reserving a Campsite. Open year-round.

Directions: From Washington Island, take the passenger ferry to Rock Island and the campground.

Contact: Rock Island State Park, W4N1924 Indian Point Rd., Rt. 1, Box 118A, Washington Island, WI 54246-9728 or 920/847-2235 or 920/847-3156.

Trip Notes: This primitive Lake Michigan island, which was visited by LaSalle and Hennepin in the Griffon in 1679, is accessible only by ferry from Washington Island. The stone buildings that were built by a wealthy inventor who owned the island between 1910 and 1945 now house exhibits. There is only primitive walk-in camping. Wheeled vehicles are not allowed.

12 Island Camping and Recreation

Location: Washington Island in Lake Michigan at the tip of the Door Peninsula, map 2, grid F1.

Campsites, facilities: There are 101 campsites. Facilities include electric hookups, water, flush toilets, showers, disposal station, grocery store, mini-golf, tennis court, hiking trail, and playground. Nearby are lake boating, canoeing, fishing, and swimming.

Reservations, fees: The daily fee ranges from $18 to $21. Open from mid-May through mid-October.

Directions: Take the car ferry (920/847-2526 or 800/223-2094) from North Port. From the ferry

landing, go one and three-quarter miles northeast on Lobdells Point Road. Then go one-third mile north on Main Street, then two miles east on Lake View Road, and one-half mile south on East Side Road to the campground entrance.

Contact: Island Camping and Recreation, John and Pat Fumner, RR1 Box 144, Washington Island, WI 54246, 920/847-2622.

Trip Notes: While on Washington Island be sure to visit the Jackson Harbor Maritime Museum (920/847-2522) to see old maritime and fishing artifacts, and Jacobsen's Museum (920/847-2213) to view the Indian artifacts and local history in a log cabin museum.

13 Happy Hollow Camping Resort

Location: DePere, south of Green Bay and near the Fox River, map 3, grid E8.

Campsites, facilities: There are 130 campsites. Facilities include electric hookups, water, sewer, flush toilets, showers, disposal station, laundry, grocery store, separate tent area, restaurant, swimming pool, pond and stream fishing, and planned activities. River boating, canoeing, and fishing are nearby. Pets are allowed.

Reservations, fees: The daily fee ranges from $19 to $32. Credit cards are accepted. Open year-round. Facilities are fully operational from mid-April through mid-October.

Directions: From the junction of U.S. Hwy. 41 and County Road U, go one-quarter mile west on County Road U to the campground entrance.

Contact: Happy Hollow Camping Resort, Dave and Judy Boldt, 3831 County Road U, DePere, WI 54115, 920/532-4386, fax 920/532-4944, email: happyhollow@greenbaynet.com, website: www.happyhollowcamping.com.

Trip Notes: The Neville Public Museum of Brown County in Green Bay (920/448-4460) provides two floors filled with changing history, art, and science exhibits related to northeast Wisconsin and the Upper Peninsula of Michigan. It traces its roots back to 1915. In 1983, the current 58,000-square-foot facility opened to the public. "On the Edge of the Inland Sea" takes visitors on a trip through history beginning in a simulated glacier representing the last Ice Age and ending with a look at how Green Bay developed into a modern city. The Frankenthal Gallery gives a panoramic view of the Fox River and Green Bay's skyline.

14 Potawatomi State Park

Location: Sturgeon Bay on the southern coast of Door Peninsula, map 4, grid B5.

Campsites, facilities: There are 123 campsites. Facilities include electric hookups, showers, disposal station, wheelchair access, boat ramp and dock, and swimming beach. There are also biking, hiking, cross-country ski and snowmobile trails. Also available are boating, canoeing, and fishing. Pets are allowed. In winter eight sites with electric hookups and water (hose required) are open.

Reservations, fees: Reservations are accepted. Campsite reservations are available. See State Park Camping Fees and Reserving a Campsite. Open year-round.

Directions: From Sturgeon Bay, go 1.5 miles west on County Road C, then one mile north on Park Road to the park entrance.

Contact: Potawatomi State Park, 3740 Park Dr., Sturgeon Bay, WI 54235, 920/746-2890 or 920/746-2891.

Trip Notes: On a clear day, the view from the park's observation tower reaches 16 miles across Green Bay to Menomonee, Michigan, and Chambers Island, 20 miles to the northeast. The two-mile shoreline is dotted with granite boulders, brought from Canada by the glacier. Be sure to visit Whitefish Dune State Park (920/823-2400) in Sturgeon Bay, too. It boasts 6,000 feet of Lake Michigan shoreline, massive sand dunes, and winter sports.

15 Door County Jellystone Park

Location: Sturgeon Bay on the southern shore of Door Peninsula, map 4, grid B6.

Campsites, facilities: There are 275 campsites. Facilities include electric hookups, water, sewer, flush toilets, showers, disposal station, laundry, grocery store, swimming pool, shuffleboard courts, hiking trail, and playground. Boating, canoeing, and fishing are nearby. Seasonal campsite rentals are available. Pets are allowed.

Reservations, fees: The daily fee ranges from $25 to $27. Credit cards are accepted. Open from mid-May to mid-September.

Directions: From Two Rivers take Hwy. 42 north to Sturgeon Bay. Turn left on County Road C, and then right on I-29. Turn left onto I-42, and then make a sharp left on County Road C.

Contact: Door County Yogi Bear's Jellystone Park, Sylvia and Dick Himes, 3677 May Rd., Sturgeon Bay, WI 54235, 920/743-9001.

Direction: From the junction of Hwy. 42/57 and County Road C, go one mile north, three miles west on County Road C, and then one mile north on County Road M. Then travel two miles west on Sand Bay Road to the campground entrance.

Trip Notes: If you want to experience Great Lakes

ship handling, visit the new 20,000-square-foot Door County Maritime Museum (920/743-5958) and take the helm of the Steamer Elba in the reconditioned pilot house. You can also see the decompression chamber used in raising the Str. George M. Humphrey.

16 Quietwoods North Camping Resort

Location: Sturgeon Bay, on the southern shore of Door Peninsula, map 4, grid B6.

Campsites, facilities: There are 250 campsites. Facilities include electric hookups, water, sewer, flush toilets, showers, disposal station, laundry, grocery store, RV storage, separate tent area, swimming pool, mini-golf, hiking trail, and playground. Boating, canoeing, and fishing are available nearby. Bike, trailer, and cabin rentals are available. Pets are allowed.

Reservations, fees: The daily fee ranges from $22 to $30. Credit cards are accepted. Open May through mid-October.

Directions: From the junction of Hwy. 42/57 and County Road PD, go one and one-quarter miles north on County Road PD. Then drive one mile east on County Road C and three-quarters of a mile north on Grondin Road to the campground entrance.

Contact: Quietwoods North Camping Resort, the McClelland family, 3668 Grondin Rd., Sturgeon Bay, WI 54235, 920/743-7115 or 800/986-2267, fax 920/746-1140, email: quietwoods@gocampingamerica.com, website: www.quietwoodsnorth.com.

Trip Notes: For a break from the outdoors, drive to Green Bay and tour the NFL's Green Bay Packer Hall of Fame (920/499-4281); website: www.packerhalloffame.com).

17 Quietwoods South Camping Resort

Location: Brussels, in the southeast area of Door Peninsula, map 4, grid B4.

Campsites, facilities: There are 155 campsites. Facilities include electric hookups, water, flush toilets, showers, disposal station, laundry, grocery store, swimming pool, pond fishing, mini-golf, playground, and planned activities. Boating, canoeing, and fishing are available nearby. RV rentals and storage are available. Pets are allowed.

Reservations, fees: The daily fee ranges from $18 to $21. Open May through mid-October.

Directions: From the junction of Hwy. 57 and County Road C, go two miles north on County Road C, then 1.5 miles east on County Road K. Finally, drive one-half mile north on Lovers Lane to the campground entrance.

Contact: Quietwoods South Camping Resort, 9245 Lovers Ln., Brussels, WI 54204, 920/825-7065.

Trip Notes: Take a spin a few miles north on Hwy. 57 to visit the Door Peninsula Winery (920/743-7432) or 800/551-5049) at Carlsville. It features wines produced from Door County orchards. You can even do a little tasting.

If wine isn't to your taste, the Outagamie County Historical Society (330 E. College Ave., Appleton, WI 54911, 920/733-8445) shares its building with the Houdini Historical Center. The Houdini Center features the Sidney H. Radner collection of Houdini memorabilia, as well as a history of magic.

18 Bayshore Campground

Location: Dyckesville, on the northern coast of Door Peninsula, map 4, grid C2.

Campsites, facilities: There are 115 campsites in this Brown County park. Facilities include electric hookups, water, flush toilets, showers, disposal station, laundry, boat ramp and dock, hiking trail, swimming, and playground. Boating and fishing are available. Pets are allowed.

Reservations, fees: First-come, first-served. The daily fee ranges from $15 to $19. Credit cards are not accepted. Open from mid-April through mid-October.

Directions: From Green Bay, take Hwy. 57 north about 15 miles to the county park entrance.

Contact: Bayshore Campground, 5637 Sturgeon Bay Rd., New Franken, WI 54229, 920/866-2414 or 920/448-4466.

Trip Notes: Drive south to Green Bay and visit the Green Bay Botanical Garden (920/490-9457). There are formal flower gardens and, for youngsters, a new children's garden with tree house, maze, and frog pond.

19 Ahnapee River Trails Campground

Location: Near Algoma on the Ahnappe River, map 4, grid D5.

Campsites, facilities: There are 65 campsites. Facilities include electric hookups, water, flush toilets, showers, disposal station, laundry, swimming pool, boat ramp, river fishing, canoeing, hiking trail, and a playground. Lake swimming, boating, and fishing are nearby. Boat rentals are available. Pets are allowed.

Reservations, fees: The daily fee ranges from $15 to $18. Credit cards are accepted. Open from mid-April through mid-October.

Directions: Take Hwy. 42 and go two miles north to Washington Road, turn left and go one mile on Washington Road. Finally, drive one mile east, following the signs to the campground entrance.

Contact: Ahnappe River Trails Campground, Joe and Sandy Weimer, E6053 W. Wilson Road, Algoma, WI 54201, 920/487-5777, email: ahnapee@itol.com.

Trip Notes: This is a favorite Lake Michigan port for sport anglers. Many fishing groups hold weekend outings here, virtually taking over the town. Here, too, is the Von Stiehl Winery (800/955-5208 or 920/487-5208), the state's oldest licensed winery. It's two blocks east of Hwy. 42 and housed in the former Ahnapee Brewery built in the 1850s. Take the 30-minute guided tour that takes you through all the steps of wine making. Be sure to sample the apple or cherry wine.

After spending time touring the winery, go next door to The Grapevine. It features more than 20 different fudge flavors and hand-dipped candies.

Behind the winery, breathe in a little lakeshore mist and take a stroll down the scenic harbor walkway that leads along the Ahnapee River to the Algoma Marina. From there, a harbor walkway leads along the Algoma beach.

20 Timber Trail Campground

Location: Near Algoma, on the Ahnapee River, map 4, grid D5.

Campsites, facilities: There are 70 campsites. Facilities include electric hookups, water, flush toilets, showers, disposal station, laundry, grocery store, separate tent area, RV storage, swimming pool, river and lake boating, canoeing, fishing, boat ramp, hiking and jogging nature trails, rental bikes, playground, and planned activities. Pets are allowed.

Reservations, fees: The daily fee ranges from $18 to $20. Credit cards are accepted. Open from mid-April through mid-October.

Directions: From the junction of Hwy. 54 and Hwy. 42, go one-half mile north on Hwy. 42, then one mile west on County Road S. Finally, drive three-quarters of a mile north on County Road M to the campground entrance.

Contact: Timber Trail Campground, Mike and Alisa Herrick, N8326 County Road M, Algoma, WI 54201, 920/487-3707, email: timbertrail@itol.com.

Trip Notes: Have you ever seen furniture being made? Stop by Svoboda Industries on Hwy. 42 just north of town to see the world's largest grandfather clock (35 feet tall and eight feet wide) and watch masters of wood from a viewing platform that overlooks the manufacturing area.

21 Big Lake Campground

Location: Algoma, on the southern coast at the base of the Door Peninsula, map 4, grid D5.

Campsites, facilities: There are 86 campsites. Facilities include electric hookups, water, sewer, disposal station, laundry, hiking trail, and playground. Lake fishing is available. Lake Michigan swimming, boating, canoeing, and fishing are nearby. Pets are allowed.

Reservations, fees: The daily fee ranges from $14 to $18. Open from mid-April through mid-October.

Directions: From the junction of Hwy. 54 and Hwy. 42, go one mile south on Hwy. 42 to the campground entrance.

Contact: Big Lake Campground, 2427 Lake St., Algoma, WI 54201, 920/487-2726.

Trip Notes: Need a red lighthouse to add to your photo collection? This oft-photographed red lighthouse stands at the entrance to Algoma's Harbor. Early in the morning or late in the afternoon, you'll be more likely to capture a sportfishing boat leaving or entering the harbor. Farther inland, you might be able to photograph an old commercial fishing boat.

22 Kewaunee Village Camping Resort

Location: Kewaunee, on the Kewaunee River, a mile from Lake Michigan, map 4, grid E4.

Campsites, facilities: There are 90 campsites. Facilities include electric hookups, water, sewer, flush toilets, showers, disposal station, laundry, snack bar, separate tent area, swimming pool, lake and river boating and fishing, canoeing, boat dock, mini-golf, shuffleboard courts, playground, and planned activities. Boat, cabin, and seasonal campsite rentals are available. Pets are allowed.

Reservations, fees: The daily fee ranges from $20 to $27. Credit cards are accepted. Open May though mid-October.

Directions: From the junction of Hwy. 29 and Hwy. 42, go three-quarters of a mile north on Hwy. 42 to the resort entrance.

Contact: Kewaunee Village Camping Resort, Warren Clark and Dean Kulm, 333 Terraqua Dr., Kewaunee, WI 54216, 920/388-4851, email: info@kewauneevillage.com, website: www.kewauneevillage.com.

Trip Notes: Although peak activities at the C. D. "Buzz" Besadny Anadromous Fishing Facility is spring, summer, and fall when spawn is collected to raise salmonid fingerlings to stock Lake Michigan, there's something fascinating to see all year long. There are two large viewing ports to let you look under the water's surface to see the fish follow the primordial urge to jump the ladder (920/388-1025).

23 Cedar Valley Campground

Location: In Kewaunee on the Kewaunee River, map 4, grid E4.

Campsites, facilities: There are 130 campsites. Facilities include electric hookups, water, flush toilets, showers, disposal station, laundry, grocery store, swimming pool, river fishing and canoeing, mini-golf, playground, and planned activities. Nearby you can access Lake Michigan boating, canoeing, fishing, and swimming. Pets are allowed.

Reservations, fees: The daily fee ranges from $17 to $19. Open May through mid-October.

Directions: From the junction of Hwy. 42 and Hwy. 29, go three-quarters of a mile west on Hwy. 29, then five miles northwest on County Road C. Finally, drive three-quarters of a mile north on Cedar Valley Road to the campground entrance.

Contact: Cedar Valley Campground, 920/388-4550.

Trip Notes: Drive up to Green Bay and visit the Bay Beach Wildlife Sanctuary (920/391-3671). This is a 700-acre wildlife refuge with 6.2 miles of trails and the Nature Center Observation and Rehabilitation Building with live birds of prey exhibits.

24 Kewaunee Marina Campground

Location: In Kewaunee on Lake Michigan, map 4, grid E4.

Campsites, facilities: There are 36 campsites in this city park. Facilities include electric hookups, water, flush toilets, showers, and disposal station. The campground offers lake swimming, boating, canoeing, and fishing. Pets are allowed.

Reservations, fees: The daily fee ranges from $17 to $19. Open May through September.

Directions: From the junction of Hwy. 42 and Hwy. 29, go one-quarter of a mile north on Hwy. 42 to the park entrance.

Contact: Kewaunee Marina Campground, 920/388-4550.

Trip Notes: You don't want to go to jail, but you will enjoy visiting the Kewaunee County Museum and Old Jail (920/388-4410). The museum is filled with local and maritime history.

25 Mapleview Campsites

Location: In Kewaunee on a private lake, map 4, grid E4.

Campsites, facilities: There are 75 campsites. Facilities include electric hookups, water, flush toilets, showers, disposal station, laundry, RV storage, separate tent area, lake swimming, and playground. Lake Michigan boating, canoeing, fishing, and swimming are nearby. Pets are allowed.

Reservations, fees: The daily fee ranges from $18 to $21. Open May through mid-October.

Directions: From Kewaunee, travel five miles south on Hwy. 42, then three miles on Hwy. G, and 500 feet south on Norman Road to the campground.

Contact: Mapleview Campsites, Stan and Joyce LaCrosse, N1460 Hwy. B, Kewaunee, WI 54216, 920/776-1588 or 920/388-2910 during the off-season.

Trip Notes: Go downtown and take the Marquette Historic District Walking Tour (800/666-8214). It's a self-guided tour with map and brochure available. You can also stop and see the tugboat Ludington in Kewaunee Harbor (920/388-5000). The craft is a 225-foot World War II seagoing tug built in 1943. It was used during the D-Day invasion of Europe.

26 Devils River Campers Park

Location: In Maribel, south of Green Bay on the Devil's River, map 4, grid F2.

Campsites, facilities: There are 146 campsites. Facilities include electric hookups, water, flush toilets, showers, disposal station, laundry, grocery store, swimming pool, river fishing, playground, hiking trail, and planned weekend activities. In nearby Green Bay, you can find access to lake boating, canoeing, and fishing. Pets are allowed.

Reservations, fees: The daily fee ranges from $20 to $22. Credit cards are accepted. Open May through September.

Directions: From the junction of Hwy. 96 and I-43, go six miles south on I-43 and take exit 164. Then drive one-third mile east on Hwy. 147/County Road Z and one-half mile north on County Road R to the entrance.

Contact: Devil's River Campers Park, the Lyman family, 16612 County Road R, Maribel, WI 54227, 920/863-2812.

Trip Notes: Everyone loves a choo-choo. The National Railroad Museum (920/437-7623; website: www.nationalrrmuseum.org) in Green Bay will entertain the entire family. It is America's oldest and largest railroad museum, located in a new 26,000-square-foot exhibit hall (2285 S. Broadway St.).

An alternate side trip to the Gordon Bubolz Nature Preserve (4815 N. Lynndale Dr., Appleton, WI 54913, 920/731-6041) offers educational and recreational opportunities. You can walk, jog, hike, or ski eight miles of scenic trails weaving through diverse habitats, including meadow, cedar swamp, forest, prairie, and pond.

27 Point Beach State Forest

Location: Near Two Rivers on Lake Michigan, map 4, grid G4.

Campsites, facilities: There are 127 campsites. Facilities include electric hookups, showers, disposal station, grocery store, interpretative center, and lake swimming and fishing. The park also has hiking, mountain bike, and cross-country skiing trails. Pets are allowed. In winter, 10 sites with electric hookups and water are open.

Reservations, fees: Reservations are accepted. Campsite reservations are available. See State Park Camping Fees and Reserving a Campsite. Open year-round.

Directions: From the junction of Hwy. 42 and County Road O, go four miles northeast on County Road O to the entrance.

Contact: Point Beach State Forest, 9400 County Road O, Two Rivers, WI 54241, 920/794-7480.

Trip Notes: This is a terrific spot for beachcombing. The campground is on a point that juts seven miles out into Lake Michigan. Occasionally, the six-mile-long beach produces pieces of 19th-century ships that sank nearby.

Another interesting spot is in Menasha, at the Barlow Planetarium at the University of Wisconsin-Fox Valley (1478 Midway Rd., Menasha, WI 54952). It features a 48-foot projection dome with a realistic night sky and 3D effects that pull you into a virtual world.

28 Rainbows End Campground

Location: In Reedsville, northwest of Manitowoc, map 4, grid G1.

Campsites, facilities: There are 48 campsites. Facilities include electric hookups, water, flush toilets, showers, disposal station, pond swimming, mini-golf, and hiking trail. In Manitowoc, there's Lake Michigan boating, canoeing, and fishing. Pets are allowed.

Reservations, fees: The daily fee ranges from $14 to $18. Open May to mid-October.

Directions: From the junction of Hwys. 57/32 and U.S. Hwy. 10, go 11.5 miles east on Hwy. 10 to the campground entrance.

Contact: Rainbow's End Campground, Norman and Marlene Gill, 18227 U.S. Hwy. 10, Reedsville, WI 54230, 920/754-4142.

Trip Notes: Drive to Manitowoc and tour the fascinating Wisconsin Maritime Museum (920/684-0218; email: maritime@lakefield.net; website: www.wimaritimemuseum.org), one of the finest on the Great Lakes. See the many exhibits of the history of Great Lakes shipping, fishing, and other artifacts and take a tour of the USS Cobia, a World War II submarine that sank 13 Japanese vessels.

29 Seagull Marina and Campground

Location: In Two Rivers on Lake Michigan, map 4, grid G4.

Campsites, facilities: There are 100 campsites. Facilities include electric hookups, water, sewer, disposal station, grocery store, boat ramp and dock, lake swimming, boating, canoeing, and fishing. Pets are allowed.

Reservations, fees: The daily fee ranges from $13 to $17. Open year-round. Facilities are fully operational from mid-April through October 30.

Directions: From the junction of Hwy. 147 and Hwy. 42, go two-thirds of a mile south on Hwy. 42 to the campground entrance.

Contact: Seagull Marina and Campground, 1400 Lake St., Two Rivers, WI 54241, 920/794-7533.

Trip Notes: Two Rivers is the birthplace of the ice cream sundae. Be sure to stop at the Washington House Museum and Soda Fountain (920/793-2490) for a delicious frozen treat and enjoy a stroll through the Rogers Street Fishing Village to see the 1886 lighthouse and Great Lakes Coast Guard Museum (920/793-1103).

30 Kohler-Andrae State Park

Location: Near Sheboygan on Lake Michigan, map 5, grid C3.

Campsites, facilities: There are 106 campsites. Facilities include electric hookups, showers, disposal station, laundry, lake swimming, nature center, and access to boating, canoeing, and fishing. There are also bike, hiking, horseback riding, and cross-country ski trails. Pets are allowed. In winter, 45 sites with electric hookups and water are open.

Reservations, fees: Reservations are accepted. Campsite reservations are available. See State Park Camping Fees and Reserving a Campsite. Open year-round.

Directions: From I-43 take exit 120 and go three miles south of town and follow the signs on County Road K to the park entrance.

Contact: Kohler-Andrae State Park, 1020 Park Beach Ln., Sheboygan, WI 53081, 920/451-4080.

Trip Notes: This 924-acre state park is located on the shores of Lake Michigan and features wooded campsites. There are two miles of beach and two nature trails. The park is also adjacent to a 200-acre wildlife refuge.

HIDDEN VALLEY

Hidden Valley

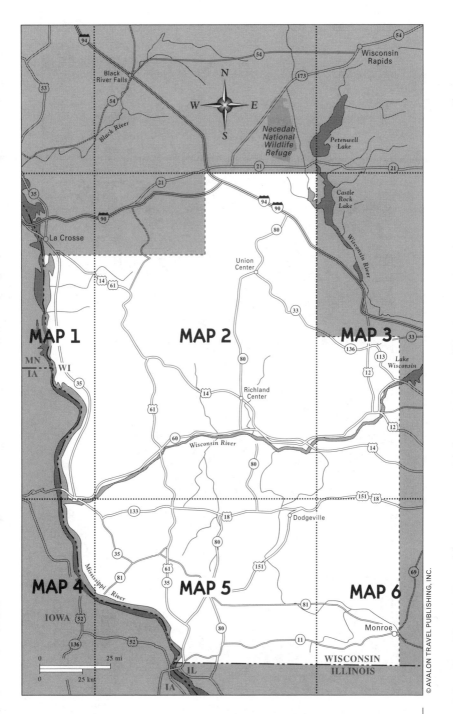

Map 1

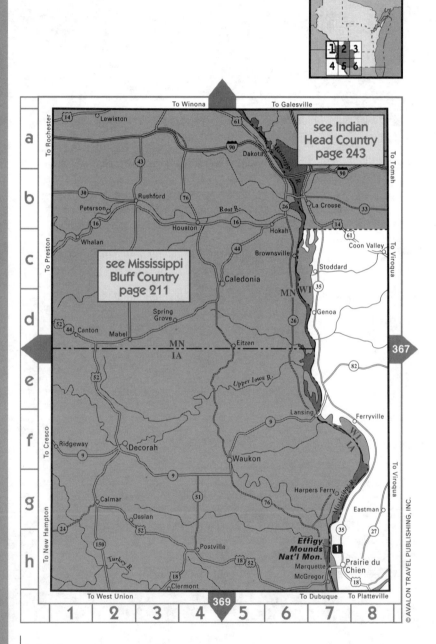

see Indian Head Country page 243

see Mississippi Bluff Country page 211

To Winona

To Galesville

To Rochester

Lewiston

Dakota

To Tomah

To Preston

Rushford

Peterson

Root R.

La Crosse

Whalan

Houston

Hokah

Coon Valley

To Viroqua

Brownsville

Stoddard

Caledonia

MN WI

Spring Grove

Genoa

Canton

Mabel

MN

Eitzen

IA

Upper Iowa R.

To Cresco

Ridgeway

Decorah

Waukon

Lansing

Ferryville

WI

IA

To Viroqua

Harpers Ferry

To New Hampton

Calmar

Eastman

Ossian

Postville

Effigy Mounds Nat'l Mon.

Turkey R.

Marquette

Prairie du Chien

McGregor

Clermont

To West Union

To Dubuque

To Platteville

367

369

© AVALON TRAVEL PUBLISHING, INC.

Map 2

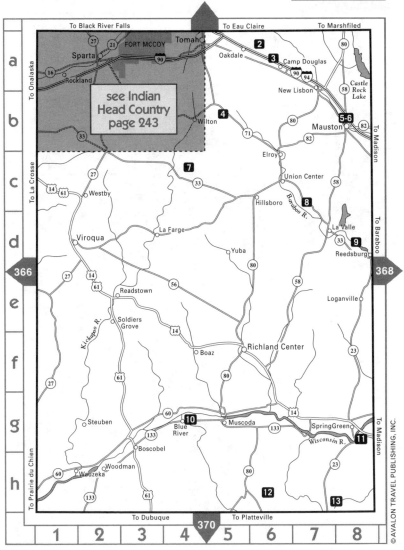

To Black River Falls
To Eau Claire
To Marshfiled

a

To Onalaska

(27) (21) **FORT MCCOY** Tomah
Sparta **2**
(16) Oakdale **3**
Rockland Camp Douglas
(90) (94)

see Indian
Head Country
page 243

Castle
Rock
Lake

New Lisbon (58)

b

(33)
Wilton **4**
(71)
(80)
Mauston **5-6** (82)

To Madison

(82)

Elroy

c

To La Crosse

(27)
Union Center
(14) (61) Westby
(33)
Hillsboro **8**
Baraboo R.

La Farge La Valle

d

Viroqua
Yuba
(33) **9**
Reedsburg

To Baraboo

366
(27) (14)
(61) Readstown
(56)
(80)
(58)
368

e

Soldiers
Grove
Loganville
(14)

Kickapoo R.

f

(27)
Boaz
Richland Center
(61)
(80)
(23)

g

To Prairie du Chien

Steuben
(60) **10**
Muscoda
(133) SpringGreen
(133) Blue
River
Wisconsin R. **11**

To Madison

Boscobel
(23)
Woodman
(60) Wauzeka
(80)
12
13

h

(133) (61)

To Dubuque
To Platteville

1 **2** **3** **4** **370** **5** **6** **7** **8**

© AVALON TRAVEL PUBLISHING, INC.

Hidden Valley 367

Map 3

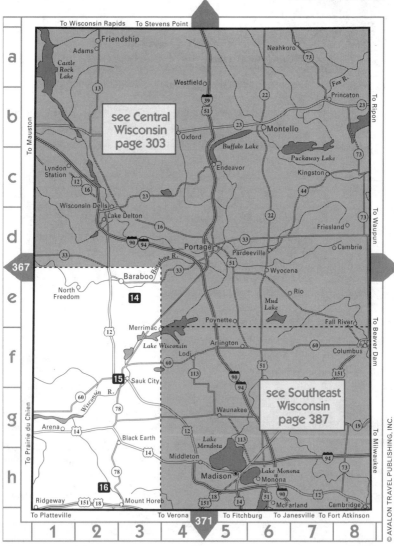

To Wisconsin Rapids   To Stevens Point

a Friendship
Adams
Castle Rock Lake
Neshkoro
73
Westfield
13
22
Fox R.
Princeton
To Ripon
23

b To Mauston
see Central Wisconsin page 303
39 51
23
Montello
Oxford
Buffalo Lake
Puckaway Lake
73

c Lyndon Station
12
16
Endeavor
Kingston
44
23
Wisconsin Dells
Lake Delton
16
22
Friesland
73
To Waupun

d 90 94
33
Portage
Pardeeville
Cambria
33
Baraboo R.
33
Wyocena
51

367 **e** 33
North Freedom
14
Merrimac
12
Poynette
Mud Lake
Rio
Fall River
To Beaver Dam

f Lake Wisconsin
Lodi
60
Arlington
Columbus
60
15 Sauk City
113
90 94
51
151

g To Prairie du Chien
60 Wisconsin R.
78
Waunakee
see Southeast Wisconsin page 387
19
To Milwaukee
Arena
14
Black Earth
12
Lake Mendota
113

h 14
78
Middleton
Madison
Lake Monona
Monona
94
73
16
Ridgeway
151 18
Mount Horeb
151
18
14
51
McFarland
12
Cambridge

To Platteville   To Verona   371   To Fitchburg   To Janesville   To Fort Atkinson

1   2   3   4   5   6   7   8

© AVALON TRAVEL PUBLISHING, INC.

Map 4

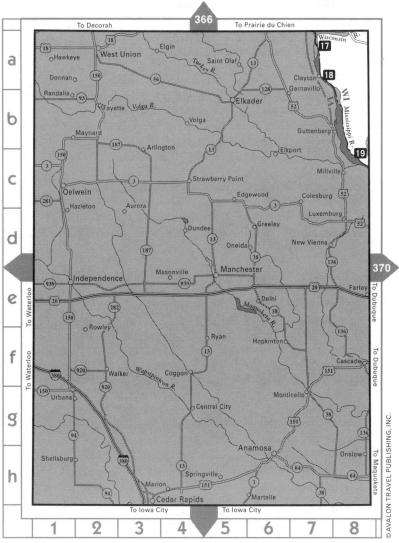

Wisconsin R.

17

18
WI Mississippi R.

19

18
Hawkeye
West Union
Elgin
Saint Olaf
13

Donnan
150
56
Clayton
Garnavillo

Randalia
93
Fayette
Volga R.
128
Elkader
52

Volga

Guttenberg

Maynard
187
Arlington
13
Elkport

150
3
Strawberry Point
Millville

Oelwein
3
Edgewood
Colesburg
52

281
Hazleton
Aurora
3
Luxemburg
52

Dundee
13
Greeley

Oneida
New Vienna

187
38
136

Masonville
Manchester
370
To Dubuque

Independence
939
20
939
20
Farley

150
282
Delhi

Rowley
Maquoketa R.
136

Ryan
Hopkinton
Cascade

920
Walker
Wapsipinicon R.
Coggon
151

150
Urbana
Monticello

94
Central City
151
38

380
136

Shellsburg
Anamosa
Onslow
To Maquoketa

13
Springville
64
64

Marion
151
1

94
Cedar Rapids
Martelle
38

To Waterloo
To Waterloo
To Dubuque

1 2 3 4 5 6 7 8

a b c d e f g h

© AVALON TRAVEL PUBLISHING, INC.

Map 5

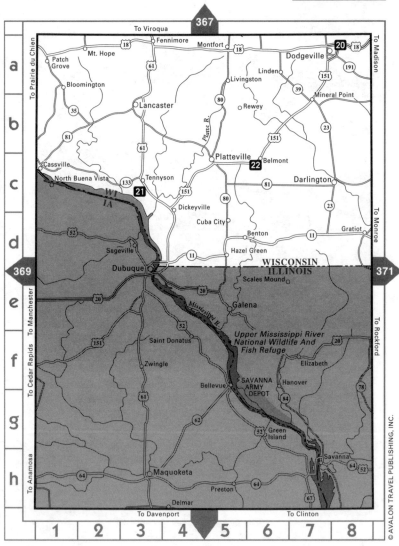

Map 6

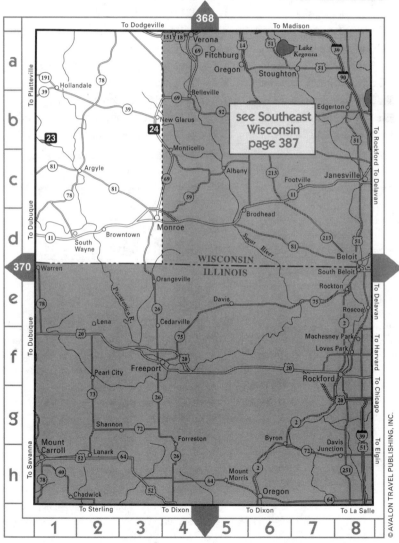

To Dodgeville
To Madison
368

a

To Platteville
191
Hollandale
78
39

Verona
151 18
69
Fitchburg
14
51
Lake Kegonsa
39
Oregon
Stoughton
51
90

b

23
39
New Glarus
24
Belleville
69
92
Monticello

see Southeast Wisconsin page 387

Edgerton
51

To Rockford To Delavan

c

81
Argyle
78
81
69
Albany
59
213
Footville
11
Janesville

d

To Dubuque
11
South Wayne
Browntown
Monroe
Brodhead
Sugar River
81
213
Beloit
51

WISCONSIN
ILLINOIS

370

To Dubuque
Warren
78

Orangeville
Davis
Pecatonica R.
26
Cedarville
75
Lena
20

South Beloit
Rockton
75
Roscoe
2
Machesney Park
Loves Park

To Delavan

e

f

Pearl City
Freeport
20
20
Rockford

To Harvard To Chicago

g

73
Shannon
72
26
Forreston
26
Byron
2
72
Davis Junction
39
51

To Elgin

h

Mount Carroll
52
Lanark
64
Mount Morris
64
2
Oregon
251
40
78
Chadwick
52
64

To Savanna

© AVALON TRAVEL PUBLISHING, INC.

To Sterling
To Dixon
To Dixon
To La Salle

1   2   3   4   5   6   7   8

Hidden Valley

This southwest corner of Wisconsin is fascinating partly because it's somewhat off the well-traveled highways of the state. But make no mistake: there's plenty to see and do throughout this region. The small towns offer rural hospitality, scenic routes, historic sites, and cottage industries.

For example, the area around Platteville was among the first settled by Europeans attracted by the rich lead deposits. Mt. Horeb, Blue Mounds, and Barnveld have remnants of their Scandinavian heritage. The Swiss settled in New Glarus in 1845 and today the community is called "Little Switzerland." Richland Center, meanwhile, is the birthplace of famous architect Frank Lloyd Wright and where he returned to build Tallesin, his dream home.

1 Sports Unlimited Campground

Location: Prairie du Chien, on the Mississippi River, map 1, grid H7.

Campsites, facilities: There are 350 campsites. Facilities include electric hookups, water, sewer, seasonal rentals, laundry, grocery store, marina, restaurant, swimming pool, boat ramp and dock, river boating, canoeing, river fishing, mini-golf, tennis, and shuffleboard courts.

Reservations, fees: The daily fee ranges from $16 to $20. Open from mid-April through October.

Directions: From the junction of U.S. Hwy. 18 and Hwys. 35/60/27, go 2.5 miles north on Hwy. 35. Then, drive one-half mile west on Limery Road and one-half mile north on Frenchmen Road to the campground entrance.

Contact: Sports Unlimited Campground, P.O. Box 210, Prairie du Chien, WI 53821, 608/326-2141.

Trip Notes: Be sure to tour the Villa Louis Historic Site (608/326-2721; website: www .shaw.wisc.edu/sites/villa). It's an 1870 Victorian mansion built by the family of Hercules Dousman, an entrepreneurial frontiersman who made a fortune. The mansion is restored to its British Arts-and-Crafts-style elegance. It's on St. Feriole Island in Prairie du Chien. Also visit the Prairie du Chien Museum at Fort Crawford (608/326-6960) and learn more about local history.

If you love nature, you should see the Kickapoo Indian Caverns and Native American Museum (608/875-7723).

❷ Oakdale KOA

Location: Oakdale, northeast of LaCrosse, map 2, grid A6.

Campsites, facilities: There are 84 campsites. Facilities include electric hookups, water, sewer, flush toilets, showers, disposal station, laundry, grocery store, swimming pool, and playground. Boating, canoeing, and fishing are available nearby at the Petenwell and Castle Rock Flowages. Cabin rentals are available. Pets are allowed.

Reservations, fees: The daily fee ranges from $16 to $22. Credit cards are accepted. Open year-round. The facility is fully operational from mid-May through September.

Directions: From the junction of I-90/94 and Country Road PP (Oakdale exit 48), go one block north on County Road PP to Woody Drive and turn right. Then, drive two blocks to Jay Street, turn right and go one block to the entrance.

Contact: Oakdale KOA, William Rood, P.O. Box 150, Oakdale, WI 54649, 608/372-5622.

Trip Notes: It may not be Thanksgiving, but in nearby Warrens be sure to visit the Cranberry Expo (608/378-4878; website: www.cran berryexpo.com), a museum and gift shop that is dedicated to cranberries. It's six miles east of I-94. Take exit 135.

Or, you can drive to nearby Sparta and see the world's largest bike—an old-fashioned high-wheeler formed out of fiberglass. It welcomes visitors to the town, which dubs itself the "Bicycling Capital of America." Sparta offers ready access to several nationally known bike trails, including the Elroy-Sparta State Trail, the first rails-to-trails bicycle route in the country. Sparta itself has a lovely historic downtown district you can tour.

❸ Mill Bluff State Park

Location: Camp Douglas, west of the Castle Rock Flowage, map 2, grid A6.

Campsites, facilities: There are 21 campsites. There are no hookups or showers, but there are vault toilets, pond swimming, and hiking trails. Nearby Castle Rock Flowage offers boating, canoeing, and fishing. Pets are allowed.

Reservations, fees: Reservations are accepted. Campsite reservations are available. See State Park Camping Fees and Reserving a Campsite. Open from late May through mid-August.

Directions: From Camp Douglas, go three miles northwest on U.S. Hwy. 12 and Hwy. 16 to the park entrance.

Contact: Mill Bluff State Park, P.O. Box 99, Ontario, WI 54651, 608/427-6692 summer; 608/337-4775 off-season.

Trip Notes: This park is part of the Ice Age National Scientific Reserve and offers a spectacular view of picturesque rock formations.

A nice side trip is a drive to the Paul and Matilda Wegner Grotto (608/269-8680; website: www.spartan.org/historyroom/), which is locally known as the "Glass Church." You can get directions at the Monroe County Local History Museum in the Masonic Temple, which has been designated a state and national historic site. It's located at 200 W. Main Street, across the street from the county court house.

4 Tunnel Trail Campground

Location: Wilton, south of Tomah, map 2, grid B5.

Campsites, facilities: There are 75 campsites. Facilities include RV pull-through sites, electric hookups, water, flush toilets, showers, disposal station, laundry, grocery store, swimming pool, hiking trail, mini-golf, and playground. Bike and cabin rentals are available. The campground is adjacent to the Elroy-Sparta Bike Trail, with canoeing and fishing in the nearby Kickapoo River.

Reservations, fees: The daily fee ranges from $17 to $19. Credit cards are accepted. Open year-round. The facility is fully operational from April through mid-October.

Directions: From the junction of Hwys. 131 and 71, go one mile east on Hwy. 71 to the campground entrance on the right.

Contact: Tunnel Trail Campground, Scott and Julie Grenon, 26983 Hwy. 71, Wilton, WI 54670, 608/435-6829 or 920/294-3742 off-season.

Trip Notes: The Kickapoo River offers 120 miles of twists and turns for canoeists; the Elroy-Sparta Bike Trail, which is the old Chicago-Northwestern railroad bed, provides 32.5 level miles of biking or hiking through the scenic countryside. The trail travels through three century-old tunnels and the beautiful hills of the Coulee Region.

5 Castle Rock Park

Location: Mauston, southeast of Tomah, map 2, grid B8.

Campsites, facilities: There are 200 campsites in this county park. Facilities include electric hookups, flush toilets, showers, disposal station, lake swimming, boat ramp and dock, canoeing, hiking trail, fishing, and playground.

Reservations, fees: The daily fee ranges from $10 to 12.50. Open May through October.

Directions: From the junction of I-90/94 and Hwy. 82, take exit 69 and go one-half mile west on Hwy. 82, then 10 miles northeast on County Road G to the park entrance.

Contact: Castle Rock Park, Juneau County Forestry and Parks, 650 Prairie St., Mauston, WI 53948, 608/847-7089 or 608/339-7713.

Trip Notes: Located by two of Wisconsin's largest bodies of water—Castle Rock and Petenwell Flowages—you'll find the best fishing for walleye, northern pike, bass, and a variety of panfish.

If you're looking for something different, drive to Sparta to the M and M Ranch (608/486-2709; website: www.centuryinter.net/mmranch), which is the largest exotic animal ranch in the Midwest. It boasts some 700 animals. From I-90, take County Road J south to Jackpot Avenue and turn left to the ranch at 4494 Jackpot Avenue.

6 Bavarian Campsites

Location: Mauston, on Castle Rock Flowage, map 2, grid B8.

Campsites, facilities: There are 70 campsites. Facilities include electric hookups, water, flush toilets, showers, disposal station, grocery store, and swimming beach. Seasonal campsite rentals are available. Pets are allowed.

Reservations, fees: The daily fee ranges from $11 to $17. Open year-round. The facility is fully operational from April through mid-October.

Directions: From Mauston, take Hwy. 58 north for seven miles to County Road G. Turn right and drive three miles to the campground entrance.

Contact: Bavarian Campsites, Castle Rock Lake, Mauston, WI 53948, 608/847-7039.

Trip Notes: This campground is on the Castle Rock Flowage, the fourth largest body of water in Wisconsin. Covering 26 square miles, the flowage was created between 1949 and 1951. It's regarded as one of the best fishing lakes in the state for walleye, northern pike, and bass.

The Lower Wisconsin River basin includes the river from the flowage dam to its confluence with the Mississippi near Prairie du Chien and all the tributary streams. The basin spans all or parts of 12 counties: Adams, Columbia, Crawford, Dane, Grant, Iowa, Jackson, Juneau, Monroe, Richland, Sauk, and Vernon.

◼ Wildcat Mountain State Park

Location: Ontario, south of Tomah, map 2, grid C4.

Campsites, facilities: There are 54 campsites. There are no hookups or showers, but facilities include pond boating, canoeing, and fishing. Boat ramp, swimming, hiking, horseback riding, and cross-country ski trails are nearby.

Reservations, fees: Reservations are accepted. Campsite reservations are available. See State Park Camping Fees and Reserving a Campsite. Open April through November.

Directions: From Ontario, go three miles east on Hwy. 33 to the park entrance.

Contact: Wildcat State Park, 33E Box 99, Ontario, WI 54651, 608/337-4775.

Trip Notes: This park, which has an excellent observation point overlooking the Kickapoo Valley and the village of Ontario, is a good spot to canoe the winding Kickapoo River. The campground also offers 15 miles of horseback riding trails. You can rent a horse at Jo's Rent-N-Ride (608/337-4739) and take a guided trail ride through the park.

◼ Chapparal Campground and Resort

Location: Wonewoc, southeast of Tomah, map 2, grid C7.

Campsites, facilities: There are 73 campsites and separate areas for tents and horseback riders. Facilities include electric hookups, water, flush toilets, showers, disposal station, laundry, grocery store, restaurant, swimming pool, biking and hiking trails, and shuffleboard courts. Bike and cabin rentals are available.

Reservations, fees: The daily fee ranges from $20 to $24. Credit cards are accepted. Open April through October.

Directions: From the junction of Hwys. 58 and 33, go 3.5 miles west on Hwy. 33 to the campground entrance on the right.

Contact: Dennis Plantenberg, S320 Hwy. 33, Wonewoc, WI 53968, 888/283-0755, email: chap@mwt.net, website: www.chapparal.com.

Trip Notes: This campground is located on the "400 Trail," a 22-mile rail-bed biking, hiking, skiing, and snowmobile trail that runs between Reedsburg and Elroy. It links up with the Elroy-Sparta, Hillsboro, and Omaha Trails. Features along the route include rock outcroppings along the Baraboo River.

9 Lighthouse Rock Campground

Location: Reedsburg, west of Baraboo, map 2, grid D8.

Campsites, facilities: There are 96 campsites. Facilities include electric hookups, sewer, flush toilets, showers, disposal station, laundry, grocery store, boat dock, lake boating (no motors), canoeing, fishing, swimming, hiking trail, mini-golf, and playground. There is a biking trail nearby.

Reservations, fees: The daily fee ranges from $19 to $23. Open April through October.

Directions: From Hwy. 22/33, go 2.5 miles north on County Road V (Walnut Street) to the campground entrance.

Contact: Faye Hedrington, S2330 County Hwy. V, Reedsburg, WI 53959, 608/524-4203.

Trip Notes: The campground is on a private lake and on one end of the "400 Trail," a bike trail that meanders between Reedsburg and Elroy.

If you loved the covers of "Saturday Evening Post" or any of the many other places where Norman Rockwell's famous paintings appeared, you'll enjoy a visit to the Museum of Norman Rockwell Art (608/524-2123). It's housed in a quaint old church and contains paintings, prints, videos, and many other items that cover his more than 65-year career.

10 Eagle Cave Natural Park

Location: Blue River, east of Prairie du Chien, map 2, grid G4.

Campsites, facilities: There are 50 campsites. Facilities include electric hookups, water, flush toilets, showers, disposal station, lake and river boating, canoeing, fishing, swimming, hiking and horseback riding trails, and planned weekend activities. Canoe rentals are available.

Reservations, fees: The daily fee ranges from $10 to $12. Open year-round.

Directions: From the junction of Hwys. 193 and 60, go three miles west on Hwy. 60, then 2.5 miles north on Eagle Cove Road to the campground entrance.

Contact: Eagle Cave Natural Park, 16320 Cavern Ln., Blue River, WI 53518, 608/537-2988.

Trip Notes: Eagle Cave is claimed to be Wisconsin's largest onyx cave, containing stalactites, stalagmites, and fossils. It has marked trails, and you can take a tour of the cave. In addition, two-day canoe and horseback-guided tour packages are offered.

11 Tower Hill State Park

Location: Spring Green, northwest of Madison, map 2, grid G8.

Campsites, facilities: There are 15 campsites. There are no hookups or showers. Facilities include vault toilets, river boating, canoeing, fishing, hiking trails, and nature center.

Reservations, fees: Reservations are accepted. Campsite reservations are available. See State Park Camping Fees and Reserving a Campsite. Open from mid-April through October.

Directions: From Spring Green, go three miles southeast on U.S. Hwy. 14 and Hwy. 23 to the park entrance.

Contact: Tower Hill State Park, 5805 County Road C, Spring Green, WI 53588, 608/326-2141 or 608/588-2116.

Trip Notes: Visit the park's unique restored shot and melting house to see exhibits and a film on lead shot-making from the 1800s. Here, two men used picks and crowbars to tunnel 120 feet down and 90 feet horizontally through the rock. Enjoy the challenging bluff trails and panoramic views.

12 Blackhawk Lake Recreation Area

Location: Highland, southeast of Prairie du Chien, map 2, grid H6.

Campsites, facilities: There are 135 campsites. Facilities include electric hookups, water, flush toilets, showers, disposal station, boating on a 223-acre lake, canoeing, fishing, swimming beach, hiking trails, 1,500 acres of hunting grounds, planned activities, and playground. Boat rentals are available. In winter, there are cross-country ski and snowmobile trails, and ice fishing.

Reservations, fees: The daily fee ranges from $10 to $14. Open year-round.

Directions: From the junction of Hwy. 80 and County Road BH, go 2.5 miles east on County Road BH to the recreation area's entrance.

Contact: Blackhawk Lake Recreation Area, 2025 County Road BH, Highland, WI 53543, 608/623-2707.

Trip Notes: Have you been curious about how wine is made? You can take a guided tour of the Spurgeon Vineyards and Winery and even do a little tasting (608/929-7692; website: www.spurgeonvinyards.com) at the 16-acre winery nestled in the rolling countryside west of Highland. Call ahead for tour times.

13 Governor Dodge State Park

Location: Dodgeville, southwest of Madison, map 2, grid H8.

Campsites, facilities: There are 270 campsites. Facilities include electric hookups, showers, disposal station, lake boating, canoeing, swimming, and boat ramp. There are also bike, hiking, horseback riding, snowmobile, and cross-country ski trails. In winter, there are 15 to 20 campsites, all with water and some with electric hookups.

Reservations, fees: Reservations are accepted. Campsite reservations are available. See State Park Camping Fees and Reserving a Campsite. Open year-round.

Directions: From Dodgeville, go three miles north on Hwy. 23 to the park entrance.

Contact: Governor Dodge State Park, 4175 State Rd., 23 North, Dodgeville, WI 53533, 608/935-2315.

Trip Notes: More than 5,000 scenic acres of steep hills, bluffs, and deep valleys, plus two lakes and a waterfall, make this park a family favorite.

A nice side trip is a drive to Doby Stables (608/935-5205) at 4228 Hwy. 23N and its Museum of Minerals and Crystals, a display of rocks, minerals, crystals, and fluorescent stones from around the world.

14 Devil's Lake State Park

Location: Baraboo, south of the Wisconsin Dells, map 3, grid E3.

Campsites, facilities: There are 406 campsites. Facilities

include electric hookups, showers, disposal station, grocery store, boat ramp, lake boating (electric motors only), canoeing, fishing, and swimming. There are also bike, hiking, and cross-country ski trails. In winter, there are 12 plowed and 12 backpacking campsites with electric hookups and water.

Reservations, fees: Reservations are accepted. Campsite reservations are available. See State Park Camping Fees and Reserving a Campsite. Open year-round.

Directions: From Baraboo, go two miles south on Hwy. 123 to the park entrance.

Contact: Devil's Lake State Park, S5975 Park Rd., Baraboo, WI 53913, 608/356-8301.

Trip Notes: The park's campground is situated along the Ice Age Trail where 500-foot bluffs tower above the 360-acre lake. Spectacular scenery, a full range of recreational activities, and a full-time naturalist make this a very popular park.

15 Snuffy's Campsite

Location: Sauk City, northwest of Madison, map 3, grid F3.

Campsite, facilities: There are 145 campsites. Facilities include RV pull-through sites, electric hookups, water, sewer, flush toilets, showers, disposal station, river boating, boat ramp, canoeing, fishing, swimming, and playground. Seasonal campsite rentals are available.

Reservations, fees: The daily fee ranges from $15 to $16. Open from mid-April through mid-October.

Directions: From the junction of Hwy. 60, Hwy. 78, and U.S. Hwy. 12, go one-half mile south on U.S. 12/Hwy. 78 to the campground entrance.

Contact: Snuffy's Campsite, 608/643-8353.

Trip Notes: On the Wisconsin River, the campground is a terrific spot if you enjoy canoeing. If you don't have one, there are three places where you can rent one: Bender's Bluff-View Canoe Rental (608/643-8247), Blackhawk River Runs (608/643-6724) and Sauk Prairie Canoe Rental (608/643-6589).

16 Blue Mounds State Park

Location: Blue Mounds, west of Madison, map 3, grid H2.

Campsites, facilities: There are 78 campsites. Facilities include electric hookups, flush toilets, showers, disposal station, swimming pool, and bike, hiking, and cross-country ski trails. In winter, there are four plowed campsites and 78 backpack sites. All have water.

Reservations, fees: Reservations are accepted. Campsite reservations are available. See State Park Camping Fees and Reserving a Campsite. Open year-round.

Directions: From Hwys. 18 and 151 in Blue Mounds, drive one mile northwest on Mounds Road to the park entrance.

Contact: Blue Mounds State Park, 4350 Mounds Park Rd., Box 98, Blue Mounds, WI 53517-0098 or 608/437-5711.

Trip Notes: Perched atop the highest point in southern Wisconsin, the park offers spectacular views, as well as unique geological features. It is also the only Wisconsin state park with a swimming pool, equipped with a lift for disabled people, as well as a cabin for the wheelchairped.

You should not leave the area without touring the Cave of the Mounds (608/437-3038; website: www.caveofthemounds.com), a registered National Natural Landmark. It is 20 miles west of Madison on U.S. Hwys. 18/151. Exit Cave of the Mounds Road, midway between Madison and Dodgeville.

17 Wyalusing State Park

Location: Bagley, south of Prairie du Chien, map 4, grid A7.

Campsites, facilities: There are 110 campsites. Facilities include electric hookups, flush toilets, showers, disposal station, river boating, canoeing, and fishing. There are also bike, hiking, and cross-country ski trails. In winter, there are six plowed campsites and 55 backpack sites. All have electric hookups and water.

Reservations, fees: Reservations are accepted. Campsite reservations are available. See State Park Camping Fees and Reserving a Campsite. Open year-round.

Directions: From Bagley, travel seven miles north on Country Road X and then one mile on County Road X. Finally, drive one mile on County Road C.

Contact: Wyalusing State Park, 13081 State Park Ln., Bagley, WI 53801, 608/996-2261, website: www.wyalusing.org.

Trip Notes: You can camp 500 feet above the confluence of the Wisconsin and Mississippi Rivers. This is one of Wisconsin's oldest state parks with Indian burial mounds, canoe trails, and plenty of opportunities for bird-watching.

Take a drive to Boscobel on the Wisconsin River and tour the Boscobel Depot Museum (608/375-6010; website: www.boscobelwisconsin.com), which was built in 1857. It served as the marshalling point of more than 2,000 enlisted men of the Union Army and again during World Wars I and II. Its interior has been converted into a turn-of-the-century railroad and early rural America walk-through museum.

18 Yogi Bear Jellystone Park

Location: Bagley, south of Prairie du Chien, map 4, grid A8.

Campsites, facilities: There are 204 campsites, including a separate tent area. Facilities include electric hookups, water, sewer, flush toilets, showers, disposal station, restaurant, swimming pool, mini-golf, shuffleboard courts, and playground. There are also bike and hiking trails. Cabins and seasonal campsite rentals are available. River boating, canoeing, and fishing can be found nearby.

Reservations, fees: The daily fee ranges from $23 to $28. Open year-round. Facilities are fully operational from April through mid-October.

Directions: From the junction of County Road A and County Road X, go one mile north on County Road X to the campground entrance.

Contact: Yogi Bear Jellystone Park, Mike and Kim Esler, 11354 County Hwy. X, Bagley, WI 53801, 608/996-2201, email: yogibagley@mail.tds.net, website: wwwjellystonebagley.com.

Trip Notes: In Boscobel, which is on the Great River Road/National Scenic Byway, is the Stonefield Historic Village and State Agricultural Museum (608/725-5210; website: www.shsw.wisc.edu/sites/stone). Owned by the State Historical Society of Wisconsin, the site includes a re-created turn-of-the-century village, museum, and the estate of Wisconsin's first governor.

19 Nelson Dewey State Park

Location: Cassville, south of Bagley, map 4, grid C8.

Campsites, facilities: There are 45 campsites. Facilities

include electric hookups, showers, disposal station, bike and hiking trails, and nearby river boating, canoeing, and fishing. In winter, there are four campsites with electric hookups and water is available.

Reservations, fees: Reservations are accepted. Campsite reservations are available. See State Park Camping Fees and Reserving a Campsite. Open April through October.

Directions: From the junction of Hwy. 133 and County Road VV, go one mile northwest on County Road VV to the park entrance.

Contact: Nelson Dewey State Park, Box 658, Cassville, WI 53806, 608/725-5374.

Trip Notes: Take in a panoramic view of the Mississippi from a campsite atop the river bluffs.

Not far from here, Nicholas Perrot discovered southwestern Wisconsin's first lead mine in what is now Potosi. By 1850, the area had more than 10,000 hand-dug lead mines, supplying more than half of the nation's supply. This region also produced virtually all of the lead shot for the Union Army during the Civil War. One of our favorite tours was to crawl through the St. John Mine (608/763-2121) in our hard hats. Originally a natural cave worked by Native Americans, you can learn how miners toiled to extract the mine's lead.

20 Tom's Campground

Location: Dodgeville, southwest of Madison, map 5, grid A8.

Campsites, facilities: The campground has 96 campsites. Facilities include electric hookups, flush toilets, showers, disposal station, grocery store, and playground. Lake boating, canoeing, fishing, and swimming and hiking, biking, horseback riding, snowmobiling, and cross-country ski trails are available at Governor Dodge State Park. Cottage rentals are also available.

Reservations, fees: The daily fee ranges from $11 to $19. Open April through October.

Directions: From the junction of U.S. Hwys. 18 and 151, go four miles east on U.S. 18/151, then 2.5 miles south on County Road BB and one-quarter mile east on Hwy. 191 to the entrance.

Contact: Tom's Campground, Robert and Twila Thomas, 2751 County Road BB, Dodgeville, WI 53533, 608/935-5446.

Trip Notes: Military Ridge State Trail goes through Dodgeville to Verona and offers some 40 miles of biking, hiking, and cross-country ski trails.

In Highland, you can try A to Z Percherons (608/623-2888; website: www.atozpercherons .com), which offers year-round hayrides and, in winter, sleigh rides. There also are two sledding hills. Reservations are required. From Dodgeville, take U.S. Hwy. 18 to Cobb and go north to Highland.

21 Grant River (Coe Lock and Dam 11) Campground

Location: Potosi, east of Cassville, map 5, grid C3.

Campsites, facilities: There are 73 campsites. Facilities include electric hookups, disposal station, boat ramp, river boating, canoeing, fishing, playground, and planned weekend activities.

Reservations, fees: The daily fee ranges from $10 to $16. Open from mid-April through late October.

Directions: From Hwy. 133 south of town, go two miles east on the local road to the campground entrance.

Contact: Grant River Recreation Area, U.S. Army Corps of Engineers, Hwy. 133, Potosi, WI 53820, 319/582-0881.

Trip Notes: This campground on the Grant River is an excellent place to fish for small-mouth bass, but the most popular species is the channel catfish. Other species include walleye, bluegill, crappie, and northern pike.

This site has also become one of Wisconsin's greatest archaeological finds. The riverbanks revealed a large burial site that belonged to the Woodland Indians who lived here 1,000 years ago. Discovered here were copper instruments and jewelry.

22 Lake Joy Campground

Location: Belmont, east of Cassville, map 5, grid C6.

Campsites, facilities: There are 239 camp-sites. Facilities include electric hookups, water, flush toilets, showers, disposal station, laundry, grocery store, boat ramp and dock, lake boating, canoeing, fishing, swimming, hiking trail, planned weekend activities, and playground. Boat rentals are available.

Reservations, fees: Reservations are requested. The daily fee ranges from $16 to $20. Open April through mid-October.

Directions: From Belmont, go four miles northeast on U.S. Hwy. 151, then one-half mile east on Burr Oak Road and one-half mile south on Bethel Grove Road to the entrance.

Contact: Lake Joy Campground, Barb and Lee Fender, 24192 Lake Joy Ln., Belmont, WI 53510., 608/762-5150.

Trip Notes: Belmont was the site of the first capitol (608/987-2122; website: www.shsw .wisc.edu/sites/firstcap/). In October 1836, 39 legislators held the first legislative ses-

sion for the Wisconsin Territory here. Two of the buildings used have survived and the exteriors have been restored. The interiors, meanwhile, contain modern exhibits on early territorial Wisconsin and the first legislature.

Here, you are also close to Mineral Point (888-POINT-WI), a restored Cornish village of the area's early miners. You'll discover artisans and craftsmen who do all types of work.

23 Yellowstone Lake State Park

Location: Blanchardville, southwest of Madison, map 6, grid B1.

Campsites, facilities: There are 128 camp-sites. Facilities include electric hookups, vault toilets, showers, disposal station, grocery store, lake boating, canoeing, fishing, swimming, and playground. There are also bike, hiking, snowmobile, and cross-country ski trails. In winter, there are 22 campsites with electric hookups. Water is available.

Reservations, fees: Reservations are accepted. Campsite reservations are available. See State Park Camping Fees and Reserving a Campsite. Open year-round.

Directions: From Blanchardville, go eight miles southwest on County Road F to the park entrance.

Contact: Yellowstone Lake State Park, 7896 Lake Rd., Blanchardville, WI 53516, 608/ 523-4427.

Trip Notes: Yellowstone Lake, one of the few lakes in southwestern Wisconsin, is a popular recreation area all year. The 450-acre body of water features fishing, swimming, and boating. Campsites are set on the top of a bluff.

Nearby Monroe is a cheese-lover's paradise. One fun place to visit is the Historic Cheesemaking Center (608/325-4636;

website: www.greencounty.org). At 2108 7th Avenue, it tells the history of cheese making in the county.

24 New Glarus Woods State Park

Location: New Glarus, southwest of Madison, map 6, grid B3.

Campsites, facilities: There are 32 campsites. There are no hookups or showers, but there are vault toilets, hiking trails, and nearby biking and snowmobiling trails. In winter, there are four plowed and 28 backpack campsites with electric hookups. Water is not available.

Reservations, fees: Reservations are accepted. Campsite reservations are available. See State Park Camping Fees and Reserving a Campsite. Open year-round.

Directions: From the junction of Hwy. 69 and County Road NN, go one-eighth of a mile west on County Road NN to the park entrance.

Contact: New Glarus Woods State Park, W5446 County Hwy. NN, New Glarus, WI 53574, 608/527-2335.

Trip Notes: Here, you are close to the Sugar River State Trail (608/527-2334) that offers 23 miles of bike, hiking, and snowmobile trails from New Glarus to Brodhead. Built on part of the Milwaukee Road rail right-of-way, it's part of the Ice Age National Scenic Trail. You can find quiet, wooded campsites, and enjoy a replica of the Clarence covered bridge and historic New Glarus.

SOUTHEAST WISCONSIN

Southeast Wisconsin

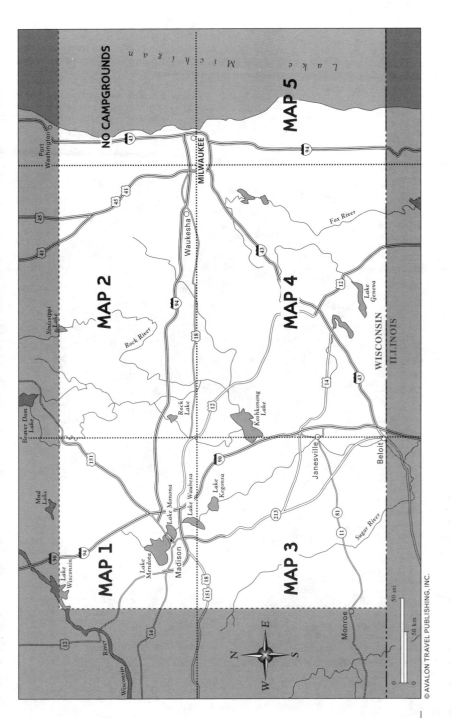

© AVALON TRAVEL PUBLISHING, INC.

Map 1

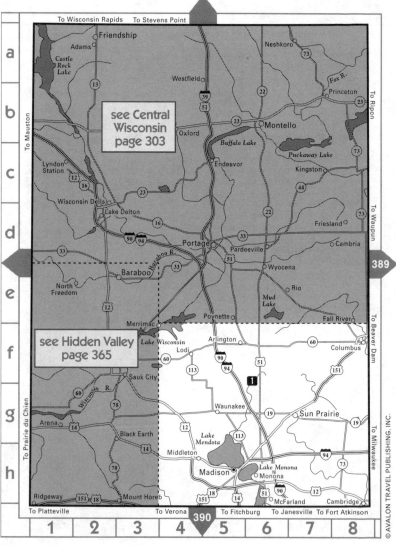

To Wisconsin Rapids   To Stevens Point

a

Friendship
Adams
Castle
Rock
Lake
(13)
Westfield
Neshkoro
(73)

b

To Mauston

see Central
Wisconsin
page 303

(39)
(51)
(22)

Fox R.
Princeton
(23)

To Ripon

(23)
Montello

Oxford
Buffalo Lake
Puckaway Lake

c

Lyndon
Station
(12)
(16)
(23)
Endeavor
Kingston
(44)

Wisconsin Dells
Lake Delton
(16)
(22)
Friesland
(73)

To Waupun

d

(33)
(90)(94)
Portage
(33)
Pardeeville
Cambria

389

Baraboo
(33)
(51)
Wyocena

North
Freedom
Rio

e

(12)
Mud
Lake
Fall River

To Beaver Dam

Merrimac
Poynette

see Hidden Valley
page 365

f

To Prairie du Chien

Lake Wisconsin
Arlington
(60)
Columbus

Lodi
(90)
(51)
(94)
(151)

(60)
(113)
1

Sauk City

g

(60)
Wisconsin R.
(78)
Waunakee
(19)
Sun Prairie
(19)

Arena
(14)
(12)
Lake
Mendota
(113)

To Milwaukee

Black Earth
(14)
Middleton
(94)
(73)

h

(78)
Madison
Lake Monona
Monona

Ridgeway
(151)(18)
Mount Horeb
(18)
(151)
(151)
(18)
(14)
(51)
(90)
McFarland
(12)
Cambridge

To Platteville
To Verona
390
To Fitchburg
To Janesville To Fort Atkinson

1   2   3   4   5   6   7   8

© AVALON TRAVEL PUBLISHING, INC.

388 Wisconsin

Map 2

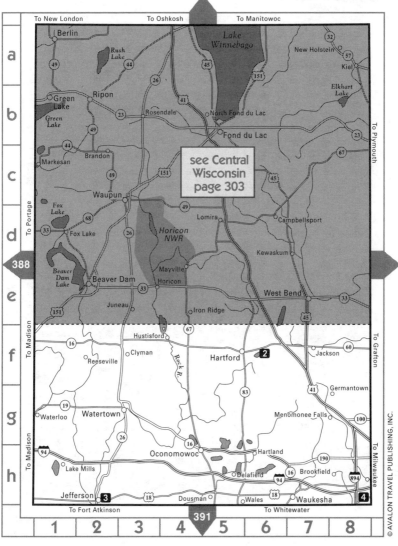

Map 3

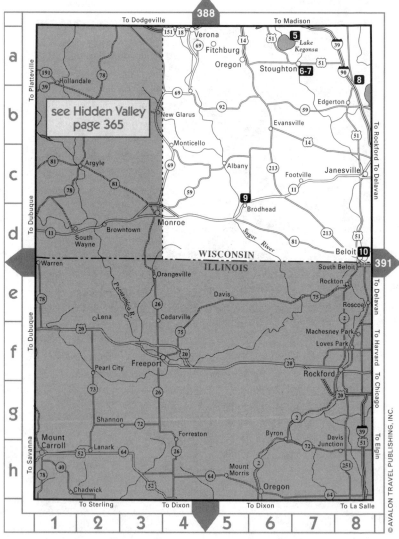

see Hidden Valley
page 365

Map 4

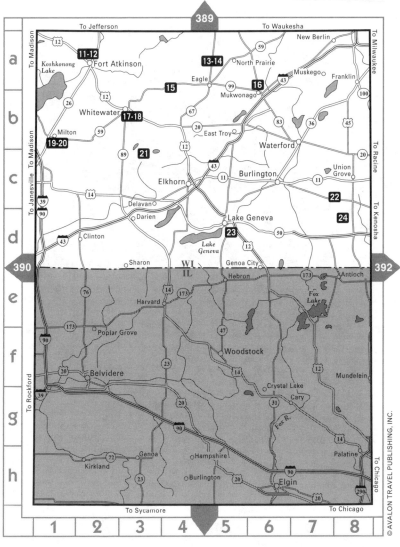

Map 5

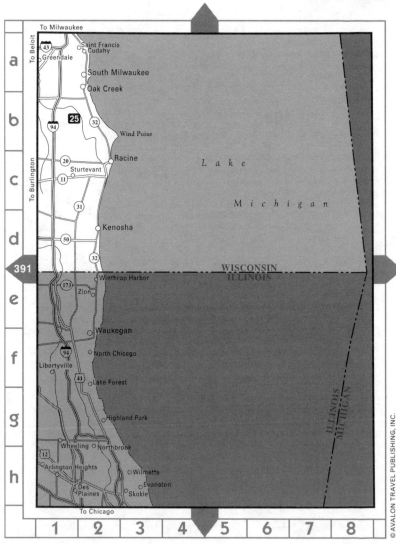

To Milwaukee

To Beloit

Saint Francis
Cudahy
Greendale
South Milwaukee
Oak Creek

Wind Point

To Burlington

Sturtevant
Racine

Kenosha

Winthrop Harbor
Zion

Waukegan
North Chicago
Libertyville
Lake Forest

Highland Park

Wheeling Northbrook
Arlington Heights
Des Plaines
Wilmette
Evanston
Skokie

To Chicago

Lake

Michigan

WISCONSIN
ILLINOIS

ILLINOIS
MICHIGAN

© AVALON TRAVEL PUBLISHING, INC.

Southeast Wisconsin

Southeast Wisconsin boasts the two largest cities in the state—Milwaukee and Madison, the capital. Milwaukee is rich in ethnic neighborhoods and heritage. Home of the Miller Brewery and Harley Davidson motorcycles, it's a place to go for a mix of diversion. The beautiful Lake Michigan shoreline is host to a variety of summer and winter activities.

Stretching northwestward is Eagle, nestled against the eastern edge of the Kettle Moraine State Forest, where at Old World Wisconsin you can take a walk back into time and see how early settlers lived. Waukesha and Oconomowoc preserve the rural charm of quaint small communities, and Honey Acres at Ashippun will amaze you with its bee tree coming right into the museum.

Madison, nestled on a narrow isthmus between two lakes, is one of the country's top canoe towns. Besides the Capitol Building and the University of Wisconsin campus, there is plenty to see and do—the Dane County Farmer's Market, Henry Vilas Zoo, Olbrich Botanical Gardens—to name a few.

Southeast of Madison, small towns have fascinating stories to tell. Cambridge is famous for Rowe Pottery; at Fort Atkinson you can view a replica of the fort built in 1832 or the mansion of W. D. Hoard, the father of dairy farming, which houses a museum and diary shrine. Near the Illinois border, you can enjoy all the activities at Lake Geneva, a resort developed after the Civil War by wealthy families desiring a summer home. There you can take a historic walking tour, enjoy a cruise on the large lake, or just shop until you drop.

◻ KOA-Madison

Location: De Forest, northeast of Madison, map 1, grid G6.

Campsites, facilities: There are 81 campsites. Facilities include RV pull-through sites, electric hookups, water, sewers, flush toilets, showers, disposal station, laundry, grocery store, and playground. Seasonal campsite rentals are available.

Reservations, fees: The daily fee ranges from $18 to $30. Open April through October.

Directions: From the junction of I-94/90 and County Road V, take exit 126 and go one-quarter mile east on County Road V to the entrance on the right.

Contact: KOA-Madison, 4859 County Rd. V, De Forest, WI 53532, 608/846-4528 or 800/562-5784.

Trip Notes: Always interesting is a visit to Madison where you can tour the Capitol Building (608/266-0382) and spend the afternoon at the Henry Vilas Zoo (608/266-4732; website: www.vilaszoo.org) at 702 S. Randall Avenue, where the youngsters can get a free camel ride during the summer. The entire family can also stroll through the Olbrich Botanical Gardens and Tropical Conservatory (608/246-4550) and its 14 acres of outdoor gardens and glass indoor tropical conservatory. The gardens are at 3330 Atwood Avenue.

◻ Kettle Moraine State Forest-Pike Lake State Park Unit

Location: Hartford, northwest of Milwaukee, map 2, grid F6.

Campsites, facilities: There are 32 campsites. Facilities include electric hookups, flush toilets, showers, disposal station, picnic area, lookout tower, lake boating, fishing, and swimming. There are also biking, hiking, cross-country ski, and snowmobiling trails.

Reservations, fees: Reservations are accepted. Campsite reservations are available. See State Park Camping Fees and Reserving a Campsite. Open from early May through late October.

Directions: From Hartford, go two miles east on Hwy. 60 to the campground entrance.

Contact: Pike Lake State Park, 3544 Kettle Moraine Rd., Hartford, WI 53027, 262/670-3400.

Trip Notes: Powder Hill, a 1,350-foot glacial kame, offers panoramic views of the 678-acre park's unique glacial topography.

◻ Bark River Campground

Location: Jefferson, east of Madison, map 2, grid H2.

Campsites, facilities: There are 295 campsites. Facilities include RV pull-through sites, electric hookups, water, sewers, disposal station, laundry, grocery store, restaurant, swimming pool, river canoeing, fishing, and swimming. Biking, hiking, and snowmobile trails are available nearby.

Reservations, fees: The daily fee ranges from $15 to $19. Open year-round. The facility is fully operational from mid-April through mid-October.

Directions: From the junction of Hwy. 106 and County Road F, go three-quarters of a mile north on County Road F and then one-half mile west on Hanson Road.

Contact: Bark River Campground, 2340 W. Hansen Rd., Jefferson, WI 53549, 262/593-2421, email: hd@jdcnet.com.

Trip Notes: The Glacial Drumlin State Trail East (920/648-8774), which runs from Jefferson to Waukesha, and the Glacial Drumlin State Trail West, which runs from Jefferson to Cottage Grove, both provide more than 20 miles each of biking, hiking, and snowmobiling trails.

4 Wisconsin State Fair RV Park

Location: West Allis, west of Milwaukee, map 2, grid H8.

Campsites, facilities: There are 70 full-service (electric, water, sewer) campsites and 100 electric hookup-only sites. Tents are not permitted. Facilities include RV pull-through sites, flush toilets, showers, laundry, and disposal station. Lake swimming, boating, fishing, tennis, and golf are available nearby. Pets on leashes are allowed.

Reservations, fees: The daily fee ranges from $20 to $25. For auto race events, there is a three-day minimum ($25 to $40); for the Wisconsin State Fair, there is an 11-day minimum ($25 to $40). Credit cards are accepted. Open year-round.

Directions: From I-94, take exit 306 (84th Street) and go straight to the park entrance at the fairgrounds.

Contact: Recreational Vehicle Park, Wisconsin State Fair Park, P.O. Box 14990, West Allis, WI 53214, 414/266-7035, website: wi statefair.com.

Trip Notes: You won't be at a loss for something to do in Milwaukee. You can enjoy walking tours of the various ethnic sections of the city, a tour of the Capt. Frederick Pabst Mansion (414/931-0808), and the Pabst Brewing Company (414/223-3709). You can also enjoy the beauty of the Mitchell Park Horticultural Conservatory (414/649-9800).

5 Lake Kegonsa State Park

Location: Stoughton, southeast of Madison, map 2, grid A7.

Campsites, facilities: There are 80 campsites. Facilities include a few electric hookups, disposal station, showers, picnic area, boat ramp, fishing, and swimming beach. There are also hiking, nature, and cross-country ski trails.

Reservations, fees: Reservations are accepted. Campsite reservations are available. See State Park Camping Fees and Reserving a Campsite. Open May through October.

Directions: From the junction of I-90 and Country Road N, take exit 147 and go one-quarter mile south on County Road N and then 2.5 miles west on Koshkonong Road. Then drive 1.25 miles south on Door Creek Road to the park entrance.

Contact: Lake Kegonsa State Park, 2405 Door Creek Rd., Stoughton, WI 53589, 606/873-9695.

Trip Notes: One of the best-kept secrets of southern Wisconsin, Lake Kogonsa State Park offers a variety of recreation and good fishing on a 3,200-acre glacial lake. In fact, Kogonsa means lake of many fishes. Here, you'll see prairie, forest, and marsh habitats. In addition, the park's White Oak Nature Trail's strange earthen structures are of mysterious origin.

6 Viking Village Campground and Resort

Location: Stoughton, southeast of Madison, map 3, grid A7.

Campsites, facilities: There are 78 campsites, including a separate tent area. Facilities include electric hookups, water, sewer, disposal station, flush toilets, showers, laundry, restaurant, swimming pool, mini-golf, and playground. Lake boating, fishing, and swimming are available nearby. Seasonal campsite rentals are available. Pets are allowed.

Reservations, fees: The daily fee ranges from $23 to $27. Open May through September.

Directions: From I-90, take exit 147 and go south four miles on County Road N to the campground entrance.

Contact: Viking Village Campground and Resort, Sherry Bibro, 1648 County Rd. N, Stoughton, WI 53589, 608/873-6601, email: vikingboss@aol.com, website: www.in stoughton.com/vikingvillage.htm.

Trip Notes: Take a stroll down Historic Main Street in Stoughton and visit the antique store, coffee shops, and other shops.

In nearby Madison, you might enjoy the Wisconsin Veterans Museum (608/267-1799; website: museum.dva.state.wi.us) in Capitol Square next to the Madison Children's Museum and across the street from the Wisconsin Historical Museum. The Veterans museum uses exhibits, displays, and presentations to the story of the Wisconsin citizens who served in America's conflicts from the Civil War to the Persian Gulf War.

⑦ Kamp Kegonsa

Location: Stoughton, southeast of Madison, map 3, grid A7.

Campsites, facilities: There are 100 campsites, including a separate tent area. Facilities include electric hookups, water, disposal station, grocery store, lake swimming, boating, canoeing, and fishing. Hiking trail and golf are available nearby. Pets are allowed on a leash.

Reservations, fees: RV reservations are recommended. The daily fee ranges from $17 to $23. Open from mid-April through mid-October.

Directions: From I-90, take exit 147 and go 1.5 miles south. Then turn right on Circle Drive and go three-quarters of a mile to the campground entrance on the left.

Contact: Kamp Kegonsa, Doug and Sandy Gerber, 2671 Circle Dr., Stoughton, WI 53589, 608/873-5800.

Trip Notes: If history excites you, the Wisconsin Historical Museum (608/264-6555; website: www.shsw.wisc.edu/museum) in Capitol Square in Madison is worth several hours. It features Wisconsin exhibits from prehistoric Indian culture to contemporary social issues.

⑧ Hickory Hills Campground

Location: Edgerton, on Rice Lake southeast of Madison, map 3, grid A8.

Campsites, facilities: There are 290 campsites. Facilities include electric hookups, water, sewer, flush toilets, showers, disposal station, grocery store, swimming pool, boat ramp and dock, fishing, mini-golf, shuffleboard courts, playground, and planned weekend activities. Bike, boat, and cabin rentals are available. Pets are allowed.

Reservations, fees: The daily fee ranges from $23 to $28. Open May through mid-October.

Directions: From junction I-90 and Hwy. 73, take exit 160 and go one-half mile north on Hwy. 73, then three-quarters of a mile east on Hwy. 106. Drive three-quarters of a mile north on Hillside Road to the entrance.

Contact: Hickory Hills Campground, Richard and Cynthia Poff, 856 Hillside Rd., Edgerton, WI 53534, 608/884-6327.

Trip Notes: Take a self-guided tour of Edgerton History and Tobacco farming in Wisconsin at the Tobacco City Museum (608/884-4319).

9 Crazy Horse Campground

Location: Broadhead, south of Milwaukee, map 3, grid D5.

Campsites, facilities: There are 196 campsites in this riverside campground. Facilities include electric hookups, water, flush toilets, showers, disposal station, laundry, grocery store, swimming pool, river swimming, fishing, boating, canoeing, mini-golf, and playground. Canoe and seasonal campsite rentals are available. Biking and hiking trails are available nearby. Pets are allowed.

Reservations, fees: The daily fee ranges from $27 to $31. Open from mid-May through mid-October.

Directions: From Broadhead, go one mile west on County Road F and then one-half mile south to the campground entrance.

Contact: Crazy Horse Campground, Stacy Baumgartner, W741 County Rd. F, Broadhead, WI 53520, 608/907-2207.

Trip Notes: The Sugar River State Trail (608/527-2334) offers 24 miles of biking, hiking, and snowmobiling trails to historic New Glarus. The route gently meanders along the Sugar River and lets you enjoy a replica of the Clarence covered bridge.

10 Turtle Creek Campsite

Location: Beloit, near the Illinois border, map 3, grid D8.

Campsites, facilities: There are 100 campsites. Facilities include RV pull-through sites, electric hookups, water, flush toilets, showers, disposal station, swimming pool, river canoeing, fishing, and hiking trail.

Reservations, fees: The daily fee is $15. Open from mid-May through September.

Directions: From the junction of I-90/43, go two miles north on I-90 and take exit 183 (Shopiere Road). Then drive 500 feet east on County Road S to the entrance.

Contact: Turtle Creek Campsite, 3513 E. County Rd. S, Beloit, WI 53511, 608/362-7768.

Trip Notes: Angels are the subject of one of the newest museums—the Angel Museum (608/362-9099) at 656 Pleasant Street in Beloit. It displays the largest private collection of angel figurines in the United States, including many donated by TV personality Oprah Winfrey.

11 Yogi Bear Jellystone Park-Fort Atkinson

Location: Fort Atkinson, southeast of Madison, map 4, grid A2.

Campsites, facilities: There are 569 campsites. Facilities include electric hookups, water, flush toilets, showers, disposal station, laundry, swimming pools, pond fishing, hiking trail, mini-golf, shuffleboard and tennis courts, and playground. Lake boating, canoeing, and fishing are available nearby.

Reservations, fees: The daily fee is $22. Open from mid-May through mid-September.

Contact: Yogi Bear Jellystone Park-Fort Atkinson, Steve Kline, N551 Wishing Well Dr., Fort Atkinson, WI 53538, 920/568-4100, website: www.bearsatfort.com.

Directions: From Fort Atkinson, take Hwy. 26 about four miles south, then three-quarters of a mile to Lake Koshkonong Road. Drive one-quarter mile south on Wishing Well Road to the park entrance.

Trip Notes: After a day of fishing for a great variety of panfish on Lake Koshkonong or walleye and bass on Rock Lake, why not take the cook in the camper out to a dinner show at Fort Atkinson's famous Fireside Restaurant and Playhouse (800/477-9505)?

12 Pilgrim's Campground

Location: Fort Atkinson, southeast of Madison, map 4, grid A2.

Campsites, facilities: There are 83 campsites, including a separate tent area. Facilities include electric hookups, water, sewer, flush toilets, showers, disposal station, grocery store, and swimming pool. Boating, canoeing, fishing, horseback riding, and cross-country skiing are available nearby at Aztalan State Park.

Reservations, fees: The daily fee ranges from $18 to $22. Open May through October.

Contact: Pilgrim's Campground, Bart and Kim Kincannon, W7271 County Rd. C, Fort Atkinson, WI 53538, 800/742-1697, email: pilgrim@idcnet.com.

Directions: From Hwy. 26, go west on U.S. Hwy. 12, then left on County Road C to Kunz Road. Then turn left at the campground entrance.

Trip Notes: At Aztalan State Park, 12 miles north, is one of the most important archaeological sites in the 12th-century Native American Village (920/648-8774).

13 Kettle Moraine State Forest-Ottawa Lake Campground

Location: Near Eagle, on Ottawa Lake in the Kettle Moraine State Forest, map 4, grid A5.

Campsites, facilities: There are 100 campsites. Facilities include electric hookups for 49 sites, no hookups for 51 sites, vault toilets, disposal station, lake boating, canoeing, fishing, and swimming beach. Biking, hiking, cross-country ski, and snowmobile trails are available. In winter, there are 40 sites with electric hookups and hand-pumped water.

Reservations, fees: Reservations are accepted. Campsite reservations are available. See State Park Camping Fees and Reserving a Campsite. Open year-round.

Directions: From the junction of Hwy. 99 and Hwy. 67, go five miles north on Hwy. 67 to Country Road ZZ to the campground entrance.

Contact: Kettle Moraine State Forest, Southern Unit, SO1 W3909 Hwy. 59, Eagle, WI 53119, 262/594-6200.

Trip Notes: The glacier left 21,000 acres of rolling hills and many lakes in the Kettle Moraine.

While in the area, you will want visit Eagle to take a step back in time and visit Old World Wisconsin (414/594-6300), a 600-acre living history museum with 65 historical buildings in five ethnically-themed villages. By the way, the first diamond found in Wisconsin was discovered in Eagle in 1876.

14 Kettle Moraine State Forest-Pinewoods Campground

Location: Near Eagle, in the Kettle Moraine State Forest, map 4, grid A5.

Campsites, facilities: There are 97 campsites. Facilities include vault toilets, disposal station, and hiking trails. Pets are not allowed.

Reservations, fees: Reservations are accepted. Campsite reservations are available. See State Park Camping Fees and Reserving a Campsite. Open May through mid-October.

Directions: From Eagle, go five miles north on Hwy. 67 to County Road ZZ, then three miles north on County Road G to the campground entrance.

Contact: Kettle Moraine State Forest, Southern Unit, SO1 W3909, Hwy. 59, Eagle, WI 53119, 262/594-6200.

Trip Notes: In nearby East Troy, you can tour the extensive trolley collection of the East Troy Electric Railroad Museum (414/548-3837) and take the ll-mile round-trip from the historic depot.

15 Horserider's Campground

Location: Palmyra, in the Kettle Moraine State Forest, map 4, grid A4.

Campsites, facilities: There are 64 campsites for horse campers only. Facilities include vault toilets, and horseback and hiking trails.

Reservations, fees: Reservations are accepted. Campsite reservations are available. See State Park Camping Fees and Reserving a Campsite. Open from mid-April through November.

Directions: From the junction of U.S. Hwy. 12 and Hwy. 67, go five miles northeast on Hwy. 67, then four miles west on County Road NN/EW to the campground entrance.

Contact: Kettle Moraine State Forest, Southern Unit, Hwy. 59, Eagle WI 53119, 262/594-6200.

Trip Notes: Take a closer look at the Kettle Moraine. In Palmyra, about six miles from Eagle, drive on County Road H, where Hwy. 59 turns right. On your right, you'll see cropland in a shallow valley. The surrounding terrain is a glacial outwash plain, formed when fine glacial particles were washed out of the glacier by running water. The valley itself is called a "spillway," where a smaller meltwater stream cut through the already sandy plain. Turn right on Kettle Moraine Drive, cross the spillway, and go through the outwash plain. The wooded ridge on the right is the moraine you've been following. It marks the spot of a significant pause in the final retreat of the Lake Michigan Lobe of the glacier.

16 Country View Campground

Location: Mukwonago, southwest of Milwaukee, map 4, grid B6.

Campsites, facilities: There are 159 campsites. Facilities include RV pull-through sites, electric hookups, water, sewer, flush toilets, showers, disposal station, laundry, grocery store, swimming pool, and playground. Lake fishing and hiking trails are available nearby. Pets are allowed.

Reservations, fees: The daily fee ranges from $19 to $22. Credit cards are accepted. Open from mid-April through mid-October.

Directions: From the junction of I-43 and Hwy. 83, take exit 43 and go one-quarter mile southeast on Hwy. 83, then 1.5 miles east on Maple Avenue. Drive 1.5 miles south on Craig Avenue to the campground entrance.

Contact: Country View Campground, Dan and Coleen Jax, S110 W26400 Craig Ave., Mukwonango, WI 53149, 262/662-3654.

Trip Notes: Have you ever wondered what the wind-driven schooners that carried the cargoes on Lake Michigan in the early days looked like? A visit to the Wisconsin Lake Schooner at the foot of Harbor Drive and the Milwaukee lakefront (414/276-7700) to see the 137-foot, three-masted schooner built to honor Wisconsin's Sesquicentennial will answer your questions.

17 Scenic Ridge Campground

Location: Whitewater, on Whitewater Lake south of Fort Atkinson, map 4, grid B3.

Campsites, facilities: There are 250 campsites. Facilities include electric hookups, water, flush toilets, showers, disposal station, grocery store, lake swimming, boating, canoeing, fishing, hiking trail, and playground. Golf courses and state biking trail are available nearby.

Reservations, fees: The daily fee is $19. Open from mid-April through mid-October.

Directions: From the junction of Hwy. 59 and U.S. Hwy. 12, go one mile east on Hwy. 12, then five miles south on County Road P. Drive one mile west on Town Line Road to the entrance.

Contact: Scenic Ridge Campground, Julie Michaels, W7991 R and W Town Line Rd., Whitewater, WI 53190, 608/883-2920.

Trip Notes: Campers at this campground, on 900-acre Whitewater Lake, will enjoy the Minnieska Ski Show on Saturday nights, and theater-goers are only 15 minutes away from the Apple Valley Theatre.

18 Kettle Moraine State Forest-Whitewater Lake Campground

Location: Near Whitewater, in the Kettle Moraine State Forest, map 4, grid B3.

Campsites, facilities: There are 62 sites. Facilities include vault toilets, disposal station, hiking trails, lake boating, canoeing, fishing, and swimming.

Reservations, fees: Reservations are accepted. Campsite reservations are available. See State Park Camping Fees and Reserving

a Campsite. Open from mid-May through mid-October.

Directions: From the junction of U.S. Hwy. 12 and Country Road P, drive southeast on County Road P to Kettle Moraine Drive, then go one mile west on Kettle Moraine Drive to the campground entrance.

Contact: Kettle Moraine State Forest, Southern Unit, Hwy. 59, Eagle, WI 53119, 414/594-6200.

Trip Notes: The Kettle Moraine is a geologic corridor that provides a "snapshot" of the collision of two glaciers thousands of years ago. As you drive or hike around the area, you can see the hundreds of hills, or drumlins, supporting dense forest. In between are hollows—the kettles—filled by marshes or clear lakes. Narrow bridges, known as esker, slice through the landscape.

19 Hidden Valley RV Resort and Campground

Location: Milton, southeast of Madison, map 4, grid B1.

Campsites, facilities: There are 128 campsites for RVs. Tents are not permitted. Facilities include electric hookups, water, sewer, flush toilets, showers, disposal station, grocery store, and swimming pool. Boating, canoeing, fishing, and hiking trail are available nearby. Pets are allowed.

Reservations, fees: The daily fee ranges from $24 to $29. Credit cards are accepted. Open from mid-April through mid-October.

Directions: From the junction of I-90 and Hwy. 50, take exit 163 and go three-quarters of a mile east on Hwy. 59 to the entrance.

Contact: Hidden Valley RV Resort and Campground, Jim and Marcia Kersten, 872 E. Hwy. 59, Milton, WI 53563, 608/868-4141 or 800/469-5515 for reservations, website: www.hiddenvalleyrvresort.com.

Trip Notes: History stays alive in Milton, including the days when it was a stopover on the "Underground Railroad." At the junction of Hwys. 26 and 59 visit the Milton House Museum and view the unique hexagonal stagecoach inn and the secret, hand-dug tunnel beneath it that provided a safe haven for runaway slaves.

20 Blackhawk Campground

Location: Milton, southeast of Madison, map 4, grid B1.

Campsites, facilities: There are 430 campsites. Facilities include RV pull-through sites, electric hookups, water, sewer, flush toilets, shower, disposal station, laundry, grocery store, boat ramp and dock, swimming beach, fishing, hiking trail, shuffleboard courts, and playground. Boat rentals are available. Pets are allowed.

Reservations, fees: The daily fee is $23. Credit cards are accepted. Open from mid-April through mid-October.

Directions: From the junction of Hwy. 26 and Hwy. 59, go 2.5 miles northwest on Hwy. 59, then one-half mile west on Clear Lake Road and Blackhawk Road to the campground entrance.

Contact: Blackhawk Campground, Rt. 2, Box 125, Milton, WI 53563, 608/868-2586, email: camp@blackhawkcampgrounds.com, website: www.blackhawkcampgrounds.com.

Trip Notes: The nearby Rock River is a great place to fish for northern, walleye, and catfish.

Nearby, in Janesville, you can visit the Helen Jeffris Wood Museum Center (608/756-4509) housed in the 1912 Prairie-style residence of Stanley Dexter Tallman. The museum, maintained by the Rock County Historical Society, features a changing exhibit gallery and children's interactive activity area. From I-90, exit at 175A (Hwy. 11, Janesville). Turn right on Franklin Street. The museum is 1.5 blocks past the railroad bridge with a parking lot on the left.

Another option is the Janesville General Motors Assembly Plant (608/756-7681; website: www.gm.com/index.cgi). There is a 90-minute tour via tram. The 3.5 million-square-foot complex is the largest GM plant under one roof in the U.S. There are more than 600 robots on the sport utility line. After leaving exit 175A, turn left at the first stoplight onto Beloit Avenue. Then, turn right at the first stoplight onto to East Delavan Drive. Go 1.5 blocks. The plant is on the left.

21 Snug Harbor Inn Resort

Location: Delavan, on Turtle Lake southwest of Milwaukee, map 4, grid C3.

Campsites, facilities: There are 63 campsites. Facilities include electric hookups, water, flush toilets, showers, disposal station, grocery store, boat ramp and dock, canoeing, fishing, swimming beach, and playground. Boat and seasonal campsite rentals are available. Pets are allowed.

Reservations, fees: The daily fee ranges from $25 to $30. Open year-round. The facility is fully operational from mid-April through mid-October.

Directions: From the junction of Hwy. 11 and Country Road P, go 7.5 miles north on County Road P and three-quarters of a mile west on County Road A. Then drive one-quarter mile south on Holiday Drive and 200 feet east on Wisconsin Parkway to the entrance.

Contact: Snug Harbor Inn Resort, Linda Friedman, W7772-2C Wisconsin Pkwy., Delavan, WI 53115, 608/883-6999, email:

turtle vc@idnet.com, website: www.turtle-valleyd cove.com.

Trip Notes: Between 1847 and 1894, Delavan was headquarters for 28 different circuses. The original P. R. Barnum circus was organized there during the winter of 1870-1871. Be sure to visit the 50-acre Circus World Museum (608/356-8341; website: www.circusworld museum.com) in nearby Baraboo. It's at 426 Water Street (Hwy. 113), the Ringling Bros. Circus original winter quarters and a national historic landmark.

22 Bong State Recreation Area

Location: Kansasville, southwest of Milwaukee, map 4, grid C7.

Campsites, facilities: There are 217 campsites. Facilities include electric hookups, water, flush toilets, disposal station, boat ramp, canoeing, fishing, swimming beach, and visitor center. There are also 27 miles of biking, hiking, snowmobiling, and cross-country ski trails.

Reservations, fees: Reservations are accepted. Campsite reservations are available. See State Park Camping Fees and Reserving a Campsite. Open year-round.

Directions: From the junction of Hwys. 75 and 142, go one mile west on Hwy. 142 to the campground entrance.

Contact: Bong State Recreation Area, 26313 Burlington Rd., Kansasville, WI 53139, 414/878-5600.

Trip Notes: About 4,515-acres await visitors to the Bong State Recreation Area (262/878-5600; website: www.wiparks.net), a multiuse recreation area in Kenosha County. It's eight miles southeast of Burlington on Hwy. 142. In spring, be sure to bring your binoculars to spot migrant and resident birds.

If birds are your thing, don't miss the International Crane Foundation (608/356-9462) at E11376 Shady Lane Road, only about five miles away in Baraboo. Here, you can see the world's most complete collection of cranes, the tallest flying bird.

23 Big Foot Beach State Park

Location: Lake Geneva, southwest of Milwaukee, map 4, grid D5.

Campsites, facilities: There are 100 campsites. Facilities include vault toilets, lake boating, canoeing, fishing, swimming beach, and hiking trails.

Reservations, fees: Reservations are accepted. Campsite reservations are available. See State Park Camping Fees and Reserving a Campsite. Open from mid-May through October.

Directions: From Lake Geneva, drive 1.5 miles south on Hwy. 120 to the park entrance.

Contact: Big Foot Beach State Park, 1452 Hwy. H, Lake Geneva, WI 53147, 262/248-2528.

Trip Notes: Located on the shore of 5,230-acre Lake Geneva, the park offers wooded campsites and a sandy beach. The lake provides a variety of game fish, including largemouth and smallmouth bass. For winter sports enthusiasts, the Grand Geneva Resort (262/248-8811) and Wilmot Mountain (262/862-2301) offer excellent skiing.

24 Happy Acres Kampground

Location: Bristol, southwest of Milwaukee, map 4, grid D8.

Campsites, facilities: There are 179 campsites. Facilities include electric hookups, water, flush toilets, showers, disposal station, laundry, grocery store, pond canoeing, fishing, swimming beach, mini-golf, hiking trail, playground, and planned weekend activities. Pets are allowed.

Reservations, fees: The daily fee ranges from $27 to $31. Open May through September.

Directions: From the junction of Hwy. 50 and U.S. Hwy. 45, go two miles north on Hwy. 45 and 1.5 miles west on Country Road NN to the entrance.

Contact:

Trip Notes: Located within the 341-acre Bristol Woods County Park is the Pringle Nature Center (262/857-2688; website: www.pringle nc.htmlplanet.com.) There are four miles of hiking trails through upland hardwood forests, lowland marshes, and oak savannah remnants. The center offers environmental programs, bird-watching opportunities, wildflower viewing, and, in winter, cross-country skiing. Go to 9800 160th Avenue.

25 Yogi Bear Jellystone Camp-Resort

Location: Caledonia, south of Milwaukee, map 5, grid B1.

Campsites, facilities: There are 247 campsites, including a separate tent area. Facilities include RV pull-through sites, electric hookups, water, sewer, flush toilets, showers, disposal station, laundry, grocery store, swimming pool, pond fishing, hiking trail, mini-golf, and playground. Lake Michigan boating, canoeing, fishing, and swimming are available nearby. Pets are allowed.

Reservations, fees: The daily fee ranges from $24 to $34. Open from the end of April to early October.

Directions: From I-94, take exit 326, and drive two miles east on Seven Mile Road, then one-quarter mile north on Hwy. 38 to the campground entrance.

Contact: Yogi Bear Jellystone Camp-Resort, Don and Robyn Votaw, 8525 Hwy. 38, Caledonia, WI 53108, 414/835-2565, email: Yogi park@aol.com, website: www.jellystone-cale donia.com.

Trip Notes: Want to exercise your brain? Visit Discovery World: The James Lovell Museum of Science, Economics, and Technology (414/765-9966; website: www.braintools.org) and you'll be able to do just that. You can interact with 140 exhibits and displays for "kids" of all ages.

MICHIGAN
UPPER PENINSULA

Michigan Regions

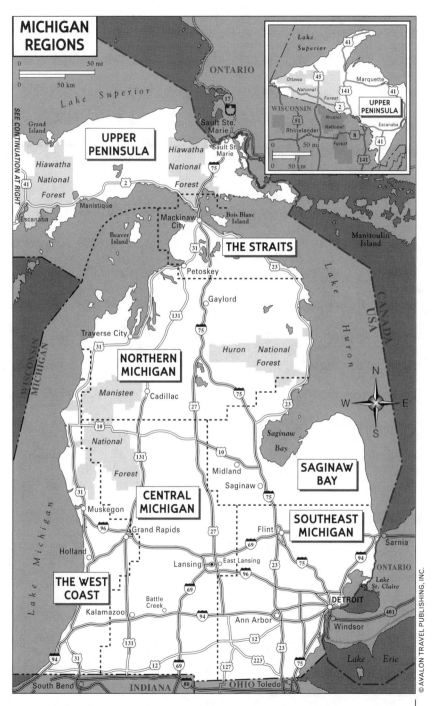

Upper Peninsula

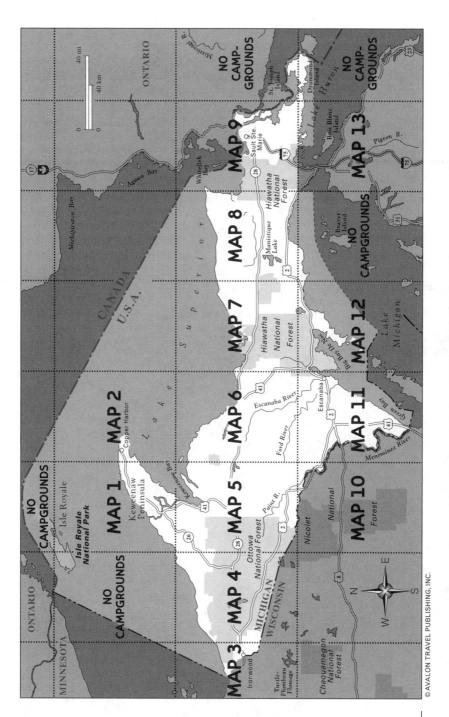

Map 1

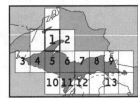

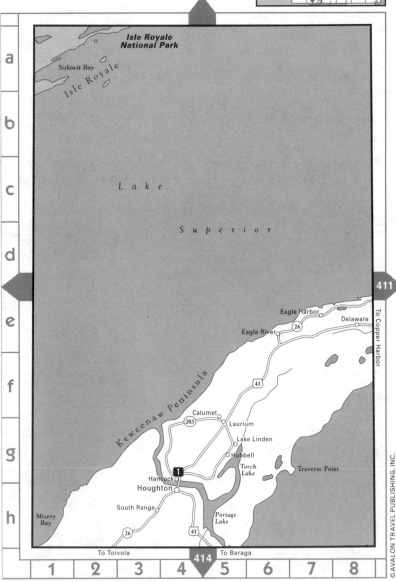

Isle Royale
National Park

Siskiwit Bay

Isle Royale

Lake

Superior

411

To Copper Harbor

Eagle Harbor

Eagle River

26

Delaware

41

Keweenaw Peninsula

Calumet

203

Laurium

Lake Linden

Hubbell

Torch
Lake

Traverse Point

1

Hancock

Houghton

Misery
Bay

South Range

Portage
Lake

26

41

To Toivola

414

To Baraga

a b c d e f g h

1 2 3 4 5 6 7 8

© AVALON TRAVEL PUBLISHING, INC.

Map 2

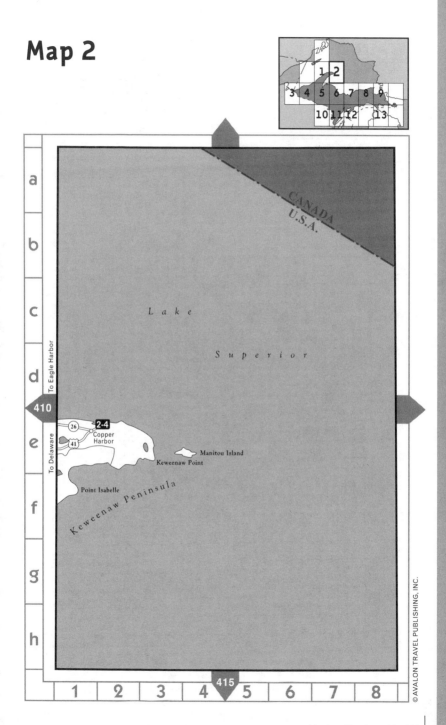

© AVALON TRAVEL PUBLISHING, INC.

Map 3

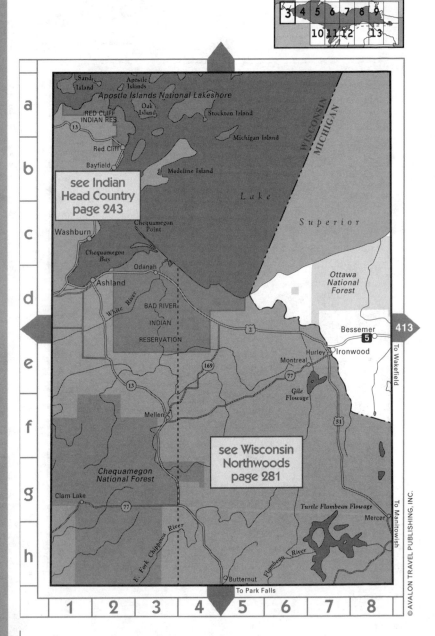

a

Sand Island
Apostle Islands
Apostle Islands National Lakeshore
RED CLIFF INDIAN RES.
13
Oak Island
Stockton Island
Michigan Island

b

Red Cliff
Bayfield
Medeline Island
see Indian Head Country page 243

WISCONSIN
MICHIGAN

Lake

c

Washburn
Chequamegon Point
Chequamegon Bay

Superior

d

Odanah
Ashland
White River
BAD RIVER
INDIAN
RESERVATION
2

Ottawa National Forest

Bessemer
5
413
To Wakefield

e

169
13
Hurley Ironwood
Montreal
77
Gile Flowage
51

f

Mellen
see Wisconsin Northwoods page 281

g

Chequamegon National Forest
Clam Lake
77
Turtle Flambeau Flowage
Mercer
To Manitowish

h

E. Fork Chippewa River
Flambeau River
Butternut
To Park Falls

1 2 3 4 5 6 7 8

© AVALON TRAVEL PUBLISHING, INC.

Map 4

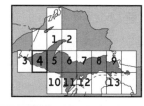

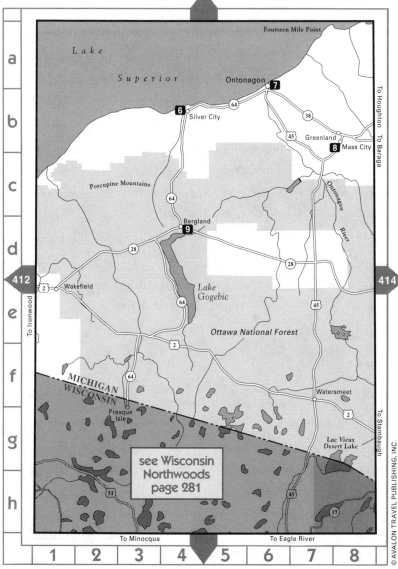

Fourteen Mile Point

Lake

Superior

Ontonagon **7**

To Houghton

To Baraga

64

6 Silver City

38

45

Greenland

8 Mass City

Porcupine Mountains

64

Ontonagon River

Bergland
9

28

28

412

414

To Ironwood

2

Wakefield

64

Lake Gogebic

45

Ottawa National Forest

2

MICHIGAN
WISCONSIN

64

Watersmeet

2

To Stambaugh

Presque Isle

Lac Vieux
Desert Lake

see Wisconsin
Northwoods
page 281

51

45

17

To Minocqua

To Eagle River

1 2 3 4 5 6 7 8

© AVALON TRAVEL PUBLISHING, INC.

Map 5

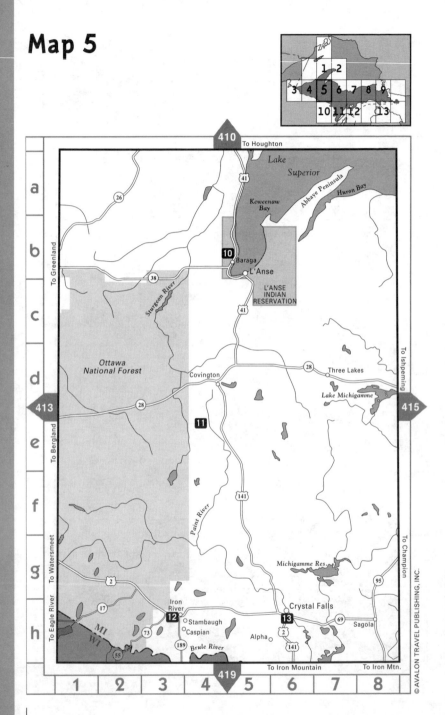

Map 6

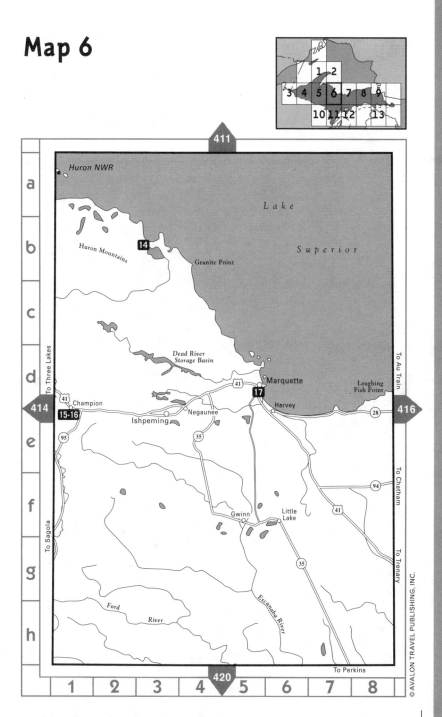

Map 7

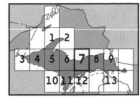

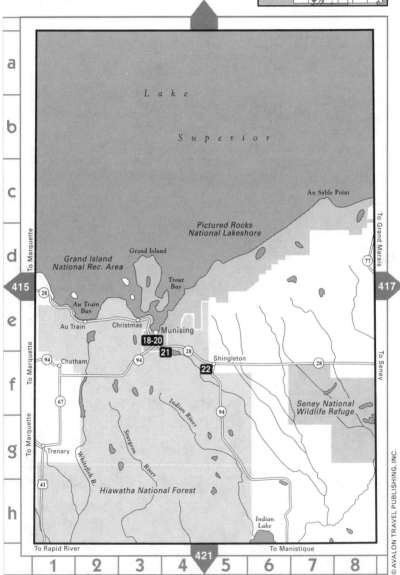

Map 8

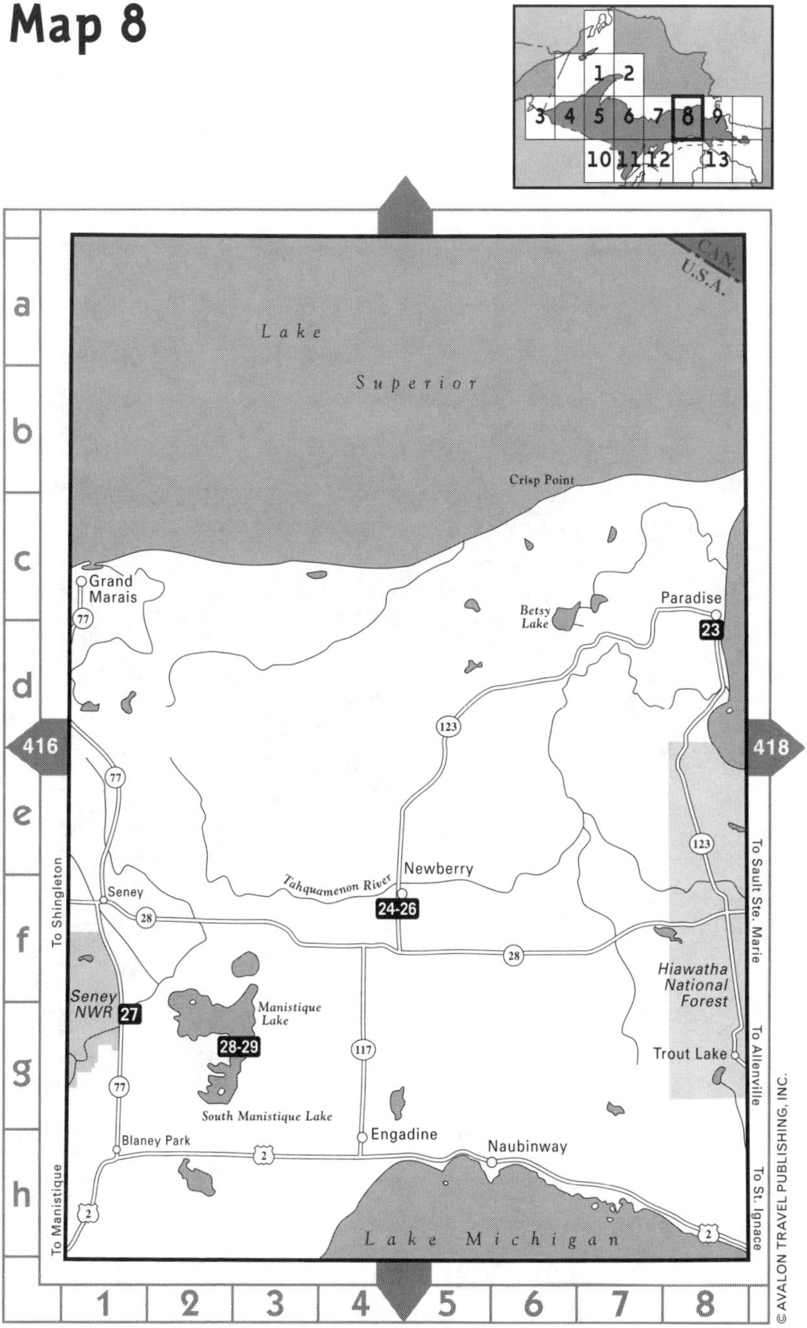

Map inset showing Upper Peninsula grid with regions 1-13, with region 8 highlighted.

Lake Superior

CAN.
U.S.A.

a

b

Crisp Point

c

Grand Marais
77
Betsy Lake
Paradise
23

d

123

416

418

77

e

123

To Sault Ste. Marie

Tahquamenon River
Newberry
Seney
24-26

To Shingleton

f

28
28
Hiawatha National Forest

Seney NWR
27
Manistique Lake
28-29
117
Trout Lake
To Allenville

g

77
South Manistique Lake

To Manistique

Blaney Park
2
Engadine
Naubinway
2

h

To St. Ignace

Lake Michigan

2

© AVALON TRAVEL PUBLISHING, INC.

1 2 3 4 5 6 7 8

Map 9

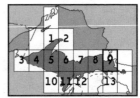

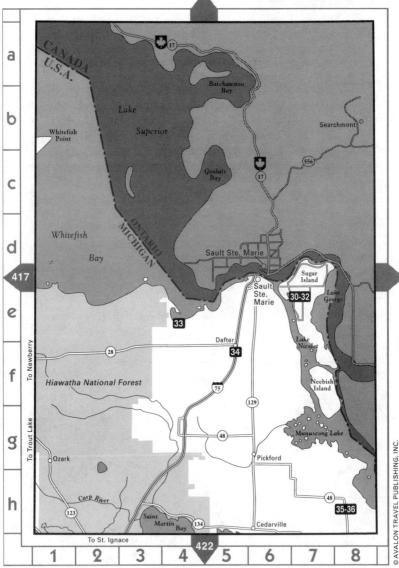

© AVALON TRAVEL PUBLISHING, INC.

Map 10

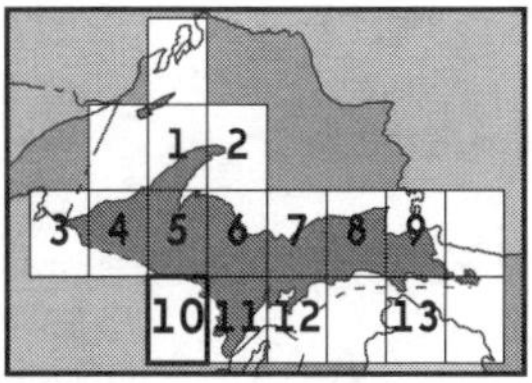

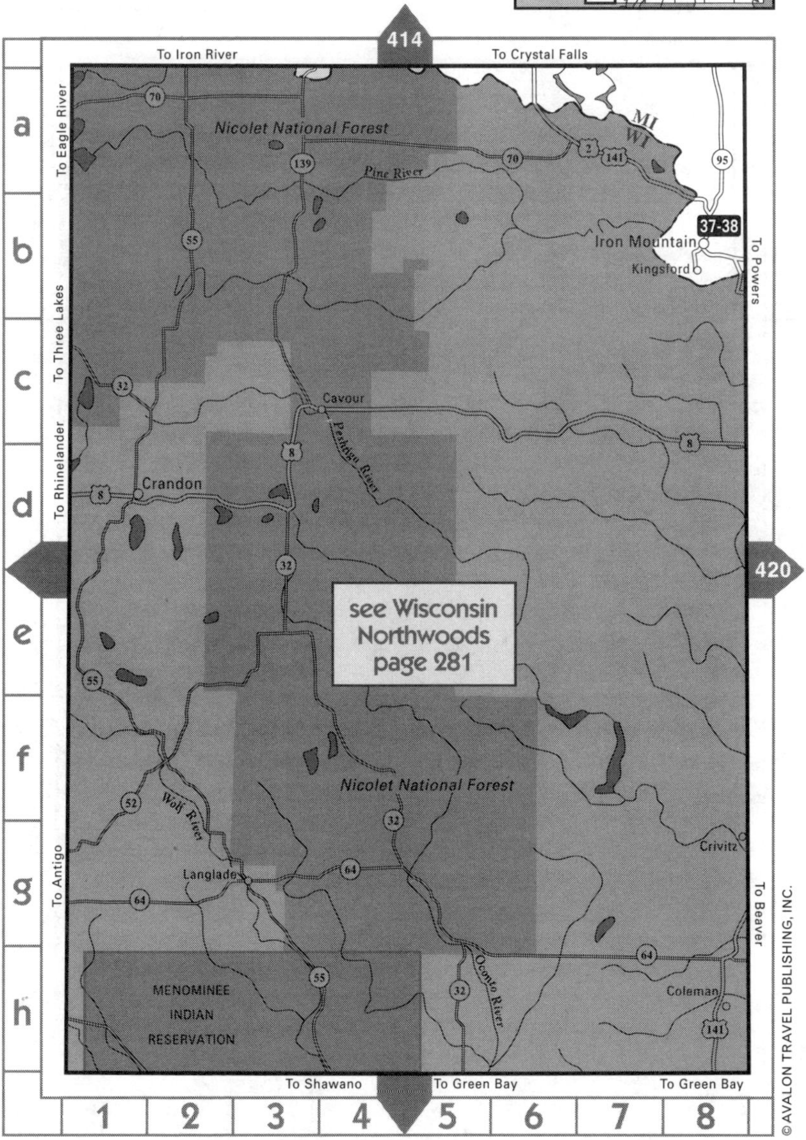

To Iron River
To Crystal Falls

a

To Eagle River
Nicolet National Forest

70

139

Pine River

70

2 141

MI
WI

95

b

To Three Lakes

55

Iron Mountain
Kingsford

37-38

To Powers

c

To Rhinelander

32

Cavour

8

Pestigo River

8

d

To Rhinelander

8

Crandon

32

see Wisconsin
Northwoods
page 281

420

e

55

f

52

Wolf River

Nicolet National Forest

32

Crivitz

g

To Antigo

52

Langlade

64

64

32

To Beaver

64

h

55

MENOMINEE
INDIAN
RESERVATION

32

Oconto River

Coleman

141

To Shawano
To Green Bay
To Green Bay

1 2 3 4 5 6 7 8

© AVALON TRAVEL PUBLISHING, INC.

Map 11

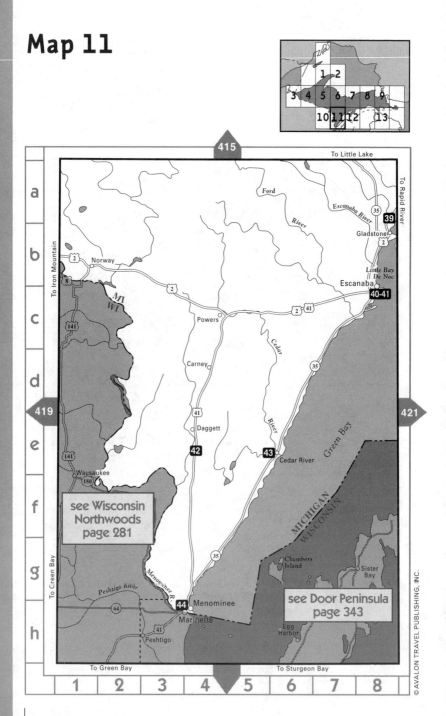

Map 11

To Little Lake

Ford

Escanaba River

Gladstone

To Iron Mountain

Norway

MI
WI

Powers

Carney

Little Bay
De Noc

Escanaba

40-41

Cedar

Daggett

42

Cedar River

43

Green Bay

35

141

Wausaukee

180

see Wisconsin
Northwoods
page 281

To Green Bay

Peshtigo River

Menominee R.

Menominee

44

Marinette

Peshtigo

41

MICHIGAN
WISCONSIN

Chambers
Island

Sister
Bay

see Door Peninsula
page 343

Egg
Harbor

To Green Bay

To Sturgeon Bay

To Rapid River

39

35

2

2

41

35

8

141

64

© AVALON TRAVEL PUBLISHING, INC.

Map 12

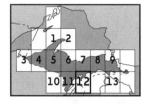

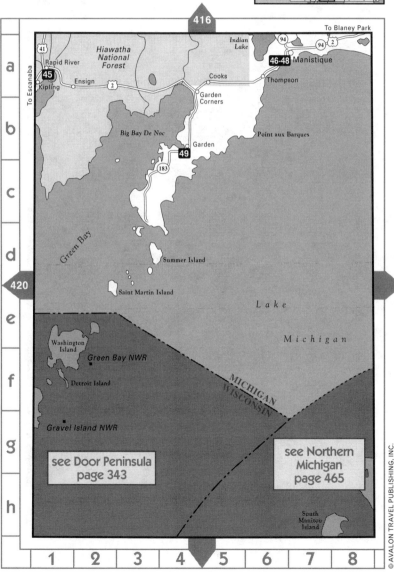

To Blaney Park

Indian Lake

94

46-48 Manistique

94 2

41

Hiawatha National Forest

Rapid River

Cooks

Thompson

45

Ensign

2

Kipling

Garden Corners

To Escanaba

Big Bay De Noc

Point aux Barques

Garden

49

183

Green Bay

Summer Island

420

Saint Martin Island

L a k e

M i c h i g a n

Washington Island

Green Bay NWR

Detroit Island

MICHIGAN
WISCONSIN

Gravel Island NWR

see Door Peninsula
page 343

see Northern
Michigan
page 465

South Manitou Island

© AVALON TRAVEL PUBLISHING, INC.

Map 13

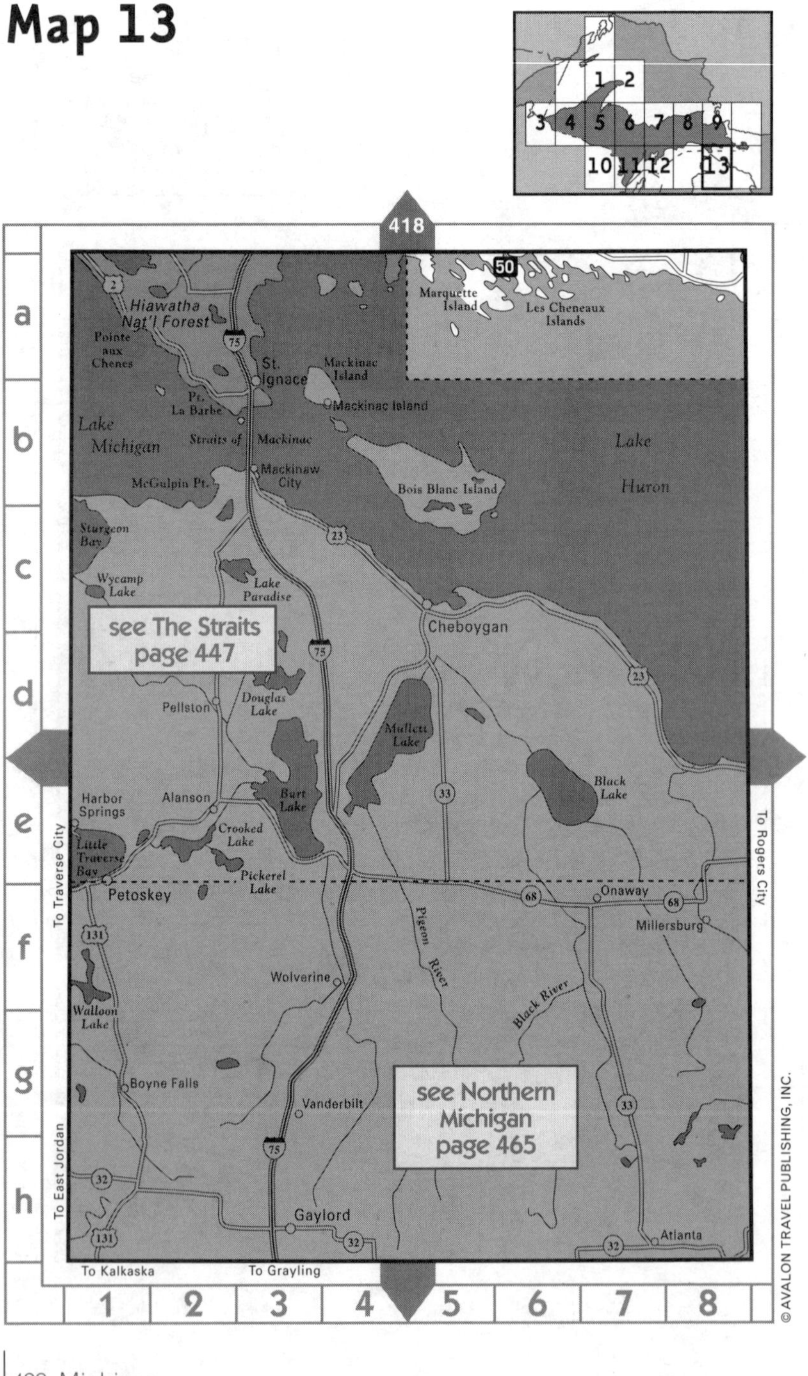

1
2
3
4
5
6
7
8
9
10
11
12
13
418
a
b
c
d
e
f
g
h
Hiawatha Nat'l Forest
Pointe aux Chenes
St. Ignace
Mackinac Island
Mackinac Island
Marquette Island
Les Cheneaux Islands
Pt. La Barbe
Lake Michigan
Straits of Mackinac
Mackinaw City
McGulpin Pt.
Bois Blanc Island
Lake Huron
Sturgeon Bay
Wycamp Lake
Lake Paradise
Cheboygan
see The Straits page 447
Pellston
Douglas Lake
Mullett Lake
Black Lake
Harbor Springs
Alanson
Burt Lake
Crooked Lake
Little Traverse Bay
Pickerel Lake
Petoskey
Onaway
Millersburg
To Traverse City
To Rogers City
Pigeon River
Black River
Wolverine
Walloon Lake
Boyne Falls
Vanderbilt
see Northern Michigan page 465
To East Jordan
Gaylord
Atlanta
To Kalkaska
To Grayling
© AVALON TRAVEL PUBLISHING, INC.

Upper Peninsula

(CONTINUED ON NEXT PAGE)

Simply put, the Upper Peninsula of Michigan is beautiful. There are 1,700 miles of shoreline lapped by three massive bodies of water—Lakes Superior, Michigan, and Huron. The UP is bigger than Connecticut, Delaware, Massachusetts, and Rhode Island combined, and has plenty of room for campers. Here, you can traverse the longest bridge, visit the largest islands, and climb the highest peaks in the Midwest. Of the state's 152 major waterfalls, all but two tumble to earth here. There are also miles of sandy beaches, towering dunes, and old-growth forests, as well as thousands of inland lakes and thousands of miles of sparkling trout streams.

The UP's romance and allure is reflected in the ethnic mix of its people, heritage, and historic towns, born of mining and forestry that opened the region to settlement more than 150 years ago.

1 Hancock Recreation Area

Location: Hancock, on the west coast of Keweenaw Peninsula, map 1, grid G4.
Campsites, facilities: There are 70 sites at this city park. Facilities include electric hookups, flush toilets, showers, disposal station, laundry, lake swimming, fishing, boat ramp and dock, hiking trail, and playground. Pets are allowed.
Reservations, fees: The daily fee ranges from $8 to $14. Open from mid-May to mid-October.
Directions: From the junction of U.S. Hwy. 41 and Hwy. 203, go two miles west on Hwy. 203 to the park entrance on the left.
Contact: Hancock Recreation Area, M-203, Hancock, MI 49930, 906/482-7413.
Trip Notes: Take the family to see the Quincy Steam Hoist (906/482-6200), Shaft House, and Underground Mine for a guided tour and tram rides one mile north of town on U.S. Hwy. 41.

Another deep place is the Sturgeon River Gorge Wilderness (906/852-3500 or 906/524-7444) in Baraga and Houghton Counties, three miles north of Sidnaw and 35 miles south of Houghton. The Sturgeon, a National Wild and Scenic River, and Little Silver Rivers and their tributaries form rugged, steep-sided gorges up to 300 feet deep and one-half to one mile wide.

2 Fort Wilkins State Park

Location: Copper Harbor, on the west coast of the Keweenaw Peninsula, map 2, grid E1.
Campsites, facilities: There are 165 campsites. Facilities include electric hookups, flush toilets, showers, disposal station, grocery store, boat ramp, and fishing. Hiking, mountain biking, and cross-country ski trails are available.

Reservations, fees: The daily fee is $14. Open from mid-May to mid-October.

Directions: From the junction of U.S. Hwy. 41 and Hwy. 26, go one mile east on Hwy. 41 to the park entrance.

Contact: Fort Wilkins State Park, P.O. Box 71, Copper Harbor, MI 49918, 906/289-4215.

Trip Notes: Fort Wilkins portrays military life in the mid-1800s. Costumed guides demonstrate the old Army lifestyle. Take the 20-minute boat ride and guided tour.

The Copper Harbor Lighthouse Museum (906/289-4966) depicts Lake Superior shipping, shipwrecks, and lighthouse living conditions. It's located a quarter of a mile west of the intersection of U.S. Hwy. 41 and Hwy. 26 on Hwy. 26.

3 Lake Fanny Hooe Resort and Campground

Location: Copper Harbor, on the west Coast of the Keweenaw Peninsula, map 2, grid E1.

Campsites, facilities: There are 64 campsites. Facilities include electric hookups, water, sewer, flush toilets, showers, disposal station, laundry, boat dock, lake and stream fishing, lake swimming, and playground. Bike, hiking, and cross-country ski trails, and boat, canoe, and motor rentals are available. Pets are allowed.

Reservations, fees: Reservations are recommended. The daily fee ranges from $16 to $20. Open year-round.

Directions: Go two blocks east on U.S. Hwy. 41 and then one block south on 2nd Street. The office is on the left and the park entrance is on the right.

Contact: Lake Fanny Hooe Resort and Campground, Alan and Grace Catron, 505 Second St., P.O. Box 31, Copper Harbor, MI 49918, 800/426-4451 or 906/289-4451, email: fanny hoe@up.net, website: www.fannyhooe.com.

Trip Notes: There is plenty to see and do in this quaint little town. You can visit the Astor House (906/289-4449) and see items from the early mining boom-days and hundreds of antique dolls. Take the underground guided Delaware Mine Tour (906/289-4688), or take the ferry to beautiful Isle Royale National Park and spend the day.

4 F.J. McLain State Park

Location: Hancock, on the west coast of the Keweenaw Peninsula, map 2, grid E1.

Campsites, facilities: There are 103 campsites. Facilities include electric hookups, flush toilets, showers, disposal station, lake swimming, boating, canoeing, and fishing. You can enjoy the park's many hiking and snowmobile trails. There is also hunting in season. Pets are allowed.

Reservations, fees: The daily fee is $14. Open from mid-May to mid-October.

Directions: From Hancock, go 10 miles north on Hwy. 203 to the park entrance.

Contact: F.J. McLain State Park, Rt. 1 Box 82, M-203, Hancock, MI 49903, 906/482-0278.

Trip Notes: Situated on Lake Superior, the campground has a beautiful view of Michigan sunsets and the lighthouse. It's also a great place to swim, fish, hike, snowmobile, and cross-country ski at the Maasto Hilhto Ski Trail's 9.5-mile groomed trails.

5 Ottawa National Forest: Black River Harbor Campground

Location: Bessemer, on the Black River north of Ironwood, map 3, grid E8.

Campsites, facilities: There are 40 campsites.

Facilities include vault toilets, disposal station, swimming beach, boat ramp and dock, lake and river fishing, and hiking trails. Pets are allowed.

Reservations, fees: The daily fee is $10. Open from mid-May through mid-October.

Directions: From the junction of U.S. Hwy. 2 and County Road 513, go north for 15 miles on County Road 513 to the entrance.

Contact: Ottawa National Forest, Bessemer Ranger District, Black River Harbor Campground, 500 N. Moore St., Bessemer, MI 49911, 906/667-0261 or 906/932-1330.

Trip Notes: The Black River National Scenic Byway features five spectacular waterfalls with varying access that should not be missed in any season. In winter, they are partially frozen. In spring, they are thunderous with melting ice. In summer, the mist rises upward in bright sunlight. In fall, they reflect nature's color.

⑥ Porcupine Mountains Wilderness State Park

Location: Silver City on Lake Superior and north of Wakefield on the Presque Isle River, map 4, grid B4.

Campsites, facilities: At the park's campground in Silver City, there are 100 campsites. Facilities include electric hookups, rustic cabin rentals, flush toilets, showers, disposal station, laundry, swimming beach, boat ramp and dock, lake and river fishing, hiking, and cross-country ski trails and ski runs.

The park's Presque Isle unit has 80 sites with disposal station, flush toilets, showers, swimming beach, lake and river boating, fishing, and hiking trails. Pets are allowed.

Reservations, fees: The daily fee is $14. Open May through mid-October (Silver City Unit); Mid-April through mid-November (Presque Isle Unit).

Directions: To the Silver City Unit, take Hwy. 107 three miles west of Silver City. To the Presque Isle Unit, take County Road 519 north of Wakefield for 16 miles.

Contact: Porcupine Mountains Wilderness State Park, 412 S. Boundary Rd., Ontongon, MI 49953, 906/885-5275.

Trip Notes: The Silver City Unit is on the shores of Lake Superior with 60,000 acres of land filled with towering old-growth forests, cliff-top scenic vistas, waterfalls, more than 90 miles of hiking trails, miles of cross-country ski trails, and 15 ski runs along a 641-foot vertical drop. The park also contains four lakes, including the impressive Lake of the Clouds. The visitor center is a necessary stop to get oriented to the park facilities and programs.

The Presque Isle Unit is on a bluff overlooking Lake Superior. It is a short walk from the campground to spectacular waterfalls, cascades, and rapids of the Presque Isle River.

⑦ River Pines RV Park and Campground

Location: Ontonagon, on the west Coast of the Keweenaw Peninsula, map 4, grid B6.

Campsites, facilities: There are 32 campsites. Facilities include RV pull-through sites, electric hookups, water, sewer, disposal station, laundry, grocery store, boat dock, and lake and river fishing. There are also hiking, snowmobiling, and cross-country ski trails. Boat rentals are available. Pets are allowed.

Reservations, fees: The daily fee ranges from $17 to $19. Credit cards are accepted. Open year-round.

Directions: From the junction of U.S. Hwy. 45 and Hwy. 64, go one-quarter mile south on Hwy. 64, and then one-half mile east on River Road to the entrance on the right.

Contact: River Pines RV Park and Campground, Dot Phillips and Gladys Chamberlain, 600 River Rd., Ontonagon, MI 49953, 906/884-4600 or 800/424-1520.

Trip Notes: Within a 60-mile radius, there are some 500 miles of snowmobile trails and five major ski hills for winter fun. There is also easy access to the Ontonagon River and Lake Superior for year-round activities.

8 Twin Lakes State Park

Location: Mass City, on Roland Lake east of Ontonagon, map 4, grid B8.

Campsites, facilities: There are 62 sites. Facilities include electric hookups, vault toilets, swimming beach, and fishing. There are also boating, hiking, and snowmobile trails.

Reservations, fees: The daily fee is $11. Open from mid-April through mid-October.

Directions: From the junction of Hwys. 26 and 38, go 20 miles north on Hwy. 26 to the park entrance.

Contact: Twin Lakes State Park, Rt. 1 Box 234, M-26, Toivola, MI 49965, 906/482-0278.

Trip Notes: The most popular feature is warm, sandy, inland Lake Roland that is shallow enough for young children. It offers anglers good fishing for walleye, crappie, bass, and an occasional hybrid tiger muskie. This park is also a good starting point for many attractions, including historic Fort Wilkins, the copper mines near Hancock and Delaware, and the area's historic and mineralogical museums.

9 Lake Gogebic State Park

Location: Bergland, on Lake Gogebic southeast of Ontonagon and Silver City, map 4, grid D4.

Campsites, facilities: There are 127 campsites. Facilities include electric hookups, flush toilets, showers, disposal station, swimming beach, boat ramp and dock, and hiking and cross-country ski trails. Pets are allowed.

Reservations, fees: The daily fee ranges from $9 to $11. Open from mid-May through mid-October.

Directions: From Bergland, go 11 miles south on Hwy. 64 to the park entrance.

Contact: Lake Gogebic State Park, H.C. 1 Box 139, Marenisco, MI 49947, 906/842-3341.

Trip Notes: The park offers lakefront campsites on the shore of Lake Gogebic, the largest inland lake in the Upper Peninsula. The lake's 13,380 acres of prime fishing water is home to walleye, smallmouth bass, northern pike, perch, and whitefish.

10 Baraga State Park

Location: South of Baraga on Lake Superior on the Keweenaw Peninsula, map 5, grid B5.

Campsites, facilities: There are 119 sites. Facilities include electric hookups, flush toilets, showers, disposal station, swimming beach, boat ramp, fishing, and hiking trails. Pets are allowed.

Reservations, fees: The daily fee ranges from $9 to $11. Open May through mid-October.

Directions: Take Hwy. 41 south of Baraga. It is less than one mile to the park entrance.

Contact: Baraga State Park, 1300 U.S. Hwy. 41, South Baraga, MI 49908, 906/353-6558.

Trip Notes: Situated on the Keweenaw Bay of Lake Superior with easy access to the water, the park is centrally located to many attractions in the western Upper Peninsula. The bay offers anglers good action on salmon, steelhead, lake and brown trout.

11 Ottawa National Forest: Lake Ste. Kathryn Campground and Norway Lake Campground

Location: Sidnaw, on Lake Ste. Kathryn and Norway Lake, south of Baraga, map 5, grid E4.

Campsites, facilities: At Ste. Kathryn Campground there are 25 campsites. Facilities include vault toilets, swimming beach, boat ramp and fishing.

At Norway Lake, there are 28 campsites. Facilities include vault toilets, swimming beach, boat ramp, and fishing.

Reservations, fees: The daily fee ranges from $7 to $9. Both campgrounds are open May through November.

Directions: To Lake Ste. Kathryn from the junction of Hwy. 28 and County Road 137, go eight miles south on County Road 137 to the entrance.

To Norway Lake from the junction of Hwy. 28 and County Road 137, go six miles south on County Road 137 to the entrance.

Contact: Ottawa National Forest, Lake Ste. Kathryn Campground and Norway Lake Campground, Kenton Ranger District, 4810 E. M-28, Kenton, MI 49943, 906/852-3500.

Trip Notes: If you like to view or photograph waterfalls, drive a few miles over to Kenton and view Jumbo and disposaly Falls (906/358-4724).

12 Ottawa National Forest: Lake Ottawa Campground

Location: Iron River, on Lake Ottawa, map 5, grid H3.

Campsites, facilities: There are 32 campsites. Facilities include water, flush toilets, disposal station, swimming beach, boat ramp, fishing, and hiking trail. Pets are allowed.

Reservations, fees: The daily fee ranges from $7 to $12. Open from mid-May to mid-September.

Directions: From the junction of Hwy. 189 and U.S. Hwy. 2, go just over 1.25 miles west on Hwy. 2, and one-half mile southwest of Hwy. 73. Then drive four miles west on Forest Road 101.

Contact: Ottawa National Forest, Lake Ottawa Campground, Iron River Ranger District, 990 Lalley Rd., Iron River, MI 49935, 906/265-5139.

Trip Notes: About a half-hour drive south to Laona, Wisconsin, will take you to the Camp 5 Museum where you can board the Lumberjack Special Steam Train (800/774-3414) and go to the original site of the 1870s logging camp. Tour the museum and blacksmith shop, visit the country store, nature center, and farm corral, and take a guided tour through the forest in a motorized surrey.

13 Bewabic State Park

Location: Crystal Falls, northwest of Iron Mountain, map 5, grid H6.

Campsites, facilities: There are 144 campsites. Facilities include electric hookups, flush toilets, showers, disposal station, grocery store, swimming beach, boat ramp and dock, fishing, hiking trail, picnic area, and playground. Pets are allowed.

Reservations, fees: The daily fee is $11. Credit cards are accepted. Open from mid-May through mid-October.

Directions: From the junction of Hwys. 2 and 141, go four miles west on Hwy. 2 to the park entrance.

Contact: Bewabic State Park, 1933 U.S. Hwy. 2 West, Crystal Falls, MI 49920, 906/875-3324.

Trip Notes: The park is located on a chain of lakes providing prime fishing opportunities and a sandy swimming beach. A modern campground is shaded by the surrounding virgin hardwood forest. This is the only state park with tennis courts.

14 Perkins Park

Location: Big Bay, on the shores of Lake Superior, map 6, grid B1.

Campsites, facilities: There are 72 campsites in this Marquette County Park. Facilities include electric hookups, water, sewer, flush toilets, showers, disposal station, swimming beach, boat ramp, and fishing. Pets are allowed.

Reservations, fees: The daily fee ranges from $9 to $15. Open from mid-May through mid-September.

Directions: From Big Bay, take County Road 550 to the park entrance.

Contact: Perkins Park Campground, Big Bay, MI 49808, 906/345-9353.

Trip Notes: The lighthouse at Big Bay Point, which was built in 1896, is being restored by its new private owner and guided tours are available from May to September (906/345-9957). Visitors must park at the gate and walk a short distance to the lighthouse. From town, follow the red and white lighthouse signs three miles to the lighthouse.

15 Van Riper State Park

Location: Champion, on Lake Michigamme west of Marquette, map 6, grid D1.

Campsites, facilities: There are 189 campsites. Facilities include electric hookups, flush toilets, showers, disposal station, swimming beach, boat ramp, fishing, and hunting. There are also hiking, snowmobiling, and cross-country ski trails. Pets are allowed.

Reservations, fees: The daily fee is $12. Open from mid-May through October.

Directions: From the junction of U.S. Hwy. 41 and Hwy. 95, go five miles west on Hwy. 41 to the park entrance.

Contact: Van Riper State Park, P.O. Box 88, Champion, MI 49814, 906/339-4461.

Trip Notes: Located in a conifer and hardwood forest, Van Riper State Park provides a sandy beach, hiking trails, and fishing spots in the heart of moose country. It also offers rustic camping.

16 Michigamme Shores

Location: Champion on Lake Michigamme, west of Marquette, map 6, grid D1.

Campsites, facilities: There are 80 campsites. Facilities include electric hookups, water, sewer, flush toilets, showers, disposal station, laundry, grocery store, swimming beach, boat dock, lake and river fishing, hiking trail, and playground. Bike, boat, canoe, and motor rentals are available. Pets are allowed.

Reservations, fees: The daily fee ranges from $18 to $24. Open year-round.

Directions: From the west edge of Champion, go 2.5 miles west on U.S. Hwy. 41 and Hwy. 28 to the entrance.

Contact: Michigamme Shores, Woody and Pat Taylor, Box 6, Champion, MI 49814, 906/339-2116.

Trip Notes: Do you like antiques? If so, take a drive over to Negaunee and visit the Old Bank Building Antiques (906/475-4777) with 25 large rooms of antiques housed in an old triangular bank building built in 1874.

17 Gitche Gumee Campground and RV Park

Location: Marquette, near Lake Superior's southern shore, map 6, grid D5.

Campsites, facilities: There are 66 campsites. Facilities include RV pull-through sites, electric hookups, water, flush toilets, showers, disposal station, hiking trail, and playground. Lake swimming, boating, canoeing, fishing, boat ramps, and cross-country ski trails are nearby. Cabin rentals are available. Pets are allowed.

Reservations, fees: The daily fee ranges from $16 to $28. Open year-round. Winter reservations requested.

Directions: From the junction of U.S. Hwy. 41 and Hwy. 28, go six miles east on Hwy. 28 to the entrance.

Contact: Gitche Gumee Campground and RV Park, Ranger Jeff and Mrs. Fudge, 2048 M-28 East, Marquette, MI 49855, 906/249-9102.

Trip Notes: Directly across the street from Lake Superior you can enjoy Presque Isle Park's water slide, swimming facilities, boating, nature trails, and bog walk, which features 4,000 feet of plant walkways and 10 observation decks. The campground also has a fudge factory with different flavors of homemade fudge made with real cream.

18 Buckhorn/Otter Lake Campground

Location: Munising, on Otter Lake east of Marquette, map 7, grid E3.

Campsites, facilities: There are 72 campsites. Facilities include electric hookups, flush toilets, showers, disposal station, laundry, grocery store, swimming beach, boat ramp and dock (no motors allowed), and lake fishing. Hiking, snowmobile, and cross-country ski trails are in the area. Boat rentals are available. Pets are allowed.

Reservations, fees: The daily fee is $15. Open year-round.

Directions: From the junction of Hwys. 28 and 94, go six miles west on Hwy. 94, then 2.5 miles southeast on Buckhorn Road to the entrance.

Contact: Buckhorn/Otter Lake Campground, Richard Beckwith, HC 50 Buckhorn Rd., Munising, MI 49862, 906/387-4648 or 906/387-3559.

Trip Notes: You can enjoy hiking and scuba diving in the summer; hunting in season; snowshoeing, and snowmobiling and cross-country skiing on groomed trails.

19 Wandering Wheels Campground

Location: Munising, east of Marquette, map 7, grid E3.

Campsites, facilities: There are 89 campsites. Facilities include RV pull through sites, electric hookups, water, sewer, flush toilets, showers, disposal station, laundry, grocery store, heated swimming pool, and playground. Bike and camping cabin rentals are available. Lake fishing, canoeing, and hiking trail are nearby.

Reservations, fees: The daily fee ranges from $19 to $24. Credit cards are accepted. Open May through mid-October.

Directions: From Munising, drive 3.5 miles east on Hwy. 28 to the campground entrance.

Contact: Wandering Wheels Campground, P.O. Box 419, Munising, MI 49862, 906/474-7044.

Trip Notes: Take the three-hour Pictured Rocks Boat Cruise and experience the breathtaking beauty of the Pictured Rocks National Lakeshore (906/387-2379). The lakeshore facilities are open in June through early October.

20 Hiawatha National Forest: Bay Furnace Campground and Island Lake Campground

Location: Munising, on Bay Furnace east of Marquette, map 7, grid E3.

Campsites, facilities: Bay Furnace has 50 campsites. Facilities include water, vault toilets, disposal station, grocery store, historic site, swimming beach, boating, canoeing, fishing, and hiking trail.

Island Lake Campground has 45 sites. Facilities include water, vault toilets, swimming beach, boating, canoeing, and lake fishing.

Reservations, fees: The daily fee is $10. Both campgrounds are open from mid-May through September.

Directions: To Bay Furnace from the junction of Hwys. 94 and 28, go nearly five miles northwest on Hwy. 28 to the entrance.

To Island Lake from the junction of Hwys. 28 and 94, go just over six miles southeast on County Road 2254, and then one-third of a mile south on FR 2557 to the entrance.

Contact: Hiawatha National Forest, Bay Furnace Campground and Island Campground, Munising Ranger District, 400 E. Munising Ave., Munising, MI 49862, 906/387-2512.

Trip Notes: Colorful sandstone formations, waterfalls, sand dunes, agate beaches, and hiking trails are features of the Hiawatha National Forest and Pictured Rock National Lakeshore.

21 Hiawatha National Forest: Pete's Lake Campground and Widewaters Campground

Location: Wetmore, southeast of Munising, map 7, grid E4.

Campsites, facilities: Pete's Lake has 41 campsites and 20 picnic units. Facilities include water, vault toilets, disposal station, swimming beach, fishing, boat ramp, hiking trail, and wheelchair access.

Widewaters has 34 campsites. Facilities include water, vault toilets, boat ramp, fishing, and hiking trail. Pets are allowed.

Reservations, fees: The daily fee at Pete's Lake ranges from $8 to $14. The fee at Widewaters is $9. Both campgrounds are open from mid-May through September.

Directions: To Pete's Lake from the junction of Hwy. 94 and County Road H13, go 10 miles south on County Road H13 and then one-half mile east on FR 2173. Drive one-half mile south on FR 2256.

To Widewaters from the junction of Hwy. 94 and FR 13, go just over 11.5 miles south on FR 13, then one-third mile northwest on FR 2262 to the entrance.

Contact: Hiawatha National Forest, Pete's Lake, Munising Ranger District, 400 E. Munising Ave., Munising, MI 49862, 906/387-2512.

Trip Notes: Are you interested in seeing shipwrecks, but don't want to dive to the bottom to see them? Head to Munising and take a Glass Bottom Shipwreck Boat Tour (906/387-4477) and discover the shipwrecks of the Alger Underwater Preserve. A narrated, two-hour tour describes the history of these turn-of-the-century wrecks. It is presented on board "Miss Munising," a 60-foot Coast Guard-certified steel vessel equipped with through-the-hull glass viewing areas.

② Hiawatha National Forest: Colwell Lake Campground

Location: Shingleton, on Colwell Lake southeast of Munising, map 7, grid E5.

Campsites, facilities: There are 35 campsites. Facilities include water, vault toilets, swimming beach, boat ramp, fishing, and hiking trail. Pets are allowed.

Reservations, fees: The daily fee ranges from $7 to $35. Open from late May through November.

Directions: From the junction of Hwys. 28 and 94, go south 10 miles on Hwy. 94 and then one-half mile east on County Road 2246 to the park entrance.

Contact: Hiawatha National Forest, Colwell Lake Campground, Manistique Ranger District, 4990 E. Lake Shore Dr., Manistique, MI 49878, 906/474-6442.

Trip Notes: Do you want to really do some hiking? Starting at the Munising Visitors Center a few miles northwest is the trailhead for the Lakeshore Trail (906/387-3700). It's a 42-mile route running the length of the Pictured Rocks National Lakeshore that features waterfalls, beaches, dunes, and cliffs. If you'd rather bike somewhere, take the Coalwood Trail (906/341-5010) on Hwys. M-94 and M-28. This is a 24-mile trail at Shingleton.

② Tahquamenon Falls State Park and Tahquamenon Falls State Park Rivermouth Unit

Location: Paradise, near Whitefish Point, map 8, grid C8.

Campsites, facilities: The main unit has 174 campsites; the river unit has 136 campsites. Facilities include electric hookups, water, flush toilets, showers, disposal station, swimming beach, river and lake boating, canoeing, fishing, and hiking and cross-country ski trails. Boat rentals are available. Pets are allowed.

Reservations, fees: The daily fee ranges from $6 to $14. Open from mid-April through October.

Directions: To reach the main unit, take M-123 and go 25 miles north of Newberry or 12 miles west of Paradise. To get to the river unit, take M-123 five miles south of Paradise.

Contact: Tahquamenon Falls State Park, 41382 W. M-123, Paradise, MI 49768, 906/492-3415.

Trip Notes: The Upper Falls is one of the largest waterfalls east of the Mississippi, with a drop of 50 feet and width of 200 feet. The Lower Falls is a series of smaller waterfalls cascading around an island. This park is a hiker's paradise with 25 miles of forest trails that meander through its 40,000 acres of wilderness.

The river unit is a scenic, secluded campground with both modern and rustic campsites, as well as a launch ramp for canoeists and boaters. While camping in the park be sure to visit Whitefish Point to experience the gripping tales of ships and men told through underwater films. See the artifacts from ships that went to the bottom of this inland sea.

24 Muskallonge Lake State Park

Location: Northwest of Newberry, between Lakes Muskallonge and Superior, map 8, grid F4.

Campsites, facilities: There are 177 campsites. Facilities include electric hookups, flush toilets, showers, disposal station, swimming beach, boat ramp, fishing, hiking trail, and playground. Pets are allowed.

Reservations, fees: The daily fee is $11. Open from mid-April through mid-October.

Directions: From the junction of Hwys. 28 and 123, go 33 miles north on Hwy. 123 and County Road 407 to the park entrance.

Contact: Muskallonge Lake State Park, Rt. 1, Box 245, Newberry, MI 49868, 906/658-3338.

Trip Notes: Situated between Lakes Muskallonge and Superior, this park is well known for its forests, lakes, and streams. Rock hunters frequent the Lake Superior shoreline in search of agates.

25 KOA Newberry-Tahquamenon

Location: Newberry, map 8, grid F4.

Campsites, facilities: There are 148 campsites. Facilities include RV pull-through sites, electric hookups, water, disposal station, laundry, grocery store, swimming pool, sauna, whirlpool, gift and antique shop, minigolf, and planned activities. Cabin rentals are available.

Reservations, fees: The daily fee ranges from $21 to $25. Open from mid-May through mid-October.

Directions: From the junction of Hwys. 123 and 28, go one-quarter mile east on Hwy. 28 to the campground entrance.

Contact: KOA Newberry-Tahquamenon, Rob and Margaret Pike, Rt. 4 Box 783, Newberry, MI 49868, 906/293-5762.

Trip Notes: Fall comes early in the UP and Newberry is one of the stops for a picture-perfect autumn color journey, which could take you 150 miles to Seney, Grand Marais, Deer Park, Paradise, and Whitefish Point.

26 North Country Campground and Cabins

Location: Newberry, southwest of Whitefish Point, map 8, grid F4.

Campsites, facilities: There are 50 campsites. Facilities include RV pull-through sites, electric hookups, water, flush toilets, showers, disposal station, laundry, hiking trail, and a playground. Lake and river boating, canoeing, and fishing are nearby, as are snowshoeing, snowmobiling, and cross-country skiing. Log cabin and lodge unit rentals are available. Pets are allowed.

Reservations, fees: The daily fee ranges from $13 to 18. Open May through mid-March.

Directions: From the north edge of Newberry, go 4.5 miles north on Hwy. 123 to the campground entrance.

Contact: North Country Campground and Cabins, Dan and Cathy Clementz, R.R. 1 Box 94, Newberry, MI 49868, 906/293-8562 or 800/471-0111, email: cclementz@sault.com.

Trip Notes: In addition to the year-round sports that are available in the area, be sure to visit the Tahquamenon Logging Museum on North M-123. It features artifacts from early lumber days, a cook shack, an original CCC building, and music pavilion, as well as picnic area, nature trail, and boardwalk.

27 Big Cedar Campground and Canoe Livery

Location: Germfask, on the Manistique River south of Grand Marais, map 8, grid G1.

Campsites, facilities: There are 53 campsites. Facilities include electric hookups, water, sewer, flush toilets, showers, disposal station, grocery store, boat dock, fishing, and hiking trail. Boat rentals are available. Pets are allowed.

Reservations, fees: The daily fee ranges from $13 to 15. Credit cards are accepted. Open May through November.

Directions: From the junction of Hwys. 44 and 77, go one-half mile south on Hwy. 77 to the campground entrance.

Contact: Big Cedar Campground and Canoe Livery, Barry and Tanya Peters, P.O. Box 7, Germfask, MI 49836, 906/586-6684.

Trip Notes: This former CCC Camp #3626 is located on the beautiful Manistique River where you can enjoy canoe trips through the Seney National Wildlife Refuge (906/586-9851). The refuge boasts more than 200 species of birds, as well as beavers, black bear, coyotes, mink, muskrats, otters, and white-tailed deer. A slide presentation is offered at the visitor center and self-guided walking tours will take you through the refuge.

28 Lake Superior State Forest: South Manistique Lake Campground

Location: Curtis, on South Manistique Lake, map 8, grid G3.

Campsites, facilities: There are 29 campsites. Facilities include vault toilets, swimming beach, boating, and fishing. There are

also hiking, cross-country ski, and snowmobile trails nearby.

Reservations, fees: The daily fee is $6. Open May 1 through mid-December.

Directions: From Curtis, go three miles west on South Curtis Road and two miles south on Long Point Road. Then drive one-half mile southeast on the west side of the lake to reach the campground.

Contact: Lake Superior State Forest, South Manistique Lake Campground, Box 428, South M-123, Newberry, MI 49868, 906/293-5131 or 906/293-3293.

Trip Notes: The Curtis Area Trails provide excellent cross-country skiing, and there is unlimited snowmobiling on groomed trails and on all roads around Curtis.

29 Log Cabin Resort and Campground

Location: Curtis, on Manistique Lake, map 8, grid G3.

Campsites, facilities: There are 42 campsites. Facilities include electric hookups, water, sewer, flush toilets, showers, disposal station, laundry, swimming beach, boat ramp and dock, lake fishing, and playground. Boat and cabin rentals are available. Pets are allowed.

Reservations, fees: The daily fee ranges from $15 to $19. Open from mid-May through mid-October.

Directions: From the junction of Hwys. 33 and 42, go three miles west and north on Hwy. 42 to the entrance.

Contact: Log Cabin Resort and Campground, Ken and Marg Host, P.O. Box 9, Curtis, MI 49820, 906/586-9732, email: logcabin @mail.portup.com, website: www.exploringthenorth.com/logcabin/log.html.

Trip Notes: On Manistique Lake in the 15,000-acre Manistique Recreation Area, which has a trio of lakes surrounded by forest, you can experience terrific fishing for walleye, northern pike, bass, and muskie. You can also hunt in season. In addition, there are loads of other activities, including dogsled races and a snowmobile safari.

30 Soo Locks Campground

Location: Sault Ste. Marie, on the St. Marys River, map 9, grid G7.

Campsites, facilities: There are 100 campsites. Facilities include electric hookups, water, flush toilets, showers, disposal station, laundry, grocery store, boat dock, and fishing. Lake boating and fishing are located nearby. Pets are allowed.

Reservations, fees: The daily fee ranges from $19 to 23. Credit cards are accepted. Open May through mid-October.

Directions: From the junction of I-75 and Easterday, take exit 394 and go three-quarters of a mile east on Easterday. Then drive three-quarters of a mile north on Ashum Street and two miles east on Portage Avenue to the entrance.

Contact: Soo Locks Campground, Bob and Helen Collia, 1001 E. Portage, Sault Ste. Marie, MI 49783, 906/632-3191.

Trip Notes: Whether you ever wanted to be a sailor or not, you will enjoy every minute of a guided tour through the "Str. Valley Camp" Maritime Museum (906/632-3658). You'll see everything from the engine room to the pilot house of this 550-foot freighter, as well as a video presentation about Great Lakes life and artifacts from ships in the museum.

31 Chippewa Campground

Location: Sault Ste. Marie, near the St. Marys River, map 9, grid G7.

Campsites, facilities: There are 100 campsites. Facilities include RV pull-through sites, electric hookups, water, sewer, disposal station, laundry, hiking trail, and playground. River swimming at Bell's Point Beach on the Canadian side, and river boating, fishing, and snowmobiling are nearby. Pets are allowed.

Reservations, fees: The daily fee ranges from $18 to $20. Open year-round.

Directions: From I-75, take exit 392 and drive go one-half mile east to the second traffic light. Then go 100 feet south and one-half mile east on Three Mile Road to the entrance.

Contact: Chippewa Campground, Ed and Shirley Patrick, E. Three Mile Rd., P.O. Box 786, Sault Ste. Marie, MI 49783, 906/362-8581.

Trip Notes: While in this area visit the Tower of History (906/632-3658) at 326 E. Portage Ave. Take the express elevator to the observation platforms at the top of this 21-story tower where you can see more than 20 miles. The lobby features exhibits of local historical sites.

32 Aune-Osborn RV Park

Location: Sault Ste. Marie, on the St. Marys River, map 9, grid G7.

Campsites, facilities: There are 101 campsites. Facilities include electric hookups, water, flush toilets, showers, disposal station, river and lake boating, and fishing. A boat ramp and swimming beach are nearby.

Reservations, fees: The daily fee is $17. Open from mid-May through mid-October.

Directions: From the junction of I-75 and Easterday Road, take exit 394 and go one block west on Easterday Road. Then drive 3.75 miles northeast on Portage Road to the park entrance.

Contact: Aune-Osborn RV Park, 1225 Riverside Dr., Sault Ste. Marie, MI 49783, 906/632-3268.

Trip Notes: It's one thing to watch the freighters from your campsite or from the U.S. Army Corps of Engineering Visitors Center, but it won't take the place of cruising through the locks. Go on a Soo Locks Boat Tour that leaves from Dock #1 or #2 on Portage Avenue or from the foot of Water Street. It is a thrill the entire family won't forget.

33 Brimley State Park

Location: Brimley, on Lake Superior's Whitefish Bay, map 9, grid E4.

Campsites, facilities: There are 270 campsites. Facilities include electric hookups, water, flush toilets, showers, disposal station, swimming beach, boating, canoeing, fishing, and lakeshore hiking. Cabin rentals are available. Pets are allowed.

Reservations, fees: The daily fee is $12. Open from mid-April through October.

Directions: From the junction of I-75 and Hwy. 28, go eight miles west on Hwy. 28, and then two miles north on Hwy. 221. Drive one mile east on Lakeshore Drive to the park entrance.

Contact: Brimley State Park, 9200 W. 6 Mile Rd., Brimley, MI 49715, 906/248-3422.

Trip Notes: The state park features large grassy campsites with a swimming beach on Lake Superior's Whitefish Bay. Brimley has the warmest swimming water of any state park located on usually frigid Lake Superior. Anglers fish the bay for northern pike

and walleye. A scenic view of the Canadian highlands can be seen to the north.

34 Clear Lake Campground

Location: Dafter, south of Sault Ste. Marie, map 9, grid F5.

Campsites, facilities: There are 80 sites. Facilities include RV pull-through sites, electric hookups, water, flush toilets, showers, disposal station, laundry, grocery store, swimming beach, boating (no motors permitted), canoeing, and fishing. Pets are allowed.

Reservations, fees: The daily fee is $12. Open from mid-May through September.

Directions: From the junction of I-75 and Barbeau, take exit 379 and go 1.5 miles north on Country Road H63 to the campground entrance.

Contact: Clear Lake Campground, John and Charlene Meehan, 13301 S. Mackinaw Trail, Dafter, MI 49724, 906/645-0201 or 906/632-3043.

Trip Notes: Do you like unique little shops? It's just 14 miles to Sault Ste. Marie and the Mole Hole (906/632-3540). Many of the gifts are made by outstanding artists and craftsmen.

35 Glen's Resort

Location: Goetzville, at the southeastern tip of the UP, map 9, grid H8.

Campsites, facilities: There are 15 campsites. Facilities include electric hookups, water, sewer, flush toilets, showers, disposal station, grocery store, boat ramp, and fishing. Golf and cross-country skiing and snowshoeing are available nearby. Boat, canoe, and cottage rentals are available.

Reservations, fees: Reservations are recommended. The daily fee ranges from $7 to $14. Open from mid-May through mid-October.

Directions: Take I-75 north to exit 369 right to the center of Cedarville. At blinking light, turn left at 129 to the center of Pickford. Drive 11 miles to blinking light, turn right, and go 13 miles to campground entrance.

Contact: Glen's Resort, HC-55, Box 396, Goetzville, MI 49736, 906/297-5042.

Trip Notes: Take the ferry across to Drummond Island and enjoy the best in golfing at The Rock at Woodmore Resort in spring and summer, or cross-country skiing and snowshoeing in winter.

❸❻ Raber Bay Landing

Location: Goetzville, on Raber Bay, map 9, grid H8.

Campsites, facilities: There are 30 campsites. Facilities include RV pull-through sites, electric hookups, water, vault toilets, showers, grocery store, boat ramp and dock, and river fishing. Boat, canoe, and cottage rentals are available. Pets are allowed.

Reservations, fees: Reservations are recommended. The daily fee is $15. Open year-round.

Directions: From Goetzville, go one mile north on Hwy. 48, and four miles north on Raber Road. Then drive two miles east on Mike's Landing Road to the entrance at the end.

Contact: Raber Bay Landing, 26816 S. Raber Bay Rd., Goetzville, MI 49736, (888/846-3923 or 906/297-5812.

Trip Notes: Raber Bay is noted for its excellent walleye, northern pike, and smallmouth bass fishing.

❸❼ Rivers Bend Campground

Location: Iron Mountain, map 10, grid B8.

Campsites, facilities: There are 155 campsites. Facilities include electric hookups, water, sewer, flush toilets, showers, disposal station, laundry, river or pond swimming, boat ramp and dock, river fishing, and playground. Boat, canoe, and seasonal campsite rentals are available. Pets are allowed.

Reservations, fees: The daily fee ranges from $14 to 16. Open from mid-April through mid-October.

Directions: From the west junction of U.S. Hwy. 2 and Hwy. 95, go one-half mile west on Hwy. 2, and one-half mile south on Pine Mountain Road to the entrance.

Contact: Rivers Bend Campground, P.O. Box 652, Iron Mountain, MI 49801, 906/779-1171 or 906/774-2664.

Trip Notes: You should not overlook a visit to the Iron Mountain Iron Mine and Museum (906/563-8077) at Vulcan. Everyone will be awed when they don raincoats and ride the miner's train on a guided tour through 2,600 feet of underground drifts and tunnels.

❸❽ Iron Mountain Campground

Location: Iron Mountain, near the Wisconsin border, map 10, grid B8.

Campsites, facilities: There are 70 campsites. Facilities include RV pull-through sites, electric hookups, water, sewers, flush toilets, showers, disposal station, laundry, and swimming pool. Many lakes and rivers for boating, canoeing, and fishing are nearby. Pets are allowed.

Reservations, fees: The daily fee ranges from $19 to $16. Open May through October.

Directions: From the junction of U.S. Hwy. 2 and Hwy. 95, go 1.25 miles north on Hwy. 95, then one-quarter mile west on Twin Falls Road to the campground entrance.

Contact: Iron Mountain Campground, Gregory Scott, W8576 Twin Falls Rd., Iron Mountain, MI 49801, 906/774-2807.

Trip Notes: This was iron mining country its reminders are everywhere. The Menominee Range Historical Museum and the Cornish Pumping Engine and Mining Museum (906/774-4276 or 906/774-1086) are well worth your time.

39 Gladstone Bay Campground

Location: Gladstone, on Lake Michigan, map 11, grid B8.

Campsites, facilities: There are 60 campsites in this city park. Facilities include RV pull-through sites, electric hookups, flush toilets, showers, disposal station, swimming beach, boating, and fishing. Pets are allowed.

Reservations, fees: The daily fee is $8 to $15. Open May through October.

Directions: From U.S. Hwy. 2/41, take the Delta Avenue exit and go one mile east on Delta Avenue to the entrance at the end.

Contact: Gladstone Bay Campground, c/o City Hall, P.O. Box 32, Gladstone, MI 49837, 906/428-2311.

Trip Notes: If you're a biking enthusiast, the Days River Pathway (906/428-2311) is a four-mile trail from Gladstone to Rapid River that you'll enjoy riding.

40 O. B. Fuller and Pioneer Trail Parks

Location: Escanaba, on Lake Michigan and on Escanaba River, map 11, grid C8.

Campsites, facilities: O. B. Fuller county park has 25 modern campsites (no primitive sites). Facilities include electric hookups, flush toilets, showers, disposal station, laundry, swimming beach, boat ramp, and lake and river fishing. Pets are allowed. Pioneer Trail county park has 58 modern and 25 primitive sites.

Reservations, fees: The daily fee ranges from $15 to $17 at O. B. Fuller and from $10 to $15 at Pioneer Trail. Open from mid-May through mid-September.

Directions: To reach O. B. Fuller from the junction of U.S. Hwy. 2 and Hwy. 35, go 14 miles south on Hwy. 35 to the entrance. Pioneer Trail Park is north of Escanaba on the Escanaba River.

Contact: O. B. Fuller Park and Pioneer Trail Park, 6822 U.S. Hwy. 2 and 41, M-35, Gladstone, MI 49837, 906/786-1020.

Trip Notes: Make a visit to Sand Point Lighthouse (906/786-3763) on the west shore of Little Bay De Noc. Although it's no longer in service, it has been restored to its original condition and is a public museum open for tours.

41 Bayside Resort and Campground

Location: Escanaba, on Lake Michigan, map 11, grid C8.

Campsites, facilities: There are 31 campsites. Facilities include electric hookups, water, sewer, flush toilets, showers, grocery store, swimming pool, swimming beach, boat ramp, nature trail, and fishing. Cottage, kitchenette, and motel room rentals are available.

Reservations, fees: The daily fee ranges from $20 to $25. Open May through November.

Directions: From Escanaba, go 16 miles south on Hwy. 35 to the campground entrance.

Contact: Bayside Resort and Campground, 376 Highway M-35, Bark River, MI 49807, 906/786-7831.

Trip Notes: Escanaba boasts great fishing from the shore and from a charter fishing boat, but if you'd rather hit a little ball around a great course, play the Escanaba Country Club (906/786-1701) or Dergrand Country Meadows (906/786-1565).

42 Shakey Lake Park

Location: Stephenson, on Shakey Lake, map 11, grid E4.

Campsites, facilities: There are 103 campsites in this Menominee County park. Facilities include electric hookups, flush toilets, showers, disposal station, laundry, grocery store, swimming beach, boat ramp, hiking trail, cross-country skiing, and snowshoeing. Boat rentals are available.

Reservations, fees: The daily fee ranges from $10 to $14. Open year-round.

Directions: From the junction of U.S. Hwy. 41 and County Road G12, go 12 miles west on County Road G12 and follow the signs to the park entrance, which is on the right.

Contact: Shakey Lake Park, N8390 County Park Rd., Stephenson, MI 49887, 906/753-4582.

Trip Notes: Snowshoeing is becoming a popular sport. Both cross-country skiing and snowshoeing can be enjoyed at the Cedar River Path (906/753-6317).

43 J. W. Wells State Park

Location: Cedar River, on Lake Michigan, map 11, grid E6.

Campsites, facilities: There are 178 campsites, with 30 sites on Green Bay. Facilities include electric hookups, flush toilets, showers, disposal station, swimming beach, boat ramp, fishing, playground, biking and hiking trails, snowmobiling, and cross-country skiing. Boat rentals are available. Pets are allowed.

Reservations, fees: The daily fee is $12. Open May through mid-October.

Directions: From the junction of County Road G-12 and Hwy. 35, go one mile south on Hwy. 35 to the park entrance.

Contact: J. W. Wells State Park, N7670 Hwy. M-35, Cedar River, MI 49813, 906/863-9747.

Trip Notes: There are waterfront campsites and rustic cabins on Green Bay with three miles of shoreline to explore. Wildlife is abundant here. J. W. Wells is an ideal getaway for biking and hiking enthusiasts, and for enjoying the old-growth forest from a seven-mile network of trails.

44 River Park Campground

Location: Menominee, on Green Bay and the Menominee River, map 11, grid H4.

Campsites, facilities: There are 58 campsites in this city park. Facilities include electric hookups, water, sewer, flush toilets, showers, disposal station, swimming beach, boat ramp, lake and river boating and fishing. Pets are allowed with restrictions.

Reservations, fees: The daily fee is $22. Open from mid-May through mid-October.

Directions: The park is in Menominee on U.S. Hwy. 41.

Contact: Menominee City Hall, Recreation Dept., 2511 10th St., Menominee, WI 49858, 906/863-2656.

Trip Notes: Make a visit to the Historic Waterfront District (906/863-2679), which is being restored along scenic Green Bay and Lake Michigan. Call for information on scheduled activities.

45 Vagabond Campground Resort

Location: Rapid River, on Little Bay De Noc, map 12, grid A1.

Campsites, facilities: There are 58 campsites. Facilities include electric hookups, flush toilets, showers, disposal station, laundry, swimming beach, boat dock, fishing, and biking, hiking, snowmobile, and cross-country ski trails. Boat and cabin rentals are available. Pets are allowed.

Reservations, fees: The daily fee ranges from $12 to $19. Open year-round.

Directions: From the junction of U.S. Hwys. 2 and 41, go three miles east on Hwy. 2 and then three miles south on County Road 513 to the entrance.

Contact: Vagabond Campground, County 513 T Rd., Rapid River, MI 49878, 906/474-6122.

Trip Notes: This campground is near Lighthouse Point National Park. If you want to go biking, the seven-mile Rapid River Biking Trail is just north of Rapid River. If you want to ski, there is the 22-mile Rapid River Trail (906/474-6442).

46 Indian Lakes State Park-Main and West Units

Location: Manistique, on Indian Lake, map 12, grid A7.

Campsites, facilities: The main unit has 158 campsites. Facilities include electric hookups, flush toilets, showers, disposal station, and laundry. The west unit has 144 campsites. Its facilities include electric hookups, vault toilets, showers, and disposal station. Both units offer swimming beach, boat ramp and dock, and hiking trails. Boat rentals are available. Pets are allowed.

Reservations, fees: The daily fee ranges from $9 to $15. Open from mid-April through October (main unit); from mid-June through mid-September (west unit).

Directions: To reach the main unit from the junction of U.S. Hwy. 2 and Hwy. 94, go five miles west on Hwy. 2 and Hwy. 149 to the entrance. To reach the west unit from the junction of Hwy. 2 and Hwy. 94, go six miles west on Hwy. 2, and then eight miles northwest on Hwy. 149 to the entrance.

Contact: Indian Lakes State Park, Rt. 2, Box 2500, Manistique, MI 49854, 906/341-2355.

Trip Notes: The main unit is located on a mile of sandy beach and offers recreation for swimmers, anglers, and campers. The west unit provides secluded, sheltered campsites about one-half mile from the lake. On Hwy. 149, about 11 miles north of Hwy. 2 is Palms Book State Park (906/341-2355), known as the "Mirror of Heaven" by Native Americans. This park is a photographer's delight. You will enjoy riding the self-propelled observation raft to view the crystal-clear mineral waters of the "Kitch-Iti-Kipi" (The Big Spring), which is 40 feet deep and 200 feet across. You can see more than 16,000 gallons of water bubble from the spring each minute into pools of constant

45-degree F. water that never freezes in the winter or warms up in summer.

47 Indian Lake Travel Resort

Location: Manistique, on Indian Lake, map 12, grid A7.

Campsites, facilities: There are 58 campsites. Facilities include electric hookups, water, sewer, flush toilets, showers, disposal station, grocery store, boat ramp and dock, swimming beach, and hiking trails. Boat rentals are available. Pets are allowed.

Reservations, fees: The daily fee is $15. Open May through mid-October.

Directions: From the junction of U.S. Hwy. 2 and Hwy. 149, drive 3.75 miles northwest on Hwy. 149, and then one-half mile north on County Road 455 to the entrance.

Contact: Indian Lake Travel Resort, L.V. Ellis and Dick Ellis, Mgr., HC01, Box 3286, Manistique, MI 49854, 906/341-2807.

Trip Notes: For lighthouse buffs, there is a double treat while camping here. Just off Hwy. 2 is Lakeview Park where you can get a view of the Manistique East Breakwater Light. On clear days you can see this 35-foot red steel tower that stands on a concrete crib. Take a half-hour drive east on Hwy. 2 to Gulliver to visit the Seul Choix (sis shwah, meaning "only choice") Point Lighthouse Park and Museum. The white tower is 79-feet, 9 inches high and you'll enjoy a climb to the top for a breathtaking view of Lake Michigan. The museum and restored keeper's quarters offer considerable information about the lighthouse and the job of the keeper. The lighthouse is still fully operational.

48 Hiawatha National Forest: Camp 7 Lake

Location: Manistique, on Camp 7 Lake, map 12, grid A7.

Campsites, facilities: There are 41 campsites and 15 picnic units. Facilities include water, vault toilets, swimming beach, fishing, bike and hiking trails, boat ramp, and wheelchair access. Cross-country ski trail is nearby.

Reservations, fees: The daily fee ranges from $8 to $12. Open from late May through November.

Directions: From Manistique, drive 9.5 miles west on County Road 442, and then 7.5 miles north on County Road 437. Then go four miles west on County Road 443, and one-quarter mile north on Forest Road 2218 to the entrance.

Contact: Hiawatha National Forest, Camp 7 Lake, Manistique Ranger District Office, 499 E. Lake Shore Dr., Manistique, MI 49854, 906/341-5666.

Trip Notes: There is excellent biking on Ashford Lake Pathway north of Manistique, and Bruno's Run, which can be reached from Widewaters Campground during the spring and summer. There are also cross-country ski trails at Ashford Lake Pathway and Indian Lake Trail (906/341-5010).

49 Fayette State Park

Location: Garden, on Big Bay De Noc, map 12, grid B4.

Campsites, facilities: There are 80 campsites. Facilities include electric hookups, vault toilets, swimming beach, boat ramp and dock, fishing, and hiking trail. Pets are allowed.

Reservations, fees: The daily fee is $9. Open from mid-April through mid-November.

Directions: From Garden, go eight miles southwest on County Road 483 to the park entrance.

Contact: Fayette State Park, 13700 13.25 Lane, Garden, MI 49835, 906/644-2603.

Trip Notes: This park features three miles of shoreline on Big Bay De Noc and a restored iron smelting company town (1867-1891). It also has cross-country ski trails and seven miles of bike trails.

50 Cedarville RV Park Campground

Location: Cedarville, on Cedarville Bay, map 13, grid A6.

Campsites, facilities: There are 77 campsites. Facilities include electric hookups, water, sewer, disposal station, laundry, swimming beach, boat ramp and dock, hiking trail, and snowmobiling. Golf course is nearby. Boat and cabin rentals are available.

Reservations, fees: The daily fee ranges from $18 to $22. Open May through November.

Directions: From the junction of I-75 and Hwy. 134, take exit 359 (Cedarville-Hessel, Les Cheneaux Island) and go east for 17 miles through Cedarville. Go one block south to Grove Street and follow the signs to the entrance.

Contact: Cedarville RV Park, Sharrie and Jon Steinbach, Box 328, Grove Street, Cedarville, MI 49719, 906/484-3351 or 800/906-3351.

Trip Notes: Located on Lake Huron, the Les Cheneaux Islands provide many year-round activities, including the Les Cheneaux Islands/Hessel, Cedarville, Pickford route —107 miles of connected trails for snowmobiling.

THE STRAITS

The Straits

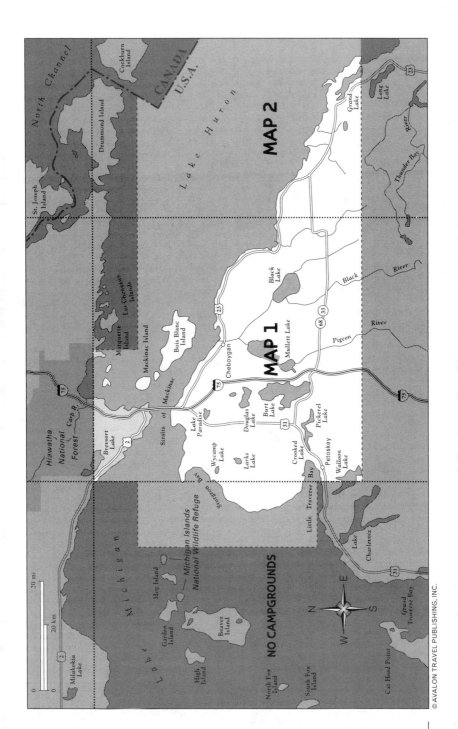

© AVALON TRAVEL PUBLISHING, INC.

Map 1

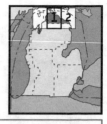

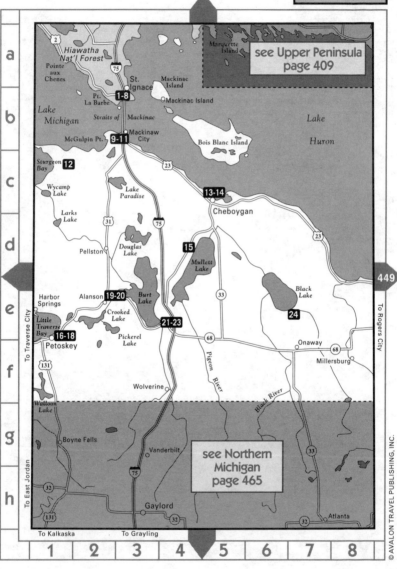

see Upper Peninsula page 409

see Upper Peninsula
page 409

a

Hiawatha
Nat'l Forest

Pointe
aux
Chenes

Lake
Michigan

Pt.
La Barbe

St.
Ignace

1-8

Mackinac
Island

Mackinac Island

Marquette
Island

b

Straits of   Mackinac

McGulpin Pt.

9-11

Mackinaw
City

Bois Blanc Island

Lake

Huron

c

Sturgeon
Bay

12

Wycamp
Lake

Lake
Paradise

13-14

Cheboygan

Larks
Lake

d

Pellston

Douglas
Lake

15

Mullett
Lake

Black
Lake

Harbor
Springs

Alanson

19-20

Burt
Lake

449

e

Little
Traverse
Bay

16-18

Petoskey

Crooked
Lake

Pickerel
Lake

21-23

24

Onaway

Millersburg

f

Wolverine

Pigeon River

Black River

g

Walloon
Lake

Boyne Falls

Vanderbilt

see Northern Michigan page 465

see Northern
Michigan
page 465

h

Gaylord

Atlanta

To Traverse City

To East Jordan

To Rogers City

To Kalkaska

To Grayling

© AVALON TRAVEL PUBLISHING, INC.

Map 2

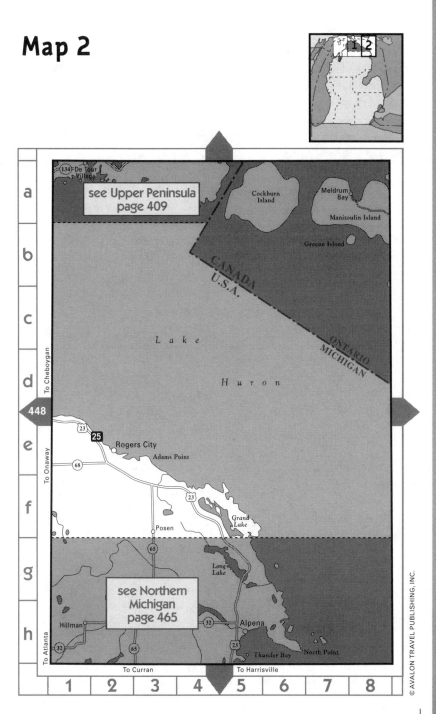

see Upper Peninsula page 409

see Northern Michigan page 465

134 De Tour Village

Cockburn Island

Meldrum Bay

Manitoulin Island

Greene Island

CANADA
U.S.A.

ONTARIO
MICHIGAN

L a k e

H u r o n

To Cheboygan

To Onaway

23

25 Rogers City

Adams Point

68

23

Grand Lake

Posen

65

Long Lake

To Atlanta

Hillman

32

65

32

Alpena

23

Thunder Bay

North Point

To Curran

To Harrisville

1 2 3 4 5 6 7 8

448

© AVALON TRAVEL PUBLISHING, INC.

The Straits

The Straits region of Michigan—spanned by the Mackinac Bridge, the world's longest suspension bridge—is one of the state's most historic areas. Mackinac Island, a limestone hump rising from Lake Huron, was called "Michilimackinac," (great turtle) by the Native Americans. It's the site of an ancient Indian burial ground, British and American trading posts, supply center for fishing and lumbering during the 19th century and, since the mid-1800s, a tourist treasure.

Mackinac State Historic Parks include four parks in the Straits region: Fort Mackinac and Mackinac Island State Park on Mackinac Island, and Colonial Michilimackinac and Historic Mill Creek in Mackinaw City.

These parks, as well as the region's forests, lakes, wildlife areas, lighthouses, and other attractions, could occupy a camper for a week or two.

1 Hiawatha National Forest: Foley Creek Campground

Location: North of St. Ignace, near Hay Lake and Lake Huron, map 1, grid B3.

Campsites, facilities: There are 54 campsites at this rustic campground. Facilities include water, vault toilets, fishing, and hiking trail. Nearby there is lake swimming, boating, and fishing in Hay Lake or Lake Huron.

Reservations, fees: The daily fee is $10. Open from late April through September.

Directions: From St. Ignace, take I-75 north three miles to County Road H-63 (Old Mackinac Trail) into the left lane. Make a sharp-left U-turn onto H-63 (sign provided) and go 2.4 miles to the entrance.

Contact: U.S.D.A. Forest Service, 1798 W. U.S. Hwy. 2, St. Ignace, MI 49781, 906/643-7900, fax 906/643-8759.

Trip Notes: Take in the view overlooking the Straits of Mackinac from the Father Marquette National Memorial and Museum (906/643-8620) in Straits State Park. The memorial and museum interpret the 17th-century missionary and explorer Jacques Marquette and the meeting of French and Native American cultures in the North American wilderness. There's an excellent photo opportunity here.

❷ Hiawatha National Forest: Carp River Campground

Location: North of St. Ignace on the Carp River near Lake Huron, map 1, grid B3.

Campsites, facilities: There are 44 campsites. Facilities include water, vault toilets, boat ramp, fishing, canoeing, and hiking trail. Lake Huron boating, fishing, and swimming are available nearby. Pets are not allowed.

Reservations, fees: The daily fee is $10. Open late May through November.

Directions: Go eight miles north of St. Ignace off the Old Mackinac trail (H-63).

Contact: Hiawatha National Forest, 2727 N. Lincoln Rd., Escanaba, MI 49829, 906/786-4062. The St. Ignace Ranger District is at 1798 W. U.S. Hwy. 2, St. Ignace, MI 49781, 906/643-7900, fax 906/643-8759.

Trip Notes: This is a small, quiet, rustic campground on the Carp River and near Lake Huron. It is a perfect home base for anglers.

In Saint Ignace, you might visit the Mystery Spot (906/643-8322; website: www.stignace.com/attractions/mysteryspot/#spot). In the

early 1950s, three surveyors discovered an area of about 300 feet in diameter where their instruments did not appear to work properly. They were also constantly light-headed. A tall person seems smaller by comparison and you can climb a wall and tilt precariously into the air without falling. It's on U.S. Hwy. 2, five miles west of the Mackinac Bridge and I-75.

❸ Hiawatha National Forest: Brevoort Lake Campground

Location: About 17 miles northwest of St. Ignace on Brevoort Lake, map 1, grid B3.

Campsites, facilities: There are 70 campsites. Facilities include water, flush toilets, disposal station, boat ramp, fishing, swimming, picnic area, hiking trail, and grocery store.

Reservations, fees: The daily fee ranges from $12 to $14. Open from early May through October.

Directions: From junction I-75 and U.S. Hwy. 2, go 17 miles northwest on Hwy. 2, then 1.5 miles north on FH 3108. Then drive one-half mile northeast on FH 3473 to the entrance.

Contact: Hiawatha National Forest, 2727 N. Lincoln Rd., Escanaba, MI 49829, 906/786-4062. The St. Ignace Ranger District is at 1798 W. U.S. Hwy. 2, St. Ignace, MI 49781, 906/643-7900, fax 906/643-8759.

Trip Notes: This is a great place to kick back and relax on your wooded site or enjoy swimming or fishing on the lake.

❹ Tiki Travel Park

Location: St. Ignace, north of the Straits of Mackinac, map 1, grid B3.

Campsites, facilities: There are 104 campsites. Facilities

include electric hookups, water, sewer, flush toilets, showers, disposal station, laundry, and grocery store. Lake boating, fishing, and swimming are nearby. Pets are allowed.

Reservations, fees: The daily fee ranges from $15 to $18. Credit cards are accepted. Open from mid-May through mid-October.

Directions: From the junction of I-75 and Business I-75, take exit 344A and go three miles north on Business I-75. In town, go about 400 feet west on Airport Road to the entrance on the left.

Contact: Tiki Travel Park, 200 S. Airport Rd., St. Ignace, MI 49781, 888/859-4258 or 906/632-8581.

Trip Notes: This is the closest campground to the Mackinac Island Boat Dock and offers free shuttle service to the ferries and casino.

On Mackinac Island, you can walk through the Butterfly House (906/847-3972) at 1308 McGulpin Street. It's the white building on the north side of the street. The Butterfly House features more than 250 live butterflies and over 1,000 flowers. Here you can see the life cycle of the butterflies and their role in our ecosystem.

5 Castle Rock-Mackinac Trail Campark

Location: North of St. Ignace on Lake Huron, map 1, grid B3.

Campsites, facilities: There are 80 campsites. Facilities include electric hookups, water, sewer, flush toilets, showers, swimming, laundry, grocery store, swimming beach, boating, fishing, and playground. Pets are not allowed.

Reservations, fees: Reservations are recommended. The daily fee ranges from $16 to $18. Credit cards are accepted. Open from mid-May through mid-October.

Directions: From I-75, take exit 348 and make a right turn. After one-quarter mile, turn left on the Mackinac Trail Loop. Go three blocks north on Mackinac Trail and make a right at the Campark sign to the entrance.

Contact: Castle Rock-Mackinac Trail Campark, Charles and Delores Muscott, 2811 Mackinac Trail, St. Ignace, MI 49781, 800/333-8754 or 906/643-9222, website: www.stignace .com/lodging/castlecamp/index.html.

Trip Notes: Five miles north of the Mackinac Bridge, you'll discover Castle Rock (906/643-8268 or 906/643-6712), a 200-foot outcropping. If you have the stamina, you can climb 170 steps to the top. It's a long way, but gives you an excellent view of Mackinac Island.

6 St. Ignace-Mackinac Island KOA Kampground

Location: West of the Mackinac Bridge, map 1, grid B3.

Campsites, facilities: There are 200 campsites. Facilities include RV pull-through sites, electric hookups, water, sewer, flush toilets, showers, wheelchair access, laundry, disposal station, grocery store and gift shop, swimming pool, mini-golf, and playground. Lake swimming, boating, and fishing are nearby. Cabin rentals are available. The campground offers free shuttles to Mackinac Island ferries. Pets are not allowed.

Reservations, fees: Reservations are recommended. The daily fee ranges from $19 to $26. Credit cards are accepted. Open May through October.

Directions: From I-74, take exit 344 and go west on U.S. Hwy. 2 for 2.5 miles to the entrance.

Contact: St. Ignace-Mackinac Island KOA Kampground, 1242 U.S. Hwy. 2 West, St, Ignace, MI 49781, 906/643-9303. email: simi koa@sault.com.

Trip Notes: Take an auto tour (maps are available) of the areas where the Civilian Conservation Corps (CCC) planted trees, built roads, constructed campgrounds and made wildlife habitat improvements between 1933 and 1942. Several CCC camps are located in the St. Ignace area. A memorial to their efforts is at the trailhead of the Sand Dunes Cross-country Ski Trail (906/643-7900).

7 Lakeshore Park

Location: Northwest of the Mackinac Bridge in St. Ignace, map 1, grid B3.

Campsites, facilities: There are 100 campsites. Facilities include RV pull-through sites, electric hookups, water, sewers, flush toilets, showers, laundry, wheelchair access, disposal station, picnic area, gift and grocery stores, lake swimming, boating, and fishing. It offers a free shuttle to Mackinac Island ferries. Pets are not allowed.

Reservations, fees: Reservations are recommended. The daily fee ranges from $19 to $21. Credit cards are accepted. Open May through mid-October.

Directions: From northbound I-75, take exit 344B. From southbound I-75, take exit 344 and then go west on U.S. Hwy. 2 about two miles. Turn south on Pte. LaBarbe Road. Then go 1.5 miles to campground. Coming from the west on Hwy. 2, look for signs and turn right on Pte. LaBarbe Road, driving 1.5 miles to the entrance.

Contact: Lakeshore Park, Bob and Kay Steward, 416 Pte. LaBarbe Rd., St. Ignace, MI 49781, 800/643-9522 or 906/643-9522, email: lakeshoi@oneqol.com, website: www.members.aol.com/lakeshoi.

Trip Notes: At the historic St. Ignace downtown waterfront is the Huron Boardwalk

(800/338-6660 or 906/643-6950), connecting shops, restaurants, parks, and museums. Outdoor displays include a rudder from a 1,212-ton wooden steamer sunk in 1894, a windlass from the wreckage of a ship that sank in 1891, and an original Mackinaw Boat, built in the city in about 1899.

8 Straits State Park

Location: East of the northern end of the Mackinac Bridge on Lake Huron, map 1, grid B3.

Campsites, facilities: There are 275 modern campsites in the 334-acre park. Facilities include electric hookups, flush toilets, showers, disposal station, and laundry. The campground provides lake swimming, boating, fishing, hiking and walking trails, cross-country skiing, picnic area, and playground. There is also an overlook platform offering a stunning view of the Mackinac Bridge and Straits of Mackinac.

Reservations, fees: Reservations are accepted. The daily fee ranges from $8 to $10. Credit cards are accepted. Open year-round.

Directions: Take I-75 to U.S. Hwy. 2 and exit on Church St. Go south on Church St. for one-quarter mile to the park entrance.

Contact: Straits State Park, 720 Church St., St. Ignace, MI 49781-1729 or 906/643-8620, fax 906/643-9329.

Trip Notes: There is a boat launch in downtown St. Ignace, one-half mile away. Fishing is allowed on the Lake Huron shore, but the water in front of the park is too shallow for good shore fishing. The best angling is west of the Mackinac Bridge.

9 Tee Pee Campground

Location: Near Mackinaw City on Lake Huron, map 1, grid B3.

Campsites, facilities: There are 96 campsites. Facilities include electric hookups, water, flush toilets, showers, wheelchair access, disposal station, grocery store, lake swimming, boating, fishing, and playground. There are also hiking and cross-country ski trails. There is a free shuttle. Pets are not allowed.

Reservations, fees: Reservations are recommended. The daily fee is about $20. Credit cards are accepted. Open from mid-May through mid-October.

Directions: From I-75, take exit 337 (northbound) or exit 338 (southbound) and go one mile southeast on U.S. Hwy. 23 to park entrance.

Contact: Tee Pee Campground, Gene and Jo Cooley, 11262 W. U.S. Hwy. 23 and Lake Huron, P.O. Box 10, Mackinaw City, MI 49701, 231/436-5391.

Trip Notes: Visit or travel the Mackinac Bridge (906/643-7600; website: www.mackinacbridge.org). It's the longest suspension bridge in the Western Hemisphere with 7,400 feet of road suspended over the Straits. Its total length, including approaches, is about five miles.

10 Mackinaw Mill Creek Camping

Location: South of the Mackinac Bridge on Lake Huron, map 1, grid B3.

Campsites, facilities: There are more than 600 campsites. Facilities include electric hookups, water, sewer, flush toilets, showers, wheelchair access, disposal station, grocery store, swimming pool, swimming beach, boating, fishing, mini-golf, and playground. Bike and cabin rentals are available. Pets are allowed.

Reservations, fees: Reservations are recommended. The daily fee ranges from $13 to $15. Open May through October.

Directions: Follow the signs near Mackinaw City south to Mill Creek State Historic Park. From there, take U.S. Hwy. 23 one mile north to the entrance.

Contact: Mackinaw Mill Creek Camping, Dick and Rose Rogala, 9730 U.S. Hwy. 23 and Lake Huron, Box 728 M, Mackinaw City, MI 49701, 231/436-5584, email: office@campmackinaw.com, website: www.campmackinaw.com.

Trip Notes: The whole family will enjoy Historic Mill Creek (231/436-5564). You'll think you've been transported back to lumbering days when trees were felled, logs were split in the saw pit and milled in the 18th-century water-powered mill, and turned into boards and shingles. Kids are invited to participate in demonstrations. You can also get a snack at the cookhouse.

11 KOA Mackinaw City

Location: In Mackinaw City, map 1, grid B3.

Campsites, facilities: There are 110 campsites. Facilities include RV pull-through sites, electric hookups, water, disposal station, laundry, grocery store, swimming pool, and playground. Cabin rentals are available. Lake swimming, boating, and fishing are nearby. Pets are allowed.

Reservations, fees: The daily fee ranges from $21 to $25. Open May through mid-October.

Directions: From I-75, take exit 337 to Hwy. 108. Go one block south to Trailsend Rd. and drive one-half mile west to the entrance on the right.

Contact: KOA Mackinaw City, 566 Trailsend Rd., Box 616, Mackinaw City, MI 49701, 800/562-1738.

Trip Notes: No trip to Mackinaw City is complete without a ferry trip out to Mackinac Island. There, you can walk, bike, or take a carriage ride around the island because cars aren't allowed. Visit Old Fort Mackinac and hear the cannons boom. See the buildings used by the British during the 1780s.

12 Wilderness State Park

Location: West of Mackinaw City on Lake Michigan, map 1, grid C1.

Campsites, facilities: There are 250 modern campsites in two campgrounds (the Lakeshore and the Pines). Facilities include electric hookups, flush toilets, showers, disposal station, swimming beach, boat ramp on Big Stone Bay, fishing, hunting, picnic area, and playground. Rustic cabin rentals are available. There are also 16 miles of hiking and 12 miles of cross-country ski trails.

Reservations, fees: The daily fee is $15. Open April through November.

Directions: From Mackinaw City, take Wilderness Park Drive west for 11 miles to the park entrance.

Contact: Wilderness State Park, 898 Wilderness Park Dr., Carp Lake, MI 49718, 231/436-5381.

Trip Notes: The 8,286-acre park, formed 2,000 years ago by shifting sand dunes, boasts 26 miles of Lake Michigan shoreline. There is excellent hunting for deer and snowshoe hare. Other game includes grouse, waterfowl, and squirrel. In addition, there is hunting for bear and bobcat.

13 Cheboygan State Park

Location: Southeast of Mackinaw City on Lake Huron, map 1, grid C5.

Campsites, facilities: There are 73 modern campsites. Facilities include electric hookups, flush toilets, showers, wheelchair access, disposal station, and grocery store. The campground provides lake swimming, boating, and fishing on Duncan Bay, and a playground. There are also hiking and cross-country ski trails. Rustic cabin rentals are available. Pets are not allowed.

Reservations, fees: The daily fee is $11. Credit cards are accepted. Open May through mid-October.

Directions: From Mackinaw City, take U.S. Hwy. 23 south and go four miles past Cheboygan to Beach Road and the entrance.

Contact: Cheboygan State Park, 4490 Beach Rd., Cheboygan, MI 49721, 800/447-2757 or 231/627-2811.

Trip Notes: Located on the Straits of Mackinac, this 932-acre park has a scenic Lake Huron shoreline and views of historic lighthouse ruins, including Cheboygan Point Light, originally built in 1851. Anglers can fish for speckled brook trout in Little Billy Elliot Creek. There are also wooded hiking and cross-country ski trail systems nearby.

14 Waterways Campground

Location: Southeast of Mackinaw City on the Cheboygan River, map 1, grid C5.

Campsites, facilities: There are 50 campsites. Facilities include electric hookups, water, sewer, flush toilets, showers, wheelchair access, disposal station, grocery store, fishing, boat ramp and dock, hiking trail, planned weekend activities, and a playground. Boat rentals are available. Pets are allowed.

Reservations, fees: The daily fee ranges from $18 to $20. Open May through October.

Directions: From southbound I-75, take exit 313. From northbound I-75, take exit 326 or 322 to the junction of Hwys. 27 and 33. Go south one-quarter mile on Hwy. 33 to the entrance on the Cheboygan River.

Contact: Waterways Campground, Ron and Jan Ramsey, P.O. Box 262, Cheboygan, MI 49721, 888/882-7066 or 231/627-7066.

Trip Notes: Check the turning basin on the east side of the Cheboygan River. You may spot the U.S. Coast Guard Cutter "Mackinaw" when it is in port.

In nearby Charlevoix, tour the Harsha House Museum (231/547-0373), an 1891 restored Queen Anne-styled home. It contains unique local history, including photographs, documents, books, and artifacts of the area. Go to downtown Charlevoix on U.S. Hwy. 31 (Bridge Street) and then go one block west to the 100 block on State Street.

15 Aloha State Park

Location: South of Mackinaw City on Mullett Lake, map 1, grid D4.

Campsites, facilities: There are 287 modern campsites in the 106-acre park. Facilities include electric hookups, flush toilets, showers, disposal station, swimming beach, boat ramp, fishing, and playground. Boat rentals are available. Cross-country ski and snowmobile trails are nearby. Pets are not allowed.

Reservations, fees: Reservations are recommended. The daily fee is $14. Credit cards are accepted. Open May through mid-October.

Directions: Take Hwy. 33 seven miles south of Cheboygan and then turn west for one mile on Hwy. 212 to the entrance.

Contact: Aloha State Park, 4347 Third St., Cheboygan, MI 49721, 231/625-2522, fax 231/625-8180.

Trip Notes: Aloha State Park is on beautiful Mullett Lake, known as the heart of the Inland Waterway. This is part of a 40-mile water route from Lake Huron to Lake Michigan. In 1974, a 193-pound sturgeon was caught in the lake. Anglers, however, usually seek northern pike, yellow perch, smallmouth bass, walleye, and lake trout. As for the unusual park name, "Aloha" was the name given to a village next to the park by a president of the Detroit and Mackinac Railroad after his return from Hawaii.

16 Petoskey State Park

Location: Petoskey, on Lake Michigan's Little Traverse Bay, map 1, grid F1.

Campsites, facilities: There are two separate campgrounds in the 304-acre park. Tannery Creek offers 98 campsites and Dunes has 70 campsites. Both offer electric hookups, flush toilets, showers, swimming beaches, boating, fishing, two hiking trails (Old Baldy and Portage), picnic areas, and playgrounds. There are also cross-country ski, snowshoe, and winter hiking trails, but snowmobiling is prohibited. Boat ramps are located in Harbor Springs and Petoskey.

Reservations, fees: The daily fee is $15. Open April through November.

Directions: Take U.S. Hwy. 31 north of Petoskey to Hwy. 119 and go 1.5 miles west to the park.

Contact: Petoskey State Park, 2475 M-119, Petoskey, MI 49770, 231/347-2311.

Trip Notes: The park is prime "pickings" for Michigan's Petoskey stones. Found on the beach, they aren't actually stones, but pieces of fossilized coral that lived at least 350 million years ago.

17 KOA Petoskey

Location: Near Petoskey close to Lake Michigan, map 1, grid F1.

Campsites, facilities: There are 206 campsites. Facilities include electric hookups, water, sewer, flush toilets, showers, laundry, wheelchair access, disposal station, grocery store/gift shop, swimming pool, hot tub, and playground. Cabin and cottage rentals are available. Swimming, boating, and fishing are nearby. Pets are not allowed.

Reservations, fees: The daily fee ranges from $22 to $32. Credit cards are accepted. Open from late April through early October.

Directions: From Petoskey, take U.S. Hwy. 31 north for two miles to the entrance.

Contact: Petoskey KOA, H. Wayne and Lorene Rose, 1800 N. U.S. Hwy. 31, Petoskey, MI 49770, 231/347-0005, fax 231/347-6999, email: petkoa@msn.com. website: www.petoskey koa.com/petoskey.

Trip Notes: After considerable time on land and water, try the air. Grand Traverse Balloons (231/947-7433) offers sunrise and sunset hot-air-balloon rides all year over the Grand Traverse Bay area. FAA-certified pilots take you for a panoramic journey of northern Michigan. The rides, however, are not wheelchair accessible.

18 Magnus Municipal Park

Location: In downtown Petoskey on Little Traverse Bay, map 1, grid F1.

Campsites, facilities: There are 75 campsites. Facilities include RV pull-through sites, electric hookups, water, sewer, flush toilets, showers, wheelchair access, disposal station, swimming beach, boating, fishing, hiking trail, and playground. Pets are not allowed.

Reservations, fees: The daily fee ranges from $12 to $16. Credit cards are accepted. Open May through mid-October.

Directions: Take U.S. Hwy. 31 to Ingalls Avenue and go one block. Turn left on Lake Street and drive one-half mile to the park entrance.

Contact: Magnus Municipal Park, 901 W. Lake St. (summer address), 101 East Lake St. (winter address), Petoskey, MI 49770, 231/347-1027 (summer), 231/347-2500 (winter).

Trip Notes: Want something different? How about sailing out of Traverse City on a two-hour cruise aboard a two-masted, gaff-rigged, topsail schooner? You can at the Traverse Tall Ship Co. (800/678-0383 or 231/941-2000). The vessels take up to 46 people for an excursion or dinner cruise. The cost is less than $40 per person and reservations are required.

19 El Rancho Alanson RV Resort

Location: Alanson near Crooked River, northeast of Petoskey, map 1, grid E2.

Campsites, facilities: There are 137 campsites. Tents are not permitted. Facilities include electric hookups, water, sewer, flush toilets, showers, swimming, pool, pond fishing, tennis and shuffleboard courts, hiking trail, and weekend planned activities. Seasonal campsite rentals are available. River and lake boating and fishing are nearby.

Reservations, fees: The daily rate is $22. Credit cards are accepted. Open May through October, but all year for seasonal campsites.

Directions: From the junction of U.S. Hwy. 31 and Hwy. 68, go one-half mile east on Hwy. 68 to the entrance on the right.

Contact: El Rancho Alanson RV Resort, 6732 M-68, #139, Alanson MI 49706, 231/548-2600.

Trip Notes: If you like to pick your own vegetables, drive about 20 miles north to Carp Lake to the Just A Plain Farm (231/537-2302) during July and August or in October to pick pumpkins and apples. Ask about their hayrides and other activities.

20 Crooked River RV Park

Location: In Alanson, on the Crooked River north of Petoskey, map 1, grid E2.

Campsites, facilities: There are 17 campsites. Facilities include RV pull-through sites, electric hookups, water, sewer, flush toilets, showers, river fishing and boating on the Crooked River or lake swimming, boating, and fishing in nearby Crooked or Burt Lakes. There are also nearby hiking and ski trails.

Reservations, fees: Reservations are recommended. The daily fee is $15. Open year-round.

Directions: From Petoskey, go eight miles north on U.S. Hwy. 31 to Hwy. 68 and then drive east on Hwy. 68 to the village of Alanson. The park is one-quarter mile east of the highway.

Contact: Crooked River RV Park, Scott Rehmann, 7384 Cheboygan St., P.O. Box 406, Alanson, MI 49706, 888/564-5534 or 231/548-5534.

Trip Notes: Take U.S. Hwy. 31 and go north about 20 miles to Just A Plain Farm, 5055 Gill Road, Carp Lake (231/537-2302; website: www.justaplainfarm.com), during the summer to pick vegetables or in October to pick pumpkins and apples. You can also get a hayride.

21 Burt Lake State Park

Location: West of Indian River on Burt Lake, map 1, grid E2.

Campsites, facilities: There are 374 campsites. Facilities include electric hookups, flush toilets, showers, disposal station, grocery and gift store, swimming beach, boat ramp, lake and river fishing, hiking trail, nature programs, and playground. Boat rentals are available.

Reservations, fees: The daily fee is $12. Credit cards are accepted. Open April through October.

Directions: From I-75, take exit 310 and go one-quarter mile west into Indian River. Turn left at the stoplight and go one-quarter mile to the campground entrance on the right.

Contact: Burt Lake State Park, 6635 State Park Dr., Indian River, MI 49749, 231/238-9392, fax 231/238-4603.

Trip Notes: Attractions in and around Mackinaw City are about 30 miles north on I-75. Elk may be spotted in and around the nearby Pigeon River State Forest. In addition, there are many other hiking, cross-country ski, and snowmobile trails in the area.

22 Yogi Bear's Jellystone Park Camp-Resort

Location: Near Indian River, map 1, grid E2.

Campsites, facilities: There are 173 campsites. Facilities include electric hookups, water, sewer, flush toilets, showers, wheelchair access, disposal station, laundry, grocery and gift store, swimming pool, mini-golf, shuffleboard courts, hiking trail, planned activities, and playground. Cabin rentals are available. Lake swimming, boating, and fishing are nearby.

Reservations, fees: Reservations are recommended. The daily fee ranges from $22 to $32. Credit cards are accepted. Open from mid-May through mid-September.

Directions: From I-75, take exit 310 and go four miles east on Hwy. 68 to the campground entrance.

Contact: Yogi Bear's Jellystone Park Camp-Resort, Clark and Barbara Tallman and Fred Jana, 2201 E. M-68, Indian River, MI 49749, 800/375-6067 or 231/238-8259.

Trip Notes: During your stay, visit the Cross in the Woods (231/238-8973), a wooden, 55-foot crucifix and outdoor shrine one mile west of I-75 on Hwy. 68.

23 Indian River RV Resort and Campground

Location: North of Indian River near Mullett and Burt Lakes, map 1, grid E2.

Campsites, facilities: There are 144 campsites. Facilities include RV pull-through sites, electric hookups, water, sewer, flush toilets, showers, wheelchair access, laundry, grocery store, swimming pool, walking trail, and a playground. Cabin rentals are available. Swimming beach, boating, and fishing are nearby. Pets are not allowed.

Reservations, fees: The daily fee ranges from $19 to $25. Credit cards are accepted. Open April through September.

Directions: From I-75, take exit 313 and go one mile north on Hwy. 27. Follow the signs to the entrance.

Contact: Indian River RV Resort and Campground, Don and Nancy Schlickau, 561 N.

Straits Hwy., Indian River, MI 49749, 888/792-2267 or 231/238-0035, fax 231/238-0036, email: iregresort@email.msn.com, website: www.michcampground.com/indianriver.

Trip Notes: If you haven't done so yet, consider taking the Star Line Mackinac Island Ferry (800/638-9892 or 906/643-7635) from St. Ignace or Mackinaw City to Mackinac Island. Be prepared to spend most of the day.

24 Onaway State Park

Location: North of Onaway on the southeast shore of Black Lake, map 1, grid E7.

Campsites, facilities: There are 85 semi-modern campsites in the 158-acre park. Facilities include electric hookups, flush toilets, showers, disposal station, swimming beach, boat ramp, fishing, nature trail, and playground.

Reservations, fees: The daily fee is $9. Credit cards are accepted. Open from mid-April through November.

Directions: From Onaway, take Hwy. 211 six miles north to the park entrance.

Contact: Onaway State Park, 3622 N. M-211, Onaway, MI 49765, and fax 517/733-8279.

Trip Notes: Onaway became a state park in 1921, one of Michigan's oldest and home to some of the last lake sturgeon in the state. The highest waterfalls in lower Michigan are only 10 miles to the east. A variety of natural sinkholes are 15 miles to the south. Old Mill Creek Historic State Park and Fort Michilimackinac, a 1700s community, are only about 45 miles to the north.

25 P.H. Hoeft State Park

Location: North of Rogers City on Lake Huron, map 2, grid E1.

Campsites, facilities: There are 142 campsites in the 301-acre park. Facilities include electric hookups, flush toilets, showers, disposal station, swimming beach, boating, fishing, hiking and cross-country ski trails, hunting area, picnic area, and playground. The park is not wheelchair-accessible. Pets are not allowed.

Reservations, fees: The daily fee is $11. Credit cards are accepted. Open from mid-April through November.

Directions: From Rogers City, take U.S. Hwy. 23 northwest for five miles to the park.

Contact: P.H. Hoeft State Park, 5001 U.S. Hwy. 23 N., Rogers City, MI 49779, 517/734-2543, fax 517/734-7051.

Trip Notes: The park is a popular staging area for anglers who fish for Lake Huron's trout and salmon by launching their boats at nearby ramps or by using local charter services. About half the park is opened for hunting. Nearby public lands also offer hunting for deer, bear, or small game. You'll also enjoy the gently rolling mixed hardwood and conifer forest. Many wildflowers bloom in spring, some of them endangered species.

NORTHERN MICHIGAN

Northern Michigan

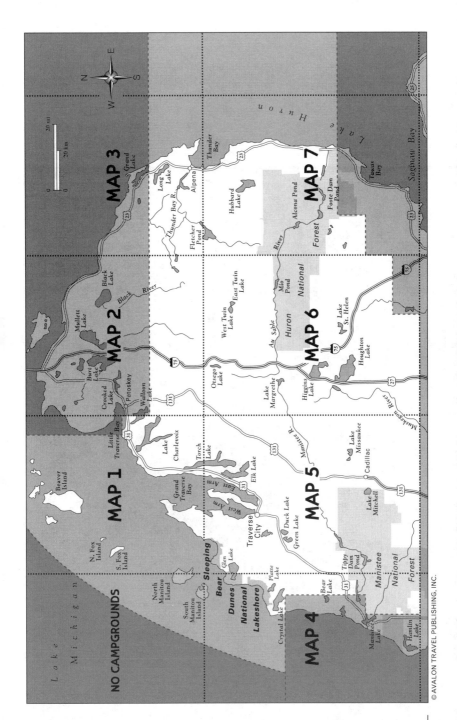

Map 1

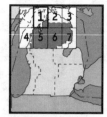

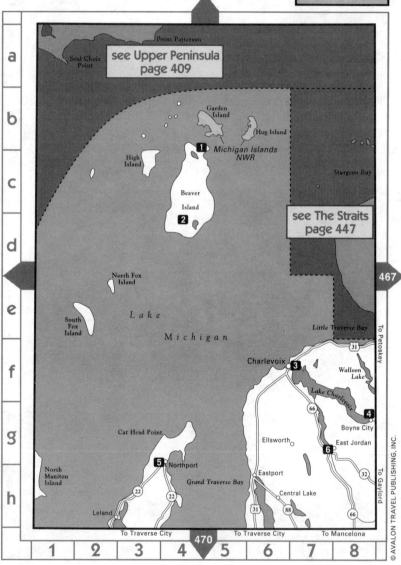

Point Patterson

see Upper Peninsula page 409

Seul Choix Point

Garden Island

Hog Island

1 Michigan Islands NWR

High Island

Sturgeon Bay

Beaver Island

2

see The Straits page 447

North Fox Island

467

South Fox Island

Lake

Michigan

Little Traverse Bay

To Petoskey

Charlevoix **3**

Walloon Lake

Lake Charlevoix

4

Boyne City

Cat Head Point

Ellsworth

6 East Jordan

North Manitou Island

5 Northport

32

To Gaylord

Eastport

Grand Traverse Bay

22

Central Lake

Leland

22

31

88

66

To Traverse City

To Traverse City

To Mancelona

470

© AVALON TRAVEL PUBLISHING, INC.

Map 2

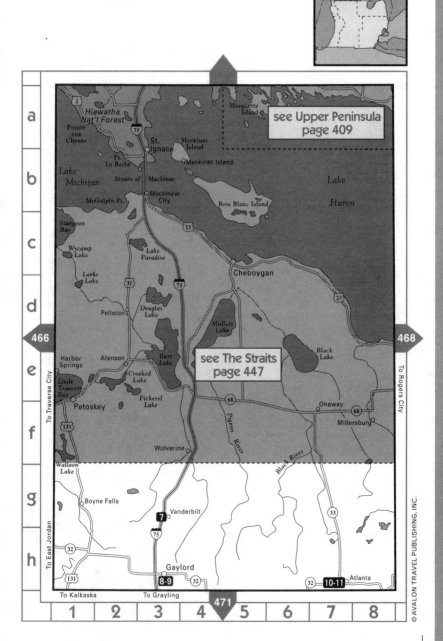

see Upper Peninsula
page 409

see The Straits
page 447

a

b

c

d
466   468

e

f

g

h

1 2 3 4 5 6 7 8

471

To Traverse City

To Rogers City

To East Jordan

To Kalkaska   To Grayling

Hiawatha Nat'l Forest
Pointe aux Chenes
Lake Michigan
St. Ignace
Pt. La Barbe
Mackinac Island
Marquette Island
Mackinac Island
Straits of Mackinac
McGulpin Pt.
Mackinaw City
Bois Blanc Island
Lake Huron
Sturgeon Bay
Wycamp Lake
Lake Paradise
Larks Lake
Cheboygan
Pellston
Douglas Lake
Mullett Lake
Harbor Springs
Alanson
Burt Lake
Black Lake
Crooked Lake
Little Traverse Bay
Pickerel Lake
Petoskey
Onaway
Millersburg
Pigeon River
Wolverine
Black River
Walloon Lake
Boyne Falls
Vanderbilt
Gaylord
Atlanta
7
8-9
10-11

© AVALON TRAVEL PUBLISHING, INC.

Map 3

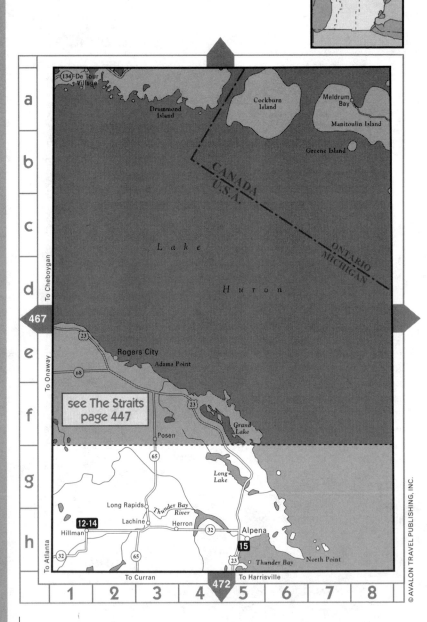

see The Straits
page 447

Map 4

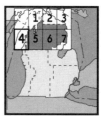

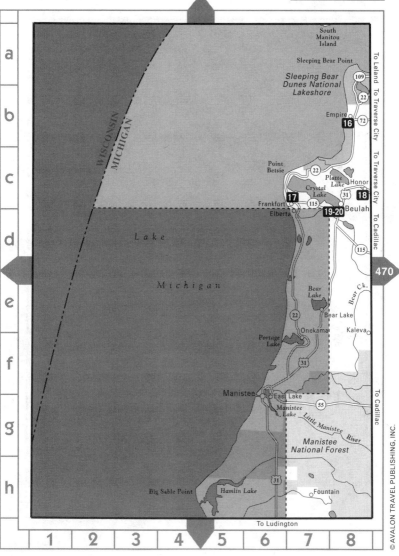

© AVALON TRAVEL PUBLISHING, INC.

Map 5

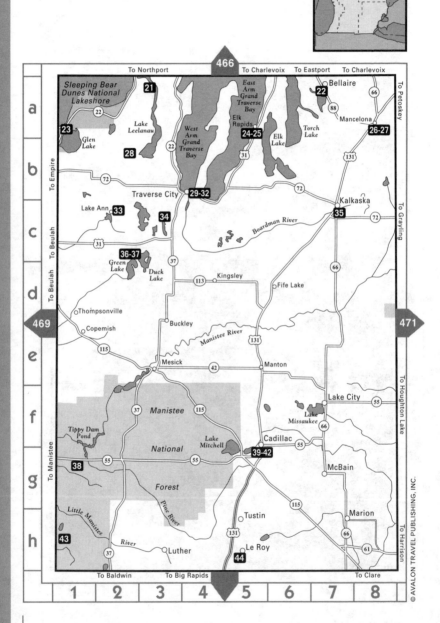

Map 6

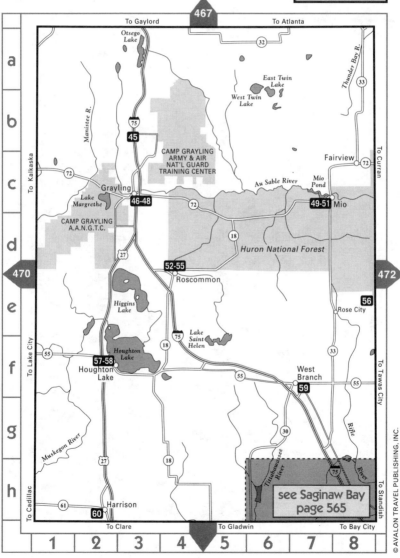

To Gaylord — 467 — To Atlanta

a

Otsego Lake

32

East Twin Lake

West Twin Lake

Thunder Bay R.

33

To Curran

b

Manistee R.

I-75

45

CAMP GRAYLING ARMY & AIR NAT'L GUARD TRAINING CENTER

Fairview

72

c

To Kalkaska

72

Grayling

46-48

72

Au Sable River

Mio Pond

49-51 Mio

Lake Margrethe

CAMP GRAYLING A.A.N.G.T.C.

d

27

52-55

18

Huron National Forest

470 — 472

Roscommon

e

Higgins Lake

Rose City

56

f

To Lake City

55

57-58

Houghton Lake

18

Lake Saint Helen

55

West Branch

59

55

To Tawas City

33

g

Muskegon River

27

18

30

Rifle River

h

To Cadillac

61

60

Harrison

Tittabawassee River

I-75

see Saginaw Bay page 565

To Standish

To Clare — To Gladwin — To Bay City

1 2 3 4 5 6 7 8

© AVALON TRAVEL PUBLISHING, INC.

Map 7

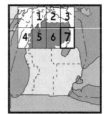

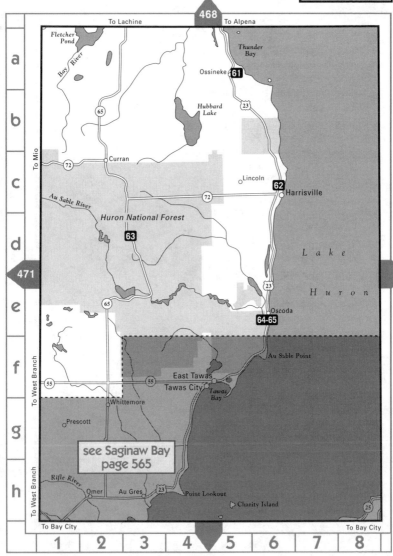

Northern Michigan

(CONTINUED ON NEXT PAGE)

F ire, wind, and water have had a significant impact on northern Michigan. The area's climate is softened by moisture-laden breezes across the waters of the Great Lakes, which has made it the world's top cherry producer and a noted wine region.

From Traverse City, at the base of the twin arms of Grand Traverse Bay, you not only have access to the historic sites of the Straits, but also to this region's dozens of challenging golf courses, hundreds of miles of streams, the arts and music mecca of Interlochen, and on the Lake Michigan shore, vast expanses of dunes.

1 Bill Wagner Memorial Campground

Location: Beaver Island, on Lake Michigan, map 1, grid C4.

Campsites, facilities: There are 25 campsites. Facilities include vault toilets, boat ramp, fishing, swimming beach, and hiking trail.

Reservations, fees: No reservations are accepted. The daily fee is $5. Register at the campground before setting up your tent. Open year-round.

Directions: Take the ferry from Charlevoix to St. James on Beaver Island. From St. James, go seven miles south on East Side Road to the campground entrance.

Contact: Chamber of Commerce, P.O. Box 5, Beaver Island, MI 49782, 231/448-2505.

Trip Notes: This 58-square mile island is the most remote inhabited island on the Great Lakes and is linked to the mainland by a 32-mile ferry ride. There are about 350 year-round residents on the island.

2 The Township Campground

Location: Near St. James, on Beaver Island in Lake Michigan, map 1, grid D4.

Campsites, facilities: There are 12 campsites for tents only. Facilities include vault toilets, picnic area, lake boating, fishing, swimming, and hiking trail.

Reservations, fees: No reservations are accepted. The daily fee is $5. Register at the campground before setting up your tent. Open year-round.

Directions: Take the ferry to St. James on Beaver Island. From town, go less than one mile on Donegal Bay Road, then take the long driveway of the road to the entrance.

Contact: Chamber of Commerce, P.O. Box 5, Beaver Island, MI 49782, 231/448-2505.

Trip Notes: In the late 1830s, the North West Trading Company built a post on the island's north shore. In 1847 James Jesse Strang founded a small Mormon colony near the trading post. The Mormons hoped to isolate themselves from the rest of society and by 1852 non-Mormans had been crowded off the island. In the mid-1850s, after Strang was murdered by two of his followers due to friction in the colony, the Mormons were forcibly removed from the island by a mob. Irish fishermen began resettling the island. The community flourished until 1960, when there were only about 150 people living on the island. There are many interesting remnants of these colonists that can be seen at the Beaver Island Historical Society, the Mormon Print Shop Museum, and the Protar Home (616/448-2254).

❸ Fisherman's Island State Park

Location: South of Charlevoix on Lake Michigan, map 1, grid F6.

Campsites, facilities: There are 90 rustic sites. Facilities include vault toilets, picnic area, three trout streams, hiking trail, swimming beach near Inwood Creek, boating, hunting area, and cross-country ski and winter hiking trails.

Reservations, fees: The daily fee is $6. Credit cards are accepted. Open April through November.

Directions: From Charlevoix, take U.S. Hwy. 31 south to Bells Bay Road and turn west to the park.

Contact: Fisherman's Island State Park, P.O. Box 456, Bells Bay Rd., Charlevoix, MI 49720, 231/547-6641.

Trip Notes: Visit the Friske Orchards (231/588-6185; website: www.friske.com) where you can, if you wish, pick your own apples, cherries, peaches, and other fruits or buy them at its farm market. The orchard, in business for nearly 40 years, is 10 miles south of Charlevoix on U.S. Hwy. 31.

❹ Young State Park

Location: Northwest of Boyne City on Lake Charlevoix, map 1, grid G8.

Campsites, facilities: The 2,678-acre park has 240 modern sites in three campgrounds—Terrace, Oak, and Spruce. Facilities include electric hookups, flush toilets, showers, disposal station, grocery store, picnic area, swimming beach, boat ramp, fishing, and nearly five miles of hiking trail. In winter, cross-country skiing is popular.

Reservations, fees: The daily fee is $15. Credit cards are accepted. Open April through November. The facilities are fully operational from mid-May through October.

Directions: From U.S. Hwy. 131, go west on Hwy. 75 through Boyne City and continue west for two miles on Boyne City Road.

Contact: Young State Park, 00280 Boyne City Rd., Boyne City, MI 49712, 231/582-7523.

Trip Notes: Located on beautiful, 17,260-acre Lake Charlevoix with depths to 122 feet, the park is terrific for sailing, power boating, water-skiing, and fishing. It offers access to Lake Michigan, too. Annually, the lake is stocked with rainbow, brown, and lake trout.

Mirror Pond, stocked with sunfish and rock bass, provides good fishing for youngsters.

5 Leelanau State Park

Location: Northport, at the tip of the peninsula on the west arm of Grand Traverse Bay, map 1, grid H4.

Campsites, facilities: There are 82 rustic sites. Facilities include wheelchair-accessible restrooms, vault toilets, swimming beach, fishing, hiking and cross-country ski trails, gift shop, and playground. Pets are allowed with restrictions.

Reservations, fees: The daily fee is $6. Credit cards are accepted. Open April through November.

Directions: From the junction of Hwys. 201 and 22, go one mile north and then 1.5 miles northeast to the end of the peninsula.

Contact: Leelanau State Park, 15310 N. Lighthouse Point Rd., Northport, MI 49670, 231/386-5422 or 231/922-5270, fax 231/386-7036.

Trip Notes: Tour the Grand Traverse Lighthouse and Museum (231/922-5270; website: www.geocities.com/Yosemite/4278/grandtraverse.html). The historic lighthouse in the Manitou Passage has guided ships for nearly 150 years, making it one of the oldest on the Great Lakes. The museum resembles a lighthouse keeper's home of the 1920s and 1930s.

6 East Jordan Tourist Park

Location: Southeast of Charlevoix on the south arm of Lake Charlevoix, map 1, grid G8.

Campsites, facilities: This municipal campground has 101 sites. Facilities include electric hookups, water, sewers, flush toilets, showers, disposal station, boat ramp, river or lake fishing, swimming beach, tennis courts, and playground. Pets are not allowed.

Reservations, fees: The daily fee ranges from $9 to $16. Credit cards are accepted. Open from mid-April to mid-October.

Directions: From the junction of Hwys. 66 and 32, go one-tenth of a mile north on Hwy. 66 to the southern end of Lake Charlevoix to the corner of Hwys. 66 and 32. The entrance is on the right.

Contact: East Jordan Tourist Park, 418 N. Lake St., East Jordan, MI 49727, 231/536-2561.

Trip Notes: With hands-on displays, the Raven Hill Discovery Center (231/536-3369; website: www.nature.org.) links science, history, and the arts. It includes a museum area, live exotic animals, a one-room school, and an art center. The center is between East Jordan and Boyne City just off Hwy. 48 (Boyne City-East Jordan Road) at Peargall Road.

7 Mackinaw State Forest: Pickerel Lake Campground

Location: Vanderbilt, on Pickerel Lake southeast of Charlevoix, map 2, grid G3.

Campsites, facilities: There are 43 rustic sites. Facilities include wheelchair-accessible sites and restrooms, vault toilets, swimming beach, boat ramp (no motors are permitted) fishing, and 1.9-mile hiking trail. Pets and horses are not allowed.

Reservations, fees: The daily fee is $6. Open year-round.

Directions: From U.S. Hwy. 131, turn east on Rabourn Road (Manistee Lake Road) north of Kalkaska past Darragh. Continue west on County Road 612 to Sunset Trail N.E. Then turn north to Pickerel Lake.

Contact: Pickerel Lake Campground, Pickerel Lake Rd., Kalkaska, MI 49646, 231/258-2711.

Trip Notes: Visit one of the more than 100 nature preserves in Charlevoix and other northern Michigan counties established by the Little Traverse Conservancy (231/347-0991; website: www.lantruss.org). Many have nature trails or beach access. A guide with maps is available by phoning or writing the organization at 3264 Powell Rd., Harbor Springs, MI 49740.

🞸 KOA-Gaylord Michaywe' Wilderness Resort

Location: South of Gaylord on the Au Sable River, map 2, grid H3.

Campsites, facilities: There are 120 campsites. Facilities include RV pull-through sites, electric hookups, water, flush toilets, showers, camping cabins and cottages, laundry, disposal station, grocery store, gift shop, swimming pool, river swimming, fishing, tennis courts, mini-golf, bike and hiking trails, and playground. Lake boating and fishing are nearby. Pets are allowed.

Reservations, fees: The daily fee ranges from $21 to $28. Credit cards are accepted. Open from mid-April to mid-October.

Directions: From I-75, take exit 279 and go south for two miles on Old Hwy. 27 to Charles Brink Road. Then go one mile east to the campground.

Contact: KOA-Gaylord Michaywe' Wilderness Resort, 5101 Campfires Pkwy., Gaylord, MI 49735, 800/562-4146 or 517/939-8723.

Trip Notes: An unusual attraction is the Bottle Cap Museum (517/732-1931). It houses the largest Coca-Cola collection in northern Michigan. Travel one mile east of I-75 on Hwy. 32. At the edge of Gaylord, take F-44 left and follow it for five miles to 4977 Sparr Road next to Sparr Mall.

🞩 Otsego Lake State Park

Location: South of Gaylord on Otsego Lake, map 2, grid H3.

Campsites, facilities: There are 155 campsites in two locations in this 62-acre park—the North Campground and the South Campground. Sites in the former are slightly higher and overlook the lake; the latter sites are lower and closer to the lake. Facilities include electric hookups, flush toilets, showers, disposal station, laundry, grocery store, swimming beach, beach house, fishing, boat ramp, picnic area, and two playgrounds. There are no designated hiking trails, but there are paths through a wooded area where you can pick blueberries or look for the rare, protected wild orchid, the Lady's Slipper. Boat rentals are available.

Reservations, fees: The daily fee is $14. Credit cards are accepted. Open April through November. The facilities are fully operational May through October.

Directions: From I-75 and the village of Waters, go one-half mile west to Old Hwy. 27 and then go north on Hwy. 27 for about five miles to the park.

Contact: Otsego Lake State Park, 7136 Old Hwy. 27 S., Gaylord, MI 49735, 517/732-5485.

Trip Notes: An easy drive south down I-75 takes you to the Grayling Historical Museum (517/348-4461). It consists of six buildings housing railroad, logging, military, trapping, fire fighting, and farm memorabilia. It's wheelchair accessible. Take exit 254 and the Business Loop to the second stoplight. Turn left and go one block to 97 Michigan Avenue.

🔟 Clear Lake State Park

Location: North of Atlanta on Clear Lake, map 2, grid H7.

Campsites, facilities: There are 200 modern sites on the north shore of Clear Lake in this 290-acre park. Facilities include electric hookups, flush toilets, disposal station, swimming beach, boat ramp, fishing, picnic areas, hiking trails, and playground.

Reservations, fees: The daily fee is $12. Credit cards are accepted. Open from mid-April through November.

Directions: From the junction of Hwys. 32 and 33, go eight miles north on Hwy. 33 to the park.

Contact: Clear Lake State Park, 20500 M-33, Atlanta, MI 49709, 517/785-4388.

Trip Notes: From the park, you have access to more than 70 miles of biking and hiking trails. A 4.5-mile groomed cross-county ski trail runs from the park to Canada Creek. Near the park, there are snowmobile trails, too. There's also excellent canoeing in the nearby Au Sable and Thunder Bay Rivers.

🔟🔟 Mackinaw State Forest: Jackson Lake Campground

Location: North of Atlanta near Jackson Lake, map 2, grid H7.

Campsites, facilities: There are 25 primitive sites. Facilities include vault toilets, swimming beach, boating (no motors are permitted), fishing, and biking and hiking trails. Pets are not allowed.

Reservations, fees: No reservations are accepted. The daily fee is $6. Open year-round.

Directions: From the junction of Hwys. 32 and 33, go north for six miles on Hwy. 33.

Contact: Jackson Lake Campground, M-33, Atlanta, MI 49709, 517/785-4251, fax 517/785-3513.

Trip Notes: Tour the Alpena flour mills, a Michigan Historic Site built in 1914. Much of the original equipment is still in place, but it now houses the Bayviewer Chair Co. (517/356-0438), makers of handcrafted cedar outdoor furniture. Just take Hwy. 32 to Alpena and Ripley, turning south on Ripley to Campbell. Then turn east on Campbell and go two blocks.

🔟🔟 Lyons' Landing and Travel Trailer Park

Location: Hillman on Fletcher Pond, map 3, grid H1.

Campsites, facilities: There are 35 campsites. Facilities include RV pull-through sites, electric hookups, water, flush toilets, showers, disposal station, boat ramp and dock, fishing, swimming beach, and hiking trail. Boat rentals are available. Pets are allowed.

Reservations, fees: The daily rate is $12. Open year-round.

Directions: From town, go four miles southwest on Hwy. 32, then one mile east on Landing Road to the entrance.

Contact: Lyons' Landing and Travel Trailer Park, tel. 517/742-4756.

Trip Notes: The campground is only minutes away from the port town of Alpena. Be sure to visit one of the many festivals at Alpena, such as Log Cabin Days in June, or the Michigan Brown Trout Festival or the Art on the Bay Festival in July (800/4-ALPENA; website: www.oweb/upnorth/cvb/home.html).

13 Long Lake Resort and Campgrounds/RV Park

Location: Hillman, west of Alpena, map 3, grid H1.

Campsites, facilities: There are 27 campsites. Facilities include RV pull-through sites, electric hookups, water, flush toilets, showers, partial wheelchair access, disposal station, grocery store, gift shop, swimming beach, hiking trail, and playground. Boat, fishing gear, and seasonal campsite rentals are available.

Reservations, fees: The daily fee is $17. Credit cards are accepted. Open May through October.

Directions: From I-75, exit on Hwy. 32 and go east to Hillman. Go north through Hillman to County Road 459 and west to North Shore Drive. Turn left and go two miles to the entrance.

Contact: Long Lake Resort and Campgrounds/RV Park, 20510 North Shore Dr., Hillman, MI 49746, 517/742-4347, website: www.fishwebb.com.

Trip Notes: Take a two-hour, 10-mile-long, stern-paddlewheel boat cruise (517/739-7351) on the Au Sable River aboard the "River Queen," which carries up to 173 passengers. The boat is wheelchair accessible. The dock is on River Road, six miles west of U.S. Hwy. 23.

14 Jack's Landing Resort and Restaurant

Location: Hillman, west of Alpena, map 3, grid H1.

Campsites, facilities: There are 24 campsites. Facilities include electric hookups, water, flush toilets, showers, grocery store, restaurant, boating, canoeing, fishing, and playground. Boat and cabin rentals are available. Pets are allowed.

Reservations, fees: The daily fee ranges from $12 to $22. Open May through November and January through March.

Directions: From Hillman, go two miles east on Hwy. 32 to Jack's Landing Road and drive five miles south to the campground. Follow the signs.

Contact: Jack's Landing Resort and Restaurant, Dean and Ann Robinson, 20836 Tennis Rd., Hillman, MI 49746, 517/742-4370.

Trip Notes: Be sure to sample the angling. The resort is on the north shore of Fletcher Pond floodwaters, one of Michigan's largest inland waters—8,600 acres of warm water habitat that is noted for its northern pike, bass, yellow perch, and panfish.

15 Campers Cove RV Park

Location: Alpena on Lake Wynich near Lake Huron, map 3, grid H5.

Campsites, facilities: There are 80 campsites. Facilities include RV pull-through sites, electric hookups, water, sewer, flush toilets, showers, disposal station, laundry, grocery store, indoor swimming pool, boat ramp, fishing, mini-golf, and shuffleboard courts. RV and tent rentals are available. Pets are allowed.

Reservations, fees: The daily fee ranges from $14 to $24. Open May through October.

Directions: From Hwy. 32, take U.S. Hwy. 23 in north Alpena and turn west on Long Rapids Road to the campground.

Contact: Campers Cove RV Park, Bruce and Joann Canady, 5005 Long Rapids Rd., Alpena, MI 49707, 517/356-3708 or 888/306-3708,

website: www.michcampgrounds.com/campers
cove.

Trip Notes: There's a lot to do around Alpena—charter fishing on Lake Huron, diving to preserved shipwrecks in Thunder Bay, and touring the Old Presque Isle Lighthouse and Museum. You can also feed the resident wildfowl on Island Park and at the Alpena Wildfowl Sanctuary, or golf at many nearby courses.

16 Sleepy Bear Campground

Location: Near Empire, map 4, grid B8.
Campsites, facilities: There are 191 campsites. Facilities include RV pull-through sites, electric hookups, water, sewer, flush toilets, showers, wheelchair access, laundry, grocery store, heated outdoor swimming pool, hiking trail, and playground. Cabin rentals are available. Pets are allowed.
Reservations, fees: The daily fee ranges from $20 to $30. Open from mid-May through mid-October.
Directions: From Traverse City, take Hwy. 72 west for 18 miles or three miles east of Empire to the campground.
Contact: Sleeping Bear Campground, Ray and Mary Savage, 6760 W. Empire Hwy. (M-72), Empire, MI 49630, 231/326-5566, fax 231/326-5711.
Trip Notes: This facility is just north of Sleeping Bear Dunes National Lakeshore (231/326-5134) and its outdoor opportunities. Another option is to drive to Maple City a few miles east to visit Westover Market (231/228-5514). During berry season you can pick your own blueberries, black and red raspberries, and gooseberries, and enjoy many homemade products. Call for time and crops available.

17 Betsie River Campsite

Location: Frankfort, on Lake Michigan, map 4, grid C7.
Campsites, facilities: There are 100 campsites. Facilities include RV pull-through sites, electric hookups, water, flush toilets, showers, disposal station, grocery store, hiking trail, lake boating, fishing, swimming beach, and playground. Some RV and seasonal campsite rentals are available. Pets are allowed.
Reservations, fees: The daily fee ranges from $15 to $17. Credit cards are accepted. Open April through November.
Directions: From the junction of Hwy. 115 and U.S. Hwy. 31, go one block on Hwy. 31 and then five miles west on Traverse Avenue/River Road/Hwy. 608 to the entrance on the left.
Contact: Betsie River Campsite, Wilbert and Barbara Lavely, 1923 River Rd., Frankfort, MI 49635, 231/352-9535, email: brcs@benzie.com.
Trip Notes: Frankfort is known for its excellent salmon, trout, and perch fishing in Lake Michigan or off Frankfort's piers. There are also several other inland lakes nearby. The campground provides fish-cleaning stations and freezing of your catch. There is a spectacular fall color tour, excellent hunting, and ice fishing in the area.

18 Sleeping Bear Dunes National Lakeshore: Platte River Campground

Location: Near Empire, on Lake Michigan, map 4, grid C8.
Campsites, facilities: There are 179 campsites. Facilities include RV pull-through

sites, walk-in tent sites, electric hookups, flush toilets, showers, disposal station, river swimming, boating, fishing, hiking trails, and ranger-led campfire programs during the season. Crystal Mountain Resort for downhill skiing, snowboarding, cross-country skiing, and entertainment is nearby. Pets are allowed.

Reservations, fees: Only 48 sites can be reserved. The daily fee ranges from $10 to $19 plus a park pass. Open year-round.

Directions: From Traverse City, take U.S. Hwy. 31 south and west to County Road 679 north and west to Hwy. 22, turning south to the campground at Peterson Road.

Contact: Sleeping Bear Dunes National Lakeshore, 9922 Front St., Empire, MI 49630, 231/325-5881.

Trip Notes: The lakeshore park's lakes and rivers offer you plenty of opportunities for swimming, boating, and fishing. Canoes can be rented on the Platte and Crystal Rivers. Anglers can fish for trout, northern pike, bass, and salmon. In winter, about 50 miles of trails are marked for cross-country skiing. Get a map at the visitor center. Snowmobiling, however, is prohibited except on rights-of-way along some state and county roads.

19 Timberline Campground

Location: Benzonia, east of Frankfort, map 4, grid D8.

Campsites, facilities: There are 189 campsites. Facilities include RV pull-through sites, electric hookups, water, flush toilets, showers, disposal station, swimming pool, and playground. River boating and fishing are nearby. Seasonal campsite rentals are available. Pets are allowed.

Reservations, fees: The daily fee ranges from $14 to $18. Open year-round.

Directions: From the junction of U.S. Hwy. 31 and Hwy. 115, go north on Hwys. 31/15 to the entrance on the left.

Contact: Timberline Campground, 2788 Benzie Hwy., U.S. Hwy. 31, Benzonia, MI 49616, 231/882-9548.

Trip Notes: The campground is minutes from the Betsie and Platte Rivers, Crystal Lake, and Lake Michigan for some excellent fishing and boating.

While in the area, visit the Northwest Michigan Maritime Museum and Manitou Underwater Preserve (231/352-6106). It's one of the state's largest maritime facilities and offers an exhibit gallery, theater, research library, and archives. The museum is one-half block north of the Hwy. 115 west and Hwy. 31 intersection on the hill in Benzonia.

20 Vacation Trailer Park

Location: Benzonia, east of Frankfort, map 4, grid D8.

Campsites, facilities: There are 100 campsites. Facilities include electric hookups, water, flush toilets, showers, disposal station, laundry, grocery store, swimming pool, river and lake boating, fishing, hiking trail, and playground. Boat, cabin, and RV rentals are available. Pets are allowed.

Reservations, fees: The daily fee ranges from $19 to $21. Credit cards are accepted. Open March through November.

Directions: From the south junction of Hwy. 115 and U.S. Hwy 31, go one mile north on Hwy. 31 at the Betsie River Bridge to the entrance on the left.

Contact: Timberline Campground, Bill and Betty Workman, 2080 Benzie Hwy., Benzonia, MI 49616, 231/882-5101 or

800/482-5101, fax 231/882-4687, website: www.vacationtrailer.com.

Trip Notes: This facility provides campers with a complete sporting goods/RV supplies/RV dealership store. You can enjoy trout and steelhead fishing or canoeing and kayaking in the Betsie River.

21 Lake Leelanau RV Park

Location: Northwest of Traverse City on Lake Leelanau, map 5, grid A2.

Campsites, facilities: There are 196 campsites. Facilities include RV pull-through sites, electric hookups, water, sewer, flush toilets, showers, laundry, disposal station, swimming beach, fishing, boat ramp and dock, children's programs, and playground. Boat rentals are available. Pets are allowed.

Reservations, fees: The daily fee ranges from $26 to $32. Open May through mid-October.

Directions: From Traverse City, take Hwy. 22 north to Sutton's Bay and turn west on Hwy. 204 for four miles to Lake Leelanau. Turn south at Dick's Pourhouse (Lake Shore Drive) and go 3.5 miles to the campground.

Contact: Lake Leelanau RV Park, Donald and Marilyn Wilson, 3101 Lake Shore Dr., Lake Leelanau, MI 49653, 231/256-7236, email: donrrman@aol.com.

Trip Notes: Because the campground is on 18-mile-long Lake Leelanau, it offers excellent opportunities for all water sports.

22 Chain O'Lakes Campground

Location: Near Bellaire, northeast of Traverse City, map 5, grid A7.

Campsites, facilities: There are 78 campsites. Facilities include RV pull-through sites, electric hookups, water, sewer, flush toilets, showers, laundry, disposal station, swimming pool, and hiking trail. Creek and lake boating, canoeing, fishing, and cross-country and downhill skiing are nearby. Cabin and RV rentals are available. Pets are allowed.

Reservations, fees: The daily fee ranges from $18 to $22. Open year-round.

Directions: From Bellaire, go four miles south on Hwy. 88.

Contact: Chain O'Lakes Campground, Greta and Louis Zaka, 7231 S. M-88, Bellaire, MI 49615, 231/533-8432.

Trip Notes: This campground is just minutes away from five nice golf courses, a number of good fishing lakes, and two ski resorts. During the season, you can hunt for morel mushrooms or visit Clam Lake Orchard (231/533-6497) where you can pick more than 30 varieties of apples from dwarf and semidwarf trees. Call for picking times.

23 Sleeping Bear Dunes National Lakeshore: D.H. Day Campground

Location: Near Empire on Lake Michigan, map 5, grid A1.

Campsites, facilities: The 71,187-acre national lakeshore has 88 rustic campsites. Facilities include flush toilets, some wheelchair access, disposal station, swimming beach, boating, fishing, hiking trails, and ranger-led campfire programs during the season. Pets are allowed with restrictions.

Reservations, fees: No reservations are accepted. The daily fee is $10 plus a park pass. Open from early May through mid-October.

Directions: From the junction of Hwys. 22 and 109, go one mile west on Hwy. 109.

Contact: Sleeping Bear Dunes National Lakeshore, 9922 Front St., Empire, MI 49630, 231/326-5134.

Trip Notes: Explore the dunes. Climbing to the top at the Dune Climb is strenuous, but rewarding. From the crest, you can see Glen Lake. You also can hike the Dunes Trail, a 3.5-mile round-trip or walk a 2.8-mile loop trail to Sleeping Bear Point. Watch the youngsters; it's easy to get lost here! Wear shoes to protect your feet and stay on designated trails to prevent erosion and damage to vegetation. Bikes are not allowed off the roads.

Be sure to visit the Sleeping Bear Point Maritime Museum, too. It's one mile west of Glen Haven on Hwy. 209 in the restored U.S. Coast Guard Station.

24 Honcho Rest Campground

Location: Near Elk Rapids on Bass Lake, map 5, grid A5.

Campsites, facilities: There are 50 modern campsites. Facilities include RV pull-through sites (no tents allowed), electric hookups, water, sewer, flush toilets, showers, laundry, partial wheelchair access, disposal station, swimming beach, boat dock, fishing, and playground. Boat rentals are available. Pets are not allowed.

Reservations, fees: Reservations are recommended. The daily fee is about $22. Credit cards are accepted. Open from late May through mid-October.

Directions: In Elk Rapids, go east at the stoplight (Ames Street). After 1.25 miles, it becomes Cairn Hwy. Watch for the sign on the left to the campground, which is on the east shore of Bass Lake.

Contact: Honcho Rest Campground, Robert and Johanna Wilder, 8988 Cairn Hwy., P.O. Box 65, Elk Rapids, MI 49629, 888/358-8695 or 231/264-8548, fax 231/264-6849.

Trip Notes: You might stop at the Brumm Galleries in Charlevoix (231/547-4085). It features plates, enamel sculpture, and sun-catchers. Other items include rocks, minerals, and a large variety of jewelry. It's one mile from Charlevoix Airport on U.S. Hwy. 31 going south and is on the left side of the road.

25 Vacation Village Waterfront Campground

Location: In Elk Rapids on Bass Lake, map 5, grid A5.

Campsites, facilities: There are 80 campsites. Facilities include RV pull-through sites, electric hookups, water, sewer, flush toilets, showers, disposal station, swimming beach, boating, canoeing, fishing, and playground. Boat rentals are available. Pets are allowed.

Reservations, fees: The daily fee ranges from $17 to $21. Open from mid-May through September.

Directions: In Elk Rapids turn east at the stoplight (Ames Street) and go one mile to the entrance on the left across from the golf course.

Contact: Vacation Village Waterfront Campground, 509 Lake St., Elk Rapids, MI 49629, 231/264-8636.

Trip Notes: If you love to golf or fish, this is the spot for you. There's fishing in Bass Lake and in Lake Michigan, and a public golf course is just across the road.

26 Rapid River Campground

Location: Mancelona, northeast of Traverse City, map 5, grid A8.

Campsites, facilities: There are 63 campsites. Facilities include RV pull-through sites, electric hookups, water, flush toilets, showers, wheelchair access, laundry, disposal station, grocery store, river boating, canoeing, fishing, snowmobiling, and playground. Golfing and cross-country and downhill skiing are nearby. Cabin rentals are available. Pets are allowed.

Reservations, fees: The daily fee ranges from $15 to $17. Credit cards are accepted. Open year-round.

Directions: From Kalkaska, take U.S. Hwy. 131 five miles to the campground on the right.

Contact: Rapid River Campground, Rick and Linda Legue, 7182 U.S. Hwy. 131, Mancelona, MI 49659, 231/258-2042 or 888/246-2267, email: rapidv@freeway.net.

Trip Notes: This 27-acre campground is next to public land and home of the National Trout Festival. You can camp at the lower campground near the river in your tent or the upper campground in your RV. In winter, you can snowmobile from your site.

27 Antrim 131 RV Campground

Location: Near Mancelona, northeast of Traverse City, map 5, grid A8.

Campsites, facilities: There are 23 campsites. Facilities include RV pull-through sites, electric hookups, water, flush toilets, showers, disposal station, and laundry. Opportunities to hunt, fish, and golf are nearby. Pets are not allowed.

Reservations, fees: The daily fee ranges from $14 to $17. Open from mid-April through mid-October.

Directions: In Mancelona, go one mile south of the stoplight on U.S. Hwy. 131 to E. Elder Road to the entrance.

Contact: Antrim 131 RV Campground, Alfred and Joyce Cannarile, 764 E. Elder Rd., Mancelona, MI 49659, 231/587-5665.

Trip Notes: Here, you're about one hour south of the Mackinac Bridge, near Schuss Mountain and Shanty Creek Resorts, and a great area for mushrooming.

28 Leelanau Pines Campground

Location: Near Cedar, on Lake Leelanau, map 5, grid B2.

Campsites, facilities: There are 152 campsites. Facilities include electric hookups, water, flush toilets, showers, disposal station, laundry, grocery store, gift shop, boat ramp, swimming beach, hiking trail, and playground. Boat rentals are available. Pets are not allowed.

Reservations, fees: The daily fee ranges from $21 to $30. Credit cards are accepted. Open May through mid-October.

Directions: From Traverse City, take Hwy. 72 to County Road 651. Turn right, going through the village of Cedar, and turn right on County Road 645. Go one-half mile to County Road 643 and turn right, driving another 3.5 miles to the campground.

Contact: Leelanau Pines Campground, Carol and David Novak, 6500 E. Leelanau Pines Dr., Cedar, MI 49621, 231/228-5742, fax 231/228-4393.

Trip Notes: Check with the Traverse City Convention and Visitors Bureau (231/947-1120 or 800/872-8377) for the exact dates of the National Cherry Festival in July and plan to camp during the event.

29 Traverse City South KOA

Location: Near Traverse City, map 5, grid B3.

Campsites, facilities: There are 110 campsites. Facilities include RV pull-through sites, electric hookups, water, flush toilets, showers, disposal station, laundry, grocery store, gift shop, heated outdoor swimming pool, wagon rides, petting farm, and playground. Cabin rentals are available. Lake boating, canoeing, and fishing are nearby. Pets are not allowed.

Reservations, fees: The daily fee ranges from $21 to $30. Credit cards are accepted. Open May through mid-October.

Directions: From Buckley, 15 miles of Traverse City, go three miles on Hwy. 37 to the entrance on the right.

Contact: Traverse City South KOA, David and Cathy Kuebler, 9700 S. M-37, Buckley, MI 49620, 800/562-0280 or 231/269-4562, email: gtcamping@coslink.com.

Trip Notes: Take the scenic drive along the Old Mission Peninsula to the tip; it's claimed to be midway between the North Pole and the equator. Stop to see the Old Mission Lighthouse and have some refreshment at the Old Mission Tavern before touring the 15,000-square-foot art gallery, featuring local artists and some from around the world.

30 Yogi Bear's Jellystone Park-Traverse City

Location: Near Traverse City, map 5, grid B3.

Campsites, facilities: There are 212 campsites. Facilities include RV pull-through sites, electric hookups, water, flush toilets, showers, wheelchair access, disposal station, laundry, grocery store, heated outdoor swimming pool,

mini-golf course, and hiking trail. Cabin rentals are available. Lake boating, canoeing, and fishing are nearby. Pets are not allowed.

Reservations, fees: The daily fee ranges from $25 to $42. Credit cards are accepted. Open May through mid-October.

Directions: From the junction of U.S. Hwy. 31 and Hwy. 72, go five miles east to Four Mile Road and go two miles south to Hammond Road. Drive two miles east on Hammond Road to the entrance on the left.

Contact: Yogi Bear's Jellystone Park-Traverse City, 4050 Hammond Rd., Traverse City, MI 49684, 800/909-2327 or 231/947-2770.

Trip Notes: Looking for adventure? Take a cruise on the Tall Ship "Malabar," a 105-foot, two-masted topsail schooner or the 114-foot "Manitou" (800/968-8800 or 231/941-2000).

31 Traverse City State Park

Location: East of downtown Traverse City on Grand Traverse Bay, map 5, grid B3.

Campsites, facilities: The 45-acre park has 342 campsites. Facilities include electric hookups, flush toilets, showers, disposal station, swimming beach, boating, canoeing, fishing, picnic area, and paved bike trail. Rustic cabin rentals are available. Pets are allowed with restrictions.

Reservations, fees: The daily fee is $15. Credit cards are accepted. Open year-round.

Directions: Take U.S. Hwy. 31 three miles east of downtown Traverse City to the park.

Contact: Traverse City State Park, 1132 U.S. Hwy. 31 North, Traverse City, MI 49686, 231/922-5270, fax 231/922-5323.

Trip Notes: With one-quarter mile of sandy beach along the east arm of Grand Traverse Bay, this urban state park, once home to the Ottawa branch of the Algonquin

Indians, is an ideal getaway spot for swimming, sunbathing, boating, fishing, and camping.

③② Pere Marquette State Forest: Arbutus Lake Number 4

Location: Traverse City, map 5, grid B3.

Campsites, facilities: There are 33 campsites. Facilities include water, vault toilets, swimming beach, boat ramp, fishing, and hiking and cross-country ski trails. Pets are allowed with restrictions.

Reservations, fees: Reservations are accepted. The daily fee is $6. Open from late May through late August.

Directions: From Traverse City, take County Road 611 (Garfield Road), about 10 miles southeast to Potter Road and go east for 2.5 miles. Drive one-half mile south on 4 Mile Road and one-half mile east on N. Arbutus Lake Road.

Contact: Arbutus Lake Number 4, Garfield Rd. and Potter Rd., Traverse City, MI 49684, 231/922-5280, fax 517/373-2443.

Trip Notes: Visit the Interlochen Center for the Arts (231/276-7203, recorded, fax 231/276-7600; website: www.interlochen.org). The facility presents some 750 concerts, visual art exhibits, and theater and dance productions annually. The center is 16 miles southwest of Traverse City on Hwy. 137.

③③ Pere Marquette State Forest: Lake Ann Campground

Location: Lake Ann, west of Traverse City, map 5, grid C2.

Campsites, facilities: There are 30 rustic sites. Facilities include vault toilets, swimming beach, boat ramp (no motors are permitted), fishing, and a 5.8-mile hiking trail good for cross-country skiing. Pets are allowed.

Reservations, fees: The daily fee is $6. Open year-round.

Directions: From Hwy. 72, go south on County Road 667 (Reynolds Road) to the campground entrance.

Contact: Lake Ann Campground, County Road 667 (Reynolds Rd.), Lake Ann, 49650, 231/775-9727.

Trip Notes: The story of hunting and fishing in Michigan from the early days of the Native Americans to the present can be traced at the Johnson Hunting and Fishing Center (231/779-1321, recorded). You can see multimedia programs at the auditorium and a freshwater aquarium. The center is on Hwy. 115, one-half mile north of the junction with Hwy. 55, just north of Clam Lake Canal in Cadillac.

③④ Holiday Park Campground

Location: South of Traverse City on Silver Lake, map 5, grid C3.

Campsites, facilities: There are 154 campsites. Facilities include RV pull-through sites, electric hookups, water, sewer, flush toilets, showers, wheelchair access, disposal station, laundry, grocery store, gift shop, swimming beach, boat ramp, fishing, hiking trail, and playground. Boat rentals are available. Pets are allowed.

Reservations, fees: The daily fee ranges from $21 to $32. Credit cards are accepted. Open April through November.

Directions: From Traverse City, take U.S. Hwy. 31 six miles south to the campground.

Contact: Holiday Park Campground, 4860 U.S. Hwy. 31 South, Traverse City, MI 49684, 231/943-4410, website: www.michcampgrounds.com/holidaypark.

Trip Notes: Visit the Music House (231/938-9300) and see the extensive collection of some of the world's most fascinating automated musical instruments and experience an hour-long program.

35 Kalkaska Family Campground

Location: Near Kalkaska, midway between Traverse City and Grayling, map 5, grid C7.

Campsites, facilities: There are 88 campsites. Facilities include RV pull-through sites, electric hookups, water, flush toilets, showers, disposal station, laundry, grocery store, heated outdoor pool, biking and hiking trails, and playground. Lake swimming, boating, canoeing, fishing, and golfing are nearby. Cabin rentals are available.

Reservations, fees: The daily fee ranges from $18 to $21. Credit cards are accepted. Open year-round.

Directions: From Kalkaska, take U.S. Hwy. 131 south to Hwy. 72. Turn east on Hwy. 72 and go one mile to the entrance on the right.

Contact: Kalkaska Family Campground, Dan and Jodie White, 580 East M-72, Kalkaska, MI 49646, 231/258-9863, fax 231/258-9873, email: kalcamp@freeway.net.

Trip Notes: Take Hwy. 72 east to Grayling to visit Wellington Farm Park (517/348-5187; website: www.wellingtonfarmpark.org), a 60-acre environmental, historical, and educational complex. It depicts a mid-American farm of 1932. Farming is conducted daily using vintage equipment, tools, and practices. Take exit 251 and go west to the end of the road, turn left, and go less than one mile to the park on the right.

36 Interlochen State Park

Location: Near Interlochen, between Duck Lake and Green Lake south of Traverse City, map 5, grid C2.

Campsites, facilities: There are 490 modern or rustic sites. Facilities include electric hookups, flush toilets, showers, disposal station, grocery store, swimming beach, boat ramp, fishing, self-guided interpretive Pines Nature Trail, picnic area, and playground. In winter, cross-country skiing and smelt fishing on Green Lake are popular activities. Boat rentals are available. Pets are allowed.

Reservations, fees: The daily fee is $14. Open from mid-April through November.

Directions: From Traverse City, take U.S. Hwy. 31 west seven miles to Interlochen and go south on Hwy. 137 for two miles.

Contact: Interlochen State Park, M-137, Interlochen, MI 49643, 231/276-9511.

Trip Notes: Situated in one of the few remaining stands of virgin pine between Duck and Green Lakes, the 187-acre park is next to the Interlochen National Music Camp (231/276-6230 or 231/276-9221), which offers nightly musical performances by world-renowned artists from June through August.

37 Pere Marquette State Forest: Lake Dubonnet

Location: Near Interlochen, south of Traverse City, map 5, grid C2.

Campsites, facilities: This state forest campground has 50 rustic sites. Facilities include vault toilets and boat ramp (motors are not allowed). Pets are allowed with restrictions.

Reservations, fees: Reservations are accepted. The daily fee is $6. Open year-round.

Directions: From Interlochen, take U.S. Hwy. 137 west for 1.5 miles to Wildwood Road and go north one mile to the campground.

Contact: Lake Dubonnet, U.S. Hwy. 31 and Wildwood Rd., Interlochen, MI 49643, 231/775-9727, fax 231/775-9671.

Trip Notes: Near Lake Dubonnet, you can use Lost Lake Pathway, a 16.3-mile trail with flat to slightly rolling terrain for hiking or cross-country skiing.

38 Manistee National Forest: Sand Lake Campground

Location: South of Wellston on Sand Lake, map 5, grid G1.

Campsites, facilities: There are 45 campsites. Facilities include flush toilets, showers, wheelchair access, lake swimming, boat ramp, fishing for bass and bluegill, and sailing. Pets are allowed.

Reservations, fees: The daily fee is $14. Open from late May through late September.

Directions: From Wellston, take Seaman Road 3.9 miles south through Dublin. Just beyond the grocery store, the road turns right. Stay on Seaman Road for one-half mile to Sand Lake Road (Forest Road 5728) and the campground sign. Turn onto Sand Lake Road and go 0.6 mile to the campground.

Contact: Sand Lake Campground, Manistee Ranger District, 1658 Manistee Hwy., Manistee, MI 49660, 231/723-2211.

Trip Notes: Trek the one-mile Arboretum Trail, a self-guided route along Pine Creek. It meanders through stands of European, U.S., and Asian trees planted in 1940 to study their growth potential in this climate. The trail is southwest of Wellston on Pine Lake Road.

39 Camp Cadillac

Location: Near Cadillac, map 5, grid G5.

Campsites, facilities: There are 100 campsites. Facilities include RV pull-through sites, electric hookups, water, sewer, flush toilets, showers, laundry, disposal station, grocery store, outdoor swimming pool, hiking trail, petting zoo, barrel train rides, planned activities, and playground. Several large lakes for boating, canoeing, and fishing are nearby. Cabin rentals are available. Pets are allowed.

Reservations, fees: The daily fee is about $23. Open from mid-April through mid-October.

Directions: From Cadillac, go north on U.S. Hwy. 131 to 34 (Boon Rd.) and turn right and go two miles to the entrance.

Contact: Camp Cadillac, Tim and Angie Vaughan, 10621 E. 34 Rd. (Boon Rd.), Cadillac, MI 49601, 800/927-3124 or 231/775-9724, email: ves@netone.netoncom.net.

Trip Notes: Take the kids to Johnny's Game and Fish Park where they are sure to catch a rainbow trout (no license required and no limit) for a moderate fee. They can also watch the tame or wild animals and the 75-foot-long elevated "goat walk."

40 Birchwood Resort and Campground

Location: South of Cadillac one block from Lake Cadillac, map 5, grid G5.

Campsites, facilities: There are 28 campsites for RVs. Tents are not permitted. Facilities include electric hookups, water, sewer, flush toilets, showers, shuffleboard courts, and playground. One block away there is lake swimming, boating, and fishing. Golfing, hunting, snowmobiling, and cross-country and downhill skiing are nearby at Caberfae Peaks. Pets are allowed.

Reservations, fees: The daily fee ranges from $18 to $24. Credit cards are accepted. Open year-round.

Directions: From the junction of Hwys. 55 and 115, go one block south. Or from U.S. Hwy. 131, take exit 176 and go two miles north of the Hwy. 131 and Hwy. 115 junction to the entrance on the right side of Hwy. 115.

Contact: Birchwood Resort and Campground, Patricia and Harold Fairbrother, 6545 E. M-115, Cadillac, MI 49601, 800/299-9190 or 231/775-9101.

Trip Notes: Cadillac is home of the North American Snowmobile Festival, usually held in early February. More than 600 routes fan out from this old lumber town, curving along the shore of Lake Cadillac.

41 Cadillac KOA Kampground

Location: Southeast of Cadillac, map 5, grid G5.

Campsites, facilities: There are 50 campsites. Facilities include electric hookups, water, flush toilets, showers, laundry, disposal station, grocery store, swimming pool, hiking trail, mini-golf, and playground. Lake swimming, boating, canoeing, fishing, snowmobiling, cross-country skiing, and downhill skiing are nearby. Cabin and RV rentals are available. Pets are allowed.

Reservations, fees: The daily fee ranges from $19 to $22. Open May through October.

Directions: From Cadillac, take U.S. Hwy. 131 south about two miles to Hwy. 115 and

go about six miles southeast on Hwy. 115 to the entrance.

Contact: Cadillac KOA Kampground, Paul and John Stack, 23163 M-115, Tustin, MI 49688, 800/562-4072 or 231/825-2012, email: cadillac koa@prodigy.net.

Trip Notes: This area also offers the camper fishing on three lakes, canoeing on three rivers, golfing on nine courses, horseback riding, and hunting for morel mushrooms.

42 William Mitchell State Park

Location: West of Cadillac between Cadillac and Mitchell Lakes, map 5, grid G5.

Campsites, facilities: There are 215 campsites in the 334-acre park. Facilities include electric hookups, flush toilets, showers, disposal station, lake swimming, boat ramps on Lakes Mitchell and Cadillac (connected by a historic canal), hiking trails, picnic area, and playground. In winter, the area also features ice fishing, snowmobiling, snowshoeing, and cross-country skiing. Pets are allowed with restrictions.

Reservations, fees: The daily fee is $15. Credit cards are accepted. Open year-round.

Directions: From the junction of U.S. Hwy. 131 and Hwy. 115, go 3.5 miles northwest on Hwy. 115 to the park entrance.

Contact: William Mitchell State Park, 6093 E. M-115, Cadillac, MI 49601, 231/775-7911.

Trip Notes: The Heritage Nature Trail starts at the Carl T. Johnson Hunting and Fishing Center and is about 2.5 miles in length. It's actually a study area that supports a variety of plants and wildlife, including whitetail deer, wild turkeys, beavers, great blue herons, and other waterfowl. The trail is mostly a woodchip path with bridges and boardwalks for an easy hike around wetland areas.

43 Leisure Time Campground

Location: Near Irons, on Seaman Lake, east of Manistee, map 5, grid H1.

Campsites, facilities: There are 100 campsites. Facilities include electric hookups, water, sewer, flush toilets, showers, laundry, disposal station, swimming beach, boat dock (only electric motors are permitted), fishing, and playground. Boat and trailer rentals are available. Pets are allowed.

Reservations, fees: The daily fee ranges from $15 to $20. Open April through November.

Directions: From Baldwin, go north for 10 miles on Hwy. 37 and turn west on 4 Mile Road (Peacock). Then go 7.5 miles to the entrance.

Contact: Leisure Time Campground, Jim and Stacie Wolfe, 9214 W. 5 Mile Rd., Irons, MI 49644, 800/266-8214 or 231/266-8214, email: leisuretimecamp@carrinter.net.

Trip Notes: The campground is on Seaman Lake, where the 1973 and 1985 state record largemouth bass were caught. This body of water offers good fishing and there are other popular fishing lakes, as well as the Pere Marquette River, nearby. In winter, you can enjoy snowmobiling at nearby major trails or ski at Caberfae Peaks Ski Resort.

44 Rose Lake Park

Location: Le Roy, on Rose Lake south of Cadillac, map 5, grid H5.

Campsites, facilities: There are 200 campsites in this Osceola County Park. Facilities include electric hookups, water, flush toilets, showers, disposal station, grocery store, swimming beach, boating, canoeing, fishing, and mini-golf course. Pets are allowed.

Reservations, fees: The daily fee ranges from $11 to $13. Open from mid-May through mid-September.

Directions: From Le Roy, go two miles north on Old U.S. Hwy. 131, then four miles east on 18 Mile Road to the park entrance.

Contact: Rose Lake Park, 17726 Youth Dr., Le Roy, MI 49655, 231/768-4923.

Trip Notes: It may not be time to cut your own Christmas tree, but a trip to the Duddles Tree Farm (231/832-2731) just south of Le Roy in Reed City will give you a lot of information on tree farming and you can bring home some of their maple syrup.

45 Happi Days Campground and Diner

Location: Near Frederic, north of Grayling, map 6, grid B2.

Campsites, facilities: There are 40 campsites. Facilities include RV pull-through sites, electric hookups, water, flush toilets, showers, disposal station, laundry, and restaurant. Numerous lakes and rivers for boating, canoeing, and fishing are nearby. The campground is also near an area of public land hunting, and cross-country ski, downhill skiing, and snowmobile trails. Cabin rentals are available. Pets are allowed.

Reservations, fees: The daily fee ranges from $12 to $16. Open year-round.

Directions: From I-75, take exit 259 and go 1.5 miles west on Hwy. 93, then four miles north on Old Hwy. 27. Then go one block west on Batterson Road to the entrance on the right.

Contact: Happi Days Campground and Diner, Gilmar and Gail Smith, 7486 W. Batterson Rd., Frederic, MI 49733, 517/348-6115, email: hapidays@hotmail.com.

Trip Notes: Treat the family to a home-cooked breakfast or lunch at the campground's 1950s diner and enjoy the display of memorabilia. If it's winter, drive north to the Sno-Kist Tree Co., in Cheboygan (231/627-9744), where you can select and cut your own Christmas tree or take a sleigh ride. Take I-75 north to exit 322 (Riggsville Road). Go east for 3.25 miles. It's on the left side with a sign in the yard.

46 Yogi Bear's Jellystone Camp Resort-Grayling

Location: South of Grayling, map 6, grid C3.
Campsites, facilities: There are 218 campsites. Facilities include RV pull-through sites, electric hookups, water, sewer, flush toilets, showers, laundry, disposal station, grocery store, swimming pool, hiking trail, mini-golf, and playground. Cabin rentals are available. Pets are allowed.
Reservations, fees: The daily fee is $28. Open May through September.
Directions: From I-75, take exit 251 (Four Mile Road) and go four miles east to the entrance.
Contact: Yogi Bear's Jellystone Camp Resort-Grayling, Gregory and Marlene Schoo, 370 W. Four Mile Rd., Grayling, MI 49738, 517/348-2157, website: www.michcampgrounds.com/yogi bears.
Trip Notes: The Empire Area Museum (231/326-5568, recorded) to the northwest near Lake Michigan is worth a morning or afternoon. It features a turn-of-the-century saloon, blacksmith shop, sail and rail displays, lumbering exhibit, parlor, old kitchen, and a complete one-room school. There's also a barn with horse-drawn equipment. The museum is three blocks north of the Hwys. 72 and 22 intersection in Empire.

47 River Park Campground and Trout Pond

Location: Near Grayling on the east branch of the Au Sable River, map 6, grid C3.
Campsites, facilities: There are 53 campsites. Facilities include electric hookups, water, flush toilets, showers, laundry, disposal station, grocery store, river and pond fishing, and snowmobiling. Cross-country and downhill skiing are available nearby. Pets are allowed.
Reservations, fees: The daily fee ranges from $14 to $18. Open year-round.
Directions: From I-75, take exit 259 (Hwy. 93) and go three miles northeast to a dirt road (Bobcat Trail). Turn right and go two miles to the entrance. Follow the signs.
Contact: River Park Campground and Trout Pond, Dennis and Maureen Fyock, 2607 Peters Rd., P.O. Box 448, Grayling, MI 49736, 517/348-9092 or 888/517-9092, fax 517/348-1638, email: RVpark@freeway.net.
Trip Notes: For an unusual day trip, there's the Kaleva Bottle House Historic Museum (231/362-2080), a home built in the 1940s with more than 60,000 bottles. From Cadillac, take Hwy. 115 northwest to Yates Road, just before Copemish. Turn south down Yates Road and turn east to Kaleva. Watch for the signs.

48 Hartwick Pines State Park

Location: North of Grayling, map 6, grid C3.
Campsites, facilities: The park has 100 modern campsites. Facilities include RV pull-through sites, electric hookups, flush toilets, showers, disposal station, river boating, canoeing, fishing, playground, and three

hiking, cross-country ski, and snowshoe trails. Pets are allowed.

Reservations, fees: The daily fee is $14. Open May through October.

Directions: From I-75, take exit 259 turn east on Hwy. 93. Go about two miles north to entrance.

Contact: Hartwick Pines State Park, 4216 Ranger Rd., Grayling, MI 49738, 517/348-7068.

Trip Notes: The park has one of the few remaining tracts of virgin pines in the Midwest, the Michigan Forest Visitor Center, and a logging camp museum. The 9,762-acre park offers hiking, mountain biking, and fishing opportunities on two inland lakes and the east branch of the Au Sable River. The Logging Museum is open from daily, from Memorial Day to Labor Day. It's closed from November through April.

49 Mio Pine Acres Campground

Location: In Mio, east of Grayling, map 6, grid C7.

Campsites, facilities: There are 75 campsites. Facilities include RV pull-through sites, electric hookups, water, flush toilets, showers, laundry, disposal station, grocery store, and playground. River swimming, boating, canoeing, fishing, snowmobile trails, cross-country skiing, and downhill skiing are available nearby. Cabin and cottage rentals are available. Pets are allowed.

Reservations, fees: The daily fee ranges from $14 to $18. Open year-round.

Directions: From Hwy. 33, go one mile west through Mio on Hwy. 72 to the entrance.

Contact: Mio Pine Acres Campground, Wayne Purchase, 1215 West 8th St., Mio, MI 48647, 800/289-2845 or 517/826-5590, email: miocamp@northland.lib.mi.us.

Trip Notes: Located in the heart of the Huron National Forest just one-quarter mile from the Au Sable River, the surrounding area offers a variety of recreational opportunities. You can also take an Au Sable Valley Railroad Train Ride nearby. This county is home to the Kirtland's warbler, an endangered species, and this is the only known place in the world that you can take a tour and possibly spot one.

50 Oscoda County Park

Location: Mio, on the Au Sable River, east of Grayling, map 6, grid C7.

Campsites, facilities: There are 153 campsites. Facilities include electric hookups, water, flush toilets, showers, disposal station, river swimming, boating, canoeing, lake and river fishing, and hiking trail. Pets are allowed.

Reservations, fees: The daily fee ranges from $14 to $17. Open April through November.

Directions: From the junction of Hwy. 33 and Hwy. 72, on the south side of the Mio Dam.

Contact: Oscoda County Parks Dept., 1110 Jay Smith Dr., Mio, MI 48647, 989/826-5114.

Trip Notes: Mio is a city of festivals that you won't want to miss. In May, it is the Kirtland's Warbler Festival; in June, the Kids Free and Northeast Michigan Sportsmen's Club Fishing Tournaments; in both May and September, the community stages the Mio mud drag races.

51 Huron National Forest: Mack Lake Campground

Location: Near Mio, east of Grayling, on Mack Lake, map 6, grid C7.

Campsites, facilities: There are 42 campsites. Facilities include vault toilets, disposal station, boating (no motors are permitted), canoeing, and fishing.

Reservations, fees: The daily fee is $10. Open from late April through November.

Directions: From Mio, take Hwy. 33 south for 5.7 miles to County Road 604. Turn left on County Road 604 and go 3.4 miles to the campground sign. Turn left and go one mile to stop sign. Turn left on County Road 489 to the campground.

Contact: Mack Lake Campground, Mio Ranger Station, 401 Court St., Mio, MI 48547, 517/826-3252.

Trip Notes: Mack Lake, 124 acres, is a shallow body of water with a muck bottom. It's stocked with bass. Anglers can also fish for yellow perch, northern pike, bullheads, and sunfish.

52 Paddle Brave Canoe and Campground Resort

Location: North of Roscommon, on the Au Sable River, map 6, grid E4.

Campsites, facilities: There are 43 campsites, including some rustic sites. Facilities include electric hookups, water, flush toilets, showers, disposal station, grocery store, gift shop, boat ramp, river fishing, snowmobile trails, and playground. Boat and cabin rentals are available. Pets are allowed.

Reservations, fees: The daily fee is $16. Credit cards are accepted. Open year-round.

Directions: From I-75, take exit 239 (Hwy. 18) through Roscommon, to the first road past the river. Turn left on Lancewood (Steckert Bridge Road) and go two miles to the campground.

Contact: Paddle Brave Campground and Canoe Livery, 10610 Steckert Bridge Rd., Roscommon, MI 48653, 800/681-7092 or 517/275-5273.

Trip Notes: This is a terrific place to stay and paddle a canoe down the south branch of the Au Sable River.

53 Higgins Lake Family Campground

Location: Southwest of Roscommon near the Au Sable River, map 6, grid E4.

Campsites, facilities: There are 60 campsites. Facilities include electric hookups, water, sewer, flush toilets, showers, disposal station, grocery store, hiking trail, and playground. The campground is only minutes away from lake and river swimming, boating, canoeing, and fishing. Horseback riding and a golf course are also nearby. Bike rentals are available. Pets are allowed.

Reservations, fees: The daily fee is $17. Open from mid-May through mid-October.

Directions: From the junction of I-75 and Hwy. 18, take exit 239 and go south one-tenth mile on Hwy. 18 to County Road 103 (Robinson Lake Road). Go west for three miles to County Road 100 and north for one mile to the entrance on the right.

Contact: Higgins Lake Family Campground, Ed and Monica Worman, 2380 W. Burdell, Roscommon, MI 48653, 517/821-6891.

Trip Notes: If you're there for the last weekend in July, drive to Grayling to see the start of the International Canoe Marathon as the racers begin their 122-mile paddle to Oscoda on Lake Huron.

54 North and South Higgins Lake State Park

Location: Roscommon, near Higgins and Houghton Lakes, map 6, grid E4.

Campsites, facilities: The North Park has 218 campsites. The South Park has 436 campsites. Facilities include electric hookups, water, flush toilets, showers, grocery store, disposal station, swimming beach, boat ramp, fishing, biking and hiking trails, Nordic skiing, and playground. Boat rentals are available. Pets are allowed with restrictions.

Reservations, fees: The daily fee is $15. Credit cards are accepted. North Higgins is open year-round; South Higgins is open from mid-April through October.

Directions: To reach North Higgins Lake, take exit 244 from I-75 and go six miles west, following the signs to the park entrance. To reach South Higgins Lake, exit from U.S. Hwy. 27 and go six miles east to the park entrance.

Contact: North Higgins Lake State Park, 11747 N. Higgins Lake Dr., Roscommon, MI 48653, 517/821-6125, fax 517/821-9120. South Higgins Lake State Park, 106 State Park Dr., Roscommon, MI 48653, 517/821-6374.

Trip Notes: Higgins Lake, 9,000 acres, boasts a cement boat ramp. It has a variety of cold-water species, including several kinds of trout. Other species include northern pike, yellow perch, rock bass, and smelt. In winter, ice fishing, cross-country skiing, and snowmobiling are popular activities.

55 Higgins Hill RV Park

Location: Roscommon, near Higgins and Houghton Lakes, map 6, grid E4.

Campsites, facilities: There are 100 campsites. Facilities include RV pull-through sites, electric hookups, water, sewer, flush toilets, showers, laundry, disposal station, grocery store, nature trail, and playground. Lake and river swimming, fishing, boating, and canoeing are available at the Au Sable River and Higgins Lake. In winter, cross-country and downhill skiing and snowmo-

biling are available, too. Cabin rentals are available. Pets are allowed.

Reservations, fees: The daily fee ranges from $19 to $24. Credit cards are accepted. Open year-round.

Directions: From I-75, take exit 244 and go one mile west. From U.S. Hwy. 27, take the Military Road exit and go 4.5 miles east to the park entrance.

Contact: Higgins Hill RV Park, Ben and Pam Carr, 3800 W. Federal Hwy., Roscommon, MI 48653, 800/478-8151 or 517/275-8151, email: snow@snowshoecenter.com.

Trip Notes: Located on 65 acres of natural hardwoods and pine trees, the campground has lots of deer and other wildlife to see. It's also home of the Michigan Snowshoe Center.

56 Rifle River State Recreation Area

Location: Lupton, on the Rifle River, west of Lake Huron, map 6, grid E8.

Campsites, facilities: There are 181 campsites in three locations; one is on Devoe Lake and the other two are on the Rifle River. Facilities include electric hookups, flush toilets, showers, disposal station, river swimming, boat ramp (no motors are permitted), hiking and cross-country ski trails, fishing, and playground. Cabin rentals are available.

Reservations, fees: The daily fee is $6. Open April through November.

Directions: From I-75, take exit 202 and go 20 miles north on Hwy. 33 to Rose City. Go east on Rose City Road for 4.5 miles to the park entrance.

Contact: Rifle River Recreation Area, P.O. Box 98, Lupton, MI 48635, 517/473-2258.

Trip Notes: The area features 10 inland lakes and ponds for fishing, canoeing, and swimming. It is an excellent spot for viewing birds and other wildlife, especially along the 14 miles of biking, hiking, cross-country ski, and snowshoe trails, many of which are groomed for skiers. Most of the park is open to hunting and trapping during designated seasons.

57 Houghton Lake Travel Park

Location: On Houghton Lake, east of Cadillac, map 6, grid F2.

Campsites, facilities: There are 60 campsites. Facilities include RV pull-through sites, electric hookups, water, sewer, flush toilets, showers, laundry, disposal station, grocery store, swimming pool, and playground. The campground is one mile away from Houghton Lake for fishing, boating, hiking, and snowmobiling. Cabin rentals are available.

Reservations, fees: The daily fee ranges from $17 to $22. Credit cards are accepted. Open April through mid-October.

Directions: Take U.S. Hwy. 27 to Hwy. 55. Turn south off Hwy. 55 at Cloverleaf Lane to the park entrance.

Contact: Houghton Lake Travel Park, Ron and Jo Seim, 370 Cloverleaf Ln., Houghton Lake, MI 48629, 800/659-9379 or 517/422-3931, email: hnlktlpk@freeway.net.

Trip Notes: If it's rainy, a visit to the Wexford County Historical Society Museum (231/775-1717) in Cadillac would be interesting. It has displays, photographs, and other material of county history. In the downtown area take U.S. Hwy. 131 north to Beech Street. Turn right at Beech and drive up the hill to the museum.

58 Wooded Acres Family Campground

Location: South of Houghton Lake, near Houghton Lake, map 6, grid F2.

Campsites, facilities: There are 100 campsites. Facilities include RV pull-through sites, electric hookups, water, sewer, flush toilets, showers, laundry, disposal station, grocery store, swimming pool, pond fishing, shuffleboard courts, and playground. The campground is just minutes away from Houghton Lake for lake swimming, boating, canoeing, fishing, and snowmobiling. Cabin rentals are available.

Reservations, fees: The daily fee ranges from $15 to $23. Credit cards are accepted. Open year-round.

Directions: From U.S. Hwy. 27, exit on Hwy. 55 east and turn right at the second stop light at Loxley Road. Go one mile south to Federal Avenue to the entrance.

Contact: Wooded Acres Family Campground, David and Tina Dietzel, 997 Federal Ave., Houghton Lake, MI 48629, 517/422-3413, email: dietzel@freeway.net.

Trip Notes: Visit 22,000-acre Houghton Lake, the state's largest inland lake and the source of the Muskegon River. It has 32 miles of shoreline and provides winter campers with 200 miles of groomed and marked snowmobile trails. If you're in the area in winter, don't miss the Tip-Up Town USA Ice Festival with ice fishing contest, games, and lots of food. It's usually held the third and fourth weekends in January.

59 Lake George Campground

Location: Near West Branch, on Lake George, west of Lake Huron, map 6, grid F7.

Campsites, facilities: There are 97 campsites. Facilities include electric hookups, water, sewer, flush toilets, showers, laundry, disposal station, grocery store, swimming beach, boat dock, fishing, mini-golf, and playground. Bike rentals are available. Pets are allowed with restrictions.

Reservations, fees: The daily fee ranges from $21 to $24. Reservations are required for hunters. An additional fee is charged for pets. Open May through mid-October.

Directions: From I-75, take exit 212 and go south on Cook Road about three miles to Channel Lake Road. Turn right and go one mile to the campground.

Contact: Lake George Campground, Jack and Carol Keller, 3070 Elm Dr., West Branch, MI 48661, 800/374-3837 or 517/345-2700.

Trip Notes: You're bound to catch something in the campground's trout-and bass-stocked lake. On some weekends, the facility sponsors an angling competition.

60 Wilson State Park

Location: Near Harrison, on Budd Lake, map 6, grid H2.

Campsites, facilities: There are 160 campsites in this 36-acre park. Facilities include electric hookups, water, flush toilets, showers, disposal station, swimming beach, boat ramp, fishing, hiking trails, picnic area, and playgrounds. Cabin and teepee rentals are available. Pets are allowed with restrictions.

Reservations, fees: The daily fee is $14. Credit cards are accepted. Open April through November.

Directions: From Harrison, go north on Business Route 27 for one mile to the park.

Contact: Wilson State Park, 910 N. First St., Harrison, MI 48625, 517/539-3021, fax 517/539-9771.

Trip Notes: The park has a quiet, shady campground with a sandy beach on 175-acre Budd Lake, well known for muskie fishing. A modern boat ramp is outside the park at the southern end of the lake.

61 Paul Bunyan Kampground

Location: Ossineke, south of Alpena, map 7, grid A5.

Campsites, facilities: There are 80 campsites. Facilities include RV pull-through sites, electric hookups, water, sewer, flush toilets, showers, disposal station, laundry, grocery store, outdoor swimming pool, and playground. Lake Huron and Hubbard Lake are nearby for boating, canoeing, fishing, and cross-country skiing and downhill skiing. Pets are allowed.

Reservations, fees: The daily fee ranges from $14 to $18. Credit cards are accepted. Open year-round.

Directions: From Alpena, go 15 miles south on U.S. Hwy. 23 and one-quarter mile north of the Paul Bunyan and Babe statues.

Contact: Paul Bunyan Kampground, Jerry and Pam Marks, 6969 N. Huron (U.S. Hwy. 23), Spruce, MI 48762, 517/471-2921.

Trip Notes: This is a great place to stay and fish Lake Huron for salmon and walleye, hunt deer and turkey in season, sit on the beach, or take a farm tour.

62 Harrisville State Park

Location: South of Harrisville, on Lake Huron, map 7, grid C6.

Campsites, facilities: There are 229 modern campsites. Facilities include electric hookups, flush toilets, showers, disposal station, lake swimming, boating, fishing, and playground. In nearby Harrisville, there is a DNR boat ramp and access to Lake Huron. There are also bike, hiking, and cross-country ski trails. Pets are allowed with restrictions.

Reservations, fees: The daily fee is $14. Credit cards are accepted. Open from mid-April through October.

Directions: From Harrisville, take U.S. Hwy. 23 one-half mile south of the Hwy. 72 intersection to the park.

Contact: Harrisville State Park, 248 State Park Rd., P.O. Box 326, Harrisville, MI 48740, 517/724-5126, fax 517/517-5330.

Trip Notes: Within walking distance of Harrisville, the 107-acre park's campground is tucked in a stand of pine and cedar trees along the sandy Lake Huron shore. There are a number of hiking trails, including the two-mile-long Cedar Run Nature Trail. Some trails start in Harrisville and run to the Huron National Forest on Hwy. 72. Other area attractions are Sturgeon Point Lighthouse and Museum and Negwegon State Park.

63 Alcona County Park

Location: Glennie, on the Au Sable River west of Lake Huron, map 7, grid D3.

Campsites, facilities: There are 470 campsites. Facilities include electric hookups, water, flush toilets, showers, disposal station, boat ramp, swimming beach, lake and river fishing, and hiking trail. Pets are allowed.

Reservations, fees: The daily fee ranges from $8 to $18. Open April through November.

Directions: From the junction of Hwy. 72 and Hwy. 65, go seven miles south on Hwy. 65, then three miles west on Bamfield Road. Then drive 1.5 miles north on Au Sable Road to the park entrance.

Contact: Alcona County Park, 2550 S. Au Sable Rd., Glennie, MI 48737, 517/735-3881.

Trip Notes: Located on 1,100 acres of water with trophy fishing, this has become a popular canoeing and kayaking spot. From Glennie you can take one of the most beautiful scenic drives in all of northeast Michigan by taking Bamfield Road west of Glennie and following the Au Sable River to Mio. This route is radiant with color in the fall.

64 Oscoda KOA Family Resort Kampground

Location: South of Oscoda near the Au Sable River and Lake Huron, map 7, grid E6.

Campsites, facilities: There are 100 campsites. Facilities include RV pull-through sites, electric hookups, water, flush toilets, showers, laundry, disposal station, grocery store, swimming pool, biking and hiking trails, and playground. Only one-half mile south is the mouth of the Au Sable River and Lake Huron for lake swimming, boating, canoeing, and fishing. Bike and cabin rentals are available.

Reservations, fees: The daily fee ranges from $21 to $25. Credit cards are accepted. Open April through November.

Directions: From Oscoda, take U.S. Hwy. 23 to Johnson Road and turn west for 1.75 miles to the campground. Follow the signs to the park entrance.

Contact: Oscoda KOA Family Resort Kampground, Bill and Sandy Bittner, 3591 Forest Rd., Oscoda, MI 48750, 800/562-9667 or 517/739-5115.

Trip Notes: In Alpena, on the Second Avenue Bridge near the junction of Hwy. 32 and U.S. Hwy. 23, is the site of the Saginaw Treaty of 1819, the state's last treaty to be negotiated. With the pact, six million acres were ceded by the Chippewa, Ottawa, and Potawatomi tribes to the U.S. government.

65 Old Orchard Park

Location: Oscoda on Lake Huron, map 7, grid E6.

Campsites, facilities: There are 525 campsites in this Iosco County park. Facilities include electric hookups, water, flush toilets, showers, disposal station, grocery store, river and lake swimming, boat ramp, fishing, and playground. Cabin rental is available. Pets are allowed.

Reservations, fees: The daily fee ranges from $12 to $16. Open year-round.

Directions: From the junction of U.S. Hwy. 23 and River Road, go eight miles west on River Road to the park entrance.

Contact: Old Orchard Park, 883 River Rd., Oscoda, MI 48750, 517/739-7814, fax 517/739-0039, email: lschneider@oldorchardpark.com.

Trip Notes: Plan to spend the day in the 427,000-acre Huron section of the Huron-Manistee National Forest. A major attraction is the Lumberman's Monument (517/739-0728), a three-figure bronze memorial to the loggers who cut the virgin timber in Michigan in the latter part of the 19th century. You'll enjoy the interpretations of the era at the visitors center. Scenic drives, beaches, swimming, streams and lakes for trout fishing, and canoe trips down the Au Sable River are all available.

THE WEST COAST

The West Coast

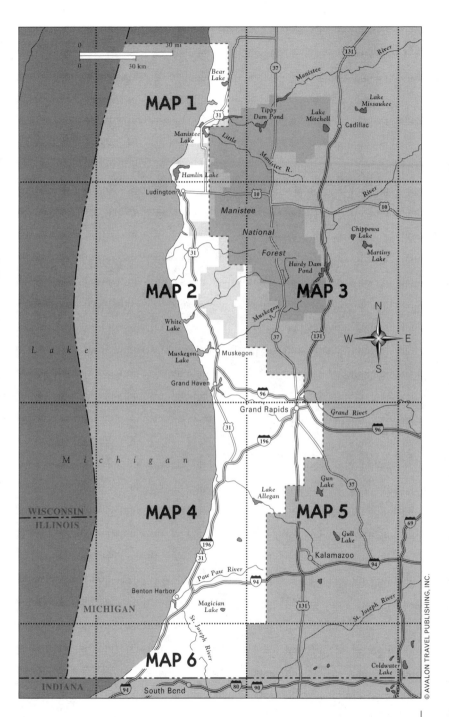

Map 1

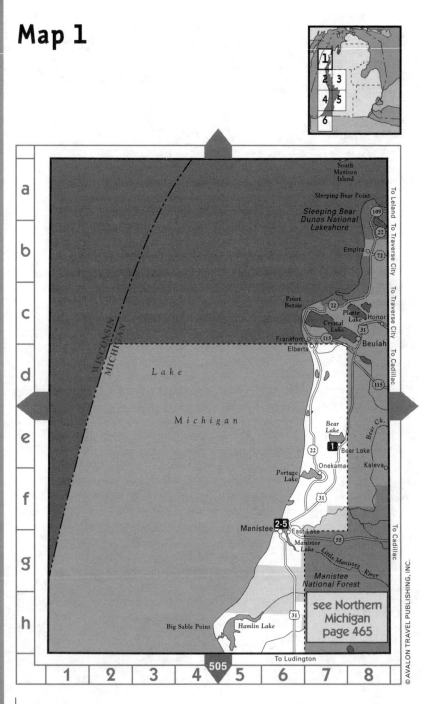

© AVALON TRAVEL PUBLISHING, INC.

see Northern
Michigan
page 465

Map 2

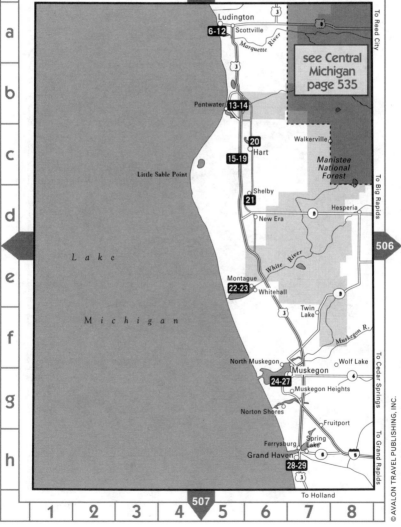

To Manistee

a

Ludington
6-12 Scottville

Marquette River

To Reed City

see Central
Michigan
page 535

b

Pentwater 13-14

20

Walkerville

c

15-19 Hart

Little Sable Point

Manistee
National
Forest

To Big Rapids

Shelby
21

d

New Era

Hesperia

506

Lake

White River

Montague
22-23 Whitehall

e

Michigan

Twin
Lake

f

Muskegon R.

North Muskegon

Wolf Lake

Muskegon
24-27

Muskegon Heights

To Cedar Springs

g

Norton Shores

Fruitport

To Grand Rapids

h

Ferrysburg Spring
Lake
Grand Haven
28-29

To Holland

© AVALON TRAVEL PUBLISHING, INC.

1 2 3 4 507 5 6 7 8

Map 3

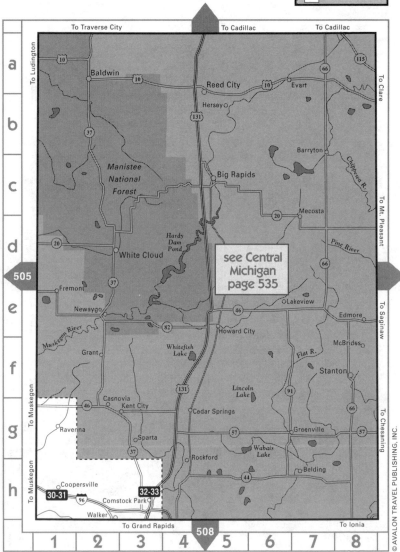

To Traverse City
To Cadillac
To Cadillac

a

To Ludington

Baldwin
Reed City
Evart
Hersey

b

Barryton
Chippewa R.

Manistee
National
Forest
Big Rapids

c

Mecosta

To Mt. Pleasant

Hardy
Dam
Pond

d

White Cloud

Pine River

**see Central
Michigan
page 535**

505

Fremont

e

Newaygo
Lakeview
Edmore

To Saginaw

Muskegon River
Grant
Whitefish
Lake
Howard City
McBrides
Flat R.

f

Stanton

Lincoln
Lake

To Muskegon

Casnovia
Kent City
Cedar Springs

g

Ravenna
Sparta
Wabasis
Lake
Greenville

To Chesaning

Rockford
Belding

h

To Muskegon

Coopersville
30-31
96
Comstock Park
32-33
Walker

To Grand Rapids
508
To Ionia

1 2 3 4 5 6 7 8

© AVALON TRAVEL PUBLISHING, INC.

Map 4

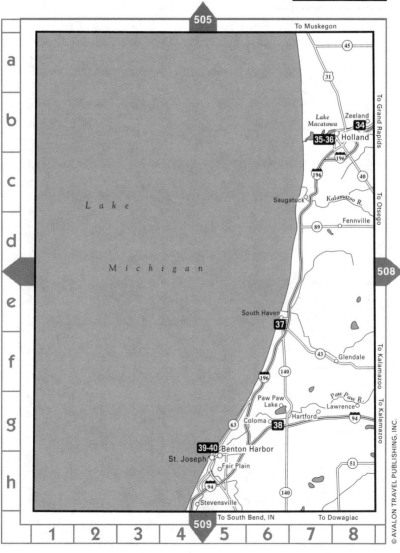

To Muskegon

To Grand Rapids

To Osego

To Kalamazoo

To Kalamazoo

505

508

509

a

b

c

d

e

f

g

h

1 2 3 4 5 6 7 8

Lake Macatawa

Zeeland

34

35-36 Holland

Saugatuck

Kalamazoo R.

Fennville

Lake Michigan

South Haven

37

Glendale

Paw Paw R.

Paw Paw Lake

Lawrence

Coloma

38 Hartford

39-40 Benton Harbor

St. Joseph

Fair Plain

Stevensville

To South Bend, IN

To Dowagiac

© AVALON TRAVEL PUBLISHING, INC.

Map 5

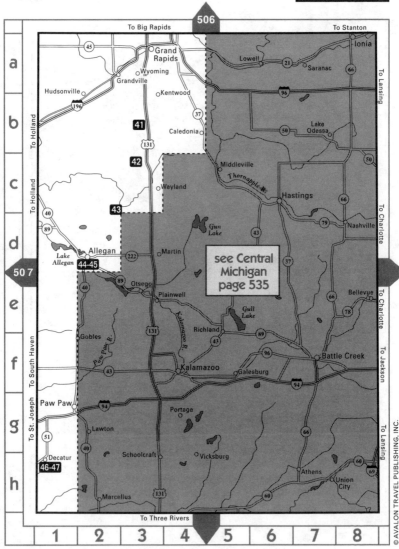

To Big Rapids **506** To Stanton

a Grand Rapids · Lowell · 21 · Saranac · Ionia · To Lansing
45 · Wyoming · Grandville · 96

b Hudsonville · 196 · Kentwood · 37 · Caledonia · 50 · Lake Odessa · 50
41 · 131

c 42 · Middleville · *Thornapple R.* · Hastings · 66
Wayland · 40 · 89

d 43 · *Gun Lake* · 43 · 79 · Nashville
To Holland · *Lake Allegan* · Allegan · 222 · Martin · 37 · 66
507 · 44-45

e 89 · Otsego · Plainwell · **see Central Michigan page 535** · Bellevue · 66 · 78 · To Charlotte
40 · *Kalamazoo R.* · *Gull Lake*

f Gobles · 131 · Richland · 89 · 96 · Battle Creek
Paw Paw R. · 43 · Kalamazoo · Galesburg · 94
43

g Paw Paw · 94 · Portage · 66 · To Lansing
To South Haven · 51 · Lawton · 40

h Decatur · Schoolcraft · Vicksburg · Athens · Union City · 69
46-47 · 131 · Marcellus · 60 · 60

1 2 3 4 5 6 7 8

To Three Rivers

© AVALON TRAVEL PUBLISHING, INC.

Map 6

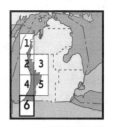

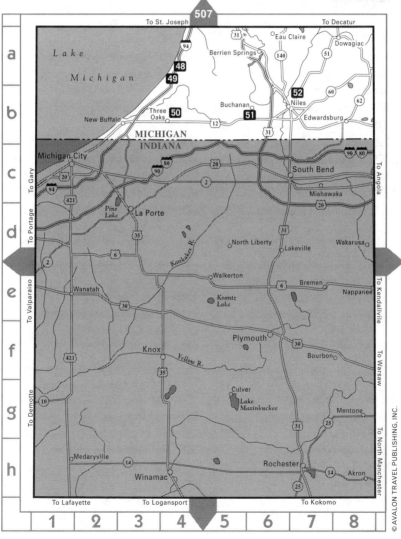

The West Coast

A journey along the Lake Michigan side of Michigan's Lower Peninsula is a fascinating adventure. Some harbor towns alone are worth the drive. In the north, set aside time for a dune climb at Sleeping Bear Dunes National Lakeshore, or even a side trip to the Manitou Islands.

This area is another of the state's wine regions and a world-class cherry producer. Northwest Michigan is also where America's summer golf capital got its start. Today, there are dozens of "designer" golf courses.

Traveling southward is Grand Rapids where you can get a taste of culture. Or, you can visit the largest Dutch community outside of Europe in the coastal community of Holland. This area has more dunes and five lighthouses to climb and explore.

Closer to Indiana, you'll see harbors filled with sailboats. Hundreds of fishing craft in each port seek the lake's abundant salmon and trout. In addition, there are more golf courses, and vast areas of dunes and orchards. North, central, or south along Michigan's "west coast," you can camp at hundreds of picturesque spots and take advantage of hundreds of miles of biking and hiking trails.

◼ Kampvilla RV Park and Family Campground

Location: Bear Lake, south of Benzonia, map 1, grid E7.

Campsites, facilities: There are 92 campsites. Facilities include RV pull-through sites, electric hookups, flush toilets, showers, laundry, heated swimming pool, mini-golf, and playground. Lake swimming, boating, canoeing, fishing, hiking, snowmobile and ski trails nearby. Pets are allowed.

Reservations, fees: The daily fee ranges from $18 to $22. Open year-round.

Directions: From U.S. Hwy. 31 at the north edge of town, go four miles north on Hwy. 31 to the entrance on the left.

Contact: Kampvilla RV Park, 16632 U.S. Hwy. 31, Bear Lake, MI 49614, 231/864-3757 or 800/968-0027.

Trip Notes: Drive to Frankfort on Lake Michigan to see the Point Betsie Lighthouse, Michigan's oldest operating lighthouse. Built in 1858 at a cost of $3,000, it has a 37-foot brick tower painted white to match the attached keeper's house. It is also Michigan's most photographed lighthouse. Follow Hwy. 22 north from Frankfort for 5.5 miles and then turn west on Point Betsie Road.

◻ Matson's Big Manistee River Campground

Location: Manistee, on Lake Michigan, map 1, grid G6.

Campsites, facilities: There are 75 campsites. Facilities include riverfront sites, electric hookups, flush toilets, showers, disposal station, laundry, grocery store, boat ramp, river fishing, fish cleaning station, weekend planned activities, and playground. Boat, canoe, cabin, and some seasonal campsite rentals are available. Pets are allowed.

Reservations, fees: The daily fee ranges from $13 to $18. Credit cards are accepted. Open from mid-April through November.

Directions: From the junction of U.S. Hwy. 31 and Hwy. 55, go just over nine miles east on Hwy. 55 and then slightly more than three miles north on Skocelas Road. Drive three-quarters of a mile west on Becker Road and three-quarters of a mile north on Bialik Road to the entrance on the right.

Contact: Matson's Big Manistee River Campground, 2680 Bialik Rd., Manistee, MI 49660, 231/723-5705 or 888/556-2424.

Trip Notes: Be sure to visit the North Pier Light and Catwalk. Go 1.6 miles west on Memorial Drive, which changes to 5th Avenue at the blinking light. Drive one mile to the parking area or you can leisurely walk along the scenic Riverwalk from downtown to the lighthouse and beach. The original lighthouse was at the mouth of the Manistee River for only a year. It was destroyed by fire in 1871. Today's 39-foot tower, constructed in 1927, boasts of having one of only four remaining catwalks on Lake Michigan's east coast.

3 Orchard Beach State Park

Location: Manistee, on Lake Michigan, map 1, grid G6.

Campsites, facilities: There are 175 campsites, including one mini-cabin. Facilities include electric hookups, flush toilets, showers, disposal station, laundry, swimming beach, boating, fishing, hiking and nature trails, and playground. Pets are allowed with restrictions.

Reservations, fees: Reservations are recommended. The daily fee is $12. Personal checks and credit cards are accepted. The campground is fully operational April through November.

Directions: From the junction of U.S. Hwy. 31 and Hwy. 110, go two miles north on Hwy. 110 to the park entrance.

Contact: Orchard Beach State Park, 2064 Lakeshore Rd., Manistee, MI 49660, 231/723-7422.

Trip Notes: The campground is situated on a bluff overlooking Lake Michigan and offers grassy picnic areas, campsites, and a stairway leading to the sandy Lake Michigan beach. There is a half-mile, self-guided nature trail, and two miles of hiking trails adjacent to the campground.

Be sure to ride the trolley on a historic tour of Manistee. It was a lumbering town that has preserved the Victorian atmosphere with its Victorian Village shopping district and lumbermen's homes.

4 Manistee National Forest: Lake Michigan Recreation Area

Location: Manistee, on Lake Michigan, map 1, grid G6.

Campsites, facilities: There are 99 campsites with a separate tent area. Facilities include water, flush toilets, disposal station, bike and hiking trails, nature programs, picnic area, swimming beach, and playground. Lake boating, fishing, swimming, snowmobile and ski trails are nearby. Pets are allowed.

Reservations, fees: Reservations are accepted. The daily fee is $10. Personal checks are accepted. Open year-round. The facility is fully operational from mid-May through September.

Directions: From the junction of Hwy. 55 and U.S. Hwy. 31, go 10 miles south on Hwy. 31, and then eight miles west on Forest Road 5629 to the entrance.

Contact: Lake Michigan Recreation Area, 412 Red Apple Rd., Manistee, MI 49660, 231/723-2211.

Trip Notes: This popular area has scenic and natural campsites. Lake Michigan is to the west and Nordhouse Dunes Wilderness Area is to the south.

In Manistee, you can visit Orchard Beach Aviation (231/723-8095) and fly along the Lake Michigan shoreline from Manistee to Portage Lake. Flights depart from Manistee Blacker Airport on U.S. Hwy. 31.

A less expensive alternative is to take the Manistee Arboretum Trail (616/723-0124), which meanders through a variety of trees planted in the 1940s as part of a tree growth experiment. The species came from Europe, Asia, and the United States. It offers wildlife viewing opportunities, too.

◳ Insta-Launch Campground and Marina

Location: Manistee, on Lake Michigan, map 1, grid G6.

Campsites, facilities: There are 180 campsites. Facilities include electric hookups, water, flush toilets, showers, disposal station, laundry, grocery store, pond swimming, boat ramp and dock, lake and river boating, canoeing, and fishing. Boat rentals are available. Pets are allowed.

Reservations, fees: The daily fee ranges from $11 to $18. Open April through November.

Directions: From the junction of Hwy. 55 and U.S. Hwy. 31, go three-tenths of a mile south on Hwy. 31, then two-tenths of a mile east on Park Avenue to the entrance on the right.

Contact: Insta-Launch Campground and Marina, 20 Park Ave., Manistee, MI 49660, 231/723-3901.

Trip Notes: Visit the Huron-Manistee National Forest, which has nearly 521,000 acres of forest and includes the Lake Michigan Recreation Area with its trails, panoramic view of sand dunes and beaches, fishing, and hiking and biking trails.

◶ Vacation Station RV Park

Location: Ludington, on Lake Michigan, map 2, grid A5.

Campsites, facilities: There are 150 campsites. Facilities include RV pull-through sites, electric hookups, water, sewer, flush toilets, showers, laundry, grocery store, heated swimming pool, whirlpool, pond fishing, boating, canoeing, hayrides, planned activities, and playground. Boat and seasonal campsite rentals are available. Pets are allowed.

Reservations, fees: The daily fee ranges from about $29 to $33. Credit cards, travelers checks, and personal checks are accepted. Open April through October.

Directions: From U.S. Hwys. 31/10, go almost a mile west on Hwy. 10 to the entrance on the left. It's across from the Wal-Mart.

Contact: Vacation RV Park, 4895 W. U.S. Hwy. 10, Ludington, MI 49431, 231/845-0130 or 877/856-0390, email: camp@vacationstationrvpark.com, website: www.vacationstationrvpark.com.

Trip Notes: This campground is in a quiet natural setting with a neighborhood feel. It has a private pond with fishing for kids and is within walking distance to shopping and restaurants, and next to a family fun park.

◷ Kibby Creek Travel Park

Location: Ludington, on Lake Michigan, map 1, grid G6.

Campsites, facilities: There are 113 campsites. Facilities include RV pull-through sites, electric hookups, water, sewer, flush toilets, showers, disposal station, grocery store, heated outdoor swimming pool, pond fishing, mini-golf, shuffleboard courts, boating (no motor permitted), hiking trail, picnic area, planned weekend activities, and playground. RV and seasonal campsite rentals are available. Pets are allowed.

Reservations, fees: Reservations are recommended. The daily fee ranges from $22 to $24. Credit cards, travelers checks, and personal checks are accepted. Open from mid-April through mid-October.

Directions: From the junction of U.S. Hwys. 10/31, go 2.5 miles south on Hwy. 31 and 4.5 miles south on Pere Marquette (Old U.S. Hwy. 31). Drive 200 yards west on Deren Road to the entrance on the right.

Contact: Kibby Creek Travel Park, Roger and Kelly Anderson, 4900 Deren Rd., Ludington, MI 49431, 231/864-3757 or 231/574-3995 or 800/574-3995, email: kibbycreek@carrinet.net, website: www.michcampgrounds.com/kibby creek.

Trip Notes: The campground is near the Ludington Ferry and Lake Michigan fishing. Whether you take the "S.S. Badger" to Manitowoc and back or just go down to the docks to see several of the retired ships docked there and visit the unique boutique across the road, this is a must on any camper's list of things to do.

8 Lakeview Campsite

Location: Ludington, on Lake Michigan, map 2, grid A5.

Campsites, facilities: There are 106 campsites. Facilities include RV pull-through campsites, electric hookups, water, disposal station, flush toilets, showers, partial wheelchair access, grocery store, outdoor swimming pool, bike and hiking trail, picnic area, playground, boat ramp and dock, and fishing on Hamlin Lake. Canoe, RV, and seasonal campsite rentals are available. Pets are allowed.

Reservations, fees: Reservations are recommended. The daily fee ranges from $11 to $18. Travelers checks and personal checks are accepted. Open from mid-April through mid-October.

Directions: From the junction of U.S. Hwys. 31/10, go 1.75 miles west on Hwy. 10 and four miles north on Jebavy Road. Then drive 2.5 miles northeast on Angling Road and continue 200 yards east on Fountain Road. Drive 1.25 miles north on Peterson Road to the entrance at the end.

Contact: Lakeview Campsite, 6181 Peterson Rd., Ludington, MI 49431, 231/843-3702, website: www.hamlinlake/lakeview.

Trip Notes: Be sure to tour the Mason County Historical White Pine Village (231/843-4808), a community of 21 buildings on 23 acres dedicated to preserving and presenting Mason County's history. It's about two miles south of Ludington. Follow the signs.

9 Ludington State Park

Location: Ludington on Lake Michigan, map 2, grid A5.

Campsites, facilities: There are 347 campsites. Facilities include electric hookups, flush toilets, showers, disposal station, grocery store, gift shop, swimming beach, fishing, fish cleaning station, boat ramp, picnic area, planned activities, and playground. There are also bike, hiking, snowmobile, and cross-country ski trails. Bike, boat, and canoe rentals are available. Pets are allowed with restrictions.

Reservations, fees: Reservations are accepted. The daily fee is $15. Credit cards, travelers checks, and personal checks are accepted. Open year-round. The facility is fully operational mid-April through October.

Directions: From the junction of U.S. Hwys. 31/10 and Hwy. 116, go eight miles north on Hwy. 116 to the park entrance.

Contact: Ludington State Park, P.O. Box 709, Ludington, MI 49431, 800/447-2757 or 231/843-8671 or 231/843-2423.

Trip Notes: The campground at this 5,300-acre park has six miles of Lake Michigan beach, and the Great Lakes Visitor Center has day and evening interpretive programs. The park features a beach, boat ramp on Hamlin Lake, 18 miles of hiking trails, 16 miles of cross-country ski trails, and a unique canoe trail along the Hamlin Lake shoreline.

10 North Woods Campground

Location: Ludington, on Lake Michigan, map 2, grid A5.

Campsites, facilities: There are 98 campsites. Facilities include RV pull-through sites, electric hookups, water, sewer, flush toilets, showers, disposal station, and playground. Lake boating, fishing, and hiking trails are nearby. Some seasonal campsite rentals are available. Pets are allowed.

Reservations, fees: The daily fee ranges from $20 to $25. Open May through October.

Directions: From the junction of U.S. Hwys. 31/10, go one-quarter mile west on Hwy. 10 to the entrance on the left.

Contact: North Woods Campground, Ron and Gary Berquist, 4565 West U.S. Hwy. 10, Ludington, MI 49431, 231/845-7106.

Trip Notes: You really shouldn't miss the Ludington Pumped-Storage Hydroelectric Plant (231/727-6381), one of the world's largest generating plants of its kind. Its 842-acre man-made reservoir offers an unguided scenic overlook for Lake Michigan viewing. From Hwy. 31 (Oceana Drive exit), drive seven miles south and go one-half mile west

to Old Hwy. 31, and north to Meisenheimer. Drive one mile west to Lakeshore Drive, then two miles north.

11 Poncho's Pond and RV Park

Location: Ludington, on Lake Michigan, map 2, grid A5.

Campsites, facilities: There are 226 campsites. Facilities include RV pull-through sites, electric hookups, water, sewer, flush toilets, showers, laundry, grocery store, two heated swimming pools, boat ramp, pond boating, fishing, fishing pond for kids, picnic area, planned activities, and playground. Bike and boat rentals are available. Pets are allowed.

Reservations, fees: Reservations are recommended. The daily fee ranges from $23 to $30. Credit cards, travelers checks, and personal checks are accepted. Open April through October.

Directions: From the junction of U.S. Hwys. 31/10, go two miles west on Hwy. 10 (behind McDonalds) to the entrance on the left.

Contact: Poncho's Pond, 5335 W. Wallace Rd., Ludington, MI 49431, 231/845-5538 or 888/308-6602, website: www.poncho.com.

Trip Notes: This campground's three-acre pond offers an abundance of activity for everyone, but it is only two miles from Lake Michigan beaches for all the water sports you can handle. It is also one mile from the renowned Pere Marquette River.

12 Crystal Lake Family Camp Resort

Location: Ludington, on Lake Michigan, map 2, grid A5.

Campsites, facilities: There are 160 campsites. Facilities

include electric hookups, water, sewer, flush toilets, showers, disposal station, laundry, grocery store, sandy walk-out swimming beach, boating, canoeing, fishing, hiking trail, mini-golf, planned weekend activities, and playground. Boat and seasonal campsite rentals are available. Pets are allowed.

Reservations, fees: The daily fee ranges from $23 to $25. Credit cards are accepted. Open April through October.

Directions: From the west junction of U.S. Hwys. 10 and 31, go three miles east on Hwys. 10/31, and then go 1.5 miles north on Stiles Road. Drive one-half mile east on Hansen Road to the entrance on the left.

Contact: Crystal Lake Family Camp Resort, the Purcell family, 1884 W. Hansen Rd., Scottville, MI 49454, 231/757-4510.

Trip Notes: This is a forested campground on beautiful Crystal Lake with a terrific beach.

The entire family can experience a small Michigan town in the late 1800s with a blacksmith shop, quaint chapel, and old-time ice cream parlor at the Ronald M. Wood (231/843-4808) historic site at 1687 Lakeshore Drive, which is two miles west of Hwy. 31 at Ludington. Exit to south Pere Marquette Hwy. and go two miles south to Iris Road. Then drive 1.5 miles west to south Lakeshore Drive.

13 Charles Mears State Park

Location: Pentwater, on Lake Michigan, map 2, grid B5.

Campsites, facilities: There are 179 campsites. Facilities include electric hookups, flush toilets, showers, disposal station, grocery store, lake fishing, boating, swimming beach, hiking trails, picnic area, and playground. Pets are allowed with restrictions.

Reservations, fees: Reservations are recommended. The daily fee ranges from $13 to $15. Credit cards are accepted. Open April through November.

Directions: From U.S. Hwy. 31, take the Pentwater exit and go west for about three blocks on Lowell Street to the park entrance.

Contact: Charles Mears State Park, P.O. Box 370, W. Lowell St., Pentwater, MI 49449, 231/869-2051.

Trip Notes: Located in the quaint village of Pentwater along the Lake Michigan shoreline, the park features paved campsites surrounded by fine sand, and a swimming beach adjacent to the harbor pier where anglers fish for yellow perch and smallmouth bass in summer. The steelhead and salmon action begins in late August, but is best done from a boat.

14 Hill and Hollow Campground

Location: Pentwater on Lake Michigan, map 2, grid B5.

Campsites, facilities: There are 150 campsites. Facilities include electric hookups, water, sewer, flush toilets, showers, disposal station, grocery store, swimming pool, hiking trail, and playground. Lake swimming, boating, and fishing are nearby. Some seasonal campsite rentals are available.

Reservations, fees: The daily fee ranges from $22 to $28. Open May through September.

Directions: From the junction of U.S. Hwy. 31 and Business 31, go 6.5 miles north on Business 31 to the entrance on the left.

Contact: Hill and Hollow Campground, Donald and Linda Becke, 8915 N. Business Hwy. 31, Pentwater, MI 49449, 231/869-5811.

Trip Notes: The whole family can have fun at the A & J's Action Territory with go-karts, adventure mini-golf, and a video arcade.

15 Hideaway Campground/ Water Slide

Location: Mears, south of Ludington near Lake Michigan, map 2, grid C5.

Campsites, facilities: There are 150 campsites. Facilities include electric hookups, water, flush toilets, showers, disposal station, grocery store, lake fishing, boating, swimming beach, swimming at a 340-foot water slide, hiking trail, and playground. Some seasonal campsite rentals are available. Pets are allowed.

Reservations, fees: The daily fee ranges from $18 to $23. Open May through September.

Directions: From the junction of Hwy. 31 and Shelby Road, go five miles west on Shelby Road, then 4.5 miles north on Scenic Drive (B-15) to the entrance on the left.

Contact: Hideaway Campground/Water Slide, Dan and Laurie Kolosci, 967 W. Silver Lake Rd., Mears, MI 49436, 231/873-4428, email: hideway@voyager.net, website: www .hideawaycampground.com

Trip Notes: After you have enjoyed a thrilling 340-foot water slide ride, be sure to take an exciting ride in a dune buggy along the Lake Michigan shore.

16 Silver City II Campground/Resort

Location: Mears, south of Ludington near Lake Michigan, map 2, grid C5.

Campsites, facilities: There are 260 campsites. Facilities include RV pull-through sites, electric hookups, water, flush toilets, showers, disposal station, and grocery store. Lake swimming, fishing, boating, golfing, and hiking and biking trails are nearby. Cabin rentals are available.

Reservations, fees: The daily fee begins at $11 per person. Open May through September.

Directions: From U.S. Hwy. 31, take the Hart exit and go two miles west on Polk Road. Follow the signs to the entrance on the left.

Contact: Silver City II Campground/Resort, Mike and Sandi Fuller, 1786 N. 34th Ave., Mears, MI 49436, 231/873-7199 or 800/359-1909.

Trip Notes: This is the closest campground to Sand Dunes Park. It is near most area attractions, including the Sand Drag Strip, restaurants, fun parks, farm market, and horseback riding stables.

17 Sandy Shores Campground and Resort

Location: Mears, south of Ludington near Lake Michigan, map 2, grid C5.

Campsites, facilities: There are 200 campsites. Facilities include RV pull-through sites, electric hookups, water, sewers, flush toilets, showers, disposal station, laundry, swimming pool, lake swimming, boating, canoeing, biking and hiking trails, fishing, and playground. Boat and canoe rentals are available. Pets are allowed.

Reservations, fees: The daily fee ranges from $25 to $28. Open May through September.

Directions: From the junction of U.S. Hwy. 31 and Shelby Road, go five miles west on Shelby Road, then four miles north on Scenic Drive. Drive one-half mile east on Silver Lake Road to the entrance on the right.

Contact: Sandy Shores Campground and Resort, 8595 Silver Lake Rd., Mears, MI 49436, 213/873-3003.

Trip Notes: This campground is on private Silver Lake and next to Silver Lake State Park where you can enjoy Mac Wood's Dune's rides

(231/873-2817) on the beautiful sand dune mountains of Silver Lake.

18 Yogi Bear Jellystone Park-Silver Lake

Location: Mears, south of Ludington on Lake Michigan, map 2, grid C5.

Campsites, facilities: There are 200 campsites. Facilities include RV pull-through sites, electric hookups, water, flush toilets, showers, laundry, disposal station, swimming pool, pond fishing, boating, and planned activities. Lake swimming is available nearby. Cabin, RV, and seasonal campsite rentals are available. Pets are allowed.

Reservations, fees: Reservations are recommended. The daily fee ranges from $27 to $32. Credit cards are accepted. Open from mid-April through mid-October.

Directions: From U.S. Hwy. 31, take the Hart exit and go 5.5 miles west on Polk Road/56th Avenue/Fox Road, then one-half mile west on Hazel Road. Follow the signs to the entrance on the left.

Contact: Yogi Bear Jellystone Park-Silver Lake, Craig and Lorie Clark, 8239 Hazel Rd., Mears, MI 49436, 231/873-4502.

Trip Notes: This campground is near Silver Lake, the dunes, and Lake Michigan for everything you will ever want to do while camping. One option is to go horseback riding at the Rainbow Ranch (231/861-4445) in nearby New Era.

19 Silver Lake State Park

Location: Mears, south of Ludington on Lake Michigan, map 2, grid C5.

Campsites, facilities: There are 196 campsites. Facilities include electric hookups, flush toilets, showers, disposal station, swimming beach, fishing, and boat ramp. Pets are allowed with restrictions.

Reservations, fees: Reservations are recommended. The daily fee is $15. Credit cards are accepted. Open April through November.

Directions: From U.S. Hwy. 31, take the Hart or Shelby exit and follow the signs to the park entrance.

Contact: Silver Lake State Park, 9679 W. State Park Rd., Mears, MI 49436, 231/873-3083.

Trip Notes: This 1,500-acre park of desert-like sand dunes can be explored on foot or by vehicle. The park's 450-acre vehicle scramble area, separate from the pedestrian area, is the only dune in Michigan that allows off-road vehicles. Also located in the park is the Little Sable Point Light, built in 1874, which can be viewed from the grounds.

20 Pine Haven Campground and Grocery

Location: Walkerville, near the west coast southeast of Ludington, map 2, grid C5.

Campsites, facilities: There are 84 campsites. Facilities include electric hookups, water, sewer, flush toilets, showers, disposal station, laundry, grocery store, lake boating, fishing, swimming, and hiking trail. Cross-country ski and snowmobile trails are nearby. Pets are allowed.

Reservations, fees: The daily fee ranges from $17 to $18. Open year-round. The facility is fully operational May through October.

Directions: Take U.S. Hwy. 31 to the Pentwater exit and go east on Monroe Road about seven miles to 126th Street. Drive one mile north on 126th to Madison, then six miles east on Madison to 176th Street. Drive two miles northeast on 176th to 186th Avenue, and one-quarter mile on 186th to the entrance on the left.

Contact: Pine Haven Campground and Grocery, 7792 186th Ave., Walkerville, MI 49459, 231/898-2722.

Trip Notes: Drive to New Era and visit the Ramey's Farm Market (231/861-5755), where you can pick strawberries, raspberries, and pumpkins in season, or shop in their market bakery and gift shop.

21 Holiday Camping Resort

Location: New Era, midway between Muskegon and Ludington, map 2, grid D6.

Campsites, facilities: There are 80 campsites. Facilities include RV pull-through sites, electric hookups, flush toilets, showers, disposal station, laundry, grocery store, swimming pool, hiking trail, and playground. Biking and horseback riding trails are nearby. Pets are allowed.

Reservations, fees: The daily fee ranges from $18 to $22. Open May through mid-October.

Directions: From the junction of U.S. Hwy. 31 and Hwy. 20, go one mile west on Stone Lake Road to the entrance on the left.

Contact: Holiday Camping Resort, Glen Holz, 5483 W. Stony Lake Rd., New Era, MI 49446, 231/861-5220, website: www.holiday-camping.com.

Trip Notes: This campground is close to the Hart-Montague Bike Trail, a paved trail on an abandoned railroad corridor between the two communities. There is also Michigan Adventure Fun Park, Sand Dune Recreation Area, and horseback riding at Rainbow Ranch (231/861-4445) where the family can also enjoy a hayride.

22 White River Campground

Location: Montague, on the White River, map 2, grid E6.

Campsites, facilities: There are 227 campsites. Facilities include RV pull-through sites, electric hookups, water, sewer, disposal station, laundry, grocery store, swimming pool, lake and river boating, canoeing, and fishing. Float trips, horseback riding, and hiking trails are nearby. Canoe, kayak, and cabin rentals are available. Pets are allowed.

Reservations, fees: The daily fee ranges from $19 to $23. Credit cards are accepted. Open from mid-April through mid-October.

Directions: From the junction of U.S. Hwy. 31 and Fruitvale Road, go five miles east on County Road B-86 (Fruitvale Road) to the entrance on the right.

Contact: White River Campground, Jim and Joy Cordray, C.P.O., 735 Fruitvale Rd., Montague, MI 49437, 231/894-4708.

Trip Notes: Be sure to visit the White River Light Station (231/894-8265). It was built in 1874 following the Civil War and today it's a museum with artifacts related to Great Lakes history. There is also a great view from the top of the station.

23 Terry's Campground

Location: Montague, midway between Ludington and Muskegon, map 2, grid E6.

Campsites, facilities: There are 55 campsites. Facilities include RV pull-through sites, electric hookups, water, flush toilets, showers, and disposal station. Boat ramp, river boating, canoeing, and fishing are nearby. Seasonal campsite rentals are available. Pets are allowed.

Reservations, fees: The daily fee is $20. Open from late April through late October.

Directions: From the junction of U.S. Hwy. 31 and Business 31, take the Whitehall-Montague exit and go 2.25 miles west on Business 31 to the entrance on the right.

Contact: Terry's Campground, 4540 Dowling St., Montague, MI 49437, 231/894-4902.

Trip Notes: The campground is directly across from the World's largest weather vane, standing 48 feet high and weighing 4,300 pounds. It features the White Lake lumber schooner "Ella Ellenwood." The campground is also close to the 22-mile Hart-Montague paved bike trail.

24 Muskegon State Park

Location: Muskegon, on Lakes Michigan and Muskegon, map 2, grid G7.

Campsites, facilities: There are 183 campsites. Facilities include electric hookups, flush toilets, showers, laundry, grocery store, swimming beach, fishing, boat ramp, hiking and cross-country ski trails, and luge run. Ski rentals are available. Pets are allowed with restrictions.

Reservations, fees: Reservations are recommended. The daily fee is $14. Credit cards are accepted. Open May through November.

Directions: From Muskegon, go five miles west on Giles Road or take Hwy. 31 to Hwy. 110 and exit in North Muskegon. Follow the signs to the park entrance.

Contact: Muskegon State Park, 3560 Memorial Dr., Muskegon, MI 49445, 201/744-0400.

Trip Notes: Featuring more than two miles of Lake Michigan shoreline and one mile on Lake Muskegon, the park provides the best in both Great Lakes and inland lake fishing, boating, and swimming. There are 12 miles of hiking trails, five miles of lighted cross-country ski trails, and one of only four luge runs in the country.

25 P. J. Hoffmaster State Park

Location: Muskegon, on Lake Michigan, map 2, grid G7.

Campsites, facilities: There are 293 campsites. Facilities include electric hookups, flush toilets, showers, disposal station, boating, fishing, swimming beach, cross-country skiing, snowshoeing, and interpretive center. Pets are allowed with restrictions.

Reservations, fees: Reservations are recommended. The daily fee is $15. Credit cards are accepted. Open April through November.

Directions: From U.S. Hwy. 31, take the Pontaluna Road exit and go two miles west on Pontaluna Road. From I-96, take exit 4 and go six miles west on Pontaluna Road to the park entrance.

Contact: P. J. Hoffmaster State Park, 6585 Lake Harbor Rd., Muskegon, MI 49441, 231/798-3711.

Trip Notes: The many attractions of this park include 2.5 miles of fine sand shoreline along Lake Michigan, towering sand dunes, and a dune climb stairway leading to the top of a high overlook. The Gillette Sand Dune Visitor Center offers interpretive programs, exhibits, and hands-on displays that the story of Michigan's sand dunes. Cross-country skiing, sledding, and snowshoeing are popular in winter.

26 Lake Sch-Nepp-A-Ho Campground

Location: Muskegon, on Lake Michigan's eastern shore, map 2, grid G7.

Campsites, facilities: There are 100 campsites. Facilities include electric hookups, water, flush toilets, showers, disposal station, laundry, grocery store, lake boating, canoeing, and fishing. Boat rentals are available. Pets are allowed.

Reservations, fees: The daily fee ranges from $19 to $21. Open May 1 through September.

Directions: From the junction of U.S. Hwy. 31 and Hwy. 120, go nearly three miles north on Hwy. 31, and then one-quarter mile south on Russell Road. Drive 100 yards east on Tyler Road to the park entrance on the left.

Contact: Lake Sch-Nepp-A-Ho Campground, 390 East Tyler Rd., Muskegon, MI 49445, 231/766-2209.

Trip Notes: There is much to see and do in Muskegon. By all means take the trolley, which runs daily year-round, from the mall down Western Avenue to Lakeshore Drive. It passes many interesting sites. For a trip back into history, visit the Hackley and Hume Homes (888/843-5661 or 231/722-7578) and see the splendor of the famous lumbering days of Michigan.

27 Muskegon KOA

Location: Muskegon, on Lake Michigan's eastern shore, map 2, grid G7.

Campsites, facilities: There are 96 campsites. Facilities include electric hookups, water, sewer, flush toilets, showers, disposal station, grocery store, swimming beach, boating, fishing, hiking trail and playground. Boat rentals are available. Pets are allowed.

Reservations, fees: The daily fee ranges from $18 to $22. Open from mid-May through mid-September.

Directions: From the junction of U.S. Hwy. 31 and Russell Road, go 50 yards north on Russell Road, one-quarter of a mile east on Bard, and one-quarter of a mile south on Strand to the entrance.

Contact: Muskegon KOA, 3500 N. Strand, Muskegon, MI 49445, 231/766-3900.

Trip Notes: The entire family will enjoy a tour aboard the World War II submarine "U.S. Silversides," and the Maritime Museum in Pere Marquette Park (231/755-1230).

28 Yogi Bear Jellystone Park-Grand Haven

Location: Grand Haven, south of Muskegon on Lake Michigan, map 2, grid G7.

Campsites, facilities: There are 235 campsites. Facilities include RV pull-through sites, electric hookups, water, sewer, flush toilets, showers, disposal station, laundry, grocery store, swimming pool, mini-golf, driving range, planned activities, and playground. Lake boating and fishing are nearby. Pets are allowed.

Reservations, fees: The daily fee ranges from $29 to $40. Credit cards are accepted. Open May through September.

Directions: From the junction of Hwy. 45 and U.S. Hwy. 31, go one-quarter of a mile south on Hwy. 31 to the entrance.

Contact: Yogi Bear Jellystone Park-Grand Haven, 10990 U.S. Hwy. 31 North, Grand Haven, MI 49417, 800/828-1453.

Trip Notes: Enjoy the performance of the Musical Fountain (616/842-2550), which is said to be the world's largest electronically-controlled musical fountain. The water, lights, and music are synchronized.

29 Grand Haven State Park

Location: Grand Haven, south of Muskegon on Lake Michigan, map 2, grid H7.

Campsites, facilities: There are 174 campsites. Facilities include electric hookups, flush toilets, showers, grocery store, swimming beach, fishing, boating, and playground. Pets are allowed with restrictions.

Reservations, fees: Reservations are recommended. The daily fee is $15. Credit cards are accepted. Open April through October.

Directions: From U.S. Hwy. 31, exit at Grand Haven and follow the waterfront signs to the waterfront and go south to the park entrance.

Contact: Grand Haven State Park, 1001 Harbor Ave., Grand Haven, MI 49417, 616/798-3711.

Trip Notes: Grand Haven State Park attracts more than one million visitors each year to its half-mile sandy beach along Lake Michigan adjacent to a boardwalk that follows the Grand River into Grand Haven. Fishing in Lake Michigan is popular here, in the Grand River Channel, and at the lighthouse pier.

30 Conestoga Grand River Campground

Location: Coopersville, southeast of Muskegon, map 3, grid H1.

Campsites, facilities: There are 81 campsites. Facilities include RV pull-through sites, electric hookups, water, flush toilets, showers, disposal station, laundry, grocery store, swimming pool, boat ramp and dock, and fishing. Seasonal campsite rentals are available. Pets are allowed.

Reservations, fees: The daily fee ranges from $22 to $25. Open year-round. The

facility is fully operational May through September.

Directions: From the junction of I-96 and 68th Avenue, take exit 16 and go three miles south on 68th Avenue, then four miles west on Leonard Street. Drive three-quarters of a mile south on 96th Avenue and one-tenth mile west on Oriole Drive to the entrance on the left.

Contact: Conestoga Grand River Campground, 9720 Oriole Dr., Coopersville, MI 49404, 616/837-6323.

Trip Notes: The campground is near an 18-hole golf course, Muskegon Harness Racing, Coopersville Train Ride, and many other activities.

31 River Pines RV Park and Campground

Location: Coopersville, southeast of Muskegon, map 3, grid H1.

Campsites, facilities: There are 109 campsites. Facilities include electric hookups, waters, sewer, flush toilets, showers, disposal station, laundry, swimming pool, boat dock, river boating, canoeing, and fishing. Seasonal campsite rentals are available. Pets are allowed.

Reservations, fees: The daily fee ranges from $20 to $23. Open year-round.

Directions: From I-96, take exit 16 (68th Avenue) and go four miles south on 68th Avenue and nearly two miles west on Warner Road to the entrance on the left.

Contact: River Pines RV and Campground, Jerry and Louise Cannon, 8275 Warner, Allendale, MI 49401, 616/895-6601.

Trip Notes: Visit some of Coopersville and Marne Railway (616/837-7000), Michigan's only tourist railroad. This all-volunteer operation is working to preserve railroad history. Enjoy the SummerTrains, GreatTrain Robbery with optional ChuckWagon Barbeque, and others.

Grand Rogue Campgrounds Canoe and Tube Livery

Location: Grand Rapids, northeast of Holland, map 3, grid H3.

Campsites, facilities: There are 82 campsites. Facilities include electric hookups, water, flush toilets, showers, disposal station, laundry, grocery store, swimming beach, boat ramp, canoeing, kayaking, canoe and tube trips, lake and river fishing, and planned weekend activities. Boat rentals are available. Pets are allowed.

Reservations, fees: The daily fee ranges from $16 to $23. Credit cards are accepted. Open May through mid-October.

Directions: From the junction of I-96 and U.S. Hwy. 131, go 1.5 miles north on Hwy. 131 and take exit 91. Go four miles east on West River Drive to the entrance on the right.

Contact: Grand Rogue Campgrounds Canoe andTube Livery, the Briggs family, 6400 W. River Dr., Belmont, MI 49306, 616/361-1053, Website: www.michcampgrounds.com/grandrogue.

Trip Notes: You will enjoy riding the train through 75 wooded acres of this campground, taking a two-or four-hour canoe trip, or taking a one-or two-hour tube trip.

Other options are to take a 10-minute drive to Grand Rapids to visit the Gerald Ford Museum (616/451-9263) or the Frederik Meijer Gardens (616/957-1580).

Tyler Creek Recreation Area

Location: Grand Rapids, northeast of Holland, map 3, grid H3.

Campsites, facilities: There are 206 campsites. Facilities include RV pull-through sites, electric hookups, water, flush toilets, showers, disposal station, laundry, grocery store, swimming, pool, river swimming, boating, fishing, hiking trail, golf course, planned weekend activities, and playground. Pets are allowed.

Reservations, fees: The daily fee ranges from $17 to $25. Open April through September.

Directions: From the junction of I-96 and Hwy. 50, take exit 52 and go 6.5 miles south and east on Hwy. 50 to the entrance on the right.

Contact: Tyler Creek Recreation Area, 13495 92nd St. S.W., Alto, MI 49302, 616/868-6751.

Trip Notes: If you're a camper who loves to golf, you will enjoy the 18-hole course on the premises or take a trip into town to visit the Blandford Nature Center (616/453-6192). You can also watch salmon leap the rapids at the unique fish ladder at the Sixth Street Dam during spawning season on the Grand River.

Dutch Treat Camping and Recreation

Location: Zeeland, north of Holland on Lake Michigan, map 4, grid B8.

Campsites, facilities: There are 105 campsites. Facilities include RV pull-through sites, electric hookups, water, sewers, flush toilets, showers, disposal station, grocery store, laundry, swimming pool, pond fishing and boating, and playground. Lake swimming, boating, and fishing are nearby. Pets are allowed.

Reservations, fees: The daily fee ranges from $13 to $20. Open April through October.

Directions: From the junction of Hwy. 31 and E-W Business I-96, go just over two miles east on I-196, then one-quarter of a mile east on Gordon. Follow the signs to the entrance on the left.

Contact: Dutch Treat Camping and Recreation, Nelson Reimersma, 10300 Gordon, Zeeland, MI 49038, 616/764-8941.

Trip Notes: Zeeland is one of the communities of Dutch settlement. A visit to the Holland Museum and Cappon House (888/200-9123) will give you 150 years of Holland's history.

Holland State Park

Location: Holland, on Lake Michigan's eastern shore, map 4, grid B8.

Campsites, facilities: There are 310 campsites in two large campgrounds. Facilities include electric hookups, flush toilets, showers, disposal station, grocery store, sandy swimming beach along Lake Michigan, fishing, and boat ramp. Pets are allowed with restrictions.

Reservations, fees: Reservations are recommended. The daily fee is $15. Credit cards are accepted. Open from mid-April through mid-October.

Directions: From westbound BR-196, take exit 55 and follow park signs to Ottawa Beach Road. From eastbound BR-196, take exit 44. The park is eight miles west of Holland.

Contact: Holland State Park, 2215 Ottawa Beach Rd., Holland, MI 49424-2344 or 616/399-9390.

Trip Notes: Do you know how wooden shoes are made or have you ever seen them used in dancing? A visit to the Wooden Shoe Factory (616/396-6513) is enlightening for the whole family. A trip to the top of the windmill on Windmill Island (616/355-1030) or watching the young women dance in their wooden shoes is a real treat, along with a ride on the 1895 musical menagerie.

Oak Grove Resort Campground

Location: Holland, on Lake Michigan's eastern shore, map 3, grid H3.

Campsites, facilities: There are 135 campsites. Tents are not permitted. Facilities include electric hookups, flush toilets, showers, disposal station, laundry, grocery store, and hiking and biking trails. Lake boating and fishing are nearby. Cabin and seasonal campsite rentals are available. Pets are allowed.

Reservations, fees: The daily fee is $35. Open May through September.

Directions: From U.S. Hwy. 31, go 1.5 miles west on Lakewood Blvd., and then 1.5 miles on Douglas Avenue. Drive three miles west on Ottawa Beach Road and follow the signs to the entrance.

Contact: Oak Grove Resort Campground, Ron and Betty, Rod and Maria VandenBerg, 2011 Ottawa Beach Rd., Holland, MI 49424, 616/399-9230, website: www.michcampgrounds.com/oakgrove.

Trip Notes: This campground is within walking distance of Lake Macatawa and Lake Michigan beaches with access to miles of paved bike trails.

Van Buren State Park

Location: South Haven on Lake Michigan's eastern shore, map 4, grid E6.

Campsites, facilities: There are 220 campsites. Facilities include electric hookups, flush toilets, showers, disposal station, grocery store, swimming beach, boating, fishing, and hiking and biking trails. Pets are allowed with restrictions.

Reservations, fees: Reservations are recommended. The daily fee is $12. Credit cards are accepted. Open April through November.

Directions: From I-96 and U.S. Hwy. 31, go five miles south on Blue Star Highway to the park entrance.

Contact: Van Buren State Park, 23960 Ruggles Rd., South Haven, MI 49090, 616/637-2788.

Trip Notes: This state park has almost one mile of Lake Michigan frontage and is six miles from the Kal-Haven Trail State Park, which offers a 34-mile limestone path from South Haven to Kalamazoo. The trail meanders through wooded areas, past farmland, and over rivers. The trail's highlights include a covered bridge.

If you're looking for an indoor treat, visit the Michigan Maritime Museum (800/747-3810 or 616/637-8078).

38 Dune Lake Campground

Location: Coloma, south of South Haven, map 4, grid B8.

Campsites, facilities: There are 86 campsites. Facilities include electric hookups, water, flush toilets, showers, disposal station, grocery store, swimming beach, hiking trail, mini-golf and shuffleboard courts. Lake boating and swimming are nearby. Seasonal campsite rentals are available. Pets are allowed.

Reservations, fees: The daily fee is $19. Credit cards are accepted. Open from mid-May through September.

Directions: From I-96, take exit 7 and go one-quarter mile west on Hager Shore Road, then 2.25 miles north on Blue Star Highway. Drive one mile east on County Road 376 to the entrance.

Contact: Dune Lake Campground, Ed Rouselle and Dan Wichman, 80783 County Rd. 376, Coloma, MI 49038, 616/764-8941, email: DuneLake@webtv.net, website: www.comunity-2webtv.net/dunelakecampground.

Trip Notes: There are beautiful pine-forested hiking trails to enjoy around this spring-fed lake. For summer fun head north to South Haven and visit the Fideland Fun Park (616/637-3123). In fall, try South Haven's Jollay Orchards (616/468-3075) to pick apples and pumpkins or enjoy a hayride.

39 House of David Travel Trailer Park

Location: Benton Harbor, south of South Haven on Lake Michigan, map 4, grid H5.

Campsites, facilities: There are 121 campsites. Facilities include electric hookups, water, sewer, flush toilets, showers, and disposal station. Lake boating, fishing, swimming, and golf courses are nearby.

Reservations, fees: The daily fee ranges from $12 to $15. Open year-round.

Directions: From the junction of I-94 and Hwy. 139, take exit 28 and go 2.5 miles north on Hwy. 139 to the entrance on the right.

Contact: House of David Travel Trailer Park, P.O. Box 1067, Benton Harbor, MI 49023-1067 or 616/927-3302.

Trip Notes: While in the area you should visit the Josephine Morton Memorial House (616/925-7011), built by Eleazar Morton who permitted the Potawatomi Indians to sleep on the porch when they were traveling to St. Joseph to sell their wares.

40 Benton Harbor-St. Joseph KOA

Location: Benton Harbor, north of St. Joseph, map 4, grid H5.

Campsites, facilities: There are 123 campsites. Facilities include RV pull-through sites, electric hookups, water, sewer, flush toilets, showers, disposal station, laundry, grocery store, swimming pool, mini-golf, and hiking trail. Lake boating, fishing, and swimming are nearby. Cabin and seasonal campsite rentals are available. Pets are allowed.

Reservations, fees: The daily fee ranges from $21 to $27. Open from mid-April through mid-October.

Directions: From the junction of I-96 and Coloma-Riverside Road, take exit 4 and go one block east of Coloma-Riverside Road to the entrance.

Contact: Benton Harbor-St. Joseph KOA, Ginter and Ursela Bansen, 3527 Coloma Rd., Box 136M, Riverside, MI 49084, 616/849-3333, email: bhstjoekoa@qtm.net.

Trip Notes: This campground is only five minutes from Lake Michigan and is in the heart of the Fruit Belt and U-Pick farms. Check with the campground to see what is in season to pick. In any case, you'll want to visit the Sarett Nature Center (616/927-4832) and enjoy the five miles of self-guided nature trails.

41 Dome World Campground

Location: Byron Center, south of Grand Rapids, map 5, grid B3.

Campsites, facilities: There are 120 campsites. Facilities include electric hookups, water, sewer, flush toilets, showers, disposal station, swimming pool, and mini-golf.

Seasonal campsite rentals are available. Pets are allowed.

Reservations, fees: The daily fee is $21. Open May through September.

Directions: From the junction of U.S. Hwy. 131 and 84th Street, take exit 74 and go 500 feet west to the entrance.

Contact: Dome World Campground, 400 84th S.W., Bryon Center, MI 49315, 616/878-1518.

Trip Notes: Take a trip to Grand Rapids to visit the Van Andel Museum Center and Chaffee Planetarium (616/456-3977) and enjoy a look at the heavens in the domed sky theater, or view the 76-foot whale skeleton and many other exhibits.

42 Hungry Horse Campground

Location: Dorr, south of Grand Rapids, map 5, grid C3.

Campsites, facilities: There are 85 campsites. Facilities include RV pull-though sites, electric hookups, water, flush toilets, showers, disposal station, laundry, grocery store, swimming pool, hiking trail, and planned weekend activities. Pets are allowed.

Reservations, fees: The daily fee ranges from $5 to $15. Open May through September.

Directions: From U.S. Hwy. 131 (12 miles south of Grand Rapids), take exit 68 (Dorr exit) and go 3.5 miles on 142nd Street to the entrance on the right.

Contact: Hungry Horse Campground, 2016 142nd St., Door, MI 49323, 616/681-9836 or 616/681-9843.

Trip Notes: If you like gardens, you're in a perfect spot to go north to Grand Rapids to visit the Frederik Meijer Gardens (616/957-1580) or west to Holland to view the Veldheer Tulip Gardens (616/399-1900).

43 East Lake Camping

Location: Hopkins, midway between Grand Rapids, Holland and Kalamazoo, map 5, grid D2.

Campsites, facilities: There are 109 campsites. Facilities include electric hookups, water, sewer, flush toilets, showers, disposal station, laundry, grocery store, swimming beach, boat ramp and dock, kayaking, fishing, and hiking trail. Boat, cabin, and RV rentals are available. Pets are allowed.

Reservations, fees: The daily fee ranges from $17 to $21. Credit cards are accepted. Open May through September.

Directions: From U.S. Hwy. 131, take exit 64 (Wayland exit) and go west three miles on 135th Avenue. Then drive south 2.5 miles on 18th Street, and west for 2.5 miles on 130th Avenue to Weick Drive (a private road). The entrance is on the right.

Contact: East Lake Camping, Greg and Catherine Miller, 3091 Weick Dr., Hopkins, MI 49328, 616/793-7177.

Trip Notes: The quiet country setting is perfect for fishing, swimming, reading, and relaxing on the campground's sandy beach or enjoying a wagon ride.

44 Tri Ponds Family Camp Resort

Location: Allegan, near Holland and South Haven, map 5, grid D2.

Campsites, facilities: There are 116 campsites. Facilities include RV pull-through sites, electric hookups, water, sewer, flush toilets, showers, disposal station, laundry, grocery store, pond swimming, fishing, hiking trail, and planned activities with a craft director. Pets are allowed.

Reservations, fees: The daily fee ranges from $16 to $25. Open May through October.

Directions: From the junction of Hwy. 222 and Hwy. 40/89, go three miles northwest on Hwy 40/89, and two miles north on 36th Street. Then drive one mile west on Dumont to the entrance.

Contact: Tri Ponds Family Camp Resort, Paul and Doty VanDrunen, 3687 Dumont Rd., Rt. #5, Allegan, MI 49010, 616/673-4740.

Trip Notes: If you're camping during the summer, take some time to visit the Conor Apiaries (616/673-3693) and sample some of the maple syrup or honey. It also features beeswax, candles, soaps, and other products.

45 Dumont Lake Campground

Location: Allegan, near Holland and South Haven, map 5, grid D2.

Campsites, facilities: There are 86 campsites. Facilities include lake-view campsites, electric hookups, water, flush toilets, showers, disposal station, grocery store, lake swimming, boat dock, fishing, no-license pond fishing, and planned weekend activities. Boat and RV rentals are available. Pets are allowed.

Reservations, fees: The daily fee ranges from $17 to $21. Open May through mid-October.

Directions: From the south junction of Hwys. 89/40, go one block north on Hwy. 89/40, then one-half mile east on Hwy. 222. Then drive five miles north on County Road A-37 (Main Street) and one-half mile west on 125th to the entrance.

Contact: Dumont Lake Campground, Pat and Susan Riley, 3106 125th Ave., Allegan, MI 49010, 616/673-6065.

Trip Notes: This is a camper's paradise. You can

stay for a day, week, month, or season. The lake has excellent muskie fishing. While in the area be sure to visit Marr Haven Wool Farm (616/673-8800) for knitting or weaving yarn from the Merino-Rambouillet sheep. You can shop for many woolen items.

46 Leisure Valley Campground

Location: Decatur, near the Indiana border, map 5, grid H1.

Campsites, facilities: There are 108 campsites. Facilities include electric hookups, water, sewer, flush toilets, showers, disposal station, laundry, grocery store, lake and pool swimming, lake canoeing, fishing, hiking trail, mini-golf, shuffleboard courts, and playground. Pets are allowed.

Reservations, fees: The daily fee ranges from $17 to $18. Open April through October.

Directions: From the junction of Hwy. 51 and George Street, go three miles south on George Street, then one-quarter of a mile west on Valley Road (County Road 669) to the entrance.

Contact: Leisure Valley Campground, Gale and Josie Congdon, 40851 County Rd. 669, Decatur, MI 49045, 616/423-7122.

Trip Notes: This campground's stocked lake is full of bass, bluegill, and yellow perch for lots of fishing fun. At Paw Paw, a few miles north, you can visit one of several blueberry farms and enjoy picking during July and August.

An alternative is to tour the St. Julian Wine Company (800/732-6002).

47 Oak Shores Campground

Location: Decatur, near the Indiana border, map 5, grid H1.

Campsites, facilities: There are 220 campsites. Facilities include electric hookups, water, sewer, flush toilets, showers, disposal station, laundry, grocery store, swimming pool, lake swimming, boating, canoeing, shuffleboard and tennis courts, planned weekend activities, and playground. Cabin and RV rentals are available. Pets are allowed.

Reservations, fees: The daily fee ranges from $23 to $24. Credit cards are accepted. Open from mid-April through mid-October.

Directions: From the junction of I-94 and Hwy. 51, take exit 56 and go 10 miles southwest on Hwy. 51. Then drive one-quarter of a mile north on County Road 215 to the entrance.

Contact: Oak Shore Campground, Joe and Mary Lou Schanz, 86882 County Rd. 215, Decatur, MI 49045, 616/423-7370.

Trip Notes: This campground is located on Lake Knickerbocker, a 75-acre private lake. Write for their brochure and listings of weekend activities so you can plan ahead to participate in their Chili Supper, Strawberry Festival, Flea Market, Hog Roast, Halloween Party, and other events.

48 Weko Beach Park and Campground

Location: Bridgman, south of St. Joseph, map 6, grid A4.

Campsites, facilities: There are 65 sites, including 22 primitive sites. There are also four log camping cabins. Facilities include electric hookups, flush toilets, showers, disposal station, large Lake Michigan swimming beach, boat ramp, children's hayrides, observation deck and boardwalk, picnic area, and playground. Pets are allowed with restrictions.

Reservations, fees: Reservations taken on cabins only. The daily fee ranges from $12 to $15. Open from early May through early October.

Directions: From I-94, take exit 16 and go north one mile on Red Arrow Hwy. Then turn left to the campground.

Contact: Weko Beach Park and Campground, Tim Kading, 5237 Lake St., Bridgman, MI 49106, 616/465-3406.

Trip Notes: Take a short drive west to Berrien Springs and visit the Apple Valley Market (800/237-7436 or 616/473-6531), said to be the largest natural and bulk foods, vitamin, and vegetarian grocery store in the northern United States. You can sample the goods at a from-scratch bakery, have lunch, or browse the card, gift, and floral shops. It's one mile west of downtown Berrien Springs across from the Berrien County Youth Fairgrounds and east of the Hwy. 31 bypass.

49 Warren Dunes State Park

Location: Sawyer, south of St. Joseph, map 5, grid H1.

Campsites, facilities: There are 200 campsites. Facilities include electric hookups, flush toilets, showers, disposal station, grocery store, swimming beach, boating, fishing, hiking trails, and playground. Pets are allowed with restrictions.

Reservations, fees: Reservations are recommended. The daily fee is $15. Credit cards are accepted. Open from mid-April through October.

Directions: From I-94, take exit 16 and go two miles south on Red Arrow Hwy. to the park entrance.

Contact: Warren Dunes State Park, 12032 Red Arrow Hwy., Sawyer, MI 49125, 616/426-4013.

Trip Notes: Warren Dunes has more than two miles of Lake Michigan shoreline with sand dunes rising 240 feet above the lake. A wide variety of natural settings, from rugged dune formations to winding streams and from forest growth to wildflowers, are featured in the park. Two-thirds of the Warren Woods Natural Area's 311 acres consist of a beech-maple forest with hiking trails that cross a suspended wooden foot bridge over the Balien River.

50 Bob-A-Ron Campground

Location: Three Oaks, north of the Michigan-Indiana border, map 6, grid B4.

Campsites, facilities: There are 334 campsites. Facilities include electric hookups, water, sewer, disposal station, grocery store, swimming beach, canoeing, fishing, hiking trail, and planned weekend activities. Boat and seasonal campsite rentals are available. Pets are allowed.

Reservations, fees: The daily fee ranges from $18 to $20. Open May through September.

Directions: From I-94, take exit 6 and follow the signs to the entrance on the left.

Contact: Bob-A-Ron Campground, 7650 Warren Woods Rd., Three Oaks, MI 49128, 616/469-3894.

Trip Notes: Three Oaks is biker's paradise. First you must stop at the Three Oaks Spokes Bicycle Museum in the Three Oaks Railroad Depot (616/756-3361) and see the collection of antique bicycles and the exhibits on cycling history. Next, plan to take one of the many Outback Trails or Backroads Bikeway self-guided tours originating from Three Oaks. Planned by the Three Oaks Spokes, they range from five to 60 miles in length. Bicycle rentals are available.

51 Fuller's Resort and Campground on Clear Lake

Location: Buchanan, west of Niles, map 6, grid B6.

Campsites, facilities: There are 176 campsites. Facilities include electric hookups, water, sewer, flush toilets, showers, disposal station, laundry, grocery store, swimming beach, boat ramp, fishing, planned weekend activities, and playground. Boat, cottage, and seasonal campsite rentals are available. Pets are allowed.

Reservations, fees: The daily fee ranges from $18 to $20. Credit cards are accepted. Open from mid-April through mid-October.

Directions: From the junction of U.S. Hwy. 12 and Bakertown Road, go two miles north on Bakertown Road, then one mile west on Elm Valley Road. Drive one mile northwest on East Clear Lake Road to the entrance.

Contact: Fuller's Resort and Campground on Clear Lake, Rene and Jeff McNeil, 1622 E. Clear Lake Rd., Buchanan, MI 49107, 616/695-3785, website: www.fullersresort.com.

Trip Notes: Clear Lake provides an excellent beach for swimming and other shoreline activities. While in the area be sure to visit the Cook Energy Information Center (800/548-2555) in Bridgman.

Another sight is Bear Cave (616/695-3050), a tufa rock cave that developed 25,000 to 30,000 years ago. In the cave is a boulder believed to be several hundred thousand years old. The cave was once part of the "Underground Railroad" for slaves and a movie location for the 1903 film, The Great Train Robbery. Bear Cave is four miles north of Buchanan and a few hundred yards east of Red Bud Trail on the west side of the St. Joseph River.

52 Spaulding Lake Campground

Location: Niles, near the Indiana border, map 6, grid B7.

Campsites, facilities: There are 98 campsites. Facilities include RV pull-through sites, electric hookups, water, flush toilets, showers, disposal station, laundry, swimming beach, lake and stream fishing, boating, hiking trail, and playground. Pets are allowed.

Reservations, fees: The daily fee ranges from $16 to $18. Open April through November.

Directions: From the junction of U.S. Hwy. 12 and Hwy. 51, go one-quarter of a mile south on Hwy. 51, and two miles east on Bell Road to the entrance.

Contact: Spaulding Lake Campground, 2305 Bell Rd., Niles, MI 49120, 616/684-1393.

Trip Notes: Visit the Fort St. Joseph Museum (616/683-4702), housed in the remodeled carriage and boiler house behind the historic Henry A. Chapin Home. You can also take a self-guided tour of the Chapin Mansion/City Hall for an informative history of the area around the St. Joseph River.

CENTRAL MICHIGAN

Central Michigan

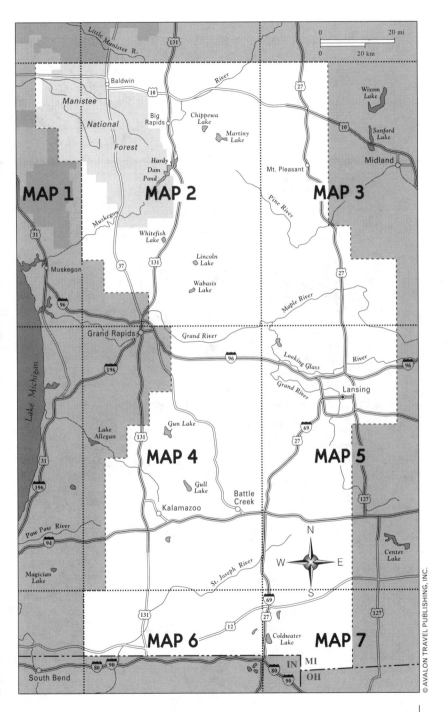

Map 1

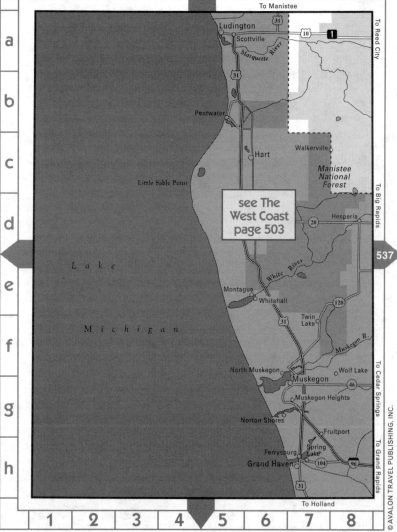

see The West Coast page 503

Map 2

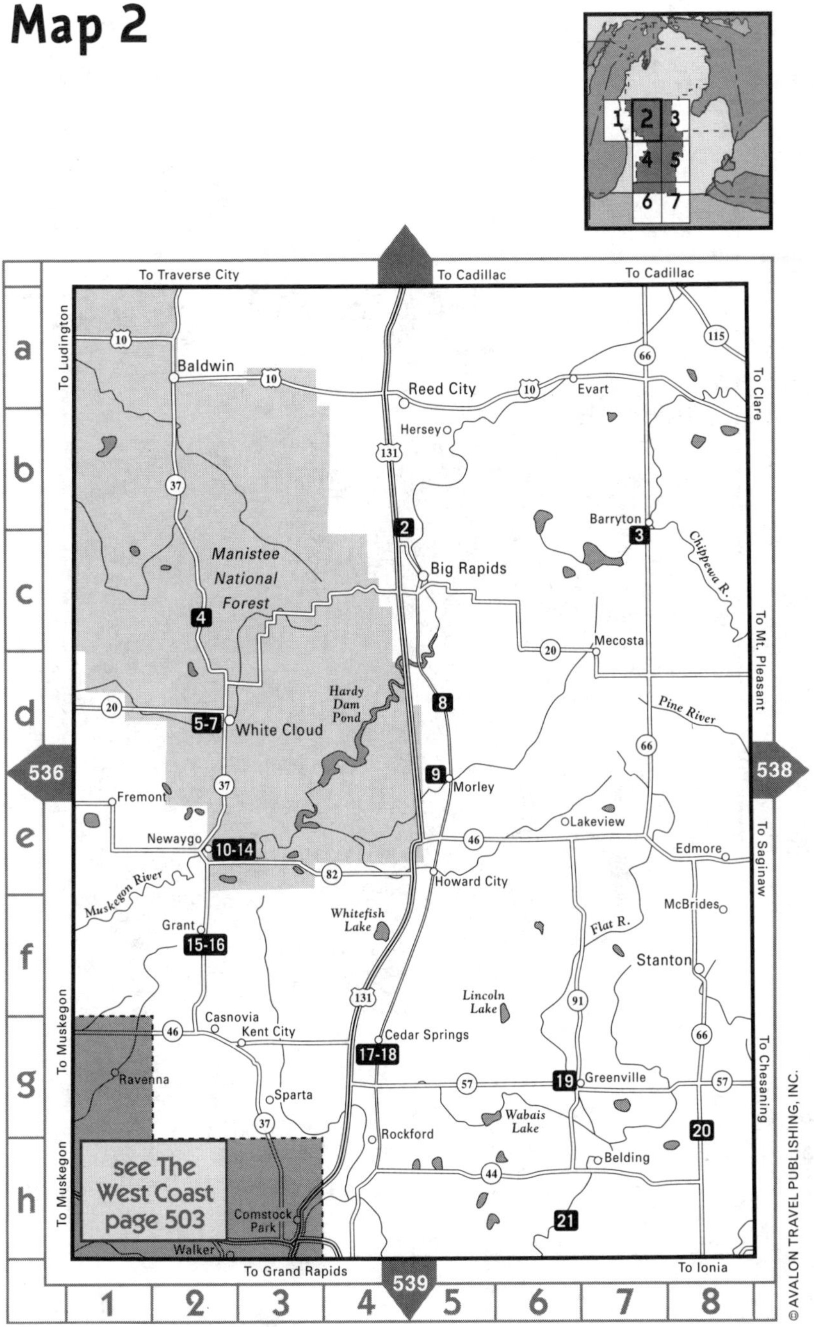

To Traverse City

To Cadillac

To Cadillac

To Ludington

To Clare

a

10

Baldwin **10**

Reed City **10**

Evart

66

115

b

37

Hersey

131

Barryton **3**

Chippewa R.

To Mt. Pleasant

c

Manistee National Forest **4**

Big Rapids

20

Mecosta

d

20

5-7

White Cloud

Hardy Dam Pond

8

Pine River

66

536

538

e

Fremont

37

9

Morley

46

Lakeview

Edmore

To Saginaw

Newaygo **10-14**

82

Howard City

McBrides

Muskegon River

f

Grant **15-16**

Whitefish Lake

Flat R.

Stanton

To Muskegon

Lincoln Lake

91

g

46

Casnovia

Kent City

Cedar Springs **17-18**

57

19 Greenville

66

57

To Chesaning

Ravenna

Sparta

37

Wabais Lake

20

To Muskegon

Rockford

44

Belding

h

see The West Coast page 503

Comstock Park

21

Walker

To Grand Rapids

To Ionia

539

1 2 3 4 5 6 7 8

© AVALON TRAVEL PUBLISHING, INC.

Map 3

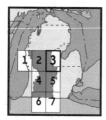

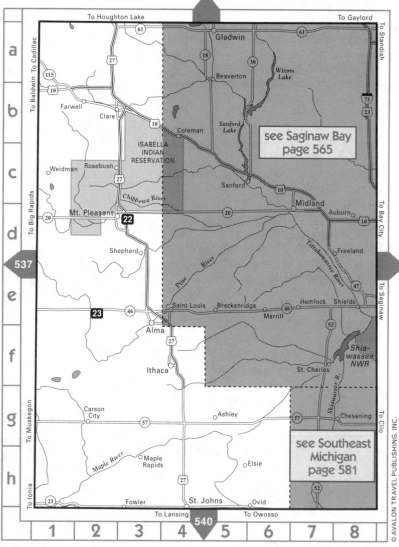

To Houghton Lake

To Gaylord

a

To Baldwin To Cadillac

115

10

Farwell

Clare

61

Gladwin

18

30

Beaverton

Wixom Lake

To Standish

75

23

b

27

10

Coleman

Sanford Lake

see Saginaw Bay page 565

ISABELLA INDIAN RESERVATION

Weidman

Rosebush

27

c

To Big Rapids

Chippewa River

Sanford

10

Midland

Auburn

10

To Bay City

20

Mt. Pleasant

22

26

d

Shepherd

Pine River

River

Tittabawassee River

Freeland

47

To Saginaw

537

23

46

Saint Louis

Breckenridge

Merrill

46

Hemlock

Shields

52

e

Alma

27

f

Ithaca

St. Charles

Shiawassee NWR

Shiawassee R.

To Muskegon

Carson City

57

Ashley

57

Chesaning

To Clio

g

see Southeast Michigan page 581

Maple River

Maple Rapids

27

Elsie

52

h

To Ionia

21

Fowler

St. Johns

Ovid

To Lansing

540

To Owosso

© AVALON TRAVEL PUBLISHING, INC.

1   2   3   4   5   6   7   8

Map 4

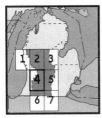

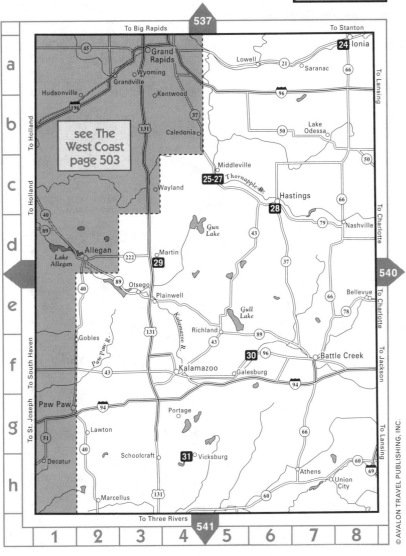

see The West Coast page 503

To Big Rapids
To Stanton
537

To Holland
To Holland
To St. Joseph
To South Haven

540
To Charlotte
To Charlotte
To Jackson
To Lansing
To Lansing

541
To Three Rivers

24 Ionia
Lowell
Saranac
Grand Rapids
Wyoming
Grandville
Hudsonville
Kentwood
Caledonia
Lake Odessa
Middleville
25-27 Thornapple R.
Hastings
28
Nashville
Wayland
Gun Lake
Bellevue
Allegan
Lake Allegan
Martin
29
Otsego
Plainwell
Gull Lake
Gobles
Richland
Paw Paw R.
Kalamazoo R.
Kalamazoo
30
Galesburg
Battle Creek
Paw Paw
Portage
Lawton
Decatur
Schoolcraft
31 Vicksburg
Athens
Union City
Marcellus

a b c d e f g h
1 2 3 4 5 6 7 8

© AVALON TRAVEL PUBLISHING, INC.

Map 5

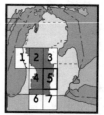

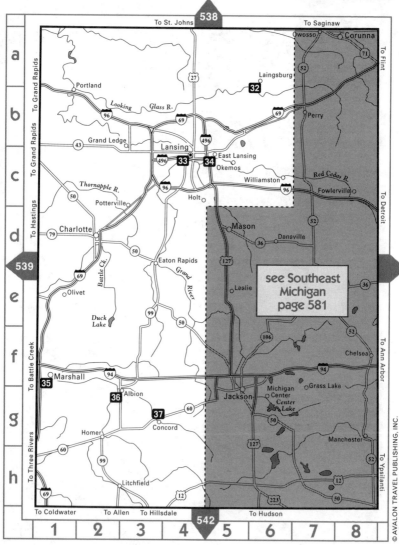

© AVALON TRAVEL PUBLISHING, INC.

Map 6

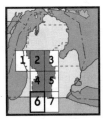

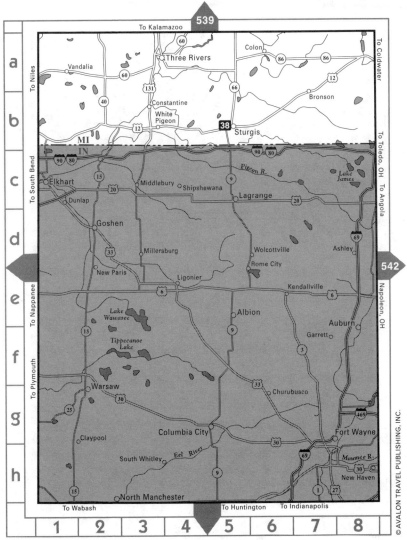

© AVALON TRAVEL PUBLISHING, INC.

Map 7

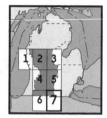

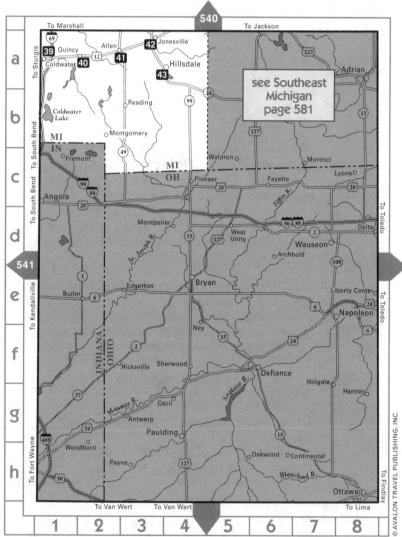

To Marshall

To Jackson

540

a

To Sturgis

69

Quincy

Allen

42

Jonesville

39

Coldwater

40

12

41

Hillsdale

43

223

Adrian

14

see Southeast
Michigan
page 581

b

To South Bend

Coldwater
Lake

Reading

99

127

52

Montgomery

49

MI
IN

Fremont

c

To South Bend

MI
OH

Waldron

Morenci

Pioneer

Fayette

Lyons

20

90

80

Angola

20

Tiffin R.

To Toledo

d

541

Montpelier

15

127

West
Unity

90 80

2

Wauseon

Delta

Archbold

108

To Kendallville

INDIANA

OHIO

1

Edgerton

Bryan

Liberty Center

6

To Toledo

e

Butler

6

24

Napoleon

Ney

15

6

f

2

Hicksville

Sherwood

24

Defiance

Holgate

Hamler

37

g

24

Cecil

Maumee R.

Antwerp

Auglaize R.

To Fort Wayne

469

Paulding

15

h

Woodburn

Payne

127

Oakwood

Continental

Blanchard R.

30

Ottawa

To Lima

To Van Wert

To Van Wert

1   2   3   4   5   6   7   8

© AVALON TRAVEL PUBLISHING, INC.

To Findlay

Central Michigan

Many rivers, most of them narrow and shallow, drain the central area of Michigan. Of the estimated 15,000 Indians living in the territory when the French arrived—mostly Chippewa, Ottawa, or Potawatomi— many lived along the river valleys of southern Michigan. Later, the mildly rolling countryside, including that of the central portion of the state, attracted early farmers and other settlers. There is a longer growing season and fertile clay soil that favor a wide variety of crops, especially grains; corn is the state's major field crop. In fact, the southern agricultural counties produce much of Michigan's agricultural wealth, but the region also includes industrial areas such as Grand Rapids and Battle Creek.

In a way, Ionia County was site of the first campground. In 1929, a county engineer built a picnic table from scrap planks used for guardrails and put it along the highway right-of-way on old U.S. Hwy. 16. It became the first highway rest area. Today, the image of a roadside table is a symbol of Michigan's hospitality.

■ Timber Surf Camping Resort

Location: Walhalla, map 1, grid A8.

Campsites, facilities: There are 68 campsites with a separate tent area. Facilities include RV pull-through sites, electric hookups, water, sewer, disposal station, grocery store, swimming beach, boat ramp and dock, fishing, fish cleaning station, and playground. Boat rentals are available. Pets are allowed.

Reservations, fees: Reservations are recommended. The average daily fee is $18. Travelers checks and personal checks are accepted. Open from early April through early December.

Directions: Go five miles north of Walhalla on the north side of Round Lake. From U.S. Hwy. 10, turn north on Benson Road for three miles and then turn west on Sugar Grove Road for 0.75 mile. Turn north on Morse Road for one mile, then turn east for 0.75 mile on Dewey Road.

Contact: Timber Surf Camping Resort, Larry and Pat Polacek, 6575 Dewey Rd., Fountain, MI, 49410, 231/462-3468.

Trip Notes: Enjoy the rustic tranquility of tall shade trees, quiet beach, and relaxed family camping in this campground near Round Lake, which has a clean sandy bottom. There are also a variety of winter activities.

If you want to canoe a terrific body of water, Ivan's Canoe Rental (231/745-3361), one mile south of Baldwin on Hwy. 37 (east side of highway), services the Pere Marquette National Wild and Scenic River with canoes and kayaks. It offers trips from three hours to three days.

■ Paris Park

Location: Paris, map 2, grid B4.

Campsites, facilities: There are 68 campsites in this county park. Facilities include electric hookups, water, flush toilets, showers, disposal station, river fishing and canoeing, gift shop, and playground. Rustic cabin rentals are available. Pets are not allowed.

Reservations, fees: Reservations are accepted. The daily fee ranges from $11 to $15. Credit cards are not accepted. Open year-round. The facility is fully operational May through September.

Directions: The campground is six miles north of Big Rapids on Old U.S. Hwy. 131. From Hwy. 131, exit at 19 Mile Road and go 1.5 miles to Old Hwy. 131, then go three miles north to the park on the east side of the street.

Contact: Paris Park, 22090 Northland Dr., Paris, MI 49338, 231/796-3420.

Trip Notes: An eight-foot concrete Indian with full headdress stands on the eastern side of Paris Park. The meaning and symbolism of the statue is yet unknown.

An afternoon in Big Rapids, six miles south of the park, will produce a lot of fun. You can visit the "Old Jail" (231/796-9507) on South Stewart Street, which served as the jail and residence of the sheriff from 1893 to 1965. Tours are by appointment. Or you can visit the Ferris State University Nature Preserve on South State Street and take a self-guided tour, use the hiking trail, and do some bird-watching.

3 Merrill Lake Park

Location: Sears, near Barryton, map 2, grid C7.

Campsites, facilities: There are 147 campsites in this Mescosta County park. Facilities include RV pull-through sites, electric hookups, water, flush toilets, showers, swimming beach, boat ramp, bike trails, picnic area, fishing, and playground. Hiking trails are nearby. Seasonal campsite rentals are available. Pets are allowed.

Reservations, fees: Reservations are recommended. The daily fee ranges from $10 to $14. Travelers checks and personal checks are accepted. Open May through September.

Directions: At the junction of Hwy. 66 and U.S. Hwy. 10, go seven miles south on Hwy. 66. Go west (left) on Evergreen. The road dead-ends into the park.

Contact: Merrill Lake Park, 3275 Evergreen Rd., Sears, MI 49679, 517/382-7158.

Trip Notes: This county park is in a great location, nestled between Merrill and Gorrel Lakes. Enjoy a visit to the Barryton Area Museum on 30th Avenue (517/382-7678). This museum has an old one-room schoolhouse attached and displays old cameras, pictures of the area, hand tools, sleigh, and organs. Admission is free.

4 Manistee National Forest: Nichols Lake Campground

Location: Brohman, on Nichols Lake, map 2, grid C2.

Campsites, facilities: There are 28 campsites. Facilities include lake swimming, boat ramp, lake fishing, and hiking trails. Pets are allowed.

Reservations, fees: The daily fee is $12. Open from mid-May through mid-October.

Directions: From Brohman, go two miles north on Hwy. 37, and then 4.5 miles west on 11 Mile Road. Then drive 0.75 mile north on Forest Road 5140 to the entrance.

Contact: Nichols Lake Campground, 412 Red Apple Rd., Manistee, MI 49660, 231/723-2211.

Trip Notes: Drive west to Big Rapids and see the brick sidewalks, antique-style lighting, park benches, and seasonal banners in the downtown area. There are more than 35 specialty shops, 10 restaurants, and four screen theaters.

While you're there, visit the Anna Howard Shaw sculpture at 428 S. Michigan. Born in 1847, she was a resident from the age of 12 and contributed her energy to the Women's Suffrage Association with Susan B. Anthony. Ms. Shaw is in the Women's Hall of Fame in Lansing.

5 Big Bend Park

Location: White Cloud, map 2, grid D2.

Campsites, facilities: There are 204 campsites with a separate tent area. Facilities include electric hookups, water, flush toilets, showers, disposal station, swimming beach, boat ramp, fishing, bike and hiking trails, planned weekend activities, and playground. In winter, there's cross-country skiing. RV and seasonal campsite rentals are available. Pets are allowed.

Reservations, fees: Reservations are recommended. The daily fee ranges from $18 to $20. Credit cards are accepted. Open year-round. The facility is fully operational from mid-April through mid-October.

Directions: From U.S. Hwy. 131, take exit 125 and go 8.5 miles west on Jefferson (36th Street). Go across the Hardy Dam and drive north on Elm Street and then east of 16th Street to the entrance.

Contact: Big Bend Park, 2000 Beech, White Cloud, MI 49349, 231/689-6325.

Trip Notes: If you're looking for something different, visit the Shelby Man-Man Gemstone Factory (231/861-2165). Take the Shelby exit from Hwy. 31, turn east and follow the blue and white signs. The factory has a 50-seat theater for shows on the creation of natural and man-made gems. The showroom features finished 14kt gold jewelry set with simulated and synthetic diamonds, emeralds, rubies, and sapphires. Naturally there's a gift shop.

6 Sandy Beach Park

Location: White Cloud, map 2, grid D2.

Campsites, facilities: There are 200 campsites in this county park. Facilities include electric hookups, water, disposal station, lake swimming, boat ramp, lake or river fishing, and hiking trail. Seasonal campsite rentals are available. Pets are allowed.

Reservations, fees: The daily fee ranges from $10 to $16. Open from mid-May through mid-September.

Directions: From the junction of U.S. Hwy. 131 and Jefferson Road, take exit 125 and go nine miles west on Jefferson Road. Then drive 0.75 mile east on 30th Street to the park entrance.

Contact: Sandy Beach Park, 6926 30th St., White Cloud, MI 49349, 231/689-1229.

Trip Notes: If you like to climb, visit the Higher Ground Rock Climbing Centre (616/774-3100). It has all your equipment needs. The store is at 851 Bond, N.W., in Grand Rapids.

7 Leisure Time RV Park

Location: White Cloud, map 2, grid D2.

Campsites, facilities: There are 86 campsites with a separate tent area. Facilities include RV pull-through sites, electric hookups, sewer, flush toilets, showers, and small lake for fishing, canoeing, and swimming. Fishing and hunting are available nearby. Cabin rentals are available. Pets are allowed.

Reservations, fees: The daily fee is $20. Open year-round.

Directions: From Newaygo, go north on Hwy. 37 to 40th Street, turn east on 40th, and go 1.5 miles to Spruce. Then turn right on Spruce and go 1.5 miles to the campground at the end of the road.

Contact: LeisureTime RV Park, Cut and Marcie Pollie, 4799 S. Spruce, White Cloud, MI 49349, 231/689-5490.

Trip Notes: If the weather turns poor, take in a performance at Western Michigan's Cherry County Playhouse at the 1,750-seat Frauenthal Center for the Performing Arts (231/722-9750) at 425 W. Western Avenue near the shore of Muskegon Lake. The theater, a downtown landmark, first opened in 1930. In 1998, an $8.2 million restoration returned it to its original Spanish Renaissance and Moorish-style splendor.

8 Brower Park

Location: Near Stanwood, north of Grand Rapids, map 2, grid D5.

Campsites, facilities: There are 230 campsites. Facilities include electric hookups, water, sewer, flush toilets, showers, disposal station, river swimming, boat ramp and dock, fishing, biking and hiking trails, tennis court, and playground. Boat and canoe rentals are available nearby. Pets are allowed.

Reservations, fees: The daily fee is $16. Open from mid-April through mid-October.

Directions: From the junction of Hwy. 46 and U.S. Hwy. 131 expressway, go 10 miles north on Hwy. 131 and 2.25 miles west on 8 Mile Road. Then drive 2.25 miles southwest on Old State Road and 1.5 miles west on Polk Road to the park entrance.

Contact: Brower Park, 23056 Polk Rd., Stanwood, MI 49346, 231/823-2561, email: park@ netonecominet.

Trip Notes: Drive to nearby Mt. Pleasant where you can visit the McIntosh Orchard (517/773-7330) and, in season, pick your own cherries and plums, and enjoy the store's other items. Another option is golfing at the St. Ives Golf Club Course (616/972-4837).

9 Tall Pines Campsites and Canoe Livery

Location: Morley, on the Little Muskegon River, map 2, grid E5.

Campsites, facilities: There are 60 campsites, about half of them rustic and on the river. Facilities include electric hookups, water, flush toilets, showers, disposal station, heated outdoor pool, swimming beach, grocery store, and playground. Canoe, rowboat, and kayak rentals are available. Charter boat fishing and a hunting area are nearby. Pets are not allowed.

Reservations, fees: Reservations recommended. The daily fee is $20 for up to four people. Open from mid-April through mid-October. It is also open during deer season.

Directions: From Grand Rapids, take U.S. Hwy. 131 north for 35 miles to exit 125 and Jefferson Road. Then go one mile east to the entrance.

Contact: Tall Pines Campground, Von and Naomi Phillips, 550 S. Talcott, Morley, MI 49336, 800/375-4672 or 231/856-4556.

Trip Notes: You might visit the nearby Amish communities or drive to Coopersville to the Coopersville and Marne Railway (616/837-7000), a specialty railroad that offers charters, summer trains, and theme rides beginning in mid-April. Take I-96 exit 16 or 19 and follow the signs to downtown Coopersville.

10 Newaygo State Park

Location: Between Stanwood and Newaygo on Hardy Dam Pond, map 2, grid E2.

Campsites, facilities: There are 99 rustic campsites, but none are directly on the water. Facilities include vault toilets, disposal station, boat ramp, pond boating, canoeing, swimming, fishing, hiking trail, and playground. Pets are allowed with restrictions.

Reservations, fees: Reservations are recommended on weekends. The daily fee is $6. Credit cards are accepted. Open April through mid-December.

Directions: Take U.S. Hwy. 131 to exit 125 and go west five miles to Beech Street. Turn right and go north on Beech about one mile to the park.

Contact: Newaygo State Park, 2793 Beech St., Newaygo, MI 49337, 231/856-4452.

Trip Notes: In addition to taking advantage of the rustic beauty of this park on the Hardy Dam impoundment, you might experience a musical adventure with the West Shore Symphony Orchestra (231/726-3231) in Muskegon. Call or send an email (info@wsso.org) for a schedule of performances. Founded in 1939, the professional orchestra serves all of western Michigan with classical and pops concerts.

▮▮ Little Switzerland Resort and Campground

Location: North of Newaygo, on Pickerel Lake, map 2, grid E2.

Campsites, facilities: There are 80 campsites. Facilities include electric hookups, water, flush toilets, showers, laundry, disposal station, grocery store, swimming beach, boat ramp and dock, fishing, and playground. Boat and cabin rentals are available. Pets are allowed.

Reservations, fees: The daily fee is $17. Open May through October.

Directions: From Newaygo, take Old Hwy. 37 to Centerline Road and go north for 1.5 miles to Pickerel Lake Drive. Turn left to the entrance.

Contact: Little Switzerland Resort and Campground, Richard and Marcia Hoffman, 254 Pickerel Lake Dr., Newaygo, MI 49337, 231/652-7939.

Trip Notes: Visit Swede Hill Settlement, originally known as the upper Big Rapids, settled by people of Swedish, Norwegian, and Danish heritage. A marker in a park on Baldwin Street names the Swede Hill pioneers.

▮▮ Croton Township Campground

Location: Newaygo, at Croton Dam, map 2, grid E2.

Campsites, facilities: There are 150 campsites with a separate tent area. Facilities include RV pull-through sites, electric hookups, water, flush toilets, showers, bike trail, swimming beach, two boat ramps and dock, picnic area, and playground. Boating, canoeing, and fishing are also nearby. Pets are allowed.

Reservations, fees: Reservations are recommended. The daily fee ranges from $11 to $15. Travelers checks and personal checks are accepted. Open from mid-April through mid-October.

Directions: From Hwy. 82, take Elm Street north to the dead end and turn right. The campground is one mile on the left, on the east side of the Muskegon River at Croton Dam.

Contact: Croton Township Campground, 5725 Croton Hardy Dr., Newaygo, MI 49337, 231/652-4642.

Trip Notes: Want to go fishing, but you don't have any tackle? Let the 5-19 "At Ease" River Charters supply everything and take you where the fish dwell (231/856-4586). This campground is located on Croton Dam backwaters.

▮▮ Ed H. Henning County Park

Location: In Newaygo, overlooking the Muskegon River, map 2, grid E2.

Campsites, facilities: There are 60 campsites. Facilities include electric hookups, water, sewer, flush toilets, showers, disposal station, swimming beach, boat ramp and dock, lake and river fishing, tennis courts, 1.25-mile nature hiking trail, and playground. Pets are allowed.

Reservations, fees: Reservations are recommended. The daily fee ranges from $10 to $15. Personal checks are accepted. Open from mid-May through mid-September.

Directions: Go north on Hwy. 37 to Newaygo. Then go one-quarter mile east on Croton Drive to the park entrance.

Contact: Ed H. Henning County Park, 500 E. Croton Dr., Newaygo, MI 49337, 231/652-1202.

Trip Notes: The park is on a beautiful plateau overlooking the Muskegon River and offers a variety of outdoor activities for the family.

If you have time to see the nearby sites, children of all ages will enjoy the Orchard Hill Farm (616/868-7229) in Lowell. At this working farm, they can pet and feed many of the animals, see a beehive in glass, the cider mill, and a maple syrup display. They can also play in a maze, visit "the spook house," eat in a picnic area, and take a hayride. From I-96, take the Hwy. 50 exit and go north one-quarter mile to Cascade Road. Drive west 2.5 miles to the farm.

14 Oxbow Park

Location: Between Newaygo and White Cloud, map 2, grid F2.

Campsites, facilities: There are 179 sites in this Big Prairie township park with a separate tent area. Facilities include RV pull-through sites, electric hookups, water, sewer, flush toilets, showers, disposal station, river swimming, boat ramp and dock, picnic area, and fishing. Biking, hiking, and cross-country ski trails are available. Pets are allowed.

Reservations, fees: Reservations are recommended. The daily fee is $18 in the campground and $20 in the RV park. Travelers checks, personal checks, and credit cards are accepted. Open year-round except holidays. The facility is fully operational from mid-April through mid-October.

Directions: Take U.S. Hwy. 131 to exit 125 and go about seven miles west on Jefferson to Chestnut. Go north on Chestnut to the entrance.

Contact: Oxbow Park, 2937 Cottonwood, Newaygo, MI 49337, 231/856-4279, email: bprairiebb@mail.riverview.net.

Trip Notes: The campground is across from the Hardy Dam and has access to 17 miles of the Big Muskegon River.

Next to the wayside park on Hwy. 66 in Barryton, northeast of Newaygo, is the Barryton Area Museum (517/382-7678). It has an attached one-room schoolhouse. The museum also has a large selection of cameras and pictures of this area of Michigan. Other items include old hand tools, a sleigh, and organs. Admission is free.

15 Chinook Camping

Location: Grant, just south of Newaygo, map 2, grid F2.

Campsites, facilities: There are 106 campsites. Facilities include electric hookups, water, flush toilets, showers, disposal station, laundry, swimming pool, boat ramp, fishing, shuffleboard courts, and playground. Boat rentals are available. Pets are allowed.

Reservations, fees: The daily fee is $18 up to a family of four and $2 for each additional person. Credit cards are accepted. Open May through mid-October.

Directions: From the junction of Hwy. 37 and 112th Street, go six miles west on 112th Street to the entrance on the right.

Contact: Chinook Camping, 5471 W. 112th St., Grant, MI 49327, 231/834-7505.

Trip Notes: If you wish to eat out one evening, you might try the Grant Depot Restaurant (231/834-7361) at 22 W. Main Street. It offers family-style dining in an authentic railroad setting in a century-old railway station that also features baked chicken, sandwiches, desserts, and homemade breads and soups. Reservations are recommended.

Need a cultural fix? Visit the Muskegon Museum of Art (231/720-2570) at 296 W. Webster Avenue in Muskegon.

16 Salmon Run Campground and Vic's Canoes

Location: In Grant, on the Muskegon River, map 2, grid F2.

Campsites, facilities: There are 238 campsites. Facilities include electric hookups, water, flush toilets, showers, laundry, disposal station, grocery store, gift shop, outdoor swimming pool, boat ramp, river fishing, hiking trail, planned weekend activities, and playground. Boat, canoe, and cabin rentals are available. Pets are allowed.

Reservations, fees: Reservations are recommended. The daily fee ranges from $17 to $21. Personal checks and credit cards are accepted. Open from mid-April through mid-October.

Directions: From Grant, go one mile north on Gordon Street to 104th Street. Turn west and go one-half mile to Felch Road. Then drive one mile north on Felch to the entrance on the right.

Contact: Salmon Run Campground and Vic's Canoes, 8845 Felch Ave., Grant, MI 49327, 231/834-5494, email: salmonrun@worldnet.att.net.

Trip Notes: In Big Rapids, drive to the Old Jail (231/796-9507), a Michigan Historic Site, at 220 S. Stewart. The building served as the county jail and sheriff's residence from 1893 to 1965. It's the community's oldest public structure. The restored jail is now used as a community center. Tours are conducted by appointment.

17 Lakeside Camp Park

Location: In Cedar Springs, north of Grand Rapids, map 2, grid G4.

Campsites, facilities: There are 162 campsites on a five-acre private lake stocked with fish (no license required). Facilities include electric hookups, water, sewer, flush toilets, showers, laundry, disposal station, grocery store, lake swimming, boat dock (electric motors only), fishing, planned weekend activities, and playground. Boat rentals are available. Pets are allowed.

Reservations, fees: Reservations are recommended. The daily fee ranges from $18 to $20 per family. Credit cards are accepted. Open May through September.

Directions: From Grand Rapids, take U.S. Hwy. 131 north to Cedar Springs at exit 104. Go east about 300 feet to first stoplight, turn right and go one-half mile to the campground.

Contact: Lakeside Camp Park, 13677 White Creek Ave., Cedar Springs, MI 49319, 616/696-1735.

Trip Notes: In Grand Rapids, spend part of a day at the John Ball Zoo (616/336-4300) at 1300 W. Fulton St. This 100-acre park has more than 700 animals and many displays.

18 Duke Creek Campground

Location: Cedar Springs, on Duke Creek, map 2, grid G4.

Campsites, facilities: There are 114 campsites. Facilities include electric hookups, water, sewer, flush toilets, showers, disposal station, laundry, grocery store, swimming pool, stream fishing, shuffleboard courts, and planned weekend activities. Cabin rentals are available. Pets are allowed.

Reservations, fees: The daily fee ranges from $16 to $20. Credit cards are accepted. Open May though mid-October.

Directions: From the junction of Hwys. 131/46, take the Cedar Springs exit 104 and go 100 yards east on Hwy. 46, then just over one mile north on White Creek Avenue to the entrance on the right.

Contact: Duke Creek Campground, 15190 White Creek Ave., Cedar Springs, MI 49319, 616/696-2115.

Trip Notes: Michigan is known for its delicious cherries. Why not pick your own one afternoon? Drive to Robinette's Apple Haus in Grand Rapids (616/361-5567) where you can pick cherries in July, buy peaches in August, or enjoy delicious treats from their bakery and lunchroom.

19 Three Season's RV Park

Location: North of Greenville, on Fish Lake, map 2, grid G6.

Campsites, facilities: There are 185 campsites. Facilities include electric hookups, water, flush toilets, showers, laundry, disposal station, grocery store, swimming pool, lake swimming, boat ramp and dock (20 hp motor limit), fishing, mini-golf, and playground. Boat rentals are available. Pets are allowed.

Reservations, fees: Reservations are recommended. The daily fee ranges from $15 to $20. Open from mid-May through mid-October.

Directions: From the U.S. Hwy. 31 exit at Hwy. 57, go east for 1.7 miles to Hwy. 91. Drive north on Hwy. 91 for 2.5 miles to Peck (County Road 506) and turn east for one mile to Fitzner. Drive north on Fitzner for one mile to Fuller. Turn east and go one mile to the entrance.

Contact: Three Season's RV Park, 6956 W. Fuller Rd., Greenville, MI 48838, 616/754-5717.

Trip Notes: If you're a racing fan, the Mount Pleasant Speedway (517/773-2387) is just northeast of Greenville. The speedway, open May through mid-September, boasts some of the most competitive dirt-track racing in Michigan. To reach it, exit U.S. Hwy. 27 at Hwy. 20 and follow the signs.

20 Snow Lake Kampground

Location: Fenwick, north of Ionia, map 2, grid G8.

Campsites, facilities: There are 246 campsites. Facilities include RV pull-through sites, electric hookups, water, sewer, flush toilets, showers, wheelchair access, disposal station, laundry, restaurant, grocery store, swimming pool, boat ramp and dock, fishing, shuffleboard courts, mini-golf, and playground. Boat rentals are available. Pets are allowed.

Reservations, fees: The daily fee ranges from $23 to $25. Open May through September.

Directions: From I-96, take exit 67 north to Ionia. Follow Hwy. 66 north of Ionia about 10 miles to Snow Lake Road. Turn east on

Snow Lake Road and drive about three-quarters of a mile to the entrance.

Contact: Snow Lake Kampground, Ronald and Marie Sellers, 644 E. Snow Lake Rd., Fenwick, MI 48834, 517/248-3224.

Trip Notes: If you have the urge to hike, observe birds, take wildlife photographs, or just relax, visit the Ferris State University Nature Preserve at 901 S. State St., in Big Rapids. The rural, mostly woodland, area is partly wheelchair accessible.

21 Double R Ranch Resort and Golf

Location: Smyrna, northeast of Grand Rapids, map 2, grid H6.

Campsites, facilities: There are 100 campsites. Facilities include electric hookups, water, sewer, flush toilets, showers, laundry, disposal station, grocery store, swimming pools, river swimming, boating, canoeing, fishing, horseback riding, hayrides, nine-hole golf course and driving range, hiking trail, and playground. Cabin and canoe rentals are available. Pets are allowed.

Reservations, fees: The daily fee starts at $23 for two people. Credit cards are accepted. Open May through mid-September.

Directions: From Grand Rapids, take U.S. Hwy. 131 to the Comstock Park exit and follow West River Drive east to Hwy. 44. Follow Hwy. 44 toward Belding and take Whites Bridge Rd. south for 2.5 miles to the entrance.

Contact: Double R Ranch Resort, Richard and Mary Reeves, 4424 Whites Bridge Rd., Smyrna, MI 48887, 800/734-3575 or 877/794-0520 or 616/794-0520, email: rrranch @pathwaynet.com, website: www.doubler ranch.com.

Trip Notes: The Grand Rapids Children's Museum (616/235-4726; website: www.grcm

.org) is an interactive hands-on environment that inspires learning, encourages self-direction, and is a good option for rainy days. The museum is at 11 Sheldon Ave., N.E., in Smyrna.

22 Coldwater Lake Family Park

Location: Mount Pleasant, on Coldwater Lake, map 3, grid D2.

Campsites, facilities: There are 95 campsites in this county park. Facilities include electric hookups, water, flush toilets, showers, disposal station, swimming beach, boat ramp and dock, picnic area, fishing, and playground. Camping cabin and seasonal campsite rentals are available. Pets are allowed.

Reservations, fees: Reservations are recommended. The daily fee ranges from $11 to $32. Credit cards are accepted. Open May through September.

Directions: From the junction of U.S. Business Hwy. 27 and Hwy. 20, go seven miles west on Hwy. 20, and then five miles north on Winn Road. Then drive two miles west on Beal City Road and a quarter of a mile south on Littlefield Road to the park entrance.

Contact: Coldwater Lake Family Park, 1703 N. Littlefield Rd., Weidman, Mi 48893, 517/772-0911.

Trip Notes: The entire family will enjoy a visit to the Center for Cultural and Natural History (517/774-3829) at Central Michigan University to view the museum gallery of 50-plus exhibits that display materials from all of the museum's collection areas, or to see the Native American gallery, which displays both traditional and contemporary creations of Native American artisans. The museum is located on the campus in Rowe Hall at the corner of Bellows and Mission Streets in Mt. Pleasant. There's no admission fee. You can enjoy a leisurely stroll, but most visitors see the museum as part of a pre-arranged tour.

Half Moon Lake Campground

Location: Riverdale, on Half Moon Lake, map 3, grid E2.

Campsites, facilities: There are 43 campsites. Facilities include electric hookups, water, flush toilets, showers, disposal station, lake swimming, boat ramp, fishing, and playground. Boat rentals are available. Pets are allowed.

Reservations, fees: The daily fee ranges from $16 to $19. Credit cards are accepted. Open May through September.

Directions: From the junction of Hwy. 46 and Lumberjack Road north of Riverdale, go 3.5 miles north on Lumberjack to the entrance on the right.

Contact: Half Moon Lake Campground, 517/833-7852.

Trip Notes: Have a yen for strawberries, black and red raspberries? Why not pick your own at Ruter's Berry Farm (517/842-3322), just west of Riverdale off Hwy. 46. is

☷ Ionia Recreation Area

Location: Near Ionia on Sessions Lake and the Grand River, map 4, grid A8.

Campsites, facilities: There are 100 campsites plus 49 sites for equestrians. Facilities include electric hookups, flush toilets, showers, disposal station, lake swimming, boat ramp, lake and river fishing, large picnic areas, and playground. Biking, hiking, and horseback riding trails are available. Pets are allowed.

Reservations, fees: The daily fee is $12. The daily horse campground fee is $10. Payment can be made by check or cash. Open April through November. The facility is fully operational May through mid-October.

Directions: From I-96, take exit 64 and drive three miles north to the recreational area entrance.

Contact: Ionia Recreation Area, 2880 David Hwy., Ionia, MI 48846, 616/527-3750.

Trip Notes: Anglers can take advantage of 140-acre Sessions Lake, a man-made body of water that's up to 60 feet deep. It has walleye, largemouth and smallmouth bass, channel catfish, crappie, and bluegill. A boat-launching facility is on the west side of the lake.

☵ Yankee Springs Recreation Area: Deep Lake Campground, Gun Lake Campground, Horseman Campground

Location: Middleville, between Kalamazoo and Grand Rapids, map 4, grid C5.

Campsites, facilities: Deep Lake has 120 sites, Gun Lake has 220 sites and Horseman has 50 sites. Facilities at Deep Lake and Horseman include vault toilets. Facilities at Gun Lake include electric hookups, flush toilets, showers, and disposal station. All three campgrounds offer lake swimming, boat ramp, fishing, and playground. Hiking, biking, snowmobiling trails, hunting area, and golf course are nearby.

Reservations, fees: Reservations are recommended. The daily fee is $12. The daily horse campground fee is $10. Credit cards are accepted. Open year-round.

Directions: Deep Lake Campground: From the junction of Hwys. 34/37, go 6.5

miles north on Hwy. 37 and 4.5 miles south on County Road 611 to the entrance. Gun Lake: From the junction of Hwys. 34/37, go 9.5 miles west on Gun Lake Road to the entrance. Horseman Campground: From the junction of Hwys. 115/37, go 6.5 miles north on Hwy. 37 and 5.5 miles south on County Road 611. Then drive one-half mile west on Duffy Road to the entrance.

Contact: Yankee Springs Recreation Area, 2104 Gun Lake Rd., Middleville, MI 49333, 616/795-9081.

Trip Notes: In Grand Rapids, you can visit a Celtic cottage like those you would see in Scotland or Ireland. The Celtic Fields Gift Cottage (888/323-5842 or 616/364-5640), which features a botanical garden, also offers guided tours. From I-96, take exit 38C (East Beltline) and go north to Three-Mile Road. Turn right and drive about one-half block. The cottage is on the left.

26 Whispering Waters Campground and Canoe Livery

Location: Southeast of Grand Rapids on the Thornapple River, map 4, grid C5.

Campsites, facilities: There are 118 campsites. Facilities include RV pull-through sites, electric hookups, water, sewer, flush toilets, showers, disposal station, grocery store, swimming pool, river swimming, boating (no motors permitted), canoeing, fishing, shuffleboard courts, hiking trail, and playground. Canoe rentals are available. Pets are allowed.

Reservations, fees: The daily fee ranges from $18 to $23. Open from late April to early October.

Directions: From Grand Rapids, take Hwy. 37 for 25 miles to just south of Woodland Mall. Go left on Irving Road. From Hastings, go four miles north on Hwy. 37 to Irving Road.

Turn right and go one-quarter mile to the entrance.

Contact: Whispering Waters Campground and Canoe Livery, Roger and Uta Vilmont, 1805 N. Irving Rd., Hastings, MI 49058, 800/985-7019 or 616/945-5166, email: whisper @iserv.net.

Trip Notes: A visit you really should make is to the Gerald R. Ford Museum (616/451-9263 or 616/451-9290) in Grand Rapids. There's a wealth of information on the 38th president's life and public service record. Take U.S. Hwy. 131 exit 85 and turn right at the third stoplight (Pearl Street). Turn right at the third stoplight and enter the parking lot.

27 Indian Valley Campground and Canoe Livery

Location: Southeast of Grand Rapids and north of Middleville, map 4, grid C5.

Campsites, facilities: There are 142 campsites. Facilities include RV pull-through sites, electric hookups, water, sewer, flush toilets, showers, disposal station, laundry, grocery store, swimming pool, river and pond swimming, boat ramp and dock, fishing, hayrides, and playground. Boat, RV, and tent rentals are available. Pets are allowed.

Reservations, fees: The daily fee ranges from about $13 to $18. Open from mid-April through October.

Directions: From Grand Rapids, take U.S. Hwy. 131 south and go east on 100th Street to Patterson. Then go south one-half mile to 108th Street and drive east for four miles to the campground near the Thornapple River.

Contact: Indian Valley Campground and Canoe Livery, 8200 108th St., Middleville, MI 49333, 616/891-8579.

Trip Notes: At Grand Rapids, you can see a herd of buffalo, try a buffalo burger, and ride a hay wagon at Buffalo Ridge Ranch (616/784-4853). You can also see a pow wow, and browse food and craft booths. It's located at 4600 N.W. Fruitridge. From I-96 west, take exit 26 at Fruitridge Avenue. Go north for two miles to the ranch. Use the north entrance.

28 Camp Michawana

Location: Hastings, on Head Lake, map 4, grid C5.

Campsites, facilities: There are 58 campsites. Facilities include electric hookups, water, sewer, flush toilets, showers, disposal station, laundry, lake swimming, canoeing, fishing, mini-golf, tennis courts, and playground. Boat rentals are available. Pets are allowed. This Christian family campground does not allow smoking or alcoholic beverages.

Reservations, fees: The daily fee ranges from $15 to $17. Open May through mid-October.

Directions: From the junction of Hwy. 37N and Hwy. 43, go six miles south on Hwy. 43 and one mile west on Head Lake Road to the entrance.

Contact: Camp Michawana, 5800 Head Lake Rd., Hastings, MI 49058, 616/623-5168 or 616/623-3035.

Trip Notes: One day you might take a picnic lunch and spend the afternoon at Carlton Park Historic Village, Museum, and Recreation Area (616/945-3775). Visit the 17 restored buildings, take the guided tour, and take a stroll through its gift shop.

29 Schnable Lake Family Campground

Location: Martin, on Schnable Lake, map 4, grid C6.

Campsites, facilities: There are 160 campsites. Facilities include RV pull-though sites, electric hookups, water, disposal station, grocery store, swimming beach, boating, canoeing, fishing, hiking trail, and playground. Boat rentals are available. Pets are allowed.

Reservations, fees: The average daily fee ranges from $15 to $19. Open May through September.

Directions: From the junction of U.S. Hwy. 131 and Hwy. 222, go one mile west on Hwy. 222 and one-half mile south on 14th Street. Then drive about one-third of a mile west on 115th Street to the entrance on the right.

Contact: Schnable Lake Family Campground, P.O. Box 222, Martin, MI 49070, 616/672-7367.

Trip Notes: In Allegan, a few miles west, is the Marr Haven Wool Farm (616/673-8800), a farm of Merino-Rambouillet sheep. Visit the gift shop for hand and machine knitting, supplies for spinning, and all types of woolen items.

30 Fort Custer State Recreation Area

Location: West of Kalamazoo near Augusta, map 4, grid F6.

Campsites, facilities: There are 219 campsites. Facilities include electric hookups, flush toilets, showers, lake and river swimming, boat ramp (3 hp motor limit), and fishing. There are also 22 miles of hiking, 20 miles of biking, and 16 miles of horse trails. The trails are open in winter for cross-country skiing. Rustic cabin rentals are available.

Reservations, fees: The daily fee is $12. Payment can be made by check or cash. Open year-round.

Directions: West of Battle Creek, take Hwy. 96 (Dickman Road) 10 miles to the area.

Contact: Fort Custer State Recreation Area, 5163 W. Fort Custer Dr., Augusta, MI 49012, 616/731-4200.

Trip Notes: This 3,000-acre area has four lakes, high rolling meadows, soggy wetland, and abundant woods offering just about anything in outdoor recreation. It provides campers with excellent hunting during the season.

31 Oak Shores Resort Campground

Location: Vicksburg, southeast of Kalamazoo, map 4, grid H4.

Campsites, facilities: There are 117 campsites. Facilities include electric hookups, water, sewer, flush toilets, showers, wheelchair access, disposal station, laundry, grocery store, swimming pool, lake swimming, boat ramp and dock (no motors are permitted), fishing, shuffleboard courts, hiking trail, and playground. Cabin rentals are available.

Reservations, fees: The daily fee ranges from $21 to $23. Open May through mid-October.

Directions: From I-94, take exit 80 and go south for 9.4 miles on Sprinkle Road to the end. Turn east on V Avenue and go two miles to 28th Street. Turn south for one-half mile to the campground.

Contact: Oak Shores Resort Campground, Warren and Janet Wright, 13496 28th St., Vicksburg, MI 49097, 800/583-0662 or 616/649-4689.

Trip Notes: You can cruise on an old-fashioned riverboat with the J and K Steamboat Line (517/627-2154), which has a big paddle-wheeler on the Grand River near Lansing. Call for directions and the schedules of the "Princess Laura" and "Michigan Princess."

32 Sleepy Hollow State Park

Location: Laingsburg, north of Lansing on Lake Ovid, map 5, grid A6.

Campsites, facilities: There are 181 campsites. Facilities include electric hookups, flush toilets, showers, disposal station, swimming beach, boat ramp and dock, and fishing. There are also biking, hiking, horseback riding, and snowmobile trails. Boat rentals are available. Pets are allowed with restrictions.

Reservations, fees: The daily fee is $12. Payment can be made by check or cash. Open April through November. The facility is fully operational May through October.

Directions: From Lansing, take U.S. Hwy. 27 north to County Road 562 (Price Road) and go east for seven miles on Price past Shepardsville Road to the park entrance.

Contact: Sleepy Hollow State Park, 7835 Price Rd., Laingsburg, MI 48848, 517/651-6217.

Trip Notes: There are good opportunities in this more than 2,600-acre park for the angler. You can fish by boat or from land on two fishing piers or from 410-acre Lake Ovid's high banks. The lake was developed from the Little Maple River that winds through the park.

33 Lansing Cottonwood Campground

Location: In Lansing, map 5, grid C4.

Campsites, facilities: There are 110 campsites. Facilities include RV pull-through sites, electric hookups, water, sewer, flush toilets, showers, wheelchair access, laundry, grocery, swimming pool, boating (electric motors only), stocked fishing ponds, and playground. Boat, canoe, kayak, and seasonal campsite rentals are available.

Reservations, fees: Reservations are recommended. The daily fee ranges from $15 to about $21. Credit cards are accepted. Open May through October.

Directions: From I-96, take exit 104 (Cedar Street) to the first stoplight. Turn right at the next stoplight on Miller Road and go east to the end of the road. Turn north on Aurelius to the campground.

Contact: Lansing Cottonwood Campground, 5339 S. Aurelius Rd., Lansing, MI 48911, 517/393-3200, email: cottoncamp@aol.com.

Trip Notes: The campground is near the Ledges, majestic, 60-foot, quartz sandstone rock formations that are more than 300 million years old. The ledges, in 78-acre Fitzgerald Park (517/527-7351), jut from the shore of the Grand River and offer a glimpse of how the earth was formed. Take exit 93A from I-96 and go six miles to Jefferson Street and turn right. The entrance is about one-half mile on the left.

34 Moon Lake Resort

Location: East Lansing, on Moon Lake, map 5, grid C5.

Campsites, facilities: There are 108 campsites. Facilities include electric hookups, water, disposal station, laundry, grocery store, lake swimming, boating (no motors are permitted), canoeing, and fishing. Boat rentals are available. Pets are allowed.

Reservations, fees: The daily fee ranges from $14 to $17. Credit cards are accepted. Open year-round.

Directions: From the junction of U.S. Hwy. 17 and I-69, go 10 miles east on I-69 and take exit 98. Then go one mile east on Lansing Road and two blocks north on Colby Lake Road to the entrance on the left.

Contact: Moon Lake Resort, 12700 Colby Lake, Laingsburg, MI 48848, 517/675-7212 or 517/675-5175.

Trip Notes: If you are in the area on Labor Day weekend, be sure to attend "Riverfest" at the Riverfront Park to see water activities, ethnic food and crafts, and a lighted float parade.

35 Tri-Lake Trails Campground

Location: East of Battle Creek near Marshall, map 5, grid F1.

Campsites, facilities: There are 272 campsites on this 300-acre campground. Facilities include electric hookups, water, flush toilets, showers, disposal station, lake swimming, boating (5 hp motor limit), fishing on three lakes, mini-golf, hiking trails, and shuffleboard courts. Pets are allowed.

Reservations, fees: The daily fee is about $16. Open May through September.

Directions: From I-94/69, go 5.75 miles south on I-69 to exit 32. Drive one mile east on F Dr. South. On Old U.S. Hwy. 27 (17 Mile Road), go a quarter of a mile south and nearly one mile west on Perrett Road to the entrance on the right.

Contact: Tri-Lake Trails Campground, 219 Perrett Rd., Marshall, MI 49068, 616/781-2297.

Trip Notes: Long ago, the nearby community of Marshall was to be Michigan's capital. You can visit the grand governor's mansion that was built. Also, go to the Honolulu House Museum (800/877-5163 or 616/781-8544) at 107 N. Kalamazoo Avenue, built by the first U.S. Counsel to the Sandwich Islands, which is now Hawaii.

36 Rockey's Campground

Location: Albion, on a chain of five lakes west of Kalamazoo, map 5, grid G2.

Campsites, facilities: There are 100 campsites. Facilities include electric hookups, water, flush toilets, showers, wheelchair access, disposal station, grocery store, mini-golf, hiking trail, and playground. The campground provides access to a five-lake chain for swimming, boat docks, and fishing. Boat rentals are available. No large dogs are allowed.

Reservations, fees: The daily fee ranges from $18 to $20. Open from mid-May through September.

Directions: From I-94, take exit 121 and go 6.7 miles north on 28 Mile Road to the entrance on the right.

Contact: Rockey's Campground, Brian and Vicki Mead, 19880 27-1/2 Mile Rd., Albion, MI 49224, 517/857-2200 or 877/ROCKEYS.

Trip Notes: In Battle Creek, everyone will find a trip to Kellogg's Cereal City, USA (616/962-6230; website: www.kelloggscerealcityusa.org) fascinating. Take the self-guided tour where you'll see how cereal is made at a simulated production line. Allow yourself at least 2.5 hours. Call for hours and fees. The facility is at 171 W. Michigan Avenue.

37 Twin Pines Campground and Canoe Livery

Location: Concord, southeast of Battle Creek, map 5, grid G3.

Campsites, facilities: There are 89 campsites. Facilities include electric hookups, water, flush toilets, showers, wheelchair access, disposal station, laundry, grocery store, river swimming, boating (no motors are permitted), canoeing, fishing, and playground. Canoe and seasonal campsite rentals are available. Pets are allowed.

Reservations, fees: The daily fee is $15 per family. Open May through October.

Directions: From I-94, take exit 136 and Hwy. 60 west to Wheeler Road to the entrance.

Contact: Twin Pines Campground and Canoe Livery, the Greiner family, 9800 Wheeler Rd., Hanover, MI 49241, 517/524-6298.

Trip Notes: Visit the 72-acre garden at the Leila Arboretum (616/969-0270). It features more than 3,000 species of trees and shrubs, many dating back to the 1920s. They're displayed in the manner of European gardens. Admission is free, but donations are accepted. Take I-94 to the Helmer Road exit and go six miles north to West Michigan Avenue. Turn right and go one mile. It's on the left side of the road.

38 Green Valley Campground

Location: Sturgis, near the Indiana border, map 6, grid B5.

Campsites, facilities: There are 220 campsites. Facilities include electric hookups, water, flush toilets, showers, disposal station, grocery store, Olympic-size swimming pool, pond fishing, mini-golf, and playground. An 18-hole golf course is next door. Pets are allowed.

Reservations, fees: The daily fee is about $17. Open May through mid-October.

Directions: From U.S. Hwy. 12 west of Sturgis, go to White School Road and turn south for one mile. Then drive one-quarter mile west on Fawn River Road to the campground.

Contact: Green Valley Campground, Bartt Nettleman, 25499 W. Fawn River Rd., Sturgis, MI 49091, 616/651-8760.

Trip Notes: Treat the family to the Kalamazoo Aviation History Museum and Air Zoo (616/382-1813; website: www.airzoo.org). It has aircraft ranging from a replica of the Wright Flyer to the advanced F-14. In all, there are about 60 aircraft on exhibit and a hands-on area for youngsters. Take I-94 to exit 78 and go south on Portage Road for three stoplights to Milham, which ends in the parking lot.

39 Waffle Farm Campgrounds

Location: North of Coldwater, on Morrison Lake, one of a seven-lake chain, map 7, grid A1.

Campsites, facilities: There are 376 campsites. Facilities include RV pull-through sites, electric hookups, water, sewer, flush toilets, showers, grocery store, lake swimming, boat ramp and dock, fishing, mini-golf, golf driving range, and playground. Boat rentals are available. Pets are allowed.

Reservations, fees: The daily fee ranges from $12 to $24. Open from mid-April through mid-October.

Directions: From I-69, take exit 16 (Jonesville Road) and go west for two miles to Union City Road. Then drive one-half mile north to the campground.

Contact: Waffle Farm Campgrounds, Loyd Green Jr., 790 Union City Rd., Coldwater, MI 49036, 517/278-4315.

Trip Notes: Learn more about how salmon and trout were stocked in Lake Michigan and other Great Lakes at the Wolf Lake Fisheries Interpretive Center (616/668-2876) in Mattawan. The center at 34270 County Road 652 also offers tours, display pond for fish feeding, walking trails, and a picnic area.

40 Cottonwood Resort

Location: Quincy, on Marble Lake, map 7, grid A1.

Campsites, facilities: There are 95 campsites. Facilities include electric hookups, water, sewer, flush toilets, showers, disposal station, grocery store, lake swimming, boat ramp and dock, fishing, and playground. Boat, cabin, and seasonal campsite rentals are available. Pets are allowed.

Reservations, fees: The daily fee ranges from $22 to $25. Open May to mid-October.

Directions: From the junction of I-69 and U.S. Hwy. 12, go 4.75 miles east on Hwy. 12 and 2.25 miles south on Main Street and Ray Quincy Road. Then drive one mile west on Wildwood Road to the entrance on the left.

Contact: Cottonwood Resort, 801 W. Wildwood, Quincy, MI 49082, 517/639-4415.

Trip Notes: Has it been many years since you and your best camper went to a drive-in movie? Drive over to Coldwater and see a double feature at the Capri Drive-In (517/278-5628).

41 Historic Marble Springs Campground

Location: Allen, map 7, grid A2.

Campsites, facilities: There are 80 campsites. Facilities include electric hookups, water, flush toilets, showers, disposal station, laundry, pond swimming and fishing, hiking trail, and playground. Lake boating and fishing are also nearby. Pets are allowed.

Reservations, fees: The average daily fee is about $15. Open May through October.

Directions: From the junction of I-69 and U.S. Hwy. 12, go 10 miles east on Hwy. 12 to the entrance on the right.

Contact: Historic Marble Springs Campground, 517/869-2522.

Trip Notes: The town of Allen (517/869-2575) claims to be the antique capital of Michigan. It has one mile of antique shopping and specialty retailers, including nine antique shops, four antique malls, an antique village, book shops, garden and herb shop, craft shop, Christmas shop, and restaurants. The stores represent more than 500 individual antique dealers.

42 Gateway Park Campground

Location: Hillsdale, southwest of Jackson, map 7, grid A3.

Campsites, facilities: There are 95 campsites. Facilities include electric hookups, water, sewer, flush toilets, showers, disposal station, swimming pool, lake swimming, boat ramp and dock on a 90-acre lake, hiking trail, shuffleboard court, and playground. Boat, log cabin, and RV rentals are available. Pets are allowed.

Reservations, fees: The daily fee ranges from $18 to $21. Open May through October.

Directions: From Hwys. 99/34, take Hwy. 99 to Bacon Road and go west for three miles to Bunn Road. Turn south and go one-half mile to Hallett and turn west into the campground entrance on the left.

Contact: Gateway Park Campground, Norm and Ginny Wilcox, 4111 W. Hallet Rd., Hillsdale, MI 49242, 517/437-7005.

Trip Notes: See the latest in automotive engineering with the guidance of Lansing Car

Assembly Tours (517/885-9676; website: my.voyager.net/vaw602/tours.html). Call for driving directions and schedule. The admission is free.

43 Wildwood Acres

Location: Jonesville, on Goose Lake, map 7, grid A3.

Campsites, facilities: There are 125 campsites. Facilities include RV pull-through sites, electric hookups, disposal station, grocery store, swimming beach on 26-acre Goose Lake, boat ramp (electric motors only), fishing, bike and hiking trails, mini-golf, and playground. Boat, canoe, and fishing tackle rentals are available. Pets are allowed.

Reservations, fees: The daily fee ranges from $15 to $16. Personal checks are accepted. Open April through mid-October.

Directions: From the junction of U.S. Hwy. 12 and Hwy. 99, go one mile east on Hwy 12 and six miles north on Concord Road. Then drive two miles west on Goose Lake Road to the entrance at the end of the road.

Contact: Wildwood Acres, 14540 Goose Lake Rd., Jonesville, MI 49250, 517/524-7149.

Trip Notes: On the east side of Maumee Street in Jonesville is the Grosvenor House Museum (517/849-9596), the renovated home of E. O. Grosvenor, a former Lt. Governor of Michigan. Grosvenor was head of the commission in charge of building Michigan's state capitol building, and his home was designed by the same architect as the capitol. A 32-room Victorian Italianate structure, the museum is open weekends. You can take a guided tour of the mansion and learn about the family and the town.

SAGINAW BAY

Saginaw Bay

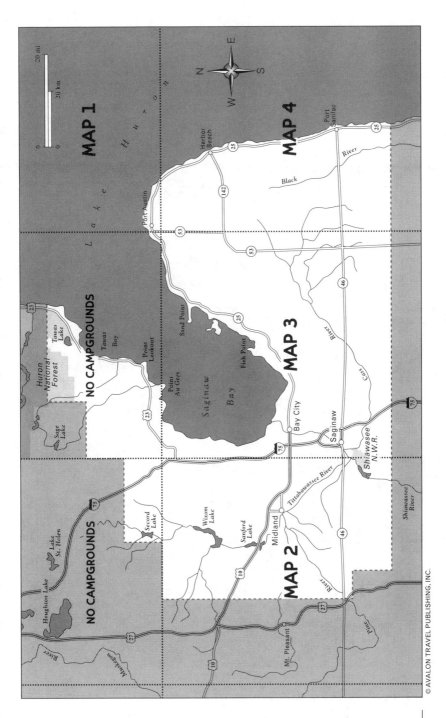

Map 1

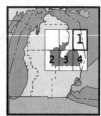

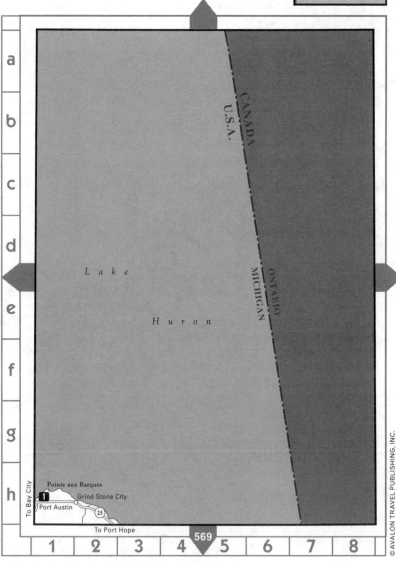

CANADA

U.S.A.

ONTARIO

MICHIGAN

L a k e

H u r o n

Pointe aux Barques

Grind Stone City

To Bay City

1

Port Austin

25

To Port Hope

569

© AVALON TRAVEL PUBLISHING, INC.

a

b

c

d

e

f

g

h

1 2 3 4 5 6 7 8

Map 2

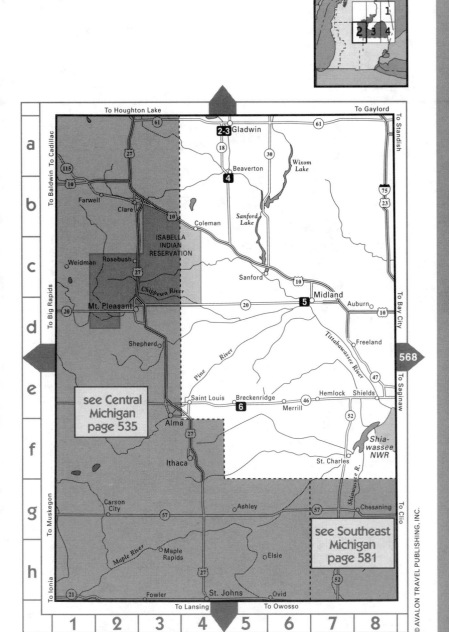

To Houghton Lake · To Gaylord

a To Baldwin · To Cadillac · 61 · **2-3** Gladwin · To Standish · 61

18 · 30 · Wixom Lake

115 · Beaverton · **4**

b 27 · 10 · Farwell · Clare · Coleman · Sanford Lake · 75 · 23

10 · ISABELLA INDIAN RESERVATION

c To Big Rapids · Weidman · Rosebush · 27 · Sanford · 10 · Midland · Auburn · To Bay City

Chippewa River · 20 · **5** · 10

d 20 · Mt. Pleasant · Shepherd · Tittabawassee River · Freeland · 568 · To Saginaw

Pine River · 47

e see Central Michigan page 535 · Saint Louis · Breckenridge · Hemlock · Shields · To Saginaw

Alma · **6** · Merrill · 46 · 52

f 27 · Ithaca · St. Charles · Shiawassee NWR

g To Muskegon · Carson City · 57 · Ashley · 57 · Chesaning · To Clio

Maple River · see Southeast Michigan page 581

h To Ionia · 21 · Maple Rapids · 27 · Elsie · 52

Fowler · St. Johns · Ovid

To Lansing · To Owosso

1 · 2 · 3 · 4 · 5 · 6 · 7 · 8

© AVALON TRAVEL PUBLISHING, INC.

Map 3

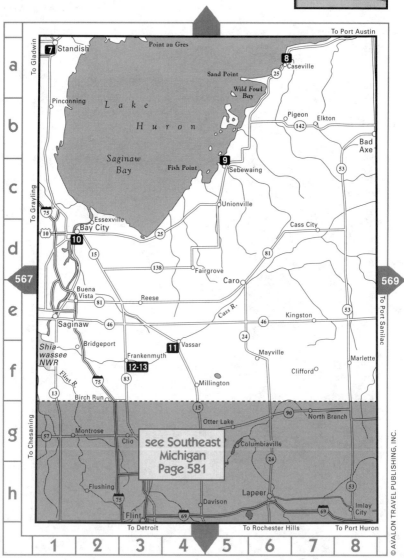

Map 4

566

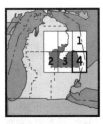

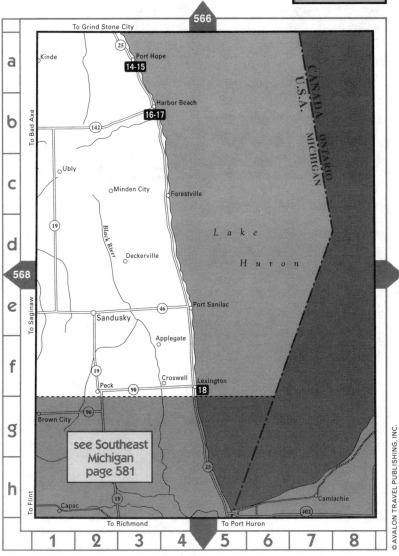

To Grind Stone City

a Kinde   25   Port Hope
14-15

b   To Bad Axe   142   Harbor Beach
16-17

c Ubly   Minden City   Forestville

d Black River   19   Deckerville   *L a k e*

H u r o n

e To Saginaw   46   Port Sanilac
Sandusky

f 19   Applegate

Croswell   Lexington
Peck   90   **18**

g 90   Brown City

see Southeast Michigan page 581

CANADA   U.S.A.
ONTARIO   MICHIGAN

h To Flint   Capac   19

25   Camlachie   402

To Richmond   To Port Huron

1 2 3 4 5 6 7 8

© AVALON TRAVEL PUBLISHING, INC.

568

Saginaw Bay

A t the upper base of Michigan's "thumb" is Saginaw Bay, which has been a major focal point on the Great Lakes.

Long ago, Ottawa and Chippewa Indians occupied the area. Leon Tromble, a trader, was the first white settler. The Saginaw River, which empties into Lake Huron at Bay City, was used to float timber in the late 1800s. Later, as lumbering declined, it became a key port for shipbuilding, steel, and agriculture, especially sugar beets.

Nearby Saginaw, which was established as a fur-trading post in 1816, was named after the Sauk Indians who inhabited the area in the 1800s. In fact, O-Sag-A-Nong means land of the Sauks. The Suaks, however, were evicted by the Iroquois and, later, the Chippewa. A few years later, it became Fort Saginaw.

Today, the communities that surround Saginaw Bay are prime recreational areas for campers pursuing boating, fishing, swimming, and other water sports.

1 Port Crescent State Park

Location: Port Austin, on Saginaw Bay, map 1, grid H1.

Campsites, facilities: There are 135 campsites. Facilities include electric hookups, disposal station, showers, flush toilets, lake swimming, boating, fishing, hiking trails, and playground. Pets are allowed with restrictions.

Reservations, fees: The daily fee is $15. Open April through November.

Directions: From the junction of Hwys. 53 and 25, go 4.5 miles southwest on Hwy. 25 to the park entrance.

Contact: Port Crescent State Park, 1775 Port Austin Rd., Port Austin, MI 48467, 517/738-8663.

Trip Notes: The campground is located on the tip of Michigan's thumb along three miles of sandy shoreline along Saginaw Bay. Some campsites offer a waterfront view of either Lake Huron or the Pinnebog River. There is a 900-foot boardwalk and five picnic decks that offer a scenic view from the top of the sand dunes. You may also enjoy a visit to the

Huron City Museum (517/428-4123) to see the nine preserved 1850-1890 buildings, which include a U.S. Lifesaving Station, general store, church, brick museum, and carriage shed.

② River Valley RV Park

Location: Gladwin, west of Saginaw Bay, map 2, grid A5.

Campsites, facilities: There are 100 campsites. Facilities include electric hookups, water, flush toilets, showers, disposal station, laundry, grocery store, shuffleboard courts, lake swimming, lake and river boating, fishing, and hiking trail. Pets are allowed.

Reservations, fees: The daily fee ranges from $21 to $22. Open May through October.

Directions: From the west junction of Hwys. 18 and 61, go seven miles west on Hwy. 61, then 2.5 miles south on Bailey Avenue to the entrance on the right.

Contact: River Valley RV Park, Bruce and Laura Schofield, 2165 S. Bailey Ave., Gladwin, MI 48624, 517/386-7844.

Trip Notes: This campground is a full family facility located in the rolling woodlands of mid-Michigan's Amish Community.

For more history about the area, visit the Gladwin County Historical Society Museum (517/426-4849), which is housed in an old Michigan Central Railroad depot. Here, you can tour two restored cabins and a schoolhouse. The museum is at 515 E. Cedar Avenue. Once you reach the city limits from Hwy. 61, it is about one-quarter mile on the north side of the road.

③ Gladwin City Park and Campground

Location: Gladwin, west of Saginaw Bay, map 2, grid A5.

Campsites, facilities: There are 61 campsites. Facilities include electric hookups, water, flush toilets, showers, disposal station, picnic area, river swimming, canoeing, fishing, bike and hiking trails, tennis courts, and playground. Call for pet restrictions.

Reservations, fees: The daily fee is $14. Open May through late November.

Directions: From the east junction of Hwys. 18 and 61, go four blocks west on Hwy. 61 to the park entrance. Enter between the courthouse and sheriff's department.

Contact: Gladwin City Park and Campground, 1000 W. Cedar, Gladwin, MI 48624, 517/426-8126.

Trip Notes: In June through December, you can visit the Yost Country Lane Orchard and Cider Mill (517/428-3971). The facility features U-pick apples, baked goods, and pumpkins. It also has a gift shop and a picnic area. It's five miles west of Gladwin on Hwy. 61.

④ Lost Haven Campground

Location: Beaverton, west of Saginaw Bay, map 2, grid B5.

Campsites, facilities: There are 100 campsites. Facilities include RV pull-through sites, electric hookup, flush toilets, showers, disposal station, laundry, pond swimming, fishing, and playground. Seasonal campsite rentals are available. Pets are allowed.

Reservations, fees: The daily fee ranges from $12 to $14. Open May through mid-October.

Directions: Take I-75 to U.S. Hwy. 10 and take it west to Hwy. 18. Then drive seven miles north to Lyle Road and three miles west to Townhall Road. Finally, go north one-quarter mile to the entrance on the left.

Contact: Lost Haven Campground, Bill and Louise Weldon, 5300 Townhall Rd., Beaverton, MI 48612, 517/435-7623.

Trip Notes: If you enjoying sailing and want to relive the old days on the Great Lakes, go to Wenonah Park marina (888/229-8696 or 517/893-4567) in downtown Bay City for a three-hour excursion aboard the "Appledore IV," a tall-ship replica.

⑤ Valley Plaza RV Park

Location: Midland, west of Bay City, map 2, grid D7.

Campsites, facilities: There are 96 campsites. Tents are now permitted. Facilities include RV pull-through sites, electric hookups, water, flush toilets, showers, grocery store, pond and pool swimming, pond canoeing and kayaking, and fishing. Kayak and seasonal campsite rentals are available. Pets are allowed.

Reservations, fees: The daily fee ranges from $25 to $32 per vehicle. Credit cards are accepted. Open year-round.

Contact: Valley Plaza RV Park, 5215 Bay City Rd., Midland, MI 48642, 517/496-2159 or 800/262-0006 (in Michigan), website: www.valleyplazaresort.com.

Directions: From westbound I-75, take exit 162B to U.S. Hwy. 10 and go 10 miles west on Hwy. 10 to the Bay City Road exit. The entrance is on the right. From the junction of U.S. Hwy. 10 and Waldo Road, go 2.5 miles south on Waldo Road, then 1.5 miles on Bay Road to the entrance on the left.

Trip Notes: Although there is lots to do at the adjacent Best Western Resort, the entire family will enjoy the architectural tour, a self-guided driving tour of buildings designed by Allen B. Dow. Maps and audiocassettes can be obtained at the Midland Center for the Arts (517/631-5930). You can also visit the Dow Gardens (517/631-2677 or 800/362-4872), which were originally the grounds of the Herbert H. Dow residence.

⑥ Pine Ridge Campground

Location: Breckenridge, south of Midland, map 2, grid E5.

Campsites, facilities: There are 98 campsites. Facilities include RV pull-through sites, electric hookups, water, flush toilets, showers, disposal station, grocery store, river and pond swimming, and fishing. Kayak and seasonal campsite rentals are available. Pets are allowed.

Reservations, fees: The daily fee ranges from $15 to $19. Credit cards are accepted. Open May through mid-October.

Directions: From the junction of Hwy. 20 and Meridian Road, go three miles south on Meridian Road and then 4.5 miles west on Pine River Road to the entrance on the left.

Contact: Pine Ridge Campground, 1989 W. Pine River Rd., Breckenridge, MI 48615, 517/842-5184 or 800/647-2267.

Trip Notes: The campground is on the scenic Pine River. While camping here you can enjoy a visit to the Chippewa Nature Center (517/631-0830) that covers more than 1,000 acres, 14 miles of marked trails with wildflower and pond walkways, and a homestead farm you can visit. Admission is free.

7 Big Bend Campground

Location: Standish, near the west coast of Saginaw Bay, map 3, grid A1.

Campsites, facilities: There are 86 campsites. Facilities include RV pull-through sites, electric hookups, water, disposal station, flush toilets, showers, laundry, grocery store, lake and river swimming, canoeing, river fishing, hiking trail, and playground. Canoe and seasonal campsite rentals are available. Pets are allowed.

Reservations, fees: The daily fee ranges from $17 to $19. Open from mid-May through mid-October.

Directions: From the junction of Hwys. 23 and 65, go 1.5 miles south on Hale Road, then one mile west on Conrad Road to the entrance on the left.

Contact: Big Bend Campground, 513 W. Conrad Rd., Standish, MI 48658, 989/653-2267.

Trip Notes: You can learn a lot about the Saginaw Bay area with a trip to the Historical Museum of Bay County (517/893-5733) at 312 Washington Avenue in Bay City. It houses seven period rooms and three changing galleries. It also has a new permanent Maritime History Gallery.

8 Albert E. Sleeper State Park

Location: Caseville, on the east coast of Saginaw Bay, map 3, grid A6.

Campsites, facilities: There are 223 campsites. Facilities include electric hookups, flush toilets, showers, disposal station, grocery store, lake swimming, boating, canoeing, hiking and cross-country skiing trails, fishing, and playground. Pets are allowed with restrictions.

Reservations, fees: The daily fee is $15. Open year-round.

Directions: From Caseville, go five miles northeast on Hwy. 25 to the park entrance.

Contact: Albert E. Sleeper State Park, 6573 State Park Rd., Caseville, MI 48725, 517/856-4411

Trip Notes: This is a tranquil, well-wooded state park with a half-mile of Huron Dunes sand beach. There are four miles of marked nature trails that traverse old dune ridges where the vegetation changes from wetland to thick forest.

9 Sebewaing County Park

Location: Sebewaing, on the west side of the "thumb" on Saginaw Bay, map 3, grid C5.

Campsites, facilities: There are 64 campsites. Facilities include electric hookups, water, flush toilets, showers, disposal station, lake and stream fishing, canoeing, boating, swimming beach, and hiking trail. Pets are allowed.

Reservations, fees: The daily fee is $12 to $17 plus a non-refundable $7 reservation fee. Open May through September.

Directions: From the junction of Hwy. 25 and Pine Street, go west on Pine Street, then south on Miller to Union Street. Turn west to the park entrance.

Contact: Sebewaing County Park, 759 Union St., Sebewaing, MI 48759, 517/883-2033.

Trip Notes: If you take a few hours to go to Bay Port, you can tour the Bay Port Fish Company (517/656-2121 or 989/656-2121; website: www.huroncounty.com). In the early 1900s, commercial fishermen shipped tons of yellow period, walleye, herring, whitefish, and carp to New York and Chicago in refrigerated boxcars.

The company is at 1008 First Street. Free guided tours are available.

10 Bay City State Recreation Area

Location: Bay City, on Saginaw Bay, map 3, grid D1.

Campsites, facilities: There are 193 campsites. Facilities include electric hookups, flush toilets, showers, lake boating, fishing, swimming, hiking, and hunting. Pets are allowed.

Reservations, fees: The daily fee is $12. Open year-round.

Directions: Take I-75 to exit 168 and go east 5.5 miles on Hwy. 247 to the entrance.

Contact: Bay City Recreation Area, 3582 State Park Dr., Bay City, MI 48706, 517/684-3020.

Trip Notes: There are five miles of trails and several overlook towers at the new Saginaw Bay Visitor's Center (517/879-2849). There is also an interpretive program on the 1,800-acre Tobico Marsh, which is known nationally for its wetland birds and wildlife.

11 Ber-Wa-Ga-Na Campground

Location: Vassar, east of Frankenmuth, map 3, grid E4.

Campsites, facilities: There are 150 campsites. Facilities include electric hookups, water, flush toilets, showers, grocery store, hiking trail, and playground. There is also a stocked pond for fishing, canoeing, or swimming. Bike and seasonal campsite rentals are available. Pets are allowed.

Reservation, fees: The daily fee ranges from $16 to $22. Credit cards are accepted. Open from mid-April to mid-October.

Directions: From the junction of Hwys. 15 and 46, go 11 miles east on Hwy. 46 to the entrance on the right.

Contact: Ber-Wa-Ga-Na Campground, 3526 Sanilac Rd. (M-46), Vassar, MI 48768, 517/673-7125.

Trip Notes: Only minutes away from historic Frankenmuth, you can also drive to Miller's Family Orchard (517/823-2891) to pick cherries, apples, or pumpkins in season. You can even pit your cherries while you are there and leave the mess behind. The orchard is open all year, seven days a week.

12 Frankenmuth Yogi Bear's Jellystone Park Camp Resort

Location: Frankenmuth, south of Bay City, map 3, grid F3.

Campsites, facilities: There are 260 campsites. Facilities include RV pull-through sites, electric hookups, water, flush toilets, showers, grocery store, laundry, heated swimming pool, whirlpool, mini-golf, planned activities, and playground. Bike and cabin rentals are available. Pets are allowed.

Reservations, fees: The daily fee ranges from $23 to $36. Credit cards are accepted. Open year-round.

Directions: If you are coming northbound on I-75, take Birth Run exit 136 (or southbound the Bridgeport exit 144) and follow the signs to Frankenmuth to the south city limits. Then take Hwy. 83 (Main Street) and go 1,000 yards north of Bronners Christmas Wonderland on Weiss Street to the entrance.

Contact: Frankenmuth Yogi Bear's Jellystone Park Camp Resort, 1339 Weiss St., Frankenmuth, MI 48734, 517/652-6668, fax 517/652-3461, website: www.frankenmuthjellystone.com.

Trip Notes: Although the campground provides activities to keep you busy, take time to visit the city, where you can enjoy the old German flavor of the community. Be sure to eat at Zehnders, (800/863-7999; website: www.zehnders.com) reputed to be America's largest family restaurant. It features a family chicken dinner. You can also visit its bakery and gift shops, and play the 18-hole golf course.

13 Pine Ridge RV Campground

Location: Frankenmuth, south of Bay City, map 3, grid F3.

Campsites, facilities: There are 157 campsites. Tents are not permitted. Facilities include RV pull-through sites, electric hookups, water, sewer, disposal station, flush toilets, showers, laundry, and playground. Pets are allowed.

Reservations, fees: The daily fee is $25. Credit cards are accepted. Open April through mid-November.

Directions: From I-75, take Birch Run exit 136 and follow the signs to Frankenmuth. Then go east on Birch Run Road to Hwy. 83 and go one-quarter mile north on Hwy. 83 (Gera Road) to the entrance on the left.

Contact: Pine Ridge RV Campground, 11700 Gera Rd., Birch Run, MI 48415, 517/624-9029.

Trip Notes: This campground is only 3.9 miles south of Frankenmuth. You should experience Bonner's Christmas Wonderland (800/ALL-YEAR), the Frankenmuth Historical Museum (517/652-9701), Michigan's Own Military and Space Museum (517/652-8005), or enjoy the sound of the Glockenspiel, a 35-bell carillon with carved wooden figures moving on a track acting out the story of the Pied Piper of Hamlin at 713 S. Main Street.

14 Stafford County Park

Location: Port Hope, on the northern side of the thumb on Lake Huron, map 4, grid A3.

Campsites, facilities: There are 99 campsites. Facilities include electric hookups, water, flush toilets, showers, disposal station, lake swimming, boating, fishing, hiking trail, tennis courts, and playground. Boat and seasonal campsite rentals are available. Pets are allowed.

Reservations, fees: The daily fee ranges from $12 to $20. Open May through September.

Directions: From the junction of Hwys. 53 and 25, go 17 miles south on Hwy. 25 and then one-half mile east.

Contact: Stafford County Park, 4451 W. Huron St., Port Hope, MI 48413, 517/428-4213.

Trip Notes: You can take a short cruise from Caseville to the light on Big Charity Island. It was named by the late mariners for its location, placed "through the charity of God" midway between the city of Au Gres and the "thumb," at the entrance to Saginaw Bay. The light was constructed in 1857 and replaced by the Gravelly Shoal Light and abandoned in 1939.

15 Lighthouse County Park

Location: Port Hope, on the northern side of the thumb on Lake Huron, map 4, grid A3.

Campsites, facilities: There are 74 campsites. Facilities include electric hookups, flush toilets, no showers, disposal station, boat ramp, fishing, swimming beach, and playground. Pets are allowed.

Reservations, fees: The daily fee ranges from $15 to $20. Open May through September.

Directions: From town, go five miles north on Hwy. 25 and then one mile east on Lighthouse Road to the park entrance.

Contact: Lighthouse County Park, 7320 Lighthouse Rd., Port Hope, MI 48468, 517/428-4749.

Trip Notes: The park is the home of Pointe Aux Barques Lighthouse and Museum (517/428-4749), which makes for a fascinating tour. It's one of the few lighthouses that is still in operation on the Great Lakes. Built in 1857, under President Polk's orders to guard ships from some of the most treacherous shoals in the Great Lakes, the lighthouse is 89 feet tall with 103 cast-iron steps to the top.

16 North Park Campground

Location: Harbor Beach, on Lake Huron, map 4, grid B3.

Campsites, facilities: There are 184 campsites. Facilities include RV pull-through sites, electric hookups, water, flush toilets, showers, disposal station, stream fishing, nearby lake boating, fishing, swimming, hiking trails, and playground.

Reservations, fees: The daily fee ranges from $13 to $16. Open year-round.

Directions: From the junction of Hwys. 142 and 25, go one-half mile north on Hwy. 25 to the park entrance.

Contact: North Park Campground, 766 State St., Harbor Beach, MI 48441, 517/479-9554.

Trip Notes: Go down to the harbor to view one of the largest man-made harbors in the world and the pier that extends out to the 1880 Harbor Beach Lighthouse.

17 Wagener County Park

Location: Harbor Beach, on Lake Huron, map 4, grid B3.

Campsites, facilities: There are 96 campsites. Facilities include electric hookups, water, pull-through sites, flush toilets, showers, disposal station, seasonal rental sites, lake boating, fishing, swimming, boat ramp, hiking trails, and playground. Pets are allowed.

Reservations, fees: The daily fee ranges from $15 to $20. Open May through mid-October.

Directions: From the junction of Hwys. 142 and 25, go five miles south on Hwy. 25 to the park entrance on the left.

Contact: Wagener County Park, 2671 S. Lakeshore, Harbor Beach, MI 48441, 517/479-9131.

Trip Notes: Take a drive 25 miles northwest on Hwy. 25 to see the 1857 Pointe Aux Barques Light in Lighthouse County Park and the marine museum (517/428-4749).

18 Lexington RV Resort

Location: Lexington, on Lake Huron, map 4, grid F4.

Campsites, facilities: There are 210 campsites. No tents are permitted. The campground accepts full-hookup RVs only. Facilities include RV pull-through sites, electric hookups, water, sewer, flush toilets, showers, laundry, swimming pool, and playground. Lake swimming, fishing, and boating are nearby. Pets are allowed.

Reservation, fee: The daily rate is $25. Open year-round.

Directions: From the junction of Hwy. 90 and U.S. Hwy. 25, go one-half mile north on Hwy. 25 to the entrance on the left.

Contact: Lexington RV Resort, 7181 Lexington Blvd., Lexington, MI 48450, 810/359-2054.

Trip Notes: Drive a few miles west of Lexington to Croswell and visit the Croswell Berry Farm (810/679-3273) to pick your own blueberries and blackberries, or buy some that they have picked.

SOUTHEAST MICHIGAN

Southeast Michigan

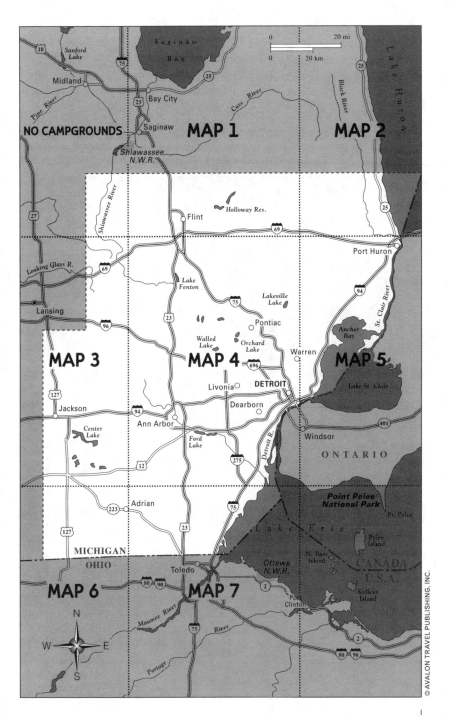

Map 1

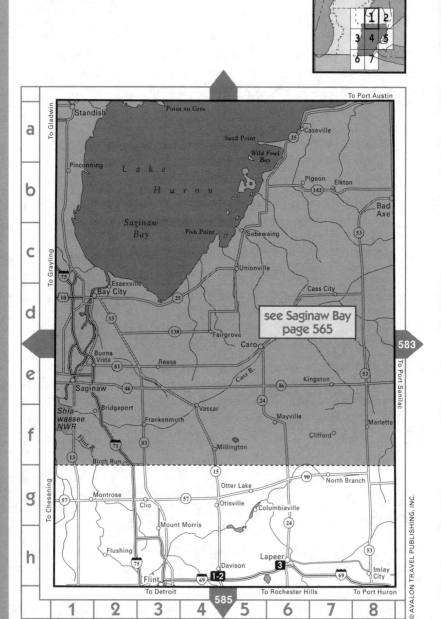

To Port Austin

a — Standish, Point au Gres, Caseville, Sand Point, Wild Fowl Bay, Pigeon, Elkton

b — Pinconning, Lake Huron, 142, Bad Axe

c — Saginaw Bay, Fish Point, Sebewaing, 53, Unionville

d — Essexville, Bay City, Cass City, 25, 138, Fairgrove, Caro, *see Saginaw Bay page 565*

e — Buena Vista, 81, Reese, Cass R., Kingston, 53, Saginaw, 46, 46

f — Shia-wassee NWR, Bridgeport, Frankenmuth, Vassar, 24, Mayville, Clifford, Marlette, Flint R., 75, 83, Millington

g — Birch Run, 13, 15, Otter Lake, 90, North Branch, Montrose, 57, Clio, 57, Otisville, Columbiaville, Mount Morris, 24

h — Flushing, 75, Davison, Lapeer, 3, Imlay City, 53, Flint, 69, I-2, 69

To Gladwin · To Grayling · To Chesaning · To Detroit · To Rochester Hills · To Port Huron

To Port Sanilac

583 · 585

© AVALON TRAVEL PUBLISHING, INC.

Map 2

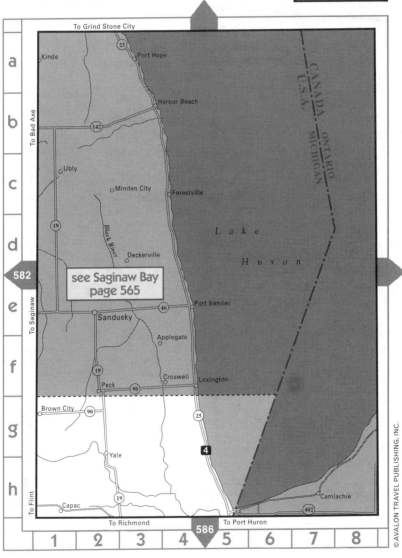

To Grind Stone City

Kinde

Port Hope
25

Harbor Beach

To Bad Axe
142

Ubly

Minden City

Forestville

19

Black River

L a k e

Deckerville

H u r o n

see Saginaw Bay
page 565

582

To Saginaw

Port Sanilac
46

Sandusky

Applegate

19

Croswell   Lexington

Peck
90

Brown City
90
25

Yale

4

To Flint

Capac
19

To Richmond   To Port Huron

586

CANADA
U.S.A.

ONTARIO
MICHIGAN

Camlachie
402

© AVALON TRAVEL PUBLISHING, INC.

Map 3

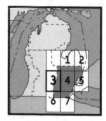

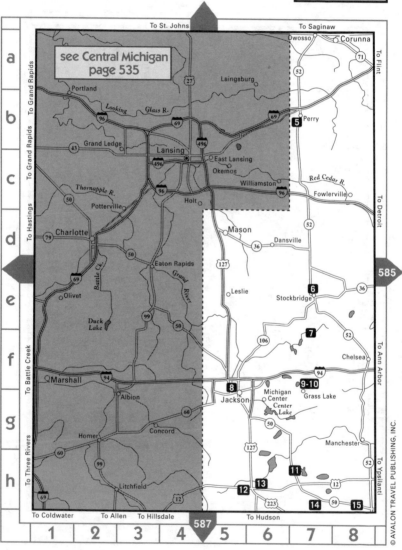

see Central Michigan
page 535

To St. Johns

To Saginaw

Owosso

Corunna

To Flint

a

To Grand Rapids

Laingsburg

27

52

71

Portland

b

To Grand Rapids

Looking

Glass R.

96

69

69

Perry

5

c

To Hastings

43

Grand Ledge

Lansing

496

496

East Lansing

Okemos

Williamston

96

Red Cedar R.

Fowlerville

To Detroit

Thornapple R.

50

Potterville

96

Holt

Mason

d

To Hastings

79

Charlotte

Battle Ck.

50

Eaton Rapids

Grand River

127

36

Dansville

52

585

e

Olivet

69

99

Leslie

Stockbridge

6

36

Duck
Lake

50

f

To Battle Creek

7

106

52

Chelsea

To Ann Arbor

Marshall

94

8

94

9-10

Jackson

Michigan
Center

Grass Lake

g

Albion

60

Concord

50

127

Center
Lake

Manchester

52

To Ypsilanti

h

To Three Rivers

Homer

60

99

Litchfield

11

12

13

12

50

14

15

To Coldwater

To Allen

To Hillsdale

To Hudson

223

69

12

587

1   2   3   4   5   6   7   8

© AVALON TRAVEL PUBLISHING, INC.

Map 4

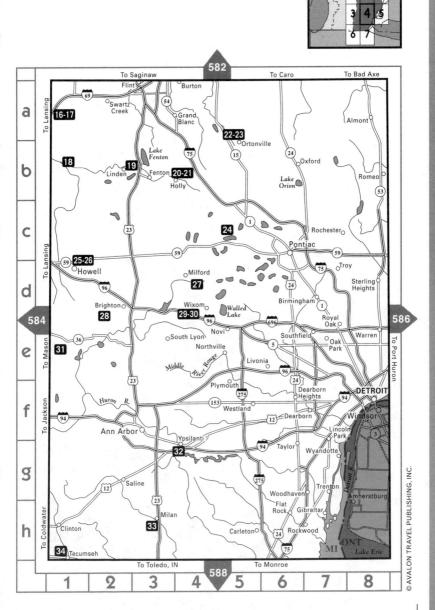

Map 5

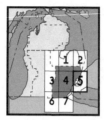

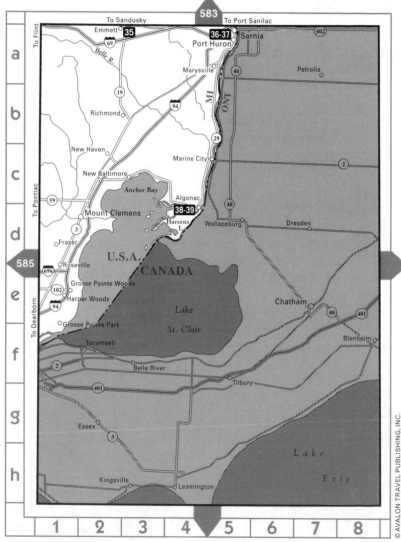

Map 6

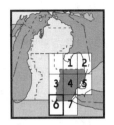

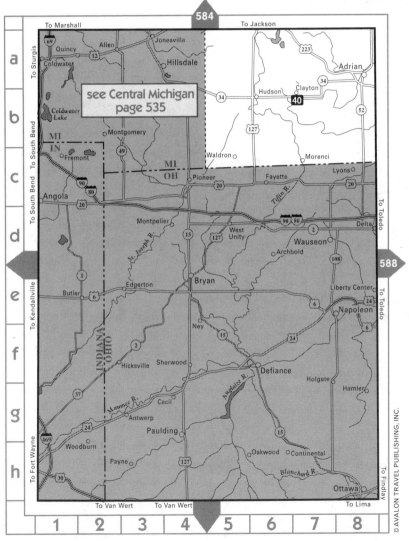

584 To Marshall / To Jackson

To Sturgis

a

To Marshall
69 Quincy
Allen
Jonesville
Coldwater
Hillsdale

223
Adrian

b

To South Bend
To South Bend

Coldwater
Lake

see Central Michigan
page 535

34
Hudson
Clayton
34
Adrian

40
52

c

MI
IN
Fremont

Montgomery
49

MI
OH

Waldron
Morenci

90
80
Angola
20

Pioneer
20
Fayette
Tiffin R.
Lyons
20

To Toledo

d

Montpelier
15
127
West
Unity
Archbold
Wauseon

90 80
2
Delta
108

588 To Toledo

e

To Kendallville

1
Butler
6
Edgerton
Bryan

6
Liberty Center
24
Napoleon
6

f

2
Hicksville
Sherwood
Ney
15
24

Defiance
Holgate
Hamler

g

37
Maumee R.
Cecil
Antwerp
Paulding
400

15
Blanchard R.

h

369
Woodburn
Payne
30
127
Oakwood
Continental
Ottawa

To Fort Wayne
To Van Wert
To Van Wert
To Lima
To Findlay

INDIANA OHIO

© AVALON TRAVEL PUBLISHING, INC.

| 1 | 2 | 3 | 4 | 5 | 6 | 7 | 8 |

Map 7

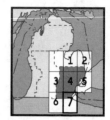

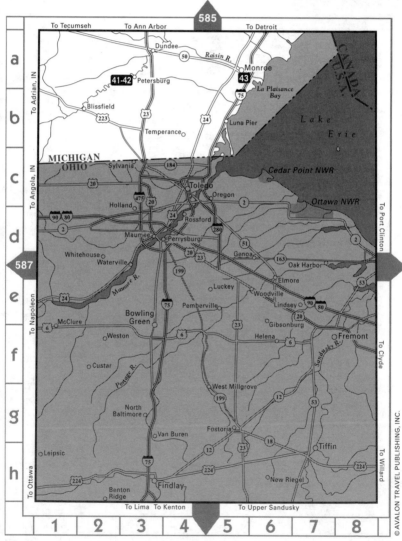

© AVALON TRAVEL PUBLISHING, INC.

Southeast Michigan

Without a doubt, the automobile has played a significant part in the lives of most Americans and no place is better suited than the cities of Detroit and Lansing as sources of automotive history. The Michigan Historical Center in Detroit or an automobile plant tour in Lansing are good places to start.

Yet, despite the imposing presence of these large Michigan cities, there's a surprising amount of outdoor adventures in store for the camper throughout this region in every season.

❶ Wolverine Campground

Location: Davison, east of Flint, map 1, grid H4.

Campsites, facilities: There are 195 campsites in this county park. Facilities include RV pull-through sites, electric hookups, flush toilets, showers, disposal station, boat ramp, fishing, swimming beach, hiking trail, and playground. Rustic tent sites are also available. Pets are allowed.

Reservations, fees: Reservations are recommended. The daily fee is $13. Credit cards are accepted. Open from late May through August.

Directions: From I-75, take the Mt. Morris Road exit, go 14.5 miles east to Baxter Road and drive south to the entrance.

Contact: Wolverine Campground, 7698 N. Baxter Rd., Davison, MI 48423, 800/648-7275 or 810/736-7100 or 810/793-6613, email: gencopks @concentric.net.

Trip Notes: On the shores of the 2,000-acre Holloway Reservoir, this campground is nestled in a pine forest. If you love apples, you'll love them even more when you pick them yourself. At the Apple Lane Orchards (810/736-7622) in Flint you can pick many varies, including Wolf River, Northern Spy, Tolman Sweet, Grimes, and others. You can also get pumpkins, squash, and other tasty produce.

❷ Timber Wolf Campground

Location: Davison, east of Flint, map 1, grid H4.

Campsites, facilities: There are 196 campsites. Facilities include RV pull-through sites, electric hookups, water, flush toilets, showers, disposal station, laundry, grocery store, boat ramp (10 hp limit), fishing, playground, and hiking trail. Pets are allowed.

Reservations, fees: Reservations are recommended. The daily fee is $13. Credit cards are accepted. Open May through September.

Directions: From I-75, take the Mt. Morris Road exit and go 10 miles east on Mt. Morris Road. Then drive one mile south on Irish Road to the campground entrance.

Contact: Timber Wolf Campground, 5045 Stanley Rd., Flint, MI 48506, 800/648-7275 or 810/736-7100 or 810/793-6613.

Trip Notes: This is a quiet campground on the Flint River. It's close to several attractions, including the Crossroads Village and Huckleberry Railroad (800/648-7275 or 810/736-7100; website: www.geneseecounty parks.org), a terrific steam railroad and a living history village of more than 30 buildings. Costumed interpreters demonstrate crafts and the skills of the 1800s. There's also live entertainment in the Opera House, vintage amusement park rides, and a paddlewheel riverboat.

❸ Hilltop Campground

Location: Lapeer, east of Flint on Lake Nepessing, map 1, grid H6.

Campsites, facilities: There are 60 campsites. Facilities include electric hookups, water, flush toilets, showers, disposal station, grocery store, swimming beach, boat ramp and dock, fishing, and playground. Pets are allowed.

Reservations, fees: The daily fee ranges from $17 to $20. Open May through mid-October.

Directions: From I-69, take exit 153 and go south for one-half mile on Lake Nepessing Road to Piper Drive. Then go one-quarter mile west on Piper Drive to the entrance.

Contact: Hilltop Campground, Les and Lisa Noblett, 1260 Piper Dr., Lapeer, MI 48446, 810/644-2782.

Trip Notes: Visit Fuhr's Valley View Fruit Farm (810/724-0314) in Imlay City and whet your appetite for lots of jams, jellies, and homemade cider. In fall, you can pick your own raspberries.

4 Lakeport State Park

Location: Lakeport, north of Port Huron on Lake Huron, map 2, grid H5.

Campsites, facilities: The park has 284 modern campsites. Facilities include electric hookups, water, flush toilets, showers, wheelchair access, disposal station, grocery store, one-mile-wide swimming beach along Lake Huron, boating, fishing, hiking trails, playground, children's activities, and nature programs. Pets are allowed with restrictions.

Reservations, fees: Reservations are recommended. The daily fee is $14. Credit cards are accepted.

Open: April through November.

Directions: From Port Huron, take U.S. Hwy. 25 north for 10 miles to the park entrance.

Contact: Lakeport State Park, 7605 Lakeshore Rd., Fort Gratiot, MI 48059, 810/327-6224.

Trip Notes: Take a trip to Sawmill City (810/982-5090) on Lapeer Rd. It's a miniature Western town featuring train rides, adventure golf, go-carts, bumper boats, basketball water wars, and other activities for the youngsters.

5 Hickory Lake Camping

Location: Near Perry, northeast of Lansing, map 3, grid B7.

Campsites, facilities: There are 108 lakeside campsites. Facilities include RV pull-through sites, electric hookups, water, sewer, flush toilets, showers, disposal station, swimming beach, fishing, boating (electric motors only are permitted), hiking trail, planned activities, and playground. Pets are allowed.

Reservations, fees: The daily fee ranges from about $16 to $17. Open May through mid-October.

Directions: From junction I-69 and Hwy. 52, take exit 105 and go one-tenth of a mile south on Hwy. 52. Then drive three miles west on Old Hwy. 78/Lansing Rd. and one-tenth of a mile west on Bath Road. Go one-quarter mile north on Beardslee to the entrance on the right.

Contact: Hickory Lake Camping, Dick and Arlene Locke, 11433 S. Beardslee Rd., Perry MI 48872, 517/625-3113, winter 517/625-7437.

Trip Notes: Learn more about the achievements of the state's women, past and present, at the Michigan Women's Historical Center and Hall of Fame (517/484-1880) at 213 W. Main St., in Lansing. It houses the Hall of Fame gallery and Belen Art gallery, which show the work of women artists and photographers. It's next to Cooley Gardens, an outstanding botanical garden. While you're in Lansing, see the Malcolm X Homesite at the Historic Marker-Vincent Court on Martin Luther King Junior Blvd.

6 P J's Family Campground

Location: Stockbridge, southwest of Howell, map 3, grid E7.

Campsites, facilities: There are 145 campsites and a separate tent area. Facilities include RV pull-through sites, electric

hookups, water, flush toilets, showers, disposal station, laundry, wheelchair access, two fishing ponds, bike and hiking trails, tennis courts, and playground. Nearby there are numerous lakes for boating, canoeing, and fishing. Pets are allowed.

Reservations, fees: Reservations are recommended. The daily fee is $17. Travelers checks and personal checks are accepted. Open from mid-April through October.

Directions: From I-94, take exit 139 and go nine miles north on Hwy. 106, then two miles north on Bunker Hill Road. Drive one-quarter mile west on Baseline Road and one-half mile north on Williamston Road to the entrance.

Contact: P.J.'s Family Campground, 5250 Williamston Rd., Stockbridge, MI, 49285, 517/565-3044.

Trip Notes: Do you like maple syrup on your pancakes? If you'd like to see how it is made, drive up to Mason to the Snow's Sugar Bush (517/676-2442) and tour the maple syrup production line. You can also have lunch in the farm restaurant, which feature pancakes (of course), French toast, and waffles. You can also let the youngsters touch the animals at the petting farm.

◼ Waterloo State Recreation Area

Location: Near Chelsea, north of Jackson, map 3, grid F7.

Campsites, facilities: There are three areas ranging from rustic to modern with 434 campsites. Facilities include no hookups in the Green Lake Unit, but there are electric hookups at the Portage and Sugarloaf Lake Units. Other facilities include water, flush toilets, showers, nature center, swimming beach, boat ramps, fishing, disabled parking,

planned activities, and playground. There are also biking, hiking, backpacking, horseback riding, cross-country ski, and snowmobile trails. Canoe rentals are available. Pets are allowed with restrictions.

Reservations, fees: Reservations are recommended. The daily fee ranges from $6 to $14. The daily fee for the horse campground is $10. Credit cards are accepted. Open year-round.

Directions: From I-94, take exits 147-157 and follow the signs north to the entrance and the visitors center.

Contact: Waterloo State Recreation Area, 16345 McClure Rd., Chelsea, MI 48118, 734/475-8307, fax 734/475-1830.

Trip Notes: This is the largest recreation area in the Lower Peninsula. It is nearly 20,000 acres and has 11 lakes, 47 miles of trails, 13 rustic cabins, and many horse trails. The Gerald E. Eddy Geology Center features year-round exhibits and nature programs on Michigan's geologic history. The Chelsea State Game Area with an abundance of rabbit, pheasant, duck, and geese is nearby.

◼ Greenwood Acres

Location: West of Jackson on Goose Lake, map 3, grid G5.

Campsites, facilities: There are 1,080 campsites. Facilities include RV pull-through sites, electric hookups, water, sewers, flush toilets, showers, laundry, disposal station, grocery store, café, swimming pool, lake swimming, boating (five hp motor limit) lake fishing, picnic area, golf and mini-golf, tennis courts, hiking trail, planned weekend activities, and playground. Pets are allowed.

Reservations, fees: The daily fee ranges from $22 to $25. Open from mid-April through November.

Directions: From I-94, take exit 147 and turn south on Race Road to Ann Arbor Road. Follow Ann Arbor Road west to Portage Road. Then go south to Greenwood Road and go east to Hilton Road. Turn north to the campground.

Contact: Greenwood Acres, Wendy Wolfinger and Sharon Kinchsular, 2401 Hilton Rd., Jackson, MI 49201, 517/522-8600, fax 517/522-5432.

Trip Notes: The facility is on 400-acre Goose Lake that features good fishing and has a swimming beach. There's also a free nine-hole golf course and nearly a dozen more courses within a 30-minute drive.

9 Apple Creek Resorts and RV Park

Location: Near Grass Lake, east of Jackson, map 3, grid G7.

Campsites, facilities: There are 167 campsites. Facilities include RV pull-through sites, electric hookups, water, flush toilets, showers, laundry, disposal station, grocery store, outdoor swimming pool, mini-golf, planned weekend activities, bike and hiking trails, and playground. Lake swimming, boating, canoeing, and fishing are nearby. Alcohol is prohibited. Bike rentals are available.

Reservations, fees: The daily fee ranges from $22 to $25. Credit cards are accepted. Open from mid-April through mid-October.

Directions: From I-94, take exit 150 south and go nearly three miles on Mt. Hope Road. At Michigan Ave., go three miles west and one-half mile south on Wolf Lake Road. Then go 0.75 mile east on Orban Road to the entrance on the right.

Contact: Apple Creek Resorts and RV Park, Roy and Ruth Felty, 11185 Orban Rd., Grass Lake, MI 49240, 517/522-3467.

Trip Notes: At the Michigan Speedway (517/592-6666; website: www.iscmotorsports.com) in Brooklyn, you might time your trip to include attending a NASCAR, ARCA, ASA IROC, or Indycar race, which are held on this two-mile oval super speedway.

10 Andry's Acres on the Lake

Location: Grass Lake, east of Jackson, map 3, grid G7.

Campsites, facilities: There are 160 campsites. Facilities include electric hookups, water, flush toilets, showers, disposal station, laundry swimming beach, boat ramp, and fishing. Seasonal campsite rentals are available. Pets are allowed.

Reservations, fees: The daily fee is $15. Open May through September.

Directions: From I-94, take exit 150 and go four miles north on Mt. Hope Road, then one-quarter mile west to the campground entrance.

Contact: Andry's Acres on the Lake, 7740 Mt. Hope Rd., Grass Lake, MI 49240, 517/596-3117.

Trip Notes: Hungry for some berries or fresh tomatoes? A quick drive over to Rowe's Produce Farm (734/482-8538) in Ypsilanti and you can pick strawberries, raspberries, peas, tomatoes, and other produce.

11 Greenbriar Campground and Golf

Location: Southeast of Brooklyn near Wampler's Lake, map 3, grid H7.

Campsites, facilities: There are 100 campsites. Facilities include RV pull-through sites, electric hookups, water, flush toilets, showers, wheelchair access, laundry, disposal station, grocery store, restaurant, swimming pool, children's pond fishing, 18-hole golf course, putting green, pro shop, and playground. Pets are allowed.

Reservations, fees: The daily fee ranges from $22 to $30 for two people. Open April through October.

Directions: From U.S. Hwy. 12 and Hwy. 124, go one mile north on Hwy. 124 to Wellwood Road. The entrance is on the right.

Contact: Greenbriar Campground and Golf, Arthur and Thelma Babian, 14820 Wellwood Rd., Brooklyn, MI 49230, 517/592-6952.

Trip Notes: The campground is near the attractions of Brooklyn/Irish Hills (517/592-8907; website: www.irishhills.com). They include year-round family entertainment, a variety of shops, an 1800s western town, petting zoo, street show, Hidden Lake Gardens, and "prehistoric forest with dinosaurs."

12 Willits Lake Family Campground

Location: Near Moscow, on Willit Lake, southwest of Jackson, map 3, grid H5.

Campsites, facilities: There are 185 campsites. Facilities include electric hookups, water, flush toilets, showers, wheelchair access, disposal station, swimming pool, boat dock (no motors permitted), fishing, and playground. Bike rentals are available. Pets are allowed.

Reservations, fees: The daily fee is about $20. Open from mid-April through mid-October.

Directions: From the east edge of Moscow, go one mile east on U.S. Hwy. 12. The entrance is on the right.

Contact: Willits Lake Family Campground, Gregg and Sue Heisler, 8291 E. Chicago Rd., U.S. Hwy. 12, P.O. Box 211, Moscow, MI 49257,

800/816-8705 or 517/688-9853, email: wlkfe@ibm.net.

Trip Notes: There are many activities in the area to choose, including the Michigan International Speedway, an antique mall, the Irish Hills Recreation Area, and numerous golf courses and theme parks. You can get directions and suggestions from the campground.

13 Irish Hills Campground

Location: Cement City, on Mud Lake, map 3, grid H6.

Campsites, facilities: There are 130 campsites. Facilities include RV pull-through sites, electric hookups, water, flush toilets, showers, wheelchair access, laundry, disposal station, grocery store, outdoor swimming pool, picnic area, boat dock (electric motors only), fishing, mini-golf, and playground. Boat rentals are available. Pets are allowed.

Reservations, fees: Reservations are required. The daily fee ranges from $17 to $25. Credit cards are accepted. Open May through mid-October.

Directions: Take U.S. Hwy. 12, south of Cement City, and go five miles west of Hwy. 50 and three miles east on U.S. Hwy. 127.

Contact: Irish Hills Campground, Bill Wild, 16230 U.S. Hwy. 12, Cement City, MI 49233, 517/592-6751.

Trip Notes: This campground is also near the restaurants, antique shops, craft stores, and other attractions of the Irish Hills.

14 W. J. Hayes State Park

Location: Near Onsted, between Wampler's Lake and Round Lake west of Clinton, map 3, grid H7.

Campsites, facilities: There are 183 semi-modern campsites (10 are wheelchair-accessible). Facilities include electric hookups, water, flush toilets, wheelchair access, disposal station, grocery store, lake swimming, boat ramp, fishing, picnic areas, and playground. Mini-cabin rentals are available. Pets are allowed with restrictions.

Reservations, fees: Reservations are accepted. The daily fee is $15. Credit cards are accepted. Open April through October.

Directions: On U.S. Hwy. 12, about nine miles west of Clinton, eight miles southeast of Brooklyn and four miles east of Hwy. 50.

Contact: W. J. Hayes State Park, 1220 Wampler's Lake Rd., Onsted, MI 49265, 517/467-7401.

Trip Notes: Located in the heart the Irish Hills, the park is bordered by a group of inland lakes popular with anglers and boaters. It has excellent sandy beaches and good boating on Wampler's and Round Lakes.

15 Ja Do Campground

Location: Near Tipton, southeast of Jackson, map 3, grid H8.

Campsites, facilities: There are 100 campsites. Facilities include electric hookups, water, flush toilets, showers, disposal station, pond fishing, hiking trail, and playground. Lake boating, canoeing, and fishing are nearby.

Reservations, fees: The daily fee ranges from $19 to $21. Open May through mid-October.

Directions: From U.S. Hwy. 12 and Hwy. 52, go 4.5 miles west on Hwy. 12. The entrance is on the left.

Contact: Ja Do Campground, Doug and Kay Miller, 5603 U.S. Hwy. 12, Tipton, MI 49287, 517/431-2111.

Trip Notes: The campground is nestled in beautiful rolling hills near the Irish Hills attractions and the Michigan International Speedway. For a seven-mile panorama of the Irish Hills, you can climb 64 feet to the top of Irish Hills Towers where you can count more than 50 lakes amid the lush woodlands and fields.

16 Walnut Hills Family Campground and Canoe Rentals

Location: Near Durand, between Lansing and Flint, map 4, grid A1.

Campsites, facilities: There are 150 campsites. Facilities include electric hookups, water, flush toilets, showers, disposal stations, grocery store, swimming beach, canoeing, kayaking, river and pond fishing, hiking trail, mini-golf, and playground. Boat and cabin rentals are available.

Reservations, fees: The daily fee ranges from $19 to $22. Open from early May through September.

Directions: From I-69, take exit 113 and go 3.25 miles south on Grand River Avenue and two miles east on Cole Road. At Cole Road, drive one mile southwest on Reed/Lehring Road. The entrance is on the right.

Contact: Walnut Hills Family Campground and Canoe Rentals, Jim and Janette Borke, 7685 Lehring Rd., Durand, MI 48429, 517/634-9782, email: walhills@hotmail.com.

Trip Notes: Kids of all ages will enjoy the Impression 5 Science Museum (517/485-8116; website: www.impression5.org) at 200 Museum Drive in Lansing. It has a terrific selection of interactive physical and natural science-related toys. The museum is in a 100-year-old building on the banks of the Grand River across from the Lansing Center.

17 Holiday Shore

Location: Near Durand, map 4, grid A1.

Campsites, facilities: There are 300 RV campsites. Tents are not permitted. Facilities include full hookups, but no restrooms. The campground provides lake boating, canoeing, fishing, swimming beach, planned weekend activities, tennis courts, hiking trail, and playground. Seasonal campsite rentals are available. Pets are allowed.

Reservations, fees: The daily fee is $20. Open from May through October.

Directions: From the junction of I-69 and Hwy 13, take exit 123 and go one mile south. Then drive one mile west on Goodall Road to the entrance on the right.

Contact: Holiday Shores, 10915 Goodall Rd., Durand, MI 48429, 517/288-4444.

Trip Notes: Be sure to visit the Potter Park Zoo in Lansing (517/363-4730) for a fun-filled day with the animals.

18 Myers Lake United Methodist Campground

Location: Near Byron, on Myers Lake between Lansing and Flint, map 4, grid B1.

Campsites, facilities: There are 126 lakeside campsites. Facilities include electric hookups, water, disposal station, laundry, grocery store, swimming beach, boating, fishing, church services, and planned weekend activities. Boat, cabin, and seasonal campsite rentals are available. Alcoholic beverages are not permitted. Pets are allowed.

Reservations, fees: The daily fee ranges from $18 to $25. Open May through October.

Directions: From the junction of U.S. Hwy. 23 and Silver Lake Road, take exit 79 (Linden-Fenton) and go 10 miles west on Silver Lake Road to the entrance on the left.

Contact: Myers Lake United Methodist Campground, Detroit Conference, United Methodist Church, 10575 Silver Lake Rd., Byron, MI 48418, 800/994-5050 or 810/266-4511, fax 810/266-6037, email: myerslak@shianet .org.

Trip Notes: The family shouldn't miss the Capitol Building (517/373-2353; website: www.milegislativecouncil.org/cfa.html). Tours cover the public areas, including visits to the House and Senate galleries. Admission is free and reservations are recommended as early as possible. Take I-69, I-496, or I-96 to the Downtown/Lansing exit and follow signs to the Capitol Loop.

19 Hide Away Park

Location: Linden, on Louise Lake, northeast of Lansing, map 4, grid B2.

Campsites, facilities: There are 163 campsites. Facilities include electric hookups, water, flush toilets, showers, disposal station, swimming beach, boat ramp and dock, shuffleboard courts, hiking trail, and playground. Boat rentals are available. Pets are allowed.

Reservations, fees: The daily fee ranges from $14 to $15. Open from mid-April through mid-October.

Directions: From the junction of U.S. Hwy. 23 and Clyde Road, go five miles west to Argentine. Then drive 4.5 miles north to Hogan Road and one-half mile west to the entrance.

Contact: Hide Away Park, 9383 Gould Rd., Linden, MI 48451, 810/735-7666.

Trip Notes: Want some fresh vegetables for dinner? Drive northeast on I-69 to Perry at Hwy. 52 and Your Garden (517/625-7774). Here you can pick your own sweet corn and other mixed vegetables, flowers, and pumpkins.

20 Yogi Bear's Jellystone Park Camp Resort of Holly

Location: Near Holly, south of Flint, map 4, grid B4.

Campsites, facilities: There are 145 campsites. Facilities include RV pull-through sites, electric hookups, water, flush toilets, showers, laundry, disposal station, grocery store, swimming pool, picnic area, mini-golf, planned activities, and playground. Bike and cabin rentals are available. Lake boating and fishing are nearby.

Reservations, fees: The daily fee ranges from $28 to $32. Open year-round.

Directions: From I-75, take exit 101 onto Grange Hall Road and go about 100 yards east. The entrance is on the right.

Contact: Yogi Bear's Jellystone Park Camp Resort of Holly, Sandy Serling, 7072 E. Grange Hall Rd., Holly, MI 48442, 800/442-YOGI or 248/634-8621.

Trip Notes: Go to Historic Battle Alley, a 19th-century street that features antiques, boutiques, and specialty shops. You can enjoy a seven-course dinner with no artificial additives at the Historic Holly Hotel and Restaurant (248/634-5208; website: www.hollyhotel.com) at 110 Battle Alley next to the railroad tracks in Holly. The restored Victorian structure is on the National Register of Historic Places.

21 Holly State Recreation Area

Location: Near Holly, south of Flint, map 4, grid B4.

Campsites, facilities: There are 161 campsites. Facilities include electric hookups, flush toilets, swimming beach, boat ramp (no motors are permitted), fishing, playground, and hiking, mountain biking, cross-country skiing, and snowmobiling trails. Canoe and mini-cabin rentals are available. Pets are allowed with restrictions.

Reservations, fees: Reservations are recommended. The daily fee is $12. Credit cards are accepted. Open April through October.

Directions: From I-75, take exit 101 and go two miles east on Grange Hall Road for one mile to McGinnis Lake Road. Take McGinnis Lake Road three-quarters of a mile to the campground entrance on the left.

Contact: Holly State Recreation Area, 8100 Grange Hall Rd., Holly, MI 48442, 248/634-8811, fax 248/634-9754.

Trip Notes: This area's rolling hills offer scenic lake overlooks and excellent viewing for fall color. Campsites vary from heavily wooded to open and sunny. It's minutes away from Holly and its annual Renaissance Festival and the Mt. Holly ski hill.

If you're looking for the unusual, drive to Lansing and the Minibeast Zooseum and Education Center (517/886-0630) at 6907 W. Grand River Ave. This unique learning center is devoted to mini-beasts—everything from worms to insects—with all of the best attributes of a zoo, museum, interpretive center, science store, and outdoor classroom.

22 Ortonville State Recreation Area

Location: Near Ortonville, map 4, grid B5.

Campsites, facilities: There are 25 rustic campsites. Facilities include vault toilets, swimming beach, boating, canoeing, fishing, and playground. There are also bike, hiking, horseback riding, cross-country ski, and snowmobiling trails.

Reservations, fees: Reservations are accepted. The daily fee is $6. The daily horse campground fee is $10. Credit cards are accepted. Open from mid-April through November.

Directions: From I-75, take exit 91 at Clarkston and go nine miles north to Oakwood Road. Turn right and go five miles to Hadley Road and go left for one mile to the area.

Contact: Ortonville State Recreation Area, 5779 Hadley Rd., Rt. 2, Ortonville, MI 48462, 248/627-3828, fax 248/627-5000.

Trip Notes: The 5,300-acre area with many small lakes offers opportunities for every outdoor enthusiast from hunting to picnicking. There is also a shooting range, but check the hours by calling the park. The original park, Bloomer #3 State Park, is a game sanctuary, and much of the rest of Ortonville Recreation Area is open to public hunting.

23 Clearwater Campground

Location: Ortonville, map 4, grid B5.

Campsites, facilities: There are 115 campsites. No tents are permitted. Facilities include RV pull-through sites, electric hookups, water, sewer (full hookup units only), laundry, grocery store, swimming beach, boat docks, canoeing, fishing, hiking trail, putting green, mini-golf, playground, and planned weekend activities. Pets are allowed.

Reservations, fees: Reservations are recommended. The daily fee is $22. Credit cards are accepted. Open from mid-April through mid-October.

Directions: From the junction of I-75 and Hwy. 15, take exit 91 and go just over six miles north on Hwy. 15 to the entrance on the left.

Contact: Clearwater Campground, 1140 Ortonville Rd., Ortonville, MI 48462, 248/627-3829.

Trip Notes: This campground on Green Lake boasts large, wooded sites.

You might visit the Cook Farm Dairy (248/627-3329) for their delicious ice cream. In October, you can also pick pumpkins.

24 Pontiac Lake State Recreation Area

Location: Near Waterford, west of Pontiac, map 4, grid C5.

Campsites, facilities: There are 176 modern campsites. Facilities include electric hookups, water, flush toilets, showers, disposal station, swimming beach, boat ramp, picnic area, disabled parking, and playground. Biking, hiking, horseback riding, and snowmobile trails are available. Horse rentals are available.

Reservations, fees: Reservations are accepted. The daily fee is $11. Credit cards are accepted. The daily fee for the horse campground is $10. Open May through October.

Directions: From I-75, go west on Hwy. 59 for 16 miles. Turn north on Williams Lake Road for one mile and go west on Gale Road into the campground.

Contact: Pontiac Lake State Recreation Area, 7800 Gale Rd., Waterford, MI 48327, 248/666-1020, fax 248/666-3883.

Trip Notes: The scenic overlooks in this area are wonderful, especially for outdoor photographers. Glacial action has left behind many ponds, marshes, fields, and rolling hills covered with forests. The park has miles of hiking, mountain biking, and horseback riding trails, as well as one-third of a mile of beach to comb.

25 Lake Chemung Outdoor Resort

Location: Howell, on Lake Chemung, map 4, grid C1.

Campsites, facilities: There are 340 sites. Tents are not permitted. Facilities include electric hookups, water, sewer (full hookup units only), flush toilets, showers, laundry, grocery store, swimming pool, swimming beach, boating, canoeing, lake or pond fishing, mini-golf, and shuffleboard courts. Seasonal campsite rentals are available. Pets are allowed.

Reservations, fees: The daily fee is $25. Open year-round.

Directions: From the junction of U.S. Hwy. 23, go three miles west on I-96 and take exit 145. Go three miles northwest on Grand River Avenue and then two miles north on Hughes Road to the entrance.

Contact: Lake Chemung Outdoor Resort, 320 South Hughes Rd., Howell, MI 48843, 517/546-6361.

Trip Notes: Planning an October camping trip to Howell? Call for the date of the Scarecrow Daze Fall Festival (517/546-3920; website: www.Howell.org) and plan to be there.

26 Taylor's Beach Camp Grounds

Location: Howell, northwest of Detroit, map 4, grid C1.

Campsites, facilities: There are 189 campsites. Facilities include RV pull-through sites, electric hookups, water, sewers, disposal station, grocery store, swimming beach, boat dock, fishing, and playground. Boat rentals are available. Pets are allowed.

Reservations, fees: The daily fee ranges from $15 to $20. Open April through October.

Directions: From the junction of I-96 and Hwy. 59, take exit 133 and go one-tenth of a mile northeast on Hwy. 59. Then drive 5.25 miles north on Burkhard Road to the entrance on the left.

Contact: Taylor's Beach Camp Grounds, the Taylor family, 6197 N. Burkhart Rd., Howell, MI 48843, 517/546-2679.

Trip Notes: Honeybees may be uninvited guests at your camping site, but they are fascinating creatures to observe at a bee farm. Visit Nectar Sweet Apiaries (517/548-5176) and watch pure honey being collected from various bee yards.

27 Proud Lake State Recreation Area

Location: On Proud Lake, north of Wixom and southwest of Pontiac, map 4, grid D4.

Campsites, facilities: There are 130 campsites. Facilities include electric hookups, water, flush toilets, showers, disposal station, swimming beach, boat ramp, fishing, disabled parking, picnic area, interpretative programs, and playground. There are also biking, hiking, cross-country ski, and snowmobile trails. Cross-country ski gear rentals are available.

Reservations, fees: The daily fee is $15. Open year-round.

Directions: From I-96, take exit 159 at Wixom Road and

follow it north for seven miles to the recreation area entrance.

Contact: Proud Lake State Recreation Area, 3500 Wixom Rd., Commerce Township, MI 48382, 248/685-2433, fax 248/864-1462.

Trip Notes: This 3,800-acre area offers a wealth of outdoor opportunities. Guided interpretive walks and other nature activities are offered at this park. A schedule is available at the park office year-round or the campground office during the summer. Powers Beach, a popular swimming spot, is a terrific area. A modern toilet building and changing courts are a short distance from the beach.

From the park, you can also make a 100-mile canoe trip on the Huron River. Along the way, you encounter a dam and must portage past rapids. There are four canoe campgrounds and frequent access to roads. The take-out point is at Point Mouilee State Game Area.

28 Brighton Recreation Area

Location: Near Brighton, west of Detroit, map 4, grid D2.

Campsites, facilities: There are 222 modern and rustic campsites. Facilities include electric hookups, water, flush toilets, showers, wheelchair access, disposal station, grocery store, swimming beach, boat ramp, fishing, interpretive program, and playground. There are also biking, hiking, horseback riding, snowmobile, and cross-country ski trails. Cabin and horse rentals are available.

Reservations, fees: Reservations are accepted. The daily fee ranges from $6 to $12. The daily fee for the horse campground is $10. Credit cards are accepted. Open April through November.

Directions: From I-96, take exit 147 at Brighton. Go west about six miles to Chilson Road and drive south 1.5 miles to Bishop Lake Road and the entrance to the recreation area.

Contact: Brighton Recreation Area, 6360 Chilson Rd., Howell, MI 48843, 810/229-6566, fax 810/229-2661, email: weissc@state.mi.us.

Trip Notes: This 5,000-acre area of rolling hills and meadows dotted with lakes, streams, and marshes is an equestrian's delight with riding stable, staging area, and 18 miles of trails. Most of the area is open to hunting, fishing, and a variety of winter activities, including cross-country skiing and snowmobiling.

29 Green Valley Park

Location: New Hudson, west of Detroit, map 4, grid D4.

Campsites, facilities: There are 112 campsites. Tents and motorcycle campers are not permitted. Facilities include electric hookups, water, sewer, disposal station, laundry, swimming beach, boating, canoeing, fishing, shuffleboard courts, and playground. Pets are allowed.

Reservations, fees: Reservations are recommended. The daily fee ranges from $20 to $24. Open May through October.

Directions: From the junction of I-96 and Milford Road, take exit 155 or 155A and go 2.25 miles south on Milford Road, and one-quarter mile west on 12 Mile Road to the entrance.

Contact: Green Valley Park, P.O. Box 298, New Hudson, MI 48165, 248/437-4136.

Trip Notes: This campground offers easy access to Detroit for shopping or sight-seeing. Be sure to visit Belle Isle and make a stop at the Zoo and Aquarium, as well as the Dossin Great Lakes Museum.

30 Hass Lake Park

Location: New Hudson, east of Lansing, map 4, grid D4.

Campsites, facilities: There are 355 campsites. Facilities include RV pull-through sites, electric hookups, water, sewer, flush toilets, showers, wheelchair access, disposal station, laundry, grocery store, swimming beach, boating (five hp limit), canoeing, fishing, picnic area, planned weekend activities, and playground. Cabin rentals are available. Pets are allowed.

Reservations, fees: The daily fee is $20 to $23 per family. Open April through mid-November.

Directions: From I-96, take exit 159, turn south and go one-quarter mile to Grand River West. Turn right and go three miles to Hass Road South. Drive to the entrance at the end of the road.

Contact: Hass Lake Park, 25800 Haas Rd., New Hudson, MI 48165, 248/437-0900.

Trip Notes: On a rainy day, a trip to the Michigan Historical Museum (517/373-3559; website: www.sos.state.mi.us) is well worth a visit. This flagship of the state museum system surrounds you with history from the prehistoric era to the present. There are 26 galleries and special exhibit areas on five levels. The museum is two blocks west of the state capitol in downtown Lansing. Follow the Capitol Loop signs. Use I-496 and exit at Logan/Martin Luther King Blvd. Go north following the Capitol Loop signs.

31 Pinckney State Recreation Area

Location: Near Pinckney, on Bruin Lake, northwest of Ann Arbor, map 4, grid E1.

Campsites, facilities: There are 245 modern and rustic campsites. Facilities include electric hookups, water, flush toilets, disposal station, swimming beach, boat ramp, fishing, picnic area, and disabled parking. There are also biking, hiking, cross-country ski, and snowmobile trails. Boat and cabin rentals are available.

Reservations, fees: Reservations are accepted. The daily fee ranges from $6 to $14. Credit cards are accepted. Open from mid-April through October.

Directions: From U.S. Hwy. 23 and Hwy. 36, go 16.5 miles west on Hwy. 36 and one mile south on Livermore. Turn west on Doyle for one-half mile, and 1.25 miles south on Unadilla. From I-94 and I-96, take Hwy. 52 and go east on North Territorial Road. Follow the signs to the entrance.

Contact: Pinckney State Recreation Area, 8555 Silver Hill, Rt. 1, Pinckney, MI 48169, 734/426-4913, fax 734/426-1916, website: www.ring.com/travel/dnr/sp_pinck.htm.

Trip Notes: This area will appeal to backpackers, mountain-bikers, anglers, and other outdoor enthusiasts. The 11,000-acre park is known for its extensive trail system and chain of fine fishing lakes. There are 26 miles of hiking trails open to mountain biking with access to five hike-in campsites along the railways. Also, some 10,000 acres are open to hunters during designated seasons.

Lakelands Trail State Park is a linear rails-to-trails park also under Pinckney Recreation Area management. About 13 miles from Pinckney to Stockbridge have been developed so far.

32 KOA-Detroit/Greenfield

Location: East of Ann Arbor, map 4, grid G4.

Campsites, facilities: There are 220 campsites. Facilities include RV pull-through sites, electric hookups, water, sewer, flush toilets, showers, laundry, disposal station, grocery store, swimming beach, boating (no motors permitted), canoeing, fishing, bike and hiking trails, mini-golf, and playground. Bike, canoe, golf, and fishing equipment, and cabin rentals are available. Pets are allowed.

Reservations, fees: The daily fee ranges from $22 to $31. Credit cards are accepted. Open year-round.

Directions: From I-94, take exit 187 and go one mile south to Textile Road, then go west one mile to Bunton Road and south on Bunton Road for one-half mile. The entrance is on the right.

Contact: KOA-Detroit/Greenfield, Thomas Chang, 6680 Bunton Rd., Ypsilanti, MI 48197, 734/482-7722.

Trip Notes: At 23 miles, this is one of the closest campgrounds to Ford's Greenfield Museum and Village (313/271-1620 or 800/343-1929), a place the whole family will enjoy. It's at 20900 Oakwood Blvd., one-half mile south of U.S. Hwy. 12 and 1.5 miles west of Southfield Road.

33 K C Campground

Location: Milan, southwest of Detroit, map 4, grid H3.

Campsites, facilities: There are 100 campsites. Facilities include electric hookups, water, flush toilets, showers, disposal station, pond swimming, and playground. Numerous lake and rivers for boating, canoeing, and fishing are nearby. Pets are allowed.

Reservations, fees: The daily fee is $18. Open May through October.

Directions: From the junction of U.S. Hwy. 23 and Plant Road, take exit 25 and go 1.5 miles southeast on Plank Road. Then drive one mile east on Sherman Road to the campground entrance.

Contact: K C Campground, 14048 Sherman Rd., Milan, MI 48160, 734/439-1076.

Trip Notes: Two very different choices for entertainment are near this campground. One is the Milan International Dragway (734/439-7368; website: www.milandrag way.com) on Plank Road, four miles east of U.S. Hwy. 23 exit 25. It's a straight drag strip that is a NHRA member track and is open from April to October.

The other is the Exhibit Museum of Natural History (734/764-0478; website: www.exhibits .lsa.umich.edu/Welcome.html), which features exhibits, workshops, tours, and planetarium. Tour reservations are required two weeks in advance. It's located 3.5 miles west of U.S. Hwy. 23, exit 37B. Take Washtenaw west to Geddes Avenue and turn left. The building is on the right.

34 Indian Creek Camp

Location: Tecumseh, southeast of Jackson, map 4, grid A1.

Campsites, facilities: There are 47 campsites. Facilities include electric hookups, electric, flush toilets, showers, disposal station, swimming beach, fishing, hiking trail, and playground. Lake boating, canoeing, and fishing are nearby. Pets are allowed.

Reservations, fees: The daily fee ranges from $18 to $25. Open April through October.

Directions: From east of the Tecumseh city limits, go 3.5 miles east on Hwy. 50, and then 2.5 miles north on Ford Hwy. to the park entrance.

Contact: Indian Creek Camp, 9415 Tangent Hwy., Tecumseh, MI 49286, 517/423-5659 or 888/412-2122.

Trip Notes: The campground is part of a 42-acre working llama ranch. And if you like animals, another place to visit is the Michigan Whitetail Hall of Fame Museum (517/522-3354), featuring deer that can be fed. Try to get there in early June when the fawns are born. The museum is at 4220 Willis Road in Grass Lake off I-94, between exits 147 and 150 on the north side of the highway.

35 Beech Grove Family Campground and RV Park

Location: Emmett, west of Lake Huron, map 5, grid A2.

Campsites, facilities: There are 100 campsites. Facilities include RV pull-through sites, electric hookups, water, flush toilets, showers, laundry, disposal station, grocery store, swimming beach, fishing, mini-golf, and playground. Pets are allowed.

Reservations, fees: The daily fee is $21. Credit cards are accepted. Open year-round, but there are limited facilities during the off-season.

Directions: From I-69, take exit 180 and go one-quarter mile north on Riley Center Road, and one-quarter mile west on Burt Road. Then go 1.5 miles north on Breen Road to the entrance.

Contact: Beech Grove Family Campground and RV Park, 3864 Breen Rd., Emmett, MI 48022, 810/395-7042.

Trip Notes: Drive just a little northeast of Emmett to Capac and the Blueridge Blueberry Farm (810/395-2245) to pick your own berries and taste their made-from-scratch baked goods and honey.

36 Fort Trodd Family Campground

Location: Port Huron, on a private lake near St. Clair River, map 5, grid A5.

Campsites, facilities: There are 185 campsites. Facilities include RV pull-through sites, electric hookups, water, sewers, flush toilets, showers, disposal station, laundry, grocery, swimming beach, canoeing, fishing, shuffleboard courts, and hiking trail. Lake and river boating and fishing are nearby. Bike, boat, cabin, and seasonal campsite rentals are available. Pets are allowed.

Reservations, fees: The daily fee ranges from $22 to $27. Credit cards are accepted. Open May through September.

Directions: From the junction of I-69 and Barth Road, take exit 194 and go 500 feet north on Barth Road to the entrance at the end.

Contact: Fort Trodd Family Campground, 6350 Lapeer Rd., Cylde, MI 48049, 810/987-4889 or 810/987-6579.

Trip Notes: A visit to the Huron Lightship Museum (810/982-0891) at Pine Grove Park, one of the few floating lighthouses constructed for the Great Lakes, will give you a glimpse of the history of the "Lakers."

Another option is to drive across the Blue Water Bridge to Canada for lunch at one of the quaint little cafes.

37 Port Huron KOA

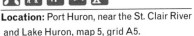

Location: Port Huron, near the St. Clair River and Lake Huron, map 5, grid A5.

Campsites, facilities: There are 346 campsites and 81 cabins. Facilities include RV pull-through sites, electric hookups, water, sewer, flush toilets, showers, disposal station, laundry, grocery store, swimming pools, hiking trail, shuffleboard courts, planned activities, and playgrounds. Lake and river boating, canoeing, fishing, and biking trail are nearby. Bike and cabin rentals are available. Pets are allowed.

Reservations, fees: The daily fee ranges from $19 to $28. Credit cards are accepted. Open April through October.

Directions: From I-69, take exit 196 and go one-half mile north on Wadhams Road, then one-quarter mile east on Lapeer Road to the entrance on the right.

Contact: Port Huron KOA, 5111 Lapeer Rd., Kimball, MI 48074, 810/987-4070 or 800/KOA-0833 for reservations.

Trip Notes: If you drive to Flint, visit the Robert T. Longway Planetarium (810/760-1181), Michigan's largest. It features programs ranging from astronomy to laser light shows. From I-475, exit at Longway Blvd., and go east for 350 yards on Longway. Turn south on Walnut Street until it ends at the planetarium.

38 Algonac State Park

Location: Algonac, on the St. Clair River, map 5, grid D4.

Campsites, facilities: There are 300 modern campsites. Facilities include electric hookups, flush toilets, showers, wheelchair access, boat ramp, river and shore fishing, picnic area, self-guided tours, and playground. There are also hiking, snowmobiling, and cross-country ski trails available.

Reservations, fees: Reservations are accepted. The daily fee ranges from $11 to $15. Credit cards are accepted. Open year-round.

Directions: From I-94, take exit 243 and go east for 19 miles to the park entrance.

Contact: Algonac State Park, 8732 River Rd., Marine City, MI 48039, 810/465-5605, fax 810/765-3808.

Trip Notes: The St. Clair River parallels the park, providing boating, shore fishing, and lake fishing in Lake St. Clair. There's also a great close-up view of passing Great Lakes and oceangoing vessels. Self-interpretive trails in the park wander through unique oak and prairie savannahs.

39 River View Campground and Marina

Location: Algonac on the St. Clair River, map 5, grid D4.

Campsites, facilities: There are 16 campsites. Tents are not permitted. Facilities include RV pull-through sites, electric hookups, water, sewer, flush toilets, showers, disposal station, wheelchair access, boat dock, fishing, and a playground. Lake swimming, boating, and fishing are available. Pets are allowed.

Reservations, fees: The daily fee is $30; $150 per week. Reservations accepted only for one week's stay or longer. Travelers checks and personal checks accepted. Open April through October.

Directions: From the center of Algonac, go one mile south and one mile west on Hwy. 29 to the entrance. The campground is right on the river.

Contact: River View Campground and Marina, 4175 Pte. Tremble Rd. (M-29), Algonac, MI 48001, 810/794-0182.

Trip Notes: If you get tired of boating or fishing the St. Clair River north channel, drive down to Auburn Hills northwest of Detroit to the Walter P. Chrysler Museum (888/456-1924; website: www.chryslerheritage.com) to see what Chrysler has manufactured, including the engine that engineers made from several six-cylinder car engines for tanks during World War II.

Lake Hudson Recreation Area

Location: Clayton, south of Jackson, map 6, grid B7.

Campsites, facilities: There are 50 campsites. Facilities include electric hookups, vault toilets, and no showers. The campground provides lake swimming, canoeing, fishing, boating, and ramp. Pets are allowed.

Reservations, fees: The daily fee is $9. Open April through November.

Directions: From Hudson, take Hwy. 34 and go six miles to Hwy. 156. Then drive one mile south on Hwy. 156 to the area's entrance.

Contact: Lake Hudson Recreation Area, 1220 Wampler's Lake Rd., Onsted, MI 49265, 517/445-2265.

Trip Notes: Lake Hudson offers campers some excellent muskie and bass fishing. There is a boat ramp to access this 700-acre body of water. Note that there is a no-wake speed limit.

In winter, ice fishing is the most popular activity, although cross-country skiing is possible if there is enough snow. If there's more than four inches of snow, snowmobiling is allowed. There are no marked trails for either activity.

Totem Pole Park

Location: Petersburg, west of Monroe, map 7, grid A3.

Campsites, facilities: There are 130 campsites. Facilities include RV pull-through sites,

electric hookups, water, flush toilets, showers, disposal station, grocery store, swimming beach, fishing, shuffleboard courts, planned weekend activities, and playground. Lake Erie boating and fishing are nearby. Cabin rentals are available. Pets are allowed.

Reservations, fees: The daily fee ranges from $18 to $22. Credit cards are accepted. Open from mid-April through mid-October.

Contact: Totem Pole Park, Carl and Joyce Laming, 16333 Lulu Rd., Petersburg, MI 49270, 734/279-2110, email: totem@cass.net, website:www.michcampgrounds.com/totempole/.

Directions: From U.S. Hwy. 23, take exit 9 and go 2.5 miles north on Summerfield Road. Then drive one-quarter of a mile west on Lulu Road to the park entrance.

Trip Notes: A trip to the new Cabela's World in Dundee (734/529-4700; website: www.cabelas.com) the "World's Foremost Outfitter of Hunting, Fishing, and Outdoor Gear" is not just a shopping spree, but a real indoor outdoor experience.

Monroe County KOA Kampground

Location: Petersburg, west of Monroe, map 7, grid A3.

Campsites, facilities: There are 249 campsites. Facilities include RV pull-through sites, electric hookups, water, sewer, flush toilets, showers, disposal station, laundry, grocery store, swimming beach, water slide, lake fishing, mini-golf, shuffleboard courts, playground, and planned activities. Bike, boat, cabin, and RV rentals are available. Pets are allowed.

Reservations, fees: The daily fee ranges from $23 to $28. Credit cards are accepted. Open from early April through mid-October.

Directions: From Hwy. 23, take exit 9 and go 200 yards southeast on Summerfield Road to the entrance.

Contact: Monroe County KOA Kampground, Ray and Donna Crots, U.S. Hwy. 23 Exit 9, Summerfield Rd., Petersburg, MI 49270, 734/856-4972.

Trip Notes: There's plenty to do around this campground, just nine miles north of the Ohio border. You can drive east to Newport and visit the Fermi 2 Nuclear Power Station (734/586-5228). Take I-75 exit 15 and go north on Dixie Hwy. to the plant's visitor center. A two-hour guided tour can be scheduled in advance. Reservations are required.

In nearby Monroe, you can go to the Monroe County Historical Museum and the George A. Custer exhibits (734/243-7137), featuring Gen. George Armstrong Custer memorabilia and displays on local French pioneers and Native Americans. It's three miles west of I-75. Take exit 11, 14, or 15 and follow the signs.

43 Sterling State Park

Location: Near Monroe, on Lake Erie, map 7, grid A6.

Campsites, facilities: There are 288 sites. Facilities include electric hookups, flush toilets, showers, wheelchair access, disposal station, swimming beach, boat ramp and dock, fishing, biking and hiking trails, and playground. Boat rentals are available. Pets are allowed with restrictions.

Reservations, fees: Reservations are accepted. The daily fee is $14. Credit cards are accepted. Open year-round.

Directions: From I-75, take the Dixie Hwy. exit 15 and go one mile northeast on Dixie Hwy. to the entrance on the east side of the road.

Contact: Sterling State Park, 2800 State Park Rd., Monroe, MI 48161, 734/289-2715.

Trip Notes: This is the only Michigan state park on Lake Erie and offers swimming, boating, and fishing on this Great Lake. You can also view wildlife near the park's lagoons and marshes.

RESOURCE GUIDE

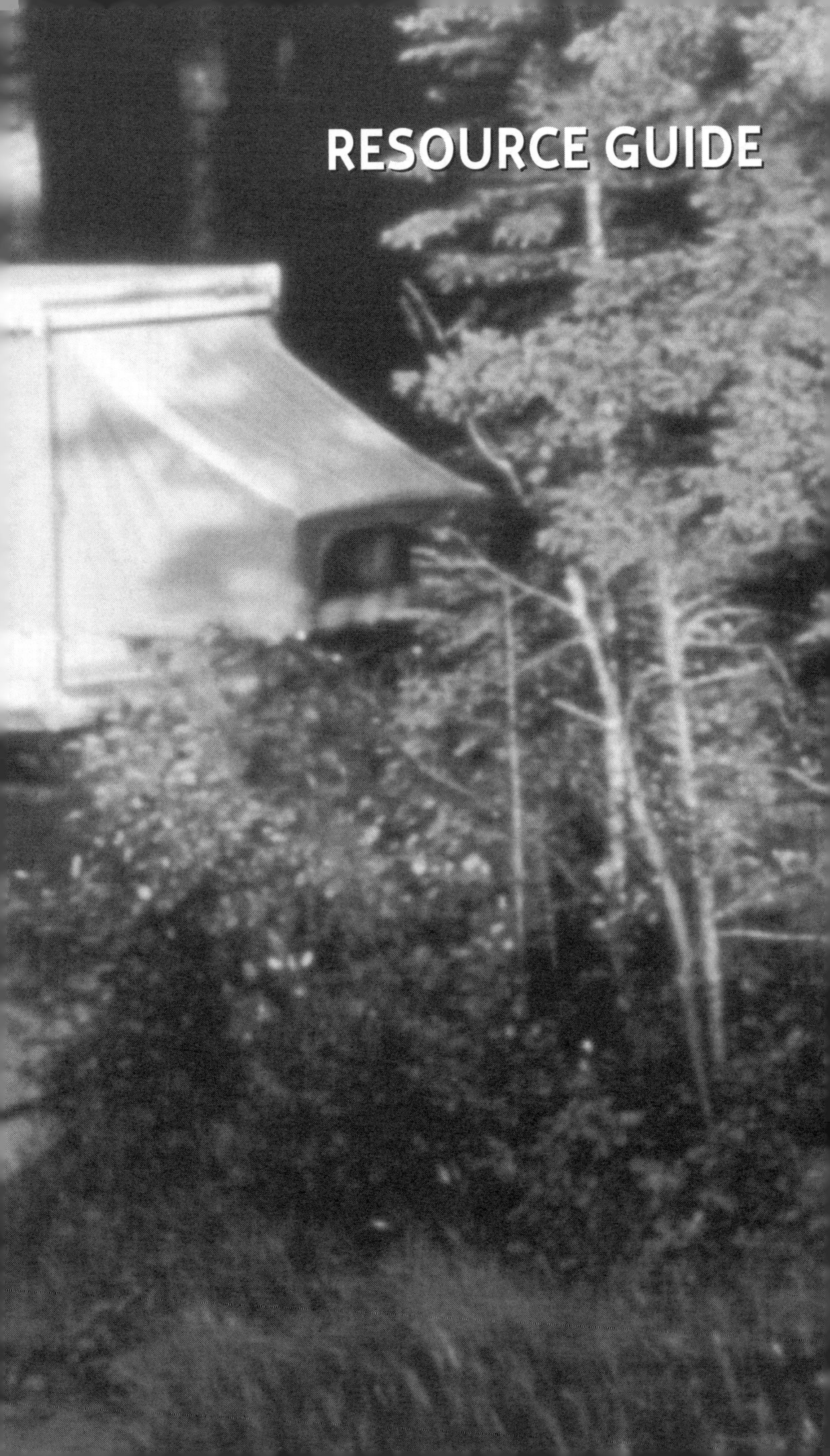

Resource Guide

Minnesota Resources

**Albert Lea Convention and
Visitors Bureau**
202 N. Broadway
Albert Lea, MN 56007
507/373-3938 or 800/345-8414
fax: 507/373-0344

**Alexandria Lakes Area Chamber
of Commerce**
206 Broadway
Alexandria, MN 56308
320/763-3161 or 800/235-9441
fax: 320/763-6857
website: www.alexandriamn.org

**Bemidji Area Convention and
Visitors Bureau**
P.O. Box 850
Bemidji, MN 56601
218/751-3540 or 800/458-2223
fax: 218/759-0810
website: www.bemidji.org

**Boundary Waters Canoe Area
Wilderness Information**
Box 338
Duluth, MN 53301
218/720-5324

**Brainerd Lakes Area Chamber
of Commerce**
P.O. Box 356
Brainerd, MN 56401
218/829-2838 or 800/450-2838,
  ext. 402
fax: 218/829-8199
website: www.brainerd.com

**Crane Lake Visitors &
Tourism Bureau**
7238 Handberg Rd.
Crane Lake, MN 55725
218/993-2901 or 800/362-7405
fax: 218/993-2281
website: www.cranelake.org

**Detroit Lakes Regional Chamber
of Commerce**
P.O. Box 348
Detroit Lakes, MN 56501
218/847-9202 or 800/542-3992
fax: 218/847-9082
website: www.detroit-lakes.com

**Duluth Convention and
Visitors Bureau**
100 Lake Place Dr.
Duluth, MN 55802
218/722-4011 or 800/4DULUTH
fax: 218/722-1322
website: www.visitduluth.com

**Elk River Area Chamber
of Commerce**
509 Hwy. 10
Elk River, MN 55330
612/441-3110
fax: 612/441-3409

Ely Chamber of Commerce
1600 E. Sheridan Rd.
Ely, MN 55731
218/365-6123 or 800/777-7281
fax: 218/365-5929
website: www.ely.org

**Fergus Falls Convention
& Visitors Bureau**
P.O. Box 868
Fergus Falls, MN 56538
218/739-0149 or 800/726-8959
fax: 218/739-0149
website: www.fergusfalls.com

**Grand Marais Chamber
of Commerce**
P.O. Box 1048
Grand Marais, MN 55604
218/387-1400 or 888/922-5000
website: www.grandmaraismn.com

**Grand Rapids Convention
& Tourist Bureau**
One N.W. 3rd St.
Grand Rapids, MN 55744
218/326-9607 or 800/472-6366
fax: 218/326-4825
website: www.grandmn.org

Gunflint Trail Association
P.O. Box 205
Grand Marais, MN 55604
218/387-2870 or 800/338-6932
fax: 218/387-2870
website: www.gunflint-trail.com

Highway, Detour Information
800/542-0220 or 651/405-6030

**Hinckley Convention and
Tourism Bureau**
P.O. Box 197
Hinckley, MN 55037
320/384-0126 or 800/996-4566
fax: 320/384-6297
website: www.hinckleymn.com

**International Falls Convention
and Visitors Bureau**
301 2nd Ave.
International Falls, MN 56649
218/283-9400 or 800/325-5766
fax: 218/283-3572
website: www.intlfalls.org

Kabetogama Lake Association
9707 Gamma Rd.
Lake Kabetogama, MN 56669
218/875-2621 or 800/524-9085
fax: 218/875-2621
website: www.kabetogama.com

**Lake Country Visitor
Information Center**
1330 U.S. Hwy. 61 East
Two Harbors, MN 55616
218/834-4005 or 800/554-2116
website: www.lakecnty.com

**Lake of the Woods Area
Tourism Bureau**
P.O. Box 518
Baudette, MN 56623
218/634-1174 or 800/382-3474
fax: 218/634-2915
website: www.lakeofthewoodsmn.com

**Leech Lake Area Chamber
of Commerce**
P.O. Box 1089
Walker, MN 56484
218/547-1313 or 800/833-1118
fax: 218/547-1338
Website: www.leech-lake.com

Lutsen-Tofte Tourism Association
Box 2248
Tofte, MN 55615
218/663-7804 or 888/61NORTH
fax: 218/663-8012
website: www.61north.com

**Mankato Area Chamber
& Convention Bureau**
112 S. Riverfront Dr.
P.O. Box 999
Mankato, MN 56002
800/657-4733
website: www.mankato.com

Mille Lacs Area Tourism
P.O. Box 362b
Isle, MN 56342
320/676-3029 or 888/350-2692,
   ext. B
fax: 320/676-4991
website: www.millelacs.com

**Minneapolis Metro North
Convention & Visitors Bureau**
6200 Shingle Creek Pkwy., Ste. 248
Minneapolis, MN 55430
763/566-7722 or 800/541-4364
website: www.justaskmn.com

Minnesota Office of Tourism
100 Metro Square
121 Seventh Place East
St. Paul, MN 55101
651/296-5029 or 800/657-3700
email: explore@state.mn.us
website: www.exploreminnesota.com

**New Ulm Convention and
Visitors Bureau**
P.O. Box 384, 1 No. Minnesota
New Ulm, MN 56073
507/354-4217 or 888/463-9856
fax: 507/354-1504
website: www.ic.new-ulm.mn.us

North Shore Drive
website: www.lakesuperiordrive.com

**North Shore Ranger
District Offices**
Gunflint District
P.O. Box 790
Grand Marais, MN 55604
218/387-1750

**Park Rapids Area Chamber
of Commerce**
P.O. Box 249
Park Rapids, MN 56470
800/247-0054
website: www.parkrapids.com

**Rochester Convention and
Visitors Bureau**
150 S. Broadway, Ste. A
Rochester, MN 55904
507/288-4331 or 800/634-8277
fax: 507/288-9144
website: www.rochestercvb.org

**St. Cloud Area Convention and
Visitors Bureau**
P.O. Box 487
St. Cloud, MN 56302
320/251-2940 or 800/264-2940
fax: 320/251-0081
website: www.stcloudcvb.com

**St. Paul Convention and
Visitors Bureau**
175 W. Kellogg Blvd., #502
St. Paul, MN 55102
651/265-4900 or 800/627-6101
fax: 651/265-4999
website: www.stpaulcvb.org

Thief River Falls Convention and
Visitors Bureau
2017 Hwy. 59 S.E.
Thief River Falls, MN 56701
218/681-3720 or 800/827-1629
fax: 218/681-3739
website: www.ci.thief-river-
falls.mn.us

Tofte District
P.O. Box 2157
Tofte, MN 55615
218/663-7981

Two Harbors Chamber
of Commerce
603 7th Ave.
Two Harbors, MN 55616
218/834-2600 or 800/777-7384
fax: 218/834-4012
website: www.twoharbors.com

Warroad Area Chamber
of Commerce
P.O. Box 551
Warroad, MN 56763
218/386-3543 or 800/328-4455
fax: 218/386-3318
website: www.warroad.org

Willmar Area Convention &
Visitors Bureau
2104 E. Hwy. 12
Willmar, MN 56201
320/235-3552 or 800/845-8747
fax: 320/231-1948
website: www.willmarcvb.com

Wisconsin Resources

Federal
Apostle Islands
National Lakeshore
Route 1, Box 4
Old Courthouse Building
Bayfield, WI 54814
email: epis_superintendent@nps.gov
website: www.nps.gov/apis

Chequamegon National Forest
1170 Fourth Ave., S.
Park Falls, WI 54552
715/762-2461
TTY 715/762-5701
website: www.fs.fed.us/r9/cnnf

Nicolet National Forest
68 S. Stevens St.
Federal Building
Rhinelander, WI 54501
715/362-1300
TTY 715/362-1383
website: www.fs.fed.us/r9/cnnf

St. Croix National Scenic Riverway
P.O. Box 708
St. Croix Falls, WI 54024
715/483-3284

State
Wisconsin Department of
Natural Resources
Bureau of Parks and Recreation
P.O. Box 7921
Madison, WI 53707-7921
608/266-2181
TTY 608/267-2752
email: wiparks@dnr.state.wi.us
website: www.wiparks.net

Wisconsin Department of Tourism
201 W. Washington Ave.
P.O. Box 7976
Madison, WI 53707
800/432-8747
website: www.travelwisconsin.com

Organizations

Beloit Convention and
   Visitors Bureau
1003 Pleasant Street
Beloit, WI 53511-4449
608/365-4838 or 800/423-5648
website: www.visitbeloit.com

Brookfield Convention and
   Visitors Bureau
16460 W. Bluemound Road
Brookfield, WI 53005-5908
262/789-0220 or 800/388-1835
website: brookfieldcvb.com

Chippewa Valley Convention and
   Visitors Bureau
3625 Gateway Drive, Suite F
Eau Claire, WI 54701
715/831-2345 or 888/523-3866
website: eauclaire-info.com

Door County Chamber
   of Commerce
P.O. Box 406
Sturgeon Bay, WI 54235-0406
920/743-4456 or 800/527-3529
website:www.doorcounty
   vacations.com

Fond du Lac Area Convention and
   Visitors Bureau
19 W. Scott St.
Fond du Lac, WI 54935-2342
920/923-3010 or 800/937-9123
fax: 920/929-6846
website: www.fdl.com

Fox Cities Convention and
   Visitors Bureau
3433 W. College Ave.
Appleton, WI 54914
920/734-3358 or 800/236-6673
fax: 920/734-1080
website: www.foxcities.org

Green Bay Area Convention and
   Visitors Bureau
P.O. Box 10596
Green Bay, WI 54307-0596
920/494-9507 or 888/867-3342
fax: 920/494-9229
website: www.greenbay.com

Hayward Area Convention and
   Visitors Bureau
c/o Spider Lake Resort Association
Rt. 1, Box 1391
Hayward, WI 54843
715/462-3766
website: www.haywardlakes.com/
   links/spider.htm

Janesville Area Convention and
   Visitors Bureau
51 S. Jackson St.
Janesville, WI 53545
608/757-3171 or 800/48-PARKS
fax: 608/757-3170
website: www.janesvillecvb.com

Kenosha Area Convention and
   Visitors Bureau
812 56th St.
Kenosha, WI 53140
414/654-7307 or 800/654-7309
fax: 414/654-0882
website: www.kenoshacvb.com

La Crosse Area Convention and
Visitors Bureau
410 E. Veterans Memorial Dr.
Riverside Park
La Crosse, WI 54601
608/782-2366 or 800/658-9424
fax: 608/782-4082
website: www.wilcenturyinter
.net/lacvb

Lake Geneva Area Convention and
Visitors Bureau
201 Wrigley Dr.
Lake Geneva, WI 53147
414/248-4416 or 800/345-1020
fax: 414/248-1000
website: www.lakegenevawi.com

Madison Convention and
Visitors Bureau
615 E. Washington Ave.
Madison, WI 53703
608/255-2537 or 800/373-6376
website: www.visitmadison.com

Manitowoc Convention and
Visitors Bureau
P.O. Box 966
Manitowoc, WI 54221-0966
920/683-4388 or 800/627-4896
fax: 902/683-4876
website: www.manitowoc.org

Milwaukee Convention and
Visitors Bureau
510 W. Kilbourn Ave.
Milwaukee, WI 53203-1402
414/273-7222 or 800/554-1448
fax: 414/273-5596
website: www.milwaukee.org/
visit.htm

Oconomowoc Convention and
Visitors Bureau
P.O. Box 27
Oconomowoc, WI 53066-0027
414/569-2185 or 800/524-3744
fax: 414/569-3238
website: www.ci.oconomowoc. wi.us

Oshkosh Convention and
Visitors Bureau
525 W. 20th Ave.
Oshkosh, WI 54901-4897
877/303-9200
fax: 920/303-9200

Racine County Convention and
Visitors Bureau
345 Main St.
Racine, WI 53403
414/634-3293 or 800/272-2463
fax: 414/634-9029
website: www.racine.org

Sheboygan County Convention and
Visitors Bureau
712 Riverfront Dr., Ste. 101
Sheboygan, WI 53081-4665
920/457-9495 or 800/457-9497
fax: 920/457-6269
website: www.sheboygan.org

State Historical Society
of Wisconsin
816 State Street
Madison, WI 53706
608/264-6400
website: www.shsw.wisc.edu

**Stevens Point Area Convention and
Visitors Bureau**
340 Division St., North
Stevens Point, WI 54481
715/344-2556 or 800/236-4636
fax: 715/344-5818
website: www.spacvb.com

**Superior-Douglas County
Convention and Visitors Bureau**
305 Harbor View Pkwy,
Superior, WI 54880
715/392-2773 or 800/942-5313
fax: 715/394-3810
websites: www.superiorwi.com and
www.visitsuperior.com

Tomah Chamber of Commerce/CVB
P.O. Box 625
Tomah, WI 54660-0625
608/372-2166 or 800/94-TOMAH

**Waukesha Area Convention and
Visitors Bureau**
233 Wisconsin Ave.
Waukesha, WI 53186-4926
414/542-0330 or 800/366-8474
fax: 414/542-2237
website: www.wauknet.cin/visit

**Wausau-Central Wisconsin
Convention and Visitors Bureau**
10101 Market St., Ste. C80
Mosinee, WI 54455
715/355-8788 or 888/948-4748
fax: 715/359-2306

**Wisconsin Association of
Campground Owners**
P.O. Box 251
Neenah, WI 54957-0251
800/432-8747
fax: 920/725-9997
email: es.rvtalk@worldnet.att.net
website: www.campgrounds.com/waco

**Wisconsin Dells Convention and
Visitors Bureau**
P.O. Box 390
Wisconsin Dells, WI 53965-0390
608/254-4636 or 800/94-DELLS
fax: 608/254-4293
website: www.wisdells.com

**Wisconsin Rapids Area Convention
and Visitors Bureau**
1120 Lincoln St.
Wisconsin Rapids, WI 54494
715/423-1830 or 800/554-4484
fax: 715/423-1865
website: www.wisconsinrapidsarea.com

No fishing tackle? No problem!

Would-be anglers have an additional incentive to "wet a line" in Wisconsin. Through its Department of Natural Resources' Tackle Loaner Program, anglers can borrow rods, reels, hooks and other fishing gear at no charge at select state parks and DNR field offices across the state. Visit the website: www.dnr.state.wi.us /org/water/fhp/fish/equip.htm.

The fishing equipment is available on a first-come, first-served basis and may be borrowed for up to one week. Most locations offer spincast and spinning rods and reels, casting lures, bobbers, hooks, line and sinkers. Special lures and live or fresh bait are not provided.

The Tackle Loaner Program is operational at the following state parks: Brunet Island (Cornell), Buckhorn (Necedah), Council Grounds (Merril), Harrington Beach (Belgium), Hartman Creek (Waupaca), High Cliff (Sherwood), Interstate (St. Croix Falls), Mill Bluff (Ontario), Mirror Lake (Baraboo), Pattison (Superior), Peninsula (Fish Creek), Perrot (Trempealeau), Whitefish Dunes (Sturgeon Bay), and Willow River (Hudson).

Michigan Resources

Federal

Hiawatha National Forest
Forest Supervisor Office
2727 N. Lincoln Rd.
Escanaba, MI 49829
906/789-4062
fax: 906/789-3311
website: www.fs.fed.us

Rapid River Ranger District
906/474-6442

Manistique Ranger District
906/341-5666

Munising Ranger District
906/387-2512

Sault Ste. Marie Ranger District
906/635-5354

St. Ignace Ranger District
906/643-7900

Ottawa National Forest
Supervisor's Office
E6248 U.S. Hwy. 2
Ironwood, MI 49938
906/932-1330
fax: 906/932-0122
website: www.fs.fed.us

Bessemer Ranger District
906/932-1330

Iron River Ranger District
906/265-9259

Kenton Ranger District
906/852-3500

Ontonagon Ranger District
906/884-2085

Watersmeet Ranger District
906/358-4724

Huron-Manistee National Forests
1755 S. Mitchell St.
Cadillac, MI 49601
800/821-6263
fax: 231/775-5551
website: www.fs.fed.us

Cadillac-Manistee Ranger District
231/723-2211

**Baldwin-White Cloud
  Ranger District**
231/745-4631

Mio Ranger District
517/826-3252

Huron Shores Ranger District
517/739-0728

State

Michigan Dept. of Natural Resources
Parks and Recreation Division
P.O. Box 30257
Lansing, MI 48909
(800) 44-PARKS (State Park
  reservations)
517/373-9900
website: www.dnr.state.mi.us

Michigan Dept. of Natural Resources
License Control Division
P.O. Box 30181
Lansing, MI 48909
517/373-1204
website: www.dnr.state.mi.us

Travel Michigan
P.O. Box 39226
Lansing, MI 48909
888/78-GREAT

Organizations

**Association of RV Parks and
  Campgrounds of Michigan**
9700 M-37 South
Buckley, MI 49620
231/269-CAMP
website: www.michcampgrounds.com

**Michigan Association of Recreational
  Vehicles and Campgrounds**
2222 Association Dr.
Okemos, MI 48864-3975
800/4222-6478
517/349-8881
website: www.marvac.org

Michigan Chamber of Commerce
800 S. Walnut St.
Lansing, MI 48933
800/748-0266
517/371-2100
website: www.michamber.com

**Michigan Festivals and
  Events Association**
P.O. Box 22
Chesaning, MI 48616-0022
517/845-2080
website: www.nfea.org

**Michigan's Sunrise Side
  Travel Association**
1361 Fletcher St.
National City, MI 48748-9666
800/424-3022
517/469-4544
website: www.misunriseside.com

Upper Peninsula Travel and Recreation Association
P.O. Box 400
Iron Mountain, MI 49801-0400
800/562-7134
906/774-5480
website: www.uptravel.com

West Michigan Tourist Association
1253 Front Ave., N.W.
Grand Rapids, MI 49504-3216
800/442-2084
616/456-8557
website: www.wmta.org

Index

Cross-Country Skiing

Historic Landmarks

Museums

Arches Museum of Pioneer Life: 232

A. Schell Museum of Brewing: 200

Aviation History Museum: 559

Bagley Wildlife Museum: 131

Bayfield Maritime Museum: 262

Bunnell House Museum: 230

Camp Ripley's military museum: 138

Christie Home Museum: 188

Circus World Museum: 333 402

Copper Harbor Lighthouse Museum: 425

Dorothy Molter Museum: 110

Ellingson Car Museum: 220

Ely-Winton History Museum: 109

Empire Area Museum: 491

Fairlawn Mansion and Museum: 256

Harsha House Museum: 456

Helen Jeffris Wood Museum Center: 401

Hibbing Historical Society and Museum: 109

Hubbard County Historical Museum: 134

Hutchinson House Victorian Museum: 316

Judy Garland Chil-

dren's Museum: 141

Kittson County History Center and Museum: 63

Koochiching Historical and Bronco Nagurski Museums: 104

La Cross Doll Museum: 276

Lake County Historical Society Depot Museum: 163

Lake of the Woods County Historical Museum: 100

living history museums: 223

Madeline Island Museum: 261

Marshall County Historical Museum: 66

Milton House Museum: 401

mining: 438 439

Minnesota Museum of Mining: 108

Museum of Minerals and Crystals: 377

Museum of Norman Rockwell Art: 376

Museum of Woodcarving: 266

Neillsville: 274

Norman County Historical Museum: 70

Northwoods Children's Museum: 290

Otter Tail County Historical Society Museum: 80

Paynesville Historical

Museum: 194

Pioneer Farm and Village: 67

Plains Art Museum: 69

Polk County Historical Museum: 68

Richland County Historical Museum: 73

Ripley's Believe It or Not! Museum: 328

Roseau County Historical Society and Museum: 67

Runestone Museum: 135

Swenson Farm Museum: 196

Tahquamenon Logging Museum: 433

Twin City Model Railraod Museum: 225

UFO and Sci-Fi Museum: 329

Wabasha County Museum: 226

Warroad Museum: 96

Washington Island: 354

Wes Westrum Baseball Museum: 129

Wild Rose Historical Museum: 317

Wilkin County Museum: 74

Wilson Place Museum: 270

Wisconsin Maritime Museum: 361

Wisconsin Veterans Museum: 396

State Parks

State Parks (cont'd)

197

Lake Wissota State
    Park: 271
Leelanau State Park:
    476
Ludington State Park:
    514
Maplewood State Park:
    79–80
Merrick State Park: 272
Michigan: 14–15
Mill Bluff State Park:
    373–374
Mill Lacs Kathio State
    Park: 143
Minneopa State Park:
    200–201
Minnesota: 4–5
Mirror Lake State Park:
    333
Monson Lake State
    Park: 192
Moose Lake State Park:
    144–145
Muskallonge Lake State
    Park: 433
Muskegon State Park:
    520
Nelson Dewey State
    Park: 379–380
Newaygo State Park:
    547–548
New Glarus Woods
    State Park: 382
North and South Hig-
    gins Lake State Park:
    493–494
Old Mill State Park:
    64–65
Onaway State Park: 459
Orchard Beach State

Park: 512
Otsego Lake State
    Park: 477
Pattison State Park: 256
Peninsula State Park:
    350
Perrot State Park: 273
Petoskey State Park:
    456, 456–457
P.H. Hoeft State Park:
    460
Porcupine Mountains
    Wilderness State
    Park: 426
Port Crescent State
    Park: 570
Roche-A-Cri State
    Park: 324
Rock Island State Park:
    353–354
Rocky Arbor State
    Park: 328–329
Sakatah Lake State
    Park: 223–224
Savanna Portage State
    Park: 141
Scenic State Park: 132
Schoolcraft State Park:
    132–133
Sibley State Park: 193
Silver Lake State Park:
    518
Sleepy Hollow State
    Park: 556
Split Rock Creek State
    Park: 202
Split Rock Lighthouse
    State Park: 161–162
Sterling State Park: 606
Straits State Park: 453
Tahquamenon Falls

State Park: 432
Temperance River State
    Park: 168
Tettegouche State
    Park: 160
Tower Hill State Park:
    376–377
Traverse City State
    Park: 485–486
Twin Lakes State Park:
    427
Upper Sioux Agency
    State Park: 196
Van Buren State Park:
    524–525
Van Riper State Park:
    429
Warren Dunes State
    Park: 529
Whitewater State Park:
    229
Wildcat Mountain State
    Park: 375
Wilderness State Park:
    455
William Mitchell State
    Park: 489
Willow River State
    Park: 264
Wilson State Park: 496
Wisconsin: 8
W.J. Hayes State Park:
    594–595
Wyalusing State Park:
    379
Yellowstone Lake State
    Park: 381
Young State Park: 475
Zippel Bay State Park:
    98

State Forests

Wildlife Refuges

Agassiz National Wildlife Refuge: 66
Bay Beach Wildlife Sanctuary: 359
camping at national: 21
Devil Track Wildlife Sanctuary: 164
Ken's Kampsite: 267
Navarino Wildlife Area: 320
Necedah National Wildlife Refuge: 311
Rice Lake Wildlife Refuge: 133
River's Edge Campground: 313
Rydell National Wildlife Refuge: 69–70
Seney National Wildlife Refuge: 434
Tamarac National Wildlife Refuge: 75–76
Trempealeau National Wildlife Refuge: 273
Vince Shute Wildlife Sanctuary: 102
Wisconsin: 9

---

ground: 67

W.J. Hayes State Park: 594–595

Waffle Farm Campgrounds: 559

Wagener County Park: 576

Wagon Trail Campground: 350

Wagon Wheel: 163

Wagon Wheel Campground: 331–332

Wahpekita tribe: 224

Wakemup Bay Campground: 107–108

Walnut Hills Family Campground and Canoe Rentals: 595–596

Wandering Wheels Campground: 430–431

Wapiti Park Campground: 147

Warren Dunes State Park: 529

Warroad City Campground: 96

Warroad Estates and RV

Court: 97

Waskos Lakeshore Campground: 257

waterfalls: Big Manitou Falls 256; Black River National Scenic Byway 426; Cascade River State Park 165; Copper Falls State Park 263; Gooseberry Falls State Park 162; High Falls 159; Minneopa State Park 200–201; Upper and Lower Falls 432

Waterloo State Recreation Area: 592

water parks: Hideaway Campground/Water Slide 517; Noah's Ark Water Park 331; Ridgewood Campground 313; Wild Waters Minnesota 78

water treating: 36–37

Waterways Campground: 455–456

Watona Park: 201

Waupaca Camping Park: 316

WE Fest: 76

Weko Beach Park and Campground: 528–529

Welles Memorial Park and Fairgrounds: 74

West End Park: 261

Westward Ho Camp-Resort: 335

Wes Westrum Baseball Museum: 129

Wheeler's Point Resort: 99

Whispering Waters Campground and Canoe Livery: 554

White Earth Traditional Pow-Wow: 71

White River Campground: 519

Whitewater State Park: 229

Wigwam Inn Campground and Marina: 143

Wildcat Mountain State Park: 375

Wilder, Laura Ingalls: 269

Wilderness Campground: 332–333

Wilderness County Park: 311–312

Wilderness Cruise: 295

Wilderness of Minnesota: 142

Wilderness State Park: 455

wildflowers: Beaver Creek Valley State Park 235; Buffalo River State Park 71–72

Wildhurst Lodge and Campground: 159

wildlife viewing: 10, 46–47; Great River Bluffs

About the Authors

Bob Schmidt has a Bachelor of Arts Degree in Journalism from Marquette University, Milwaukee, Wisconsin. He has spent more than two decades writing and editing for educational publications and texts for consumers on computers, computer software, do-it-yourself repairs, high-fidelity audio equipment, history, hobbies, financial planning and real estate. Schmidt edited more than 100 books for Publications International, Ltd. (PIL), and Consumer Guide before focusing on writing for and editing outdoors publications.

Schmidt was the first editor of *In-Fisherman* magazine and, later, the Inland Seas Angler for the Great Lakes Sport Fishing Council. Currently, he is editor of *Horizons,* the newsletter of the Association of Great Lakes Outdoor Writers (AGLOW); Foundation News, the newsletter of the Illinois Conservation Foundation; consulting editor of the *Great Lakes Basin Report,* the newsletter of the Great Lakes Sport Fishing Council (GLSFC); and owner of The Outdoor Experience, a media and public relations company for a variety of clients. Over the years, his articles for consumer outdoors publications have covered freshwater fishing, upland game hunting, the sport fishing industry, camping and travel.

He is also the co-author and editor of *The Whole Fishing Catalog* (PIL/Simon & Schuster, 1978) and *The Whole Boating Catalog* (PIL/Simon & Schuster, 1979). He is author of *Great Fishing Close to Chicago* (Contemporary Books, Inc., 1978), *Lake Michigan Salmonid Manual* (American Fishing Institute, Indiana State University, 1985), *Cub Scouts Sport-Fishing* (Boy Scouts of America, 1985), *Sport Fishing and Aquatic Resources Handbook,* Intermediate Edition (American Fishing Tackle Manufacturers Association, 1991), *Advanced Sport Fishing and Aquatic Resources Handbook,* (American Sportfishing Association, 1997), and *Great Circle Tours: Reliving History Along Lake Michigan's Great Lakes Circle Route* (Palmer Publications, Amherst Press, now The Guest Cottage, 1998).

Schmidt is an active member of the Outdoor Writers Association of America, an active member and past president of AGLOW, and co-founder of the Great Lakes Sport Fishing Council.

Ginger Schmidt holds a Bachelor of Arts Degree in Elementary Education and History from Stetson University, Florida, and a Master of General Studies in Journalism and Public Administration from Roosevelt University, Chicago.

She taught public and private school, and designed and taught creative writing courses for the Adult Education Program in Palm Beach County, Florida.

For more than a decade, her column "Camping Comforts," as well as numerous travel articles, have appeared in outdoor magazines and newspapers in the U.S.

She is also the compiler of *Freebies for Cat Lovers* (Prince Paperbacks, Crown Publishers, Inc., 1987) and publisher of *Have They Heard You, Lord?* (Ginmak Communications, Inc., 1988), and co-author of *Great Lakes Circle Tour: Reliving History Along Lake Michigan's Great Lakes Circle Route* (Palmer Publications, Amherst Press, 1998).

Today, she is co-owner of The Outdoor Experience. She is also an active member of AGLOW and a former member of its board of directors.

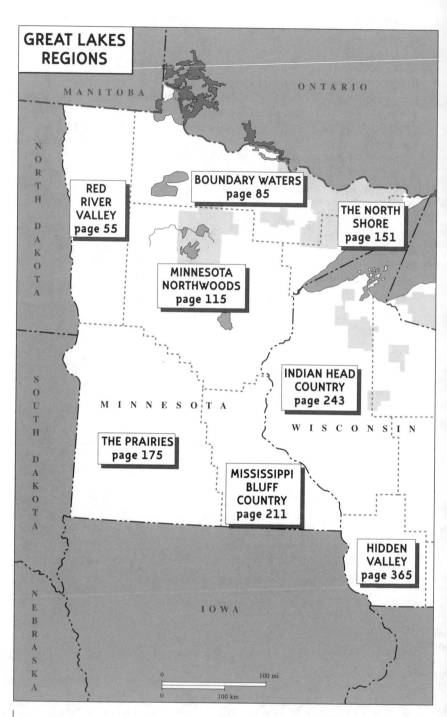

GREAT LAKES
REGIONS

MANITOBA   ONTARIO

N
O
R
T
H

D
A
K
O
T
A

RED
RIVER
VALLEY
page 55

BOUNDARY WATERS
page 85

THE NORTH
SHORE
page 151

MINNESOTA
NORTHWOODS
page 115

S
O
U
T
H

D
A
K
O
T
A

INDIAN HEAD
COUNTRY
page 243

M I N N E S O T A

W I S C O N S I N

THE PRAIRIES
page 175

MISSISSIPPI
BLUFF
COUNTRY
page 211

HIDDEN
VALLEY
page 365

N
E
B
R
A
S
K
A

I O W A

0   100 mi

0   100 km

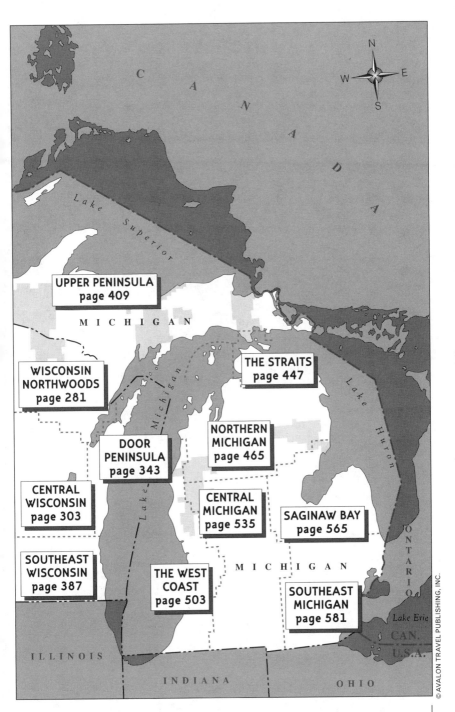

UPPER PENINSULA
page 409

THE STRAITS
page 447

WISCONSIN NORTHWOODS
page 281

NORTHERN MICHIGAN
page 465

DOOR PENINSULA
page 343

CENTRAL WISCONSIN
page 303

CENTRAL MICHIGAN
page 535

SAGINAW BAY
page 565

SOUTHEAST WISCONSIN
page 387

THE WEST COAST
page 503

SOUTHEAST MICHIGAN
page 581

CANADA

Lake Superior

MICHIGAN

Lake Michigan

Lake Huron

MICHIGAN

ONTARIO

Lake Erie

CAN.
U.S.A.

ILLINOIS

INDIANA

OHIO

© AVALON TRAVEL PUBLISHING, INC.

Notes

Notes

Notes